"Ambray is no longer my home, is it, my lord?"

"You still have a home, lady. Just remember that I am now master here, and we will deal well enough."

A quiver of distress crossed Lisette's face for the merest instant, but Raverre saw it. His eyes lost a little of their hard glitter.

"Don't make this more difficult for yourself," he advised in a softer tone. "There's no need. When you know me better you'll find I mean you no harm."

"I would rather not know you at all," she said.

D0639895

Gentle Conqueror

Julia Byrne

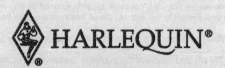

TORONTO • NEW YORK • LONDON
AMSTERDAM • PARIS • SYDNEY • HAMBURG
STOCKHOLM • ATHENS • TOKYO • MILAN • MADRID
PRAGUE • WARSAW • BUDAPEST • AUCKLAND

If you purchased this book without a cover you should be aware
that this book is stolen property. It was reported as "unsold and
destroyed" to the publisher, and neither the author nor the
publisher has received any payment for this "stripped book."

ISBN 0-373-30329-7

GENTLE CONQUEROR

First North American Publication 1999

Copyright © 1992 by Julia Byrne

All rights reserved. Except for use in any review, the reproduction or
utilization of this work in whole or in part in any form by any electronic,
mechanical or other means, now known or hereafter invented, including
xerography, photocopying and recording, or in any information storage
or retrieval system, is forbidden without the written permission of the
publisher, Harlequin Enterprises Limited, 225 Duncan Mill Road,
Don Mills, Ontario, Canada M3B 3K9.

All characters in this book have no existence outside the imagination of
the author and have no relation whatsoever to anyone bearing the same
name or names. They are not even distantly inspired by any individual
known or unknown to the author, and all incidents are pure invention.

This edition published by arrangement with Harlequin Books S.A.

® and TM are trademarks of the publisher. Trademarks indicated with
® are registered in the United States Patent and Trademark Office, the
Canadian Trade Marks Office and in other countries.

Look us up on-line at: http://www.romance.net

Printed in U.S.A.

JULIA BYRNE

lives in Australia with her husband, daughter and two overgrown cats. She started her working career as a secretary, taught ballroom dancing after several successful years as a competitor, and presently works part-time in the history department of a Melbourne university. When not writing historical romances, she enjoys reading, tapestry and playing mah-jongg.

Historical Note

In the autumn of 1068 William the Conqueror had been King of England for almost two years, but another three years were to pass before William conquered the entire country. Several uprisings centred around the Saxon Prince Edgar, last of the old English royalty. However, he was merely a boy, a figurehead, whose supporters alternately sided with William or rebelled against him, according to their fluctuating ambitions.

These rebellions effectively wiped out the Saxon nobility. Prince Edgar fled, with his mother and sisters, to Scotland, and by 1071 there was only one Saxon Earl remaining in England, the Court spoke Norman French, and, though the common folk remained relatively unaffected, the ruling minority became more Anglo-Norman than Anglo-Saxon.

The Atheling Edgar eventually returned to England and was sent to William's father-in-law in Flanders for several years. He spent the remainder of his life drifting between England and Scotland, apparently lacking the strong personality necessary to make a bid to regain his family's throne. However, the ancient royal line continued through a woman.

Prince Henry, the only child of William and Matilda to be born in England, was crowned Henry I in August 1100. He married Edith of Scotland, Edgar's niece, thereby uniting his family with the last Saxon princess.

Prologue

Romsey Abbey, near Winchester, September 1068

"'Tis of no use to argue further. I cannot help you." The black-robed woman standing by the window folded her hands over the intricately carved wooden rosary at her waist with a gesture of finality.

Her visitor's grim expression showed his intention of ignoring this remark, but the nun's face, framed by the white wimple and black veil of the Benedictine Order, remained steadfast.

"If they may not seek shelter here, Reverend Mother, where else can they go? You are their only family remaining, and you know the alternative."

"A fate shared by many," the nun answered implacably. "They could fare worse."

"Marriage to men my ladies regard as enemies?"

"Enemies," she scoffed. "The late Confessor's Queen—Harold's own sister, I would remind you—herself handed over the royal town of Winchester to William of Normandy; which proves her opinion of her brother's ambitions. When I advise my nieces to obey the King I but follow the example of a pious and noble lady. Naturally we welcome any girl who has the King's permission to dedicate her life to God. However, such true brides of Christ bring with them a dowry. Worldly goods though they are, even a large house such as ours cannot exist without funds.''

"A dowry!" the visitor exclaimed, frowning at her. He took a hasty turn about the room, the glimpse of chainmail beneath his mantle and the dagger at his waist jarringly alien in the peaceful simplicity of Reverend Mother's chamber. "My Lady Enide, what dowry can they possibly bring now their heritage has been taken from them? In truth, they are as poor as the lowliest serf.''

The nun gestured slightly with one hand. "In that case there is no more to be said. And I am no longer the Lady Enide, as you well know.''

The elderly soldier regarded her sombrely. He had not really expected the request to be granted; but he had promised to deliver it, and he would never break a promise to his lady. Even if he did happen to agree with the Prioress that continuing to treat the Normans as enemies was futile.

"Then I shall not impose on your time any longer, my Lady Prioress,'' he said, giving subtle emphasis to her title. "My apologies for disturbing you.''

He turned to open the door, not staying for her blessing.

"Wait!" The nun looked away, through the open window. She was silent for a long moment.

Though autumn was upon them, the leaves outside were still green here in the sheltered cloister, but her eyes were blind to the summer verdure. She saw instead the trees surrounding her girlhood home, already beginning their transformation to red, gold, and amber, fed by the cool air blowing across from the Welsh mountains.

"I cannot act against the King's orders,'' the Prioress

said at last, "but...we do not refuse shelter to those desperate enough to arrive at our gates with nothing."

There was another long silence. Then she added, "God go with you, Bertrand." It was dismissal.

The nun heard the door close softly, but remained by the window. A faint breeze rustled through the leafy branches, touching her face with a warm caress.

Had she done right? Her own kin, and she'd had to refuse them. But, with only four other nunneries in the whole of England, they could not take in every Saxon widow or bereft daughter who objected to the likelihood of having a Norman husband foisted upon them. Already her resources were dangerously stretched to the limit.

The wily old warrior had tried an appeal to memories of her life before the cloister by using her former title, and it had almost succeeded. But if she offered shelter to three penniless girls of her own family the Abbot would have plenty to say when he arrived for his next visit of inspection; and she had no intention of ceding her place to one of the ambitious Norman ladies who coveted her high position.

The bell tolled for Prime, recalling the Prioress to her duties. She could only pray for her nieces. Pray that they had the courage to face whatever future had been ordained by the will of God.

Or rather, she amended with wry pragmatism, by the will of the Conqueror.

Chapter One

The late afternoon sun, shining through the narrow windows set high in the walls of the great hall, sent dancing rays of golden light across the rush-strewn floor, enveloping the three girls seated near the huge stone fireplace in a soft luminous haze. Bertrand, coming in through the main door and rounding the corner from the screen passage, paused to watch them for a moment.

They presented a peaceful tableau, a little apart as they were from the bustle elsewhere in the hall as the house carls set up trestles for the evening meal. Two of the girls sat close together on a wooden bench, the fair head of the elder bent over the sewing of her younger sister and guiding a hand still unskilled and impatient.

A smile crossed Bertrand's lined and weathered face. Young Catherine would much rather be out in the stables or running through the orchard on this warm autumn day than confined indoors, wielding a needle.

Then the smile faded as his gaze rested longest on the middle sister, Lisette, who sat curled up on the floor at her sisters' feet, a large black mastiff stretched out by her side, his head in her lap. She, too, had been stitching, but her hands were now resting in the thick fur of the dog's ruff, and she sat gazing into the fire, where a small flame flickered into life against the oncoming chill of evening.

Bertrand, gazing at the pure outline of her profile etched against the dark stone, considered her the loveliest of his late master's daughters. Although they all had the fineboned, delicate features of their Celtic mother, Lisette was the only one who had inherited that lady's dark colouring, Enide and Catherine having the fair skin and hair of their father's Saxon forebears.

"She looks at ease for the first time in months," murmured Bertrand to his companion, a brawny youth garbed in the leather apron of the blacksmith.

"A fragile peace at best, my friend," the younger man answered, drawing Bertrand back into the passage. "She's been worried about you travelling alone, and now 'tis all for nought. You should have taken them with you, as I suggested."

"They were safer here," said Bertrand mildly. He and Siward had had this argument before, and it was irrelevant now.

"Do you still say so now the Norman usurper has thrown his shadow over them?" Siward's voice grew angry. "We can still fight."

"You hotheaded young fool," retorted Bertrand. "There are at least forty soldiers about to arrive against eight of us—apart from the serfs. You might be willing to throw away your life for nothing, but my lady would never permit it. You can serve her best by accepting what we've always known would happen."

Siward swore softly. Aye, they had known, he thought. Since William of Normandy had conquered England, Norman overlordship was becoming more and more the rule as the King rewarded his followers by granting them the lands and manors previously held by the Saxon Thegns who had died with King Harold in the bloody battle at Hastings. Or in the uprisings since that date. But knowing didn't make acceptance any easier.

"I was my Lord Alaric's man," he said sullenly, turning away to the door. "And I don't intend to serve his enemies."

"My lord admired William," Bertrand called after him, hoping the reminder would hold Siward's hot temper in check for a while. It was the truth, after all.

Alaric, Thegn of Ambray, had accepted the Witan's decision to crown Harold Godwinson King of England, despite the claim by William of Normandy that the English crown had been promised to him by his cousin, King Edward, known as the Confessor. Edward had no true right to will his crown away, English Kings being elected; and Harold was Saxon, the most powerful man in the land, and the late King's brother-in-law, three circumstances which made his claim a good one. But Alaric had had doubts.

He had travelled extensively in his young days, staying some considerable time in Normandy, where he had remote family connections dating back to Viking days, and had considered William to be a strong ruler. Ruthless certainly, but fair, and possibly better able to unite England under one leader than the old Cerdic line, where bitter fighting between factions and brothers divided the Saxons, weakening the country.

In fact, on Alaric's return to England years earlier, King Edward, who was half-Norman himself by birth, and had plenty of his mother's countrymen in his service, had besought Alaric to settle on his land-holdings in the west, promising him aid in building the Norman stronghold of Alaric's ambition in exchange for helping to maintain the peace on the Welsh border.

However, King Edward's death had caused more than

one claimant to the English throne to come forward. Harold Godwinson might have managed to have himself elected and crowned, but his position was not secure. When the Norwegian King, Harald Hardrada, had mounted an attack in the north, Alaric, considering himself more Saxon than anything else, had finally sworn fealty to Harold and marched with the fyrd to a resounding victory at Stamford Bridge. The Norwegians had been utterly routed, limping home in only twenty-four of the three hundred ships in which they had arrived.

But then news had come of William's landing at Pevensey on the south coast, and Alaric had found himself in the forced march back through England and in the thick of the fighting at Hastings.

The Saxons had fought bravely, but an army weakened by two long marches with a battle between, in the space of thirteen days, was no match for the disciplined Normans. Alaric had been taken prisoner, and, before being given the opportunity to transfer his allegiance to William, had died of his wounds, leaving his three daughters without the male protection needed in these troubled times, and an estate upon which more than one Norman knight had cast an acquisitive eye.

Nestling in the rolling green pasturelands of the Wye Valley, with a prosperous village clustered around a stone church, and many acres of farmland bordered by dense forest, it was a fair estate indeed. And crowned by the small though solid castle, built after the Norman style which Alaric had so admired on his travels, and which was easier to defend than the usual simple wooden dwellings favoured by the Saxons. The castle, in its still unfinished state, was more a fortified manor-house, but a tower had been added to the hall, from which an excellent view could be had of the countryside, and a stone wall protected the manor and outbuildings, replacing the original wooden palisade.

Three smaller compounds, once occupied by Alaric's retainers, completed the estate. A comfortable prize for an enterprising man with ambition.

Well, thought Bertrand, recalled to his mission, if change must come, at least the terms the King had laid down would ensure that Lord Alaric's daughters would be cared for; and the estate had been given to a man who looked as if he could be one Bertrand could come to respect, and even admire. Still, he sighed, Lisette would not take kindly to handing over her family home to a stranger, and a Norman stranger at that.

Bertrand knew well her opinion of illegitimate Dukes of Normandy who decided that a kingdom would suit them and rode roughshod over any who stood in their way, and he would not place much dependence on her meekly accepting the terms the King had ordered him to deliver. She had already been given plenty of reason to hate and fear any Norman, let alone one who now had absolute control over her future, and Bertrand was conscious of extreme reluctance to be the bearer of such tidings. But, as the subject of his message was at this very moment only about a mile behind him, he had best get on with it.

As he strode forward the sun slid further towards the western horizon, plunging the hall into sudden dimness, and he hoped it wasn't an ill omen. Then all other thoughts were forgotten as Lisette heard him and turned her head, a smile of welcome lighting up her lovely face.

"Bertrand!" She sprang to her feet with a light, graceful movement, disturbing the dog from his slumber. He rose also, whining and coming forward to snuffle at the familiar figure before flopping down again before the fire, knowing his mistress had no need of defence.

Lisette held out her hands in greeting. "I didn't look to see you so soon. What news from Winchester? Did you see my lady aunt? Will she take us into sanctuary? Has she heard any talk of the manor?"

The spate of questions tripped over each other in a breathless rush as the cares she had tried to forget in daydreaming for a few moments flooded back, causing a frown to appear on her smooth brow.

Bertrand sank to one knee at her feet. "Lady, dear, news indeed. And you must quickly prepare to meet it in the flesh, for the new lord would have me travel with him when he learned from whence I came, and is only a few minutes behind."

Lisette's face paled suddenly as she listened, Bertrand's voice seeming to come from a great distance.

"New lord?" The question was a horrified whisper.

After nearly a year of peace she had forgotten, Lisette thought. Had forgotten how sickening fear could be. But she must not give in to the numbing feeling of helplessness. Too many people depended on her. The churls...her sisters...

"Then Enide and Catherine must be got away. Hidden in the village until you can take them to my aunt..." Lisette faltered to a stop as Bertrand shook his head.

"Hear me out, mistress." His voice was grave. "I wish I could have spared you this, but the King has granted all your father's lands to one of his young officers, Alain of Raverre, a younger son of a noble family, I am told. And that is not all. He has also granted him the wardship of yourself and your sisters, so you are under his protection and not destitute or a charge on the royal household."

"You saw the King himself?" Lisette asked. "He knows of us?"

"Aye," confirmed Bertrand, rising stiffly to his feet. "I

came upon him and some of his knights the instant I set foot inside the town walls, and was promptly seized.''

"Oh, Bertrand!''

"'Twas not so bad. I had thought to mingle with the beggars, and slip unnoticed through the city gates at dawn, but there were soldiers everywhere, interrogating all who passed.''

Bertrand grimaced at the memory, but his tone held reluctant admiration for such Norman efficiency. "There is no time to tell it all now, but William remembered me from the time I asked his permission to bring your father's body home for burial. The next thing I knew, he ordered me to the palace so I could meet my new liege lord.''

"Then I left it too late to send to my aunt.'' Lisette's voice held such despair that Bertrand felt compelled to steady her with a sustaining grip on her arm.

"You mustn't blame yourself, my lady. Even had I gone earlier—''

He hesitated, trying to find the right words. He knew Lisette's concern was all for her sisters; that, despite the many tales noised abroad of manors and villeins deserted by their Thegns, she had not once considered the personal consequences of remaining in her home until the inevitable arrival of a Norman master.

"I did have some speech with the Lady Prioress, and, though she sends you her blessings, she bids you obey the King. Although she did say she would shelter any who came.''

He stopped, not wishing to add to her worries. He could not bring himself to tell Lisette of the Prioress's offer of shelter on the condition of a dowry, or unless they came alone, practically as beggars.

His news had brought the other girls to their feet, their sewing falling unheeded to the floor, and the servants crowding around, asking questions, fearful of the future. Catherine clung to Lisette's hand and Enide, although the eldest, also looked to her sister for guidance.

The load was too great for a young girl, thought Bertrand, wishing he had the power to lift some of it from her slender shoulders. Her face was so pale that he feared she might swoon. And she looked tired, as well she might, having had the running of the estate since her father's death, as well as the ordering of the household.

"A Saxon woman may hold land in her own right," she murmured, as though in puzzled denial of Bertrand's words. "The Witan would have named Enide as our father's heiress before Hastings. Do you tell me that now we own nothing, and are dependent upon a stranger and an enemy?"

A flash of anger suddenly went through her, pushing the fear aside for the moment, but there was no time now to rail against fate. Without waiting for an answer, Lisette squared her shoulders and, gently putting aside Bertrand's supporting hand, set about quieting the servants.

"Hush, all of you," she commanded firmly. "Go about your business. You are in no danger, and I am here to speak for you. When I know more, so will you, but for now we will not show frightened faces to these Normans."

Hoping that the familiar preparations for the arrival of visitors might occupy the serfs enough to keep them from panicking, she turned to old Wat, who ruled the kitchen slaves with a stern hand.

"Wat, you had best prepare plenty of food; no doubt our—" she hesitated, then took a deep, steadying breath and went on "—our guests will be hungry. The rest of you, go back to your work."

As some of the serfs scurried away to the kitchens, murmuring among themselves, Lisette turned back to the man who had served her family faithfully for so many years.

"Bertrand, can you manage? You will know what to do. How many men should be housed here in the bailey or elsewhere…"

Her voice trailed off, and Bertrand knew she was remembering the last time Norman soldiers had been in the castle and the terrible damage that had been done. He could at least set her mind at ease on this question, however.

"Lady, see to your household and don't worry your head about the soldiers. Raverre has not brought many men. Three of his own knights with their retainers, the rest merely as escort on the road, and he has them well disciplined. You need not fear for yourselves or your people. Indeed, from what speech I had with him as we travelled, Raverre intends things to go on much as before."

He paused. There was a lot more to say but it would have to wait. Bertrand, knowing of his late lord's high opinion of Duke William, had also been impressed by the young man he must now call master, and was willing to co-operate with him, but he wanted Lisette to judge for herself. He knew she was prepared to see nothing good in any Norman from the King down, but he hoped in time she would come to accept this change in her life, and not become bitter and angry.

Bertrand remembered the carefree, innocent child she had been two years before. Afraid of nothing. Facing life with happy anticipation. Eager, loving, she had seemed to carry light and laughter within her. He knew the child could never return, but he hoped the woman who emerged from the years of uncertainty and loss would still have that gift of happiness and love.

Hearing the jingling of harness and voices raised in command coming faintly through the unglazed windows, Bertrand left the hall swiftly, and Lisette sank back on to the settle for a moment to gather her strength and courage. She had to think. There was so much to do. But of the myriad thoughts jostling themselves about in her head, only one stood out clearly.

He has come.

As if sensing the tension in the air, the dog rose again, ears pricked towards the sounds outside, and would have investigated, but Lisette held him back.

"Stay, Finn," she commanded, and felt slightly comforted at the touch of the big animal under her restraining hand. Her eyes flew to her sisters.

Enide had the mindless, vacant look in her eyes that Lisette dreaded to see there, but Catherine was now looking ready to do battle with any amount of Normans, her little fists clenched and a pugnacious tilt to her chin. The sight of her made Lisette smile slightly and she quickly rallied, kneeling to gather up the forgotten threads and cloths.

"Come," she said, striving for a brisk tone, "we will show these Normans that we are not disturbed by their arrival. Fear will only make us appear weak. Sit down and at least pretend to be calm. Catherine, as soon as you can, take Enide up to our chamber and wait for me there. Whatever this Norman Baron intends, we must surely be allowed some privacy."

Catherine only had time to nod her understanding with a quick glance at the still silent Enide when firm footsteps sounded at the head of the outside stairway and a man strode into the hall. Taking in the servants huddled in one corner and the three girls seated by the fire, without breaking stride, he advanced towards them.

Tension gripped Lisette's body instantly. The Norman's quiet entrance, unattended by any soldiers, had not been at all threatening, but she felt herself brace as though about to confront an unknown, unseen danger. Her mouth went dry, and her heart beat so fast that she could scarcely catch her breath.

He was so big.

Standing well over six feet tall with broad shoulders and a deeply muscled chest, tapering to more slender but still strongly muscled hips and thighs, he was the most powerful-looking man Lisette had ever seen. And, though the power was contained, leashed by the lithe, controlled grace with which he moved, the aura of physical strength about him was palpable.

He was dressed all in dark blue, including the ankle-length mantle he wore, which seemed to add to his height, and his tunic and trousers were of fine woollen cloth, obviously the best quality and weave. Although he wore no mailcoat, a deadly-looking sword was buckled at his hip, and a visored helmet of black metal concealed his eyes, making him appear even more formidable.

This, however, he pulled off as he approached, revealing a head of thick fair hair and a strong handsome face, tanned from long campaigning in all weathers, with broad, high cheekbones, an aquiline nose, and piercing ice-blue eyes, whose cool, hard gaze clashed with Lisette's and held. For a heart-stopping moment she was aware of nothing else but him.

She rose swiftly and immediately cursed herself for doing so, remembering that she had meant to remain seated, refusing to offer this invader the courteous greeting normally given to any guest. It was as though his compelling eyes had brought her to her feet before she had had time to think about it. As he reached them Lisette lifted her chin, staring him in the face. But her widened eyes and the pulse fluttering in her throat betrayed the sudden fear his intimidating presence had aroused.

His firm mouth quirked a little at the defiant picture she made, but after a sweeping glance which took in all three girls, making Lisette feel as if a lightning bolt had shot through them, he bent his head a little in her direction and addressed her directly in fluent English.

"Lady, I am Alain of Raverre, lately Captain in the army of William, King of England and Duke of Normandy, now, by the King's grace, Baron of this manor and its lands. You are—?" He paused interrogatively.

"Lisette of Ambray," she informed him briefly, surprised at the cultured note in his deep, slightly husky, voice. "These ladies are my sisters, Enide and Catherine." Her own voice wavered a little when she saw her fear mirrored on the faces of the other girls as they gazed up at Raverre in awe, but she forced herself to go on firmly.

"I ask your permission for us to retire to our private chamber and for me to reassure our serfs that no harm will come to them, and that they may continue to go about their business until any further order from you."

Raverre watched Lisette as she spoke, hearing the breathless catch in a voice he deemed would be low and sweet when she wasn't frightened almost out of her wits. And the fear was there in her eyes, despite the defiant tilt to her chin and the determined way she looked him in the face. He couldn't remember ever seeing eyes so deep and dark a blue, so full of violet shadows. She has known suffering, he thought, as he gazed down at a face so lovely that he found himself unable to look away.

Framed by silken masses of hair the colour of bronze, her delicate facial bones were slightly more defined than they should have been, given her youth, but neither meagre food nor strain could detract from the beauty of those dark long-lashed eyes set beneath finely arched brows, or the sweet, full-lipped mouth, closed now in a firm, determined line. He noticed the faintest hint of dimples at the corners of her mouth and wondered irresistibly what the serious little face looked like when she smiled.

Colour had suddenly come into her cheeks as he continued to stare at her, and Raverre belatedly realised she was waiting for his answer. His own wits seemed to have gone a-begging, he thought, impatient with himself for staring like any callow youth. He had seen beautiful women before, for God's sake.

Seeing his quick frown, Lisette prepared to argue. She and her sisters would not sit here to be ogled or accosted by Norman barbarians, and so she would tell him. Raverre saved her the trouble.

"You may retire for the moment, my lady. However, I want you all to sup with me here in the hall tonight."

As Lisette drew in breath to speak Raverre continued quickly, forestalling the protest he knew was about to be uttered, "It will reassure the serfs. If they see you accepting this change in your state without fuss and rebellion they will do likewise, and it will make life easier for all concerned. I have no desire to be forever disciplining unruly serfs, made so by the example set them by their late masters. Or mistresses, as the case may be."

He added briskly, "You and they need have nothing to fear from me. I have had a surfeit of fighting and am heartily tired of it, but nor will I tolerate any insurrection among my serfs or in my household. I trust you understand me?"

Lisette bristled. *His* household? *His* serfs? Did he perhaps expect a speech of welcome from her? she wondered rebelliously. He hadn't even paid her the courtesy of asking her to surrender the manor, but had calmly walked in and taken possession with typical Norman arrogance.

But, as Raverre's brows rose in challenge at her continued silence, Lisette forced herself to be calm. He might speak as though he owned the place, but the unpalatable truth was that he did, and standing here arguing the finer points of conquest and surrender would be useless.

She needed some time alone to marshal her thoughts and prepare for the more important battle. Because battle it would be if this cool, self-possessed Norman Baron thought the three of them were going to remain to watch their home taken over, and acquiesce in the disposal of their persons without so much as a by-your-leave.

Lisette looked up into Raverre's stern face and spoke with icy control. "I understand you, my lord."

She gestured to Catherine and Enide, and her sisters crossed towards the screen passage where a flight of stone stairs led to the upper gallery and the tower room. As they turned the corner a young man entering the hall quickly almost collided with them. He stood back with a startled apology, looking admiringly after them as they passed, but then recollected himself and hurried forward.

Lisette started towards the servants while Raverre was distracted by the newcomer, but she had only taken two steps before he moved in front of her and laid a restraining hand on her arm. His grip was firm, though not unduly so, and she pulled away immediately, startled by the warmth of his touch.

Raverre's mouth curled in a sardonic smile at her recoil. "I will address the serfs myself, lady; it will be better so."

He glanced at the other man, who had by this time taken in Lisette's beauty and was watching her, a deeply appreciative look on his face. Raverre grimly resolved to keep the girls from causing trouble among his men at his earliest opportunity, and his voice became curt.

"You may retire, my lady. I will send for you when we dine. And until I have seen to the placement of such men as I intend to keep here, and the despatching of the others back to the army, you and your sisters will keep to the manor and not wander outside.''

''I might have known you would treat us as prisoners,'' Lisette retorted in angry resentment at this abrupt order. ''I'm only surprised that we are not to be confined to the dungeon.''

''I doubt if you have any idea of the treatment of prisoners,'' Raverre replied coldly. 'But you'll find out soon enough if you give me any trouble. I don't issue empty orders, girl, and this one is for your own safety, so you would do well to obey me.''

He sensed, rather than saw, the look of surprise that crossed the face of the young soldier next to him, and didn't wonder at it. The girls were perfectly safe and both men knew it, but Raverre, surprised at his sudden feeling of distaste at the thought of Lisette being the subject of the speculative looks and coarse jests of his men, could hardly explain that this was the real reason for his order.

God's blood! Why was he even thinking of explaining? He *never* explained his orders—except occasionally to his knights. Had those shadowed eyes, now flashing daggers of scorn, cast some spell over him?

'''Tis a shameful thing when a lady is not safe in her own home,'' she said bitterly. ''But I forget. Ambray is no longer my home, is it, my lord? Nor will be, as long as Normans are here.''

''You still have a home, lady. Just remember that I am now master here, and we will deal well enough.''

A quiver of distress crossed Lisette's face for the merest instant, but Raverre saw it. His eyes lost a little of their hard glitter.

''Don't make this more difficult for yourself,'' he advised in a softer tone. ''There's no need. When you know me better you'll find I mean you no harm.''

"I would rather not know you at all," Lisette snapped back, angry at having betrayed herself. Turning abruptly on her heel and summoning Finn, she left the hall with what dignity she could muster, sped on her way by the entrance of several more men, who shoved each other good-naturedly through the doorway and filled the hall with their noisy laughter.

Raverre watched her thoughtfully until she was out of sight, then turned his attention to his companion.

"You may remove that grin from your face, de Rohan," were his first words, but the corners of his own mouth curled in the beginnings of an answering smile.

"Spirited little armful," remarked his friend judiciously. "And beautiful enough to make taming her an extremely pleasant occupation. I know you said you mean her no harm, but if she proves troublesome, what *do* you intend to do with the wench?"

"Marry her," said Raverre succinctly. He ignored de Rohan's dropped jaw. "So keep a civil tongue in your head when you mention her."

"Aye, sir! A civil tongue, sir!" De Rohan came smartly to attention.

"Idiot," returned Raverre, cuffing him across the back. A thick cloud of dust immediately rose about them.

"Mother of God, Gilbert, you need a bath," Raverre informed his henchman. "We both do. Let's get this place sorted out, and the men settled. Then we can turn our attention to William's little problem."

"I don't know whether I'd refer to an object needing twelve men to lift it as 'little'," argued Gilbert. "But you're right about the bath. Do you want me to speak to those goggle-eyed serfs? They're looking at you as if you might spit them on the end of your sword."

"Then the sooner they learn I won't, the better," replied

Raverre, advancing on the silent group in the corner with grim determination.

Gilbert shook his head, a rueful smile on his lips at his friend's forceful methods, then turned and started bellowing orders. In less than a minute the efficient machinery of Norman occupation was set in motion.

Raverre found the main solar to be a goodly sized room at the end of the hall. It had once been comfortably furnished, and even had a fireplace with an outlet set into the wall, which didn't smoke too much unless the wind happened to blow from the wrong direction. However, a band of marauding Norman soldiers had stripped the castle of everything they could carry away, leaving a trail of devastation and death in their wake, and the room was now bare.

As Raverre stood by the empty fireplace, watching two serfs pour hot water into a big wooden tub, he sent a brief mental thanks to William for allowing him to retrieve his personal belongings from Normandy before taking possession of his new lands.

His mother, obviously believing him to be settling in a heathen land with scant amenities and fewer luxuries, had loaded his baggage wagon with such diverse objects as a sheepskin rug, a tall iron candle spike, and an illuminated psalter. Not to mention his great-grandfather's raven sword, which really should have gone to one of his older brothers.

In vain had he told his over-zealous parent that Saxon learning and craftsmanship far outstripped anything Norman. She had brought out a wall tapestry for good measure.

Raverre had laughed at her, but hadn't had the heart to unload it all again, and now he was glad. Thanks to his mother's endeavours, the lord's solar would soon be properly furnished as it should be.

The manor itself would probably take several months to bring into order, having been without a master for two years, but on the whole, Raverre considered, his plans were moving along very nicely. He had a title, his own estate and, as soon as he could arrange it, a wife.

Raverre smiled slightly as he remembered Gilbert's description of Lisette. A spirited little armful, indeed. She obviously deeply resented his arrival and made no secret of it, despite her fear. But instead of feeling anger at the way she had spoken to him in front of the serfs, Raverre had been intrigued. In his experience, such outright honesty was rare in a woman. Most would have played the obedient martyr while wanting to stab him in the back, or cowered away, treating him to female weepings and wailings.

And she was exquisite. A man could drown in those deep iris-blue eyes. Had it been her fragile beauty which had compelled him to declare his intentions to Gilbert so quickly? Or had it been the unpleasant jolt that had gone through him at the idea of Gilbert, or anyone else, taming her proud spirit?

At that moment Raverre suddenly realised, with another more violent jolt of awareness, that he'd had no thought of taming Lisette himself. She had aroused some other, until now unknown, emotion within him. He tried to recall the strange feeling that had instinctively made him want to keep her away from his men, but was distracted as another serf entered the room, carrying straw to cushion the hard wooden pallet on the floor.

Raverre shrugged, dismissing the question from his mind. Not a man who was accustomed to pondering overmuch about his own emotions, he turned his thoughts to more practical matters. One of which was making the cold, bare solar more habitable. He wondered briefly if the tower room was as cheerless, and if the ladies had retired there thinking it was safer.

Lisette had not really considered safety. Since the tower had been built its small solar had been used as a sleeping chamber by the girls, and it was to this familiar haven that she had sped after leaving the hall.

The tower was the usual example of its kind. Square and rather squat-looking, the lower level housed the guard-room and opened directly into the bailey. Then came the solar and, above that, reached by a treacherously narrow stairway in the thick castle wall, the rooftop battlements.

As Lisette had hurried along the gallery she remembered how minstrels had once played there, that fine silks had covered the walls, the sconce lights gleaming on rich gold thread. Remembered how lavish had been Alaric's hospitality whenever guests came to the castle.

Those days of extravagance were past, however, the minstrels long gone, and what few household comforts Lisette had managed to salvage from the raid now furnished the room where her sisters and their old nurse waited.

Anxious faces turned to the door as she entered, beginning to feel her trembling reaction to the encounter below. Her mind felt more confused than ever—anger, distress and fear now warring with the memory of glittering blue eyes in a handsome face, and an impression of invincible strength.

Seeing her mistress's tense, pale face, Marjory bustled forward, taking Lisette's hands and murmuring soothingly. She drew her towards the brazier in the centre of the floor, where a small fire sent a cheerful glow into the room, and hushed Catherine, who obviously had a hundred questions ready to tumble off her tongue. By contrast, Enide sat quietly on a chest by the window embrasure, her hands folded gracefully in her lap and her face as serene as a madonna's.

Only the empty look in her grey eyes as she gazed into an invisible distance betrayed the fact that her calm was not natural.

Lisette sank on to a stool by the brazier with a sigh, while Marjory fetched a comb and set about smoothing the tangles out of her hair before braiding it into two thick plaits which fell to her waist. Eventually those gentle ministrations did their work, and Lisette sat up straighter, gesturing to the others to sit also.

"We are bidden to supper this evening," she began. "And, even though I dare say the smallest morsel of food eaten at the same table as a Norman Baron will be hard to swallow, swallow it we must, along with the loss of our freedom and status."

"Are we to be slaves, then?" asked Catherine, appalled, and obviously remembering every rumour of Norman brutality that had ever been spread about.

"No, of course not," Lisette hastened to reassure her, hoping devoutly that she was right. "After all, we are daughters of Saxon nobility. Even if we don't look it," she added, glancing ruefully at their shabby homespun gowns and mantles, bare of any ornamentation.

"I intend to tell his lordship 'tis our earnest desire to enter the cloister," she went on after a moment. "I can't see why he should object. He would be rid of us, for one thing. After all, our presence will be a constant reminder to our people of one who was a fair and generous master."

"Aye," put in Marjory sceptically, who had been a shrewd witness to Raverre's long scrutiny of Lisette, "but will he wish to be rid of you, sweeting?"

She went on with the acknowledged freedom of an old servant who had nurtured her mistress from babyhood and was now her right hand in managing the household.

"He doesn't appear to be penniless, I grant you, but the

wardship of three marriageable girls is still profitable, and he would not be here accepting lands from the King if he had enough back in Normandy. As for the cloister…'' Marjory's wrinkled old face beneath her linen wimple looked rather like that of an enquiring brown wren. ''Are you so sure 'tis what you wish for? I cannot see that life for you, my dearest lady, nor for Catherine, come to that. You should both be out in the world, with husbands and children.''

Lisette jumped up violently, upsetting the stool, as her emotions broke through the restraints she had placed on herself in the hall.

''Are you suggesting we allow ourselves to be given in marriage to further the mercenary ambition of a Norman?'' she demanded angrily. ''You know that is what will happen if we stay. Is that what you wish for us? To be at the beck and call of our enemies, meekly submitting to any rough treatment they mete out to us? You saw what happened to our mother, God rest her gentle soul. Is that what we must now look towards? I will never do so, *never*, I tell you! I would rather choose the cloister!''

''You may not be given the choice, my love, and 'tis of no use to frown and toss your head at me as you did when you were a wilful child. That will not serve you now. As for enemies—well, the fighting is over. William is King, the Normans are now our masters, and surely they are not all evil. The young man below appears reasonable enough.''

''Reasonable!''

''Bertrand seems to think so, and I would trust his judgement against any man's. Your father did also, remember—''

She was interrupted again as mention of Alaric fired Lisette's temper afresh.

''Marjory, I cannot believe I am hearing you aright!''

she cried, amazed at this change in one whom she had considered to be an implacable enemy of the Norman invaders. "Have you forgotten so quickly? Did my mother's torment mean nothing to you? Must we submit to the same? I would rather take my chances in the forest with the wolves! At least I wouldn't be tortured before I died."

"Oh, Lisette, do not speak so, I beg of you," cried Catherine, distressed, and crossing herself hastily against her sister's words. "Perhaps it will not be so bad. Raverre might be pleased to see us gone, as you said." She stopped, not knowing what else to say to placate the older girl, and Marjory patted her hand.

"It shall be as Our Lord wills it," she said, firmly. But she cast a worried glance at Lisette, who was pacing restlessly about the room.

The strain of the past months is beginning to tell, Marjory thought. The child is as taut as a drawn bowstring, ready to snap at any moment, and not in the mood to listen to rational arguments, or to exercise her usual good sense. And what will become of us if she enrages the Baron? What do we know of him, after all?

Then Marjory remembered the fleeting expression on Raverre's face when he had first seen Lisette. Perhaps the future would not be as bleak as they all feared. This thought, however, Marjory kept to herself. She quietly crossed the room to rouse Enide from her reverie in preparation for supper.

"At least we may sleep soundly in our beds tonight," she said placidly. "We are unlikely to be raided, with soldiers running about all over the place."

This calm observation had its effect and the angry colour faded from Lisette's cheeks, although she gave a short laugh and said ironically, "A comfort, to be sure."

However, she bent to give Catherine a quick embrace.

"Fear not, little sister. I am not about to throw myself off the tower roof, or do anything without a deal of thought." She straightened, her eyes fiercely determined. "I intend to see this through to whatever end may be in store."

Catherine looked cheered, but inwardly felt extremely uncomfortable for harbouring the thought that a cloister wouldn't suit her in the least, and that marriage, even to a Norman, would be preferable. Especially if he was young and good-looking, like Raverre. Guiltily realising what Lisette would have to say to such a rebellious idea, she set about helping Marjory tidy the room while they waited for the summons to supper.

Darkness had fallen before the knock came at the door and Lisette had long since tired of being shut away, not knowing what was happening below. She desperately wanted to find out more from Bertrand, but, much as she was tempted to slip out, she was more afraid of encountering a Norman soldier in the dark gallery and being marched ignominiously back to the solar.

She tried to comfort herself with the reflection that, until she had further speech with Raverre, it was useless to speculate about his intentions. But on one point Lisette was determined: that Enide, with her fragile hold on reality, should not be married off to a man who would never understand or sympathise with the reason for her mental withdrawal from a world that had become too brutal for her to bear.

Marjory had opened the door to the young man who had accompanied Raverre. He smiled and bowed slightly.

"I wish you good even, ladies, and am come to escort you to supper. I am Gilbert de Rohan, at your service."

He looked so young, no more than a year or so older than her own sixteen years, Lisette judged. And so pleasant, his cheerful smile lighting his dark eyes and lending boyish appeal to his frank, open countenance, that she was disarmed in spite of herself. Smiling faintly in response and taking Enide's hand, she preceded him into the gallery, leaving him to offer a gallant arm to Catherine.

The gallery was now well-lit, every sconce holding rushes bound together and dipped in mutton fat. Remembering how they had been forced to grope their way along the gallery in near-darkness for the past several months, Lisette could not help but appreciate the difference. My Lord Raverre was obviously used to living with a good deal of comfort, she reflected, and, as if her thoughts had conjured him up, he appeared at the foot of the stairs, waiting to take them into supper.

From the seeming chaos of the Normans' arrival, order had been restored. The hall was bright with the light of many sconces and the fire blazed merrily. Trestles had been set up along both sides of the great room, with wooden trenchers and drinking horns upon them, and men were taking their places on the benches as the servants waited for the signal to bring in the food.

Lisette barely glanced at Raverre as she entered, but as a sudden hush fell over the room his hand closed around her own, his grip sure and strong.

Tingling warmth raced up Lisette's arm. Her fingers quivered in his. Startled by such an intense sensation, she instinctively pulled back, only to find herself unable to free her hand without a futile struggle.

She was forced to suffer his bruisingly possessive hold across a hall that suddenly appeared endless. Forced to suffer being seated next to him at the high table on its dais across the end of the room. Forced to suffer the bold scrutiny of what seemed to be innumerable eyes.

"Must you behave like a conqueror parading his captives

before his men?'' she demanded in a goaded voice, casting a resentful look up at him.

Raverre returned her look with a faintly challenging expression, his fingers tightening briefly before he released her.

"Would you rather have walked across the room alone, giving my men an opportunity to do more than just look?" he asked mockingly, wondering with some amusement what her reaction would be if he told her that, by taking her hand, he was indicating to his men that he claimed her for his own.

Then as Lisette tossed her head and looked away, refusing to answer, he added, "Maybe some food and wine will sweeten your temper."

"I would rather starve," she muttered, but he had turned to seat Enide at his other side and her remark went unheard.

Gilbert, who appeared to be Raverre's lieutenant, politely handed Catherine to her place, seating himself next to her, and looking very much amused at her flushed face and downcast eyes.

Lisette noticed that Bertrand had been placed at the high table, and he gave her a reassuring nod as she struggled to regain her composure. In reality, after that first interested silence, Raverre's men had quickly gone back to their talk, but Lisette was too embarrassed and angry to realise this, and her own face felt as fiery as Catherine's. Her hand still smarted from the compelling pressure of Raverre's fingers, and she told herself that rage had caused that powerful reaction to his touch. She felt as if she had just been branded as his property. As though I were a slave, she thought furiously.

Then, as Raverre signalled to the serfs, sudden memory distracted her. With the hall echoing to the sound of Norman voices, Lisette almost felt like a stranger in her own home, and yet in another way all seemed so normal. As if she had gone back to a time when the hall was full of people she knew, sitting down to a good meal with the promise of entertainment to come.

As bread was laid before her and the noise of conversation rose again Lisette imagined that if she turned her head there would be her father sitting in his great carved chair, jovially calling to some neighbouring Thegn, or arguing with Bertrand about where the best hunting could be had on the morrow.

She felt unaccustomed tears prick her eyelids at the recollection, and blinked them furiously away. Never would she show her enemies any sign of feminine weakness, and to divert her mind she glanced around at the assembled company.

Four or five men were seated above the salt, and these, Lisette assumed, were knights, although their dress was as plain and functional as those of their men-at-arms. Only Raverre and Gilbert wore tunics of finer wool, and even these were without braid or fur.

My father wore garments more richly ornamented and of finer quality, she thought with scornful satisfaction. These creatures dress like the barbarians they are.

There were other differences. Used to the long hair and full beards of her countrymen, Lisette found the bare faces and close-cropped heads of the Normans a strange contrast. Most of the men were dark and stocky in build, unlike the fairer, taller Saxons; although there was the occasional reddish tint in the colouring of both races.

She found herself wondering if Raverre's unusual height and almost silvery-blond hair had their origins in a Norse ancestor, and was instantly annoyed with herself for feeling curious about him. What difference did it make where his forefathers came from? The Devil himself, probably.

These profitless ruminations were interrupted as Raverre began carving meat from the chunks of venison roasted and brought to the table on spits. Spearing several slices on the point of his dagger, he piled the meat on to their shared trencher. Lisette's brows rose. Was he such a favourite of William's that he could hunt the King's deer with impunity?

Raverre saw the question on her face and said conversationally, "We hunted quite successfully on our way here, my lady, as you see. Not knowing what supplies you might have had, and with so many of us, it seemed prudent to make sure of our first meal under this roof. William has granted me free warren—leave to hunt game in the forest— so tomorrow I'll send some of my men out to replenish the stocks of meat. With winter coming on, it will be needed, and you appear to have little in the way of livestock. That, too, shall be remedied."

Lisette, still smarting from her embarrassment, decided he was being critical. "Our stocks are low because 'tis hardly safe for anyone to go out into the forest," she said hotly. "Let alone a woman with no one to defend her should she meet a party of Norman soldiers. They seem to be everywhere," she finished bitterly, looking about her.

"Times change, my lady, and men must therefore change with them if they would survive," Raverre answered lightly, taking a hearty bite of the venison with strong white teeth, and gesturing for her to do likewise.

She felt as if the food would choke her, but, despite her earlier angry remark, Lisette knew no good would come from starving herself. With a few helpful swallows of wine she managed to eat a little of the roasted meat. Catherine seemed to be having no trouble, she thought forlornly, and was even beginning to shyly respond to Gilbert's gentle efforts to encourage her to talk to him. On Raverre's other side Bertrand was coaxing Enide to eat also, but, though her sister complied, it was as if she were a puppet, and he pulling her strings.

After watching them for a moment Raverre turned back to Lisette.

"Indulge my curiosity, madam. Your sister Enide, I am informed, is the eldest of you all; indeed she must be at least twenty years, by my reckoning. You are very much younger but are clearly in command here. In fact I could not imagine the Lady Enide in charge of such a household. How is this?"

Gladly seizing an opportunity to put him in his place, Lisette turned flashing dark eyes on him. "My sister once was as capable as any one of us until you Normans came ravaging and killing through this part of the country," she said fiercely. "She saw our home invaded and stripped of anything they deemed of value, but even that was not enough for them. They sacked the village, killing our bailiff, though he was an old man who was no threat to them, and attacking my mother and the priest when they tried to defend him!

"My mother was beaten and used like some common street harlot! By more than one of the vile brutes. She died from her injuries when they were through with her, and my sister witnessed it all. Enide was fortunate that in the end she had swooned away, and they thought her dead. They had no respect for the fact that we were women and defenceless."

Lisette's voice shook with the memory of that terrible day, and despite herself her lovely eyes filled with tears again. She no longer cared; let him see them and know what his countrymen had done.

Raverre watched her expressive little face closely, but

whatever pity or shame she had hoped to arouse did not show on his own.

"You speak as if you were not here when this befell."

"No. Catherine and I had been driving the swine out of the forest. When we came back—" She shuddered, unable to continue.

"*You* were herding swine?" His eyes narrowed intently. "In other words, there were no men here to do such work. What was your father about, to leave his family so unprotected?"

"King Harold needed all our warriors to stand against your Duke," she replied shortly, stubbornly refusing to give William the title of King.

Raverre looked rather sceptical at this explanation, but merely asked, "Did anyone hear a name spoken that could identify the attackers?"

Lisette was surprised into looking up at him. "What difference does a name make? They were Norman wolves. Savages! What else is there to know?"

"William is not in the habit of making war on defenceless women," he answered curtly. "I do not speak of the casualties that must occur in the taking of a town or castle when the occupants will not surrender without a fight, but from what you say this was not an attack sanctioned by the King. You must know he has spared every town which has opened its gates and acknowledged him Sovereign. When, pray, did this raid occur?"

"Last winter," she admitted reluctantly, knowing full well William had been back in Normandy at the time, leaving England to the joint stewardship of his half-brother, Odo, and William fitzOsbern, Earl of Hereford.

But, rallying quickly before he could pounce on this, she added sternly, "We are not the only family to be so bereaved. There are many such. As to towns spared, what of the villages burned to the ground, the people driven from their homes or killed? And you speak lightly about innocent lives taken in battle. Soldiers at least have chosen their manner of death. Do we women have such a choice?''

Deep down Lisette knew this was unreasonable. She herself would have been willing to fight to the death in defence of her home and people, and Raverre knew it. He smiled suddenly in genuine amusement, an unexpectedly boyish grin which completely banished the stern expression his face usually wore in repose.

''Lady, I think you would be a fierce opponent indeed, whether you were given the choice or not,'' he told her, a hint of laughter in his voice.

Lisette blinked up at him. Her comfortable conviction that anger had caused her acute awareness of Raverre was shattered. His smile was devastating.

His strong features could never look soft; though handsome, he also looked tough and rather dangerous, but the smile made him appear younger and more approachable. Lisette found herself so fascinated with the question of how eyes which had seemed forbiddingly cold could now hold so much warmth that she completely forgot to be incensed by his teasing comment.

Then a burst of laughter from a nearby group of soldiers broke the spell. Lisette flushed, glaring down at her unfinished meat, which had rapidly gone cold. Say something, she told herself. Don't let that Norman predator make such a fool of you with just one smile. But, before she could think of a reply which might convince Raverre that he hadn't managed to addle her wits, Gilbert decided to enter the lists.

''Why, my lady, Raverre speaks truly. You Saxon women are no mean fighters when pushed to it. Don't you know 'twas none other than a woman who stirred up the good townsfolk of Exeter to defiance of the King earlier this year? Earl Harold's mother, no less. And, though the nobles came out to surrender to William, she rallied the common folk and held out a further eighteen days.''

"Aye, I do know," Lisette retorted, venting her frustrated anger on de Rohan's unsuspecting head. "I also know that your so honourable King ordered a man's eyes put out before the town gates in an attempt to break their spirit!"

Gilbert retired, discomfited, with a rueful look at Raverre.

"Never argue with a woman unless you have all the answers," recommended his lord, and turned back to Lisette, who was seething again at this deliberately provocative remark.

"William regretted that action, you know," he told her quietly while she was still speechless. "When the town finally surrendered he not only spared the rest, but also refused to collect the tribute owing to him."

Lisette digested this statement. She wasn't sure of her reasons, but she didn't think Raverre was lying.

"And the Lady Gytha?" she asked after a moment, her interest in the fate of Harold's mother overcoming her wrath.

Raverre shrugged. "She managed to escape to Ireland with Harold's sons by his mistress, Edith of the Swan-neck. But she need not have fled. William would have treated her with courtesy."

"Perhaps she was thinking rather of what he might do to his rival's sons," remarked Lisette shrewdly. "They are her grandchildren, after all."

"Grandchildren or not, Gytha knew the risks she was taking, and still decided to make a stand against William, though there was little chance of success. She was willing to face death if necessary. And you, my lady, though you look like a fragile little rose, would have done the same. Even today, had you the manpower to back you.''

Lisette was reduced to fuming silence again. Fragile little rose, indeed! How dared he sound so patronising? Fortunately she was spared the effort of having to think of a scathing reply to this broadside by Gilbert, who, directing a question to Raverre across her as to the activities for the following day, unwittingly gave her the chance to catch her breath and calm down. Letting this enormous oaf of a Norman goad her into arguing with him would not help her cause in the least, she reminded herself sternly.

Catherine caught her sister's eye and gave a faintly guilty smile. Lisette smiled reassuringly back. It was no use chiding Catherine just for allowing Gilbert to coax her into talking to him. At thirteen, she was still young enough to make the best of the situation now that her immediate fears for their safety had been allayed.

Maybe life would be easier for me if I could do that also, thought Lisette, but I am not made like that. I have not chosen that my home be taken away from my family, and I and my sisters perhaps married off to men of whom we know nothing, except that they are our conquerors. This thought reminded her of her resolve to speak with Raverre about sending them off to a convent, but, looking at his preoccupied expression, she decided now was not the time.

Coward, she scolded herself. But, on the other hand, there was no need to antagonise him and spoil her plans. So, fragile or not, he thought her a worthy opponent, did he? Well, she might not be capable of bearing arms, but how many times had she heard Marjory say that a woman had more powerful weapons that could be used?

The only difficulty was, Lisette felt very conscious of her inexperience in the subtle mysteries between men and women, and she had an uneasy suspicion that using such weapons against Raverre would be rather like playing with fire. Just because he hadn't had them all killed, it didn't make him any less a barbarian in other ways.

Taking another sip of wine from the plain wooden beaker reminded her of the finely crafted glass goblets her mother had prized so highly, and which had been found needlessly smashed after the raid she had spoken of. The delicate brows met in another frown as Lisette cast a glaring look at Raverre from under her lashes.

She found that he had now abandoned Gilbert, and was watching her with a light in his blue eyes which instinctively put her on guard.

"Am I wrong?" he asked, returning to their sparring and wondering if she would deny his charge. "Although the battle is over and the English crown on William's head these past two years come Christmas Day, you would still fight if you could. Tell me why."

But, instead of the feminine prevarication he had half expected, Lisette leaned forward, gripping her hands together and looking him straight in the eyes. Her voice was low, trembling with the intensity of her emotions.

"Aye, the battles are over. You have conquered our land and taken our homes. You can even make us bow our heads to Norman rule. But know this! You will *never* conquer our hearts, our minds or our souls!"

The strange light in his eyes seemed to blaze with sudden fierceness. "Lady," he instantly replied, his voice soft so that only she could hear, "your soul belongs to God, and your mind is your own. But your heart—" his voice deepened to a note that made Lisette think of darkest night "—that indeed would be a prize worth winning."

Raverre held her gaze for a deliberate minute, before Lisette managed to wrench her eyes from his, breathless and shaken. What had he meant by such an answer? Win her heart? He could never do so.

"Never," she whispered, as if trying to convince herself, unaware that she had spoken aloud.

"Never is a dangerous word," Raverre murmured, still watching her closely, "when it becomes a challenge."

Ignoring the pounding of the heart in question, Lisette steeled herself to meet his eyes again. If Raverre meant to mock or torment her she would not give him the satisfaction of seeing how easily he had reduced her defiance to trembling confusion.

"I meant no challenge, sir," she said with spirit. "But you may amuse yourself by thinking so if you wish. There is no other entertainment to be had at present."

He smiled faintly, but surprised her by saying, "Then perhaps, if you have finished your supper, you and your sisters should retire again. My men have sat down to their first civilised meal for some time and I dare say some will drink far more than is good for them. You will be more comfortable elsewhere. We shall have plenty of time to speak further tomorrow."

Lisette rose at once, glad of the respite until morning, but her docility fled when Raverre also stood. She was tremblingly aware of him, tall and powerful by her side.

"Bertrand can escort us to our chamber," she said hurriedly. "I wish to speak with him before I retire."

"Tomorrow," Raverre answered with dictatorial brevity. And, giving Lisette no time to argue, he propelled her across the hall by the simple expedient of an unbreakable grip on her arm. They were followed meekly by Enide and Catherine.

"And to think I was beginning to wonder if you might not be such a tyrant after all," she muttered furiously as soon as they were out of sight and hearing of his men.

"Oh, did you not wish to leave?" he asked, mockery in the look he slanted down at her. "I thought you seemed somewhat eager to quit the hall."

"I was *not* running away!" she enunciated through gritted teeth, trying to free herself. Raverre didn't even appear to notice her struggles.

"No." The mocking gleam disappeared. "I think there would be little you would run from, my lady," he said thoughtfully, almost to himself.

Lisette stopped fighting him. It was useless, and she was only hurting herself anyway. The man was infuriating. Arrogant, domineering, mocking. And then, when she least expected it, disturbingly perceptive.

She was glad when he said nothing further, seeming to be deep in thought, but the silence only served to make her senses more acute. Why had she never before noticed the strangely fantastic patterns in the flickering shadows of the vaulted roof above her? Or the way the voices below seemed to echo off the walls in hollow cadences?

And why did her arm tingle from shoulder to wrist? A tingle that wasn't caused by pain, for Raverre was not hurting her, but by a rapidly uncoiling heat.

Lisette was relieved when they reached the doorway to the tower room. Now he would release her. But, as her sisters entered, Raverre held Lisette back a moment, casting that quick all-seeing glance around the room as he did so.

Like those of the hall and solar, the walls were bare stone, the floor wood, the single window narrow and unglazed. But the contrast between the empty chamber where he was housed and the small comforts of table, chests and bearskin-covered bed in this room was immediately apparent. Raverre made no comment, however, merely lifting an expressive eyebrow before returning his gaze to Lisette.

She looked small and defenceless, framed in the doorway. Her eyes were cast down, watching his fingers curled around her arm. Against her slenderness Raverre thought his hand seemed large, threatening. His hold slackened as a long-forgotten instinct, buried by years of fighting, stirred within him.

"Did I hurt you?" he asked softly.

"I probably don't have a drop of blood left in that arm," Lisette complained crossly, then looked up in startled indignation when he laughed. "You think that amusing?"

Raverre smiled. "One day I'll share the jest with you," he said, the warmth in his eyes seeming to reach out and enfold her.

Lisette had a sudden vision of herself out in the freezing winter snows with Raverre, and still feeling warm. She must be afflicted by moon madness. A sane woman did not have such thoughts about her enemy.

Then, as she stepped back, his expression changed. Became serious.

"You are safely guarded now, my lady," he said very low. "Sleep well." And, sliding his hand down to her own, he raised it to his lips, with a caress so brief that afterwards Lisette wondered if she had imagined it in her flustered state.

Then Raverre was gone, gently shutting the door behind him before she had a chance to answer, even had she known what to say.

Chapter Two

The morning dawned, with the promise of bright autumn sunshine and a good day for the hunt. Lisette rose early after a night spent in puzzling about Raverre's behaviour towards her.

His arrogant possession of her home notwithstanding, she had to admit they had been treated with more consideration than she'd expected from a Norman Baron. He had even permitted Bertrand to ride ahead yesterday to warn them of his arrival, when he could just as easily have taken the manor by sheer force of arms alone, precipitating the sort of panic that could quickly lead to disaster.

And there had been his unexpected gallantry when he had left her last night. Remembering the beautifully shaped, long-fingered hand wrapped about her arm, and the unexpectedly gentle note in his deep voice, Lisette had spent hours alternately hoping that Raverre was not the barbarian she had been convinced he would be, and worrying about his plans for herself and her sisters.

Feeling the need for some fresh air after such a restless night, she dressed in her worn homespun gown, and braided her hair. Then, quietly leaving the solar, she climbed the stairs at the end of the gallery, and opened the wooden trapdoor which led to the roof of the tower.

Lisette had often sought this retreat to be alone, and to look with pride over the green fields of her father's manors, although in recent months she had usually spent the time gazing anxiously along the empty road to the east for any signs of Norman activity. There was bustle aplenty now, however, as she watched the hunting party set out, with young de Rohan in the lead.

Full of early-morning high spirits, the horses paced through the gates, heads tossing, tails pluming; made even more skittish by the gambolling of several deer-hounds between their hoofs. They were making for the woods, west of the manor, but before the riders were out of sight among the trees Lisette saw them branch off on to the path she knew would lead them around the perimeter of the manor wood to the river and greater forest beyond.

Bertrand has given them directions, she thought, and was comforted to know that he was still within the castle.

Leaning over the battlements, Lisette could see one of the kitchen girls throwing grain to the hens as they clucked and pecked busily about her feet, while across the stream outside the stone wall of the bailey the smoky haze rising in the still air from the cluster of cottages indicated that the villagers were stirring, and would soon be about their daily business.

Despite the disagreeable sight of sunlight flashing on the mailcoats of the Norman soldiers moving about the bailey, the peaceful scene tempted Lisette to linger and enjoy the rare moment of quiet solitude. Then a movement from the kitchen shed caught her eye, and, seeing two maidservants emerge bearing a covered tray, she hurriedly returned to the solar, determined to learn as much as possible before she had to face Raverre again.

She found the wooden shutters flung open to let in the light, her sisters dressed, and Marjory directing the servants to lay flat wheaten loaves and ale on the table so they could break their fast. Lisette immediately pounced on the elder of the girls for news.

"Edgith! Tell me what is happening below? You have not been ill-treated, I hope?"

"Oh, no, mistress. Those of us in the kitchen have been left to our work. But there are soldiers everywhere, so Wat refused to send me alone with your bread and ale. And as we crossed the bailey I heard the Baron send more men into the village. I think Bertrand may have been with them, but I can't be sure. We didn't want to stay longer to watch in case they noticed us."

The girl looked worried, as though she had done wrong, and Lisette hastened to reassure her.

"No, of course you must not linger outside while so many soldiers are about. My Lord Raverre has said that no one will be harmed, but we can never be sure. I warrant you, he would soon change his orders if we put up even the slightest resistance." She frowned. "And we have not. So why would he send soldiers into the village?"

"If Bertrand is with them," soothed Marjory, "you need not worry, my love."

"How can I not?" Lisette began to pace, agitatedly waving away the morning ale Catherine was offering her. Her voice rose. "I have been given no chance to speak to the village folk, and you know Siward's temper. What if there is some misunderstanding and the soldiers use force? Oh, why did I not send Bertrand with a message last night? I should have insisted."

She started impulsively for the door, but Marjory, seeing her intention, grasped her mistress's arm, holding her back.

"And where, pray, do you think you are going, child?

Not to the village, if that is in your mind. You will sit down and break your fast like a sensible girl, and wait for Bertrand. What? Would you go rushing out heedlessly, only to be stopped at the gate, and that none too gently if my lord is not by. 'Tis why he asked you to keep to the manor, after all.''

"It sounded more like an order to me, and I will not be treated as a prisoner in my own home!'' retorted Lisette stormily, shaking Marjory off.

She was interrupted by a knock on the door and they all froze.

"Bertrand!'' uttered Lisette, recovering first and darting forward.

She flung wide the door. "Thank the Saints—you've—''

The words were choked off as her heart leapt into her throat. Raverre stood before her, filling the doorway.

His brows lifted quizzically at her greeting, but when Lisette said nothing further he strode past her into the room, the impact of his size immediately causing much the same effect on its occupants as a predatory fox in the dovecote. Enide paled and retreated to the window. Catherine and Marjory both dropped rather nervous curtsies. While the two maids, seeing him at close quarters for the first time, gaped up at him in mesmerised dread.

Acutely conscious of the unmade bed, and the various articles of intimate female apparel scattered about the room, Lisette turned in time to see open amusement on Raverre's face—due as much to the fact that he was conscious of looking singularly out of place in such an atmosphere of flustered femininity as to the paralysing effect his entrance had caused—and felt temper promptly replace her nervousness.

Kicking a flimsy shift out of sight under the bed, she

demanded, "Why have you sent soldiers into the village? Surely force is unnecessary when there is no resistance?"

Raverre's brows rose again at her belligerent tone. "'Tis not a matter that needs concern you, my lady," he dismissed curtly. Deliberately ignoring her outraged gasp, he turned to address Marjory with courteous deference.

"Mistress Marjory, please don't disturb yourself," he began, with a smile Lisette angrily considered was calculated to disarm the most ferocious guardian of innocent maidens. "I am merely come to ask your lady if she will accompany me while I acquaint myself with the manor. She will come to no harm, I assure you, and—" determined to try forbearance, he turned the smile on Lisette "—I believe she is the best person to advise me on what is needed to see the household through the winter."

Lisette could think of quite a number of people who had tried charm on Marjory when they wanted something—to their subsequent discomfort. Raverre was obviously not one of them. In stunned disbelief she watched as Marjory not only dropped another curtsy, but also smiled back as she assured Raverre that she trusted him to care for her lady's safety, and that she and Lisette would be only too glad to have the fast-dwindling stores replenished.

Lisette glared at her. So the man had charm. Hadn't she felt it herself last night when he had smiled at her for the first time, practically making her forget her own name? Oh, she had no doubt at all that he had melted many a female heart, but did Marjory have to be quite so—?

"Well, my lady?"

Lisette shifted the glare to Raverre. He knew he had managed to disarm Marjory, she realised as she saw the devilish gleam he directed at her. Well, she was not about to fall a victim to his smile a second time.

"*I* am not so easily distracted, my lord," she told him

scornfully, watching a lowering frown replace the gleam with immense satisfaction.

She added emphatically, "They are my people. I have a right to know. What have they done to be guarded and constrained? They will not resist you." A bitter sound of resignation escaped her. "We have learned that lesson well, I assure you."

Raverre felt his hold on his patience slip. Lisette might have admitted defeat last night, he thought with some exasperation, but she was still far from showing him the meek, unquestioning obedience that he would have expected from any other unprotected girl in her position.

He had been hoping that this morning she might begin to see him in a different light. Since he was more annoyed that Lisette apparently hadn't changed her opinion of him than by her determination to know what was going on, his answer came out more harshly than he intended.

"Very well, my lady. I have sent Bertrand with a message to the villages, to summon all the men of the estate here today to swear fealty to me as their overlord. The soldiers are there to make sure some do not think it worth their while to disobey."

No one replied to this concise statement for a moment. Indeed, Raverre's action was only to be expected, but Lisette's temper was not placated in the least by his highhanded methods. Were all her villeins and cottars to be herded to the manor like so much cattle?

"You certainly don't waste any time," she accused.

"To what purpose, madam?" Raverre frowned down at her. To hell with patience, he thought as he caught the full force of the hostile expression in Lisette's eyes. How could he be expected to cause her as little distress as possible, when she was looking at him as if he'd crawled out from under a maggoty log?

"And I want you and your sisters to attend me in the hall this afternoon also," he ordered brusquely, adding the final goad to her temper.

They had both forgotten the others in the room.

"Why? Do we have to swear allegiance to you also, my lord?" Lisette challenged. "You'll have to imprison and torture me first, and I still would not do so!"

"That could no doubt be arranged," he countered immediately, "but it won't be necessary. You hold no land or wealth under my protection."

This brutal reminder that Raverre now held the land, and that she was totally dependent upon him, struck Lisette like a bolt from a crossbow. Every muscle in her body clenched against the pain.

"Then you had best have your soldiers accompany you about the manor this morning," she lashed back blindly. "They will be more protection for you against your unwilling slaves than a woman!"

The moment the words were out Lisette regretted them. She did not need to see Catherine's look of shocked dismay at this blatant insult to bring her back to an awareness of her surroundings. Or to know that she might have jeopardised their chances of leaving for the safety of Romsey Abbey.

And, by the expression on Raverre's face, it was useless to hope that he had not understood her. He strode forward, his eyes threatening. Grasping Lisette's wrist without another word, he yanked her out of the room with breathtaking speed, slamming the door shut behind them.

"How dare you?" Lisette fumed, refusing to give in to the quick fear churning inside her at the thought of the punishment he might inflict.

Struggling to free herself from a hold that felt like an iron shackle, she demanded, "Loose me at once! I am not some slave girl whom you can handle in any way you choose! Let me go, or—''

She found herself pushed hard against the stone wall of the gallery and released, but before she could escape Raverre placed his hands on the wall on either side of her, bending until he could look her in the face. Lisette scowled furiously back at him, unconsciously rubbing her wrist, where his fingers had gripped her.

"Be still and listen to me!" he snapped, now as angry as she. "I had no intention, this morning, of doing more than coming to a better understanding between us, but make another remark like that and I'll take my whip to you first to teach you some manners.''

"A Norman, teach a Saxon manners?" she scorned recklessly. "Impossible!"

"Try me," he said with dangerous quiet. The eyes boring into hers were like chips of ice.

Lisette was silenced.

Raverre watched defiance and doubt chase each other across her face, before adding in a forceful voice, "It will be to your advantage also if we are not continually at loggerheads.''

For a moment longer they glared at each other. Then, just as Lisette was sure she was about to swoon through lack of air, Raverre straightened abruptly. With a surprisingly jerky movement he turned away to gaze down into the hall.

Lisette released her pent-up breath in a soundless gasp of relief. But it had not been Raverre's threat to beat her that had caused the constriction in her chest, or her pulse to flutter so wildly.

She had been completely dazed by the unexpected tremors Raverre's nearness had caused her to feel, hardly able to listen to what he had said for the sudden thundering of her heart in her ears. He had been so close that Lisette could see that his thick lashes were a darker gold than his hair, and how his eyes had deepened to slate with anger, before lightening again to their usual vivid blue as he controlled the emotion.

Like his men, he was clean-shaven, and her eyes had wandered in helpless fascination from the strong line of his jaw to the beautifully drawn mouth, saved from unrelenting toughness by the slightly fuller lower lip. Lisette had felt her own lips, only inches from his, part slightly as a wild unbidden urge to know the touch of his firm mouth on hers had swept over her, shocking her into mindless immobility that held her against the wall until Raverre was several paces away.

What was the matter with her? She was behaving like a witless fool. A *wanton* fool, she corrected herself savagely. How could she have wanted a Norman to kiss her? Lisette trembled. Did he know? Had he seen? How could she ever face his scorn? she thought despairingly, not daring to raise her eyes.

Her turmoil was unnecessary. Totally preoccupied with his own reaction to Lisette, Raverre had no idea of the emotions seething in his companion's breast. For in those few brief moments when they had been standing so close, glaring aggressively at each other, he had known with a sudden gut-wrenching flash of insight that this girl, this member of an alien and only recently conquered race, had to belong to him, was the other half of himself. As necessary to him as the very air he breathed.

Oh, yes, he had been aroused enough by her beauty and pride to decide coolly that she was the one he would marry. And he had admired her courage in defying him, despite the threat of punishment. But these feelings were wholly overshadowed, eclipsed, by the blinding knowledge that now he would kill for her. Give his own life for her. Even, should her rash hostility put her in any danger from William, defy his King and liege lord for her.

There was no gain in questioning why he should feel this way or how it had occurred so quickly. Used to sizing up the unexpected, Raverre recognised what had happened and as swiftly accepted it. But straight on the heels of this acknowledgement came the realisation that Lisette's own feelings were another matter entirely.

As he turned around at the precise moment that Lisette looked up at him, their eyes met and held. Raverre could see that she was still angry, but behind the anger in her wide gaze there was a startled new awareness of him as a man. It was enough for now. First, she had to learn to trust him.

Raverre held out his hand.

"Come, my lady. Let us cry a truce. You may not want me here, but surely your people's welfare comes first? I am told your store-rooms are almost empty, and I have the means to remedy that—with your help."

Whether knowingly or not, he had made the one appeal that would reach her. Lisette could not bring herself to apologise for implying that Raverre had wanted her to accompany him for his own safety. However, drawing on every ounce of dignity she possessed, she allowed her hand to lie in his for a brief moment.

"Then I will accompany you, my lord." Profoundly thankful that he seemed not to have noticed anything amiss in her demeanour, she gestured towards the stairway. "The store-room lies beneath the hall."

Raverre stood back, allowing Lisette to precede him down to the screen passage and the outer stairs. He had to resist the temptation to take her hand again as she swept past him. The large open area in front of the hall seemed at first sight to be full of men and equipment, but this soon resolved itself into piles of weaponry, and other trappings of war, being sorted and stored under the keen supervision of a weather-beaten sergeant-at-arms who had made short entries on a piece of parchment. Lisette heard his murmured voice as she passed.

"Heavy crossbow with one hundred bolts, eight ordinary crossbows with five hundred bolts, forty lances..."

The list seemed endless.

Sternly repressing the thought of the use to which the weapons had been put, Lisette refrained from comment, and produced the key to the store-room from the girdle about her slim waist. Pushing the big wooden door wide to let in as much light as possible, she entered the cool, dim interior of the room and stood back to let Raverre pass her.

The store-room was huge. Ambray Castle having been built for defence, the hall and solar were situated on the upper floor, reached by the narrow outer stairway. The more vulnerable area at ground level was used for storing goods needed by the estate and its dependants and stretched the whole length of the building. A wooden platform, half-way up one end wall, held the table and chair at which the manor steward did his tallying and issuing of supplies. Its dusty emptiness bore grim witness to the absence of both steward and stores.

Raverre wandered around in silence for a few minutes, lifting a barrel lid here and there, and looking into the recesses formed by the buttresses of the thick stone walls, while Lisette stood waiting. Then, as she made no move to follow him, he looked back questioningly.

"I already know of what we stand in need," she explained. She hesitated, but then decided to elaborate, hoping that cool civility would prove safer than other more heated emotions.

"We are not usually so ill-provisioned. Our land is fertile and well-farmed, but last season's crops barely survived destruction by your army, and the winter which followed was the hardest for many years. Then there were the homeless, and the hungry. I couldn't turn them away and so…"

Lisette looked about the echoing space and made a resigned encompassing gesture that went to his heart.

"Were there many strangers passing through?"

"Not many." She wondered if the question was quite as offhand as it seemed.

"No bands of men, returning to their homes perhaps?" Raverre persisted.

Lisette shook her head. "The nearer towns are north of here. South there is only the forest for mile upon mile, and few manors. Those who came were mostly women and children, or old folk seeking shelter for a night on their way to find kin in the villages that were not burned. And we had to feed them." She sounded slightly defensive.

"As I would," he assured softly, coming back to lean against a large barrel near her. He lifted the lid of another smaller keg and peered into it, drawing back immediately as the pungent smell of sheep fat and wood ash assailed his nostrils.

"What the hell—?"

A mischievous dimple appeared and was ruthlessly banished.

"'Tis soap," Lisette informed him in her briskest housewifely manner. "But don't worry, we scent it with herbs before we use it."

Raverre gave her a look from under his brows and replaced the lid of the keg firmly. "I'll make sure herbs are on your list," he remarked wryly, hoping to draw the fugitive smile from her, but Lisette considered his remark quite seriously.

"There's no need, I grow them in the garden here. Well," she amended, "most of what we use. But we'll need pepper, cloves, ginger, cinnamon, almonds." She ticked them off on her fingers, warming to the task. "And then candles; I should think three pounds each of large and small—"

"Stop! No more!" he begged laughingly, holding up an imploring hand. "You may order anything you please, but no more lists."

He thought he saw an answering flash of laughter in her eyes before she quickly moved out of the light, turning her head away to indicate the small block of salt in a dark corner.

"The salterer usually calls before now, so we may cure meat for the winter when the pigs are slaughtered, but he may not come this year, if the roads are not safe."

"I think he will. Now that William is back in England, travel is becoming safer, even for a wealthy man, let alone a humble salterer. And, speaking of William..." Raverre looked at Lisette gravely. "I want to know the true reason why this place was left so undefended that fitzOsbern's men could overrun it without hindrance, causing the destruction they did. If it happened last year, as you say, your men weren't still fighting for Godwinson."

This unexpected change from light-hearted banter to serious questioning threw Lisette mentally off balance.

"I...I don't know what you mean," she stammered, desperately searching for an answer that would satisfy him.

"This isn't the usual little wooden hall," he insisted, rapping his knuckles against the stone wall for emphasis. "You could have held off a raid easily, and renegade bands of mercenaries are not equipped for a long siege. What happened?"

Lisette looked down at the floor for inspiration. Finding none, she stayed silent.

"Your mother had allowed the men to leave to help in some uprising or another, hadn't she?" Raverre prompted gently.

That brought her head up again. "If you know that much, you know that I won't tell you where or who with," she replied shortly, confirming his suspicions. "Do you think I would betray my people? Besides, 'tis finished. They were beaten yet again. Isn't that enough for you?"

"Not quite," he answered coolly. At her dismayed look, he continued, "I don't intend to punish your churls for rebellions a year old, but after today you and they had better understand that, no matter what is going on elsewhere in the country, this is where they stay unless I order otherwise."

"*Is* there something going on elsewhere?"

"Don't sound so eager," Raverre commented sardonically. "I'm not about to be displaced. I merely referred to riotings of the kind that crazy forester stirred up last year. Edric the Wild, they called him, or some such heroic name."

A betraying flush crept up Lisette's face before she could look away again.

"So!" he exclaimed. "That's where they were. Miles away to the north. Do you realise your mother signed her own death warrant by her actions, and put you all in danger? Now you have no guard and barely enough men to work the fields."

At the thought of what might have happened to the delicate girl before him at the hands of some of the commanders with whom he was only too well acquainted, Raverre's voice became harsh. "My God! Anyone could have ridden in here and killed the lot of you before you'd had time to realise you were under attack!''

"Oh, do forgive us for wishing to be rid of a plundering army of butchers and murderers,'' Lisette retorted sarcastically, her eyes flashing at his criticism. "I suppose we should have permitted them to do as they pleased without raising a hand in our own defence. 'Tis not enough for the Duke of Normandy to kill or dispossess most of the Saxon nobles, wiping out an ancient and honourable race. Now he must destroy the lesser folk as well!''

"Don't judge the *King* by his brother or his friend,'' Raverre advised, emphasising William's proper title. "He has not returned to England only to quell rebellions, but to repair some of the damage done by Odo and fitzOsbern. 'Tis why he is quick to pardon. He is no tyrant, nor does he allow his men to loot and kill needlessly as they did.''

"Bishop Odo of Bayeux was still considered suitable to be left in charge,'' Lisette argued, unconvinced by this speech. "He is supposed to be a man of the Church, and yet I have heard that he leads his men into battle himself, and—''

The rest of her sentence was abruptly drowned out by sounds of violent altercation coming from the bailey. Raverre swung round immediately, but Lisette, recognising a familiar voice through the din, darted past him.

"Oh, dear God, no,'' she uttered, halting in the doorway at the scene before her.

In the gateway three of Raverre's soldiers were engaged in a fierce struggle to subdue the Saxon on that ground beneath them. Curses and the sound of blows rent the air as one of the soldiers was sent sprawling by a well-placed kick, and the victim leapt to his feet, his muscular arms brushing the other two off like bothersome flies. They circled warily around him, waiting for an opening, egged on by their fellows, who had gathered to watch the fight.

In silent contrast, several Saxons watched uneasily from the kitchen, casting angry glares at the Normans but too afraid to venture nearer.

"Siward, no!" Lisette cried out as she saw the young blacksmith advance towards the nearer of the Normans. She started forward, but Raverre's arm shot out and circled her waist, pulling her back against him.

She briefly felt the hard strength of his body against her side before he released her, ordering, "Get back inside," as he strode forward.

Ignoring this terse command, Lisette followed.

Siward had turned at the sound of her voice, and, ignoring the Normans at his back, stood proudly defiant, waiting for the order that would send him to his death. He expected no less.

Raverre didn't even glance at him.

"What in God's name happened here, Arnulf?" he demanded, addressing the sergeant Lisette had noticed earlier. At the note of impatience in his voice, the Norman contingent of spectators began to sidle unobtrusively back to their duties.

"I don't rightly know, sir," admitted Arnulf uncomfortably. "This young fellow came through the gates and the next thing I knew, Will there was lying in the dust and a fight had broken out."

Raverre shifted his cold gaze to the soldier who had felt the toe of Siward's boot.

"The smith started it, my lord," Will accused sullenly. "He came in and asked to see the Lady Lisette, and, when I told him she was engaged with you, he went for me." He sent a furious glance in Siward's direction. "Saxon scum!"

"That's enough!"

Raverre looked at Siward, who remained silent, not bothering to hide the contempt in his eyes.

"Oh, Siward, if you have any defence you must speak," cried Lisette, wondering at the blacksmith's silence. Siward usually had plenty to say for himself.

Raverre turned, frowning even more ominously.

"I told you—"

"Let her be, Norman," rasped Siward. As Raverre swung back to him, eyes narrowing, he added quickly, "I have only obeyed my lord, and now his daughter, but I will speak if I may talk to you alone." His eyes shifted briefly to Lisette and back to Raverre's face, which was suddenly intent.

"Your loyalty does you credit, even if your methods are somewhat foolhardy," Raverre remarked evenly. "But if you have anything to say I will hear it now. And so will the lady." His face was coldly implacable.

Lisette glanced from one man to the other as they eyed each other measuringly. One fair, possessing the natural arrogance of his class and the assurance of years of command; the other darker, pride blazing from clear grey eyes. Both big men. Equal in size, if not in status. And if Siward felt any awareness of their difference in station during the silent battle of wills he did not betray it, although a flicker of respect showed in his face for a moment.

"I came to see my lady," he finally answered. "To know she was safe. That dolt at the gate said you were amusing yourself with her, and asked if I wanted to wager how long I'd have to wait until you'd taken your pleasure. I hit him to shut his foul mouth."

Something dangerous blazed in Raverre's eyes for the merest instant, but it was enough to make Siward begin to look wary.

"'Tis the truth," he said.

"Holy Saints, Siward!" exclaimed Lisette, borrowing one of her father's favourite expressions. "What were you thinking of, to risk your life for such a trifle?"

Both men looked at her in surprise. She flared back at them, annoyed at their apparent lack of comprehension.

"Well? Do you expect me to fall into a swoon because of the boorish comments of an uncivilised Norman?" she demanded impatiently, momentarily forgetting that Raverre was one of them.

"No doubt you consider we're not worth the trouble," he snapped with heavy sarcasm.

Lisette felt a sickening chill. She must not anger Raverre now, when Siward was in danger. When that danger was acute. Though Lisette might consider Siward a freeman, to the Normans he was a serf who had struck a superior, and such a crime exacted severe penalties.

Raverre gestured to Arnulf, hovering near by. "Bind this man and put him in the guard-room. Use chains if he gives you any trouble. I'll speak to him later."

Siward's hands clenched into fists at this order, but something in Raverre's expression—a flash of acknowledgement perhaps, one male to another, of his defence of a lady's honour—gave him pause. He allowed himself to be led off, ignoring his recent adversary's triumphant smile.

Raverre turned as though to speak to Lisette, then, in a lightning-swift reversal of movement, whirled and swung his arm around, backhanding Will across the mouth with a blow that nearly broke the man's jaw.

Will crumpled to the ground, dazed, but still sensible enough to obey instantly when Raverre grated, "Get back to your post until I'm ready to deal with you."

He's a barbarian, after all, Lisette thought, dismayed to find how upset she felt. A fine tremor vibrated through her limbs as Raverre turned to look down at her. If he struck his own man, what would be Siward's fate? Or hers? She stepped back a pace, eyeing him warily.

His expression gentled instantly.

"You shouldn't have had to witness that," he said, so calmly that Lisette suddenly realised his violence had been coolly deliberate. Controlled. She began to feel less frightened.

"What do you intend doing with Siward?" she ventured huskily.

"I'm not going to have the fellow killed, if that's what is worrying you," he said at once. "But his insolence can't go unpunished. He answers to me now, and I won't have divided loyalties on my estate."

"Siward loved my father." Lisette's voice was low, and soft with memory. "He was found abandoned as a child after a battle against the Welsh. My father brought him here and had him taught the trade of blacksmith. No one else cared. Siward would have died for him."

"A touching tale, my lady. But he'll find himself dying for a lot less if he doesn't learn to curb that temper."

"He was only trying to defend my honour. Against *your* men."

"I'm aware of that," he told her sternly. "However, from now on the only person with the right to defend your honour is myself. Your people have already been told that if they have any complaints against my men they must come to me to have such disputes settled properly, and I intend to be obeyed."

Lisette opened her mouth to deny that Raverre had any rights at all where she was concerned, but he swept on regardless.

"And I have just bethought me of the priest you mentioned last night. You said he had been attacked. Is he dead also?"

"No," she said, worried again. What did he want with a priest if Siward was to live? "But he is old and ill abed at this moment."

"No matter. In the hearing of disputes he should also be present, and I wanted him to attend this afternoon's ceremony. However, I have no intention of dragging a sick man from his bed. Your presence should be reassurance enough for the serfs."

Raverre paused, watching Lisette intently, and, seeing her concern, reached out to take her hand. She was so small that it was like holding some precious, fragile ornament, he thought, trying to ignore the sensations that shot through him at the feel of her soft little palm against his rougher one.

"That is why I want you there this afternoon," he explained more gently. "I would not willingly cause you distress, but it will be better for your people. 'Twould also help if I had the deeds of land so I may easily match the men to their manors."

Better for you, too, thought Lisette resentfully, but unable to refute his statement. The last part of it registered and her faced paled. Her father's deeds, granted to their family almost two hundred years before by the great King Alfred himself, to be handed over to this intruder! This foreigner!

Raverre saw Lisette's face tense with suppressed emotion and tightened his hold, drawing her attention to the fact that he still possessed her hand. Trying unavailingly to free herself, Lisette glanced quickly around the bailey, further upset by the thought of how they must appear, standing close together in deep conversation, her hand clasped warmly in his, in full view of his soldiers and her serfs. And after what had just happened.

She got her hand free at last, fighting back tears of frustrated rage.

"You may have your deeds," she informed him bitterly, taking refuge in chilly courtesy.

"I'll need a list of the goods we lack also," Raverre reminded her. "I expect you would prefer to make it up yourself than have one of my men do it for you. And don't forget to include whatever feminine gewgaws you and your sisters may lack."

"That will take some time," she managed to say through the lump in her throat. "So I ask that I may be excused from dining in the hall." If she had to witness her erstwhile free churls becoming the bondmen of a Norman Baron then she would not willingly sit at table with him as well.

Raverre's keen gaze searched her face. There was a betraying shimmer in her eyes, a tender, vulnerable curve to her mouth. He saw her throat move as she swallowed hard. She had obviously endured enough for one morning.

"Very well." He tipped her face up to his with one long finger under her chin. "But you must promise to eat something. I believe I interrupted your breakfast." He smiled.

Lisette felt her knees shake. She forgot her distress. She forgot Siward. She forgot everything, except the need to escape from an abrupt premonition of danger.

"I have no intention of starving myself," she retorted, jerking her head aside.

Turning, she walked away. Quickly. Before she succumbed to an utterly perplexing temptation to change her mind and stay with him.

"Lisette! At last. We've been worried."

Catherine hailed her sister as Lisette stepped into the screen passage, forcing her to stop.

So much seemed to have happened since her earlier confrontation with Raverre that Lisette gazed at Catherine's anxious face for several blank seconds. When she did remember, however, she found herself recalling, in shameful detail, her disturbing reaction to Raverre in the gallery. She prayed Catherine wouldn't notice the heated flush staining her cheeks.

"'Twas no cause for worry," she assured the younger girl.

"You mean Raverre didn't punish you at all? But he looked furious."

Lisette waved a hand airily. "Aye...well...he issued a few warnings. But, as you see, I'm quite unscathed."

"Marjory said she didn't think Raverre would hurt you, but I wouldn't have been in your shoes for anything. Please be careful, Lisette."

"Marjory sometimes thinks she knows a great deal more than the rest of us," Lisette retorted, unaccountably annoyed.

Catherine's eyes widened in surprise at her sister's waspish tone. Lisette was immediately contrite. Really, what *was* the matter with her? First she had forgotten Raverre was an enemy to be kept at a safe distance. Now she was snapping at her innocent sister.

"Oh, Catherine, I'm sorry. I didn't mean to speak so sharply. It's been a difficult morning."

This vague excuse sounded lame indeed, but Lisette was reluctant to go into detail. The others would find out about Siward soon enough. At the moment she simply wasn't capable of dealing with the barrage of questions and worried conjecture that would arise as soon as it was known that Siward was being held prisoner.

Fortunately, Catherine accepted the apology at its face value.

"I'm going to help Marjory take an inventory of the

linen," she announced, moving towards the hall. "If Raverre is set upon bringing the manor into order we can burn the sheets that are beyond mending."

Lisette nodded, smiling absently at her sister as she started up the stairs. She had to hastily erase a sharp mental picture of Raverre's large body sprawled between fine linen sheets. What had the man done to her that she had such unsettling thoughts about him? Never before had she been so conscious of a man that he seemed to have taken up residence in her head. Wasn't taking over her home enough for him?

By the time she reached the empty tower room Lisette had concluded that it would be far better for her sanity if she spent as little time as possible in Raverre's company. Poised to defend her rights, and those of her people, from the moment of his arrival, she found it rather difficult to maintain this aggressive stance when her disordered brain couldn't decide what to make of him.

The words "arrogant" and "intimidating" sprang immediately to mind, but she also had to admit that she trusted him to give Siward a fair hearing. Lisette knew she should be thankful that Raverre hadn't ordered Siward's tongue cut out for his defiance, but, perversely, she decided that the overbearing, loutish Baron of her imaginings would have been easier to deal with.

She only had to look at her flustered reflection in the polished copper plate which served as a mirror to see she was a mass of conflicting emotions. No wonder she felt worn out. And the day had scarce begun.

Indulging in a fit of temper rather than useless feminine tears, Lisette relieved her feelings somewhat by slamming the door, marching across the room, and flinging open the chest which contained her father's documents with such

violence that the lid hit the wall and promptly fell down
again.

So much for temper. Lifting the lid more carefully, Lisette began to pull out the parchments bearing the ancient
royal seal of Alfred, firmly suppressing the strange tearing
feeling in her heart.

The number of churls and villeins in the bailey increased
as the day wore on. They stood in wary, sullen groups,
speaking occasionally to each other, greeting new arrivals,
but on the whole silent and suspicious.

Despite their rough homespun clothing and generally un-
kempt appearance, Raverre thought they looked healthy
enough. He leaned negligently against the store-room door,
his alert gaze moving over his new domain.

The compound formed a large square, with the hall oc-
cupying the centre. Raverre considered the stone structure
thoughtfully, having no difficulty in recognising the clean,
austere lines of its architecture. Somewhere in the not too
distant past there had been a marked Norman influence here
at Ambray. A mystery he intended to solve.

The kitchen sheds, to the right of the hall, were definitely
Saxon. Built of wood and thatch, they were snug and in
good repair. As were the ovens, if the smell of freshly
baked bread was anything to go by.

Raverre wondered if the tempting aroma would entice
Lisette to eat more than she had last night. In the clear
morning sunlight she had looked so damn fragile. And,
though her spirit belied her delicate appearance, Raverre
knew that even the most courageous spirit could not survive
forever against poor food, little rest and constant fear. The
lady would never admit it, but the truth was he had arrived
not a moment too soon.

Raverre moved his eyes on to the well, making a mental note to replace the fraying rope with a chain.

He had frightened Lisette when he'd struck Will. Raverre grimaced at the memory of huge eyes looking at him as though their owner expected to be struck also. But after threatening to use his whip on her he could hardly blame Lisette for being wary of him. She was not to know the threat was now an empty one. After all, when he'd uttered it Raverre himself hadn't fully realised he would do anything to protect her from such treatment.

He'd backed himself neatly into a corner there, from which only time would extricate him. And, if the rumours of strife in the north became a reality, time might be short.

Determinedly bringing his mind back to the manor yet again, Raverre mentally retraced his recent inspection. Behind the hall lay the midden, and in the opposite corner the small garden Lisette had mentioned, abutting on to a vacant dovecote. The cote would make a passable mews if he ever found the time to indulge in a little hawking.

The only other building in the compound was the stable, also standing empty, its roof looking badly in need of thatching, and the interior musty with the odour of disuse. It needed to be repaired immediately so the horses would have shelter for the winter.

Raverre's eyes completed their circuit of the bailey, returning to the gate as Gilbert rode in with his men.

The Saxons gave way before the advancing horses, some of their dour expressions lightening at the sight of the heavy game bags hanging from the Normans' saddles.

"A successful chase, my lord," murmured Bertrand, who had come to report that all were present. "In my Lord Alaric's day that usually meant a feast."

Raverre looked at him, humour in his steady gaze. "Then

let them feast by all means. Perhaps it will sweeten their oaths of allegiance.''

"There'll be no trouble, my lord. They already know you have treated the ladies with respect, and that you upheld Siward this morning against your own man.''

"Though he still languishes in the guard-room, and Will goes free?''

"It might encourage the hothead to use his brain instead of his brawn,'' remarked Bertrand unexpectedly.

As Raverre lifted a brow in half-startled enquiry he added, "We are not all rebels, sir. Don't be misled by the people's wariness. After two years of savage defeats they only want to be left in peace, to lick their wounds and rebuild their lives.''

Raverre nodded thoughtfully. "They share that ambition with the King. He wants England and her people to prosper. So do I.''

"And my ladies?''

"You refer especially to Lisette, I think,'' remarked Raverre shrewdly.

"Aye.'' The furrowed face of the old warrior softened. "I can't help but love her most. You might think her rebellious, but—''

"She will come to no harm with me, Bertrand,'' Raverre interposed quietly.

Bertrand looked up at his new master searchingly. Raverre's words could mean anything, but there was something in that level regard which said more than mere words.

Bertrand inclined his head. "I see de Rohan giving orders to have the meat smoked and stored,'' he said, his tone businesslike again. "I'll make sure that rogue Wat keeps some aside for tonight.''

He moved off, nodding civilly to Gilbert, who was strolling towards them. Gilbert's eyes went to the open door of the store-room.

"Anything?"

Raverre knew Gilbert was not referring to food. He shook his head.

"Nothing. Not here, at any rate. I've just been all over the place and there's nowhere an object of that size could be hidden." He made an impatient gesture. "I didn't expect to find anything. Whatever William's spies might have told him, I don't believe the ingot was ever this far west; certainly not here, where the local people are all well known to each other. We can search the villages and other manors, but I'm damned if I'm going to search the whole forest."

Gilbert nodded gloomily. "Perhaps it's been taken out of the country," he suggested. "To Wales."

Raverre shrugged. "I don't think there's been enough time since the robbery, but if you're right the Saxons could have taken it by any route. Why come all this way? When you consider the problems in moving it at all, let alone any great distance, I'd wager 'tis still close to Winchester."

Gilbert nodded agreement. "No wonder the fools couldn't run the country with any accord. They can't even pull off a robbery efficiently. Imagine taking Hardrada's gold ingot, and leaving a chest full of smaller, more easily managed treasures."

"Whoever was responsible obviously decided to take the gold, not realising the value of the other pieces. That ingot must be worth a King's ransom, and even a peasant knows the value of gold."

"Are you suggesting a serf is the culprit? It doesn't seem likely." Gilbert sounded sceptical in the extreme.

"Why not?" argued Raverre seriously. "We know the guards were drugged. Who else had access to their food and wine? Saxon serfs. But I didn't mean they were acting alone. Someone with more authority ordered that robbery. And it had to be someone who knew that Godwinson seized the ingot for his treasury after Harald of Norway was killed."

"And that William then took over the treasury after Hastings," concurred Gilbert thoughtfully. "It all comes down to wealth, doesn't it? The Saxons need it to finance their rebellions, and William needs it to pay off his mercenaries."

"Well, he can't parcel out land to that lawless scum he recruited from all over Christendom. Can you picture them setting up in baronial grandeur? They'd be at each other's throats in no time."

"Aye, by God," said Gilbert feelingly. "'Twould be Normandy ten years past, all over again."

Raverre looked grim. His uncle and two of his brothers had died in the constant battles of Baron against Baron, Knight against Knight, until William had finally brought unity and law to his warlike race.

Gilbert's eyes drifted casually across the bailey. "Speaking of fighting, the fellow at the gate is nursing a swollen jaw," he observed, only the faintest hint of a question in his voice.

"He can thank the Saints that's all he's nursing," growled Raverre, reminded that he had enough problems of his own.

Gilbert looked amused. "You sound annoyed. Your little Saxon causing trouble already?" he enquired.

"No, damn it! 'Twas one of her churls exercising a misguided sense of chivalry in her defence. All *she's* done is throw out insults, argue with me and disobey my orders! Why should I be annoyed?"

Gilbert laughed outright, and Raverre gave a reluctant grin.

"I wonder if William is having as much trouble with his policy of diplomacy and conciliation?" he asked ruefully.

"He's probably not dealing with a female," suggested Gilbert. "You'd better marry the girl tomorrow. I've noticed you never have any problems with a woman once you've bedded her." He saw Raverre's face change, and flung up a hand.

"I meant no disrespect," he added hurriedly. "For God's sake, don't hit me too—I wouldn't wake up for a week."

"How tempting," said Raverre silkily.

Gilbert hastened to change the subject.

"What have you done with the churl?" he asked. 'I don't see a corpse hanging from the tower."

"Nor will you. Diplomacy and conciliation, remember. Beside, the fellow meant well. I'm leaving him to cool his temper in the guard-room for a while. After that, we'll see. The manor needs a strong reeve, and he seems intelligent enough. Loyal, too, if I can win him over."

"Aye, but a Saxon," murmured Gilbert doubtfully.

"All the better. You've seen the results on other manors where Norman bailiffs and reeves have been appointed. The word 'churlish' is taking on a whole new meaning, and I don't want that happening here."

"It might work, I suppose, but what if the fellow uses his position against you?"

"Then you'll see a corpse hanging from the tower. But I don't think he will. If I'm right about him he might use his position to argue a decision, but not to incite outright rebellion."

Gilbert looked even more doubtful. Used to the instant and implicit obedience given to a Norman Knight from those below him—an obedience the Saxons seemed most reluctant to grant—he could only hope that Raverre knew what he was doing.

Raverre did know. But he waited until the last Saxon had knelt, placed his hands between those of his new master, and vowed to become Raverre's man for life and limb and earthly worship.

None of the Englishmen looked particularly happy with the situation, but there was no overt dissension. When all were done the villeins were ushered out to the bailey, where food and ale awaited them.

Lisette prepared to follow as inconspicuously as possible. Worried by Siward's continued absence, she was hoping to find out what had befallen him. She should have known better than to think she would escape Raverre's notice.

He halted her at the screen passage, his eyes scanning the list of goods handed to him earlier by Marjory. Despite his instructions to the contrary, Lisette had not included any personal requirements.

Raverre glanced over the shabby russet gown she wore, noticing for the first time the thinness of her homespun mantle, and the roughly made bone clasp holding it together at her throat. He wondered if she'd had anything new to wear since her father's departure two years earlier.

"I see you did not avail yourself of my offer to provide whatever you might need," he said, thinking of his mother's overflowing chests back in Normandy and mentally adding their contents to the list.

"My sisters and I need nothing from you," Lisette replied shortly. Then added with some reluctance, "Although I thank you for providing the feast tonight when food is still short."

Raverre regarded her somewhat ironically. "You Saxons are a stubborn lot," he informed her. "I'm not a tyrant, you know, and I see nothing to be gained by inflicting further hardship on a community that has already suffered enough. Although anyone seeing all these sour faces would be pardoned for thinking I had done just that!''

"Giving a feast is all very well," she flashed back, springing to her people's defence, "but you have taken something far more important to them. Their freedom!"

"Freedom to do what?" he demanded impatiently. "To run about the country like disorganised rabble, leaving their families to starve and perish at home?"

"But some of them were freeman farmers, or skilled tradesmen, like Cuthred, the carpenter. They attended the shire courts with my father, and could even attain the rank of Thegn if they acquired enough land or riches."

Lisette sighed, looking up at the uncompromising expression on Raverre's face. There was no hint now of the easy charm he had shown her earlier.

"Under Norman law they'll be no better than serfs," she finished dejectedly. "That is what they were fighting to avoid."

"They are *all* serfs," Raverre answered sternly. "Whether they paid rent for their land or did week work is irrelevant. They are now united in equal status and will be protected and provided for."

"Aye, little more than slaves!" she cried, knowing the argument was useless, but unable to stop. "Answerable to you for everything, no longer to have any say in their own lives!"

"Don't exaggerate," he remonstrated. "King, Baron or serf, none of us is truly free. Aye, the serfs will have to answer to me, but I then must answer to William, and he in turn to his conscience and to God for the repose of his soul.

"Besides," he continued, trying to make her understand, "even the free churls had obligations to your father while living on his estate. The only difference for those men is that they cannot leave without my permission, which is no bad thing. I have little sympathy for a system which allowed vassals to leave their master's family defenceless.''

Lisette glared at him in baffled fury. She could not in all honesty deny this claim, but determined not to let Raverre have the last word, she seized on another grievance.

''You must still regard them as slaves,'' she accused. ''Why else would they not be eating with you here in the hall?''

Raverre parried this shift in the argument without a blink.

''I know better, at this stage, than to mix Normans and Saxons at the same table while ale is being freely imbibed,'' he retorted. ''There'll be time enough for that when—'' He stopped dead.

''When we're all cowered into obedience?'' Lisette spat, her voice shaking with anger.

''No, I was *not* going to say that, you little shrew.''

Lisette turned away, struggling to hold her temper in check. ''Whatever the words, the meaning is the same,'' she said bitterly.

Raverre took a quick step towards her.

''Sweet lady!''

Lisette glanced back, startled, not quite sure if she had heard the softly spoken endearment. Raverre was watching her. The blue flames in his eyes burned so intensely that the breath caught in her throat.

''You *will* know me better,'' he stated with a calm certainty that shook her to the core. ''And when you do you will know I never want to see you cowed. I would not demean you so.''

The silence following this pronouncement seemed to Lisette to be fraught with promise. Or was it warning? She was incapable of answering. Incapable even of movement.

Pinned by Raverre's compelling gaze until he turned away, disappearing through the door into the gathering twilight.

Lisette slowly climbed the stairs, unaware of her surroundings until she found herself outside the solar door. There she hesitated, not wanting to face the others in her bemused state.

Walking to the end of the gallery, she sat down on the bottom step of the narrow staircase. Faint grey light still showed through the cracks in the trapdoor above her, but the sconces had not yet been lit and the gallery was growing dark. Wrapping her arms about her knees, Lisette gazed broodingly into the shadows.

Did Raverre really mean to know her better? Or had he deliberately diverted her because he had changed his mind about sparing Siward? If Siward had refused to swear allegiance with the other churls Raverre could well make an example of him. Lisette doubted that two instances of defiance would go unpunished. And yet, knowing this, she had weakly allowed herself to be distracted.

She sat up straighter. Where was her fighting spirit? Was she a spineless female who mindlessly allowed others to rule her life and dictate her actions? No, she was not! She would discover why Siward was still imprisoned, and would calmly demand an explanation from Raverre, instead of wasting her energy in useless arguments with him.

Lisette jumped up, full of determination. Then abruptly sat down again. If she ventured outside immediately she would probably meet Raverre before she got halfway to the guard-room. And the bailey would be full of men, Saxon and Norman. She didn't want a repeat of this morning's scene.

There was an alternative, however. At this end of the gallery, beside the stairs leading to the roof, there was a small alcove. To the casual eye it seemed no more than

that, but closer inspection revealed a steep flight of stairs
leading off at a sharp angle, descending into darkness.

A prudent man, Alaric had not relied totally on the almost impregnable position of the hall. At the foot of the
stone staircase a small door had been cut into the castle
wall. Barely four feet high and narrow, almost concealed
by a solid buttress, it opened out to the rear of the bailey.
It had been intended as an escape route for the family
should one ever be needed, but it would serve Lisette's
purpose as well.

Her hand was seeking out the postern key before the plan
was fully formed. It wasn't late. She would not be missed
for another half-hour or so. And it was extremely unlikely
that she would encounter anyone in the garden or dovecote
at this hour.

Feeling defiantly pleased with herself, Lisette waited until the glow in the hall brightened as more sconces were lit.
Night was not far away, but there would still be enough
light to see her way to the guard-room.

Trying not to think of the repercussions should she be
caught, she groped her way carefully down the stairs.
Something small skittered out of her path. Mice, Lisette
told herself firmly as she descended further. Dense blackness pressed about her, and she shuddered as her hand en-
countered a clinging spider's web. The staircase hadn't
been used in years, and she was glad to reach the last step
and open the door.

Slipping easily through the narrow opening, Lisette
straightened and glanced cautiously about. She was outside.
Now all she had to do was reach the guard-room unseen.
Not too difficult, surely, in the half-dark? And if Siward
was still bound there might not be a guard to contend with.

She had reached the corner of the tower safely, when a
distant footfall sounded. Heart pounding, Lisette strained to

listen, trying to determine its direction. Glancing over her shoulder, she saw a light at the far corner, and held her breath. The glow flared, then dimmed, and Lisette heard the faint closing of a door.

A soldier visiting the privy, she thought, relieved. But there was still the possibility of his returning to his post in her direction. She couldn't stand here forever, gathering courage. The knowledge that she was still afraid underneath her bravado spurred Lisette to action.

As the light flared brightly again she darted quickly around the corner. And ran straight into a large, solid object.

Lisette gave a startled squeak, the impact almost knocking her off her feet, but the object reached out to grasp her arms, holding her upright. It was obviously human.

"Do I have to bind you hand and foot to keep you inside?" demanded Raverre.

The resigned amusement in his voice carried a clear message to Lisette's brain. She recovered from her fright in a hurry.

"You knew I was going to come this way," she cried indignantly. "How?"

"Never mind how," he commanded, releasing one of her arms and marching her back to the small postern so fast that her feet barely touched the ground. He held out his hand imperatively. "The key, if you please, my lady."

"I'm going to have another bruise on this arm," she accused, trying to delay the inevitable.

His punishing grip didn't slacken this time. "The key!"

Lisette glared at him, but the effort was wasted in the darkness. Fumbling with her free hand, she extracted the key and slapped it into Raverre's open palm. His fingers closed over hers.

Then, before Lisette could object to his familiarity, she was abruptly pulled into his arms.

There was one second of frozen amazement, then Lisette began to struggle. Raverre's arms tightened immediately. One large hand pressed her face into the soft expanse of wool covering his chest, effectively stifling her instinctive protest; the other arm became an iron band across her back, holding her clamped against him. She could feel the steady rhythm of his heart. In spite of her helpless position, it was oddly reassuring.

"Is all secure, sir? I thought I heard—"

The moment Lisette identified the soldier's voice her rigid muscles eased. She felt Raverre draw a breath to speak as he turned his head slightly.

"It's all right, Arnulf. I was just checking here myself. All's well."

"Aye, sir."

Lisette heard the privy door close. Another one, she thought. It must be all that ale. A giggle rose in her throat at the notion, and she wondered if she was becoming hysterical.

Then her unexpected flash of levity died away as Lisette realised that Raverre's swift action had shielded her from the disparaging gossip which would have ensued had the sergeant seen them together in this dark, secluded corner.

At the same moment she also realised that she was still clasped against Raverre's broad chest, and that he showed no inclination to release her. The wool caressing her cheek was the only soft thing about that chest, she mused vaguely. Beneath the smooth fabric was solid muscle and bone. His arms were hard also, but a subtle change seemed to have occurred. Lisette still felt their strength, but now they cradled her.

She shivered, wondering how it was possible to feel both protected and threatened at the same time.

"You see what may happen when you wander about after dark," he murmured above her as she stirred against him. "I was here to protect you from Arnulf, but who is going to protect you from me?"

Lisette's hands came up instantly to push against Raverre's unyielding frame.

He released her slowly. "I'm glad you now understand why I asked you to remain indoors," he growled. But he was unable to summon up real anger. She had felt so right in his arms. If they hadn't been out in the open—

Mortified heat swept through Lisette's entire body. Dear God, she had willingly remained nestled in Raverre's embrace, when he had only been intent on punishing her. She had even been thankful for him. It was ten times worse than this morning in the gallery. At least then he hadn't known of her feelings.

And she had forgotten poor Siward *again*. Although now, Lisette suddenly discovered, her fears for Siward had been laid to rest while she had been held fast in Raverre's arms. She decided not to question this startling conclusion.

"What if you'd run into some yokel with a skinful of ale under his belt?" Raverre continued, unlocking the postern. "Little fool."

Shame and gratitude vanished.

"I have no reason to fear my people," she declared loftily. "Besides, 'tis your own fault! I was concerned for Siward, and you wouldn't tell me anything."

"You didn't ask," he stated irrefutably. "But, as a matter of fact, I was coming to tell you what had passed. 'Twas how I knew you weren't in the castle. After seeing this door earlier, it didn't take long to realise what you were up to." His voice held amusement again.

"Very clever," she muttered.

Raverre opened the door, bending almost double to peer up the stairs. "Ingenious. I was up on the tower roof this morning, and I didn't even notice this stairway when I returned."

He glanced down at Lisette, unable to see her face clearly, but sensing the unspoken question hovering in the air. "Well?"

"Well, what?" She sounded extremely grumpy.

Raverre grinned. "Aren't you going to ask me about Siward? Nicely, I hope," he couldn't resist adding.

She ground her teeth.

"Tell me what you've done with Siward, *please*."

"I've appointed him manor reeve."

"What?" Lisette gasped, instantly forgetting her wrath. "Then he must have sworn fealty to you. How did you manage it?"

"By giving him a choice. Become my man or leave the estate. Without a safe conduct, however, he would have had to remain free for a year and a day before he could seek out work in a town. I told him I didn't think that feat beyond his capabilities."

"Merciful Saints!" uttered Lisette faintly. "What did he say to that?"

"He didn't believe me at first. He thought I'd have him killed if he refused to swear allegiance."

"Many would."

"Whether he was dead or merely gone, I would still have been without a blacksmith," Raverre explained with calm practicality. "And I also needed a reeve whom I could trust to speak as fairly for me as for the Saxons. Your Siward struck me as a man of his word, once he gave it."

"Aye," Lisette said quietly. Of all the actions she

thought Raverre might have taken, she had never considered this one.

But his leniency didn't make him less dangerous, she reminded herself. Siward was no doubt trying to make sense of the fact that, though he was no longer free, he had been given a position of some authority, but Lisette knew the blacksmith had been shrewdly manipulated. In fact she was beginning to realise that, despite his daunting appearance, Raverre was no uncivilised savage relying on brute force to attain his goals. There was a shrewd, far-sighted intelligence at work behind that cool, tough façade.

"Where is Siward now?" she enquired.

"Feasting with the others, I expect. And, as your own supper is probably growing cold, you had best return to your chamber before Marjory sends out a search party."

"Very well," she acquiesced guilelessly. "May I have my key back?"

Raverre threw back his head and laughed, startling Lisette again. She had not thought him capable of such a light-hearted gesture.

"No, you may not have your key back, my little innocent," he chuckled. "But it was a nice try."

"Ohhh! You…"

Rendered speechless, Lisette spun about and stalked to the doorway. Her pose of injured dignity was rather impaired by the fact that she had to bend considerably to negotiate the low entry.

As Raverre closed the door after her the muttered words "overgrown bully" floated down the stairway. He grinned back, pocketing the key as he walked away.

Life in England certainly promised to be entertaining.

Chapter Three

From her perch in the window embrasure Lisette could see the serfs making their way through the wasteland on the far side of the manor fields. It was the time of gathering bracken and acorns to see the swine through the winter months, and she thought wistfully of days spent roaming the woods, enjoying the last of the mild weather before winter's icy gales swept down from the north, blanketing the countryside with snow.

Surely it couldn't hurt to venture into the garden, if only for an hour. After Raverre's swift discipline of Will yesterday Lisette doubted if she would be accosted by any soldiers, and she would take Finn with her.

She stepped down into the room in time to hear Catherine complaining that if she had to set another stitch her fingers would well nigh fall from her hands.

Obviously restlessness was becoming a problem here, too.

"And how will you fare when you have a family to mend for, if you don't mind your stitching now?" scolded Marjory, brandishing a torn gown belonging to her obstinate charge.

"I shall give it to my faithful old nurse, of course," said Catherine airily, skipping nimbly out of Marjory's reach.

"Let me mend the gown, Marjory," interposed Enide's soft voice.

They all jumped, as if a ghost had suddenly addressed them.

Enide smiled gently at them and took the gown from Marjory's limp hold. "You know Catherine will make it look worse, and you will have to do it all over again. 'Tis not good for your eyes, such close work." She sat down on the stone seat in the window embrasure recently vacated by her sister, and took up her needle.

This assumption that life was going on as usual sent a shiver down Lisette's spine. Was it possible that Enide really didn't comprehend what had happened? If so, the sooner she was safely in her aunt's charge, the better. Lisette resolved to speak to Raverre about the matter that same day.

"Come, Catherine," she said firmly, turning to her rebellious younger sister. "If you scorn to sew, perhaps you would like to help gather some herbs. 'Tis time I should be making simples for the winter ills that will no doubt beset some of us. You should learn how to mix a soothing salve for chapped hands, or your faithful old nurse won't be able to wield a needle."

Armed with this innocent excuse to be out about her business, Lisette ignored a sharp look from Marjory, and cautiously opened the door. An empty gallery greeted her, but sounds from below indicated that preparations were well in hand for the main meal of the day, and she could see Raverre conferring with a number of his men. He was standing before a table covered with parchments, which, even at that distance, she had no trouble in recognising as her father's deeds of land.

"Dividing the spoils of war already," she muttered to herself. "We shall be next, no doubt."

Raverre could not have heard her, but, as if sensing her presence, he raised his head and saw Lisette watching him. Murmuring an excuse to the others, he crossed the hall to intercept her as she and Catherine reached the door to the outer stairway.

"You are going out, my lady?" he asked, politely enough, but Lisette heard the underlying steel in his voice.

"Not far, my lord," she answered with deceptive sweetness. "Just to the garden to gather some herbs. For tisanes and salves, you know." As he considered this she added, "Who knows, you may even need one yourself some day?"

Raverre's hard eyes lit with appreciation at this sally, but before he could answer his attention was diverted by the appearance in the doorway of the village priest.

Father Edwin was meant to be a fat, jolly little soul, comfortable in his faith and a comfort to his flock, but the tensions of the past few months had made him a thin, nervous creature, who devoutly hoped he would not be called upon to do anything more courageous than give solace to the womenfolk of the castle in the face of this latest invasion.

The last time he had overcome his fear of violence to intervene on behalf of those in his care he had been rendered unconscious, and had lain senseless for three days. On returning to consciousness and learning of the tragedy which had overtaken Lord Alaric's family he had been almost as much in need of consolation and gentle treatment as Enide.

There was no help to be looked for here, Lisette knew, but she was fond of the old man, and greeted him warmly, enquiring about the ague which had kept him in his bed for the past week.

"'Tis nearly cured, my lady," he answered, plucking nervously at his coarse woollen gown as he glanced up at Raverre's imposing figure. "I am only sorry that I have not been able to conduct the Mass for you, but I will do so tomorrow, you may be sure. 'Twould never do for you not to receive such comfort on the Sabbath. No, no. You may come to worship with an easy mind."

"We shall be glad of it, Father," said Lisette gravely, "and will give thanks for your recovery."

An awkward silence fell, and she turned reluctantly towards Raverre, feeling as if somehow she betrayed the memory of her father by making Raverre known to Father Edwin as the new lord of the manor. Nor, she realised, was Raverre going to make it any easier for her by introducing himself. As her eyes met the relentless expression in his Lisette knew that he was aware of her feelings, and was going to force her to acknowledge aloud his baronetcy, or appear ignoble in defeat. And that she would never be.

Her head lifted, and her voice was steady as she said, "Father, you will not have met Baron Alain de Raverre. He is the Lord of Ambray now." She deliberately used the Norman pronunciation of Raverre's name, and had the satisfaction of seeing a flash of surprise in his eyes before he greeted Father Edwin courteously.

"Your arrival is most opportune, Father. I would be pleased if you would join us at dinner so I may have speech with you. I am sure you will be most helpful in reassuring your people that I am not the Devil incarnate, and that their lives will be disrupted as little as possible, the times being what they are."

The little priest's worried expression lightened somewhat at these words, and he happily nodded his acceptance. Lisette, meanwhile, seeing that Raverre would be occupied for the moment, seized Catherine's hand and made good her escape into the bailey.

The garden in its sheltered corner was warm in the morning sun. As the girls gathered herbs in the fragrant air Catherine, with a sidelong look at her sister, observed carefully, "You seem not to be so angry this morning, Lisette. Did the night bring good counsel?"

Lisette looked up with a rueful smile, remembering how she had stormed into the solar last night, still reviling Normans in general, and Raverre in particular.

"Have I indeed been so bear-like, sweet? I am sorry. 'Tis not that I am angry so much as afraid, I think, and the anger keeps the fear at bay. But I should not be speaking of such things." She squeezed Catherine's hand. "Here I am, trying to be a good example to my little sister, and all I can do is bleat about fear like a frightened lamb."

"I was afraid, too, Lisette," admitted Catherine, her round blue eyes solemn. "The other day, I mean. When Raverre first came into the hall he made me think of a great, fierce warrior. But later, when I saw his face clearly, I was no longer afraid. I don't know why exactly, because he *is* a Norman. But he has been kind to us, after all. He reminded me a little of the master mason King Edward sent to our father when he was planning the manor. Don't you remember? He carved a little wooden horse for me; I think I have it still. He and Raverre are not like those others who came, are they?"

Lisette warmed to her sister. She had become so used to being the strong one—taking care of everything and trying not to worry the others by letting her own fears show. And all the time she had overlooked the strength and quaint woman-child wisdom that Catherine possessed beneath her urchin behaviour.

"You must try to forget those others, Catkin," she said, reverting to her sister's childish pet name with quick affection. "They were evil men, and will meet their punishment in death, even if they escape it in life. Marjory was right. The fighting is over and we must learn to make the best of our lives while we still have them."

She belatedly realised that this sound advice could as well apply to herself, and hastily dismissed the thought. 'Tis different for me, Lisette told herself stubbornly. She still had an uneasy feeling that somehow, in some way as yet unknown, Raverre posed a threat to her.

"Will we make the best of our lives in a convent?" asked Catherine doubtfully. "Would it not be better to stay here?"

"Oh, Catherine, I wish we could with all my heart. But even if we were to be married, we would have to leave. As soon as Raverre is settled he will be looking to make alliances with powerful families, with us as pawns."

"He might not," said Catherine hopefully. "You'll be needed here, Lisette. No one knows the estate as you do. Why, you've even been presiding at the manor court."

Lisette jumped up. "Blessed Saint Catherine, for sending that thought to your head!" she exclaimed. "I'd forgotten all about the court. No wonder Father Edwin is here—'tis Saturday. And we'll be lucky to finish dinner before Edric and Wulf are upon us."

"Are they still squabbling over that strip of land? I thought—"

"What else? Here, take these herbs to the store-room, sweet. I must think what to say to Raverre.

"If he lets me speak," she added to herself as Catherine left the garden, her willow basket laden with the sweet-smelling harvest.

The fact that she had been holding the weekly court hear-

ings for two years might not impress Raverre at all, Lisette
suspected, and she began to consider the best way of convincing him to let her speak for the two contentious churls.

It was Finn's low growl of warning that first alerted Lisette to danger. Glancing up, she was startled to find Siward's foe of yesterday standing a few yards away. The
garden was enclosed by a low stone wall, and Will was
effectively blocking the way out. They were also, Lisette
saw, quite alone on this side of the compound.

Unable to think why the Norman would seek her out,
she ventured a careful question.

"Have you come to summon me to dinner? I didn't mean
to linger so long, but the garden was so pleasant, and—"

"I'm no serf to be sent on such footling errands," he
interrupted. His voice was rough, the English heavily ac-
cented but understandable.

"Well…even so, it must be quite late. I should return to
the hall."

Lisette took a step forward, but her resolve faltered when
Will stood his ground, scowling at her under heavy black
brows.

Even if he'd worn a more amiable expression, Lisette
thought he would not be an attractive specimen of Norman
manhood. His blunt-featured face was coarse, almost brut-
ish, his eyes small and malevolent. The ugly bruise across
his jaw didn't improve an overall impression of vicious-
ness. He was only of average height, but still bigger and
stronger than her. Lisette felt a swift stab of fear, and struggled to control it, as Will spoke again.

"Not so fast, wench. Because of you I'm to be sent back
to the army. I don't like that."

He moved closer. Lisette backed away, watching him.
She wondered if she could manage to scramble over the
wall before Will caught her, but, at the moment, he seemed

more interested in talking. Perhaps he was only trying to frighten her. Surely the man wouldn't risk actually hurting a woman who was under his lord's protection?

"I thought I'd have a nice little post here," he went on. "Some guard duty, plenty of ale and women. No more chasing after you Saxon vermin through sodden, overgrown forests." His eyes narrowed speculatively, and a vindictive smile crossed his face. "You owe me something for ruining my plans, and I intend to see you pay up."

"Don't you come near me!" Lisette said fiercely. "I'll scream!"

Will chuckled. "A wrench with spirit. All the better. Scream all you like. I'll enjoy it. Everyone's in the hall at their dinner. You won't be heard."

Lisette felt the blood drain from her face as a helpless, nauseating weakness seemed to grip her limbs. Her nerves felt stripped raw by the menace in the Norman's slow advance.

She continued to retreat before it until she came up against the dovecote.

Will laughed evilly, but halted, still some feet away. He was relishing her fear, Lisette realised. He licked his lips. His little coal-black eyes glistened. Fingers tipped with dirt-encrusted nails reached for her.

"Raverre will punish you again," she cried desperately, shrinking back. If that filthy hand touched her she would be sick.

Finn stirred restlessly at the tense note in her voice. His low continuous growling became a full-throated snarl, his lips drawn back over fangs that could tear a man's throat out as easily as a deer's.

Will's eyes turned ugly.

"We'll get rid of that cur first," he snapped, drawing his sword and coming forward in a rush.

Lisette screamed. She flung herself to her knees, throwing her arms around the wildly barking dog. Her action stopped Will in his tracks. Unfortunately, it also prevented Finn from attacking.

"Raverre will kill you if you touch us," Lisette cried over the commotion Finn was making.

"Are you going to tell him after you've been despoiled, bitch?" Will shouted back. "I think not. Even if he does have some crazy idea of handling you Saxons with velvet gloves, you'll have no value to him after I've had you. He'll hand you over to his men."

"I don't believe you," she retorted bravely. "Raverre would never do such a thing."

She didn't have time to wonder at his confident judgement of a man she had known for scarcely two days under less than ideal circumstances.

"You're absolutely right, sweetheart," said Raverre's cool voice from behind Will.

As Will slewed around Lisette slumped to the ground in relief, her head drooping against the dog's bristling fur. Dimly she realised he was still barking deafeningly, but she couldn't seem to find enough energy to calm the animal.

"Finn, sit!" commanded Raverre quietly. The clamour subsided instantly. Finn sat.

Lisette raised her head, staring at Raverre in amazement. He stood with legs braced apart, his sword drawn, its point resting lightly on the ground between his feet. He looked relaxed, but his glittering eyes never left Will's face.

At the same moment Will broke into a torrent of Norman abuse directed at his commander, and Lisette's amazement became horror as the enraged man suddenly turned and lunged at her, sword out-thrust.

Raverre leapt to intercept him, bringing his sword around in a widely swinging arc. His swing deflected Will's attack, and, carried by the fierce momentum of Raverre's powerful arms, the blade sliced through mail and flesh, straight to the heart.

A silence that could be heard fell over the garden. Lisette rose shakily to her feet, her horrified gaze fixed on the shapeless bundle that, only seconds ago, had been a man. She wished she could look away, but she seemed to have lost control of her senses.

Raverre wiped his sword on the grass and sheathed it. Stepping over Will's body and blocking it from Lisette's view, he took her hands. They were ice-cold and trembling. Her eyes lifted to his, wide and fearful. He deliberately made his voice hard.

"Take Finn and return to your chamber. Don't speak of this to anyone. No one at all, do you understand? Go back inside and act as though nothing has happened. Here, use the postern."

He produced the key and folded her fingers over it. Lisette barely registered its presence.

"But—"

At her faltering protest, Raverre's control snapped. If he hadn't just saved her life Lisette would have shrunk from the rage blazing in his eyes. She didn't notice how pale he was beneath his tan.

"Damn it, girl, just do what you're told for once!" he grated harshly. "I don't want you involved in this. Isn't it enough that I've had to kill one of my men because you wilfully disobey my orders?"

Hot tears sprang into Lisette's eyes. "I didn't mean...I didn't know..." Her voice broke.

"Don't bother with lame excuses. Go!"

The tower room was quiet. Marjory and Enide sewed, Catherine was reading, and Lisette sat by the brazier, her

outward composure giving no hint of the turmoil within.
She had even managed to eat her dinner, while pretending
an interest in Father Edwin's gossipy conversation. Although, after one look at Raverre's forbidding expression,
she had been glad to retire immediately after the meal.

Now, however, her first shock at the violent events in
the garden had worn off, and righteous anger was beginning
to take its place. It was hardly her fault Will had decided
she was to blame for his banishment to the army. But even
if she had been the innocent cause of the man's resentment,
her mere presence in the garden didn't justify his wild attack on her life.

Lisette had just reached this conclusion when Bertrand
entered through the open door. She looked up enquiringly.

"You are summoned to the hall, my lady. And my lord
wishes you to hand over to him any documents you hold
pertaining to the manor."

Lisette rose. "He has the deeds of land. What more does
the man need?" she demanded, not disposed to be co-
operative.

Bertrand gave her a straight look. "I think you would be
well-advised to accede to this request, my lady. Raverre
has already had enough to deal with today, and he's in no
mood for more."

"Why, whatever do you mean, Bertrand?" queried Catherine idly from the floor, where she was turning the pages
of a book borrowed from Gilbert.

Lisette had been too preoccupied to enquire how her sister and young de Rohan had arrived at such good terms so
quickly.

"Nothing out of the way," Bertrand replied, neatly side-
stepping the issue of Will's untimely demise. "Merely that
he told Siward he would hear petitions today from those

who had suffered losses in the past two years.'' He turned to Lisette.

''He'll need your help with that, my lady. Father Edwin knows the men, but he hasn't been running the estate. Raverre seems bent on learning the life story of every serf who has ever been born on the place, from what I can make out.''

These words reminded Lisette of Edric and Wulf. Loath though she was to face Raverre again so soon, she could not abandon her people. Delving into a chest, she produced the household accounts and manor rolls, which she had kept for her father since well before his death at Hastings.

The memory of his pride in her ability to manage the estate whenever he was absent gave her courage.

''Then let us help, by all means,'' she told Bertrand.

He gave her an approving smile. Marjory beamed.

Curbing an impulse to tell them that their attitude bordered on traitorous, Lisette marched out of the room.

Raverre sat at the high table, flanked by Father Edwin. As Lisette laid the rolls of parchment before him he glanced up, his face hard.

''Thank you, my lady. You may return to the solar.''

Lisette's eyes widened in surprise. ''But—''

''I doubt if you can help with these matters, and I have no time to further indulge your taste for discord.''

Lisette flinched at this merciless reference to the morning's catastrophe, but recovered quickly.

''How do you expect to—?''

''My God, are you still arguing?'' Raverre demanded angrily, coming menacingly to his feet. He had looked less dangerous when facing Will. ''Get back to your proper place!''

Lisette gasped, recoiling as if Raverre had struck her. Even knowing he was still angry, she had not expected to be dismissed so cruelly, as if she were of no account, a mere woman, incapable of doing more than run a household.

She barely noticed Bertrand's look of consternation as a tremor of rage shot through her at the full significance of Raverre's words. But as Bertrand would have spoken out Lisette made a savage gesture, silencing him. With shaking hands she unfastened the girdle of plaited silks at her waist, which held her keys.

Wrenching it from her gown, she flung girdle and keys across the table with such force that Raverre had to stop them from tumbling to the rushes on the other side. He immediately looked thunderous, but Lisette forestalled any outburst.

"There, my lord," she bit out. "Now you have it all!"

Not waiting for a reply, she turned and walked swiftly out of the hall.

Her rigid control lasted along the gallery and up the stairs to the tower roof. Not until the trapdoor was safely shut on any pursuit did Lisette's façade of composure crumble, and, trembling violently, she allowed herself to fully realise what had happened.

After her struggle to keep the estate well managed she was not to be consulted, not to be permitted to speak for her people. Dismissed. Rendered powerless. All taken from her in less time than it took to think about it.

Oh, it was lost indeed. Her home, the happy life she had known with her parents gone forever. Swept out of her reach by circumstances over which she had no control; by people who, until several months ago, had not even known of her existence.

Already strained to breaking-point, the dam holding back her turbulent emotions crumbled. The green and gold view of meadow and forest blurred before Lisette's eyes as the tears she had never allowed to show fell in an uncontrollable stream, and she sank to the ground against the sunwarmed stone parapet, sobbing out her heartbreak.

The distant sound of the trapdoor slamming echoed through the hall. Father Edwin was obviously trying to find the right words to smooth over the incident, but Bertrand turned to Raverre, letting his disapproval show.

"That was ill done of you, my lord," he said roundly.

Raverre already irritated, flashed a frowning look at him. "What the hell does that mean?" he asked impatiently. "God's blood, this is not a woman's business. The household, aye, but not all these records of tithes, bond days and such. How could a young girl hope to fathom them? And without a steward, or even a bailiff to aid her? Has she bewitched you all into thinking her the master here?"

"Not master, no, my lord. But more than capable of husbanding such an estate while the master is absent. Do you think I can be of help to you here? I have been away more often than not, and am a soldier besides. What do I know of lands, villeins and the rest? Who do you think has struggled to keep the estate together these long months? Not I, nor the good Father here, but yonder maid."

The frown didn't lighten, but Raverre looked thoughtful.

"I think my lady would have explained all to you fairly had she been given the chance," went on Bertrand. At a sceptical look, he insisted, "Whatever she may feel, she has been taught to value justice and honest dealing."

"You think Lisette would deal fairly with me? she would be glad rather to see a sword in my heart, I think. Your lady has not yet laid down her arms."

Father Edwin tut-tutted deprecatingly at this, and shook his head. He was ignored.

"Had she been asked she would have surrendered the

castle to ensure peace for her people,'' argued Bertrand. ''Believe me, I know her well. 'Tis being given no choice that she cannot stomach. As to these documents—'' he fanned them out on the table ''—see for yourself. They mean nought to me, but you can say if they are well kept or not. Even so, you will still need her to explain those small day-to-day matters that must arise on any large estate.''

At this inauspicious moment a commotion at the door heralded the arrival of the claimants for the contended strip of land. Wulf, a choleric fellow with an air of self-importance, had brought along two of his fellows for support, all of them well primed with ale imbibed at their noon meal. And, not to be outdone, young Edric, a fair boy of tender years but stubborn will, had dragged his shrinking mother and sister along.

Various uncomplimentary exchanges had taken place as they had made their way from the village, and Wulf's temper was already running hot. He had been prepared to listen tolerantly to the lad before putting his own case. After all, the boy's father had fought by his side at Hastings and the two families were long-time friends, but the accusations of unfair claims had worn his patience thin.

Dishevelled beard bristling, he strode forward, already launching into a belligerent speech, hoping he would win his case before the new lord quite caught the gist of the matter.

Wulf was not to know, however, of Raverre's preoccupation with Lisette. Before he had completed the first sentence he was silenced with an imperious gesture. Raverre rose to his feet again, his awesome height and build also silencing Edric, who was protesting as volubly.

''Is this how your lady conducts the manor court?'' Raverre enquired disparagingly. "Or am I especially privileged?"

Even Wulf looked somewhat shamefaced at this. His whiskers quivered as he chomped his jaws up and down, but he prudently remained silent. Seeing his foe effectively subdued, Edric eyed Raverre with cautious approval.

Satisfied that order had been restored, Raverre turned to Bertrand.

"Tell these people to wait," he instructed. "If they have a case it had better be put to their mistress as well as myself. And, Father, I would like you to stay. I may have a further request to make of you."

Bertrand looked very thoughtful at this cryptic remark as he seated both parties at a safe distance from each other while Raverre disappeared up the stairs after Lisette. It looked as if the new master intended the girls to continue here for a while. Of course, the manor needed a mistress, and who better than a daughter of the house, but exactly what position did Raverre have in mind for her?

Lisette had not thought she could have cried so many tears as the pent-up emotions of the past year seemed to flood out in an unending, hopeless stream. It was only when she heard the trapdoor open that she made an effort to stem the flow, but she didn't look around.

"Go away, Marjory," she choked. "I must be by myself for a while more."

The only answer was the closing of the door and a firm tread. Startled, Lisette looked up to see Raverre watching her, his brows coming together in a quick frown as he saw how upset she was. Springing to her feet, she turned her back again, taking a few steps away from him. The tower roof seemed suddenly to have become very small.

"Come to gloat over your conquest, my lord?" she attacked huskily, brushing a hand across her eyes in an attempt to hide the evidence of her distress.

"No, my lady," he said seriously. Then a hint of laughter came into his voice. "Rather, 'tis your conquest. I have just been taken most soundly to task by Bertrand for my brutal treatment of you. And straight after we were interrupted by two quarrelling parties who, no doubt, will expect you to amend all, even though 'tis I who passes judgement. What else was I to do but come in search of you?"

Forgetting her reddened eyes and damp lashes, Lisette turned to face him.

Raverre leaned carelessly against the battlements, swinging her girdle in one hand. The sun glinted on his fair hair, turning it to gold, and his eyes held an expression of mingled laughter and appeal.

Lisette eyed him uncertainly, not quite trusting this sudden light-hearted manner after his biting anger.

"Are you asking for my help?" she queried hesitantly.

His expression sobered as quickly as it had lightened before, and he regarded her with a strangely considering look.

"Not only help," Raverre said slowly, knowing he must tread carefully. If his lady once suspected that he had become her slave when they had looked into each other's eyes yesterday, Raverre knew he would have lost any hope of winning her love. She would use his own feelings against him at every turn, and he could not fight them both.

Under his steady gaze, Lisette began to feel very wary. "What is your meaning, then?"

"An estate must have a strong master," he began. "I could bend the serfs to my will, but 'twould not serve my purpose to have hateful looks and rebellious mutterings follow me every time I go about my own lands. 'Twas not for conquest and loot that I came into England with William."

As a look of disbelief crossed her face he said vehemently, "I speak truth, lady! William did not win himself a crown merely for the love of conquest. He wishes to make England a great part of his lands, to have some of his sons settle here and call their line English. 'Tis what I want also, and to this end, on learning that Lord Alaric had left three daughters orphaned and still unwed, I formed the intention of taking one of you to wife, that the estate would have a mistress known to the people, that our children would unite Norman and Saxon, and mayhap the period of reconciliation be reached sooner."

"Oh, did you so intend?" Lisette interrupted indignantly, unable to keep silent any longer. "And no doubt we were to have no say in the matter at all. Take one of us to wife, indeed! Just to make your way easier! I could wish we were all ill-favoured or...or already betrothed, if only to confound you. Or did you think we might be willing to fall in with these careful plans?"

"Before I came here I knew nothing of you, lady, except what Bertrand let fall on our journey, which was little enough, God knows. In truth, I'm surprised you and Enide are still unwed. You must have had suitors aplenty, being the daughters of a landed Thegn and beautiful into the bargain."

This last was said with a caressing look that swept Lisette from head to toe and back, making her colour rise with renewed indignation at his frank appraisal. Then, as Raverre's eyes lifted to her face, she glimpsed a flash of hot desire, swiftly veiled, and her heart lurched.

Men had looked at her before now with warm appreciation, but never had Lisette felt as though her flesh had been seared wherever their eyes touched. She felt hot all over.

"Enide was betrothed years ago," she said hurriedly, despising the nervous quiver in her voice. "To the son of one of my father's friends, but he was never heard of after Hastings."

"And yourself?" Raverre persisted, having seen the quick fear in her eyes and deciding her temper was the best cure for it. She would certainly reject the other remedies he had in mind. "Don't tell me men weren't falling over themselves to court you."

Lisette's eyes flashed fire again at this. "My father needed me here to oversee the manor. He was often absent. He said I was as good as any son would have been."

"So I have just been told," Raverre answered, smiling slightly at her vehemence and the obvious implication. "I did not mean to belittle your work, my lady. At home my father has many sons to fill his shoes; my mother and sisters would not be able to manage without them."

This mention of a home and family made Lisette look at him searchingly. "So you have sisters, my lord," she said slowly. "How would you feel, I wonder, if they were in the position I and *my* sisters now find ourselves?"

He looked taken aback for a moment at this unexpected challenge, then shrugged.

"'Tis the fate of all women, I suppose, to be under the authority of one man or another—a father, a husband." The caressing gleam came back. "If it must be a husband my sisters would soon become reconciled, even to an invader, if he treated them well. A woman thinks only of her home and family, after all."

"Not all of us are so compliant," Lisette answered hotly, too annoyed at this sweeping statement to notice his expression. "We Saxon women are used to more respect and independence, even under the law. We may inherit land, a widow cannot be made to remarry against her will—'' She stopped abruptly.

"None of you is a widow," Raverre pointed out gently.

"I suppose you think that will make it easier for you?" Lisette challenged. "And which one of us did you have in mind, pray tell?"

Raverre smiled teasingly again. "Which one? Well, let us consider a moment. By rights I should choose the Lady Enide, being the eldest, and your father's heiress—"

He got no further.

"You could not!" Lisette exclaimed, missing the lighter note in his voice in her sudden anxiety. "Oh, my lord, you must see how it is with her. After what she has suffered she could not become any man's wife. Oh, how can I make you understand? She could not endure it; I think her mind would be lost forever. And Catherine is but a babe, a child."

Forgetting her pride and her resolve never to yield in her fear for her sisters, Lisette impulsively flung herself on to her knees before Raverre in a sudden, graceful movement which caused her loose gown to billow about his feet. Her dark blue eyes, the long lashes still wet from weeping, pleaded with him as her hands clasped unconsciously.

"Oh, my lord, I beg of you, of your kindness, let us retire to the cloister. We could go to my aunt at Romsey Abbey. She would take us, I know."

As he looked down into the sweet face upturned to him Raverre had to repress an almost overwhelming desire to sweep Lisette up into his arms and hold her close. Ardent words rose in his throat. Trust me. Let me care for you. Let me love you.

What was he thinking? He'd frighten her away completely.

His hand clenched on Lisette's keys in abrupt impatience at having to move so slowly with her, and he cast the girdle aside. Then, leaning down from this great height and gently grasping her arms, he drew her to her feet, releasing her immediately, but retaining the memory of the feel of silken hair against his hands.

He had to clear his throat before he could speak.

"So," he said gruffly, "you would go on your knees before me, if only for your sisters' sake. But consider. Do you truly believe the Prioress would take all three of you without a dowry to enrich Holy Church? I do not; maybe you know her better."

Lisette looked away, unable to deny this assumption, but a ray of hope gleamed. "She would at least take Enide without a dowry, I think. My sister was named for her; she is her godchild. If my aunt knew how Enide has suffered she would be glad to accept her into the Order." She turned solemn eyes on Raverre again. "I ask nothing for myself; and for Catherine only that you wait until she is full grown before giving her in marriage. But for Enide, I beg you, send her to my aunt."

The opportunity to make her his own was there, and Raverre seized it without hesitation. "And if I grant this, would *you* come to me, a willing wife?"

Chapter Four

"*Me?*" Lisette squeaked in horror, aghast at the trap she had set for herself.

"Well, if Enide is to be cloistered, and Catherine too young, who else is there?" Raverre asked, not quite able to keep the note of satisfaction out of his voice. "Besides, you would retain your position as mistress of your home, which any fool can see means a great deal to you. Your sister would be safe under your care until she reaches marriageable age, and—I promise not to beat you if you behave yourself," he finished with a wicked grin.

That grin laid the flint to Lisette's temper.

The frustrations of the past two days rushed forcibly to her mind, mingling explosively with the fact that she could not see another way out of the dilemma facing her.

Her home had been taken. Her life had been threatened. She had been lashed by a tempest of rage and grief. And, as if that were not enough, she was now conscious of a *frisson* of excitement deep inside which, illogically, upset her more than all the rest. And the cause of this tumultuous storm of emotion stood there grinning at her! It was too much.

Lisette launched herself at Raverre like a spitting wildcat, aiming a blow at his face with her open hand.

"How dare you smile like that and mock me so?" she cried furiously. "How dare you?"

As swift as a hawk striking, Raverre captured her hands. Holding them behind her back with one of his own, he imprisoned Lisette in a close embrace which lifted her easily from the ground. His other hand encircled her slender neck, forcing her head up. But, though rendered helpless, she stared defiantly into those blue eyes not six inches from her own.

The teasing light slowly died out of Raverre's eyes as they gazed at each other, to be replaced by that intense, steady flame. Lisette was suddenly acutely aware of her heart racing wildly against the strong beat of his, and the feel of his hand on her throat. And heat. The wind blew coldly up here on the tower, but she felt surrounded by his warmth. She wanted to struggle...she wanted to melt...

She could not utter a word.

"What now, my fierce little Saxon warrior?" he asked softly. "If I loose you, will you stay quietly by my side, or try to scratch out my eyes?"

His gaze lowered to her mouth. Her lips parted, and Raverre felt her tremble in his arms. He managed to resist temptation. "Well, what shall it be?"

Lisette finally located her voice again. "Would you force me to wed you?" she asked shakily.

Raverre at once lowered her to the ground, setting her free except for the grip he kept on her hands.

"I would rather not drag you before a priest," he answered with a slightly crooked smile. "But you will be my wife. And, though you know but little of me, you can see the advantages as well as I."

"Aye, but marriage..." she faltered. How could she tell

him that the very word conjured up a frightening vision of the power Raverre would hold over her? And yet he already held that power, she thought confusedly.

But marriage! She would belong to him. Would have to lie with him. A man she hardly knew. An enemy.

Desperately casting about in her mind for some alternative, Lisette had to acknowledge that she had very little choice. True, she could refuse him, but what then would become of them all? Even if, by some miracle, they managed to escape from the manor and discover the way to the Abbey, Lisette had seen enough of Raverre to know they would not get far before he caught them. And what if he took revenge on her people?

On the other hand, if she married Raverre Enide would be safe, and Catherine also, for a time. Besides, these things could not be arranged in a hurry. Some other idea might yet occur to her, but for now...

Lisette bent her head. "Very well, my lord." Her voice was so low that Raverre barely heard the words. "I will marry you."

He felt her hands quiver in his, and tightened his hold. "I swear you will have no cause to regret that decision, sweet lady," he said gently and, releasing her, stepped away.

As Raverre stooped to retrieve her mistreated girdle Lisette tried to still her shaking limbs. Not regret her decision? She was already regretting it. By what ill-begotten quirk of fate was she now committed to marrying a Norman? She must have been mad to agree. Hasty words of repeal hovered on her tongue.

They died unspoken as Raverre straightened and smiled down into her eyes. He held out her girdle, but as Lisette would have taken it Raverre suddenly captured her in the circle of his arms and Lisette felt his hands, warm about her waist, as he fastened the silks.

He seemed to be taking an inordinate amount of time to replace the girdle. Why did his nearness disturb her so? She could hardly breathe. This close, he seemed enormous. She felt overwhelmed by his size and intimidating strength.

As the familiar weight of her keys settled at her side Lisette stepped back nervously, bumping into the parapet. Raverre quickly closed the distance between them, lightly clasping her arm.

"Careful," he murmured. "I don't want you falling over the battlements." He felt her tense under his hand, and added softly, "Don't fear me, little warrior."

Lisette glanced up. Those ice-blue eyes held so much warmth. She could almost believe there was nothing to fear from him. Almost.

"Did you have to kill that man?" she blurted out, surprising herself. She had sworn to herself never to broach the subject.

Raverre also looked surprised, but he didn't appear disturbed by her question.

"Of course. Didn't you hear what Will was saying?"

Lisette shook her head. "He spoke too quickly for me to follow."

So, my little dyed-in-the-wool Saxon speaks some Norman, thought Raverre. He let this go for the moment.

"Will accused you of luring him into the garden by witchcraft," he told her. "'Twas why he attacked you, trying to redeem himself with me."

Lisette stared at Raverre in sudden dismay, realising the extent of the danger Will had posed.

"Aye, you see now, don't you? Had I merely prevented Will from killing you he would have publicly accused you to explain away his actions."

"But you didn't believe him. Did you?" she asked tremulously.

"Of course I didn't," he answered gently. "But some of my men might have been more superstitious. They'd have been within their rights to demand your trial; something your people would have protested violently against, I'm sure. We don't need such a disaster."

"Oh." Lisette's voice was very subdued. Well, what other answer had she expected?

Raverre grinned. "And I didn't fancy seeing you drowned to prove your innocence, troublesome wench though you are," he added teasingly.

Lisette flushed. He hadn't read her mind, had he? She hurried into speech again.

"Then how did you explain...?"

"Will's death? My men thought he'd attacked me in anger at losing his post. It helped that we'd clashed previously over his attitude to the Saxons, even before we arrived. But he'd sworn to obey me, and was a good fighter—"

Raverre broke off and shrugged. "The best thing you can do now is to forget the whole incident."

Good advice, he thought wryly, knowing he'd never forget the chill that had gone through him when Lisette had screamed. Or the sight of her crouched at Will's feet, trying to protect her dog. That sight alone had nearly made him strangle Will with his bare hands.

"Come," he said. "'Tis cold up here. We had best return to the hall. I fear our combatants will not have wearied of the delay; however it may have cooled their ardour somewhat. Tell me what it's about."

Lisette gathered her scattered wits, trying not to feel too grateful for Raverre's sudden businesslike approach.

"Last month Edric's father died and he laid claim to the land, as was his right. But Wulf has been accusing Edric of neglect. His land adjoins Edric's strip, so 'twould be convenient for him to add it to his own holding.'' She looked up at Raverre appealingly. ''But Edric has no other skill with which he can support his mother and sister. He doesn't want them reduced to landless slaves, and Wulf has enough for his needs.''

''From that explanation, I presume you've allowed Edric to keep the land. You realise, of course, that can't continue. I remember his record of bond work from yesterday. He's no more than a child. He'll never be able to plough three acres in spring, haul a load of wood and work two days each week as well as tend his own land. No doubt it *is* neglected. And did he pay the merchet due on taking up his inheritance?''

''Do you Normans ever think of anything but money?'' Lisette demanded, immediately put on the defensive. ''Edric will grow older and stronger, and his family can help him.''

Raverre ignored this. ''The sister looks of marriageable age,'' he said thoughtfully. ''Her mother could come here to the manor. All we have to do is find something suitable for the boy.''

''But they'll own nothing if they lose the land.''

Lisette began to worry. This was exactly what she had feared. She saw the serfs as separate beings, part of the estate, yet individuals. But would Raverre? ''Edric has his pride, you know.''

''His pride won't feed and clothe his mother and sister,'' Raverre retorted grimly. Then, as Lisette turned her head away to gaze frowningly into the distance, he gave a reluctant smile.

''I think we've argued every time we've had a conversation,'' he remarked, trying to lighten the atmosphere. Lisette didn't respond.

The smile reached Raverre's eyes and he stretched out a hand to cup her cheek, gently forcing her to face him again. "Won't you trust me to come to a fair decision in this?" he questioned softly, his voice deepening to a husky caress as his hand savoured the silky texture of her skin. Not daring to test his control by moving a step closer, he murmured, "You can, you know."

Lisette's heart seemed to stop beating the moment Raverre touched her face. Unable to move away, she gazed up into his eyes, held captive by the warm understanding she saw there. A most unaccountable urge to let him take over the burden of command swept over her.

She was barely conscious of her agreement to support whatever decision he made. The staggering idea invading her head that Raverre was just the strong, protective male her intensely feminine little heart had once dreamed of drowned out everything.

She was only distantly aware of Raverre lifting the trapdoor, of descending the stairs, of returning to the hall. But, when Wulf and Edric stood before the high table, Lisette began to worry that she had let her people down rather badly.

Fortunately for her conscience, this feeling was short-lived. Further upsetting her preconceived notions about him, Raverre decreed that Edric must relinquish his claim, but would be taken into the household as a page, to be eventually trained as a squire should he prove loyal and diligent. Astonished delight replaced the shock on the boy's face, and he turned glowing eyes on Lisette, obviously thinking he had her to thank for this unlooked-for elevation in status.

Sobered by the lengthy delay in presenting his case, Wulf was equally amenable to the edict that the land would become his on condition that a marriage be arranged between Edric's sister and one of Wulf's brawny sons. In this way

Alfrida and her mother would be provided for, without being regarded as objects of charity.

So thankful was Lisette for a solution which seemed to please everyone, and which, she admitted privately, would not have occurred to her, that she had a sudden flash of understanding of the more positive side to Norman feudalism.

Then her emotional seesaw dipped the other way again as she heard Raverre announce their betrothal. Taking her hand, he led her up to Father Edwin.

"Father, your lady has done me the honour of granting me her hand in marriage. Would you hear our betrothal vows?"

"God save you, my son. 'Tis a day for betrothals, I vow. A happy day for Ambray."

But, despite these transports of delight, the little priest avoided Lisette's eyes. Under the sconce lights a light film of sweat gleamed on his tonsure.

Father Edwin can no more refuse Raverre than I can, she thought. And who can blame him?

She started nervously as Raverre took her hand. He looked into her eyes.

"I, Alain of Raverre, plight thee, Lisette of Ambray, my troth, as God is my witness." He crossed himself.

Steadying herself with a deep breath, Lisette repeated the vow. But her voice faltered at the end, suddenly aware, as she saw the various speculative glances from those present, that a way out might not be so easy to find after all.

She was further dismayed to hear Raverre ask a startled Father Edwin to prepare for their marriage the following week. The priest drew Raverre aside.

"Next week, my lord? Surely such haste is unseemly."

"Of course 'tis unseemly," protested Lisette, following them. She glanced up at Raverre. His eyes held a strangely wary expression, but it was gone so quickly that Lisette thought she must have been mistaken. "Please, my lord. We don't...I hardly know...I need more time," she stammered.

"This is not the time for long betrothals, my lady," Raverre said curtly. "Neither of us needs approval or consent by another party, and I see no reason to wait."

"The King?" she questioned faintly, grasping at any straw.

"I had his consent before I left Winchester," he answered, putting an end to this hope for a delay. "Indeed, William will be sure to visit us before long. He is no idle ruler, but one who travels constantly, overseeing all for himself. And I would have you safely wed before he gets here," Raverre finished grimly.

The tone of voice left no doubt as to his meaning. Father Edwin looked shocked.

"Surely the King would not..." He broke off, glancing worriedly at Lisette.

"Not William, no. But he does not travel alone, and his soldiers are men like any others. Men, moreover, who have been without their wives for some time. And I don't need the added trouble of defending an unmarried girl from their attentions."

"Indeed?" asked Lisette, incensed. She turned to Father Edwin. "Go ahead and arrange for the wedding, Father," she instructed imperiously. "We certainly don't wish to cause my lord any *more* trouble."

Head high, she swept both men a regal curtsy. Ignoring Raverre's amused expression, she brushed past him and went to sit by the fire with her sisters, realising too late that she had just played into her tormentor's hands.

Catherine's artless excitement over this turn of events inwardly enraged her further. After supper that night Lisette had to bite her tongue to keep from berating her sister for gazing up at Raverre with childish hero-worship. All the way through the meal.

"And, what's more, he is not above encouraging her," Lisette said furiously to Marjory the next afternoon as they scattered fresh rushes over the floor of the hall. "She is in positive thrall that Raverre has promised her a new mare of her own to ride. 'Tis bribery, no less!"

The rushes flew about in all directions under Lisette's agitated hand, and Marjory gave her a shrewd look.

"Mayhap Catherine sees further than yourself, my sweet," she said. "You see a Norman Baron who knows what he wants and takes it. An enemy, you say, and hate him accordingly. But some of us see a man who has been fair in victory. A man who can be gentle and generous when he chooses, though fierce in anger, I have no doubt. Why, did you know that the serfs no longer have to pay to use the manor ovens? They may bake their own bread, which will mean less coin in Raverre's coffers."

Lisette remembered her gibe at Raverre about money. "They still have to bring their corn to the manor mill to have it ground," she argued perversely.

Marjory clucked impatiently, waving an admonishing finger at Lisette. "They've been doing that since your grandfather's time. And did Raverre punish Siward? Has he been harsh with you and your sisters? Is he milking the estate of what little is left? Quite the contrary!

"Besides," she added, with purely feminine satisfaction, "He is young and strong, and handsome enough to assail any maid's heart and win it. You may be sure there were many such across the sea in Normandy."

"Well, he can go back there and marry one of *them*," was the tart response to this remark. Flinging the last of the rushes down, Lisette marched outside, hoping to find some much needed solitude.

The bailey was sunny and peaceful. Two soldiers lounged idly in the gateway. A half-dozen more were gathered in the field across the stream, engaged in archery practice. The steady plunk of arrows hitting the butts was oddly soothing. Occasionally a cheer went up as one of the Normans aimed true.

At least they're practising on targets and not Saxons, thought Lisette as she wandered aimlessly towards the stables. She wondered why she felt so low.

"My lady!"

At the muffled exclamation Lisette jumped, almost tripping over a deerhound, sunning itself in the stable doorway.

"Siward? Holy Saints, how you startled me."

"Hush, my lady." Siward beckoned from the stable. "In here, where we may speak without being heard."

Lisette obeyed. "Why, what is it?" She glanced about as she spoke. The roof had been newly thatched and fresh straw laid in the stalls. This evidence of Raverre's outlay on the manor made her feel worse.

Siward was engaged in checking the hoofs of a powerful grey mare. Several other horses looked on curiously.

"Are these the only horses in the stable?" asked Lisette, surprised. "Where are the others? For that matter, where are the soldiers?"

"Out hunting, supposedly," answered Siward with a significant look.

"Supposedly? What does that mean? Are you talking in riddles, Siward? Let me tell you, I'm in no mood for them. The Normans have been hunting every day."

"Have they?"

"There you go again. What else would they be doing?"

"I'd like to know, my lady. They've ridden out each day,

'tis true. But have you noticed the number of empty game bags for so many men? Methinks 'tis unlikely they hunt game every time.''

Lisette looked up at the young giant in consternation. "What, then?''

Siward shrugged. "I know not. But I thought you should be warned. Perhaps they look for runaway slaves, or masterless men who've left the army and are still free.''

"Here?"

"Such men are everywhere, my lady. And in the forest could stay undetected and free for a long time. But I'm not saying 'tis so.'' The blacksmith's usually sombre face lightened unexpectedly in a rare smile. "Perhaps the Normans are poor hunters.''

Lisette gave him a sceptical look. "In this forest? Even Enide could hit something if it stayed still long enough. Do you know, Siward, I think I shall go riding?''

Siward looked alarmed at this thoughtful remark. "I didn't mean for you to go probing into this, my lady. 'Tis enough that you be warned. My Lord Raverre is a just man. Perhaps you could ask him what is going on.''

"Ask *him?*'' she queried incredulously, forgetting that she was referring to her future husband. "The wretch is not likely to tell me anything. Here, Siward, saddle up this horse for me.''

"Now, my lady,'' Siward began, in the minatory tones he had used when a very young Lisette had demanded to handle the bellows in the forge. "You can't just ride out of here as though on a jaunt. What of the soldiers? Besides, the horse needs shoeing.''

"Good. We'll take her to the forge, and I'll leave from there. Simple.''

"Simple? Raverre would have my head on a pike. And I wouldn't blame him,'' added Siward objectively.

Lisette looked thoughtful. "You're right," she said at last. "But at least let me walk to the forge with you, Siward. I need some exercise, and we can put our heads together and see if we can find some answers."

Siward agreeing to this, they set off. The guards at the gate, seeing her with the blacksmith, gave Lisette no more than a cursory glance, and the archers were too busy arguing about increasing the distance of the targets to pay them much heed.

Lisette wondered if Raverre would allow her to shoot at the butts some day. No wonder she felt so unlike herself. She was not used to being confined indoors with little to do.

"Things have come to a pretty pass when a short walk along this rutted track cheers me so," she commented.

Siward sent her a sympathetic glance over the horse's withers as the mare clip-clopped between them.

"Soon there won't be so many soldiers here, my lady," he assured her. "And it will be safe for you to venture out. Raverre's knights will be settled at the other villages and their men will rotate the guard duty here, I'm told. The others return to the army when they escort Lady Enide to Romsey."

"You sound content to have it so, Siward."

"'Tis difficult to despise a man as just as Raverre," commented Siward thoughtfully. "And if you can marry him to benefit the estate, my lady, then I can serve him for the same cause."

Four blasts from a horn resounded faintly from the forest.

"Well, some of the soldiers are hunting," remarked Lisette, noting the direction of the sound. "They're brought down a hart."

She thought guiltily of the scheme she was hatching. If the men really were hunting she might be courting trouble for no reason. Then determination took hold. The Normans were up to something, and she was going to find out what it was.

The day was growing cloudy, a forerunner of the colder autumn weather to come. Leaves fluttered to the ground in gently eddying circles, those still clinging to their branches creating a fiery blaze of red and amber, a brilliant contrast of colour against the brown fields and misty blue-green of the distant hills.

The grey mare pranced nervously along a well-worn forest path, unaccustomed to the light weight on her back and the strange guidance of a rope. Lisette was kept so busy preventing the horse from shying at every floating leaf that she didn't see the huge black destrier emerge from a side-path until she was nearly on top of him. The mare plunged to an abrupt stop, almost unseating her rider.

Lisette stared guiltily into angry ice-blue eyes.

"What in God's name are you doing on that horse?" Raverre thundered incredulously.

The mare side-stepped, on edge and tossing her head. Lisette grabbed a handful of mane and hung on. Raverre grabbed the rope halter and hung on.

"Sweet Jesus! You haven't even bridled Phantom, let alone saddled her. Just what do you think you're doing?" he demanded, still angry but lowering his voice. Despite his shock at seeing Lisette on the most nervous horse in the stable, sudden admiration flashed into Raverre's eyes.

"Trying to find out what *you're* doing," she retorted crossly. Why did the man have to turn up whenever she didn't want him?

"I've been inspecting the village at Wiford," he said mildly. "You knew that."

"Do you think we're all blind?" Lisette demanded.

"Your men are out hunting every day, but 'tis not game they hunt, is it, my lord?"

Raverre eyed her thoughtfully. "Siward was supposed to be shoeing this horse. Perhaps you can explain why he apparently saw fit to allow you to ride her instead." He laid one arm across his saddle, leaning forward to pin Lisette with a narrow-eyed stare. "And did my men turn their backs while you rode through the gates?" he asked in ominous tones.

Lisette tossed her head. "They were too busy showing off their marksmanship," she derided, consigning the Normans to Raverre's retribution without a qualm.

"And Siward?" he prompted forebodingly.

"'Twas not his fault. The mare was at the forge and I...I borrowed her while Siward was busy stoking the fire," she explained defiantly. "You could hardly expect him to give chase on foot."

"Borrowed?" he repeated. Then he grinned unexpectedly. "Why don't I have any trouble believing that? I can only praise the Saints that I'm on Lanzelet, or no doubt you would have borrowed *him.*"

Lisette breathed a sigh of relief. "Is that his name? What does it mean?"

"'Tis Norman for Lancelot, and aye, I've heard the legend. Come on."

"Where are we going?" she asked, curious.

"Back to the manor. Where else?" Raverre nudged Lanzelet to a walk. Phantom fell in beside him. "If you think I'm going to permit you to continue with this foolish idea of yours you can think again."

Lisette subsided into frustrated silence. Not only had she been defeated, she still didn't know what the Normans were doing out in the forest every day. Raverre had ignored her challenge about his men's activities as though it had never been uttered. Resentment drew her brows together.

Raverre glanced sideways at Lisette's frowning countenance, remembering that he had wanted to see what she looked like when she smiled. She hadn't really had a lot to smile about in the past few days, he reflected.

"I suppose you know that Bertrand set off for Winchester this morning," he remarked. "Along with your shopping list, he is carrying a message to your aunt to inform her that Lady Enide has permission to enter the cloister."

Lisette glared at him. "You're not going to tell me, are you?"

Raverre reined in at the edge of the wasteland. A distant grove of trees separated the manor fields from this rough open area, where logs and dead branches lay in scattered profusion. Hillocks of grass concealed numerous rabbit holes, and stunted bushes and brushwood abounded.

"Do *you* trust *me?*" Raverre challenged quietly.

Lisette searched his face. Did she trust him?

His mouth curled sardonically at her long silence. "No. I didn't think so."

Sensing the tension in the rider on her back, Phantom moved restlessly, and Raverre reached out a quieting hand.

"I want your promise that you won't ride my horses again," he said severely. "I've asked Bertrand to keep an eye out for good mounts. He knows what you can handle. Phantom is safe while I'm with you, but she is a strong horse and still easily startled; you couldn't hold her if she bolted."

To confusion and a strange regret that she had not answered Raverre immediately was added fiery resentment.

"Oh, you think so?" Lisette demanded, haughtily. "Watch this!" And before Raverre could stop her she wheeled the big mare, put her at the solid log immediately in front of them, clearing it with feet to spare, and took off towards the trees at a headlong gallop.

Cursing, Raverre followed suit, thundering after her. Even carrying the greater weight, Lanzelet would have caught Phantom, but Raverre had to consider the dangers of rabbit holes to his horse's legs, whereas Lisette knew the rough terrain. She bent low over Phantom's withers, revelling in the power and speed of the big horse as they seemed to fly over the ground, clearing every obstacle as if it did not exist. The wind rushed past her face, whipping colour into her cheeks, and her hair flew out behind her.

The small wood came nearer, and she pulled on the rope to slow the mare. Phantom, however, was enjoying herself. Without a bridle Lisette only just managed to pull her in to a canter before she found herself among the trees, guiding her mount unerringly until she finally succeeded in halting on the other side.

Raverre, seeing his quarry disappear into the trees, swore violently as a hideous picture of Lisette dashed against a solid oak sprang into his mind. He emerged into the field still at a gallop, almost overshooting Lisette, who sat calmly waiting, while Phantom lipped the ground as if she'd never had anything further on her equine mind.

Relief that Lisette was safe inevitably gave way to blazing anger at her recklessness. Dismounting, Raverre strode back to her, looking furious. Grabbing her arm, he yanked her off the mare's back, shaking her until her hair, already loosened by her wild ride, swirled about her face.

"You stupid little idiot!" he roared. "Don't you know better than to ride through trees at that speed? What were you trying to do, kill yourself?"

But Lisette was too elated to be chastened. Shaking her hair back out of her face, she laughed up at him. Suddenly she felt more alive than she had for months, and Raverre's fury had no power to subdue her.

Phantom, however, startled by the angry voice, flung up her head nervously, dancing away as Raverre, hurriedly releasing Lisette, made a lunge for the halter. Then, with a defiant series of snorts at him as he tried to catch her, she cantered off in the direction of her stable.

Raverre turned back to Lisette, who had collapsed in helpless mirth at the horse's antics. He eyed her ominously for a moment. Then, as she looked back at him, her eyes dancing, hair tumbled about her shoulders, and those two mischievous dimples hovering near her mouth, Raverre felt his anger melt away.

She had been lovely before, he thought, but, lit up now with the sudden glow of happiness, her radiant beauty shone so brightly that everything around her seemed to pale into insignificance.

Blind to his surroundings, forgetting every other emotion save the longing to have her love him, Raverre slowly walked back to Lisette, to stand so close that she had to tilt her head right back to look up at him. His hand lifted to lightly touch the vulnerable line of her throat.

"Well," he said, his voice husky with repressed desire, "I wanted to see you smile, and now I have. You are indeed fair, sweet mistress."

His hand fell to his side and he stepped back, before the temptation to tumble her down into the soft meadow grass grew any stronger. He couldn't destroy the faint beginnings of trust behind the questions in her eyes.

So absorbed were they in each other that both failed to sense the presence of a third. In the shadows at the edge of the wood a darker shadow stirred. So close to the protective bole of an oak that the form of a man was barely discernible. The shadow lengthened slowly as the man moved back towards the wasteland, drawing his bow.

"Can Saxon and Norman trust each other?" Raverre asked.

"I...I'm going to marry you," she stammered, wondering if that was really an answer.

Raverre heard the shaky breath she drew in. By marrying him she was going to trust him in the most intimate way a woman could trust a man, and he knew that sudden realisation had frightened her.

"My men are searching for a gold ingot," he said abruptly. "Stolen from the treasury at Winchester several weeks ago."

Lisette's eyes widened in surprise, but Raverre saw her quickly grasp the issue.

"You think this ingot will be taken to safety in Wales? No. 'Twould be there by now."

Raverre nodded. "We've orders to search the manors and villages along the border. But 'tis such an unwieldy thing that I think it unlikely to be far from Winchester. Gold is heavy. 'Twould need at least twelve men to lift it, and to transport it out of the country would be well nigh impossible. You've heard nothing of such a robbery?"

"Nothing. And we surely would if such a large group of travellers had passed through any of the villages. They'd have a wagon and horses, too. No, we've heard nothing. Nor seen any—"

A swift rush of wind was the only warning Raverre had. It was barely enough. Acting from instinct rather than knowledge, he shoved Lisette to one side.

The arrow whizzed past his left shoulder as she fell, and Raverre swung round, sword drawn, his narrowed gaze keenly searching the trees. There was no movement, and he couldn't leave Lisette to go after the sniper. Reaching

Lanzelet in three strides, Raverre grabbed his hunting horn from the saddle and blew a single deafening blast. A moment later an answering blast echoed from the forest about half a mile away.

Slinging the horn back over the saddle, Raverre turned to help Lisette to her feet. His blood froze.

She still lay where his thrust had sent her, the arrow protruding from her upper arm. Then, even as he saw that she was not fatally hit, Lisette stirred. He was beside her in seconds, tearing away the sleeve of her gown.

"Lie still, sweetheart. I'll have to get this out before the shock wears off and the pain starts."

He flicked a glance at her face. She looked dazed, but this time her eyes held utter trust.

Still speaking, Raverre laid his hand over Lisette's shoulder, bearing down strongly. She felt her arm go numb.

"Thank your Saint, whoever she is, that 'tis only a flesh wound," he said through his teeth. "The arrow was nearly spent. Only the tip of the barb broke the skin."

Grasping the shaft with his other hand, he pulled swiftly. Lisette gasped. Her face went white, but her lips parted in a shaky smile.

"'Tis St Elizabeth," she said faintly.

Raverre made a rough sound in his throat and pulled her into his arms, holding her tightly. She should object, Lisette thought, but instead she turned her face into his shoulder. Her hand came up to grip his tunic. She could feel his fingers, warm against the soft skin at her nape, stroking gently. Strange, he seemed to be shaking slightly. No, 'twas the ground shaking.

Lisette raised her head as several Normans rode across the field at the gallop. It must have been the vibration of so many hoofs causing the strange tremor she'd felt. Raverre would not tremble. The man was unshakeable. Look at him. As cool as a summer rain shower as he released her and bound her arm with her torn sleeve.

Lifting her into his arms, Raverre rose to his feet as horses slithered to a stop all around them.

"My God, sir!" exclaimed Gilbert, taking in Lisette's pale face and bloodstained gown. "What happened?"

"A sniper," said Raverre briefly, jerking his head at the arrow on the ground. "You can tell your men to search the forest, but he'll be long gone."

"I'm all right, Gilbert," assured Lisette as the young Norman turned a shocked countenance to her. "'Tis only a scratch."

Raverre growled something under his breath. It didn't sound very agreeable, but he was gentle enough as he lifted her on to Lanzelet's back. Swinging up behind her, he settled Lisette in the crook of his arm and gathered up the reins.

"There's little time before sunset," he advised Gilbert. "But see if you can find any tracks nearer the wasteland. He fired from quite a distance."

"Sir!"

With a flourish Gilbert wheeled his horse and was off. Lisette saw him raise an arm in a sweeping gesture, signalling his men to spread out, before Raverre turned Lanzelet and started at a sedate walk back to the manor.

She was glad to rest her head on his shoulder when he drew her back against him.

"All right?" he murmured. His lips brushed her hair, but Lisette was too comfortable to protest. She nodded silently, and his arm tightened. She felt safe.

That was strange. Safe with an enemy? Lisette thought drowsily of trust again. Why hadn't she felt able to tell Raverre she trusted him, when in many ways she did? She trusted him to keep his word about Enide. She would trust him with her life. But what of her heart?

Lisette shivered. Why had that thought intruded? She didn't have to trust Raverre with her heart. It was perfectly safe from him.

"Easy, little warrior," he soothed, feeling her movement. "I know your arm is probably stinging like the Devil."

"'Tis not that," she denied. "I scarce feel it."

"What, then? You tremble. Are you cold?" He drew her closer.

"No, no," she said, becoming more agitated as his warmth enfolded her. "I...I just wondered who..."

"Someone whose aim is dangerously bad. 'Twas more likely meant for me than you."

"Even so, if you hadn't pushed me..." She turned her head to look up at him. "You were so quick."

Raverre slanted an amused glance down at her. "I've had enough arrows whistling about my head to recognise one coming when I hear it," he said. "You'll always be safe with me, little warrior."

"Why do you call me that?"

He chuckled. "It suits you. But if you don't like it you'll have to lay down your arms, and obey me."

She liked him in this mood, thought Lisette. Even though he was a Norman. Her enemy. But she was too tired to worry about that now. She could be a warrior tomorrow.

"I don't want to fight any more," she said wearily, resting against his shoulder again. "I feel safe with you today."

"Considering that's what I wanted, I find myself extremely inconsistent," Raverre muttered. There was no response.

He glanced down at the dark head against his shoulder

and smiled ruefully. If he had to undergo the tortures of the damned to have Lisette as warm and trusting in his arms when she wasn't hurt, then he'd do it.

This praiseworthy intention lasted until they rode into the bailey to find Phantom standing peacefully outside the stable. Recalling his fear for Lisette's safety, Raverre fixed his men with an intimidating glare.

Siward was already exhorting the soldiers to search for Lisette, but he broke off when he saw her.

"My lady! What have you done to yourself now?" He sounded more resigned than worried. "My lord, please believe that had I—"

Raverre dismounted. "Spare me, Siward. I'm quite sure you, along with everyone else at Ambray, have absolutely no control over your lady. That situation, however, is about to change."

He lifted Lisette to the ground, smiling at her affronted expression. She was obviously starting to feel better.

But the glare returned twofold when Raverre turned on his men. "Dolts!" he began furiously.

"'Twas not their fault," admitted Lisette reluctantly. "They thought I was merely walking to the forge with Siward."

Raverre gave her a hard stare. "'Tis more than time someone took you in hand," he said grimly, picking her up.

"Put me down!" Lisette protested, annoyed at this arrogant treatment. "I can walk. My arm is not even bleeding any more."

"Go shoe the horse, Siward," instructed Raverre, ignoring Lisette. "And don't turn your back on your mistress again."

"Aye, my lord," responded Siward, grinning at Lisette's indignant face.

"And if you ever do anything so reckless again," Raverre threatened softly, carrying his betrothed up the stairs, "you won't escape so lightly. Now, do I have your pledge that you won't borrow my horses?"

Lisette studied the determined set of Raverre's mouth. "Aye, my lord," she said demurely as he set her down outside the tower room.

Marjory hurried forward, exclaiming in startled concern. Then, as she urged her mistress into the room, Lisette looked back at Raverre with an impish smile.

"But you will at least admit that I can ride."

The door shut on Raverre's resigned face.

A few miles away to the south, deep in the forest, the watcher in the trees hurried towards his secret haven. He smiled grimly to himself. He knew this forest like his own hand, and had left those thick-headed Normans going around in circles like dogs in a bear-pit.

'Twas a pity his arrow had struck the girl instead of its intended victim, but her wound had been slight. And why had she been so snug with a Norman Baron anyway? Oh, yes. He had much to tell his master of what he had seen this day.

Chapter Five

‘‘’Tis as well you mend quickly, my love,’’ remarked Marjory two days later. She rolled up the linen bandage in her hand. ‘‘You have no more need of this.’’

Lisette glanced down at her arm. She had been more stunned at being hit than badly hurt by the arrow, and only a faint puckering of the skin showed where the barb had entered. Even that would fade in time.

Lisette donned her gown. ‘‘Does this mean I may now walk farther than the hall?’’ she asked with gentle raillery.

‘‘Now, sweeting, you know ’twas for your own good that my lord confined you to the manor. He was concerned for you.’’

‘‘Hah! He was concerned that I’d find out he was interrogating every man on the estate. As if one of our serfs could lay his hand on a bow. The only good that has come of it is the delay of an indecently hasty wedding while he hunts further afield.’’

‘‘And how do you know that, pray?’’

‘‘Oswy told me.’’

‘‘That half-wit!’’ scoffed Marjory, beginning to braid Lisette’s hair. ‘‘What does he know of weddings?’’

‘‘Hush, Marjory. Oswy can’t help being simple. Why,

even Raverre saw immediately that the poor boy is harm-
less. He said such people are usually good with animals,
and put him to work in the stable.''

"Raverre sees a lot," cautioned Marjory. "So 'ware how
you flout his orders."

"I am still mistress of this manor," flashed Lisette.
"And I have every right to be in the stable talking to Oswy.
Catherine spends half her days there and Raverre doesn't
object."

Marjory tied the end of Lisette's braid with a faded ribbon, giving a rather more vigorous tug than was strictly
necessary. "Catherine wasn't hit by an arrow," she pointed
out grimly.

"Tush! A scratch. I feel perfectly well, and am off to
the village before the serfs begin to think I'm the weakling
Raverre considers me." This last was said rather defiantly.

"As you wish, my love," was the soothing reply.

Expecting an argument, Lisette stared at her old nurse
suspiciously. Marjory returned the stare with a bland smile.

Of course, as she paid a visit to the cottars every week,
perhaps Marjory had thought better of protesting the per-
formance of this duty, Lisette decided. But as she started
for the village, she puzzled, nevertheless, over her nurse's
calm acceptance. And, now she thought about it, the guards,
too, had not seemed particularly worried about her being
outside the gates, and alone. Glancing back, Lisette soon
discovered why.

She was being followed.

Several yards back, a Norman soldier trod resignedly
along the road after her. Wrapping her thin mantle more
securely around herself against the cool wind, Lisette
waited, tapping an impatient foot.

"My lady," the man greeted her politely when he
reached her.

She had noticed him at table, Lisette remembered. He was considerably older than Raverre, a stocky, grizzled Knight who had seen many years of hard service in William's army.

"You are following me," she accused.

"Escorting you, my lady," he corrected stolidly. "My lord's orders."

"Indeed?" Lisette's voice was icy. "Your name, sir?"

"Richard de Somery, mistress."

"Well, Sir Richard, you may tell your lord that I declined your escort to the village. 'Tis not needed."

"That's a matter of opinion, my lady," de Somery argued gruffly. "My lord thinks of your safety. 'Tis not known for sure whom that arrow was meant to strike."

"That is foolish talk," said Lisette scornfully. "Why would anyone wish to harm me?"

"You are marrying a Norman Baron, madam. Some might think that cause enough."

"But my people here are pleased." Lisette was indignant. "'Twould be as easy to suspect one of you Normans."

De Somery seemed unmoved by this charge. His expressionless face studied Lisette dispassionately. Rather as though she were a cockroach which had suddenly crawled on to his trencher, she thought.

"*You* seem to disapprove," she added pointedly.

"'Tis not my place to approve or not, lady. The marriage is necessary. You'll learn to respect Baron de Raverre."

De Somery didn't waste his time wondering if love was involved in the match his lord was planning. Of course, the Lady Lisette was strikingly beautiful with her delicate features, dark hair and deep iris-blue eyes, framed by those impossibly long lashes. However, a man merely considered himself fortunate if his wife was physically attractive, and closed his eyes to her imperfections or, more likely, took a mistress if she was not.

De Somery knew that Raverre would have married one of the girls to further his plans, regardless of their looks. He understood such practicalities. What he couldn't fathom was why his lord had chosen this argumentative wench instead of the more docile Enide.

"That may be," retorted Lisette, "but he will also learn to respect me. Where is he? Still hunting for your missing gold?"

"He rides the fields, my lady," explained de Somery, stoically polite. "He would have the serfs know him, and he them."

"Well, I also have business to attend to," Lisette stated firmly, determined to continue with her plans for the morning.

Voicing no objection, de Somery fell into step beside her. And remained at her side all the while she exchanged greetings and gossip with the village women.

He didn't speak to her again, but while she was occupied with the bee-keeper Lisette noticed him chatting pleasantly with Siward in the doorway of the forge. It seemed everyone was welcoming the Normans with open arms. Even the bees were producing more honeycomb, she was told with pride. Feeling strangely bereft of support, Lisette turned her footsteps homeward.

Still silent, de Somery accompanied her, leaving her with a brusque nod when they re-entered the bailey.

"Accursed soldiers," she muttered as she reached the empty stable, intending to challenge Raverre the instant he returned. "Respect Baron de Raverre indeed. How dare he have me followed, and on such a weak pretext? More likely he thinks I might run away."

Lisette found herself so hurt that Raverre might mistrust

her to the extent of having her followed that uneasiness rippled through her. It was not the first time she had felt that icy finger of warning whenever she thought of him. She had even come dangerously close to liking the man the other day, and made haste to remind herself that he was arrogant, annoyingly dictatorial and obviously thought her a weak creature in constant need of safeguarding, if de Somery's explanation had been truthful.

An insidious suspicion that she didn't altogether dislike Raverre's protectiveness sent Lisette hurrying out of the stable again. To emerge straight under the nose of Lanzelet, who, fortunately, had halted and seemed to be looking down at her enquiringly with his great brown eyes.

Raverre dismounted, running a hand down the satiny neck of his destrier.

Thinking Lisette might have been startled by almost colliding with the huge animal, he commented, ''Don't be fooled by Lanzelet's size, my lady. Fearless though he must be in battle, he has no meanness in his nature. He would carry you as safely as any lady's palfrey, though he would be too strong for you if anything upset him.''

Like his master, thought Lisette, so instantly that she hoped Raverre couldn't read her mind.

He led Lanzelet into the stable as he spoke, taking off the heavy saddle.

''Why are you having me followed?'' she demanded, his preoccupation with the horse steadying her nervousness.

She regretted this impulsive question immediately. Raverre turned his full attention on her, his face very serious. Lisette felt her heartbeat quicken. Those light, glittering eyes seemed to look straight into her soul.

''I would not keep you imprisoned, sweetheart, but I will protect my own.''

Lisette occupied herself with stroking Lanzelet's black

velvet muzzle. It was better than looking into eyes that made her want to forget who and what—

"I stand in no danger from my own people," she managed to say. Indeed, she felt more endangered at this very moment. She should leave the stable. If only her heart would not beat so fast she would be able to think, to protest at Raverre's orders.

Raverre watched Lisette murmur to Lanzelet, the big horse bending his head to her caressing hand.

Lucky devil, he thought, and a pang of longing to feel the touch of her hand himself made him move restlessly, sending a broom skidding across the floor. Lanzelet, startled by the loud clatter, threw up his head, knocking Lisette off balance. She would have fallen, but Raverre grasped her around the waist to steady her then, unable to help himself, gently drew her into his arms.

Lisette looked up in startled enquiry, her hands coming to rest against the solid wall of his chest.

"What—?"

"Hush," he murmured, holding her eyes with his. He slowly lowered his mouth to hers. "I would not have you entirely ignorant of me before we're wed, little maid."

The moment Lisette realised Raverre's intent she stiffened in alarm, but, though part of her wanted to resist, another part, deeper, hidden, was strangely reassured by his words. She remembered the warm sense of safety she had known in his arms before, and as his lips brushed hers Lisette gave in to the sudden questioning in her mind, relaxing against him. And unleashing a storm.

Raverre was lost. As he felt her slender body suddenly pliant in his arms, when he had expected resistance, his control splintered. Crushing Lisette against him in an iron hold that made her gasp, he covered her mouth with his, kissing her so deeply and fiercely that she grew faint with the waves of half-frightened excitement shaking her body. Where had safety gone? There was none in the yielding weakness seeping through her limbs. She couldn't even fight, but only cling desperately to him in an attempt to hold on to her shattered senses.

Raverre broke the kiss at last, breathing hard and staring down into her face with such naked desire blazing in his eyes that Lisette was overwhelmed with dismay. How had her innocent curiosity unleashed such barely controlled passion? How had she submitted so easily? And to a Norman. He would think her wanton, shameless.

"Don't look at me like that," he ordered hoarsely. "By the Saints, sweetheart, I'm only human."

"I'm sorry…" she faltered, only wanting to escape. He was blaming her already.

Wrenching her eyes from Raverre's with an effort, she became aware that she was still clinging to his tunic for balance, and, releasing the fabric as if it carried the plague, she whirled about and fled from the stable.

Raverre took a quick step after her, but paused, knowing reassurance would be useless. Not realising that Lisette had been more shocked by her own behaviour than his, he thought he had frightened her with the unrestrained ardour of his embrace.

He cursed as he remembered that her normal girlish apprehension of men had probably been exaggerated by the attack on her mother. But when she had remained so willingly in his arms his intention to be gentle until he had overcome her mistrust had shattered along with his control.

As he remembered how soft and yielding her body had felt against the hardness of his own an impatient groan of frustration escaped him, and he struck the stable wall with his clenched fist, making Lanzelet snort in disapproval of such foolish human behaviour.

"What is it about her?" Raverre asked the great war-horse. "She's wilful, stubborn, and argues with me when-ever she gets the chance. Yet I could no more leave her to marry some frivolous Norman wench than fly through the air." He eyed Lanzelet in sudden wry amusement. "And now she's got me talking to my horse.

"Well," he continued, after a thoughtful pause, "every man has his weakness, and that tormenting little mixture of Saxon and Celtic womanhood is mine." Lanzelet flicked an ear forward in agreement. "But one thing I know well," Raverre told the horse. "She is a woman after my own heart, and if I can win hers I will win more than a meek female who would run my household, produce my children, and would bore me in less than a se'nnight."

The memory of her helpless submission in Raverre's arms haunted Lisette constantly the next day, and she avoided him as much as possible. It wasn't difficult. Whether the Normans were searching for gold or snipers, Lisette only saw Raverre at mealtimes, where the presence of others provided a shield against any advances he might have been inclined to make.

When he seemed more disposed to ignore her Lisette was torn between relief and a strange feeling of pique. She knew Raverre was only marrying her for convenience, but did he have to make it quite so plain? The disturbing idea that he might consider her passivity to be a sign of surrender was enough to goad Lisette into lingering with him after supper during the following evenings, to prove that she wasn't afraid of him.

Which was precisely what Raverre intended.

He encouraged her to question him about his plans for the land, the castle, and anything else that came to mind. Whenever a dispute arose among the serfs or villagers, though Lisette admitted to herself that Raverre's judge-ments were fair and sound, she took a perverse delight in challenging them and arguing with him later.

Raverre let her argue and even once or twice agreed with her, lounging back in his chair with careless male grace and watching Lisette under lowered lids as she paced back and forth, propounding her father's pet theories for the management of vast land-holdings and the treatment of serfs.

However, when the disputes involved Saxons against Raverre's men, he would order Lisette to the tower room, where she had to continue her pacing, frustrated at not knowing what was going on below.

She was engaged in this fruitless exercise three days later, when Enide answered a knock on the door to find a scared-looking cook demanding entrance.

"Save you, Wat," greeted Lisette. "You look as though the very fiends of hell are on your tail."

"Worse, my lady," cried the wizened little serf agitatedly. "You must go down to the hall. They've dragged Edgith from the kitchen, accusing her of stealing food. And knocking me over the head with my own soup ladle when I protested," he added, aggrieved.

"Edgith, stealing food? By our Lady, why? You must have got it wrong, Wat."

"Not I, mistress. Go see for yourself. That de Somery fellow is foaming at the mouth, demanding trials, and—"

Lisette did not wait for more. She flew down the stairs and across the hall to find Richard de Somery standing over a ragged Saxon in shepherd's garb. Edgith was on her knees before Raverre, sobbing into her hands.

Lisette put her arms around the girl, drawing her to her feet. "What is happening here?" she demanded angrily.

Raverre flicked her a frowning glance, but said nothing.

"Your stupid slave here has been passing food and who

knows what else to this felon," de Somery stated abruptly. He turned back to Raverre. "I demand that they be punished, my lord. Their lives forfeit, or we'll have every peasant in the area walking in and taking whatever they please."

Edgith gave vent to a shriek at this and started wailing. Lisette glared at de Somery. "How dare you threaten—?"

"Wait!" Raverre interrupted her tersely. "How do you know this, Richard?"

"The wench confessed to one of my men, sir. Out of concern for your lady, she would have had him believe, but more likely in fear for her own miserable skin."

"We've always given food to those in need," protested Lisette, determined to be heard. "If that's a crime under Norman law you'll have to kill all of us."

Raverre ignored her. "Speak, girl," he ordered Edgith. "If you are truthful you need not fear for your life."

Edgith glanced at Lisette, who nodded. "I was in the wasteland, gathering kindling," the girl quavered. "The shepherd came from the forest. He had been without food for days, he said, and begged me to fetch some for him. I saw no wrong."

"Then why didn't he come openly to the gates, girl?" questioned de Somery impatiently.

"I didn't think of that 'til later, and then I remembered he had a bow, not a crook. 'Tis why I went to Geoffrey." She turned to Lisette pleadingly. "Oh, my lady, forgive me. I thought he would understand. He's not like some... I...we..."

"You have committed no crime, Edgith," assured Lisette, her expression daring Raverre to contradict this statement.

But his attention was now on the shepherd who glared back at him. "What have you to say, fellow?"

"What matters it?" the man spat, getting to his feet. "You will kill me anyway, though that wench deserves to die also for betraying me." He turned a look of hatred on Lisette. "As does this one for becoming a Norman's wh—"

He didn't get a chance to finish. Raverre's clenched fist shot out, landing with sickening impact on the Saxon's jaw. The force of the blow lifted him several inches off the floor before he fell heavily among the rushes, spitting out a tooth but still defiant.

"Aye, you have the upper hand now, Norman swine, but not for long. Your King can't pay his army without gold, and soon his wealth will be in other hands."

Three pairs of eyes stared at him intently. The shepherd laughed scornfully. "Hah! Mention gold and you Normans stiffen like dogs after a bitch's scent."

Lisette turned impetuously to Raverre. "Do you think he means—?"

"Keep silent!" Raverre snapped. His cold gaze returned to the Saxon. "A bow?" he queried softly. "Now why would a simple shepherd need a bow? And what do you know of gold?"

The shepherd sneered. "Do you think I'll tell you anything, Norman dog? I am dead away. Why should you get more from me?"

"There is more than one way of dying," snarled de Somery, advancing towards his captive. Fastening his hand around the neck of the Saxon's sheepskin mantle, he forced him to his knees. "Let me choke it out of him, my lord."

"I claim justice," the shepherd gasped. "'Tis only that fool girl's word about the bow. Do you see one now? I demand Saxon justice. Trial by iron."

Raverre frowned at Lisette. "I've heard of this trial. What is it exactly?"

Lisette felt slightly sick. Her father had never permitted such brutal methods of judgement.

"'Tis meant to show proof of guilt or innocence," she explained quickly. "An iron rod is placed in the fire until white hot. The accused must take it in his hand and walk ten paces, then the hand is wrapped for three days. When uncovered, if 'tis not blistered he is innocent."

"Superstitious savages," growled de Somery, giving another twist to the Saxon's cloak. "Are we living in the Dark Ages? It will be Norman justice for you, robber, with proper witness and judgement. And for the girl also."

"Is that what you call justice?" Lisette cried. "After Edgith warned—"

She quailed as Raverre turned on her menacingly, but held her ground. "Edgith was loyal."

A look of admiration, albeit unwilling, crossed de Somery's rugged features as Lisette faced Raverre. Something not many of his men would have cared to do in his present mood.

"Your lady speaks truly," he conceded reluctantly, his usual sense of justice overcoming his wrath. "The girl can think herself lucky to escape with a warning. As for this scum, maybe that hot iron wasn't such a bad idea. It might help him talk."

Lisette opened her mouth, but before she could protest Raverre grabbed her arms with bruising strength. "If I have to force you back to your chamber you'll regret it," he growled through clenched teeth. "Now take that snivelling girl and get upstairs. This is no sight for you."

Holy Mother, he's going to do as de Somery suggests, she thought, appalled. Stricken, she grabbed Edgith's hand and almost ran from the hall.

"My lady, wait," panted Edgith, catching sight of her Norman soldier hovering outside. "Geoffrey will take me back to the kitchen.'' She flushed. ''You are not angry with me for going to him? That shepherd frightened me and—''

''I'm not angry, Edgith. But tell me quickly, did you only speak to him the once? Did he say where he came from? Are you sure about the bow?''

Edgith looked more flustered than ever at his spate of questions. ''I only saw it from a distance, my lady. The man laid it down before he approached, but 'twas not a crook, I swear.''

''And you remember nothing else? Think, Edgith! He must have come from somewhere.''

''I don't think— Stay, he wanted a light, too, my lady. Perhaps for his shepherd's hut.''

''Perhaps,'' murmured Lisette. ''Go now, Edgith. You are safe enough, I think.''

She barely heard Edgith's fervent thanks through the clamour of her thoughts. She needed time to sort them out, but it was not to be granted her.

Lisette had scarcely closed the tower room door when it was flung open again without ceremony and Raverre strode purposefully into the room. He didn't waste words.

''Out!'' he ordered the others, his voice so commanding that even Catherine, whom he always treated with affectionate indulgence, obeyed in a hurry, scurrying through the door he held open. It was immediately slammed after them.

''If you ever again question my authority before one of my men,'' he began in a quiet voice that nevertheless sent a quiver of alarm through Lisette, ''you'll wish 'twas you in that convent and not your sister. I will not have any woman, even my wife, interfering in matters of which she knows nothing. Your father might have allowed you a free rein, but he is dead and you would do well to remember that.''

This brutal reminder stung. "I didn't question—"

"Do you think me so incapable of justice?" he overrode her, his voice roughening.

"There's no justice in torture," Lisette retorted angrily.

"So you think me capable of that, too," he said with sudden quiet bitterness. "I had thought these past days you were coming to know me better." He turned away and strode over to the window, staring through the narrow split. "Come here."

Lisette approached warily, feeling strangely guilty.

"You see those soldiers out there?" Raverre asked. "They're searching for a bow." He glanced down at her. "When faced with two conflicting stories I deal in hard evidence, my lady."

She couldn't meet his eyes, her anger fading. "And if you find it?"

"Then there's every chance that man knows something about the robbery, unless he can prove otherwise by producing a master who can vouch for him. Any ideas?"

This abrupt question, coming on top of too many ideas, flustered Lisette immediately. "There is another manor," she blurted out. Then gazed up at Raverre in dismay.

The only man to whom the shepherd might belong was a neighbouring Thegn. A very old man who had been a lifelong friend of her father, he had often expressed his view that William's claim was legitimate, and had even fallen out over this question with his only son, Leofwin, who had been killed with Harold, as far as anyone knew. But would Raverre believe that?

Her eyes pleading, she finished in a breathless rush, "But the Thegn is an old, sick man. He could not have ordered that robbery. He's never even taken up arms against William."

"Where is this place?" he demanded, his voice hard.

"Oh, please, he wouldn't—"

"Where?" he roared suddenly, losing patience under the stinging lash of her doubt.

Lisette flinched. "About fifteen miles to the north," she faltered. "His name is Godric." Then, as Raverre turned without another word and opened the door, Lisette felt anger return. "And I am not yet your wife," she flung after him.

Several hours later a definite air of constraint hung over the hall.

Raverre sat frowning at the bow lying on the table before him as if it might hold the answers he hadn't received from Godric. Everyone else seemed uneasily aware of their lord's displeasure. Even Gilbert looked unusually stern.

Lisette watched in silence as the shepherd was marched out to the guard-room between four soldiers. Father Edwin brought up the rear. After passing sentence of death Raverre had told the priest to hear the man's confession. No amount of questioning had made the Saxon divulge any information about the missing gold, but when he had been confronted with the bow his own words had convicted him of firing the arrow at Raverre. From that moment his death had been certain.

Wondering why Raverre had insisted she be present, Lisette rose from the table.

Raverre was instantly on his feet. Lisette had to make a conscious effort not to flinch away from his overpowering aura of strength, but he saw her almost imperceptible movement and took her hand in a gentle clasp. She could easily have escaped it, and wondered why she didn't.

"Your friend Godric sent you a message," Raverre said as they walked across the hall. "He hopes you continue in good health, and your sisters also. And would like to see you again if it can be arranged."

Was she supposed to pretend that their previous clash had never taken place? "'Twas kind of him to remember us," she whispered.

Raverre sent her a quick glance as they mounted the stairs. "His own health is not good, but he seemed coherent enough and certainly no conspirator. In fact he intends to swear allegiance to William. I've promised to send for him when William visits us."

"Oh?"

Raverre stopped at the solar door. "The trial upset you," he murmured. "But you had to see that justice was done. The man had every chance to defend himself and refused. You realise what I'll have to do now?"

"Aye," she said curtly, beginning to open the door. Raverre clamped a hand over her wrist.

"Hate me if you must," he said very low. "But promise me you'll stay inside tomorrow morning."

Lisette raised a surprised face. He had sounded almost...regretful.

Raverre met her eyes steadily. "You shouldn't have to witness more violent death. You're haunted enough."

In utter astonishment Lisette watched him stride away down the gallery.

She was still wondering how Raverre had known of her demons of memory the following afternoon as she sat stitching by the fire in the hall, vaguely listening to Marjory's familiar scolding.

"The felon was no more a shepherd than I am. He deserved to hang. Can we have rogues wandering the countryside, loosing off arrows at all and sundry?"

"No, Marjory."

"Well, at least you agree." Marjory shifted her frown to Catherine. "And where have you been, miss?"

"In the stable. Bertrand is back with the loveliest mares I've— Ah, here he is now."

Lisette looked up with a warm smile of welcome, which wavered slightly at the sight of Raverre entering the hall with Bertrand. Did he think she hated him when he'd had no choice but to hang the Saxon? Her father would have done the same, and a lot sooner. Not knowing how to tell him this, she now felt awkward in his presence.

As Raverre set down a heavy chest he caught Lisette's shy glance and smiled at her.

"See, my lady, what Bertrand has brought back from Winchester." He flung back the lid.

"Blessed Saints!" ejaculated Marjory. "I do believe the man has purchased from every stall at St Giles's Fair."

"Oh, do look, Lisette," cried Catherine, delving her hands into the chest. "New linen, warm wool for winter gowns, lengths of lapin and sable trimming. We shall look so fine. And here is a girdle of silver links."

Unable to resist such feminine delights, Lisette glanced down as Raverre lifted out a length of the finest blue silk. He shook it out to reveal a gown of delicate workmanship.

"Here, my lady." He held out the garment to Lisette. "You must have a new gown for our wedding tomorrow."

"Tomorrow?" she repeated, dismayed, her interest in the clothes evaporating.

Raverre held her wide-eyed gaze. "Bertrand tells me there is talk in Winchester of rebellion in the north. If I have to leave I want your position here secured."

Still dazed by Raverre's announcement, Lisette slowly reached out to take the gown. The blue silk whispered, rippling and sliding through her fingers like flowing water.

"'Twas brought from the Holy Land by a Knight for his daughter," explained Bertrand, cheerfully unaware of any undercurrents. "But the lass up and entered a convent before her father returned, and he'd no one else on whom to bestow it, so I purchased it from him.''

"You have an eye for colour, Bertrand,'' murmured Raverre. "It matches my lady's eyes exactly.''

Lisette looked up at him. Raverre smiled that slow, beguiling smile that brought warmth leaping to his eyes. "But there's more.''

"Oh, Lisette,'' burst out Catherine. "I was coming to tell you. The sweetest, daintiest bay mares, with matching white stars on their foreheads and—''

Raverre laughed indulgently at Catherine's transports. "Catherine would have ridden off there and then,'' he told Lisette. "But I persuaded her to wait until you could come with us.'' He took Lisette's hand and raised it to his lips. "Would you like that, sweet lady?'' he asked against her soft palm.

Tingling heat shot straight up Lisette's arm. Shaken, she opened her mouth to refuse. Then caught Catherine's pleading eyes.

"Very well,'' Lisette found herself agreeing weakly. She knew she was blushing hotly. The feel of Raverre's mouth against her palm made her legs turn to water. She would be lucky to stay on a horse. Oh, why did that formidable charm have such an unsettling effect when she knew Raverre was only teasing her?

This puzzling question occupied Lisette's mind as she guided her horse up the steep path leading to a plateau high above the forest.

The gusting wind caught both horses and riders, snatching their breath away, tossing silky manes and tails. The river was a mere silver thread far below them, tumbling through the rocky gorge to emerge, stately and serene again, into the forest. Far to the north-west the mountains of Wales loomed dark and forbidding.

"See how this lovely creature tosses her head against the wind, making her mane fly," called Catherine. "Just like that long-haired star we saw flying across the sky the year of King William's coming."

Lisette shuddered, remembering it was also the year her father had ridden off to battle and his death. Many had said the fiery comet had presaged disaster. William, of course, had taken the star's direction towards England as a favourable omen.

"Perhaps you could name her Flying Star," she said somewhat absently.

Catherine hailed this suggestion with delight, but Raverre brought Lanzelet up closer to Lisette.

"What troubles you, sweetheart?" he asked softly, reaching across the small space between the horses and laying a strong hand over hers.

Lisette snatched her hand away. "I think I'll name mine Viking Princess," she said hurriedly to her sister as the mare lifted her nose to snuff the wind.

"She certainly carries herself like one," agreed Catherine.

"Very appropriate," growled Raverre's sardonic voice in Lisette's ear. "Are we discussing the horse still, or her mistress?"

Lisette refused to look at him. He had flustered her enough for one day. Calm civility, she told herself firmly.

"You can see for miles across the forest," she announced unnecessarily. "King Edward used to hunt here, you know."

Raverre gave her a thoughtful look. "William also, when he manages to have a little leisure. Hunting is his favourite pastime."

"Why, that makes him sound quite human," said Catherine wonderingly.

Raverre smiled at her. "Of course he's human. Did you picture some kind of monster? Complete with a tail and horns perhaps?"

Catherine blushed guiltily, having done just that.

Raverre glanced at Lisette. "Surely you don't believe such tales any more?"

"A man does not need a tail or horns to be a monster," she answered coolly, moving her horse away from him.

"Will you ever stop fighting me?" he demanded, a rush of frustration giving the question an unexpected edge. "Or do I have to wait until you meet William and judge for yourself?"

Lisette laughed suddenly at the exasperation in his voice, her spirits lifting at this evidence that she could disturb him also. It was strange that she only felt really alive when she was fighting him. Except for the other day in the stable—

Lisette threw her hood back impatiently, letting her hair fly out in a dark cloud behind her, revelling in the feeling of freedom the wind evoked. She wanted to be free. Free of the disturbing thoughts that had plagued her lately. Free of the constant fear that she could lose more than her home and her independence.

Raverre caught his breath at her look of wild, untamed beauty, feeling desire rip through him as he sensed the unawakened passion within her.

As if she felt his intense stare, Lisette turned her head, her own eyes widening as she saw the urgent hunger in Raverre's. She quickly pulled her hood forward again, hiding her face and retreating instantly behind a wall of wary reserve.

Catherine's exclamation was a welcome diversion.

"Look!" she cried, pointing across to the golden forest below them.

Alert to the slightest hint of danger from force of habit,

Raverre swung round, reaching for his sword, then relaxed as a flock of pheasants took to the air in panic-stricken flight, their harsh cries reaching them on the wind.

"There must be something prowling about over there," he remarked idly. "A fox perhaps. Come, we'd better be on our way before the wind turns colder."

"There might be a den," replied Catherine as they started back. "There are caves not far from where the birds are settling. Do you remember the fox cub we found there as children, Lisette?"

Lisette looked at her sister sharply, but Catherine chattered unconcernedly to Raverre. In seconds their voices faded into the background as Lisette's thoughts churned furiously.

Missing gold, the mention of long-forgotten caves, that sudden appearance of an unknown Saxon, seemingly from nowhere, and the fact that Godric had never received definite word of his son's death on the bloody battlefield at Hastings—all came together to settle into a picture that was extremely disquieting.

Lisette shook her head as though to clear it of her startled suspicions. Godric's son, Leofwin, had been a childhood playmate. He had spent several weeks at a time with them, under Alaric's tutelage, the two older children allowing the younger Lisette and Catherine to tag along with them and occasionally join in their games of damsels in distress and knightly rescuers. Eventually Enide and Leofwin had been betrothed, and Leofwin had ridden off to war.

The caves, deep in the forest and a relic of the ironworks of Roman times, had been a favourite haunt. Lisette had not thought of them for years, but was it possible that Leofwin had returned secretly, and was now using the spot as a safe refuge from which to conduct forays against the Normans in the district?

But why? Leofwin could not hope to do much alone, or with a small band of men, and surely the rift with his father was not so deep that he could not return openly to his home?

Yet, try as she might, she could not believe the startled flight of pheasants had been caused by a poacher or predatory fox. Poaching went on, of course, but not at a time when every available serf was engaged in the autumn harvest and would be missed. Also, predators, whether they be of the two- or four-legged variety, usually moved under cover of darkness. But a man desperate for food...

Lisette frowned worriedly. She could do nothing about her suspicions at the moment, however, and had to be content with making a resolution to ride through the forest alone as soon as she could escape Raverre's close watch. As it was, her long silence had already made him send her several penetrating glances, Lisette realised, coming back to the present to see the fields of the manor stretching before them, peaceful and welcoming in the soft grey stillness of the late afternoon. They were almost home and she could remember nothing of the ride.

As they trotted sedately past the church Lisette saw Father Edwin waving from the porch and, on impulse, reined in Princess outside the wicker gate leading to the graveyard.

"I would speak with Father Edwin a moment," she explained, at Raverre's questioning look. "About tomorrow," she added, hoping he would think the wedding had been the cause of her preoccupation.

He nodded after a second's hesitation and dismounted, intending to lift Lisette down, but she forestalled him, springing gracefully to the ground.

"I'll take the mare," he said, "and come back for you when I've seen Catherine safely indoors."

"There's no need," Lisette answered hurriedly. "Father Edwin will escort me."

Raverre gave her another long, unsmiling stare, but then mounted Lanzelet again without a word. Lisette watched as she and Catherine rode towards the manor. Had that been a flicker of hurt in Raverre's eyes just before he had turned away? No, impossible. And yet—

"God's greetings, my lady," piped Father Edwin beside her. "So I am to marry you tomorrow."

Lisette turned with a start, remembering her purpose in stopping. "Good day, Father." She hesitated, frowning, wondering how to put the question.

"There is something...?" Father Edwin paused discreetly.

"Aye, Father. It concerns the shepherd."

"Ah, Tostig. Poor unrepentant creature." Father Edwin crossed himself and shook his head.

"I know you may not betray the seal of the Confessional, Father," persevered Lisette. "But did the man say anything you could repeat to me? Mention of a master perhaps?"

"Nary a word, my lady. Nor during his Confession, such as it was. 'Twould not help you even if I repeated it word for word. A lost soul indeed, held fast by the Evil One."

Father Edwin seemed inclined to gloomy contemplation of his failure to extract proper repentance from the shepherd, but Lisette's thoughtful silence eventually bestirred him to speak again.

"My Lord Raverre has already asked me this same question, my lady. I wish I could have answered differently, for he is a good man. Your father would have liked him, I think, if they had not been on opposing sides in a conflict I pray God will soon be done."

This idea had not occurred to Lisette before, but Father

Edwin prattled on, distracting her, and it slipped from her mind as she refused his offer of escort back to the manor.

"I would sit by my mother's grave for a moment," she explained, and Father Edwin saw her off with a cheerful wave.

He might not have been so content had he heard Lisette's whispered words as she crouched in the soft grass where her mother lay at peace. By rights a proper tomb should have been erected in the church, but, with no stonemason on the estate at the time of her father's death, a simple grave had become the final resting place of both her parents.

At least it was consecrated ground, she thought gratefully, and sent up a quick prayer for the repose of her parents' souls.

"Oh, sweet Lady Mother," she whispered, "am I doing wrong? I am about to be married to one who is your enemy and mine. How do I know 'twas not he who delivered the fatal blow to my father? And since then, how many of our people has he killed or caused to be driven from their homes? And yet, dear God in Heaven, what else can I do? I have thought and thought." She bowed her head, mentally exhausted by the constant questioning and emotional struggle, and stayed so for a long time.

When she finally rose to her feet Lisette was surprised to find that twilight was falling, and the tiny graveyard looked still and mysterious in the half-light. A twig cracked behind her and she whirled with a frightened gasp, to see Raverre detach himself from the shadows of the trees by the road and come towards her.

Ignorance of how long he had been watching her, possibly a witness to her grief, didn't improve Lisette's mood. She could feel the wetness of tears on her cheeks, and yet she hadn't even been aware of crying.

Irrationally blaming him for that as well, she flared defensively, "You didn't have to come looking for me as if you feared I might run away."

Raverre ignored the tone and came up to her. "'Tis getting dark; there are other dangers beside human ones, you know."

"Human dangers are the only ones I fear," Lisette said significantly, backing away a pace or two. "See here—" gesturing to the grave at her feet "—is where my parents lie before their time. And for what? A crown, squabbled over by selfish humans who think only of themselves."

"There would have been no need of fighting if Harold had been true to his oath to support William's claim. William has only taken what was his by right."

"By right!" she exclaimed. "How dare you say so? He had no right."

"He had the right granted by the Pope, for one," Raverre countered. "Such things as a consecrated Papal banner are not given lightly. Also a bull of excommunication against Harold for breaking a vow made on sacred relics—"

"A vow made under duress!" Lisette interrupted angrily. "And achieved by trickery. William must have known his claim was not strong, to resort to such methods. He has no English blood, and there are others more nearly related to the old royal house."

"Aye," he agreed, his voice taking on a sarcastic note as he became annoyed at her persistence. "A child not much older than Catherine. That would have been a great asset to the country. Did you see any rallying to his banner after William entered London? Of course not! Edgar swore fealty to William along with many another. As your own father would have done, had he lived."

"He would never have done so!" she exclaimed hotly, stamping a little foot in her agitation.

"By the Holy Rood, let us have an end to this once and for all," Raverre growled impatiently, taking Lisette by the shoulders and giving her a little shake. "Your father was part-Norman himself, and don't try to tell me otherwise," he ordered as Lisette opened her mouth to protest. "My God, Girl, I only have to look at yonder castle to see where his ancestors came from. There were only three other such strongholds in the whole country before William came, garrisoned by Normans put there by King Edward. You even know a little of the language, so don't keep telling me of your pure Saxon blood. I know better."

Furious at being unable to deny this, she flashed, "At least my blood is legitimate, which is more than can be said for your precious William. He is base. No wonder he behaves so. What else could one expect from a low-born bastard?"

Raverre's face darkened, and he shook Lisette again, harder this time. "If you value your soft skin," he threatened, his voice rough, "you won't even whisper such a thing before William. He has had men maimed, and even killed for it before, and the fact that you are a woman won't save you."

"No," she scorned, recklessly ignoring the increasing anger on his face. "I wouldn't expect it to, when I know he beat the Queen for having the courage to speak the truth."

"I'm beginning to think a beating wouldn't do you any harm as well," Raverre muttered, wondering how the argument had become heated so quickly. "If I'd done it earlier this ridiculous conversation wouldn't even be taking place!"

"Go ahead, then!" was her defiant answer. She wrenched out of his hold and stepped back, eyes flashing. Lisette knew she was courting danger, but couldn't seem to stop herself. Dimly realising that anger would protect her against the other emotions torturing the edges of her mind, she deliberately fed her rage. She wanted to despise Raverre for what he was! Fight him! Hate him! Not...

"Why should you behave differently from any other Norman barbarian?" she taunted bitterly.

This didn't have quite the effect she expected. Raverre burst out laughing.

"You know I haven't behaved like a barbarian, you little shrew," he chided. Then his eyes gleamed wickedly. "But if that's what you would prefer I dare say I could oblige you."

This provocative remark and his laughter proved too much. Incoherent with rage, Lisette swung her arm up and slapped him across the face before he had any warning.

She was instantly aghast at what she had done, but before she could speak Raverre hauled her against him with a grip that made Lisette fear her bones would break at any moment.

"You little vixen," he ground out, his own temper swiftly fuelled by the bitter scorn in her voice and frustrated desire. "I can see I've been too patient with you, my lady. So you think me no better than a barbarian, do you? Then, by God, I'll show you a barbarian!"

Swiftly transferring her wrists to one hand, he held her face up to his with the other. Then, before Lisette had time to draw breath, Raverre's mouth crushed hers, kissing her with a ruthless anger that fired her own again.

Unable to struggle against the iron strength of the arms imprisoning her, Lisette kicked out at his legs, eventually landing a blow hard enough to make Raverre step back on the uneven ground to avoid her. She immediately renewed her attempts to escape, throwing them both off balance, but even as the earth rose dizzily to meet her, Raverre twisted, taking the brunt of the fall.

Half dazed by the force with which they landed, and the stinging of her mouth where her lips had been cut, Lisette barely realised that Raverre still held her before he rolled, using his weight to subdue her.

"Now," he said, glaring down at her, "are you ready to calm down?"

With a cry of mingled pain and rage Lisette lashed out with her arms, only to have her wrists captured again. She turned her head and tried to bite him.

"Stop it, you little fool," Raverre grated. "You'll hurt yourself."

"You're the one who's hurting me," she cried, writhing beneath him as she tried to free her arms.

"Damn it, stop that! You don't know what you're doing. Christ!" The last exclamation was smothered against her lips as Raverre brought his mouth down hard on hers again.

When he finally raised his head Lisette had stopped fighting. Her breast heaved as she struggled to catch her breath. She could feel the threatening pressure of his desire against her body.

"Now do you know what you're doing to me?" he rasped. "If you provoked another man like this you'd find yourself raped."

The brutal statement made her flinch. "If you think I'm going to marry you after this you're wrong," she choked.

Raverre went still. Lisette saw the intent in his eyes even before he spoke.

"Then I'll just have to make sure of you," he said with cold menace. "I didn't want it like this, but you're not going to find it so easy to break your promise, my lady." His long legs parted hers with frightening ease, and his free hand lowered to her breast.

A whimper of pure terror escaped her.

"Don't worry," he said bitterly against her mouth. "I'm not going to be rough with you, even if you are as false as any woman. But after tonight you'll know you belong to me."

The quiet tone was threatening, but Lisette grabbed on to the hope that his anger seemed to have died.

"If you take me here," she gasped, fighting to draw breath against the fear gripping her throat, "over my mother's grave, you'll be no better than the brutes who put her there!"

Raverre gave a mirthless laugh, the bitter note more pronounced. "Then your opinion of me shouldn't change, should it?" His hand swept her gown up to her thighs.

Lisette barely heard him. The distant roaring in her ears grew louder, and rushing wings of blackness swept over her. As the forceful weight of Raverre's body drove the breath from her lungs she lost consciousness, going limp beneath him.

Chapter Six

It took Raverre a full minute to realise that Lisette was no longer fighting him. When the knowledge finally penetrated the red mist of bitter rage aroused by her threat, and he drew back to see her lying senseless, her limbs spread-eagled in the grass, ice-cold fear washed over him.

He searched for her heartbeat with a hand that shook, only partially relieved to feel the uneven fluttering in her breast, and to know that Lisette had merely fainted. She seemed so small and fragile that for a sickening instant Raverre thought the uncontrolled strength he had used to subdue her might have been sufficient to end her life.

As sanity returned Raverre quickly swung the mantle off his shoulders. Wrapping the warm garment around her unconscious form, he gathered Lisette into his arms. Then, whispering words of reassurance and love, barely aware of what he was saying, he began to murmur soothingly as she stirred against him, willing his voice to stay soft and even.

Lisette returned slowly to her senses, to find herself still in Raverre's arms, and began to struggle weakly. Then his deep voice penetrated the confusion in her dazed mind and, though too distraught to understand the words, she was calmed by the tone. With shuddering relief she realised that

Raverre was no longer the terrifying stranger she had provoked so blindly. She tried to speak, but her throat seemed to have closed up and she could not utter a word, trembling uncontrollably in his arms for several minutes before he helped her to stand.

"Come," he said, his own voice sounding strained, "they'll be wondering where we are—it must be almost suppertime. Can you walk alone? It will arouse comment if I carry you."

"Aye," Lisette managed in barely above a whisper. She felt as if her legs would not take her more than one step before collapsing beneath her.

However, she did begin to feel stronger as Raverre guided her along the road and through the gates. By the time they reached the outer stairway Lisette started to feel more herself, and, realising she wore Raverre's mantle, put up a shaky hand to return the garment.

She would have spoken then, but he laid a gentle finger over her lips, and guided her silently around the stairway and into the empty guard-room, closing the door behind them.

The room was dark and cold. "Wait," he said as Lisette hesitated by the door.

Raverre quickly lit one of the rush sconces on the wall, and came back to her, seeing for the first time her torn lip and the dark shadows beneath her eyes. He had never asked any man's forgiveness in his life, let alone a woman's, but, looking into Lisette's eyes at that moment, Raverre would have done anything to remove the hurt he saw there.

"I'm sorry," he said abruptly, awkwardly. Then as her swollen lip quivered he took her in his arms, cradling her close, but ready to release her if she wished it. "Forgive me," he murmured more naturally, closing his eyes as his mouth caressed her hair. "You were right, I would have been no better than the men you spoke of."

She shouldn't let him hold her like this, Lisette thought. Only minutes ago Raverre's powerful body had made her terrifyingly aware of her helplessness compared to his superior muscular strength. And yet now she only wanted to stay in those same strong arms, resting her head on his broad shoulders and holding on to a suddenly peaceful feeling of having found a safe harbour after weeks on a storm-tossed sea. She was too exhausted, however, to puzzle over this conflict, and besides, she too had an apology to make.

Lisette drew gently out of his embrace. "'Twas not your doing," she said very low, "I was at fault. What I said to you, I regret. 'Twas untrue and unjust. I know you are not like them. You have shown me nothing but courtesy when you could have been so different. I didn't mean—" She took a deep breath. "I promise I will be a dutiful wife, my lord."

Raverre took her hands in a light clasp. "Dutiful?" he repeated, smiling faintly at her fervent tone.

"Aye," Lisette insisted, determined to make amends. "I do know my duty. I remember my mother telling Enide."

"What did she tell Enide?" he questioned gently, brushing a stray lock of hair from her cheek.

Lisette drew in another deep breath, like an obedient child about to recite a lesson learned by heart. She fixed her gaze on Raverre's tunic.

"That men are different from women and a husband's carnal nature must be tolerated. 'Tis a wife's duty to submit, no matter...no matter how unpleasant...she may find..."

She faltered, her fears returning twofold at the memory of her mother speaking of a distasteful duty. And there had been love between her parents. Without love, surely it must be terrible.

Raverre smiled crookedly. "And now you think you've just seen undisputed evidence of a man's carnal nature," he said. "God, I wish—" He glanced away, then back again, gazing earnestly into her face as Lisette looked up, surprised at his hesitation.

"I suppose 'twould be useless for me to tell you of a woman's carnal nature, as you put it? I prefer to call it desire."

Lisette looked shocked. "Ladies don't have such desires," she protested. She thought of the last half-hour and shuddered. "I couldn't imagine any woman enjoying... wanting...*that!*"

"Not that," Raverre said swiftly, gently cupping her face with warm hands. "This. No, sweet, don't shrink away. Let me show you how it should be. How it will be."

His mouth brushed hers, then he drew back immediately, smiling into her eyes. Her face showed wariness, but she didn't pull away. Raverre lowered his head again.

Lisette felt the gentle touch of his mouth. On her temple, in a series of tiny kisses across her cheekbone and down to the corner of her mouth. Her eyes drifted closed. She should protest. This same man had almost taken her in anger. But it was so sweet. She'd never known such warm sweetness. She felt weak again. But this time it was not the weakness of forced submission; rather a willing, melting surrender.

Raverre repeated the delicate caresses on the other side of her face, coming near her mouth, but never touching it. And then, unthinking, instinctively, Lisette turned her face slightly and their lips met in a kiss of heart-stopping tenderness. She felt the briefest touch of Raverre's tongue lightly caress her bruised mouth, then he was straightening away from her.

"There," he said huskily as her eyes flew open, dark and wondering. "You see? Was there anything to fear in my kisses?"

"No, but..."

He smiled." And you liked them."

This was too much to confess, but Lisette blushed. "I have said I will be dutiful," she stammered. "What more do you want? You are forcing me to wed you...you have taken my home...we are enemies."

"No," Raverre denied instantly. His eyes hardened. "Don't start that again. I am no enemy of yours. Your home was lost to you when your father swore for Harold, but by marrying me you will regain it. You do not lose by our bargain, my lady."

Lisette edged to the door. "I will keep my promise to wed you," she whispered, "but there can be no more than a bargain between us."

She had reached the doorway and was halfway through it, when Raverre spoke again.

"I wouldn't have forced you." The words were clipped and harsh. "I know you'll keep your promise."

Lisette hesitated. Then, glancing back with a timid smile, she slipped into the night.

Cool, pearly grey fingers of dawn crept over the horizon, heralding her wedding-day.

Unable to sleep, Lisette had been crouched in the window embrasure for hours, wrapped in a new red woollen cloak Bertrand had brought from Winchester. Paid for by Raverre, she reminded herself. It was another item on the account she owed him.

The improvements to the manor she could argue away—

they were to Raverre's advantage, after all. But by marrying her and sending Enide to the Church's protection he had forfeited two possibly valuable alliances. And, apart from that, he was supporting all of them from his own funds until the manor became fully self-sufficient again.

Of course, there were advantages to him also in marrying her. Lisette tried to concentrate on those, because if she didn't she would think about the way she had behaved last night. But the memories kept coming back.

Of herself lashing out at Raverre like a wild creature, threatening to break her vow to marry him. Lisette wondered if that demented girl had really been her. She had behaved as one possessed by demons. And why? Because she had wanted to despise Raverre and couldn't? Because she wanted to fight him and needed a reason? Even in his anger, he still hadn't given her real cause for hatred.

He had used his strength to subdue her, but the bruises on her body he had been provoked into inflicting. Lisette knew there were plenty of men who would have beaten her unmercifully in answer to such provocation, and not apologised for it later.

She huddled further into the cloak at the memory of Raverre's tenderness in the guard-room. And later. At supper he had seen her hand shake on the wine cup and had steadied it with his own. His gentle concern had almost brought her to the brink of tears, and she had clenched her teeth until her jaw ached, determined not to shame herself any further.

And nor would she shame herself by betraying how nervous the thought of becoming Raverre's wife made her. She would be dutiful if it killed her. At this inconvenient moment she remembered how her mother had died, broken and bleeding, after being raped and beaten by Norman soldiers.

"Lisette? Are you feeling all right?"

It was Enide, looking worried, her fair hair tousled from sleep. With a start Lisette realised that full daylight had come while she'd been so engrossed in her thoughts.

Catherine was sitting up in the big bed, rubbing her eyes and yawning. Marjory grumbled at the cold air blowing in through the shutters Lisette had opened. Just another morning.

If only it were.

Lisette summoned up a smile. If nothing else, her sister would be safe. Already Enide looked more animated than she had for months, knowing she was to be permitted to retire to the cloister.

"I was wondering how our mother felt on her wedding-day," she improvised.

"Relieved to get out of that fever-ridden swamp the Celts had retreated to, I imagine," said Marjory tartly. "And, if you must open the shutters before a decent time of day, at least put on some warm clothes."

Lisette couldn't help laughing. "Oh, Marjory, what would we ever do without your good sense?" she cried, flinging her arms about her old nurse.

"Tush," returned Marjory sternly. But she stroked Lisette's cheek lovingly, her gaze softening. "Your mother told me she sat up to watch the dawn, and wondered if her husband would ever come to love her as she loved him. As she found later, he already adored her." Marjory smiled complacently. "You and Raverre are not so different, I think."

Lisette's mouth fell open. She was quite unable to speak, however. Taking advantage of having had the last word for once, Marjory steered her favourite nurseling over to a stool.

"Now, sit and let me comb out your hair. I ordered hot

water and the tub to be brought first thing, and here is a
bowl of freshly perfumed soap. We shall have you bathed
and scented, and as pampered as any new bride should be.''

Marjory was true to her word. When Raverre finally saw
his bride enter the churchyard on Bertrand's arm his breath
caught at her beauty.

Her dark hair had been left loose and hung to her waist
in a shining bronze cloud, threaded with autumn daisies.
The blue silk gown, made in the Norman fashion, clung to
her still girlish figure, outlining her small breasts and slender waist, before flaring below her hips to fall in graceful
folds to the ground. Marjory had stitched a trim of dark
sable fur at the hem and around the full sleeves to add a
touch of luxury, and a heavy girdle of chased silver, set
with garnets, gave her a look of delicate fragility.

Lisette saw the crowd of churls and soldiers, heard the
appreciative murmurs paying tribute to her beauty, but they
seemed to remain at a hazy distance. She felt as though she
watched another girl walking along the road and through
the wicker gate.

And she still clung to that cool, protective distance as
she stepped into the porch entrance of the church, where
Raverre awaited her.

So, she was now a Norman's lady, Lisette told herself,
gazing over the hall from her seat at the high table.

The ceremony was over. The feasting was over. People
were gathering in their accustomed groups, exchanging
gossip, and some of the younger folk had started an extremely noisy game of hoodman blind. Lisette saw a timid
Edgith coaxed into the game by a young, fresh-faced soldier who hovered over her protectively.

This is the beginning of a Norman England, she realised
suddenly. A stronger England perhaps. The notion startled
her, but she couldn't erase it. I'm tired, she thought. But

she was feeling more at ease now after several draughts of wine and very little food.

She wasn't the only one. A burst of loud laughter made Lisette glance up to see Gilbert dancing about with a harp, his actions becoming more and more suggestive of an ardent suitor pursuing a most reluctant maiden.

Raverre grinned, but turned to Lisette. "I think perhaps your sisters should retire. This feast is about to become most unsuited to delicate maidenly sensibilities."

Catherine giggled. "Don't worry, Alain," she advised cheekily. "Saxons are the most hardened drinkers in the world. You should have seen some of my father's celebrations."

"I dare say," he answered, with a shrewd glance from her flushed countenance to the empty drinking horn in her hand. "But I doubt if *you* stayed until everyone fell asleep where they sat. Be off with you before I have Marjory after me for corrupting her chicks."

He stood and held out a hand to Lisette, drawing her up beside him. "Come, sweetheart, 'tis time we retired also."

Lisette blushed wildly, barely managing to bid goodnight to her sisters with any coherence as she and Raverre were surrounded by jostling well-wishers. Robust advice on how to keep a husband—or wife— content in the marriage bed was laughingly shouted out from all sides.

Dazed by the noisy confusion, Lisette shrank against Raverre. Instantly she was swept up into his arms and cradled against his chest. Quite unconsciously she clasped her arms about his neck, hiding her face against his tunic.

"Don't be alarmed," he murmured in her ear. "'Tis only fun." He strode towards the solar, shouldering the door closed on the boisterous, applauding crowd.

There was blissful silence. The air felt wonderfully cool

after the close, smoky atmosphere in the hall. Lisette wondered why Raverre hadn't moved from the door.

"You can look now," he said, laughter in his voice. "We're alone."

Wishing she could hide her face until the night was over, Lisette looked. The first thing to meet her gaze was Raverre's amused face. But behind the smile in his eyes a glittering elation burned. Lisette's heart began to race.

Trying to hide her nervousness, she glanced about the room. The solar had been transformed. Newly acquired tapestries, with a distinctly Norman look about them, softened the chilly appearance of the stone walls. A table and chair occupied the space between the two window embrasures, and two solid chests flanked the fireplace.

A fat candle burned in solitary splendour atop its iron spike, and more light was cast by the wall sconces. There was even a thick sheepskin rug on the floor, and Lisette was illogically relieved to see a prie-dieu in the corner by the bed.

Naturally she hadn't believed those rumours that Normans were the spawn of the Devil, but it was comforting nevertheless to see proof of it. Then her gaze fell on the newly constructed bed, with its bearskin cover turned back and a fresh linen sheet laid over the straw mattress. Thoughts of comfort fled.

Seeing her eyes skitter nervously away from the bed, Raverre strode forward to set Lisette down by the fire.

"I expect the solar looks somewhat different to you," he remarked with deliberate casualness, moving back to the door to drop a wooden bar into the brackets on either side. It landed with what, to Lisette, sounded like an ominous thud.

Why hadn't anyone told her what she was supposed to do now? Did a dutiful wife just blithely throw off her clothes and climb into bed like some willing sacrifice? Lisette suddenly remembered Raverre's fiercely burning passion when he had kissed her in the stable, and how helpless she had felt in the churchyard in the face of his overwhelming strength. She decided she could put off being dutiful for a few moments longer.

Starting to shiver, she moved closer to the fireplace and sat down on the small stool there, holding her hands to the warmth.

"It does look different," she agreed. Was conversation proper at a time like this? "But I like it. The tapestries are very good."

"My mother did them," Raverre replied, striding over to the windows and fastening the wooden shutters. "There. Warmer now, sweet?" He returned to the fireplace, hunkering down on his heels with his back to Lisette and reaching for a small jug.

She hadn't noticed it before, but now Lisette breathed in the spicy aroma of mulled wine.

"I must try to send my parents word of our marriage," Raverre commented. "My father would like to know our line will continue here in England."

"They won't mind that you've married a Saxon?" Lisette queried cautiously.

Raverre grinned at her over his shoulder as he held the dark liquid close to the flames, swirling the wine jug gently with his wrist. "My mother will be so overjoyed to know I'm married that it wouldn't matter if you were Saxon, Dane or Saracen. I've been the despair of her for years."

Oh, dear, she was starting to like him again, Lisette thought. When those blue eyes smiled with such male wickedness it was impossible not to smile back. And he was being so kind, letting her get used to being alone with him in the quiet privacy of the solar.

She thought of all the other occasions when he had shown her gentleness, even understanding, and tried to banish her fears. Then Raverre rose to his feet, immediately looming over her. Lisette's heart jumped, but he merely crossed to the table and poured some wine into a drinking horn.

"I had this mulled earlier, and it's been keeping warm here by the fire." Raverre came back to Lisette and handed her the drinking horn.

She had already drunk a lot of wine this evening, Lisette remembered, but on the other hand the fresh air in the solar had now blown away her slight dizziness, so perhaps a bit more would help.

Unable to meet the intense look in Raverre's eyes, Lisette grabbed the drinking horn and tilted it to her mouth far too quickly. Warm wine splashed her nose, and what managed to find her mouth went down the wrong way. Lisette choked.

Raverre rescued the drink and placed it on the hearth, then took her hands, drawing her to her feet. "There's no need to be so afraid," he murmured, wiping wine drops away with his fingers. "I'm not going to hurt you."

Lisette looked up. He was so big. She barely reached his shoulder. "You're not?" she quavered doubtfully.

One corner of Raverre's mouth quirked in a wry smile. He hadn't expected to spend his wedding-night explaining to his wife what she should have heard from another female.

He caressed her cheek with his knuckles. "Sweetheart, I'll be very careful with you, but the first time…" His mouth lowered to hers. "If I hurt you it will only be for a moment, I swear." Their lips met.

Lisette had no real time to absorb his words before she was caught up in the sweetness of Raverre's kiss. He had kissed her in passion and in anger, and she had managed to resist both, but this gentle seduction of her senses threatened to make her forget her fear, forget their bargain, forget everything except a gradually more insistent need to respond.

Before she could, however, Raverre suddenly released her mouth. Sweeping her off her feet, he carried Lisette to the bed and sat her down on the bearskin. Then he knelt and drew off her soft leather shoes.

"God's bones, your feet are like ice!" he exclaimed, chafing them briskly.

It seemed such a commonplace, practical thing to do that Lisette felt herself relax a little. Her eyes wandered to the fair head so close to her. In the light his hair shone like gold. Unable to resist wondering how it would feel, she put out a timid hand and touched him. His hair felt soft.

Raverre glanced up quickly and Lisette snatched her hand back, flushing.

He rose and propped one knee on the bed beside her, capturing her face between his hands. "Don't be afraid to touch me, Lisette," he said softly.

Her name, spoken in that deep, husky voice, sent a strangely pleasurable shiver through her. One long-fingered hand began to thread through her hair. A daisy fluttered to the floor.

"See? It feels good, doesn't it? Your hair feels like silk, almost as soft as your skin." Another daisy fell into Lisette's lap. Raverre's soft voice murmured reassuringly as he continued to remove the flowers. "These looked very pretty today, but I fear they will be sadly squashed if they stay where they are."

Suddenly he nuzzled the side of her throat, his lips caressing through the silky strands of hair. "Your scent reminds me of a rose garden I once saw in Aquitaine. 'Twas beautiful, but empty." He drew back to gaze into her eyes. His had darkened to slate. "Now I can picture you there, as soft and lovely as one of the roses."

The huskily murmured words were as seductive as the caress of his mouth, Lisette thought hazily. Her head fell back under the growing pressure of his kisses and the sweet weakness she had known before began to flow through her limbs.

Without knowing how, she found herself lying across the bed, encircled in Raverre's arms, his mouth gentle on hers as he brushed the tiniest of kisses across her lips. Her heart fluttered wildly. It wasn't enough. She wanted...

Her lips parted. Instantly he accepted the silent invitation, deepening the kiss until all her senses seemed filled with him. The feel of his mouth, the gentle invasion of his tongue, the sweet taste of wine, the clean masculine scent of him. The unfamiliar touch of his hand against the bare skin of her shoulder.

Lisette's eyes flew open. He had unfastened her gown. She gasped in shock as his mouth left hers, and his eyes shifted, gazing into anxious blue depths for several long seconds.

"Would you rather undress yourself?" he asked gently.

Lisette nodded quickly. She couldn't speak. Would he be angry?

"Such big eyes," he said, smiling down at her. "It's all right, my shy little bride. "The smile turned devilish. "This time."

Dropping a quick kiss on her lips, Raverre rose from the bed. Lisette sat up slowly, one hand holding her gown in place. She was grateful for Raverre's understanding, but did he expect her to undress while he watched? Suddenly the room seemed far too brightly lit.

Then, as though in answer to the unconscious appeal in

her eyes, Raverre circled the room, snuffing out the sconce
lights. He even doused the candle which normally burned
day and night. Blessed darkness fell over the solar, broken
only by the flickering of the rapidly dying fire.

Lisette hurriedly pulled off the blue gown and her shift.
Letting them fall in a silken heap to the floor, she leapt into
bed, pulling the bearskin up to her chin. Only then did she
risk a glance at Raverre.

He stood with his back to her, stripping off his tunic and
undershirt. Corded muscles flexed across his shoulders and
back as he flung the garments aside. His arms were strongly
sinewed, and when he turned the same powerful ripple of
muscle showed across his chest and flat stomach. The fire-
light flickered over his skin, burnishing it, and his gold hair
fell across his brow in ruffled disorder, softening the hard
planes of his face.

He's beautiful, thought Lisette, startled. She had never
realised a man could be considered beautiful, but Raverre
was. A beautiful male animal in the prime of his strength
and power. She was suddenly acutely aware of her own
slender softness, her femininity.

He sat on the edge of the bed, unwinding the thongs from
his boots and leggings. Lisette hurriedly averted her gaze,
sliding down in the bed until the bearskin covered her to
the eyes. When Raverre turned to climb in next to her she
saw his teeth gleam in an irrepressible smile. He peeled the
bearskin back a few inches, drawing Lisette close to him.

She was immediately enveloped by heat, her senses spinning in a dizzying whirlpool of fear, shyness and the sheer
physical presence of Raverre's naked body leaning over
hers.

He was so close that she could feel the violent pounding
of his heart, the knotted tension in his whole body. Could
feel how much he wanted her, and yet his hands were warm

and gentle as they stroked her hair, spreading it over the linen pillow until it framed her face like a dark halo.

"My beautiful wife," he murmured. "Mine." He bent to kiss her, his hand sweeping in a long caress down the side of her body and up to rest just below her breast.

Lisette trembled. She had never felt so vulnerable.

"I'm only going to touch you," he whispered. "Don't be afraid. I'll be so gentle with you, my love."

Lisette dimly remembered her resolve not to betray her fear. Somehow it no longer mattered.

"I...I feel so strange," she stammered in a tiny voice. "Not really afraid, but...we scarcely know...two weeks ago I didn't even..." Oh, how could she ever explain?

A flash of tender protectiveness went through Raverre. He hung on to it, knowing it was the only thing preventing him from burying himself in her, possessing her until she could never be apart from him again. He knew he would lose her completely if he frightened her, nor could he bear the thought of hurting her.

"I know, little one, I know," he murmured reassuringly. "You don't know how you find yourself flying in the arms of your enemy."

"Aye," she gasped thankfully. "Oh, please don't be angry. I will try to—"

"Shhh." His hand lightly stroked her breast.

Lisette made a small sound of shock at the intimate caress. Her hands came up to push against his arms, but instead she felt herself gripping Raverre's shoulders as waves of heat seemed to dissolve her vague feeling of outrage. Suddenly his touch was no longer alien, an intrusion. It felt right.

The tremors shaking her body increased. Confusion and apprehension fought with tremulously awakening desire.

Raverre held her close. "Don't fight me, sweetheart. Just

for tonight, forget about Norman and Saxon. Here, between us two, there's no need for conquest or surrender, but only a man and a maid.'' His voice deepened to a low, husky murmur that Lisette heard in the deepest part of her heart. ''Trust me, darling. For tonight, let yourself trust me.''

She was his. Though there had been no word of love spoken between them, Lisette knew she belonged to Raverre on some deep, primitive level that lay beyond words.

And the knowledge frightened her intensely. Far more than the simple fear of the unknown she had felt earlier.

Had Raverre taken her roughly, or even carelessly, she could have escaped this sense of belonging, could have remained apart from him, only yielding her body. But no lover could have been more patient with her innocence, more passionately tender. She had barely felt the brief, stinging pain at the moment of his possession, so utterly overwhelming had been the sensation of becoming one with him.

Raverre had held her so tightly, rigidly still while her body had struggled to adjust to his, that she had felt totally surrounded, enveloped by him. And then he had moved.

Lisette stirred in Raverre's arms, and he reached down to pull up the bearskin, cocooning them in its dark warmth. He nestled Lisette against his side, holding her securely in his arms.

''Are you hurting, sweetheart?'' His voice was a soft growl in the darkness.

Lisette considered the question. She was aware of a slight unfamiliar soreness inside, but deeper still a restless ache was making itself felt. It made her want—

Then, even as she questioned, the ache slipped away. She could not hold on to the feeling; its memory eluded her.

''No, you did not hurt me,'' she said. Then, as though compelled by the warm intimacy of the moment, added in a voice that was still uncertain, faintly questioning, "'Twas not…distasteful."

Raverre brushed her cheek in a tender caress. "It will be better next time, love. 'Twas too new for you tonight—" he gave a soft laugh "—and I wanted you too much. Next time there'll only be pleasure, I promise."

That was it, Lisette realised, eyes wide open and staring into the dark. That feeling. An elusive promise of pleasure, and completeness with another, such as she had never known. And there, also, lay the danger, lay the threat she had sensed from the very moment of seeing Raverre.

Instinctively Lisette thrust the thought away. "I wonder why my mother told Enide…" she began, saying the first thing that came into her head.

"Enide is not like you, sweetheart," he answered. "Even before your mother's death, for her 'twould be no more than a wifely duty." Feeling the sudden tension in her body, Raverre bit off his next words, cursing himself.

She was not ready to face the passion within herself, though he knew it was there. He had seen it directed at him in anger, but to have it directed at him in love he would have to move slowly, until Lisette no longer saw him as an enemy.

Turning on his side, Raverre gathered Lisette against the comforting warmth of his body. "Go to sleep now, little wife," he murmured into her hair. "I'll keep you safe."

Lisette remained silent, but as she heard Raverre's breathing deepened into slumber her mind continued to question for long hours afterwards; until weariness finally overtook her as the first pale light of dawn crept over the misty countryside.

The fire had been lit, and someone had brought her clothes from the tower room. Her simple homespun gowns hung from a rod across one corner of the solar, alongside

Raverre's tunics and his long dark blue mantle. She was alone.

Lisette sat up, her eyes resting thoughtfully on her wedding gown, still lying in a silken puddle on the floor, and the wilted daisies scattered by the bed.

He is no longer my enemy.

The words flashed into Lisette's mind and refused to be banished. She tried to deny them, but the questions kept coming. Would an enemy have soothed her fears last night? Or gently coaxed her past her shyness? Would an enemy have held her so protectively afterwards that she felt as though nothing could ever harm her again?

Suddenly restless, Lisette climbed from the bed and flung open the shutters. Bright daylight streamed into the room with a rush of cool morning air. She had slept quite late.

Her linen shifts lay folded on the table. Lisette slipped one over her head. Had Raverre placed them there? she wondered, tying the ribbons at the neck. The thought of his big hands touching the delicate garments brought warmth to her face, and was immediately followed by the memory of those same hands caressing her body. Strong hands, slightly calloused, and yet his touch had been so gentle. The warmth spread as far as her toes.

"'Tis the fire which is so hot," Lisette grumbled, conscious of a sudden urge to know the touch of his hands again, now that she was no longer afraid.

'Tis only curiosity, she scolded herself. And look where curiosity had led before. To a confrontation with male desires that she hadn't been able to control. Of course, she hadn't exactly been in control last night either, she remembered uneasily. Raverre had been the one in command of both of them. Recalling the tensely leashed power in the hard muscles beneath her hands, Lisette realised for the first time how truly formidable had been his control.

It meant nothing, she told herself sternly. If Raverre had married Enide he would have treated her as patiently. But then why did she recall so vividly the incredible feeling of oneness with him—such closeness—the beckoning promise of unimagined delight?

She hurriedly reminded herself that Raverre had taken over her home. For the first time, it did no good. Her inherent honesty argued that it had been granted to him after victory in honourable battle. Such things had happened from time immemorial.

And while she was being honest, Lisette thought, she might as well admit that her churls' loss of freedom had its more positive side. It *was* a relief to know the manor was constantly protected, that the harvest would be gathered safely, that men would be available for the wood-carrying in November, and that even the poorest serf would enjoy the free logs and bonfire which followed.

And, on a more personal level, she knew Raverre was honourable and just. He had been kind to her sisters, and as for herself—

Lisette grabbed the nearest gown and pulled it on. She was back at the start of the argument. But if Raverre was no longer her enemy, then what?

How could she forget that her parents had died at the hands of Norman soldiers? No matter what she thought of Raverre, how could she forget that he was still one of them? An invader? A conqueror? And how could she willingly lie with such a man, except when she must keep her side of their agreement? An agreement, Lisette reminded herself sternly, into which he had forced her.

She began to feel better. Raverre had virtually blackmailed her into marrying him; there was no argument about *that*. Well, she would hold to their bargain, but that would be all. Last night she had been unsure and afraid, and Raverre had been kind. No wonder she felt drawn to him. But he had only married her for practical reasons, after all. She would be dutiful, but distant.

Dragging a bone comb ruthlessly through her tangled hair, Lisette continued to expound along these lines. She had finally succeeded in quelling a nagging little voice that kept asking why she should need to be so determined, when the door opened and Raverre appeared.

Slamming the door behind him, he reached Lisette in three long strides, swung her up into his arms and kissed her warmly on the mouth. Her resolve tottered.

Setting her down again, he said teasingly, "Well, I see you are no worse for being married, sweet lady. How do you find yourself this morning? Hungry? I am come to tell you that dinner is on the table and awaiting. And about time—I could eat an ox whole."

Lisette sank back on to the chair by the table, wondering why her legs felt so shaky. "I must just braid my hair," she managed, but her fingers were all thumbs. The braid was going to be hopelessly loose; it would probably fall apart at the first puff of wind.

Suddenly Raverre's hands covered hers. "I think you need some help," he murmured, a smile in his voice.

Lisette glanced at him over her shoulder, surprised laughter bubbling up through her nervousness. "You?" she asked incredulously.

He grinned down at her. "Oh, I have other skills besides fighting." He propped a plate of beaten copper on the table and turned her face toward it. "Let me show you."

Two seconds later Lisette realised Raverre's intent. Ignoring her squeak of protest, with deft fingers he quickly unravelled the braid, spreading her hair over her shoulders. Her hands came up to stop him.

His eyes capturing hers in the mirror, Raverre gently

returned her hands to her lap. "Wait," he instructed. "I haven't finished."

There was a quick flash of light as he carefully lowered a gold circlet to Lisette's head. Her lips parted in surprise. It was the most exquisite thing she had ever seen. Beautifully crafted, the delicate band was engraved with dragons, whose precious sapphire eyes reflected the colour of Lisette's own. Raverre adjusted the circlet so the dragons' glowing eyes met above the centre of her brow.

"Where did that come from?" she managed weakly.

"Wales, judging by the dragons, but just lately Winchester."

Lisette had to smile. "You know that's not what I meant."

He grinned. That wicked male grin that was totally irresistible. "I've been keeping it for you. Your bride-gift, my lady." Raverre drew Lisette to her feet, wrapping his arms around her. Their eyes met in the mirror. "Do you like it?"

Lisette gazed wide-eyed at their reflections. The circlet was the loveliest piece of jewellery she had ever owned, but that was not what held her attention.

How tiny and fragile she appeared against Raverre's powerful frame, and how devastatingly handsome he looked with the morning light slanting sharply across his cheekbones, touching his firm mouth. His eyes were lowered. Following their direction, Lisette saw the telltale pulse beating in her throat.

"'Tis very beautiful," she whispered.

His arms tightened gently. "So are you," he said huskily. "That circlet makes you look like a pagan Celtic princess." His gaze lifted again to hers.

Dizziness washed over Lisette. She was mesmerised by the suddenly smouldering look in Raverre's eyes. She couldn't move, couldn't breathe. His eyes were burning her. If he had looked at her like this last night she would have died of fright. She still might if she didn't do something, say something.

"I...I really...should wear a coif...now I'm married," she whispered breathlessly.

"I know," he agreed, but he made no move to release her. One hand caressed her silky hair. "You can cover this during the day." He turned her to face him. "But not yet...not yet." His mouth came down on hers in a kiss of absolute possession.

A wild thrill of excitement shot through Lisette's entire body. If Raverre hadn't been holding her so tightly she would have fallen. She could do nothing to stop herself sagging against him, could not stop her arms from clinging to him as if he was her only support.

Still kissing her, Raverre shifted his hold. Lisette found herself swept off her feet and carried to the bed. Releasing her mouth, Raverre flung back the bearskin, and went absolutely still. Confused, Lisette looked around, her eyes falling to the small bloodstain on the sheet.

Reality rushed back with a vengeance. Blushing hotly, she glanced away. "Put me down. Please," she begged, unable to look at him.

Raverre lowered her to the floor, but he captured her face, his eyes now searching troubled.

"Did I hurt you so badly," he asked urgently. "Oh, sweetheart. I'm sorry."

His concern completely undermined what was left of her defences.

"'Twas only a slight hurt," she whispered, feeling strangely impelled to reassure him. "Truly I barely noticed..." Lisette faltered, blushing again at the expression that flashed into his eyes. How could she be distant and dutiful when he looked at her like that?

Then, as his mouth lowered again, she panicked. "They'll be waiting for us in the hall," she quavered.

Raverre hesitated. Then, with a swiftness that left her gasping, he picked Lisette up and deposited her on the bed, flinging himself down beside her and throwing an arm across her as she went to leap up.

"Oh, no," he said softly, leaning over her, his eyes fixed on her face with glittering intensity. "I have you now, my lovely wife, and I intend to hold you. For the rest of our lives."

Lisette gazed up at him, wondering what she was meant to say to this possessive statement. It seemed safer to stay silent. She doubted if she could speak anyway, because the only words she could think of were distant and dutiful. She kept repeating them over and over to herself as though they were a magic incantation which would protect her.

She didn't want to ask why she needed protection.

"You're still afraid of me," Raverre murmured, stroking her cheek with his knuckles. "I'll never hurt you again, love, I swear it."

He'd misunderstood her panic, Lisette realised thankfully. But before she could speak he pressed his mouth gently to the fluttering pulse in her throat.

"Your heart is beating like a trapped bird's," he said softly. "Relax, sweet." He raised his head, puzzled. "You were less—"

Deliverance came in the form of a knock at the door.

Raverre flicked a glance across the room. "Our dinner must be getting cold," he remarked, slanting a wry smile down at Lisette. "Wouldn't you think they'd know better than to—?"

The knock came again.

Muttering something under his breath, Raverre swung himself off the bed. He strode over to the door and yanked it open. *"What?"*

Gilbert and Siward both stepped back in a hurry.

"Sorry, sir," apologised Gilbert, recovering first. "But I thought you should know. A band of serfs turned up in the village just now. Siward says they're asking for shelter."

"Wonderful timing," growled Raverre. He looked a question at Siward.

"Five men, my lord," the blacksmith elaborated. "They say their master has fled. They've been living in the forest, but they have women and children who will not survive another winter in the open. The leader says they're willing to swear fealty to you. I have him out in the bailey."

"Very well, bring him in. I'll see him shortly." Raverre started to close the door. "Feed them," he added curtly. The door slammed.

Gilbert and Siward looked at each other. "I think I'll go hunting this afternoon," announced Gilbert. "And if I were you, Siward, I'd find plenty of work to do elsewhere for the rest of the day."

"We won't see those two for the rest of the day," remarked Raverre, turning to Lisette.

He gave a somewhat reluctant smile when he saw that she had lost no time in leaving the bed. Her hair was now arranged in the most haphazard braid he had ever seen, and she was replacing the circlet over a white linen coif. Then she turned, and the wary relief on her face wiped the smile from his own.

There was a long, uncomfortable silence. Finally Raverre turned and held open the door.

"Come, my lady," he said, his voice very cool. "Dinner awaits."

* * *

Harness jingled. Horses stamped, snorting cloudy breaths into the frosty air. The wind blew coldly, bending the bare branches of the trees standing sentinel along the road. Far to the west storm clouds were gathering in a slowly eddying grey mass.

And Raverre was angry with her.

Since yesterday he had scarcely addressed two words to her. Lisette had retired early, falling into a surprisingly deep sleep, and if she hadn't seen the indentation left by Raverre's head on the pillow next to her she would not have known that he had shared her bed last night.

Lisette eyed her husband as he issued instructions to the soldiers accompanying Enide and three serfs to Romsey. The serfs had been chosen for Enide's comfort and security—Alfrida to see to her needs, and two men to accompany the girl back to Ambray. Raverre trusted them to return, Lisette realised. Why did that realisation make her feel worse? Feel this sudden need to tell him—?

Lisette stopped her thoughts, concentrating fiercely on the farewell between her sisters. With the usual buoyancy of youth Catherine looked as cheerful as if she were merely seeing Enide off on a short jaunt, instead of parting with her forever.

Annoyed at her own tearful emotions, Lisette embraced her older sister briskly. Enide drew back to look into Lisette's face.

"It should be I standing in your place, I know," she began in a low voice. She went on quickly as Lisette made to protest. "No, please hear me. I had not the courage, though I have long known that your husband would not treat a woman harshly.

"Oh, Lisette, forgive me! I shall pray every day that you find the happiness you deserve with him, that I have not done you a terrible wrong. And do not judge Raverre too hardly. He is sending a dowry with me so I may not be taken in on sufferance. Few men would do as much, when he has already permitted me to retire to the cloister.''

Lisette felt tears well in her eyes. She blinked them rapidly away, embracing her sister. ''There is nought to forgive, dearest sister. Go with God and be content.''

Enide turned away quickly, and in a flurry of mounting riders and shouted farewells they were through the gates, disappearing down the road in a slowly subsiding cloud of dust.

''Well, that's one less for you to worry about,'' muttered Raverre behind her.

Lisette turned from her contemplation of the empty road. ''I didn't see Enide as a burden,'' she protested, guiltily remembering the times she had felt impatient with her sister. ''She suffered terribly.''

''No much more than you,'' Raverre stated bluntly. ''You might not have witnessed the attack, as she did, but you still saw the results. Bertrand told me your mother died later in your arms. And then you had to cope with the other deaths and sack of the manor.''

''I...''

''Do you think I don't know why you're so afraid of me—that you feared I would treat you as brutally?''

''No, I didn't—''

''I think Enide would have thrown herself from the tower rather than marry a Norman for the sake of her people. I hope she realises how fortunate she is in her sister.''

''No, you mustn't be so hard. Enide couldn't help—''

''Being weak.''

Was she never to get a word in? ''I wasn't going to say—''

''Do you wish 'twas yourself riding away to a life of

dedication to God?'' he asked suddenly, his gaze intent on her face.

Lisette looked away towards the road. A gust of wind sent a pile of dead leaves dancing in twirling abandon after the riders. She recognised the absolute truth of her answer before she spoke.

''No, I have never wanted that. Even when I thought it the only alternative to—''

''Marriage to me,'' he finished for her grimly.

Lisette gazed up at Raverre, confused by the rather bleak look on his face. She felt an inexplicable urge to say that marriage to him was what she now wanted. But, unwilling to do so far down a path whose destination lay shrouded in a fog of jumbled emotions and unknown consequences, she could only shake her head, clutching gratefully at Enide's words.

''I must thank you, my lord, for providing my sister with a dowry,'' she said, faltering a little as he continued to look so stern and cold. '''Twas a great kindness.''

The coldness disappeared instantly, to be replaced by such raging anger that Lisette stepped back involuntarily as Raverre's eyes went violent.

''Damn it, I don't want your gratitude!'' he snapped harshly, before turning and striding away, aggression in every line of his body.

And he stayed angry. Remaining aloof whenever their paths crossed during the day, retiring hours after Lisette and leaving her bed before she awoke. He made no attempt to claim a husband's rights, and after several days of being ignored Lisette was dismayed to find that duty had given way to longing.

A longing to be close to him that was achingly increased whenever she awoke in the night to find that, despite Rav-

erre's puzzling behaviour, he held her tightly in his arms
while he slept.

Did he know? Did he mean to hold her so possessively?
Not knowing how to approach him when he continued so
cold, nor even fully understanding that her own emotions
were changing, Lisette struggled to prevent herself betraying her distress at the loss of the fragile companionship they
had sometimes shared before their marriage.

And Raverre, tormented by the suspicion that, by taking
her body before he had won her heart, she would only feel
polite gratitude and duty towards him, kept his distance,
treating Lisette with a cold courtesy that withered at the
outset any attempt she might have made to reconcile her
guilt and respond to him.

Lisette pondered over a depressing future indeed as she
lingered over a substantial supper of venison stew three
evenings later. Raverre had thrown a meaty bone to Finn,
but the dog now turned his head towards the door as one
of the men-at-arms ushered a young Norman soldier into
the hall. While the man paced down the length of the room
Lisette had plenty of time to notice that he had ridden long
and hard; his face was lined with weariness and the dust
of the road lay thick on his clothes.

Raverre and Richard de Somrey, whose men were on
guard duty at the manor, had suspended their conversation
at first sight of the visitor, and Raverre rose to his feet as
the young man reached the table. Barely acknowledging the
girls with a slight bow, he addressed Raverre in a hoarse,
breathless voice, swaying with the effort of remaining upright until his message was safely delivered.

"My lord, I am Ralf de Pictou, squire in the army of our
lord King, and bring you greetings from William and news
that will make unpleasant hearing but must be told."

"Take your time, de Pictou," recommended Raverre

firmly, having had plenty of experience with over-eager young men burdened with a responsible errand. "A few moments to catch your breath will make no difference, whether the news be ill or not."

De Pictou steadied himself with an obvious effort.

"My lord, ill news indeed, for young Edgar the Atheling is now forsworn, and has escaped from the King's custody. Together with his mother and sister, he has taken refuge with King Malcolm of Scotland. There is rumour abroad that a marriage has been arranged between Malcolm and the Saxon princess, but 'tis not known for sure."

A startled murmur swept the hall at this announcement and some of the men leapt to their feet, but the messenger continued without a pause.

"Also, that traitor Morcar of Northumbria has broken his vows to William, and is busy stirring up a rebellion in the Midlands with the new Earl, Gospatric—another Englishman, God rot them all, who bought his Earldom from William and now has the effrontery to turn his hand against his benefactor.

"The King has sent me to warn you of his coming. He intends to personally direct the campaign against these traitors and will be travelling north as soon as he has seen all settled here on the borders."

"Then he will not be far behind you," decided Raverre, looking grim at the news. "William moves fast. Even with the whole court at his back, he'll be here in two days.

"We'll make all ready tomorrow," he announced in a louder tone for the benefit of his listening men. "To meet whatever need of men and arms the King may have."

Gesturing for them to resume their seats, he looked thoughtfully down at his guest. "But for the moment you must sit and take food." Raverre eyed the younger man shrewdly. "When did you last eat, my friend?"

Ralf swayed tiredly again and shrugged. "I ate something as I rode. To say truth, my lord, I barely remember it. And tomorrow I must be off again to warn the Earl of Hereford at Eywas Harold."

"No matter. You will have proper food and rest tonight at least."

He turned to Lisette, but she had already sent a serf hurrying to the kitchen to bring more hot food and, as their guest seated himself thankfully between Raverre and de Somery, she gestured to Edric to bring the finger basin so that Ralf could wash his hands.

She didn't dare catch Raverre's eye. After her brave talk of Saxon nobility she was now faced with the turncoat activities of two of the country's once most powerful Earls. For if Morcar had betrayed William's trust then it was fairly safe to assume that his brother, Edwin, Earl of Mercia, would not hesitate to join him. The only possible plea she could make on their behalf would be the one King Harold had used—that their oaths of allegiance had been extracted under duress.

Clasping her hands tightly together in her lap for courage, she leaned forward and ventured an innocuous question while Raverre waited for Ralf to appease some of his hunger.

"Sir, my Lord Raverre spoke of the court. Do you know if the Queen and her ladies will be travelling with the army?"

"Aye," Ralf answered briefly, his mouth full. He turned and looked at Lisette directly for the first time, suddenly aware that a lady who looked as if she had stepped out of a book of romantic poems had addressed him, and that he had answered in a rather surly fashion.

His eyes widened and a handful of bread halted halfway

to his mouth as he took in Lisette's lovely face, framed by her white coif.

He was speedily brought back to earth by Raverre.

"In that case, I look forward to presenting my wife and her sister to the King *and* the Queen," he said conversationally, but with a hint of steel in his voice.

Ralf flushed hotly as he realised that he had been staring at his host's lady like a bumbling yokel. But, emboldened by the downcast look on her face at her husband's tone, he dared to enlarge on his answer.

"You will be pleased to see other ladies with whom to exchange gossip no doubt, madam. Queen Matilda intends to accompany the King to York, where she will no doubt have her lying-in."

"The Queen is with child?" Lisette asked, interest in this snippet of information making her forget her nervousness at displeasing Raverre.

However, he also seemed interested, and began to question Ralf closely about the court, and then the activities of the army, thereby ousting Lisette effectively from the conversation.

She sat back and glared at his unresponsive left shoulder, but could not think of another opening that would lead to the information she hoped for. Catherine, however, had no such qualms. Listening intently to the discussion between the men when they returned to the subject of the Saxon Earls, she seized the first opportunity to question young Ralf herself.

"Do you think, sir, that my Lord Morcar and the Prince were perhaps scoffed at in William's court? Or ill-treated perhaps, to have fled to Scotland?" she asked innocently, not wishing to believe that her countrymen could have behaved so dishonourably without good reason.

De Somery gave a derisive snort, but Ralf answered politely enough, although he directed his response to Lisette rather than Catherine.

"Not at all, my lady. Quite the contrary. When the Atheling and his company landed in Normandy with William last year they were fêted and made much of; respected for their learning and noble appearance, and treated with all courtesy and the honour due to their rank. And William brought them back to England with him, even allowing them to return to their estates. No, 'tis undisguised treachery on their part," he finished more angrily.

The girls exchanged dismayed glances, but Raverre, sensing their disquiet, softened the blow by remarking, "Edgar won't be much of a problem. I warrant the boy will come running back to William's heels when he grows tired of the Scottish court. Malcolm, too, will need more incentive than the promise of Edgar's sister in marriage to antagonise William. Border skirmishes are more his style, not a confrontation with the whole Norman army. 'Tis Morcar and Edwin who need to be taught a lesson—they surrendered to William of their own accord, remember."

"Aye," growled de Somery. "Those two weanling Earls have never met William in battle. They need a taste of Norman warfare."

The dour knight sounded so gratified at this prospect that Lisette almost expected him to lick his lips in anticipation.

If de Somery's attitude echoed the King's, she quaked at the thought of the lesson the Earls were likely to be taught, but Ralf apparently thought William would be more inclined to be lenient.

"We didn't expect him to execute his own half-brother, even after the trouble Odo stirred up within the army," he said after remarking on the King's behaviour. "But we did think he would be imprisoned at least. However, all William did was send the Bishop back to Normandy, and still in a position of some authority. William's mercy to his enemies is becoming something of a byword. Even the common folk are not treated hardly. Take the case of the butcher—''

He caught sight of de Somery's expression, which clearly mirrored his desire to get on with talk of war. ''But I weary you with such irrelevant tales.''

''Oh, no,'' protested Lisette, not seeing Raverre's quick frown in her eagerness to hear news of the outside world. ''Please do tell us, sir. We have not had any visitors for so long.''

Ralf flushed with gratified pleasure at being so eagerly addressed by such a beautiful lady. Sending her a glowing look, he launched enthusiastically into his tale.

''Well, my lady, it came about when the butcher who supplied the court, one Siegbert, sold the panterer bad meat. Fortunately the man realised the stuff was unfit to be eaten and went straight to the King to complain, thinking the butcher might have intended some deliberate harm. But apparently he was only interested in making the most money for the least value.'' In spite of his indignation, Ralf began to laugh.

''The punishment was fitting at least, if some thought it too mild. The rogue was put in the pillory and the foul stuff burnt under his nose. He could not move his head, of course, and his grimaces were something to behold, I can tell you. The crowd enjoyed the sight, in any event, and added to the wretch's discomfort with their jeers. 'Twas more like a show of mummery than a penalty, but I swear he won't try to cheat his customers again.''

Even Raverre smiled in appreciation of the story. Lisette, relieved that he didn't seem to be angry with her for wishing to hear it, rose from the table.

''An amusing tale, sir,'' she said, smiling warmly at Ralf,

whose chest swelled visibly. "Thank you for indulging a female's curiosity. But you will no doubt have much to talk about with my lord, and we ladies shall only be in the way," she added gracefully, preparing to retire with Catherine.

"Must you go indeed, my lady?" asked Ralf, looking crestfallen at the thought of losing such a charming audience. "There are many more tales of town life which—"

But Raverre had also risen, and slanted a cool look down at the younger man.

"My lady will have a busy day or two ahead of her, and you, sir, will have to leave in the early morning to reach the Earl of Hereford with William's message," he stated unequivocally. "There is still much I would like to discuss with you, so the ladies do well to retire early."

Ralf was abashed, but couldn't resist pressing an ardent kiss on to Lisette's hand as she wished him Godspeed, or a lingering look as Raverre escorted her to the solar. Barely giving her time for the briefest of goodnights to her sister, he handed Lisette through the door.

"It will be late when I join you, my lady," he said tersely. "Sleep well." And, turning away before she could answer, he strode back to the table without another glance.

Lisette closed the solar door with something of a snap. Really! What had she done now? she wondered crossly, not recognising that Raverre's behaviour sprang from jealousy. Not having had the slightest intention of attracting young Ralf, nor even noticing his reaction to her interest, so eager had she been to hear news of life outside their own small community, Lisette could only surmise that her husband's cavalier treatment of her this evening was just part of his recent change of heart.

The lowering suspicion that Raverre felt he no longer needed to give her any extraordinary degree of attention now they were married could not be ignored. Wistfully remembering the times when he had teased her or tried to coax her into a better understanding of him, and forgetting that she had repulsed any warmer advances, Lisette felt miserably on the verge of tears. Only her scornful dislike of such feminine weakness prevented her from giving way to them as she prepared for bed.

Chapter Seven

Several hours later Lisette awoke to the sound of thunder growling overhead. The ominous storm clouds hovering in the west over the past few days seemed finally to have come to a head directly above them.

A brilliant flash of lightning illuminated the room, followed seconds later by a cacophony of thunder claps which almost shook the solid foundations of the castle. In the glaring light Lisette saw that she had forgotten to fasten the shutters across the window.

With a quick glance at Raverre she slipped from the bed, meaning to remedy her oversight. However, the scene that met her eyes as she glanced outside made her pause, spellbound.

The countryside lay in dense blackness, but the darkness of the upper sky was lifted by the eerie moonlight which showed through the violent, constant shifting of the clouds as they streamed across the sky like galloping wraiths, their voices the shrieking of the wind, lightning the spur driving them on.

"The Wild Hunt," Lisette whispered, awed, unaware that Raverre, also awakened by the storm, had come up behind her.

"Hunt?" he questioned, making her jump.

As Lisette turned he wrapped his cloak about her shoulders, and she clutched gratefully at its warmth. So enraptured had she been by the war of elements outside that she had quite forgotten that she was standing totally naked in the cold draught.

"The Wild Hunt," Lisette repeated, still gazing out at the sky. "The souls of the damned, riding through the storm. Don't you hear them?"

A flash of tenderness went through Raverre at the solemn conviction in her voice. He wrapped his arms about her and pulled her back against the solid strength of his body.

"'Tis only a storm," he murmured, his breath stirring her hair.

"Oh, no!" she persisted fervently. "Why, even monks have seen them. Holy men! They've told of seeing ghostly hunters riding their black deer through the sky, and of hearing the blasts of their horns."

He did seem to have heard some similar tale, remembered Raverre vaguely, but, though he was a true son of the Church, he was also much too practical a man to believe in such superstitions as phantom riders whenever a storm struck.

Intending to reassure her, he tipped Lisette's face up to his, and was instantly still, reassurance forgotten, as a flash of lightning lit up her expression.

She was not afraid, he realised at once, his heart beginning to pound, but excited. A responsive surge of desire went through him as his gaze took in her shining eyes and softly parted lips. The cool draught lifted her hair slightly and he remembered how she had looked on the cliff-top—burningly, intensely alive.

Driven by passionate instinct, all rational thought forgotten, Raverre's hand moved convulsively to grip Lisette's hair. Holding her still, he took her mouth in a searing, invading kiss that caused her own lightning to flash through her body, igniting every nerve-end.

When he felt her instant response in the soft yielding of her body as she seemed to melt against him Raverre tore his cloak from her and lifted Lisette into his arms, pressing their naked flesh together as if he would absorb her into himself. He reached the bed in two long strides, hot desire slicing through him again at the soft moan of longing which came from her throat when his weight followed her down to the mattress.

Taken completely unawares by the unexpected fierceness of Raverre's embrace, Lisette could only surrender helplessly. The drugging pressure of his mouth, the sure, possessive touch of his hands swept her beyond thought. The small voice at the back of her mind, telling her she would regret this in the morning, was silenced beneath the cascade of sensations bursting through the barriers she had imposed on her own passionate nature.

She was unable to stop herself from pressing against Raverre as tumultuous waves of pleasure broke over her again and again, unable to stop her hands from probing the hard muscles of his back, feeling them tense under her caresses as he fought for control, the urgent movements of her body beneath his driving him to the edge of insanity.

"Dear God," he whispered against her breast. "I love you. Lisette…Lisette…I love you."

But the hoarsely muttered words were in Norman and Lisette only heard the urgent male desire in his voice. She responded to it instinctively, her own aching need becoming more insistent as she abandoned herself totally to Raverre's mouth and hands.

Then she felt him move over her, gathering her into his arms. Her heart raced wildly in breathless anticipation as he parted her legs with his own. She could feel his breath short and fast against her cheek, but he held back.

"Lisette, say my name."

"What?" Oh, why was he waiting?

"You've never said it. Say my name." His voice was rough, tense with restraint, but the compelling demand reached her.

"Alain?" she whispered, confused, but willing to give him what he wanted if he would only satisfy the throbbing ache inside her. And then she repeated it more surely, longingly, "Oh, Alain."

With an almost feral growl of triumph he surged forward.

Lisette immediately forgot the tacit admission Raverre had forced from her. This was what she wanted…needed. The heat of him—the hard strength of his arms—the unleashed male hunger that burned away resistance and left the utterly consuming need to be joined with him. One heart…one body…one soul. And then she was swept into a spiralling whirlwind of pleasure so intense that Lisette cried out, ceasing to think at all.

Raverre felt the tremors shaking her body, heard her cry of completion, and his control shattered instantly. He was pulled violently into the fiery whirlwind with her. Lost in her…possessing her…possessed.

She was retreating from him. He could feel it. Feel tension replace the languid softness of her body as she lay beneath him. And he didn't know how to stop it. He didn't even want to relinquish his possessive hold, but he knew his weight must be crushing her.

Slowly, reluctantly, Raverre rolled to the side, turning Lisette into the circle of his arms. Stroking damp tendrils of hair from her face with a hand that shook slightly, he tried to see her face. But just as their own wild storm had passed, bathing them in a trembling aftermath, so too had the tumult outside, and the night was still and dark again.

Damn it, he wouldn't let her retreat now. He would never be able to leave her alone after tonight, despite his intention to wait until he'd won Lisette's love before taking her again. Under the goad of hot jealousy aroused by de Pictou's interest in her that intention had dissolved like snow in the spring thaw.

And if he had to use his power to arouse the passionate response Lisette had just given him then he'd do it, if it would make her love him. But he wouldn't damage her pride, Raverre vowed silently as he heard her take in a shuddering breath. She needed time. Time to admit she had wanted him as much as he wanted her.

Raverre held Lisette closer, stroking her hair gently. "Go to sleep, love," he murmured. "And don't regret this." He kissed her with devastating tenderness. "Don't ever regret this."

Aye, sleep, Lisette told herself. Don't think. Don't think at all. The morning and its inevitable recriminations would come soon enough.

"'Twas the storm, for sure."

"Aye," agreed Lisette firmly. She and Catherine were in the garden, repairing the ravages of the night before. "After all, people do behave strangely when under the influences of nature's forces. Remember that poor woman who ran amok in the village last year at the full of the moon? Tearing her hair and scratching her face and screaming that the Normans were really demons from hell who were going to devour us all?"

Catherine stared at her sister in bewildered astonishment. "Holy St Elizabeth save you, Lisette. What has that to do with the damage to the garden?"

Lisette flushed hotly, quickly bending over a flattened lavender bush. "Well...nought...but..." She let the sentence die away.

She really was losing her mind. She hadn't even been listening to Catherine's chatter, but had been wholly occupied in convincing herself that the primitive elements of nature had touched off an answering chord within herself last night. How else could she explain her wanton response to Raverre?

"I think we've finished here," she said hurriedly. "And I have to speak to Wat."

"Lisette, are you feeling quite—?"

"I'm perfectly well, sweet sister. Come, there's still much to do."

"Well, there are plenty of serfs to do it," observed Catherine practically as they rounded the corner of the tower. "I'm going to watch the huts being built."

"Huts?"

"Aye. Didn't you hear Raverre say we needed two or three huts to house some of the guests? Look, they've started already."

Lisette glanced across the bailey. Against the sheltered north wall, men were erecting the framework of a small beehive-shaped cruck, attempting to bend one of the oak branches which would form the curved walls and roof. Some rather impious language wafted across the open space towards the girls as one of the men lost his grip and the branch sprang smartly upright again.

Then Lisette noticed Raverre. He had stripped to his leggings, and now lent his formidable strength to the task of bending the solid branch. The sunlight caressed his fair hair and the play of muscles across his broad shoulders, and Lisette instantly remembered the feel of both beneath her hands the night before. The sudden sharp stab of desire she experienced to touch him again startled her. Then Raverre turned and their eyes met.

"You go on," Lisette said breathlessly to Catherine. "I've forgotten the herbs Wat asked me to bring him."

Wheeling about, she fled back to the garden, appalled that the sight of Raverre half-naked had made her weak with longing to lie in his arms again.

What was happening to her? She had woken this morning to find herself alone again, and had been shocked at the pang of disappointment that had lanced through her. And now this. One look from him and she melted inside. How could she have such feelings for a man who was showing only too clearly that he had married her for the sake of expediency? Why did she have to wonder what it would be like if Raverre loved her? It shouldn't matter. She didn't love him. She didn't!

"Good morning."

At the sound of the deep, husky voice behind her Lisette froze. She could not face him. She couldn't bear it if he was cold again. Or, worse, triumphant. Did he think he had conquered her heart, despite her brave words that first night at supper? She had to salvage her pride. She would not surrender so easily. Raverre had overwhelmed her last night, but she had only yielded her body. Not her mind. Not her heart.

Her brain in total confusion, Lisette grabbed the willow basket she had left on the wall. Kneeling, she blindly grasped a bunch of thyme and pulled. The entire plant came away in her hand.

She glared at the inoffensive herb in vexation, which quickly turned to dismay as Raverre took the plant from her, tossed it into the basket and brought her upright with a strong grip on her arms. Shifting his hands to Lisette's waist, he lifted her to sit on the wall, trapping her between his braced arms.

Through her indignation at this demonstration of easy masculine strength, she was conscious of relief that he'd donned his tunic again.

"Good morning," Raverre repeated. His voice was soft, but Lisette saw the determined gleam in his ice-blue eyes.

"Good morning," she whispered back, helpless under that compelling demand.

Immediately the ice melted into shimmering warmth. "Should I warn the King that his dinner is going to be highly spiced?" he asked with a smile that was totally irresistible.

Lisette's thoughts of salvaged pride promptly flew out of her head. She smiled shyly back at him.

Raverre leaned forward, his hands still resting on the wall, and pressed a gentle, sensuous kiss to her mouth, which immediately set her insides fluttering. But before Lisette could give in to the desire to return the slight pressure of his lips he drew back to gaze into her eyes.

Lisette's lashes fluttered down in confusion. He didn't seem to be triumphant at her utter lack of resistance to him, she thought. Rather, there had been a strangely searching look in his eyes. But what did he seek? And why?

With an abruptness that made Lisette's eyes fly back to his face Raverre straightened.

"I came to tell you that I must ride to Godric to inform him of William's coming. You will be pleased to see the old man, I expect."

Both voice and expression were calm, but there was something in the forced stillness of his body that gave Lisette an impression of precarious control. It made her nervous.

"Aye, but...must you go yourself, my lord?"

Raverre's eyes blazed with sudden light. "I'll return to-day, sweetheart. Do you think I would let you spend the night alone?"

Hot colour flooded Lisette's cheeks. Holy Saints, what had made her say that?

Unable to look at him, she stammered, "I...I mean...'tis a long ride, and if the King should arrive..."

"William won't be here until tomorrow," Raverre answered, watching her like a hawk. In fact, Lisette realised with a shiver, she was beginning to feel distinctly hunted.

"I go myself as a courtesy to Godric," he added, still not taking his eyes from her. "But I'll take some men should Godric decide to postpone the journey until tomorrow; he is an old man and may wish for a stronger escort than a few serfs. Let us hope he is in reasonable health, as I think 'twould put his mind at rest to swear allegiance to William. He told me that he and your father often argued about who would be better for England—William or Harold. And I believe he fell out with his son over the same question."

Lisette nodded in uneasy agreement, but couldn't resist saying, "My father chose Harold because he was English and had been elected by the Witan and King Edward."

"An unfortunate choice, as it turned out," Raverre commented. "William also claimed that Edward promised him the crown of England, and he is too direct a man to lie about such things." His voice hardened slightly. "And, since we're on the subject, I ask you not to anger William by arguing Harold's lost cause or bringing up the King's bastard blood. For your own safety, Lisette, if not for my sake."

"But you are his friend," she pointed out, wondering how far Raverre would go to ensure she didn't antagonise his King. "Would William punish his friend's wife for her loyalty to her people, or for stating the truth if he is so honest himself?''

Raverre shrugged. '''Tis difficult to say. William is usually even-tempered and he appreciates loyalty, but his mother's origins are a sore point with him. You would have to know more of his earlier life to understand. He has had to get used to discarding friends who seemed to betray him.''

He hesitated a moment, then took her hands. "You probably won't want to hear this," he warned softly, "but your father would have sworn to William after Harold was killed. Both Godric and Father Edwin have said as much. I would have told you sooner, but I thought it likely you wouldn't believe me. Now, however, you have to know if it will obtain me your promise to be careful.''

Feeling outnumbered and outmanoeuvred, Lisette promised. There was not much else she could do when Raverre spoke so convincingly and at the same time held her with that compelling gaze. She was rewarded with the warm, intimate smile he had given her before, but, feeling that this time he was using his considerable charm to manipulate her, she refused to respond. Pulling her hands away, Lisette jumped down from the wall. She felt oddly hurt.

"I must see things put to rights inside," she said curtly. "You will not be shamed before your King, my lord."

"Last night you called me Alain," Raverre murmured before he could stop himself.

He saw Lisette go still. Then his heart leapt as he watched her lips silently form his name. Taking a quick step forward, he reached for her...a moment too late.

Lisette had fled.

The minute Raverre rode out of sight on his way to Godric's manor, Lisette acted. All through an interminable dinner she had been making plans as the realisation had dawned on her that here was the only opportunity she might have to investigate the caves in the forest.

Raverre would be gone for several hours, and, although some might think it strange for the lady of the manor to go riding when they were expecting visitors, she was confident that her serfs would not ask questions. The Normans were another matter entirely, and Lisette set her mind to thinking of a plausible tale that would satisfy whoever was on duty at the gate.

First she would need protection. Preferably unsuspecting, silent protection, so she enlisted Oswy's help. That presented no difficulties. It seemed perfectly logical to his simple mind that he should escort his mistress, since she was going to visit his mother, and he happily saddled up Lisette's horse to be ready whenever she wished to leave.

Catherine was next. That, too, was easy. Knowing how her sister would receive an invitation to call on a respectable cottar's wife who had known her since she was an infant, and would bemoan her hoydenish behaviour at great length, Lisette issued it. Catherine declined with haste, only too happy to be asked to direct the house carls in binding up fresh rush lights for every sconce in the castle, and completely forgetting to ask why Lisette felt it necessary to pay such a visit now.

Marjory was supervising the laying of clean linen on the beds and generally keeping an eye on things in the kitchen, much to its master's annoyance. Overhearing an acrimonious debate about the merits of using larks in a pie as opposed to pigeons, Lisette was confident that Marjory would be kept well occupied for some time.

Luck, almost deserted her, however, when she led Viking Princess to the mounting block and saw, with a sinking heart, that Richard de Somery was speaking to the soldiers at the gate. By his casual attitude he looked as if he had all the time in the world to stand talking to his men, and Lisette knew she couldn't afford to wait until he had business elsewhere.

Relying on her father's oft-expressed theory that a confident attitude carried the day, she rode boldly up to the gate, Oswy by her side. As she expected, de Somery halted her with an enquiry about her purpose in riding out, politely enough but determined upon an answer.

"I go to visit Oswy's mother, sir," she answered composedly. "To ask for her help at the castle while our visitors are here."

"Can the lad not go by himself?" questioned de Somery. To his credit, the man's concern was mainly for Lisette's safety while Raverre was absent from the manor, but she turned her haughtiest look on him.

"I dare say he could, but I consider it a courtesy to go myself," she stated, borrowing Raverre's words. "Besides," she added, lowering her voice, "he may not deliver my message correctly and I want all to go well during the King's visit."

De Somery could find no fault with this. After eyeing Oswy, who was gazing dreamily off into the distance, he nodded acquiescence.

"Very well, my lady. But I know my lord would wish you to take some men as escort. That young fellow may be big enough, but he's none too quick in his reasoning."

"Nonsense!" she remonstrated briskly. "Oswy is all the protection I need on our own land. My errand will only take a short time, *if* I am permitted to start immediately," she glanced pointedly at his hand, which still held her horse's bridle.

Not a man to be easily intimidated, however, de Somery stood his ground. "Do I have your word to return before dusk, then, my lady?" he insisted.

"Of course," Lisette answered, fervently hoping she could keep her promise. The very thought of Raverre's reaction should he return home to find her missing was enough to add complete conviction to her tone. "I have no wish to be out riding after dark, I assure you."

After a tense moment of contemplation de Somery nodded and stepped back, obviously not entirely satisfied, but unable to think of a valid reason to order Lisette to abandon her errand.

Keeping her face impassive, she trotted through the gates, Oswy obediently keeping pace at her stirrup.

As soon as they were out of sight of the manor Lisette changed direction. Fervently praying she would have enough time to search the caves and carry out her hastily manufactured errand, she urged Viking Princess to a faster pace, but one which Oswy could match, not stopping until they reached a spinney in the depths of the forest without hindrance.

There Lisette left Oswy guarding her horse, and slipped through the trees. The forest here was thickly wooded and dim in the fading afternoon light. She would have to hurry. Though Raverre would not return until after dark, she must be back at the manor herself before nightfall or a hue and cry would begin.

De Somery had still looked as if he doubted her flimsy story, and Lisette suspected he had only let her go because he had not received any specific order to keep her inside the castle walls. That would not stop him, however, from instigating a search should she not return in good time for supper.

Freeing her mantle from a clinging branch and stepping carefully over a tangle of impeding roots, Lisette sped onwards, hoping her memory would not lead her astray. It had been years since she had played here, peopling the caves and the wood with magical creatures and heroic knights. Remembering her girlish dreams of one particular handsome knight who would rescue her from some un-named terror, fall instantly in love with her, and spirit her away to everlasting happiness with him, she was annoyed to find herself picturing Raverre in that role.

Resolutely suppressing the thought, she brought her wandering mind back to the present. A flurry of wings above her head made her jump and she scolded herself for her nervousness. There was no reason to be afraid. Oswy was only a short distance away, though the density of trees made her feel as if she were quite alone, it was still daylight, and she had given up imagining nameless terrors long ago.

Had the caves been this far from the spinney? She could not remember and, pausing, anxiously peered about, wondering if she had passed by them unnoticing. No, surely that gnarled old oak looked familiar, with its thick cloak of moss spreading along its roots and up the immense trunk.

Moving faster now as memory rushed back, Lisette took a straight line from the mossy side of the ancient tree, and was rewarded moments later by the pile of rocks which marked the entrance to the old Roman ironworks.

It was not surprising that Raverre's men had not mentioned the caves, Lisette realised as she approached. Over the years the hanging branches of the surrounding trees had encroached on the entrance, and even to a keen eye the haphazard pile of rocks merely had the appearance of a simple cairn erected by some long-forgotten tribe.

Lisette pushed her way through the almost leafless branches, ignoring the scratches her hands received, and felt her way along the ancient stones until her searching fingers slid into the crevice which she knew led into the several chambers excavated by the efficient Romans.

She hesitated, suddenly nervous at the thought of leaving the comparative light of the forest. What if her instinct was wrong and some other fugitive, unknown and threatening, had taken refuge in this lonely, forbidding place?

Leofwin had a comfortable home to return to, after all, even if he had disagreed with his father as to which side to take. When she stopped to think Lisette could not imagine why Leofwin would choose to stay in a cave at all, let alone for any length of time, and she began to feel rather foolish for risking possible danger or Raverre's wrath should he ever find out what she was doing.

Then she recalled the sniper and steeled herself. She had not come this far only to draw back now. If Leofwin was here and she could persuade him to return home then she would do so. And she would also have to explain what had happened to Enide.

Squaring her shoulders, Lisette squeezed through the crevice, stopping just inside the first small chamber as inky blackness embraced her, and cursing herself for not thinking to bring a candle.

The caves were much darker than she remembered, but then years ago the entrance had been fully exposed, and they had only played in the full light of midday.

Lisette took a shaky breath and called into the sombre gloom, "Leofwin?"

Her voice sounded tremulous and hesitant in the extreme. Mentally giving herself an impatient shake, she called more loudly, "Leofwin, are you there? 'Tis Lisette."

Dark silence pressed about her for what seemed like several minutes, and Lisette was about to slide thankfully back into the daylight, when a footfall sounded. A second later faint light flickered against the rock wall ahead of her.

Her heart thumping violently, Lisette watched a hand appear around the angle of a jutting rock.

The hand was followed by its owner, a ragged individual, barely decently covered by his torn clothes, his gaunt, pale face glowering at her through a rough, untrimmed beard and long, shaggy hair. Lisette thought she was about to swoon away for the second time in her life, before she let out a gasp of relief as the apparition came closer, and she recognised the man she was seeking.

Slumping against the side of the rock chamber with relief, she tried to steady her racing pulse.

"Lisette?" the creature questioned cautiously, holding the light higher. "Holy Mother, it really *is* you! Why are you...how did you know?"

"Never mind that now," she answered, swiftly regaining control of herself with the sharp awareness of passing time. However, as her eyes adjusted to the gloom, his pitiful condition distracted her.

"Oh, Leofwin, look at you!" she cried, distressed. "To what lengths have you gone to be living like an animal in a cave, waiting to starve or be captured? Why have you not returned to your father, or sent word to Enide?"

"You think 'tis that easy?" Leofwin asked, his wonder at seeing her quickly changing to harsh bitterness. "There's a price on my head. I've risked all, coming back to this district, but I needed money. I would have had it, too, if those fools hadn't bungled... But never mind that. Tostig was to steal some from my father's manor but the fool has either been caught or deserted me and I dare not wait much longer."

"Then he *was* your man!" Lisette exclaimed, fixing on the one thing that made sense to her. "Oh, Leofwin, don't you see? 'Tis what made me think you might be here, and, if I think of it, others will too. You must go home! Reconcile with your father. He has mourned you as dead these two years—do you think he would not welcome you, forgetting past disputes?''

"Just a minute, Lisette! Never mind my doddering fool of a father, what do you know of Tostig?''

"He is dead," she answered baldly, too shaken by his callous description of his parent to choose her words. Had Leofwin said *steal* money from the old man? And what bungling fools? Lisette began to wonder how wise she had been in coming here so impulsively. Was this the boy who had shared those long-ago sunlit days of her childhood, the man her gentle sister had sworn to love?

"How did he die?" Leofwin asked in a hard voice, bringing her attention back to the present.

"He tried to kill the man who has been granted my father's lands," she answered more carefully this time. "If your own father dies your lands will also be forfeit, Leofwin, but if you return you may yet claim your rightful place."

"Aye, by swearing fealty to the Norman bastard!" he retorted angrily. "Why do you think I'm in hiding, girl? I've been trying to rally our people to rebellion, but the spirit has been beaten out of them. I had hopes of my lords of Northumbria and Mercia, but they were only interested in their own gain, and sided with William. We needed money and would have had it if the idiots I hired hadn't been blinded by that ingot."

"*You* arranged that robbery?" gasped Lisette.

Leofwin didn't seem to notice her shock. "So you know about it. Aye, but the plan went awry. When I saw they'd stolen the gold instead of coin and jewels I thought at first we could take the ingot down river to the Thames and across the Channel to France. The French King has little love for William, and there we could have melted it down. But the others took fright, and Tostig and I couldn't handle it alone. Do you know how much the damn thing weighs? 'Tis still hidden underwater in the Itchen,'' Leofwin finished bitterly.

"But you, Lisette." He gave her a hard stare, seeming to realise he might have said more than he should. "How are you living at Ambray if a Norman Baron now holds the land? I suppose you're ekeing out a living on a miserable strip of land that no one happened to want, like so many others."

"Not quite," she hedged, unwilling after what she had just heard to inform him of the exact nature of her circumstances. "But Enide. Don't you wish to hear word of her?"

Leofwin gave a harsh laugh. "Aye, my gentle betrothed," he jeered, as if only just remembering. "Do you think she would be willing to cross the country with me, hiding like escaped slaves, and then take ship for so far a place as Constantinople?"

Lisette flinched from his sarcasm, but could not remain silent.

"But you love Enide," she faltered. "I remember how you argued with my father before he would consent... Did you say Constantinople?"

"I have to leave the country," he answered, as if that explained everything. "Many Thegns have joined the Varangian Guard of the Byzantine Emperor, where, let me tell you, we'll be accorded the respect we deserve! But first I need money and clothing. Some food would not come amiss either. You'll have to bring me some, Lisette."

She shook her head, but not in bewilderment than refusal. "But—"

"Ah, Enide," he remembered. "Well, you may tell her to consider herself free of me. She is no use without her inheritance. I notice she didn't accompany her little sister, but then she was always the shrinking one of you three, wasn't she?'' His scorn was unmistakable.

"But you loved her!'' insisted Lisette, feeling stupidly repetitive, but unable to reconcile the Leofwin she remembered with the contemptuous stranger before her.

"And you were always the romantic,'' he scoffed. "Enide was the eldest—your father's heiress, you little fool. Of course I asked for her. But,'' he continued in a thoughtful voice, "I often wished you had been in her place. You always had twice her spirit and you've grown quite lovely, little playmate. I thought you would, and I had plans. Still, you can hardly carry your lands with you, so your lack of dowry doesn't really matter now.''

Without warning Lisette was conscious of a new danger. She could not name it, but it seemed to hover in the air between them, almost taking tangible form as Leofwin continued to speak, almost to himself.

"You wouldn't hesitate to flee the country with the man you loved, whatever the dangers, would you, my pretty? You used to act out such fantasies, didn't you? In this very place. And what remains for you here? A life of poverty? Slavery to a Norman Baron? Or do you think to retire to watch your beauty fade away in some cloistered nunnery? No, I don't think we can allow that.''

Lisette straightened her spine to its fullest extent. She had to stop this right now.

"Leofwin, listen to me!'' she ordered, her voice an unconscious feminine echo of Raverre's when he was issuing commands. "Why should you leave England? Surely you don't really wish to—?''

"Haven't you heard a word I said?'' he demanded impatiently. "If someone blabs about that robbery I'll be outlawed. Unless I can leave the country I might as well be dead.''

"But you know where the ingot is hidden," Lisette argued eagerly. "Don't you see? If it's as valuable as everyone says and 'twas returned you would be pardoned."

"Aye, and penniless, knowing William's liking for wealth and lands—may he rot in hell."

"You won't lose your lands. Your father is going to swear fealty to the King and may be able to intercede for you. Why, even now my husband is on his way to your manor to inform Lord Godric of William's arrival."

Or more likely on his way back by now, she thought to herself, anxiously wondering what time it was.

"The Duke is coming here?" Leofwin queried sharply, his attention momentarily diverted from their argument. "Jesu, what an opportunity. But what can I do about it alone?"

"Don't even think of doing anything!" said Lisette firmly. "Do you imagine for one moment that William travels unprotected? And in this instance most of the army will be with him."

Leofwin's brows rose in interrogation.

"He is mustering soldiers to put down a rebellion in the north," she explained. "So you see how careful you must be. Leofwin, I beg you, go home."

Lisette began to edge towards the entrance, where a reassuring sliver of daylight still showed.

"I must return also," she added, hoping he wouldn't try to detain her. "Before dark."

"Lisette, wait!"

As she hesitated, looking worried, Leofwin put out a hand. His teeth showed in a smile, but the light was too dim for Lisette to see the coldly calculating expression in his eyes.

"I've shocked you with all this talk of robbery, but remember 'twas done for our people. And I'll think about going to my father.''

This sounded so much more like the Leofwin she had known that Lisette smiled at him for the first time. The effect was unfortunate.

His voice and gaze sharpened. "You spoke of a husband. Who?"

"You would not know him," she quickly evaded, foreseeing more precious time wasted in explanations if she named Raverre.

"Tostig told me he had seen a dark-haired lady with a Norman Baron. As thick as thieves, he said, although I found it difficult to believe. Perhaps I was wrong. Who is your husband, Lisette?"

"Please, Leofwin, I can tell you about it another time. I must go before I'm missed! Oswy is waiting for me."

He hesitated at this, then nodded. "Very well, but first I'll make sure no one is lurking about outside."

He brushed past her and cautiously eased through the crevice, returning a minute later to the entrance, where Lisette waited, casting an anxious look at the sky.

"All clear," he reported. "Where's your horse?"

"In the spinney," she said hurriedly. "Leofwin, think on what I've said, but if you still wish to leave England I may not see you again, so—"

"We'll see if we meet again or not," he said enigmatically, giving her another hard stare before sliding back through the hanging foliage.

For a moment Lisette could only gaze at the spot where Leofwin had been, wondering at his meaning. Then she felt the chill breeze rustling through the trees as the wood seemed to settle down for the coming night.

Whirling about, Lisette made for the spinney as fast as she could. Apart from the urgency of getting home before de Somery became suspicious, the forest, with its air of eerie mystery as the light dimmed and a barely discernible mist swirled across the ground, was the last place she wanted to be when night fell.

Raverre himself did not return until well after everyone had retired to bed. Thinking Lisette deep in slumber, he stretched out beside her, gathered her into the curve of his body and promptly fell asleep.

Sleep did not come so readily to Lisette. For some time she went over her conversation with Leofwin, worrying about what he might do and still feeling distressed at his involvement in the robbery. She had been so shocked, she recalled, that she had completely forgotten to tell him of Enide's whereabouts, although in view of his attitude this oversight hardly seemed to matter.

And for herself? How could she send to his death a man she had known all her life? She had to give Leofwin time. If he did not come with Godric to the King then she could think again.

Having reached this decision, Lisette felt better. Snuggling down under the bearskin, she allowed her tense muscles to relax. And so protected did she feel lying in Raverre's arms that Leofwin's vague mention of past plans concerning her vanished entirely from her mind.

The following morning all was bustle and activity. Word had come that the King and his retinue were well on the way and would arrive in time for a late dinner.

Serfs were sent scurrying in all directions, making sure every corner of the manor was looking its best. The hall was swept free of old rushes and their accumulated litter before fresh ones were scattered, mixed with herbs to counteract the unavoidable odours of daily life. Raverre's carved chair was polished until the wood gleamed, and Wat's frequently shouted imprecations echoed from the kitchen.

Lisette herself gathered a bouquet of late-autumn blooms from the garden to place in the solar in honour of the Queen, and it was here that Raverre found her, absorbed in the arrangement of the flowers.

"There's really no need for all this fuss," he assured her as she stood back, anxiously surveying her handiwork. "Matilda will be only too pleased to spend a night in the comfort of a civilised manor instead of a tent, or the crude wooden castles William builds as he travels."

He lifted one of Lisette's hands to his lips, intending to take his leave of her to meet William on the road, but paused as his eyes caught the deep scratch across the backs of her fingers.

"And I certainly don't expect you to injure yourself preparing for our guests, my sweet," he scolded gently, obviously assuming she had received the slight hurt in the garden. "Have you a salve to put on this?"

"'Tis only a scratch; there's no need," Lisette murmured, head bent and flushing guiltily. Prevaricating to de Somery was one thing, she now discovered. Having to lie to Raverre, if only by omission, made her feel shamefully deceitful.

When he let her hand fall abruptly her lips parted as the longing to confide in him almost overcame her. Then an image of Leofwin, gaunt and desperate, rose in her mind. How could she betray a man she had called friend? For another day at least she *must* remain silent.

Steeling herself against Lisette's obvious reluctance, Raverre turned her face to his and kissed her briefly on the lips.

"I'll be back soon," he said, more curtly than he had intended. Then, turning with a swirl of his cloak, he disappeared through the door, leaving her wondering anxiously if his brusque tone betokened suspicion.

"'Tis only guilt making you think so, Lisette told herself sternly, and decided to pacify her scruples by behaving like the perfect hostess when William arrived. It would be worth it just to see Raverre's face, she thought with a sudden burst of mischief.

This made her feel so much more like her old self that Lisette willingly joined Catherine on the tower roof an hour later to watch the arrival of King, Court and army.

They easily picked out the King's standard-bearer, the pennons flying from tall wooden staffs, just behind the lead riders.

"Do you think the man riding next to Raverre is the King?" asked Catherine. "See how rich are the trappings on his steed. He doesn't look to be as tall as Alain, but they say he is so strong that no one else can bend his bow."

"Men always tell such tales of Kings," said Lisette sceptically, but watching the riders with interest.

"Goodness, what a number of baggage wagons!" exclaimed Catherine as more lumbering vehicles appeared at the rear of the train. "That one with the drawn curtains must be the Queen's, or maybe the litter behind it. I can see a lady looking out. What a tedious way to travel—I would much rather ride."

"They do look uncomfortable," agreed Lisette. "Come. They've reached the village; we must go down and wait in the bailey."

She took a last look across the stream and saw Raverre glance up as if he sensed their observation. Impulsively Lisette waved, her long sleeve fluttering in the breeze, and he lifted an arm in a return salute before turning to speak to the man at his side, who had obviously seen the exchange.

As they hurried down to the hall Lisette felt a quick rush of gladness to know that Raverre was back. Whether it was his cool leave-taking this morning or merely his absence, she suddenly realised how secure she had come to feel with him there.

There was no time now, however, to wonder why she was so happy to see him return when she had resented his presence so much. Pushing this puzzle to the back of her mind, already overcrowded with unanswered questions, Lisette hurried out to the bailey.

An air of anticipation hung over the compound as serfs and soldiers alike craned to see the man once called William the Bastard, and now called the Conqueror.

Instructing Edric to bring the welcome cup, Lisette and Catherine waited at the foot of the outer stairway as Raverre and William rode in through the gates.

Her first sight of the son of a humble tanner's daughter who had united Normandy and conquered England gave Lisette a brief glimpse of a man above medium height and solidly built, with a face pleasant enough but rather remote and stern, before she sank into a graceful curtsy, eyes lowered.

As she rose, remembering her promise to Raverre to treat William with respect, Lisette offered him the welcome cup, but, aligning herself to her own people, said, "Welcome, sir, to my husband's manor."

If William heard the distinction he gave no sign. He took a deep draught of the mulled wine and handed the cup back to her, saying, "God's greetings, my lady. 'Tis a fair place you have here. We shall be glad to rest a night and to know you better."

Lisette handed the cup to Raverre, giving him a brilliant smile as she did so. He smiled wryly back at her, the wary look in his eyes disappearing.

"You did not exaggerate your lady's beauty, my friend,"

commented William, noticing this byplay. "No wonder you wasted no time in marrying her."

Lisette glanced at Raverre curiously, but her attention was quickly diverted by the commotion announcing the Queen's arrival.

Matilda was alighting from her litter, and William himself went at once to assist her. As he led his wife towards the group by the stairway Lisette thought they made a strange-looking pair.

Matilda was so short that she appeared almost childlike against her much taller husband. Only four feet in height, she was dressed in a burgundy wool gown, chosen more for serviceability than elegance. An over-tunic of soft grey, as plain as the gown, could not fully conceal her pregnancy, which made her look heavy and ungainly, and yet she had the presence only achieved by those of very strong personality.

As Lisette sank into another curtsy she wondered if she had been wrong to wear her blue silk gown. The Queen was obviously as frugal as William was reputed to be, but Matilda greeted her hostess with friendly interest, and Lisette felt her slight awkwardness dissipate in the warmth of the Queen's smile.

Returning the greeting, she ushered Matilda and her ladies into the solar, shyly inviting them to ask for anything they might require.

"My ladies and I will be glad to wash the dirt of the road from our faces," said the Queen, her eyes falling on the bowl of hot water on the table. "Although I must say your English roads are a sight better than the rough tracks we have to endure in Normandy."

Unsure what to answer to this forthright statement, Lisette curtsied slightly and was about to inform Matilda that dinner would be served as soon as their guests were ready, when the door opened and William entered with Raverre.

It was as though a sudden gust of wind had blown into the solar, thought Lisette. For the first time she understood why men, even Saxons, had been drawn to William's cause. The man exuded an air of determination, an implacable will to succeed, that was almost visible.

"Ah!" the King exclaimed, looking about the room approvingly. "This is more what you are used to, is it not, my love?"

His voice was quite harsh, and seemed to ring out in the confines of the solar, used to carrying over distances or above the noise of battle.

"'Tis indeed comfortable here, Alain," he went on, turning to Raverre. "And we shall be happy to repay you with some entertainment at dinner." A piercing gaze was turned on Lisette. "I believe you have no minstrel or bard, my lady."

This man would miss nothing, she thought as she confirmed his statement.

"Then 'tis fitting that we have both. My lady *would* bring them with her from Normandy when she joined me," he finished, with a quizzical look at his wife.

"One must have some amenities, even in a foreign land, William," remonstrated Matilda with a calm smile.

"So you say, my dear," he agreed good-naturedly. "You ladies must be amused while we men labour. Isn't that so, my lady?"

"I think after *both* men and women labour they *both* like to be amused, sir," Lisette replied demurely, but with a twinkle in her eyes.

The King gave a delighted guffaw and clapped Raverre on the shoulder.

"You've done well for yourself, Raverre, my friend. A

lady who is quick-witted as well as beautiful is rare indeed. I wish you joy of her. Just now, however, I see a look in her eye that betokens housewifely concern. You are thinking that dinner will be spoiling if we do not make haste, my lady.''

Startled, Lisette could not help laughing at his perspicacity. ''Tis true,'' she confirmed, ''but dinner will await your pleasure, sir.''

''Then let us away to table, my lady,'' William replied, offering a gallant arm to her.

By the Rood, thought Raverre, preparing to escort Matilda into the hall, I verily believe she's bewitched even William. I haven't seen him in such a benign mood for months. If Lisette did say something he disliked I swear he'd merely try to convince her otherwise by force of argument alone.

Chapter Eight

Roast suckling pig, baked partridge and the controversial larks in a pie had been devoured with gusto, and washed down with wine, cider and ale. Already replete, dogs squabbled lazily for bones among the rushes. And, fully aware that Raverre was trying to keep an ear tuned to her conversation with William, while forced to present a façade of courtesy to his other guests, Lisette put herself out to charm the King.

In fact it was not a hardship for her. William paid her the compliment of listening carefully to her halting Norman, helping her when she hesitated for the right word, and she was pleasantly surprised to find that he had a good deal of sympathy for the common folk, caught up in a war they had not wanted.

"'Tis why I believe so strongly in our way of life, my lady," he explained earnestly. "Your people might have had the freedom to move from one master to another, or work independently in a town guild, but many are so poor that such a way of life was impossible for them anyway. The great wealth was divided between a scant five or six too-powerful Earls, who behaved like rulers of petty kingdoms. I fear my cousin Edward kept his throne merely through the respect they had for his age and piety. Look at the quarrels that broke out the minute he was dead.

"There was no unity, your land torn apart by ambitious men who were only interested in their own gain. If a country is to keep pace with the rest of the world there must be strength and a common aim and protection of the weak. This is what I see for England. She could be a great nation one day, your Saxon tradition and learning allied to our Norman cohesion and initiative."

William was certainly convincing, Lisette thought, impressed by his argument. But she could not suppress a sigh.

"It seems a pity that such things cannot be brought about without warfare and suffering," she remarked.

"Ahh. You say so because you are a lady and gentle, and shrink from these things. Which is as it should be," he answered, but so charmingly that she could not take offence.

Just then a diversion was caused by the entrance of Wat's masterpiece. A large swan, roasted to a turn, and then restored to the full glory of its plumage by the painstaking pasting on of its feathers. It was borne in on a large platter, ensconced on a sea of fruits and nuts, and caused quite a sensation among the company.

Matilda complimented Lisette on her cook, and the conversation became more general.

Glancing down the length of the hall, Lisette assured herself that her guests were enjoying themselves. Matilda's ladies appeared to be indulging in mild flirtations with some of Raverre's men, the royal couple looked relaxed and pleased, and at the end of the high table Catherine prattled happily away to Gilbert as though she had known him for years instead a few scant weeks.

However, as William clapped his hands to summon a troop of tumblers Lisette caught a glance from Matilda's youngest lady, a pretty girl with dark hair and eyes, which seemed to hold a degree of resentment. Surprised, she stared at the girl more closely, but the other had turned her face away and Lisette thought she must have been mistaken. She did not think the Norman ladies disliked her merely because she was Saxon, for they had followed their Queen's example of civility.

A burst of applause echoed around the hall and drew her attention to the nimble antics of the tumblers as they leapt about the floor and twisted themselves into fearful contortions.

Then one fellow ran forward and began to juggle with a handful of brightly coloured balls, assisted by a tiny furred creature wearing a blue jacket, which caught the balls and tossed them quickly back to its master.

"Oh, the darling little thing," cried Lisette in delight, clapping her hands. Turning shining eyes to Raverre, she asked, "Pray, what is it, my lord?"

"Why, my lady," interposed a husky feminine voice before he could answer, "have you never seen a monkey before? What a dull life you must lead here, I vow!" Matilda's lady-in-waiting finished with a tinkle of scornful laughter.

There was no mistaking the animosity this time. Feeling like an ignorant country bumpkin, Lisette sat back in embarrassment, wondering if Raverre also considered her simple pleasure in the entertainment to be childish and naïve.

Matilda came unexpectedly to her rescue. "Tush, Judith," she scolded. "I warrant my Lady of Raverre has had little time for such frivolity these past several months."

She turned her back on Judith and applauded vigorously as the little monkey climbed nimbly up to its master's shoulder, where it gave the company a quaint bow before being carried out.

Lisette, avoiding Raverre's eye by concentrating on the bard who had come to sit on the floor in front of the high table, also failed to see the languishing gaze Judith cast at her husband. Stung by the Queen's rebuke and Lisette's obvious success with the King, the girl decided she would soon show this rustic Saxon wench how her own more worldly attractions would better suit a Norman Baron. And my Lord Raverre, with his magnificent physique and those piercing ice-blue eyes, was certainly a man worthy of her attention.

The bard was strumming a few random notes on his lute while he waited for his audience to make a choice.

"Would you like to hear a tale of Saxon courage in battle, my lady?" queried William politely.

Upon Lisette's agreeing to this, he signalled to the man to begin, and a hush fell over the hall as the story unfolded of the final stand of the fyrd.

Tears glittered in Lisette's eyes as Harold's personal guard were lauded as the most dauntless of warriors as they stood to the last man, ever ready with their steel in defence of their King, the only movement in their ranks the dropping of the dead.

William had been victorious that day at Hastings, Lisette reflected, but he still granted his fallen enemies respect and honour.

The end of the tale was greeted with polite applause from the Norman company, but Lisette turned impulsively to William, thanking him warmly for allowing her to hear it.

Seeing the King's indulgent pleasure in her unfeigned thanks, Raverre felt a flash of jealousy. Why couldn't Lisette smile so freely at him? he wondered angrily, watching her dimples deepen the corners of her mouth in a way that made him want to drag her into the solar and kiss her sense-

less. There they were, the two of them, getting on famously
on the strength of a few hours' acquaintance, while he—

"Where are your wits gone begging, my friend?" exclaimed William jokingly. "I ask what you would like to
hear now my fellow has caught his breath, and all you can
do is sit there in a daze. Dreaming of your lovely wife, I
doubt not."

Lisette flushed hotly, but fortunately Raverre seemed not
to notice. In fact, after he had given William a non-
committal answer, his whole attention now seemed to be
centred on Judith, who was speaking animatedly, gesturing
with her hands and bringing a smile to his handsome face.

"Why not allow the ladies to hear the saga of Norman
settlement in Gaul, sir?" asked Gilbert, seeing Lisette's discomfort and tactfully giving her time to recover.

"A good thought, de Rohan," declared William, nodding to the bard, and settling back in his chair to listen.

Lisette found herself caught up in the saga. It told of one
Rolf, son of a noble of Harold Fairhair, King of Norway,
who had been banished from the court and had sailed with
his followers to the Hebrides—those remote mystical is-
lands off the coast of Scotland. From there they had again
set sail in their *drakkars*—the great dragon ships—to Gaul,
rowing many miles up the Seine to Jumièges, where they
had prepared to attack the cathedral city of Rouen.

Alarmed by the fierce demeanour of the invaders, the
people of Jumièges, had begged their Archbishop to negotiate with the Norsemen, offering them no resistance if
they would allow the town to remain unscathed. Accepting
this, Rolf had entered Rouen as its conqueror.

The Viking war spirit still ran hot in the blood of the
victors, however, and for many a year they had plundered
the French countryside, defeating every army the King had
sent against them, until the long-suffering monarch had fi-

nally sued for peace. Promised the title of Count of Normandy if he would become the King's vassal, Rolf had converted to Christianity, married the King's daughter Gisele, and had settled down to rule his domain, his successors becoming Dukes in the course of time.

Lisette enjoyed the romantic ending to the tale, but the high point for the Normans came during the telling of the ceremony of allegiance that made Rolf the French King's bondman. On being ordered to kneel and kiss the King's foot, Rolf had refused point-blank and it had looked as though the whole business was doomed to failure. However, the huge Norseman had solved the problem by grasping the King's foot and lifting it up to his lips to bestow the kiss of allegiance while still remaining upright. The King had promptly been tripped over and had landed flat on his back.

The hall resounded to roars of approval as the bard finished. He retired to recruit his energies with some refreshing draughts of cider, and the feast grew louder as men, inspired by the heroic sagas, thundered out songs of war and adventure.

Lisette became increasingly conscious that Raverre seemed to be ignoring her. And there was little consolation in the fact that he now appeared to restrict his talk to the other men at the table, apparently deaf and blind to the attentions Judith was attempting to bestow upon him.

The wench was certainly doing her best to attract him, Lisette thought indignantly. Look at her, giving him those sidelong glances, and leaning forward so that she was all but falling into his lap.

Deciding that if she couldn't see what was going on she would be less upset, Lisette turned to the Queen, suggesting they walk in the garden for a while as their husbands now seemed to be involved in more serious discussion. Matilda

accepted graciously and the ladies withdrew from the hall,
but not before Lisette noticed the proprietorial hand Judith
placed on Raverre's arm as he and William rose politely.

Compared to her buoyant spirits earlier, she now felt
quite low as she and Matilda paced slowly around the small
garden. The wind bit keenly, prompting Matilda to remark
that she hoped they would be settled in York before winter.

"This would make a comfortable pleasance in the colder
months, my lady, if the wall was a little higher," she suggested. "A sheltered spot to sit outside can be a relief after
days spent indoors."

Lisette agreed, but the remark didn't make her feel any
better. She loved her home and had never noticed any lack
of comfort, but now she wondered if it looked small and
crude to Raverre, compared to the great fortress keeps
across the Channel. And did he think her ignorant and simple, compared to the more experienced Norman ladies?

Self-doubt haunted Lisette for the rest of the day, making
her so miserable that she didn't even bother to wonder why
she cared about any comparisons Raverre might care to
make. Only long force of habit kept her veneer of gracious
hostess in place. But by the time she had seen her female
guests settled for the night after a supper in the privacy of
the solar—the men still occupied in the hall with discussions of war—she was thankful to seek her own bed, where
she could sort out her feelings and talk herself into a better
frame of mind.

Unfortunately, worse was to come. Lisette remembered,
through her preoccupation, that Godric had not put in an
appearance. Thinking that he might have arrived late and,
too weary to see William tonight, retired to one of the huts
reserved for his use, she went outside to investigate.

He had not yet arrived, however, and, wondering if his
delay had been caused by Leofwin's appearance, Lisette

returned to the hall. She had just started up the stairway to the tower room when a low murmur of voices made her turn her head.

Lady Judith stood in the light of one of the sconces, out of sight of the hall in the screen passage, gazing appealingly up at the man before her. His back was towards Lisette, but there was no mistaking that height or those broad shoulders, and, as Lisette watched, Judith put up her hands to Raverre's chest, lifting her face in unmistakable invitation.

Unable to bear any more, Lisette fled up the stairway and into the tower room, only halting when she saw her sister's look of astonishment at her abrupt entrance.

"Hush, Lisette," admonished Catherine, indicating Marjory, snoring gently on her pallet. "You'll wake Marjory, bouncing into the room like that. What ails you?"

"The stairs were so dark," Lisette explained lamely, not surprised when Catherine continued to look at her strangely.

"I thought Raverre would bring you upstairs," she said. "He was looking for you a few moments ago."

Pain slashed through Lisette at the mention of his name. She walked stiffly over to the bed, wondering if Raverre would indeed seek her out that night.

To her profound relief Catherine turned away and climbed under the blankets on the pallet next to Marjory's, yawning widely, too tired to question further.

"What an exhausting day," she mumbled sleepily. "Goodnight, Lisette."

"Goodnight," Lisette returned, controlling her voice with an effort. Blowing out the candle and removing only her shoes and coif, she curled up in a tight ball on the bed, hugging her arms close to her body as she fought against acknowledging the cause of the sharp pain piercing her heart.

Nothing had prepared her for this, she now realised. Not
the loss of her parents or the ravages of war. She had
grieved, yes, but the grief had been bearable. Now she felt
that if she took her arms away her heart would shatter like
brittle glass into a thousand tiny fragments that could never
be repaired, and she would die from the agony of it.

Oh, why had she not seen what was happening to her?

She loved Raverre! Had loved him for a long time and
had tried to ignore all the signs, so that her love had grown
stronger in that dark, secret place in her heart that she had
thought to suppress. But you didn't, she berated herself,
and now you must bear the torment of loving a man who
only sees you as a means to an end, and probably a troublesome one at that.

But he desires me, her heart pleaded. Does that mean
nothing?

Less than nothing, her mind told her inexorably. Look
how quickly and easily he is beguiled by another woman.
One who has more experience in pleasing a man than you
will ever have. You have shown him nothing but cold duty,
and—as an image of the ungainly figure of the Queen came
to mind—do you think he will still want you when you are
awkward with child? You fool yourself. The only thing left
to you now is your pride. Or do you think to abandon that
as well and shame yourself forever?

No, she thought determinedly, staring into the darkness.
After what I told him that first night when we met I can
only survive this if he never knows how complete his conquest has been. Or, worse, if he felt only pity for me out
of kindness.

Shielding the raw, throbbing wound in her heart with this
resolve, Lisette carefully added another layer of protection.
She would do her utmost to give Raverre a son so that her
position as his wife was secure. If he was unfaithful to her

she would just have to bear it, but at least she would be able to stay with him.

Cringing at the thought of what Raverre would make of this admission after her determined resistance to him, Lisette lay unmoving in the darkness like a wounded animal, her eyes remaining dry but burning with the abrasive heat of her unshed tears.

So benumbed did she feel that she barely registered Raverre's presence when he entered the room some hours later.

He pulled the curtains closed around the bed for privacy, stripped, and climbed under the covers. Reaching for Lisette, he was surprised to find her lying on top of the bearskin, still fully clothed. Raverre raised himself on one elbow, leaning over her.

"Sweetheart?" he questioned softly, concern momentarily causing him to forget his earlier jealousy.

How can he call me that after coming from the arms of another woman? she thought.

Raverre drew a caressing hand along her arm, but when she didn't stir Lisette felt him leave the bed. Was he going to spend the remainder of the night elsewhere? she wondered, almost wishing he would. Then she felt the mattress dip when he returned and the light weight of a blanket as he drew the covering over her.

Dear God, don't let him be kind now, she pleaded silently. If Raverre showed her tenderness Lisette knew she would be unable to resist him. Her emotions were so vulnerable, a raw, open wound which ached unbearably, that one gentle word from him and she would turn and fling herself against him, begging him to hold her until she felt whole again.

But the word was not spoken. Raverre, thinking she must be worn out by the stresses of the day and acutely conscious that they were not alone in the small room, lay back, arms folded behind his head.

Frustration gnawed at him as he could see the progress he had made on the night of the storm fast disappearing. This realisation was made all the more bitter after watching her enjoyment of William's players. That was how she must have looked two years ago, carefree, happy—and so beautiful that a man would risk his very soul to win her.

He recalled the impulsive way Lisette had turned to him when she had asked about the juggler's monkey, her face aglow with delighted enquiry. Until that little bitch of a lady-in-waiting had thrown a damper over her. Was that why she had been lying here, still fully clothed? Or—he had to consider it—had she thought to keep him at a distance?

He should have woken her last night. Damn it, he should wake her now, he thought impatiently. God knew, he wanted her so badly that he ached with it. But, with her sister and nurse in the room, what kind of a response did he think he'd get? He wanted a passionate woman, not a frozen statue, and she'd probably hate him forever.

Thank God William had given him that licence to build. Another tower would take care of the question of privacy when the castle was full of guests, and the building of a tower and a proper barbican over the gate would keep him at home for some time. He hadn't even had to mention the subject. The King needed men he could trust to hold the borders for him while he was fighting elsewhere, and those men needed strong fortresses. William had commandeered several men-at-arms and ordered Raverre to stay put.

"I'll take William fitzOsbern north with me," the King had said, "where his propensity for fighting can be put to good use against that short-sighted fool Morcar instead of simple villagers. I need you here in case any threat comes from the west.''

Which was precisely what he had wanted. Although it wasn't doing him much good, he thought, turning restlessly. The move brought him facing Lisette and, although Raverre couldn't see her, the faint aroma of the rose water she used wafted towards him, evoking images of this mouth against her warm, scented flesh. His body hardened instantly.

So much for distracting himself with building plans. Turning over again, Raverre resigned himself to sleeplessness for what was left of the night.

Lisette awoke in the same cramped position in which she had eventually fallen asleep. She wondered tiredly why the light was muted, then her eyes focused on the closed curtains and memory came rushing back, bringing pain in its wake. She turned over abruptly, almost landing in Raverre's arms.

"Good morning," he drawled in a deep, caressing voice that sent a shiver of apprehension mingled with longing down her spine.

Lisette gazed back at him in perturbed silence, then thankfully remembered where they were. She was safe enough, she thought, glancing towards the curtains; they weren't alone.

"They've gone," Raverre said, correctly interpreting her expression. "At first light. Tactful of them, wasn't it?"

Alerted by the intent look in his eyes, Lisette leapt from the bed as though propelled from a catapult. Wrenching open the bed curtains, she saw that they were indeed alone, and turned to gaze at Raverre, her eyes wide with consternation.

He sat up, pushing the covers aside, the muscles of his chest and stomach rippling with the movement, and Lisette retreated a couple of paces, averting her gaze in sudden confusion. Since their wedding-night, when she hadn't looked, darkness had hitherto cloaked their nakedness, and she was conscious of an unexpected twinge of curiosity, which brought a blush to her face.

"Coward," he said, still in that soft voice, which now held more than a hint of amusement.

"I am not!" Lisette denied, trying to instil some firmness into her voice and sounding very nervous instead. Forcing herself to meet Raverre's gaze, she tried again. "But I have guests to attend to and—"

"Come here," he interrupted, smiling lazily across at her with those glittering blue eyes.

She was immediately rendered speechless. How could he look at her with such undisguised lust—for that was exactly what it was—when he had been with another woman last night? She could not have been mistaken. She had seen them with her own eyes. It had been almost dawn when he had come to bed, and now he wanted her as well!

A healthy bolt of rage surged through Lisette, making her forget both her unhappiness and last night's resolutions.

"How dare you?" she gasped, turning pale with anger. She felt quick satisfaction at Raverre's look of utter disbelief following her outburst, but his own temper flared just as quickly, dispelling the expression.

"What?" he barked, a black scowl descending on his face as he came to his feet. Completely unconcerned by his state of undress, he advanced on Lisette, looking so savage that she hurriedly put the table between them.

Taking hold of the nearest corner, Raverre upended the barrier with one powerful movement of his arm, hurling it out of the way. Ignoring the resounding crash as table and contents fell to the floor, he grabbed Lisette by the shoulders.

"How dare I do what?" he demanded furiously, glaring

down at her. "Dare to lie with my wife? Is that such a felony that you look at me as if I had just committed murder and come to you with blood still on my hands?"

It was an unfortunate choice of words. Lisette had felt herself start to soften towards him as trembling weakness had overcome her at his touch. He was so big and strong that she had longed to melt against the hard warmth of his body and give in to the deliciously primitive thrill that had coursed through her at his violent reaction to her retreat.

His last question, however, effectively brought a rapid return to cold sanity.

"You have murdered!" she accused breathlessly. "Do you deny that you have killed? Do you deny that you have the blood of innocent people on your hands?"

"Of course I deny it!" he roared, further enraged at this unjust charge. "I have never raised my sword against any man except in open battle. My God! I thought we had gone beyond that old argument."

Raverre's hands clenched on her shoulders, starting to shake her, but as her fragile bones quivered under his grip he pushed Lisette away, realising, even in his anger, how easily he could hurt her.

Goaded, however, by sharp pain at her accusation and the thwarted hunger of the past two days, he added bitingly, "My supposed victims didn't appear to worry you the other night."

Lisette flinched. But, as she saw Raverre's face register her pain, desperation made her rally quickly.

"Aye. For a moment I forgot who you are and what you have done. But that will never happen again, I assure you."

"Oh, won't it?" he retorted, angry again. But now the anger had a hard, controlled edge to it, and Lisette sensed danger. Raverre's eyes narrowed in mocking enquiry. "That's a challenge if ever I heard one. Are you sure you wish to take the consequences of throwing down the gaunt-let, my lady?''

She would not let him see how nervous this question made her. Shrugging with a show of indifference, Lisette turned her back on him. "I suggest you get dressed," she answered coldly. "In case you have forgotten, we have guests who—"

Raverre had heard enough. He spun Lisette around, and jerked her against him so hard that the breath left her lungs in a startled gasp. Holding her head still, he brought his mouth down hard on hers, kissing her with a sensual male dominance which aroused every feminine instinct of sur-render that she possessed.

Then his free hand began to unfasten her gown with a swift efficiency that told its own tale of his experience, and fury rescued her yet again.

Feeling her yield, Raverre had relaxed his hold, and now Lisette managed to wrench away from him, clutching at the front of her gown as her forceful movement caused it to slip from her shoulders. She had not retreated more than one pace, however, before Raverre recovered fast. Hauling her back into his arms, he pinioned her own by yanking the close-fitting gown down to her waist. Then, hoisting her over his shoulder, he carried Lisette across to the bed and tossed her on to the mattress. A grim smile curled his mouth as he watched her strive to free her arms.

"Shall I help you, sweet wife?" he asked silkily as she turned and twisted ineffectually, half blinded by her hair as it fell across her face in wild disorder.

Lisette glared up at him, forgetting his nakedness and her embarrassment, forgetting that she had almost given herself up to the demands of that beautiful, hard mouth. At that moment white-hot rage flared so fiercely in her that it cauterised every other emotion.

"Aye, you can help me!" she spat at him. "But only so I can fight you! Or do you prefer to take your women while they're helpless?"

Raverre gave a savage laugh. Bending, he stripped the gown away from her, tossing it to the floor and preventing Lisette's instant scramble for freedom by the sheer force of his body over hers.

"Oh, no," he said with soft menace. "Not this time, my lady."

With Lisette held captive between his arms, his eyes dropped to her fine linen shift, the only flimsy barrier remaining between them. She wondered with defiant fury how Raverre was going to get the shift over her head, ready to fight him every inch of the way, and he smiled grimly again as he saw the determination in her eyes.

"Do you really think a few paltry pieces of clothing will keep me from taking what is mine?" he derided. "My innocent little wife, you have much to learn." And, hooking his fingers into the neck of her shift without any further warning, he ripped the fragile garment from neck to hem.

Lisette cried out in shock, trying to shield herself from his gaze, but Raverre grabbed her hands and pinned them out to the sides, his eyes roaming heatedly over the sweet curves and shadows of her body.

"Mother of God," he breathed, his anger instantly swamped by a surge of desire so violent that he didn't dare move for fear of losing control completely and hurting her with the driving force of his need. She was so delicate. So beautiful. And he needed her with a hunger that was causing him to shake as much as she did. Raverre's mind froze on the thought as he realised how helplessly Lisette was trembling, his eyes flashing to her face.

She had turned away, her eyes tightly shut, her lower lip caught between her teeth, trying to conceal her distress.

Remorse stabbed through him like a dagger, restoring some of his control.

"Don't," he whispered, his voice hoarse. "Don't turn from me, sweetheart. I'm not going to hurt you. I could never hurt you." His mouth lowered to the tender curve of her neck, savouring the warm fragrance of her skin as he pressed hot kisses across her throat and down to her shoulder. The taste of her went to his head like strong wine. He groaned with desperate longing. "You're so lovely. So small and soft. Let me love you, darling—my sweet love— I want you so much."

Lisette heard the words of need and desire, but was deaf to the note of yearning love. Lacerated in quick succession by anger, outraged modesty, fright and her own need, she could bear no more.

"I can't! I can't! Oh, please—" Her voice broke on a despairing sob.

Raverre felt the breath leave his lungs as though he had been hit across the back by a battering-ram. He was incapable of movement for several seconds, his only conscious thought that he had all but told Lisette how much he needed her, how much he loved her, and she had thrown it back in his face.

Unable to bring himself to break down her resistance by force, he sought release from the pain of her rejection with the only other alternative.

Flinging himself off the bed, he threw the blanket over Lisette with a jerky, violent movement that in no way assuaged the agony spearing through him.

"You must pardon me for not knowing you think it shameful to lie with a Norman husband, madam," he grated with biting sarcasm, tormented by the memory of the way she had willingly charmed William and Ralf de Pictou. "Your behaviour last night with the King led me to believe you were more than content with our company. And I must have been mistaken in your response to me a few nights ago. Or perhaps 'twas the thought of that young soldier which aroused your passion.''

"Don't confuse me with your Norman whore," Lisette flung back, goaded into a retort by this unfair barb.

Raverre paused in the act of throwing on his clothes. "What?" he questioned, his voice dangerous.

Lisette sat up, clutching the blanket.

"That wanton you had last night!" she cried recklessly. "Don't bother to deny it. I saw you and the Lady Judith with my own eyes. 'Twas hours before you—"

Her voice was abruptly cut off as Raverre strode forward, reaching down to grip her face with one hand. "Don't say another word," he snarled, his eyes so ferocious that she shrank back in alarm.

"Just so there's no mistake," he gritted, his teeth clenched, "I was with the King most of the night. Whatever you saw obviously didn't include me telling Judith that I already have my hands full with a blind, stubborn little—"

"I may be blind and stubborn," Lisette cried angrily, "but I don't trifle with another woman's husband."

Raverre released her and strode to the door. "She may have been a wanton," he yelled back, "but at least she was willing. I was a fool to have pushed her away!" The door slammed behind him, leaving his parting words to echo in Lisette's brain.

He hadn't been with the Norman girl last night. Raverre might have thrown the words at her in anger, but Lisette recognised the truth when she heard it. Holy Mother, what have I done? she wondered in despair, falling back on the bed. In her frantic snatch for any weapon that would prevent Raverre making love to her in the light of day, when

he would see the response she could no longer hide, had
she now driven him away altogether?

Turning her face into the goosedown pillow, Lisette gave
way to the tears of bitter regret which had burned behind
her eyes all night.

Matilda was seated by the window where the morning
light fell on the skeins of wool in her lap. As Lisette entered
the solar the Queen took another strand of wool from one
of her ladies, holding it up to compare the colour. Hearing
the door open, she looked up and smiled.

"Good morrow, my lady," she greeted Lisette. "Come.
Talk with me while our husbands are occupied with business."

Waving away her woman, who retired to the group of
ladies on the other side of the room, Matilda herself drew
up a stool and patted it invitingly.

Lisette sat, facing away from the light. "You enjoy tapestry, madam?" she ventured timidly. Still suffering from
her raw emotions, she felt more awkward than ever in the
face of the Queen's composed dignity. She wondered what,
if anything, the two of them could have in common.

"Indeed," Matilda answered, giving the girl by her side
a shrewd glance. "I cannot sit with idle hands, and it passes
the time pleasantly when I have no household to attend to.
The King insisted that I rest this morning. He wants this
child safely delivered. It will be our first born in England,
another boy if our blessed Mother is kind."

"Then you will not be witnessing the ceremony later?"
questioned Lisette, remembering Godric with a guilty start.
She wondered if the old man had arrived.

"In truth, my dear, I am happy not to be surrounded by
noise and people for a while. Although even another ceremony of allegiance would be preferable to getting back

into that extremely uncomfortable litter. But not a word to William, mind. He thinks it gives me a respite from riding, and you know how stubborn husbands are when they think they are doing one a favour.''

This very human observation made Lisette smile, albeit a trifle wanly, and Matilda remarked shrewdly, ''You seem somewhat distraite, my dear.'' She lowered her voice. ''And you've been weeping. Never tell me that Judith's attempts to captivate your husband last night have caused trouble between you?'' She smiled at Lisette's startled expression. ''Never have I seen a man less interested. 'Twas most amusing to watch. Foolish girl.''

''I am not so foolish that I would let him see I was jealous!'' Lisette retorted, hoping devoutly that Raverre hadn't had time to put such a construction on her last angry words. ''Which I wasn't!'' she added unconvincingly, then flushed as she remembered to whom she was speaking.

Matilda chuckled. ''I meant Judith was foolish, silly child. Anyone with a farthing of sense can see your lord has eyes only for you. Well, if 'twas not the antics of my maid that has upset you, what is it?''

She waited a moment, but as Lisette stayed silent, grappling with Matilda's surprising description of Raverre, the Queen continued in her forthright way, ''Your mother is no longer here to advise you, I believe, but perhaps I may be of help.''

An urge to confide in the older woman swept through Lisette as she suddenly recalled the tales she had heard of William's courtship of his wife. Perhaps the Queen *could* help, she thought, rushing impulsively into speech before her courage deserted her.

''Oh, madam, the situation is not as you think. My Lord Raverre forced me to marry him. Not because he cares for me, but to further his own ends, and I thought I hated him for it, for taking my family's home, my people's freedom, but—''

"But now you have fallen in love with him. Is it not so?"

"Aye," uttered Lisette, in such a tragic voice that Matilda smiled to herself. Lisette gripped her hands together. "How can I, after what he has done? And yet he can be kind also, I know that, and now you say he looked only at me last night, though—''

She took a deep breath and tried to sound more coherent. "If only I knew what to do! Oh, madam, I think you might understand how I feel, for the King was not always so concerned for *your* feelings, and—''

She stopped as Matilda, in her turn, looked startled. Holy Saints, what have I said? Lisette thought, appalled at her indiscretion.

Quickly kneeling at Matilda's feet, she stammered in sudden fright. "Oh, forgive me, my lady. I should not have said such a thing to you."

But Matilda merely looked thoughtful. "So, even old news travels far," she mused. Then briskly, "Get up, child, I am not offended."

She clapped her hands to gain the attention of her chattering ladies. "Go into the hall, all of you," she ordered, waving them towards the door. "I would speak privately with my Lady of Raverre."

They rose obediently and left, with curious glances at Lisette, who had resumed her seat.

"What version of the old tale have you heard, child?" Matilda asked as the door closed again.

"Why, that the King beat you once," Lisette answered cautiously. "Because you had refused his offer of marriage."

The Queen smiled, a reminiscent look on her face.

"Well, as far as it goes, you heard truthfully enough. Aye, he beat me." She gazed into the distance as memory took her back to her girlhood. "William had come to my father's court in Flanders to ask for help in subduing his Norman Barons, and after he left he sent a courtier to ask for my hand in marriage. My father was not really in favour of the match. William's position as Duke of Normandy was precarious indeed; he had been surrounded by treachery and deceit most of his life, not knowing whom to trust. A friend today might turn out to be an enemy tomorrow. But my father left the choice up to me."

She smiled wryly at the listening girl. "You know that I refused him?"

Lisette nodded.

"I was young, only fifteen, and unversed in the ways of men. William had seemed so cold to me, so remote, as if he didn't care about me one way or the other. But I had been drawn to the strength in him, and wanted to goad him into a show of feeling. So I sent back a message saying I could never marry one of bastard blood and low-born into the bargain."

Matilda chuckled. "He would probably have beaten me there and then, before my father and the whole court, had he been present, but he had to wait, which fed his anger.

"It happened as I was leaving the church one day with my maid. As we stood there William rode into the square, dismounted, and without uttering a word, set about me with his hands, tearing at my clothes and finally throwing me to the ground before mounting again and riding off. I swear to you, child, I could not believe he had left me there. He could have abducted me, forcing me into a position where I would have to marry him or be shamed, for there was no one to gainsay him. But he didn't, and finally I understood. He still wished to wed me in all honour, but would teach

me who had the stronger whip-hand, and when he sent
again to my father I accepted him. You wonder why, I
suppose.''

Lisette shook her head. ''I think because you loved him
from the beginning, madam. But weren't you angry after
he had treated you so roughly? And in public!''

Even as she spoke, though, Lisette remembered that after
Raverre's attack on her in the graveyard she had not felt
anger, only regret that she had so provoked him. Matilda's
laugh brought her back to the present.

''Of course I was angry. I swore that William would not
come near me again, but as soon as I calmed down I
changed my mind. After all, I had sent him a message
which I knew would anger him beyond reason, and in the
years that followed while we waited for the Pope's dispen-
sation I realised that I loved him.''

She leaned forward and patted Lisette's hand. ''You see,
my dear, we are strong women, you and I, and therefore
we are only truly happy with a man who shows himself as
strong or more so. As William proved to me, earning my
respect, and, I think, as Raverre has done also with you.
Think, child. What would you say to a man who hung about
your skirts, doing nothing but sigh all day, and thrown into
extravagant displays of rapture whenever you deigned to
give him a smile or kind word?''

Lisette grimaced.

''Exactly so. And what did you think of Raverre when
you first saw him? Be honest now.''

''To say truth, Your Grace, I was afraid of the force in
him,'' admitted Lisette. ''But when we were married he
was so...''

Matilda nodded wisely. ''Aye. That union of strength
and tenderness in a man is what most women can only
dream of finding.''

It was true, thought Lisette. Raverre had used his power to take her home and marry her, but his gentleness had conquered her heart. She saw Matilda smile knowingly.

"But he does not love me, and, as if that is not bad enough, I feel so disloyal for loving *him*," Lisette answered, agitatedly wringing her hands again. "I understand what you are saying, my lady, but you at least did not see the King as an enemy of your people."

"No," agreed Matilda, "but why torment yourself with regrets for what cannot be changed? Instead, look towards the time when Norman and Englishman may live side by side, though it may take a generation or two. Who knows, maybe this first child of mine to be born on English soil will take part in such a future? After all, do you see me as an enemy?"

"Oh, no," said Lisette fervently, then gave a shaky laugh.

"You see? We are merely two women, sitting here gossiping about our husbands. And as to Raverre not loving you, what makes you think so?"

"Well, he has never said—"

Matilda tut-tutted in exasperation. "Foolish child. Men are not so easy with words as we women, but you say he treats you with kindness? And, judging by the way he watched you last night, like a dog guarding a bone, I would wager my best cloisonné brooch that he comes eagerly to your bed and is as reluctant to leave it."

Lisette felt herself blushing, but she couldn't help smiling as a tiny bud of hope burgeoned in her wounded spirit. The Queen's words reminded her of the nights she had awoken to find herself in Raverre's arms, and how protected she had felt there.

"That's better," approved Matilda as she saw Lisette's expression brighten. "Put the past behind you, child. Now

go and put on that lovely circlet I saw you wearing yesterday and but smile at Raverre. He won't be able to get rid
of us fast enough.''

Lisette giggled at the thought of Raverre hustling the
King off the premises, but rose with alacrity.

Smiling at her eagerness, Matilda dismissed her, asking
Lisette to send her ladies back to the solar.

When Lisette hurried into the hall she sensed at once that
something untoward had occurred. Several men were gathered in the room but there was no murmur of conversation.
Even Matilda's ladies, standing by the fireplace, were quiet,
and the silence hung in the air, ominous, waiting.

As she stepped around the carved oak screen which hid
the solar door the first men she saw clearly were Godric
and Leofwin. The elderly Thegn and his son were standing
before the high table, behind which sat William, with Raverre on his left. All four looked tense and, in Godric's case,
anxious.

Lisette motioned to Matilda's ladies, wondering if she
also should retire with the other women, but as she hesitated William saw her.

''Ah, my lady,'' he greeted, beckoning imperiously.
''Your arrival is most timely. You have long been acquainted with Lord Godric and his son, I believe.''

''Aye, my lord,'' she replied, and turned to smile warmly
at Godric. Her speech of welcome died on her lips, however, as William continued.

''We have weighty matters to consider. Leofwin Godricson stands accused here of rebellion, but now wishes to
acknowledge us as his Sovereign. As his father has done
of his free will. The son throws himself on our mercy and
has proof of his good intent. We are waiting to hear it.''

William leaned over to confer with Raverre in a low
voice, and Lisette had a chance to wonder at the change in

the King from the previous night's charming indulgent guest to this morning's sternly calculating monarch, before he motioned her to a bench near the table.

"You may stay, madam, in case I need to question you. Firstly, sir—" he addressed Godric, "—we will hear your son and judge on his own words."

"That is fair," answered Godric, bowing and stepping back a pace.

William gestured to Leofwin. "Speak."

"My lord, I heard talk one night of missing gold. 'Twas from a man I chanced to meet in a tavern, a mean place. The fellow was far gone in his ale cup and bragging." Leofwin paused. "He might have been lying."

William's face remained impassive. "Continue."

"I thought myself the wretch was lying when he spoke of great wealth. He looked as mean as the inn itself. But when I scoffed at him he grew angry as only the cup-shotten can and told me where this wealth was hidden. If he spoke truly 'tis there still, tied fast to the supports of the main bridge over the Itchen."

"God's bones, still in Winchester itself," muttered William. He regarded Leofwin thoughtfully. "You didn't consider taking the gold yourself?"

Lisette didn't listen to Leofwin's reply or the interrogation that followed. What was she to do? If she hadn't heard Leofwin's previous story she would have believed his explanation today, but he had omitted all mention of his own involvement. In fear for his life probably. And how could she betray him?

Lisette glanced up to meet Leofwin's intent stare. Though still gaunt and pale, he certainly looked more like his old self, but the memory of his bitter anger drifted uneasily at the edges of her mind. He looked away again to answer another question from William.

Leofwin had not betrayed their earlier meeting, and he had come openly to the King with the knowledge of the ingot's whereabouts. If he was truly reconciled to the Norman invasion she could not destroy him merely to placate her own desire to be rid of the secrets between herself and Raverre.

Risking a glance at her husband's stony countenance, Lisette doubted if he would believe in Leofwin's sincerity should she admit the truth. He still looked so savage that even the thought of smiling at him, as Matilda had suggested, was daunting.

With a start Lisette saw that Leofwin was kneeling before William, giving the oath of allegiance, and realised that he must have been pardoned. The knowledge seemed to decide the issue in her mind, but as Leofwin stood he sent her a glance from under his lashes that stirred a *frisson* of doubt once again.

Then he was bowing in her direction prior to retiring. Lisette looked anxiously at the King.

"'Tis as well you're staying here at Ambray, Alain," William was saying quietly as they watched Leofwin solicitously assist his father from the hall. "You can keep a watch on that young man. He seemed sincere enough, but there's something…"

There certainly is, thought Raverre grimly. He could hardly keep his eyes off Lisette long enough to make his peace with William. Despite the hurt anger that still burned in his veins, however, his innate sense of justice had to acquit her of a similar charge. She had sat with head bent as if divorced form the whole proceedings, and he had found himself wondering what she felt at seeing her friend again. Would she have sought shelter with Leofwin had he returned earlier? Had his appearance made her regret their marriage more than she seemed to already?

Realising the futility of tormenting himself with such questions, Raverre brought his attention back to William. The King was speaking to Lisette.

"So you see why I am more inclined to pardon such men, my lady. They are not felons merely because they chose one side over another, but men who are valuable to the welfare of England and therefore of value to me if they can be won over. My belief has been justified—in this part of the country at least."

Unable to ignore the oblique reference to the Atheling Edgar and the rebellious northern Earls, Lisette ventured, "The people of the Welsh Marches are perhaps more used to Norman rule, sir. There had been Normans here for many years. In truth…" she smiled suddenly as words Raverre would understand came into her mind, feeling the weight of her past conflict lift from her shoulders as she made the confession "…one of my father's ancestors came from Normandy."

Holy Mother of God, fumed Raverre. *I* had to find that out from Bertrand, and even then Lisette would have denied it if she could. She spends a few hours with William and comes out with it as willingly as you please. Why, in God's name, can't she speak to me like this?

Scowling furiously, he looked up, his eyes colliding with Lisette's with a shock that made his heart jolt and then start pounding against his ribs as he realised that she was in fact speaking to him. The actual words were directed to the King, but her eyes gazed, unflinching, into his.

"Is it so indeed?" asked William, interested. He glanced at Raverre's arrested expression. "Then you did not object to marrying one of us?"

"I am proud to be Raverre's lady," Lisette said softly. Her face was suffused with shy colour and her lashes quivered slightly, betraying her nervousness, but she continued to hold his gaze, her dark eyes softly glowing.

Then, as Raverre half rose from his seat, William broke the spell. "Good!" he pronounced, coming to his feet, and, as if his movement released the others in the hall from their hypnotic stillness, there was sudden talk and activity.

Slaves hurried into the solar and emerged with bundles ready to be reloaded into the baggage wagons, William's knights bellowed orders to their pages, and Matilda sallied forth from the solar, accompanied by Catherine. Guiltily realising that she hadn't even noticed her sister that morning, Lisette was recalled to her duties as hostess.

In the bustle of the King's departure she had little time to wonder about the consequences of her statement. Duty kept her and Raverre apart for some time, and it was not until the royal guests were about to leave that she found herself standing next to him.

Acutely conscious of his intent gaze, Lisette knelt before the Queen, impulsively kissing Matilda's hand.

Matilda leaned forward. "I wish you good fortune, child," she whispered, before mounting into her litter.

William was already mounted and waiting for Raverre to join him as escort for part of the way, but when Lisette turned to her husband, expecting the formal salute customary for such public occasion, Raverre clasped her about the waist. Pulling her against him, he lowered his head and kissed her long and hard on the mouth.

His body still bent protectively over hers as he broke the kiss, Raverre looked down into Lisette's eyes, his heart leaping in response to the soft surrender in their depths.

"When I get back…" he said huskily. And, releasing her as abruptly as he had seized her, he strode to Lanzelet, mounted, and rode out through the gate without a backward glance.

Lisette remained standing in the bailey, gazing after the riders until they disappeared past the village. No doubt she looked like a love-struck fool, she thought, but she didn't care. The tentative bud of hope, awakened by the Queen's encouragement, had burst into full bloom at the promise in Raverre's unfinished sentence.

Suppressing a sigh of impatience at the delay before he returned, Lisette turned to see Catherine descending the outer stairway with Leofwin and Godric, who were also preparing to depart.

She sent up a heartfelt prayer of thanks for her sister, and hurried forward, holding out both hands to Godric. He bent to kiss her gallantly on the cheek.

"Sir, I must beg your forgiveness for being absent when you arrived, and my shameful neglect of you since. But you are not leaving, surely? Won't you stay and dine with us and rest for the night before you undertake to return home, and allow us to show you a proper welcome?"

"Nothing would please me more, dear child," he answered, "but I am an old man who can only sleep at ease in his own bed these days. It does my heart good to see you again, however, and mayhap your husband will bring you to visit us soon. For now, he knows I did not intend to tarry once we had seen the King, and will understand that I shall be glad to see a long journey over."

Lisette, noticing the yellowish pallor of the elderly Thegn's face that told of constant illness, could see that Godric was anxious to be gone, not wishing to be laid up with sickness in another man's home, and forbore to persist with her invitation.

She turned to Leofwin and smiled, holding out her hand.

"Leofwin, I am so glad to see you here."

"Thanks to you," he answered softly. Then, as Lisette glanced warningly at Catherine, he said more loudly, "Our serfs are waiting with the horses, Father. Why don't you start? You will travel slowly and I shall easily catch you up. I would like to speak with Lisette a moment, but do not wish to delay you.''

''As you please,'' answered the old man, and, bidding farewell to the girls, mounted with Leofwin's help. Flanked by four serfs, he started slowly down the road.

''Why don't you both come with me part of the way?'' suggested Leofwin, turning to Lisette. ''I haven't had a good horse under me for months, and we could enjoy a gallop across the fields before I rejoin my father.''

She hesitated, but Catherine clapped her hands with delight. ''Aye,'' she cried. ''Do let us, Lisette. It will seem so dull indoors now everyone has gone.''

Knowing she was far too restless to settle to some sedentary occupation such as needlework, Lisette allowed herself to be persuaded. A ride would pass the time until Raverre returned, and she was naturally curious to know what had passed between Godric and his son. Memories of the companionable rides they had all shared in the past came to mind, and Lisette put aside her slight feeling of unease at leaving the manor.

By the time they had penetrated about a mile into the forest, Lisette was glad she had come. Letting Catherine ride a little ahead, Leofwin had excused his behaviour at their last meeting on the score of the wretched existence he had been obliged to lead, thinking the estrangement with his father had been too deep to be mended. His apology had been a little terse, that was true, but Lisette, full of excited anticipation, was feeling too happy to be critical.

He had refrained from commenting about her marriage, and had received the news of Enide's retreat to Romsey Abbey with admirable understanding. He still appeared rather grim-visaged, however, only responding briefly and unsmilingly to Catherine's attempts to engage him in conversation, but Lisette concluded that this manner was merely the natural taciturnity engendered by his recent solitary existence, and bade Catherine not to plague him with questions.

"I swear you chatter more than any jackdaw," she said, smiling at her sister. "But I must confess I was grateful for it this morning. Thank you, little sister, for being such an able deputy."

Catherine flushed with pleasure at this praise. "I enjoyed it. The Queen is a most gracious lady, don't you think? And the King is much more...but we can speak of that later," she amended hastily as Leofwin scowled.

"Aye, we should turn back now, Leofwin," suggested Lisette, reining Viking Princess to a halt. "We seem to be a long way from the road."

"Very well," he agreed. "But dismount a moment, Catherine, your saddle girth looks a little slack. I don't want you suffering a fall because of some careless stable lad. Perhaps I'd better check yours as well, Lisette."

"Oswy is usually very careful," said Catherine doubtfully. But, springing to the ground nevertheless, she peered under her horse's belly. "Everything looks secure enough to me."

Leofwin was tying Catherine's horse to a tree. "Does it?" he asked in a voice that held an unusually high note of elation.

Lisette looked at him quickly, a sudden premonition of danger brushing her skin like a cold wind, but before she had time to act Leofwin grasped Catherine's arm.

"Then we can be on our way. Over here!"

"What are you doing?" cried Catherine sharply as Leofwin pulled her across to Lisette.

"Making sure of my future. Now hold your tongue and get on the horse."

"Leofwin, have you lost your mind?" demanded Catherine, ignoring these instructions.

"Catherine! Do as he says!" cried Lisette quickly as Leofwin's expression turned ugly, and she glimpsed the dagger that appeared from its concealment beneath his mantle.

Shocked disbelief at Leofwin's unexpected behaviour seemed to suspend all her faculties while Catherine scrambled up behind her, but she forced back the panic rising in her throat and tried to think. She did not have any idea what Leofwin intended, but calm reason had worked before and might again if he would only listen to her.

"Very wise," he remarked, leading Viking Princess over to his own horse and mounting. He handed the reins back to Lisette.

"We'll travel faster if I don't have to lead you," he informed her, his eyes so cold that she shuddered. "But if you fall back I'll take the reins again, and if you try to turn and run your sister will be the worse for a sword in her back. Do you understand me?"

"Aye," she whispered, and he nodded in satisfaction.

They started off again, Lisette giving her sister's hand a reassuring squeeze as her mind searched for a way to delay their progress, giving Raverre time to catch them.

That he would come after them Lisette had no doubt whatsoever, but it could be several hours before he returned to discover their disappearance, and Leofwin seemed to be leading them deeper into the forest. Raverre would waste precious time searching for them on the road to Godric's manor, and panic churned in her stomach again at the thought of spending the night in Leofwin's company.

They now appeared to be heading in a southerly direction, away from the army to the north, and, remembering his talk of leaving the country, Lisette wondered if Leofwin intended taking ship from one of the nearer ports. But in that case, why take her and Catherine?

Glancing back at Catherine and motioning her to keep silent, Lisette brought Viking Princess up closer to Leofwin's mount.

"Why are you doing this?" she asked in a voice that she strove to keep steady and calm. "You must know we would not inform against you if, as it seems, you do not intend to honour your vow to William.

"Why, Leofwin?" she persisted quietly as he continued to stare stonily ahead. "I want to understand. You could have left England without anyone knowing, except maybe your father. Why go through all that ceremony earlier? At least tell me that much."

"How else was I to get to you, Lisette, my dear?" he asked in a conversational voice that was strangely at variance with the expression in his eyes. "I did warn you earlier, but you chose not to hear. Which I consider rather strange now that I find your husband is indeed the Norman Tostig described to me. You should be grateful to be removed from such a shameful alliance. You say you don't understand me! *I* cannot understand how you could be so disloyal to your people."

"She did it to protect Enide and me!" exclaimed Catherine, unable to bear this criticism of her beloved elder sister in silence. "And besides—"

"Hush, sweet," admonished Lisette as Leofwin turned to glare at the younger girl. "'Tis a convenient marriage for both of us. No more than that," she told him calmly, hoping he would make the assumption that her marriage was in name only.

She did not think Leofwin had witnessed Raverre's embrace in the bailey—he had not appeared outside until some moments later—but he sent her a sardonic look which held a good deal of disbelief.

"Do you think I'm blind? Even if he has not claimed you yet, how long do you think you will keep your precious virtue? Or do you expect honour from a Norman who has waded through the blood of your people to get to you?"

"He has more honour than you will ever possess!" she flashed, her temper momentarily getting the better of her. "He would never break a sacred vow as you have done. Leofwin, have you no fear for your immortal soul? And you will only make matters worse for yourself by taking us. Raverre will come after you and we'll only slow you down."

This was the wrong thing to have said, she realised immediately as Leofwin gave her an ice-cold stare.

"If you do," he stated with deadly quiet, "I'll kill your sister. But I have other plans for you, my pretty creature, and I doubt you would think death preferable to becoming my mistress. And if your husband comes after us I'll kill him also. Then, who knows, I may even marry you?"

He laughed suddenly at her appalled expression. "Didn't you think I meant what I said to you the other day? My little simpleton, still blinded by the fact that I asked for Enide. She would have been easy to dispose of, and then I would have asked for you. I had my plans well laid until the Norman bastard set his foot in England. You still look surprised. Don't you know what that innocent beauty of yours does to a man?"

He laughed again, a high uncontrolled sound that froze Lisette's blood, and she allowed Viking Princess to drop back a pace.

"He has run mad," whispered Catherine behind her, sounding as terrified as Lisette felt. "Lisette, we have to get away. He'll never be able to throw his sword among these trees if we run. We have to try.''

"No!" Lisette whispered back emphatically. "He'll catch us easily while Viking Princess is carrying both of us. But—'' she thought hard "—if I can persuade Leofwin to dismount on some pretext, you might escape. You'll ride faster alone and I don't think he'll risk losing me to go after you.''

"But I can't leave you!" protested Catherine. "He'll kill you!''

"No. You heard what he said. 'Tis you he would kill if he's enraged. I think I am safe enough for the moment, but you must get back to the manor and tell Raverre which way to follow before it's too late.''

Even as she spoke, though, Lisette felt qualms shake her. If they went much further before Catherine tried to flee she might lose her way. Both girls knew the countryside around the manor for some miles, but already the woods were taking on an unfamiliar aspect, and when the sun went down there would be other dangers.

If some accident happened to her sister Lisette knew she would never forgive herself. But she had to weigh that risk against the certainty that Leofwin would kill Catherine sooner or later. He had only taken them both because he knew Lisette would not have accompanied him alone.

"The river can't be very far from us," breathed Catherine in Lisette's ear, and even as she spoke the glitter of clear water showed through the bare trees, where the Wye cut a wide path through the forest on its slowly meandering way to the Severn estuary.

Knowing this might be their only opportunity, Lisette halted her mount. Here, at least, Catherine could follow the river until she found herself on more familiar ground.

As Leofwin stopped also, glancing around, she gestured to the smoothly flowing water.

"May we not rest just a moment to drink and water the horses?" she suggested, letting him hear a tremor in her voice. She didn't have to try very hard. It was all she could do to keep her hands steady on the reins at the thought of what they were about to do. She and Catherine could both die right here by the river if their scheme failed.

Leofwin cast a glance up at the clear sky, estimating the time, then nodded. "Aye, but don't take too long, and stay together," he ordered as Lisette slipped from the saddle.

She led Viking Princess to the river, her heart plummeting when Leofwin remained mounted, keeping pace with her until he allowed his own horse to put its head down to drink.

Kneeling down on the bank, Lisette looked up at him. "You may as well take a drink, too, Leofwin," she suggested reasonably. "What can we do? We are only women and unarmed."

He laughed scornfully, but, to her relief, dismounted and joined her. "I admire your calm, my dear," he said, but his tone was unpleasant. "I'm going to enjoy the challenge of breaking it down—when we're alone."

"You will get no pleasure from me," Lisette retorted, rising and moving away from him. His tacit admission that Catherine would not survive much longer hardened her resolve, and she added, "I would rather kill myself than let you touch me."

As she had hoped, at her deliberate provocation Leofwin rose and followed her. The minute he was several paces away from the horses, Catherine acted. Hauling on the reins, she jerked a startled Viking Princess's head up and drove her heels hard into the animal's flanks. Unused to such treatment, Lisette's horse squealed in fright and took off into the trees at a gallop before Leofwin had done more than spin around at the sound of the first startled whinny.

Leofwin immediately sprang for his horse, but Lisette ran after him and grabbed his arm, trying to use all her slight weight to slow him down.

"No!" she cried, hoping that if Catherine got a good start Leofwin would choose to put more distance between himself and the manor.

With a snarl he threw her off, shoving her to the ground and reaching for his reins, but then paused as the echo of hoofbeats rapidly died away and he realised pursuit would be useless. Turning, he strode back to Lisette and hauled her to her feet. A detached part of her mind watched the angry red colour surge into his face. She wondered if she was about to die. He looked wild enough to kill her here and now.

Holding Lisette with one hand to prevent her from falling, Leofwin swung his free arm back and struck her hard once, twice, across the face. Almost losing consciousness from the force of the blows, she only half heard him snarl. "You treacherous bitch!" as he hit her again, before letting her slump to the ground.

Through a swirling mist she watched him retrieve his horse and lead it up to her. Then he pulled her upright again by grabbing a handful of her hair. The sharp pain stung Lisette back to full awareness as Leofwin mounted and hauled her up into the saddle before him. Wheeling the horse, he spurred it in the opposite direction to Catherine's flight.

"You may well wish yourself dead when I've finished with you," he grated with chilling menace. "A man quickly forgets the civilised conduct you're accustomed to after two years of the life I've led. An unpleasant fact from which I shall derive a great deal of enjoyment in teaching you.''

Shaking from the inevitable reaction to what had just passed, still dizzy with the stinging pain of her bruised face, Lisette was unable to answer him. Now that Catherine was safely away, sick fear held her in its cruel grip, clawing at her stomach and sapping her ability to think clearly.

The only constant in her mind was that she would never let Raverre be dishonoured by allowing Leofwin to do the things he was describing in such detail. She would die first. Fortunately for her, this resolve, repeating itself over and over again in her head, prevented her from hearing most of what Leofwin was saying.

Eventually, getting no response from her, he fell silent, and the hours and miles slipped away as he kept the horse to a steady canter.

Chapter Nine

Spurred by the strong human instinct for self-preservation, Lisette at last began to free her mind from the clinging tentacles of panic. How ironic, she thought, that when I had to submit to Raverre's possession I never once thought of death as preferable, but now, faced with the same threat from one of my own people, I would gladly embrace it.

And yet...

The thought of never seeing Raverre again, of never being able to tell him she loved him, of never again knowing the fierce ardour of his embrace, was almost more than she could bear. Somehow, if deliverance didn't appear by nightfall, she would try to gain her freedom before facing the ultimate escape offered by death itself.

Another long hour passed in bleak consideration of such an escape, and Lisette began to wonder if Leofwin intended to ride through the night. He had avoided any sign of human habitation, and she had long since abandoned the hope of enlisting aid from passing travellers or villagers. Now, with sunset not far away, even a lonely shepherd's hut would have been a welcome sight.

Then, as they traversed an open meadow, moving slowly on the tired horse, Lisette, desperately listening for the sounds of rescue, at last heard the thud of hoofs behind them. Lost in his thoughts, Leofwin seemed oblivious, and she was afraid to turn her head in case he was warned.

Holy Mother, let it be Raverre, she prayed as her hands tensed on the saddle.

Judging the distance to the woods on their left in case she needed to seek their shelter, Lisette cautiously moved a little away from Leofwin, ready to jump the instant he realised they were being chased. The movement, slight though it was, penetrated his abstraction, and he frowned down at her.

"Hold still, woman," he growled. "We stop when I say and not before."

As Lisette turned her head to answer him she looked past his shoulder and almost swayed with relief. Raverre at last, but still some distance away and alone. Hoping to distract Leofwin from the growing sounds of pursuit, she said, "The horse will not travel much farther. Are we to spend the night in the open, a prey to any marauding animal?"

"Be silent," he commanded harshly, and she realised he was trying to listen over the sound of her voice.

Turning swiftly in the saddle, he saw Raverre, riding hard, and spurred his own horse to a faster pace. However, the animal was exhausted and barely responded. Leofwin cursed viciously and hauled on the reins, so suddenly that the horse reared, wheeling about. Lisette, seizing her chance, sprang from the saddle while he had his hands full controlling the frightened animal.

She landed hard, falling to the ground, but, unheeding of any bruises, leapt instantly to her feet. Grabbing up the loose folds of her gown, she began to run like a hare back towards Raverre. It was purely instinctive. Forgetting the nearer safety of the trees where Leofwin would find it difficult to follow, she fled to Raverre as any terrified female creature fled to the protection of her more powerful mate.

With a bellow of rage Leofwin immediately spurred after her, and Lisette realised that she could never outrun the horse or reach Raverre before she was recaptured. Then she remembered the woods and swerved wildly to her right, giving Raverre the opportunity he had been hoping for.

As soon as Lisette had jumped from the saddle he had urged Lanzelet to a faster gallop, but then with a pang of chilling fear had seen that he wouldn't be in time to intercept Leofwin's frenzied pursuit of her. There was only one alternative. Pulling Lanzelet to a slithering halt, Raverre drew his short bow and prayed for an opening in the rapidly diminishing gap between Lisette and the man determined to ride her down. He saw her change direction, making for the woods, and fired instantly, aiming at his adversary's horse.

The arrow whizzed past Leofwin's mount, missing its face by less than an inch, and the horse shied violently, unseating his rider. Leofwin rolled several times, but sat up, unhurt. Then, cursing under his breath, he climbed unsteadily to his feet as Lanzelet slithered to a halt.

As Lisette fought to regain her breath, sinking to her knees and gripping her side, Raverre dismounted and advanced slowly towards her. Lisette felt as though she gazed at a stranger. A stranger who moved with leashed menace, watching Leofwin with an expression in his eyes not even his men would have recognised.

She had seen Raverre impatient and angry, even furious, but never like this. Now Lisette saw clearly the terrifying, unstoppable ferocity that was the legacy of his Viking ancestors. He looked ready to commit murder, but he was still controlled, and therefore all the more dangerous.

Raverre reached her side and, without taking his eyes

from Leofwin, asked through clenched teeth, "Has he touched you?"

"No," she gasped. And then, more firmly, "I swear it."

He reached down to help her to stand, still with that cold, deadly gaze fixed on Leofwin, who had drawn his sword and stood waiting for the confrontation he knew could not be avoided.

"Wait here," Raverre said briefly, taking his own sword from its sheath on Lanzelet's saddle.

Lisette still held his arm. "Take care," she whispered, "he has lost all reason, I think. He will not fight fairly, my lord."

Raverre glanced down in quick surprise at her warning and saw, for the first time, the livid bruise across her cheek. His eyes narrowed, and an expression of such ruthless savagery crossed his face as his control slipped for a moment that Lisette gasped, stepping back.

"Fair or no, he won't live long enough to profit by anything he may choose to do," Raverre ground out in a voice she barely recognised as his. He moved away from her to the centre of the meadow, circling around to keep the westering sun out of his eyes. Leofwin followed.

Lisette watched, praying desperately, as the two men suddenly came together in a simultaneous attack which sent a vicious echo ringing into the stillness of the late afternoon.

They were fairly evenly matched. What Leofwin lacked in Raverre's great strength and reach he made up with a sure swiftness of movement that seemed to escape his opponent's blows by a hair's breadth, and enabled him to retaliate in kind, both men swinging their great two-handed swords with lethal intent, their breathing audible with the tremendous effort. Had they been jousting it would have been an interesting competition. But this was in earnest. To the death. And it gradually became obvious that Leofwin, blinded by his insane rage and the frustration of his plans, would tire before Raverre, who fought with a disciplined fury that few adversaries could have survived.

Blind rage had its own strength, however, and was not so easily defeated. Lisette gave a hastily smothered scream as Leofwin's blade suddenly flashed under Raverre's guard, slashing his left arm across his wrist. Blood gushed from the wound, but Raverre fought on, unheeding, sending his opponent reeling backwards under a series of tremendous blows that finally sent Leofwin to the ground.

Raverre leapt back. "Get up," he ordered curtly, ignoring the blood that continued to spurt from his wrist.

Lisette pressed her hands against her mouth in an attempt not to cry out again as Leofwin struggled to his feet and returned to the attack.

Raverre now seemed to keep him at bay with almost insolent ease, a contemptuous smile on his lips as he tormented Leofwin, playing with him as a cat did a mouse before the kill. Not attacking, but letting Leofwin feed his own rage at not being able to again wound his enemy, or finish him. The Saxon's face now had the desperate look of a man who saw his own death approaching, inexorable, inevitable. He was tiring quickly, but there was fight in him yet, and finally Raverre knew he would have to end it, or risk Lisette's life by collapsing through loss of blood.

Changing his tactics with a suddenness that took Leofwin by surprise, Raverre launched into an attack that unleashed the full strength of his fury. Slashing relentlessly at the man he had sworn to kill, forcing him backwards with every blow, he sent Leofwin's sword flying through the air to land several yards away. Leofwin's hand went instantly to his dagger, but he froze as Raverre's sword-point rested against his throat.

"You should have thought twice before you abducted my wife, Godricson," he bit out, shortening his arm for the final thrust.

"Maybe so, but I've had her first!" Leofwin hissed maliciously.

Raverre's arm stayed. His eyes went the colour of ice and his mouth curled in a deadly smile. "Not so, Saxon. She's mine. She was always mine. She always will be."

He watched as Leofwin's face registered the absolute certainty in his voice. Raverre laughed.

At the sound of his opponent's derision, Leofwin's face shattered into raging insanity. Lips drawn back from his teeth in a snarl of pure hatred, he pulled his dagger, but Raverre was quicker.

His sword entered Leofwin's throat with a thrust that drove it to the spine, and the two men stood frozen for a moment. Then Leofwin crumpled forward, death freezing the snarl on his face into a ghastly mask.

Raverre pulled his sword free and stepped back, breathing deeply and swaying slightly as dizziness washed over him. He was suddenly acutely aware of the silence and the slight chill in the air that warned of the coming night, and turned his head as Lisette flew towards him, tears of mingled fright and relief running down her face.

She slowed her pace as Raverre remained still, making no move towards her. Then, gathering all her courage, she stepped forward and took his hand, instantly feeling the warm stickiness of his blood.

All lesser worries fled. "Your arm! Oh, my lord, why did you go on fighting? You could have killed him a hundred times instead of letting your wound bleed so."

Raverre looked down vaguely at the blood, which continued to spurt from the ugly wound. "'Tis not as bad as it looks," he murmured, and promptly staggered against her, his weight bearing Lisette to the ground with him as he sank into unconsciousness.

"Oh, God!" she cried, momentarily panicked, then pulled herself together. This was no time for feminine hysterics. She had to stop the bleeding.

Hurriedly lifting her gown, Lisette pulled at the hem of her shift until it tore and she had a wide strip to use as a bandage. As she peeled back Raverre's sleeve to expose the long gash he stirred.

"Tie a knot tightly above the elbow," he instructed softly. "As tight as you can make it. Then bind my wrist."

Not wasting words, Lisette set about following his instructions, pulling the knot tight with her capable little hands and pressing a pad of cloth hard over the place on his wrist where the blood still seeped. Though now, she was relieved to see, it came sluggishly instead of the steady spurts that had weakened him.

Raverre watched her face as she worked, his eyes skimming over the tear-stained and bruised cheek nearest him.

"I wanted to make him suffer for that," he said, lifting his other hand to her face.

"I spoke truly, my lord," she said meeting his eyes steadily. "No matter what Leofwin said, this—" she touched her cheek "—was all he did."

"I know," he said, but his face was tense, his eyes searching. "I had to kill him," he went on, a strangely desperate note in his voice. "He was your friend, but I killed him."

"I know," Lisette answered, as he had done. "Leofwin was insane. You had to kill him as one would kill a rabid animal."

Raverre seemed to relax a little and his eyes closed again.

"Is it still bleeding?"

"Just a little."

"My men are following," he told her when Lisette had finished tying a firm strip of cloth around the pad on his wrist. She held his arm against her breast, keeping the pressure firm. "We split up, hoping to find you sooner, but some of them should be here shortly." He felt the faintness creep on him again, and fought against it. "If they are not here by nightfall take Lanzelet and ride for the castle."

"No!" she exclaimed. "I will not leave you."

"You'll do as I say," he commanded abruptly, reaching up to grip her arm.

"I will not leave you," Lisette repeated emphatically. "But, if I help you, we can both mount Lanzelet. He will have to go slowly, but we will at least come up with your men sooner and—"

"You'd never be able to take my weight if I lose my sense," Raverre interrupted and, as if to prove his point, slipped into unconsciousness, his hand falling from her arm. Lisette looked about her in despair.

The sun slipped below the horizon even as she watched it, and she cast a worried glance at the shadowy woods. Come nightfall there would be wolves, she knew, and, though it was unlikely they would attack a human at this season of the year, they might be drawn by the scent of blood and the corpse, lying exposed in the grass. Lisette looked back at Raverre, holding his arm closer, her hand starting to become numb with the pressure she was still exerting on his wrist.

"Don't die!" she ordered fiercely. "Don't die!"

Leaning forward, she stroked the sweat-darkened hair from his brow with her free hand, letting it lie for a moment against his cheek. He felt slightly cool, and she wondered if she should get his cloak from Lanzelet's saddle to keep him warm, but dared not release her hold in case the bleeding started again. As she watched him Lisette felt her heart fill with such love for Raverre that she wondered how she could have remained ignorant of her feelings for so long.

If he lives, she vowed, I will tell him. I don't care if he loves me not, if he only pursued me for his own honour. Oh, blessed Mother in Heaven, please let him live. I love him so.

Suppressing a sob, she bent over him, whispering, "Oh, my love, my lord, you *must* live."

She stopped with a sudden shock as she saw that Raverre's eyes were open. But as she took a shaky breath he said, "Call Lanzelet, then, and we'll try your plan. He'll stand quietly enough." And Lisette realised he had no recollection of the time that had elapsed since her suggestion.

It took them three attempts, but eventually Raverre managed to stand upright long enough to get into the saddle. Lisette mounted in front of him, bracing herself to take his weight against her back, as she nudged Lanzelet into a slow walk.

Raverre passed his good arm about her waist, pressing his hand into the saddle to take some of his weight off Lisette.

"At least I've stopped bleeding like a stuck pig," he murmured in her ear. "But the gash will have to be cauterised."

Lisette's stomach clenched at the thought of a treatment that was more like torture than cure.

"Maybe not," she said, thinking she would try anything rather than see Raverre's flesh seared by a hot iron. "If the cut is clean it can be stitched. Bertrand knows how. He saw it done in Spain when he travelled with my father, and once when a slave cut his hand in the kitchen Bertrand sewed the edges together. When it had healed there was only a thin line to show for it."

Raverre leaned more heavily on her as his senses swam. "Cauterising is quicker."

"But it does so much damage to the surrounding flesh, especially if left to clumsy hands," she argued. "And I know how to make you sleep while your arm would be stitched, so there wouldn't be any pain."

Raverre was silent for so long that Lisette thought he had swooned away again, but after a while he said, "Keep talking to me, sweetheart. How can you make a person sleep?"

"You need hemlock, opium, mulberry juice, hyoscyamus, ivy, mandragora and lettuce. The mixture is dried on a sponge and moistened. Then the patient inhales it and falls asleep."

"Does he wake up again?" Raverre demanded with a touch of humour.

"Aye, by fennel juice applied to the nostrils."

"Sounds disgusting," he said, the words slurring together.

But even as he seemed to slump against her, Lanzelet gave a soft whinny, and Lisette's straining ears caught the sounds of hoofs almost immediately afterwards. Peering into the rapidly deepening twilight, she saw several riders, their Norman clothing easily recognisable, and released a long breath of relief.

Gilbert reached them first, flinging himself out of the saddle almost before his horse had plunged to a stop.

"My lady, thank the Saints you are safe! But Alain—" He broke off suddenly as Raverre swayed.

"You must dismount, my lady. Quickly, while I have him!"

Lisette slid thankfully to the ground.

"He was wounded in the arm. Oh, Gilbert, he has lost so much blood. I have bandaged it, but he fought for so long with it bleeding terribly, and it will take hours yet to get him home…''

Her voice broke on a sob, and leaving Raverre to the other men who had come up with them, Gilbert gripped her hands.

"Do not give way now, my lady," he said firmly. "We shall do well enough. I have seen Raverre take deeper wounds than this scratch and survive. He is strong; 'tis merely loss of blood that has made him lose his senses, but that shall soon be remedied. I should think he will recover his wits before we are halfway home. Now, if you will allow me to help you on to my horse, we shall be on our way."

These bracing words made the helpless, sickening feeling of panic recede again, and Lisette nodded. Stumbling slightly with the chill and stiffness in her body, she began to feel her bruises and was glad to be gently lifted into the saddle of a tall chestnut, and to wait as Raverre was made secure by the man who mounted behind him. She was thankful to leave it all to Gilbert's capable direction, and could see why Raverre had so much trust in his young knight.

He strode over to her. "We must ride slowly, my lady, but you may go ahead with some of the men. You can trust them to keep you from harm, and the sooner you are safe home, the better. The others will be anxious."

"Catherine!" she uttered, conscience-stricken. "Oh, how could I have forgotten? Is she safe?"

"Safe, and back at the castle under Bertrand's escort by now," Gilbert replied reassuringly. He smiled unexpectedly. "She came up with us on the road to Godric's manor, where some of the serfs thought you may have been taken, riding like a wild creature from a Norse legend. I verily believe she would have ridden with us but that Raverre sent her back home. She has a great deal of courage for one so young," he finished admiringly.

"Aye," Lisette agreed thankfully. Then, as he would have mounted, she stayed him with a gesture. "Gilbert, we cannot leave Leofwin's body for the wolves. Base though his actions were, they were also the actions of a man out of his mind with madness, and his father has done nothing wrong. Let him at least have his son's body returned for Christian burial. After all, I am unharmed but for a bruise or two," she added coaxingly.

Gilbert hesitated, wondering what Raverre would say to this, but he wasn't proof against Lisette's pleading eyes.

"Very well, my lady," he said reluctantly, and gave the order for some of the men to go back for Leofwin, and for his body to be taken to Godric.

"The responsibility is mine," she assured Gilbert as they started and he came up to ride with her. "I will answer to my lord if need be."

"You could do no wrong in his eyes, my lady," was his surprising reply to this.

Lisette looked at him in quick enquiry, but Gilbert refused to say more, and wheeled his horse away to ensure that his captain and friend was secure and not losing more life-blood.

It was almost morning when they filed wearily into the bailey, and the torches at the gate were burning low in their sconces. Lisette had refused to go on ahead, but, overcome with exhaustion, had finally agreed to ride double with Gilbert, and had been half asleep for the last few miles. She also fell into Bertrand's arms, but anxiety for Raverre, who had drifted in and out of consciousness during the long night, kept her from letting Marjory lead her away to her bed.

"I must see him tended to," she insisted, swaying

against Bertrand as serfs came running to carry Raverre into the hall. "Bertrand, don't let them use a hot iron on him."

"What you must do is rest," scolded Marjory. "You can nurse him all you like tomorrow, but now you will probably swoon with hunger and exhaustion, and then be in the way."

Lisette would have protested at this brutal truth, but Bertrand, having taken a look at Raverre's arm, agreed with Marjory. "Mistress Marjory speaks wisely, my lady," he told her. "I can stitch the arm, but 'tis not a sight for your eyes. The best thing you can do is rest. The manor needs you while my lord is unable to command."

"I will rest when my lord has had the proper care," Lisette protested. "After last year, do you think I will swoon at the sight of a cut arm? Who do you think bound it up? Now, no more of such foolish arguments. Marjory, fetch me food and have a pallet set up in the solar, so I may be near Raverre."

As they hesitated Lisette sensed victory. She smiled suddenly at their mutinous faces. "Besides, you want to hear what happened, don't you?"

Lisette pulled the bearskin over her sleeping husband, carefully avoiding his injured arm. He stirred slightly but did not waken, and she went to sit in the window embrasure, where she could watch him in comfort.

Resting her head against the wall, she sighed wearily. For a day and a night Raverre had slept, only waking when she tended his arm or coaxed him to take some nourishment. At first she had been frightened by his utter stillness as he lay in the bed. He had barely seemed to breathe, and to see such a big, powerful man so helpless had torn at her heart. But Bertrand had assured her it was the deep sleep

of healing, and Bertrand had been right. Lisette's vigil had
been rewarded in the early hours of the morning.

She had been changing the bandage on Raverre's arm
when he had opened his eyes and looked straight at her,
his vivid blue gaze disconcertingly aware. Feeling her
heartbeat quicken under his steady regard, Lisette had bent
her head and concentrated on applying the healing salve of
her own making as gently as possible, knowing the slightest
touch must be painful. Bertrand might have congratulated
himself on a neat piece of sewing, but she looked at the
bruised skin where the needle had entered and almost felt
the pain in her own body.

As she had wrapped a protective covering over the
wound a faint smile had come into Raverre's eyes. "You
said I might need one of your brews one day," he had
reminded her softly.

Feeling suddenly shy in the intimate atmosphere of the
dim, quiet room, Lisette had only smiled back in answer,
but, unable to resist touching him, laid her hand on his brow
to check for fever. Raverre had brought his right hand up
to clasp hers.

"Stay with me," he had murmured, his eyes beginning
to close again. And the unexpected vulnerability in his
voice had restored her powers of speech.

"For the rest of our lives," she had quoted softly, remembering his words on the morning after their wedding.

She had not been sure if Raverre had heard her, for he
had turned his head and fallen into sleep again, but this
time the sleep had been more natural.

Since then he had woken several times to eat a little and
to drink the warmed milk mixed with wine that Lisette kept
ready. And each time as he had fallen back into slumber
he had murmured, "Stay with me."

As she watched the regular rise and fall of his chest, and

let her eyes roam over the strong lines of his handsome face, softened now in sleep, Lisette felt so much tenderness for him that the emotion threatened to overwhelm her. In the past Raverre had frightened her, angered her, and forced a physical response from her—all violent emotions in their way, over which she'd had little control. Raverre had been the one in command, self-possessed, contained.

But now this giant of a man who had faced undaunted the Danes of the fyrd swinging their battleaxes with terrifying accuracy, who had undertaken to settle in a land still hostile to his face, and who had never seemed to depend on anyone other than himself, had shown that he needed her.

The sound of the door opening interrupted Lisette's reflections and she looked up to see Gilbert enter quietly, carrying a tray, which he set down on the table.

Glancing at Raverre, he said, "Marjory said I might see Alain for a moment if I made myself useful by bringing in your supper, my lady. How is he?"

Lisette smiled and rose. "Much better," she said, amused to see how ill at ease he looked. Gilbert had probably gazed on the most hideous scenes of battle carnage without flinching, she thought, but, like most men, was as helpless as a babe when it came to nursing.

"There is no sign of fever," she assured him, "and the wound is clean. It should heal quickly, thanks to Bertrand."

"Aye," Gilbert answered. "Though I must say I was doubtful at the time. There we were, wasting time arguing, some of the men all for using a tried and true method and Bertrand saying that if he didn't get started he wouldn't have a patient to work on. I know the Moors have used stitching on wounds for years, but *I'd* never seen it done, and Raverre was no help, lying there senseless. If you hadn't told the men you'd hold them responsible to the King if Raverre died I don't know where we'd have been."

"What an interesting scene I missed," said an amused voice from the bed, and they both jumped, spinning around.

Lisette moved quickly across the room as Raverre began to sit up.

"No, no! You must lie still," she admonished, placing her hand lightly on his chest just as he came upright.

At the contact of her palm against his warm skin they both froze, staring into each other's eyes. Lisette felt as if every faculty became suspended. She was barely conscious of breathing as she gazed into the blue depths so close to her, their expression as searching as her own.

"Gilbert," said Raverre softly, his eyes never leaving Lisette's, "go and count the weapons in the armoury."

Gilbert grinned in quick comprehension and, convinced of his friend's recovery, left the room in double-quick time.

As if the closing of the door released her from the strange spell of Raverre's gaze, Lisette snatched her hand back, flushing slightly. However, her legs were shaking so much that she didn't dare try to step away from the bed.

"You must rest," she said faintly. She had felt so confident while he had been asleep, but now, faced with what appeared to be the full return of his senses, shyness overcame her again.

"I've been resting," Raverre answered inarguably, propping himself against the end of the bed. "Now that the room has stopped spinning around my head I feel a great deal better. Or I would if I could eat something more substantial than that pap you've been forcing down me all day."

Lisette couldn't help smiling at the aggrieved note in his voice. He sounded like a disgruntled little boy, she thought, feeling some composure return.

She found she was able to walk quite calmly over to the table. "Well, you may have some bread with your broth, if you like, and a slice or two of meat. But not too much," she scolded, as if he were in truth the child her imagination had conjured up.

She glanced up, still amused at the thought, and her shaky composure, disintegrated instantly. Raverre was still watching her, and the expression in his eyes was all adult male.

"Come and sit down," he invited, his voice lowering to that soft growl which seemed to come from deep in his throat.

Her heart starting to race, Lisette armed herself with the tray and complied, placing the meal between them. Raverre gave her a quizzical look, but began to eat.

"There's enough for two," he pointed out when she didn't follow his example.

"I'm not hungry," she said. She would never be able to get any food past the nervous lump in her throat. She could hardly speak. All she really wanted to do was reach out her hand and touch him again, to reassure herself that he was warm and alive.

Raverre finished his meal and went to place the tray on the floor, but the movement pulled his left arm and he paused, grimacing slightly. Glad of the excuse to move away from the bed, Lisette returned the tray to the table.

"Do the stitches pain you very much?" she asked, hating the thought of him suffering.

"Not as much as the memory of you leaping from that horse," he said rather grimly. "You could have broken your neck!"

Lisette rearranged the tray with intense concentration. "Are you very angry?" she managed.

"That depends," he returned, his expression suddenly

probing. There was a thoughtful pause. "Why did you do it?"

"I...I didn't want Leofwin to have an advantage over you once he saw you were so close. He was already dishonoured, so I knew he would not meekly let you kill him without a fight." She sent Raverre a quick, nervous glance. "He could have used me to disarm you, and I thought, whatever you felt for me, you wouldn't risk my life."

"Whatever I felt for you?" he questioned, his voice suddenly so rough that she looked up in surprise. "Lisette, come here."

Oh, the temptation of the strong male demand in his voice. But there were still secrets between them. Lisette gripped her hands together.

"I have a confession to make first,"she said desperately.

Raverre eyed her anxious expression and his brows rose. He leaned back against the bedpost again, propping one arm over a raised knee and tilting his head in amused enquiry.

"Well? What dreadful sin have you committed?" he asked indulgently.

Oh, would he still smile at her like that when he learned how she had gone looking for Leofwin?

"The other day wasn't the first time I had seen Leofwin," Lisette admitted in a rush. Unable to face the sudden frown in his eyes, she dropped her own. "'Twas the sniper—"

"What of him?"

"You searched for others and found nothing, but I remembered some caves deep in the forest where we all played as children, and when you went to Godric I decided to look for myself."

She thought Raverre drew in his breath sharply and looked up, but whatever emotion he felt was hidden beneath half-lowered lids, and as her glance dropped to his other hand, clenched on the bearskin, he deliberately relaxed his fingers. Keeping her gaze fixed on his hand, she said simply, "He was there."

"What happened?" Raverre asked, his tone revealing nothing more than mild curiosity.

Relieved that no outburst of rage had been forthcoming, Lisette ventured to look at him again. Raverre's face was expressionless, but a muscle quivered in his jaw once and was stilled.

"We talked. I had only half expected Leofwin to be there,"she explained, "but when Godric denied knowing that shepherd I could think of no one else who would need to hide in these parts. Then he told me about planning the robbery, though others had carried it out, and I begged him to return home, to confess and make his peace with the King. Oh, my lord, I wanted to tell you, but I thought to give him time to surrender."

"And after you spoke he let you go without hindrance?"

"Aye."

There was an ominous silence.

"I swear it!" Lisette added vehemently when Raverre didn't say anything. "Leofwin didn't know of my marriage then. We were only together a short time. I had to get back here before dark and—"

"I believe you," he interrupted softly, and she went limp with relief.

Then he exploded. "God's blood!" he roared, abandoning his relaxed façade. "He could have killed you! Reckless little fool! I could strangle you myself for taking such a risk."

An echo of his voice reached the hall. The door opened and a serf looked nervously into the room.

"Get out!" bellowed Raverre. The door was closed hurriedly. "What in God's name is a serf doing right outside our door?" he demanded, but in a less wrathful tone.

"In case I need anything during the night," she faltered.

"Get rid of him," he snapped. His eyes closed and his head fell back against the bedpost. Lisette, seeing the look of weariness that passed over his face, decided it would be wiser to obey.

"You mustn't tire yourself," she said, after complying with his order. Somehow the knowledge that Raverre had not fully regained his strength calmed her nerves, and she came back to stand by the bed.

"Don't forget I had known Leofwin all my life," she explained reasonably. "He had been like a brother to me, and I wanted to help him. There was no danger from him...or so I thought until he started speaking in that strange way," she mused, remembering.

Raverre's eyes snapped open, their expression grim. "Oh, so he was strange even then, was he?" he asked sardonically. "And yet you and Catherine still went off with him. I might have known you'd do something rash the minute my back was turned, but I didn't expect you to risk your life twice over!"

"I'm sorry," she placated, hanging her head.

At his derisive, "Hrmmph," Lisette felt her old spirit revive.

"How could I see anything wrong in his asking us to accompany him for a while?" she demanded indignantly. "You saw for yourself that he swore allegiance to the King, and he even begged my forgiveness for his earlier behaviour. What was I supposed to do?"

"Stay here and wait for me!" he shot back.

"Well, I would have," she retorted crossly, "but I was too impatient and excited to just sit and...wait."

The last word came out as a whispered breath as Lisette

realised what she had just said. Raverre's whole body seemed to stiffen. His eyes fixed on her face with a look of such glittering intensity that she took a nervous step back, not sure whether his stare betokened anger. But when he flung off the covers to come after her she rushed forward again.

"No! You mustn't get up. You're not strong enough yet."

Snaking his good arm around her waist, Raverre fell back on the bed, taking Lisette down with him. She landed sprawled over his massive chest, gazing wide-eyed into the twin blue flames of his eyes.

"I know," he said, with a devilish grin. "And you wouldn't fight a wounded man, would you?"

"Oh, your arm!" she exclaimed

"To hell with my arm. Look at me!"

Unable to obey this peremptory command while she was lying all over him, Lisette looked at her fingers instead as they softened their hold on his shoulders. The temptation to let her palm lower to his chest, to savour the feel of hard muscle, warm skin and curling hair, was too strong to resist.

"Alain," she whispered.

"Oh, God, sweetheart, come here!" With a ragged sound deep in his throat Raverre moved his hand to Lisette's head, bringing her mouth down to his.

Her body went soft against him, melting with heated longing, and he groaned again into her mouth, deepening the kiss until Lisette forgot her shyness and kissed him back for the first time. Her mouth opened over his in exquisite surrender, letting him feel the love she had repressed for so long.

Raverre broke the kiss abruptly, pressing Lisette's head into his shoulder and rolling her on to the bed so she was held protectively against his side. Still submerged in the sensual spell their kiss had woven, she murmured a soft protest, and he held her closer.

"I know, sweetheart. I need you too." His lips stroked across the soft tendrils feathering her brow, and Lisette felt his mouth curve in a smile.

"Tell me you love me," he murmured, trying to see into her eyes. But, feeling vulnerable, when Raverre himself had only mentioned need, she tucked her face into his shoulder.

"You must know I do," she whispered, feeling the ripple of the powerful muscle under her cheek.

Raverre held her for a moment in silence, then spoke suddenly in a voice which held such anguish that Lisette looked up again.

"Dear God, do you know what I thought when I got back here to find you gone?"

She shook her head, her eyes widening at the expression of remembered pain in his.

"I thought you had taken my parting words as a threat, and could no longer bear to live as my wife." His voice dropped to barely above a whisper. "After what happened that morning…you were afraid I would force you. And then later you were so quiet while Leofwin was here. I wondered what you were thinking about at the time, and when you disappeared I thought I knew."

"Oh, no," she said, lifting a hand to touch his face.

After hearing the tormented note in his voice Lisette could no longer doubt Raverre's feelings, and, loosed from the bonds of uncertainty and constraint, her own love illuminated her face with a radiance that caused him to catch his breath as the glowing warmth reached out to him.

"Lisette," he murmured. "Tell me."

"I love you," she said, her voice very clear and soft. "Oh, Alain, I love you."

"At last!" Raverre growled in fierce triumph, catching

Lisette in a one-armed embrace, which nevertheless threatened to crack her ribs.

But, instantly realising how strongly he gripped her, he relaxed his possessive hold a little and his voice held a more tender note as he murmured, "I love you so much, Lisette. You don't know how long I've waited to hear you say that."

"You love me," she repeated wonderingly, savouring the words.

"From the first moment of seeing you," he affirmed, smiling down at her. "You looked so small and fragile and yet so defiant, and all I could think of was how much I wanted to make you love me."

"I think I did even then," Lisette admitted. "When I saw you for the first time I thought you looked like one of the Viking warriors my father used to tell us about. So tall and fierce and strong. You were the hero of all my dreams, and yet I was afraid."

"I know," he groaned, remembering. "And all I seemed to do was give you reason to fear me. I was so desperate for you, Lisette. I'd never felt like that about any woman before, but with you..." He gave a self-mocking laugh. "I only had to be near you and I lost all control, driving you away."

She shook her head. "You didn't drive me away. 'Twas myself I feared. I was afraid to love you, to have such feelings for one I thought was an enemy."

"I have never been an enemy of yours, sweetheart. I tried to tell you that, but all you seemed to do was resent my presence. If you only knew how often I wished we had met differently. And then when I thought you had run away with a man who was Saxon and a friend, one whom perhaps you loved, I almost wished we'd never met at all."

"And yet you came after me? Even thinking I might love another?"

Lisette felt every muscle in Raverre's body become rigid with primitive aggression. "Do you think I would let another man touch you?" he demanded roughly. "You belong to me. Even at the risk of making you hate me, I would have brought you back. I'll never let you go, Lisette. Never!"

I would have called that Norman arrogance and resented it a few weeks ago, she thought, smiling inwardly, but now she thrilled to the fierce possessiveness in Raverre's voice.

"Besides," he went on, his eyes gentling with softer emotion, "after that first shock, when I began to think clearly, I knew you couldn't possibly do anything dishonourable. You had made a vow, and even if you didn't love me I knew you would never break it willingly."

"I do love you," she whispered. "I belong to you. I thought you had understood what I meant by my answer to the King the other morning." She peeped up at him through her lashes. "Even though you were still angry with me."

"I wasn't angry," he replied, holding her close again. "Not really. 'Twas the only way I could get out of the room that morning without begging you to let me make love to you. I wanted you so much. I kept remembering the night of the storm when you were suddenly so sweet and yielding. God—" he pressed his mouth to hers in a quick, ardent caress "—you don't know what your response that night did to me. I had such hopes that you might at last be coming to care for me, only to find later that you couldn't seem to bear me near you."

"I didn't mean it like that," Lisette cried softly, snuggling closer in remorse for the pain which, even now, echoed in his voice as he remembered the agony of her rejection. "I was such a coward. I thought you had only married me for convenience and I was afraid that if you…if we…"

"Made love," he supplied, his voice very deep and tender with amusement at her shy hesitation.

"Aye." Lisette pretended to frown. "Don't laugh at me. I was afraid I would betray how much I loved you when you only desired my body and not my heart."

"My sweet love, don't you remember what I said to you the first night when we sat at supper together? Your heart *was* the prize I longed for."

Raverre kissed the frown away, then drew back with a devilish twinkle.

"However," he added wickedly, "your delectable little body would turn a monk from his path of chastity."

Lisette blushed fierily, and Raverre moved his mouth across the warmth in her cheek. "I adore you when you look so innocent and shy," he murmured, laughing softly. "You don't know yet what that does to me. Especially when I know of the fire beneath your shyness."

His words stirred an uncomfortable memory. Leofwin had said almost the same thing, Lisette remembered uneasily. Did all men see something in her which she herself had never suspected? Raverre sensed her reaction immediately.

"What is it?" he asked sharply, drawing back to look at her face. "I've upset you."

"No," she assured quickly. "But Leofwin said something—" Lisette struggled to remember the words "—about what innocence does to a man." She looked at him, troubled. "What does it do to you?"

"It makes me want to love you," Raverre replied instantly, looking deeply into her eyes. "In every way I can. To cherish you, care for you, protect you with my life if need be."

Lisette gave a sigh of pure happiness, which quickly

changed to a tiny sound of feminine excitement when Raverre suddenly raised himself on his good arm, leaning over her. He was so much bigger than her that Lisette felt herself tremble in thrilling anticipation of his strength, knowing it was leashed by his tenderness.

"And it makes me want you more than my next breath," he growled softly, beginning to unfasten her gown.

"But your arm…" It was a very half-hearted protest.

Raverre smiled that wicked, utterly irresistible smile. "We'll improvise," he murmured huskily, lowering his mouth to hers.

The last thing Lisette saw clearly before Raverre swept her into a swirling vortex of exquisite sensation was the expression of passionate love in his glittering blue eyes.

A long time later Lisette stirred in Raverre's arms.

"You make me feel so…I don't know…wild, I think," she whispered, wondering if she ought to be shocked at the abandoned response Raverre had drawn from her.

"Good," he growled, a smile in his voice. "Because the instincts you arouse in me aren't exactly civilised either. I've never wanted anyone so much in my life." Suddenly his voice held a note of concern. "I wasn't too rough with you, was I, sweetheart?"

"Never," she murmured, brushing a kiss against his shoulder. "My gentle conqueror."

Raverre laughed softly, sleepy male satisfaction in the sound.

"I love you," he said, kissing her tenderly. "Whatever happens in the future between our people, always remember that."

"Always," Lisette answered from the heart. "As I will love you."

Chapter Ten

Early summer, 1071

Lisette sat down in her favourite corner of the garden, carefully laying the snugly wrapped infant on the ground beside her and settling her back comfortably against the stone wall. Lifting her face to the sun, she closed her eyes, a smile of contentment deepening the corners of her mouth as she savoured the memory of last night's passionate reunion with Raverre. He had been gone five long months and she had missed him every minute of that time.

Her mind went back to the arrival of the King's messenger the previous year, bringing news of a major rebellion led by a Lincolnshire Thegn known as Hereward the Wake. The man had chosen his time well to conduct sudden raids against the nearer Norman settlements.

That Easter of 1070 William had finally disbanded the army. The northern Earls had surrendered and been pardoned after two insurrections, the last of which had been brutally crushed when the King had finally lost patience.

Almost insane with rage, William had ordered such wholesale destruction of the north that the entire countryside was now a barren waste. No crops grew, no cattle grazed, and those people who had survived the savagery of the army had fled. His action had been a blot on an otherwise brilliant and noble career and Lisette had thanked God that Raverre had not taken any part in the "Harrying of the North", as it had come to be known.

However, when Hereward had gathered what few rebels remained and retreated into a secret camp in the fastness of the marshes surrounding the Isle of Ely, William had called for men and arms from those of his Barons and Knights who had settled in England. Hearing that Earls Morcar and Edwin had once again joined forces against him, the King had sworn that there would be no more pardons.

Raverre had had to answer the call to arms, leaving Lisette expecting their first child. He had hoped the rebellion would be put down quickly, but the months had dragged on, his son had been born, and Lisette had heard nothing until a messenger had arrived with the welcome news that Raverre was on his way home.

A serf had been keeping watch on the road all that week, and Lisette had been waiting in the bailey as Raverre and his men had ridden in under the barbican. She had been shaking so much with excitement that Catherine, with one look at Raverre's face as he had stridden towards them, had rapidly removed the welcome cup from her hand. Lisette hadn't even noticed its disappearance as Raverre had taken her hands in a painfully hard grip, staring down into her face as if he didn't quite believe she was standing before him in the flesh.

Her speech of welcome was forgotten as she had gazed longingly up at him, wishing the etiquette governing public greetings didn't prevent her from flinging herself at him.

Raverre had had no such inhibitions. Releasing her

hands, he had swept Lisette into his arms, holding her against his heart, his face buried in her silky, fragrant hair.

They had clasped each other tightly in the close, word-less communication of lovers. So intense had been their silent embrace that some of Raverre's soldiers had turned away, as though they gazed on something not meant for the eyes of other men. Then, recollecting himself, Raverre had set Lisette back on her feet and swept her into the hall, where Marjory had been waiting with a squalling bundle.

"Your son, my lord," Lisette had announced softly, her dark eyes glowing with love and pride. "We had him bap-tised William Geoffrey for the King and your father, if it please you."

Raverre had smiled into her eyes. "It pleases me very well, my love." And, taking the child, he held him up to the men, who had crowded into the hall after them. "A sturdy son for the house of Raverre," he had announced, and a resounding cheer had rung to the rafters.

The plaintive wail piercing the quiet of the garden brought Lisette back to the present moment with a start. Picking up the baby, she quickly loosened her gown and guided the hungry little mouth to her breast, shielding the child from the sun with her shawl. The wonder she felt at nursing Raverre's child filled her heart every time she held the tiny baby in her arms. So absorbed was she in the sweet bonding that Raverre, coming into the garden in search of her, was able to watch them unheard for several minutes.

Then as he moved his shadow fell over Lisette, and she looked up, her face lighting with all the love he had once longed to see there. Sitting down beside her, he said softly, "Motherhood suits you, my lovely wife, but should you not have a wet-nurse?"

"I like it," she answered, smiling up at him. "Besides, the Queen told me that when Prince Henry was born she insisted on nursing him herself, and look how he has thrived.''

Raverre caressed her cheek with his hand. "So long as you don't tire yourself, sweet. At least you won't have the manor to worry about now that Gilbert and I are back." He stretched out beside her. "Ah, 'tis good to be home, I vow."

Until the next time, Lisette thought with a sudden pang. Raverre saw the worry in her face.

"I'll not leave you again, love," he reassured her. "When duty calls me from home I want you with me. There won't be any question of danger. All England is William's now. Did you hear nothing of what happened?"

"No. We thought the King might pardon Morcar yet again in his penitence for what happened in the north. And I swear I never thought to hear myself say this, but, until the man is killed, how will there ever be any peace in England?"

"He is not dead, but imprisoned," answered Raverre. "For life this time. The man's a fool. He could have kept his lands, held his high position under William, and prospered. But no! He has to keep us kicking our heels around the dampest swamp you can ever imagine for the better part of a year. If it hadn't been for one of the monks on the island betraying the secret path to Hereward's stronghold, I swear we'd be there still."

"And Hereward himself?"

"He escaped during the fighting, but has now surrendered to William and had his lands restored. The fellow was acquiring quite a reputation for heroism—William knows there is little glory in killing such a man, better to win him over. As for Edwin, Morcar's brother, he was slain by his own men, trying to escape to Scotland."

"The Atheling is still there, is he not?"

"Aye. William says Edgar is welcome to Malcolm's court. He bears the boy no ill will. 'Twas William's intention to rule through Earls of English birth as well as Norman. The Saxon courts of law remain unchanged and he always admired Saxon craftsmen and learning, but, thanks to all the rebellions, 'tis no longer possible.

"However," he continued on a lighter note, "William intends that young imp, Henry, to be reared here in England, so at least one of his sons will be more English than Norman, even if he's unlikely to come to the throne with three older brothers before him. And, speaking of family matters, my love, I have had an offer of marriage for Catherine."

Lisette carefully settled the baby. "Oh?" she questioned cautiously.

"From Gilbert." Raverre grinned at her obvious relief. "Did you really think I would give your sister in marriage to a stranger who did not care for her?"

"'Twould be common enough," she admitted, "but I know how fond you are of her and Gilbert. I'm so glad he has shown his feelings for her. She has been quite in despair these past months, hearing no word from him."

"He felt she was still too young last year, though he loved her then. However, I believe she managed to convince him of her newfound maturity last night after we had retired. The poor fellow didn't stand a chance. What was I to do but give them my blessing?"

He smiled across at Lisette, already anticipating her reaction to his next statement. "As well as deeding him Godric's manor. I thought you would like them near enough to visit often."

He got his reward when Lisette flung herself into his arms, her face aglow with happiness. Raverre wrapped her in a tight embrace, his eyes a vivid blue as they roamed over her delicate features, framed by the curtain of her dark hair.

"You are the most wonderful man in the world!" she exclaimed joyously.

"And despite being a Norman, too," he stated with smug satisfaction. He dodged the swipe Lisette laughingly aimed at him, catching hold of her hand and bringing it to his lips. "'Twas the practical thing to do, love. The manor has been standing empty since the old man died, and William granted me the land, and—"

"I still think you are wonderful," she interrupted firmly. "And I missed you so much," she added softly, laying her head on his shoulder, revelling in the strength of his arms.

Approaching footsteps intruded on her lazy contentment and Lisette raised her head, but Raverre tightened his hold, refusing to release her.

"Fine goings on!" declared Marjory, coming upon them in her search for her infant charge.

"Most valued Marjory," Raverre said, grinning up at her unrepentantly. "Have I thanked you yet for taking such good care of my wife and son?"

"Aye," snapped Marjory, refusing to be placated. "'Tis as well someone is around to keep things running smoothly. There is Catherine, having nothing better to do this morning than sit gazing at that impudent rascal de Rohan. And he is as bad. And now I find my lady with her hair hanging loose and sporting in the garden like any farm lass and her swain."

"Sweet Marjory, would you begrudge a weary soldier the solace of a loving wife and a sunny garden?" Raverre winked at Lisette.

Marjory saw the wink and frowned direfully. She bent to pick up the happily gurgling baby. "Come, my little lordling," she crooned. "You shall sleep in your proper place, though others may forget their dignity."

Little William stared up at her solemnly for a moment and then yawned hugely in answer. Raverre began to laugh.

"You are outnumbered, Marjory," he told her. "Retreat is the only defence."

Marjory stalked towards the gate, muttering to herself. "Just like his father," they heard her say. It wasn't a compliment.

"I should hope so," murmured Raverre wickedly, determined to have the last word.

"Oh, hush," pleaded Lisette, trying not to laugh. "She'll be disapproving for days now, and you know we can't do without her."

"I know I can't do without you," he replied, letting his fingers play through the bronze cloud of her hair. "Have I told you yet how much I love you?"

She dimpled at him. "Several times last night," she began, counting on her fingers. "And again this morning when you gave me that set of garnet veil pins and then refused to let me wear them because you wanted to see my hair loose, thereby bringing Marjory's wrath down upon me."

"It reminds me of the first time I saw you," he explained, and kissed her.

When they reluctantly drew apart both were breathless.

"Perhaps we also should retire to our proper place, my sweet lady," Raverre suggested, springing to his feet and helping Lisette up.

Hand in hand, they strolled towards the hall. At the top of the stairway Raverre paused and looked out across the bailey and through the gate to the fields, lying golden and peaceful under the summer sun.

"Thank God all the fighting is done," he murmured.

"This land is too beautiful to be stained forever by the blood of its people. Our sons should inherit peace and prosperity, not war and privation."

"Perhaps they will," Lisette answered softly, seeing in their own happiness the promise of the unity and strength William of Normandy had dreamed of for England. "Perhaps they will."

* * * * * *

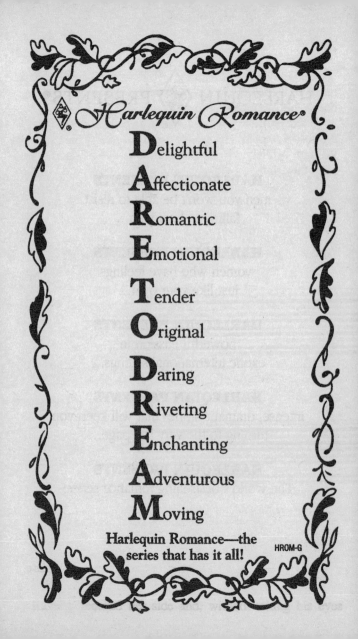

Harlequin Romance®

Delightful

Affectionate

Romantic

Emotional

Tender

Original

Daring

Riveting

Enchanting

Adventurous

Moving

Harlequin Romance—the
series that has it all!

HROM-G

HARLEQUIN ✦ PRESENTS®

HARLEQUIN PRESENTS
men you won't be able to resist
falling in love with...

HARLEQUIN PRESENTS
women who have feelings
just like your own...

HARLEQUIN PRESENTS
powerful passion in
exotic international settings...

HARLEQUIN PRESENTS
intense, dramatic stories that will keep you
turning to the very last page...

HARLEQUIN PRESENTS
The world's bestselling romance series!

PRES-G

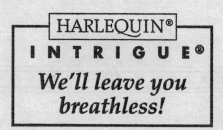

HARLEQUIN®

I N T R I G U E®

We'll leave you breathless!

If you've been looking for thrilling tales of
contemporary passion and sensuous love stories
with taut, edge-of-the-seat suspense—
then you'll *love* **Harlequin Intrigue!**

Every month, you'll meet four new heroes
who are guaranteed to make your spine tingle
and your pulse pound. With them you'll enter
into the exciting world of Harlequin Intrigue—
where your life is on the line
and so is your heart!

THAT'S INTRIGUE—DYNAMIC
ROMANCE AT ITS BEST!

HARLEQUIN®

I N T R I G U E®

INT-GENR

LOOK FOR OUR FOUR FABULOUS MEN!

Each month some of today's bestselling authors bring
four new fabulous men to Harlequin American Romance.
Whether they're rebel ranchers, millionaire power brokers
or sexy single dads, they're all gallant princes—and
they're all ready to sweep you into lighthearted fantasies
and contemporary fairy tales where anything is possible
and where all your dreams come true!

You don't even have to make a wish…
Harlequin American Romance will grant your every desire!

Look for Harlequin American Romance
wherever Harlequin books are sold!

HAR-GEN

HARLEQUIN SUPERROMANCE®

...there's more to the story!

Superromance. A *big* satisfying read about unforget-
table characters. Each month we offer
four very different stories that range from family
drama to adventure and mystery, from highly emotional stories to romantic comedies—and
much more! Stories about people you'll
believe in and care about. Stories too
compelling to put down....

Our authors are among today's *best* romance writ-
ers. You'll find familiar names and
talented newcomers. Many of them are
award winners—and you'll see why!

If you want the biggest and best
in romance fiction, you'll get it
from Superromance!

Available wherever Harlequin books are sold.

Look us up on-line at: http://www.romance.net

HS-GEN

COLL

10,000 FRENCH WORDS

D0571012

HarperCollins*Publishers*

First published in this edition 1993

© HarperCollins Publishers 1993

Latest reprint 1995

ISBN 0 00 470951-9 Paperback

---

editor
Megan Thomson

contributor
Cécile Aubinière-Robb

editorial staff
Linda Chestnutt, Diane Robinson,
Sheilagh Wilson

computing
Linda Able

editorial management
Vivian Marr

Based on 5000 French Words © 1979,
compiled by Barbara I. Christie MA (Hons)
and Màiri MacGinn MA (Hons)

A catalogue record for this book
is available from the British Library

All rights reserved

Typeset by Tradespools Ltd, Frome, Somerset

Printed in Great Britain by
HarperCollins Manufacturing, Glasgow

We are delighted you have decided to buy the **Collins Pocket 10,000 French Words**, which forms part of our range of French Study Pockets. Based on the extremely popular Collins Gem 5000 French Words, this new text offers you a considerably extended guide to modern everyday French vocabulary.

You can benefit from using the graded wordlists if you are revising for school exams, as the topics covered are those included in the syllabuses of a cross-section of international examination boards. However, if you are an adult user wishing to brush up and update your French vocabulary, you will find the book's content equally valuable.

USING YOUR COLLINS POCKET 10,000 FRENCH WORDS

To help you find words and expressions as easily as possible, the information is presented by topic, and the material in each topic is set out in a consistent manner for quick reference. After a key to the abbreviations and phonetics used in the text, followed by a list of contents, the main part of the book contains over 60 topics of carefully selected vocabulary. The areas covered by the topic wordlists range from Animals to the Weather and from Careers to Youth Hostelling.

Vocabulary lists

Vocabulary within each topic is divided into the relevant nouns for that topic, in alphabetical order. Vocabulary within the noun sections is graded to help you concentrate on material that suits your particular needs or interests. For example, ESSENTIAL vocabulary includes the basic words that are considered necessary for you to talk or write about a specific subject. IMPORTANT items expand on these and help to improve the level at which you will be able to express yourself in French. Finally, USEFUL material increases your understanding of French by widening the range of words whose meaning you will recognize.

Colour highlighting

The arrangement of graded material is extremely helpful for exam revision, as ESSENTIAL vocabulary covers the major school exam syllabus requirements. Words which appear in this category and are highlighted in red are those that are absolutely vital for exam purposes.

Use of symbols

Two symbols are used in the topics sections. The book symbol ⊞, which you will see in the ESSENTIAL and IMPORTANT categories, indicates words which you should be able to recognize and translate into English without necessarily being able to use yourself in French. However, at a more advanced level, you should also have an active knowledge of these words, meaning that you are able to use them when you write or speak French.

HOW TO USE THIS BOOK

The arrow symbol ⬦ indicates that words marked in this way can have another meaning, either in the same topic or in a completely different area. You will find a list of these words at the end of the book, entitled HOMONYMS, together with the page numbers on which the word appears with its different meaning or meanings.

Phrases and idioms

Expressing yourself in a foreign language involves much more than memorizing large quantities of individual words. Another advantage of your **Collins Pocket 10,000 French Words** is that it includes sections of appropriate phrases and idioms within each topic. These enable you to use the types of genuine French expressions you are likely to hear in everyday situations.

Parts of speech section

Supplementary wordlists in the second section of the book group words according to the following parts of speech – adjectives, conjunctions, adverbs, prepositions, nouns and verbs. You will be able to use the words listed here with most or sometimes all of the subject topics.

Grammatical information

The feminine form of all adjectives is shown where this varies from the masculine form (e.g., **ennuyeux, -euse, doux, douce**). Irregular plurals are given (e.g., **le bureau** (*pl* **-x**)) as well as plurals of compound nouns. The swung dash (~) is used to indicate the basic elements of the compound and the appropriate endings are added (e.g., **le wagon-lit** (*pl* **~s~s**), but **le sous-sol** (*pl* **~s**)).

Also covered are certain French nouns which have only one form whether they are referring to a male or a female. These are indicated with (*m+f*), e.g., **le professeur** (*m+f*) and **la vedette** (*m+f*).

English index

The English index gives page references for all the ESSENTIAL and IMPORTANT English nouns listed under the individual topics.

French index

Finally, there is a French index which gives the page references for all the ESSENTIAL and IMPORTANT French nouns.

We hope you will enjoy using your **Collins Pocket 10,000 French Words**. Its practical, everyday vocabulary will help you to understand and to express yourself effectively in written and spoken French.

ABBREVIATIONS

adj	adjective	*n*	noun
adv	adverb	*pl*	plural
conj	conjunction	*prep*	preposition
f	feminine	*qch*	quelque chose
inv	invariable	*qn*	quelqu'un
m	masculine	*sb*	somebody
m+f	masculine and	*sth*	something
	feminine form	*subj*	subjunctive

PHONETICS

i	as in vie, lit	ɛ̃	as in matin, plein
e	as in blé, jouer	ɑ	as in sans, vent
ɛ	as in merci, très	ɔ̃	as in bon, ombre
a	as in patte, plat	œ̃	as in brun, lundi
ɑ	as in bas, gras	j	as in yeux, pied
ɔ	as in mort, donner	ɥ	as in lui, huile
o	as in mot, gauche	ɲ	as in agneau, vigne
u	as in genou, roue	ŋ	as in English -ing
y	as in rue, tu	ʃ	as in chat, tache
ø	as in peu, deux	ʒ	as in je, gens
œ	as in peur, meuble	ʀ	as in rue, venir
ə	as in le, premier		

A colon : precedes words beginning with an aspirate h (**le :hibou** as opposed to **l'hippopotame**).

ANIMALS

le caneton	duckling
le caniche	poodle
le castor	beaver
le chacal	jackal
le chaton	kitten
le chenil	kennels
le chevreuil	roe deer
le chimpanzé	chimpanzee
le chiot	puppy
le clapier	(rabbit) hutch
le croc [kRo]	fang
le dauphin	dolphin
le dompteur de lions	liontamer
le dressage	taming; training
le dromadaire	dromedary
un élan	elk, moose
un éléphant de mer	elephant seal
un éléphanteau (pl -x)	baby elephant
un empailleur	taxidermist
un épagneul	spaniel
un éperon	spur
un équidé	member of the horse family
un escargot	snail
un étalon	stallion
un étrier	stirrup
le faon [fã]	fawn (deer)
le fauve	wildcat
le félin	(big) cat
le fer à cheval	horseshoe
le flair	sense of smell
le furet	ferret
le galop [galo]	gallop
le glapissement	yelping
le gorille	gorilla
le grognement	growl; grunt, snort

un serpent venimeux a venomous snake
des animaux empaillés stuffed animals
j'ai entendu un aboiement I heard a dog bark

USEFUL WORDS (f) (cont)

la laie	wild sow
la laisse	lead, leash
la licorne	unicorn
la limace	slug
la litière	litter
la loutre	otter
la louve	she-wolf
la mamelle	teat
la mangouste	mongoose
la marmotte	marmot
la meute	pack
la minette	pussycat
la morsure	bite
les moustaches	whiskers
la muselière	muzzle
la niche	kennel
une otarie	sea lion
une ourse	she-bear
la panthère	panther
la pouliche	filly
la progéniture	offspring
la proie	prey
la race	breed
les rênes	reins
la ruade	kick (*of horse*)
la sangsue	leech
la selle ◊	saddle
la SPA (Société Protectrice des Animaux)	RSPCA
la tanière	den, lair
la taupinière	molehill
la tauromachie	bullfighting
la truffe	nose (*of dog*)
la truie	sow
la vipère	viper, adder

tenir en laisse to keep on a lead
une exposition canine a dog show
beugler to low, moo; **gaver** to force-feed

ANIMALS

le groin [gʀwɛ̃]	snout
le guépard	cheetah
le :harnais	harness
l'hennissement	neighing, whinnying
l'hippodrome	racecourse
le :hongre	gelding
le jaguar	jaguar
le jappement	yap, yelp
le lapereau (pl -x)	young rabbit
le lapin de garenne	wild rabbit
le léopard	leopard
le lévrier	greyhound
le lézard	lizard
le lionceau (pl -x)	lion cub
le loir	dormouse
le louveteau (pl -x)	wolf-cub
le mâle	male
le mammifère	mammal
le mammouth	mammoth
le maquignon	horse-dealer
le marcassin	young wild boar
le marsouin	porpoise
le matou	tom (cat)
le miaou	miaow
le miaulement	mewing
le minet	pussycat
le morse	walrus
le mugissement	bellowing; lowing, mooing
le mulot	fieldmouse
le naseau (pl -x)	nostril
un orang-outan (pl ~s~s)	orang-utan
un ouistiti	marmoset
un ourson	bear cub
le panda	panda
le pedigree	pedigree
le pelage	coat, fur
le pis	udder
le poitrail	breast (of horse etc)
le porc-épic [pɔʀkepik] (pl ~s~s)	porcupine
le pur-sang (pl inv)	thoroughbred, purebred

USEFUL WORDS (m) (cont)

le putois	polecat
le rat [Ra]	rat
le raton laveur	raccoon
le renardeau (pl -x)	fox cub
le renne	reindeer
le repaire	den, lair
le reptile	reptile
le rongeur	rodent
le ronronnement	purr(ing)
le rugissement	roar, roaring
le sanglier	(wild) boar
le serpent à sonnettes	rattlesnake
le taurillon	bull-calf
le teckel	dachshund
le terrier	burrow, hole
le têtard	tadpole
le torero	bullfighter
le trappeur	trapper, fur trader
le venin	venom, poison
le vison	mink

aboyer to bark; **miauler** to mew
hennir to neigh, whinny; **rugir** to roar
mugir to bellow; to low, moo

ART AND ARCHITECTURE

ESSENTIAL WORDS (m)

un **architecte** [aRʃitɛkt(ə)]	architect
l' **art** [aR]	art
le **peintre**	painter
le **photographe**	photographer
le **portrait**	portrait; photograph
le **sculpteur** [skyltœR]	sculptor
le **tableau** ⬦ (pl **-x**)	painting

IMPORTANT WORDS (m)

un **autoportrait**	self-portrait
le **faux** 📖	fake (*painting etc*)
le **musée** ⬦	museum; art gallery
le **recueil** 📖	collection

USEFUL WORDS (m)

un **appareil-photo** (pl ~**s**~**s**)	camera
un **atelier**	workshop; studio
le **bas-relief** [baRəljɛf] (pl ~**s**)	bas-relief
les **beaux-arts** [bozaR]	fine arts
le **cadre** ⬦	frame
le **chevalet**	easel
le **dessin**	drawing
le **dôme**	dome
un **édifice**	building, edifice
le **folklore**	folklore
le **fronton**	pediment
le **fusain**	charcoal
le **grand-angle** (pl ~**s**~**s**)	wide-angle lens
le **graveur**	engraver
un **instantané**	snapshot
le **mécène**	patron
le **monument** ⬦	monument
le **négatif**	negative
un **objectif**	lens
le **pastel**	pastel
le **paysagiste** ⬦	landscape painter
le **pinceau** (pl **-x**)	(paint) brush

l' architecture [aʀʃitɛktyʀ]	architecture
une œuvre (d'art)	work (of art)
la peintre	painter
la peinture ◊	painting
la photographe	photographer
la photographie	photography
la sculpture [skyltyʀ]	sculpture

une aquarelle	watercolour
une exposition	exhibition
l' huile	oil painting
la reproduction	reproduction

la chambre noire	darkroom
la copie	copy
la coupole	dome
l' eau forte	etching
une ébauche	rough outline
une épreuve	print (*photo*)
une esquisse	sketch
une estampe	print, engraving
la fresque	fresco
la frise	frieze
la gargouille	gargoyle
la gravure	engraving; print; plate
la litho(graphie)	litho(graphy)
la marqueterie	inlaid work, marquetry
la nature morte	still life
la portraitiste	portrait painter
la restauratrice	restorer
la sculpture sur bois	wood carving
la tapisserie ◊	tapestry
la tourelle	turret
la vente aux enchères ◊	auction sale
la voûte	vault

ART AND ARCHITECTURE

le pochoir	stencil
le portraitiste	portrait painter
le relief [Rəljɛf]	relief
le restaurateur ◇	restorer
le romantisme	the Romantic Movement
le téléobjectif	telephoto lens
le vernissage	preview (*of an exhibition*)
les vers	verse (*poetry*)
le vitrail	stained-glass window

flou(e) blurred
faire de la photographie to have photography as a hobby

le casque 🕮	helmet
le cyclisme ◇ 🕮	cycling
le cycliste 🕮	cyclist
le frein ◇ 🕮	brake
le pneu	tyre
le sommet ◇	top (*of hill*)
le Tour de France ◇	Tour de France cycle race
le vélo ◇	bike; cycling

le catadioptre 🕮	reflector
le cataphote 🕮	reflector
le cuissard	cycle pants *or* shorts
le garde-boue (*pl inv*)	mudguard
le guidon	handlebars
le moyeu (*pl* -**x**)	hub
le pare-boue (*pl inv*)	mud flap
le porte-bagages (*pl inv*)	luggage rack
le rayon ◇	spoke
le réflecteur	reflector
le timbre ◇	bell
le vélo tout terrain	mountain bike

un antivol	padlock
le cambouis	dirty oil *or* grease
le cyclomotoriste	moped rider
le cyclotourisme	cycle touring
le motard	biker; motorcycle cop
le phare	headlight
le tandem	tandem
le tendeur	chain-adjuster
le tricycle	tricycle
le vélomoteur	moped

marcher to walk; **aller à pied** to go on foot
aller à bicyclette, aller à *or* **en vélo** to go by bike

BIKES AND MOTORBIKES

ESSENTIAL WORDS (f)

la bicyclette 📖	bicycle
la crevaison	puncture
la lampe ✧	lamp
la roue	wheel
la vitesse ✧	speed; gear

IMPORTANT WORDS (f)

la barre	crossbar
la chaîne ✧	chain
la côte ✧	slope, hill (*on road*)
la dynamo	dynamo
la pédale	pedal
la pente	slope
la piste cyclable	cycle path
la pompe	pump
la sacoche ✧ (de bicyclette)	saddlebag, pannier
la selle ✧	saddle
la sonnette	bell
la trousse de secours pour crevaisons	puncture repair kit
la valve	valve

USEFUL WORDS (f)

la béquille ✧	stand
la chambre à air	(inner) tube
la cyclomotoriste	moped rider
la mobylette ®	moped
la moto	(motor) bike
les pinces de cycliste	bicycle clips
la rustine	repair patch
la trottinette	(child's) scooter

---

monter à bicyclette to get on one's bike
faire une promenade à *or* **en bicyclette** to go for a bike ride
être à plat to have a flat tyre
réparer un pneu crevé to mend a puncture
la roue avant/arrière the front/back wheel
gonfler les pneus to blow up the tyres

ESSENTIAL WORDS (m)

le canard	duck
le ciel ◇ ▭	sky
le coq	cock
le dindon ◇	turkey
un insecte	insect
un oiseau (pl -**x**)	bird
le perroquet	parrot
le poulet	chicken

IMPORTANT WORDS (m)

un aigle	eagle
le bec	beak
le cafard	beetle
le choucas ▭	jackdaw
le coq de bruyère ▭	grouse
le corbeau (pl -**x**)	raven
le coucou	cuckoo
le criquet	cricket
le cygne [siɲ]	swan
un étourneau (pl -**x**)	starling
le faisan	pheasant
le faucon	falcon, hawk
le flamant (rose)	(pink) flamingo
le frelon ▭	hornet
le goéland	(sea)gull
le grillon	cricket
le :hibou (pl -**x**)	owl
le mainate ▭	mynah bird
le martin-pêcheur ▭ (pl ~**s**~**s**)	kingfisher
le merle	blackbird
le moineau (pl -**x**)	sparrow
le moucheron	midge
le moustique	mosquito
le nid	nest
le paon [pɑ̃]	peacock
le papillon	butterfly
le papillon de nuit	moth
le phasme ▭	stick insect

BIRDS AND INSECTS

le pic ◇	woodpecker
le pigeon	pigeon
le pingouin	penguin
le roitelet	wren
le rossignol	nightingale
le rouge-gorge (*pl* ~**s**~**s**)	robin (redbreast)
le serin	canary
le vautour	vulture
le ver ◇	worm
le ver à soie	silkworm

USEFUL WORDS (m)

le bourdon	bumblebee
le bourdonnement	buzzing, buzz
le bouvreuil	bullfinch
le canari	canary
le chant	singing, warbling; chirp(ing)
le cocorico	cock-a-doodle-doo
le coin-coin (*pl inv*)	quack
un échassier	wader
un épervier	sparrowhawk
un essaim	swarm (*of bees, insects*)
le freux	rook
le gazouillis	chirp
le geai [ʒɛ]	jay
le :hululement	hooting, screeching
le miel	honey
le mille-pattes (*pl inv*)	centipede
les oiseaux migrateurs	migratory birds
un oiseleur	bird-catcher
un oiselier	bird-seller
un oisillon	little *or* baby bird
le perce-oreille (*pl* ~**s**)	earwig
le perchoir	perch
le perdreau (*pl* -**x**)	(young) partridge
le piaillement	squawking

ESSENTIAL WORDS (f)

la mouche	fly
une oie ▭	goose
la perruche	budgie, budgerigar
la poule ◇ ▭	hen
la queue ◇	tail

IMPORTANT WORDS (f)

une abeille	bee
une aile	wing
une alouette	lark
une araignée	spider
une autruche	ostrich
la bête à bon dieu	ladybird
la cage	cage
la caille ▭	quail
la chenille	caterpillar
la cigale	cicada
la cigogne	stork
la coccinelle [kɔksinɛl] ▭	ladybird
la colombe ▭	dove
la corneille	crow, raven
la fourmi	ant
la grive	thrush
la grouse	grouse
la guêpe	wasp
l'hirondelle	swallow
la libellule ▭	dragonfly
la mésange bleue	bluetit
la mouche à vers	bluebottle
la mouette	seagull
la perdrix [pɛRdRi]	partridge
la pie	magpie
la plume	feather
la puce	flea
la punaise ◇	bug
la sauterelle	grasshopper

BIRDS AND INSECTS

le pigeon voyageur	homing pigeon
le pigeonneau (*pl* -**x**)	young pigeon
le pigeonnier	pigeonhouse, dovecot
le pinson	chaffinch
le pivert	green woodpecker
le plumage	feathers
le pou (*pl* -**x**)	louse
le puceron	greenfly
le rapace	bird of prey
le roucoulement	coo(ing)
le scarabée	beetle
le sifflement	whistle, whistling
le taon [tã]	horsefly, gadfly
le termite	termite, white ant
le ver luisant	glow-worm

on les met en cage people put them in cages
l'abeille/la guêpe pique the bee/the wasp stings
une toile d'araignée a spider's web

USEFUL WORDS (f)

la chouette	owl
la dinde	turkey
la fiente	droppings
la fourmilière	ant hill
la lente	nit
la luciole	firefly
la mésange	tit(mouse)
la mite [mit]	clothes moth
une ouvrière ▷	worker (bee)
la ruche	hive
les serres	claws, talons
la termitière	ant hill
la tique	tick
la tourterelle	turtledove
la volière	aviary

voler to fly; **s'envoler** to fly away
les oiseaux volent dans l'air birds fly in the air
ils font des nids they build nests
ils sifflent they whistle; **ils chantent** they sing

BUSINESS AND COMMERCE

ESSENTIAL WORDS (m)

le commerce ⇨	trade, commerce
le consommateur	consumer
le contrat	contract
le créancier	creditor
le débiteur	debtor
un emprunt	loan
le fabricant	manufacturer, maker
les fonds	funds, capital
l'homme d'affaires ⇨	businessman
le marché	market
le prêt	loan
le taux d'intérêt	interest rate

IMPORTANT WORDS (m)

un actionnaire	shareholder
un associé	partner
le bilan	balance sheet, statement of accounts
un entrepôt 🕮	warehouse
un exportateur	exporter
les frais généraux	overheads
un industriel	industrialist; manufacturer
un inventaire	inventory; stock list
un investissement	investment
le monopole	monopoly
le négociant	merchant

USEFUL WORDS (m)

un à-côté (*pl* ~**s**)	extra
un abattement fiscal	tax allowance
un aboutissement	outcome, result
un accusé de réception	acknowledgement of receipt
l'acquittement	payment; settlement
l'agio	charges
les approvisionnements	supplies; stock
un arnaqueur	swindler
les arriérés	arrears
un assuré	insured person

ESSENTIAL WORDS (f)

une action	share
une affaire ◇	deal, bargain
la banqueroute	bankruptcy
la commande	order
la comptabilité	accounts, books
la concurrence	competition
la consommatrice	consumer
la créancière	creditor
la débitrice	debtor
la dette	debt
l'exportation	export
la facture	invoice
la femme d'affaires ◇	businesswoman
l'importation ◇	import
la société	company

IMPORTANT WORDS (f)

une actionnaire	shareholder
une association	partnership
une associée	partner
la caution	deposit
la dépense	outlay, expenditure
les devises étrangères	foreign currency
la gestion	management
la main d'œuvre	manpower, labour

USEFUL WORDS (f)

une annuité	annual instalment
l'assurance-vie (*pl* ~**s**~)	life assurance
l'assurance-vol (*pl* ~**s**~)	insurance against theft
une assurée	insured person
la compagnie de navigation	shipping company
la concessionnaire	agent, dealer
la confection	clothing industry
la courtière	broker
la devise	slogan
une enchère	bid

USEFUL WORDS (m) (cont)

un **attrape-nigaud** (*pl inv*)	con
le **bénéfice**	profit
le **bon de garantie**	guarantee *or* warranty slip
le **coffre-fort** (*pl~s~s*)	safe
le **commissaire-priseur** (*pl~s~s*)	auctioneer
le **concessionnaire**	agent, dealer
le **courtier**	broker
le **découvert**	overdraft
le **dégrèvement**	tax relief
le **devis**	estimate, quotation
les **échanges commerciaux**	trade, trading
un **écu** [eky]	ecu
un **emprunteur**	borrower
un **emprunt-logement** (*pl~s~*)	mortgage
la **livraison**	delivery
l'**endettement**	debts
un **enquêteur**	person conducting a survey, pollster
un **épargnant**	saver, investor
l'**excédent commercial**	trade surplus
le **fonds (de commerce)**	business
le **forfait**	fixed price; all-in deal *or* price
le **fournisseur**	supplier
le **gestionnaire**	administrator
les **honoraires**	fees
l'**import-export**	import-export business
l'**intérêt**	interest
un **investisseur**	investor
le **krach** [kʀak]	crash (*Stock Exchange*)
le **label**	stamp, seal
le **libre-échange**	free trade
le **lingot**	ingot
le **livreur**	delivery boy
le **local** (*pl* **locaux**)	premises
le **magnat**	tycoon
le **magnat de la presse**	press baron
le **marchandage**	bargaining
le **milliardaire**	multimillionaire
le **paradis fiscal**	tax haven
le **patronat**	employers

une **enquêteuse**	person conducting a survey, pollster
l'**exonération d'impôt**	tax exemption
la **fabrique**	factory
les **facilités de crédit**	credit terms
les **facilités de paiement**	easy terms
la **flambée des prix**	(sudden) rise in prices
la **fournisseuse**	supplier
la **gestionnaire**	administrator
la **:hausse**	rise, increase
l'**hypothèque**	mortgage
la **livraison**	delivery
la **milliardaire**	multimillionaire
la **paperasserie**	paperwork
la **patente**	trading licence
la **prêteuse**	moneylender
les **recettes**	receipts
la **reconnaissance de dette**	acknowledgement of a debt (IOU)
les **relations publiques (RP)**	public relations (PR)
la **vente** ◇	sale
la **vente aux enchères** ◇	auction sale
la **vente par correspondance**	mail-order selling

les affaires business
le secteur privé/public private/public sector
en rupture de stock out of stock
entreprise en plein essor firm in full expansion

le **permis de construire**	planning permission
le **porte à porte**	door-to-door selling
le **prêteur**	moneylender
le **prêteur sur gages**	pawnbroker
le **promoteur (immobilier)**	property developer
le **récépissé**	(acknowledgement of) receipt
le **troc**	barter

être en déplacement (pour affaires) to be on a (business) trip
être en faillite to be bankrupt
faire fortune to make one's fortune
s'acquitter d'une dette to pay off a debt
vendre aux enchères to sell by auction
rentable profitable; cost-effective
une tendance à la hausse/baisse upward/downward trend

le printemps	spring
l'été (*m*)	summer
l'automne (*m*)	autumn
l'hiver (*m*)	winter

au printemps in spring
en été/automne/hiver in summer/autumn/winter
l'arrière-saison late autumn

janvier	January	**juillet**	July
février	February	**août**	August
mars	March	**septembre**	September
avril	April	**octobre**	October
mai	May	**novembre**	November
juin	June	**décembre**	December

en mai *etc,* **au mois de mai** *etc* in May *etc*
le premier avril April Fools' Day
le premier mai May Day
le quatorze juillet Bastille Day (*French national holiday*)
le quinze août Assumption (*French national holiday*)

lundi	Monday
mardi	Tuesday
mercredi	Wednesday
jeudi	Thursday
vendredi	Friday
samedi	Saturday
dimanche	Sunday

le samedi *etc* on Saturdays *etc*
samedi *etc* on Saturday *etc*
samedi *etc* **prochain/dernier** next/last Saturday *etc*
le samedi *etc* **précédent/suivant** the previous/following Saturday *etc*

THE CALENDAR

le calendrier	the calendar
la saison	the season
le mois	the month
les jours de la semaine	the days of the week
le jour férié	public holiday

le dimanche des Rameaux/de Pâques Palm/Easter Sunday
le lundi de Pâques/de Pentecôte Easter/Whit Monday
Mardi gras Shrove *or* Pancake Tuesday
mercredi des Cendres Ash Wednesday
le jeudi de l'Ascension Ascension Day
le vendredi saint Good Friday
le jour de l'An New Year's Day
le réveillon du jour de l'An New Year's Eve dinner *or* party
le jour J D-Day
le jour des Morts All Souls' Day
le jour des Rois Epiphany, Twelfth Night
l'Armistice (*m*) Remembrance Day
l'Avent (*m*) Advent
le Carême Lent
Noël (*m*) Christmas
à (la) Noël at Christmas
le jour de Noël Christmas Day
la veille de Noël, la nuit de Noël Christmas Eve
le lendemain de Noël Boxing Day
Pâques (*fpl*) Easter
le jour de Pâques Easter Day
Pâque (*f*) juive Passover
le poisson d'avril April fool; April fool's trick
la Saint-Silvestre New Year's Eve, Hogmanay
la Saint-Valentin St. Valentine's Day
la semaine sainte Holy Week
la Toussaint All Saints' Day
la veille de la Toussaint Hallowe'en

ESSENTIAL WORDS (m)

un arbre ◇	tree
le bac à vaisselle ▭	washing-up bowl
le bloc sanitaire ▭	washrooms
le bol ◇	bowl
le campeur	camper
le camping	camping; camp-site
le couteau ◇ (pl -**x**)	knife
le dépôt de butane ▭	butane store
un emplacement ▭	pitch, site
le feu de camp	camp-fire
le gardien ◇ ▭	warden, attendant
le gaz ◇	gas
le lavabo	washbasin
le lit de camp	camp bed
les plats cuisinés ▭	cooked meals
le rasoir ▭	razor
le supplément ◇ ▭	extra charge
le terrain (de camping) ▭	camp-site
le véhicule ▭	vehicle
le verre ◇	glass
les W.-C. ◇ ▭	toilet(s)

IMPORTANT WORDS (m)

le matelas pneumatique	airbed, lilo
un ouvre-boîte(s) ◇ (pl **ouvre-boîtes**)	tin-opener
le réchaud	stove
le règlement ◇	rule
le sac à dos	backpack, rucksack
le sac de couchage	sleeping bag
le tire-bouchon (pl ~**s**)	corkscrew

USEFUL WORDS (m)

le camping-car (pl ~**s**)	caravanette
le pliant	folding stool, campstool

faire du camping to go camping; **camper** to camp
bien aménagé(e) well equipped
monter to set up; **mettre** to put; **débarrasser** to clear up

CAMPING

une allumette	match
une assiette ◇	plate
la boîte	tin, can; box
les boîtes de conserve	tinned food
la campeuse	camper
la caravane ◇	caravan
la carte ◇	map; card
la chaise (longue)	(deck) chair
la cuiller, cuillère ◇	spoon
la cuisinière ◇ (à gaz) ▯	(gas) cooker or stove
la douche ◇	shower
l'eau ◇ (potable)	(drinking) water
la fourchette ◇	fork
la glace ◇	mirror
la lampe électrique	torch
la machine à laver ◇ ▯	washing machine
la nuit ◇	night
la piscine ◇	swimming pool
la poubelle ◇	dustbin
la salle ◇ ▯	room; hall
la table ◇	table
la tasse ◇	cup
la tente	tent
les toilettes ◇	toilet(s)

les installations sanitaires ▯	washing facilities
la laverie	launderette, laundry
la lessive ◇	washing powder; washing
l'ombre	shade; shadow
la prise de courant ◇ ▯	socket, power point
la salle de jeux ▯	games room

la glacière	icebox

dresser une tente to pitch a tent

ESSENTIAL WORDS (m)

un **agent (de police)** ◇	policeman
un **auteur**	author
l'**avenir** ◇	future
le **bureau** ◇ (pl **-x**)	office
le **chauffeur de taxi** ▭	taxi driver
le **chef** ◇ (m+f)	boss
le **chômage**	unemployment
le **chômeur**	unemployed person
le **coiffeur** ◇	hairdresser; barber
le **collègue**	colleague
le **commerçant** ◇ ▭	tradesman
le **commerce** ◇	commerce, business
le **concierge**	caretaker; janitor
le **décorateur**	decorator
un **électricien** ▭	electrician
un **emploi**	job
un **employé** ◇ ▭	employee; clerk
un **employeur** ▭	employer
le **facteur** ◇ ▭	postman
le **garagiste** ▭	mechanic; garage owner
le **gérant** ◇	manager
l'**homme d'affaires** ◇	businessman
un **infirmier** ◇ ▭	(male) nurse
le **laitier**	milkman
le **mécanicien** ◇ ▭	mechanic; engineer; train-driver
le **médecin** (m+f)	doctor
le **métier** ▭	trade
le **mineur** ◇	miner
un **opticien** ◇	optician
un **ouvrier**	worker
le **patron** ◇	boss
le **pharmacien** ◇	chemist
le **pilote**	pilot; racing driver

---

un emploi temporaire/permanent a temporary/permanent job
être engagé(e) to be taken on
être renvoyé(e) to be dismissed; **démissionner** to resign
mettre qn à la porte to give sb the sack
intéressant(e)/peu intéressant(e) interesting/not very interesting

CAREERS AND EMPLOYMENT

ESSENTIAL WORDS (m) (cont)

le **plombier**	plumber
le **pompier** 🕮	fireman
le **premier ministre** *(m+f)*	prime minister
le **président**	president; chairman
le **professeur** *(m+f)*	teacher
le **roi**	king
le **salaire** 🕮	salary, pay, wages
le **salarié**	wage-earner
le **sapeur-pompier** *(pl ~s~s)*	fireman
le **secrétaire** ◇ 🕮	secretary
le **soldat**	soldier
le **syndicat** 🕮	trade union
les **syndiqués**	union members
le **travail**	work
le **vendeur** ◇ 🕮	salesman, shop assistant

IMPORTANT WORDS (m)

un **architecte** [aʀʃitɛkt(ə)]	architect
un **artiste**	artist
un **avocat** ◇	barrister
un **avoué**	solicitor
le **cadre** ◇	executive
le **chercheur** ◇	researcher
le **chirurgien**	surgeon
le **comptable**	accountant
le **constructeur**	builder
le **cosmonaute**	cosmonaut, astronaut
le **couturier**	fashion designer
le **député** ◇	M.P., member of parliament
un **écrivain**	writer
le **fonctionnaire** ◇	civil servant
l' **homme politique**	politician
un **ingénieur**	engineer

mettre qn en *or* **au chômage** to make sb redundant
"demandes d'emploi" ''situations wanted''
"offres d'emploi" ''situations vacant''
je vais faire une demande d'emploi I am going to apply for a job

ESSENTIAL WORDS (f)

les affaires ◇	business
une ambition	ambition
une augmentation ▭	rise
la banque	bank
la bibliothèque ◇	library
la carrière ◇ ▭	career
la coiffeuse ◇	hairdresser
la collègue	colleague
la concierge	caretaker
la cuisinière ◇	cook
la dactylo(graphe)	typist
une employée ◇ ▭	employee
une entrevue	interview
la factrice ▭	postwoman
la femme d'affaires ◇	businesswoman
la femme de ménage ◇	cleaning woman
la gérante ▭	manageress
la grève	strike
l'hôtesse de l'air	air hostess
une industrie ▭	industry
une infirmière ▭	nurse
l'intention	intention, aim
une ouvreuse	usherette
une ouvrière ◇	worker
la patronne	boss
la politique ◇	politics
la présidente	president; chairwoman
la profession ▭	profession

se mettre au travail to start work, get down to work
il est facteur, c'est un facteur he is a postman
il/elle est médecin, c'est un médecin he/she is a doctor
il est facteur de son métier he is a postman by trade *or* to trade
travailler to work; **devenir** to become
travailler pour gagner sa vie to work to earn one's living
mon ambition est d'être secrétaire, j'ai l'ambition d'être secrétaire it is my
  ambition to be a secretary
que faites-vous dans la vie? what work do you do?, what is your job?
être au chômage to be out of work, be unemployed

CAREERS AND EMPLOYMENT

IMPORTANT WORDS (m) (cont)

un **interprète**	interpreter
le **journaliste**	journalist
le **juge**	judge
le **maçon**	mason
le **mannequin** ◇ (m+f)	model (person)
le **marin** ◇	sailor; seaman
le **menuisier**	joiner
le **notaire**	lawyer, solicitor
le **personnel**	staff
le **photographe**	photographer
le **président-directeur général, PDG**	chairman and managing director
le **prêtre**	priest
le **représentant**	representative
le **speaker** [spikœR]	announcer
le **stage**	(training) course
le **traitement**	salary
le **vétérinaire** (m+f)	vet(erinary surgeon)
le **vigneron**	wine grower

USEFUL WORDS (m)

un **adjoint**	assistant
l'**adjoint au maire**	deputy mayor
un **administrateur**	director
l'**administrateur délégué**	managing director
un **aide-comptable** (pl ~s ~s)	accountant's assistant
un **aide soignant**	auxiliary nurse
un **ajusteur**	metal worker
un **ambulancier** ◇	ambulance man
un **analyste-programmeur** (pl ~s ~s)	systems analyst
les **antécédents professionnels**	record, career to date
un **anthropologue**	anthropologist
un **antiquaire**	antique dealer

entrer en fonctions to take up one's post
être de service to be on duty
être surchargé de travail to be overworked

la **réceptionniste** 💬	receptionist
la **reine**	queen
la **salariée**	wage-earner
la **secrétaire** 💬	secretary
la **situation** 💬	job, situation
une **usine** ◊	factory
la **vedette** ◊ (*m+f*)	star
la **vendeuse** 💬	salesgirl, shop assistant
la **vie**	life

IMPORTANT WORDS (f)

l' **administration**	administration
une **artiste**	artist
une **avocate**	lawyer
la **compagnie**	company
la **comptable**	accountant
la **couturière**	dressmaker
la **dispute**	argument, dispute
une **entreprise**	business
la **femme-agent**	policewoman
la **femme au foyer** ◊	housewife
la **firme**	firm
la **formation**	training
la **grève du zèle** 💬	work-to-rule
la **grève perlée** 💬	go-slow
une **interprète**	interpreter
la **journaliste**	journalist
la **maison de commerce**	firm
l' **orientation professionnelle**	careers guidance
la **religieuse** ◊	nun
la **speakerine** [spikRin]	announcer
la **sténo-dactylo(graphe)**	shorthand typist

gagner/toucher £150 par semaine to earn/get £150 a week
une augmentation de salaire a wage *or* pay rise
se mettre en grève to go on strike; **faire la grève** to be on strike
travailler à plein temps/à mi-temps to work full-time/part-time
faire des heures supplémentaires to work overtime

CAREERS AND EMPLOYMENT

les appointements	salary
un apprenti	apprentice
un apprentissage	apprenticeship
un armateur	shipowner
un arpenteur	(land) surveyor
un artisan	craftsman
l'artisanat	craft industry
un assistanat	assistantship
un assistant	assistant
un assureur	insurance agent
un aubergiste	innkeeper
un avancement	promotion
un aventurier	adventurer
le banquier	banker
le barème des salaires	salary scale
le bénévolat	voluntary work, voluntary help
le blanchisseur	launderer
le boulot	work
le cadre supérieur	senior executive
le cadre moyen	junior executive
les cadres	managerial staff
le cancérologue	cancer specialist
le candidat	candidate
le carreleur	tiler
le carrossier	coachbuilder
le chantier	(building) site
le charpentier	carpenter
le cheminot	railwayman
le chèque-restaurant (pl ~s~)	luncheon voucher
le chimiste	chemist (scientist)
le confrère	colleague
le conservateur de musée	curator
le contrat de travail	employment contract
le cours de recyclage	retraining course
le couvreur	roofer
le crémier	dairyman
le débouché	opening, prospect
le déménageur	removal man
le dessinateur	draughtsman
le documentaliste	archivist

USEFUL WORDS (f)

une adjointe	assistant
une administratrice	director
une affectation	appointment
une aide familiale	mother's help
une aide ménagère	home help
une aide soignante	auxiliary nurse
une ambulancière	ambulance woman
une analyste-programmeuse (pl ~s~s)	systems analyst
l'ancienneté	seniority
une anthropologue	anthropologist
une antiquaire	antique dealer
une apprentie	apprentice
une assistante sociale	social worker
une aubergiste	innkeeper
une aventurière	adventuress
la blanchisseuse	laundress
la bonne	maid
la caissière	cashier; check-out assistant
la cancérologue	cancer specialist
la candidate	candidate
la cardiologue	cardiologist
la chimiste	chemist (scientist)
la conservatrice de musée	curator
la consœur	(lady) colleague
la démission	resignation
la documentaliste	archivist
une éditrice	publisher; editor
une électronicienne	electronics engineer
une esthéticienne	beautician
la fiscaliste	tax specialist
la fleuriste	florist
la garde d'enfants	childminder

faire de l'intérim to temp
faire des ménages to work as a cleaner (*in people's homes*)
faire la plonge to be a dishwasher
faire les trois-huit to operate round the clock in eight-hour shifts
grimper rapidement les échelons to get quick promotion

CAREERS AND EMPLOYMENT

USEFUL WORDS (m) (cont)

un ébéniste	cabinetmaker
un éboueur	dustman
un éditeur	publisher; editor
un électronicien	electronics engineer
un encadreur	(picture) framer
un entrepreneur de pompes funèbres	undertaker, funeral director
un entrepreneur (en bâtiment)	(building) contractor
un expert-comptable (pl ~s~s)	chartered accountant
le ferronnier	craftsman in wrought iron; ironware merchant
le fiscaliste	tax specialist
le fleuriste	florist
le forgeron	(black)smith
le fossoyeur	gravedigger
les frais de déplacement	travel expenses
le gagne-pain	job
le garde du corps	bodyguard
le garde forestier	forest warden
le gréviste	striker
le groom	page
un imprimeur	printer
l'interprétariat	interpreting
le kinésithérapeute	physiotherapist
le laborantin	laboratory assistant
le caissier	cashier; check-out assistant
le cardiologue	cardiologist
le licenciement	dismissal; redundancy; laying off
le magasinier	warehouseman
le marché du travail	labour market
le marmiton	kitchen boy
le mineur ⬦	miner
un orthophoniste	speech therapist
le peintre en bâtiment	house painter, painter and decorator

débaucher to lay off, dismiss
embaucher to take on, to hire (*labour*)
pointer to clock in/out

USEFUL WORDS (f) (cont)

la **gréviste**	striker
la **:hiérarchie**	hierarchy
une **indemnité de licenciement**	redundancy payment
la **kinésithérapeute**	physiotherapist
la **laborantine**	laboratory assistant
la **mutation**	transfer
la **nourrice**	child minder, nanny
une **orthophoniste**	speech therapist
la **paye**	wages
la **politicienne** ◇	politician
la **postière**	post office worker
la **préretraite**	early retirement
la **reconversion**	redeployment
la **reliure**	(book)binding
la **romancière**	novelist
la **servante**	(maid)servant
la **société d'intérim**	temping agency
la **styliste**	designer
la **traductrice**	translator
la **vocation**	vocation, calling
la **volontaire**	volunteer

il a été licencié he was made redundant
poser sa candidature (pour un emploi) to apply (for a job)
travail à plein temps full-time work
un emploi fixe a steady or regular job
un garçon boucher/coiffeur butcher's/hairdresser's assistant
la sécurité de l'emploi job security

CAREERS AND EMPLOYMENT

le permis de travail	work permit
le piston	string-pulling
le politicien ▷	politician
le postier	post office worker
le ramoneur	(chimney) sweep
le recrutement	recruiting, recruitment
le relieur	(book)binder
le romancier	novelist
le scaphandrier	diver
le secret professionnel	professional secrecy
le serrurier	locksmith
le soudeur	welder
le styliste	designer
le traducteur	translator
le train-train	humdrum routine
le travail au noir	moonlighting
le travailleur saisonnier	seasonal worker
le videur	bouncer
le vigile	(night) watchman
le vitrier	glazier
le volcanologue	vulcanologist
le volontaire	volunteer
le volontariat	voluntary service

renvoyer to dismiss; **se surmener** to overwork (o.s.)

ESSENTIAL WORDS (m)

un **anniversaire**	birthday
un **anniversaire de mariage**	wedding anniversary
le **bal**	dance
le **cadeau** (*pl* -**x**)	present
le **cirque** ▭	circus
le **drapeau** (*pl* -**x**)	flag
le **festival**	festival
le **feu d'artifice**	firework; firework display
le **feu de joie**	bonfire
le **mariage**	marriage, wedding
le **rendez-vous** (*pl inv*)	appointment, date

IMPORTANT WORDS (m)

le **baptême**	christening, baptism
le **char fleuri** ▭	decorated float
le **cimetière**	cemetery, churchyard
les **confettis**	confetti
le **décès**	death
le **défilé** ◇	procession; march
un **enterrement**	funeral, burial
le **faire-part (de mariage)** ▭	wedding announcement /
(*pl inv*)	invitation
le **témoin du marié**	best man

USEFUL WORDS (m)

le **bicentenaire**	bicentenary
le **carnaval**	carnival
le **centenaire**	centenary
le **cercueil**	coffin

célébrer *or* **fêter son anniversaire** to celebrate one's birthday
elle vient d'avoir ses 17 ans she's just (turned) 17
le bal du Nouvel An the New Year's Eve dance
il m'a offert ce cadeau he gave me this present
je te l'offre! I'm giving it to you!
je vous remercie thank you (very much)
divorcer to get divorced; **se marier** to get married

CEREMONIES AND SPECIAL OCCASIONS

USEFUL WORDS (m) (cont)

le chant de Noël	(Christmas) carol
le convoi funèbre	funeral procession
le couronnement	coronation
le défunt	deceased
le deuil	bereavement
le discours ⊅	speech
le drapeau tricolore	the (French) tricolour
l'état civil	registry office
le forain	fairground entertainer; stallholder
l'hôte	host; guest
un invité	guest
le lampion	Chinese lantern
le Père-Noël	Father Christmas
le pétard	banger, firecracker
le réveillon	Christmas Eve *or* New Year's Eve party
le santon	ornamental figure at a Christmas crib
le sapin de Noël	Christmas tree
le tricentenaire	tercentenary, tricentennial

soyez le *or* **la bienvenu(e)** (*pl* **les bienvenu(e)s**) you are very welcome
souhaiter la bonne année à qn to wish sb a happy New Year

ESSENTIAL WORDS (f)

la date ◇	date
les festivités	festivities
la fête	saint's day; fête, fair
la fête foraine	(fun)fair
les fiançailles ⌑	engagement
la foire	(fun)fair
la mort ◇	death
la naissance	birth

IMPORTANT WORDS (f)

la cérémonie	ceremony
la demoiselle d'honneur	bridesmaid
les étrennes ⌑	New Year's gift; Christmas box
la fanfare	brass band; fanfare
la fête folklorique	festival of folk music
la lune de miel	honeymoon
les noces	wedding
la retraite	retirement

USEFUL WORDS (f)

la couronne funéraire	(funeral) wreath
la défunte	deceased
la demande en mariage	(marriage) proposal
la fève	charm (*hidden in cake eaten on Twelfth Night*)
la Fête Nationale	national holiday
la Fête des Mères/Pères	Mother's/Father's Day
les fêtes (de fin d'année)	festive season
les funérailles	funeral
la galette des Rois	cake traditionally eaten on Twelfth Night

se fiancer (avec qn) to get engaged (to sb)
mon père est mort il y a deux ans my father died two years ago
enterrer, ensevelir to bury
ma sœur est née en 1985 my sister was born in 1985
aller à la noce de qn to go to sb's wedding
les noces d'argent/d'or/de diamant silver/golden/diamond wedding

CEREMONIES AND SPECIAL OCCASIONS

la guirlande lumineuse	(fairy) lights
la guirlande de Noël	tinsel
les illuminations de Noël	Christmas lights *or* illuminations
l'inauguration	opening
l'incinération	cremation
l'inhumation	interment, burial
une invitée	guest
la kermesse	bazaar, (charity) fête; village fair
la loterie	raffle
la majorette	majorette
la Marseillaise	the Marseillaise (*French national anthem*)
les obsèques	funeral
la pièce montée	tiered cake
la tombe	grave; tomb
la veillée (mortuaire)	watch

discours/cérémonie d'inauguration inaugural speech/ceremony
porter un toast to drink a toast

SOME COLOURS	

beige	beige
blanc (blanche)	white
bleu ◇ **(bleue)**	blue
bordeaux *inv*	maroon, burgundy
brun (brune)	brown
écarlate	scarlet
fauve	fawn, tawny
gris (grise)	grey
jaune	yellow
lie-de-vin *inv*	wine(-coloured)
marron ◇	brown
mauve	mauve
noir (noire)	black
ocre	ochre
orange, orangé(e)	orange
pourpre	crimson
rose ◇	pink
rosé(e)	rosé
rouge	red
turquoise	turquoise
vermeil (vermeille)	bright red
vert (verte)	green
violacé(e)	purplish, mauvish
violet (violette)	violet, purple
violine	dark purple, deep purple
bleu clair	pale blue
bleu foncé	dark blue
bleuté	bluish
bleu ciel	sky blue
bleu marine	navy blue
bleu roi	royal blue
bleuâtre	bluish
jaunâtre	yellowish
rougeâtre	reddish
verdâtre	greenish

COLOURS AND SHAPES

SOME COLOURFUL PHRASES

la couleur colour; **changer de couleur** to change colour
la Maison Blanche the White House
un Blanc a white man; **une Blanche** a white woman
blanc comme la neige as white as snow
Blanche-Neige Snow-White
un steak bleu a very rare steak, an underdone steak
rougir to turn red; **le Petit Chaperon Rouge** Little Red Riding Hood
rougir de honte/de gêne to blush with shame/with embarrassment
pâle comme un linge as white as a sheet
bleu de froid blue with cold
tous les trente-six du mois once in a blue moon
elle brunit she is turning brown
les feuilles roussissent the leaves are turning brown
tout(e) bronzé(e) as brown as a berry
il était couvert de bleus he was black and blue
d'un noir de jais jet-black
un Noir a black man; **une Noire** a black woman
un œil poché, un œil au beurre noir a black eye
vert(e) de jalousie green with envy
il a le pouce vert he's got green fingers
de quelle couleur sont tes yeux/tes cheveux? what colour are your eyes/is your hair?
vif (vive) colourful, bright
le bleu te va bien blue suits you; the blue one suits you
peindre qch en bleu to paint sth blue
flou(e) soft; **opaque** opaque; **translucide** translucent; **transparent(e)** transparent
uni(e) self-coloured; **voyant(e)** loud, gaudy, garish
bicolore two-coloured; **multicolore** multicoloured

SOME SHAPES

le carré	square
le cercle	circle
le cube	cube
le cylindre	cylinder
le rectangle	rectangle
le triangle	triangle
la croix	cross

en losange diamond-shaped

ESSENTIAL WORDS (m)

le **micro-ordinateur** (*pl* **~s**)	PC, personal computer
un **ordinateur** ◇	computer
le **programme** ◇	program
le **programmeur**	programmer

IMPORTANT WORDS (m)

le **caractère** ◇	character, letter
le **clavier**	keyboard
le **curseur**	cursor
le **disque dur**	hard disk
un **écran**	monitor, screen
le **fichier**	file
le **jeu électronique**	computer game
le **lecteur de disquettes**	disk drive
le **listage, listing**	print-out
le **logiciel**	software
le **matériel**	hardware
le **menu**	menu
le **modem**	modem
le **moniteur**	monitor
le **pirateur d'informatique**	hacker
le **progiciel**	software package
le **software**	software
le **tableur**	spreadsheet (program)

USEFUL WORDS (m)

le **chiffre**	digit
le **contrôle orthographique**	spellchecker
le **document**	document
un **informaticien**	computer scientist
le **langage machine**	computer language
le **méga-octet (Mo)**	megabyte (Mb)
le **menu d'assistance**	help menu
le **formatage**	formatting
le **retour (automatique) à la ligne**	wordwrap
le **saut de page**	page break

COMPUTING

le terminal   terminal
le virus   virus

aimer les jeux électroniques to like (playing) computer games
j'ai eu un ordinateur pour mon anniversaire I got a computer for my birthday
portatif(ive) portable
écrire or **rédiger un programme** to write a program
augmenter la puissance to upgrade
éditer to edit

ESSENTIAL WORDS (f)

la **batterie** ◇	battery
la **souris**	mouse

IMPORTANT WORDS (f)

la **base de données**	database
la **console (de visualisation)**	VDU, visual display unit
la **disquette**	floppy disk
les **données**	data
la **fonction**	function
une **imprimante**	printer
l'**informatique** ◇ ▫	computer science; computer studies
une **interface**	interface
la **machine de traitement de texte** ◇	word processor
la **manette (de jeu)**	joystick
la **mémoire**	memory
la **mémoire morte**	ROM, read only memory
la **mémoire vive**	RAM, random access memory
la **sauvegarde**	back-up
la **touche** ◇	key
une **unité de disquettes** ▫	disk drive unit

USEFUL WORDS (f)

la **barre d'espacement**	spacebar
la **coupe et insertion**	cut and paste
l'**entrée** ◇	input
l'**erreur**	bug
E/S (entrée/sortie)	I/O (input/output)
la **fenêtre**	window
une **icône**	icon
une **informaticienne**	computer scientist
l'**informatisation**	computerization
l'**interligne**	line spacing
la **marge**	margin
la **mise à jour**	update
la **mise en mémoire**	storage
la **pagination**	pagination

57

la **PAO** (publication assistée par ordinateur)	DTP (desktop publishing)
la **police de caractères**	font
la **programmation**	programming
la **puce**	chip

introduire or **entrer les données** to enter the data
mémoriser les données to store the data
rechercher l'information to retrieve the information
effacer to delete, to erase
justifier à gauche/à droite to justify left/right
retrouver to retrieve

ESSENTIAL WORDS (m)

le Canada	Canada
le Danemark	Denmark
les États-Unis	the United States
le Luxembourg	Luxembourg
le pays ◇	country
les Pays-Bas	the Netherlands
le pays de Galles	Wales
le Portugal	Portugal
le Royaume-Uni	United Kingdom

ESSENTIAL WORDS (m) (cont)

un Allemand	a German
un Américain	an American
un Anglais	an Englishman
un Belge	a Belgian
un Britannique	a Briton
un Canadien	a Canadian
un Danois	a Dane
un Écossais	a Scotsman
un Espagnol	a Spaniard
un Européen	a European
un Français	a Frenchman
un Gallois	a Welshman
un :Hollandais	a Dutchman
un Irlandais	an Irishman
un Italien	an Italian
un Luxembourgeois	a native of Luxembourg
un Pakistanais	a Pakistani
un Portugais	a Portuguese
un Suisse	a Swiss

The forms given here and on the following pages are the noun forms (i.e. for people) and begin with a capital letter:
il est Danois, c'est un Danois he is a Dane
elle est Danoise, c'est une Danoise she is a Danish girl *etc*

They can be used as adjectives by converting the capital into a small letter:
le paysage danois the Danish countryside
une ville danoise a Danish town

COUNTRIES AND NATIONALITIES

IMPORTANT WORDS (m)

le **Brésil**	Brazil
le **Japon**	Japan
le **Liban** 📖	Lebanon
le **Maroc**	Morocco
le **Mexique**	Mexico
le **Pakistan**	Pakistan
le **Viet-Nam**	Vietnam

IMPORTANT WORDS (m) (cont)

un **Africain**	an African
un **Algérien**	an Algerian
un **Antillais** 📖	a West Indian
un **Arabe**	an Arab
un **Asiatique**	an Asian
un **Australien**	an Australian
un **Autrichien**	an Austrian
un **Brésilien**	a Brazilian
un **Chinois**	a Chinese
un **Coréen** 📖	a Korean
un **Finnois, Finlandais**	a Finn
un **Grec**	a Greek
un **Indien**	an Indian
un **Inuit**	an Inuit
un **Japonais**	a Japanese
un **Libanais** 📖	a Lebanese
un **Marocain**	a Moroccan
un **Mexicain**	a Mexican
un **Néo-Zélandais** (*pl inv*)	a New Zealander
un **Norvégien**	a Norwegian
un **Polonais**	a Pole
un **Roumain**	a Romanian
un **Russe**	a Russian
un **Scandinave**	a Scandinavian
un **Suédois**	a Swede
un **Tchèque**	a Czech
un **Tunisien**	a Tunisian
un **Turc**	a Turk
un **Vietnamien**	a Vietnamese

ESSENTIAL WORDS (f)

l'Allemagne	Germany
l'Angleterre	England
la Belgique	Belgium
l'Écosse	Scotland
l'Espagne	Spain
l'Europe	Europe
la France	France
la Grande-Bretagne	Great Britain
la Grèce	Greece
la :Hollande ⌑	Holland
l'Irlande (du Nord)	(Northern) Ireland
l'Italie	Italy
la Suisse	Switzerland

ESSENTIAL WORDS (f) (cont)

une Allemande	a German (girl or woman)
une Américaine	an American (girl or woman)
une Anglaise	an Englishwoman, an English girl
une Belge	a Belgian (girl or woman)
une Britannique	a Briton, a British girl or woman
une Canadienne	a Canadian (girl or woman)
une Danoise	a Dane, a Danish girl or woman
une Écossaise	a Scotswoman, a Scots girl
une Espagnole	a Spaniard, a Spanish girl or woman
une Européenne	a European
une Française	a Frenchwoman, a French girl
une Galloise	a Welshwoman, a Welsh girl
une :Hollandaise	a Dutchwoman, a Dutch girl
une Irlandaise	an Irishwoman, an Irish girl
une Italienne	an Italian (girl or woman)
une Luxembourgeoise	a native of Luxembourg
une Pakistanaise	a Pakistani (girl etc)
une Portugaise	a Portuguese (girl etc)
une Suisse	a Swiss (girl or woman)

une **Canadienne française** a French Canadian
je suis Écossaise – je parle anglais I am Scottish – I speak English
un **étranger (une étrangère)** a foreigner; a stranger

COUNTRIES AND NATIONALITIES

USEFUL WORDS (m)

un **Amerloque**	Yankee
un **apatride**	stateless person
un **autochtone**	native
les **flamands**	the Flemish
le **gitan**	gipsy
l'**hymne national**	national anthem
un **indigène**	native
le **méridional**	Southerner (*from the South of France*)
le **métis**	half-caste, half-breed
les **Occidentaux**	Westerners
le **patrimoine culturel**	cultural heritage
un **Peau-Rouge** (*pl* -**x**~**s**)	a Red Indian
le **permis de séjour**	residence permit
le **pied-noir** (*pl* ~**s**~**s**)	Algerian-born Frenchman

je reviens des États-Unis I have just come back from the United States
les pays en voie de développement the developing countries
un **Canadien français** a French Canadian
je suis Écossais – je parle anglais I am Scottish – I speak English
travailler/aller à l'étranger to work/go abroad
la **nationalité** nationality
je suis né(e) en Écosse I was born in Scotland
j'irais aux Pays-Bas/au pays de Galles/en Italie I would go to the Netherlands/to Wales/to Italy

IMPORTANT WORDS (f)

l'Afrique (du Sud)	(South) Africa
l'Algérie	Algeria
l'Amérique du Sud	South America
les Antilles ▭	West Indies
l'Asie	Asia
l'Australie	Australia
l'Autriche	Austria
la Chine	China
la Communauté européenne, CE	European Community, EC
la Corée (du Nord/du Sud) ▭	(North/South) Korea
la Finlande	Finland
l'Inde	India
la Norvège	Norway
la Nouvelle Zélande	New Zealand
la Pologne	Poland
la Roumanie	Romania
la Russie	Russia
la Scandinavie	Scandinavia
la Suède	Sweden
la Tchécoslovaquie	Czechoslovakia
la Tunisie	Tunisia
la Turquie	Turkey

IMPORTANT WORDS (f) (cont)

une Africaine	an African (girl *or* woman)
une Algérienne	an Algerian
une Antillaise ▭	a West Indian
une Arabe	an Arab
une Asiatique	an Asian
une Australienne	an Australian
une Autrichienne	an Austrian
une Brésilienne	a Brazilian

mon pays natal my native country
la capitale de la France the capital of France
de quel pays venez-vous? what country do you come from?
je viens des États-Unis/du Canada/de la France I come from the United States/
from Canada/from France

COUNTRIES AND NATIONALITIES

une Chinoise	a Chinese
une Coréenne ▭	a Korean
une Finnoise, Finlandaise	a Finn
une Grecque	a Greek
une Indienne	an Indian
une Inuit	an Inuit
une Japonaise	a Japanese
une Libanaise ▭	a Lebanese
une Marocaine	a Moroccan
une Mexicaine	a Mexican
une Néo-Zélandaise (pl ~s)	a New Zealander
une Norvégienne	a Norwegian
une Polonaise	a Pole
une Roumaine	a Romanian
une Russe	a Russian
une Scandinave	a Scandinavian
une Suédoise	a Swede
une Tchèque	a Czech
une Tunisienne	a Tunisian
une Turque	a Turk
une Vietnamienne	a Vietnamese

USEFUL WORDS (f)

une Amerloque	Yankee
une apatride	stateless person
une autochtone	native
la gitane	gipsy
une indigène	native
l'Indochine	Indochina
la méridionale	Southerner (*from the South of France*)
la métisse	half-caste, half-breed
la métropole	home country
la minorité ethnique	racial *or* ethnic minority
la patrie	homeland
la tribu	tribe

francophone French-speaking

ESSENTIAL WORDS (m)

l' **air** ◇	air
un **agriculteur**	farmer
un **arbre** ◇	tree
le **bois** ◇ ▭	wood
le **bruit** ▭	noise
les **campagnards**	countryfolk, country people
le **champ**	field
le **chasseur** ◇	hunter
le **château** ◇ (*pl* -**x**)	castle
le **chemin**	path, way
le **fermier**	farmer
le **fleuve** ◇	river
le **gendarme** (*m+f*)	gendarme
l' **habitant**	inhabitant
le **lac** ◇	lake
le **marché**	market
le **pays** ◇	country; district
le **paysage**	countryside, scenery
le **paysan** ◇	country man, farmer
le **pique-nique** ▭ (*pl* ~**s**)	picnic
le **pont** ◇	bridge
le **sommet** ◇	top (*of hill*)
le **terrain** ◇	soil; ground
le **touriste**	tourist
le **trou**	hole
le **village**	village

IMPORTANT WORDS (m)

le **bâton** ◇	stick
le **blé**	corn; wheat
le **buisson** ◇	bush
le **caillou** (*pl* -**x**)	pebble
le **cottage**	cottage
le **curé**	vicar, priest
un **étang**	pond
le **foin**	hay
le **fossé**	ditch
le :**hameau** (*pl* -**x**)	hamlet

IN THE COUNTRY

IMPORTANT WORDS (m) (cont)

le jonc 🔲 [ʒɔ̃]	reed
le marais	marsh
le moulin (à vent)	(wind)mill
le piège ◇	trap
le poteau (*pl* **-x**) **indicateur**	signpost
le poteau (*pl* **-x**) **télégraphique**	telegraph pole
le pré	meadow
le ruisseau (*pl* **-x**)	stream
le sentier	path

USEFUL WORDS (m)

l' alpage	high mountain pasture
le barbelé	barbed wire
le belvédère	panoramic viewpoint
le braconnage	poaching
le braconnier	poacher
le cantonnier	roadmender
le collet	snare, noose
un escarpement	steep slope
le fourré	thicket
un garde champêtre	rural policeman
le garde-chasse (*pl* ~**s**~**(s)**)	gamekeeper
le garde-fou (*pl* ~**s**)	railing, parapet
un gîte (rural)	holiday cottage
le marécage	marsh, swamp
le montagnard	mountain dweller
le permis de chasse	hunting permit
le torrent	torrent, mountain stream
le villageois	villager

agricole agricultural
paisible, tranquille peaceful
au sommet de la colline at the top of the hill
tomber dans un piège to fall into a trap
s'égarer to get lost, lose one's way
les gens du pays the local people, the locals

ESSENTIAL WORDS (f)

l'agriculture	agriculture
une auberge ◊	inn
une auberge de jeunesse	youth hostel
la barrière ◊	gate; fence
la botte (de caoutchouc)	(wellington) boot
la camionnette ◊	(small) van
la campagne	country
la canne ◊	cane, (walking) stick
la chaussée ◊	roadway
la colline	hill
la ferme	farm, farmhouse
la feuille ◊	leaf
la forêt ◊	forest
la montagne ▭	mountain
la paysanne	country woman, peasant
la pierre ◊	stone, rock
la poussière ◊	dust
la propriété	property, estate
la rivière ◊	river
la route ◊	road
la terre ◊	earth, ground
la tour ◊	tower
la touriste	tourist
la tranquillité	peace
la vallée	valley

IMPORTANT WORDS (f)

la boue ◊	mud
la bruyère	heather
la carrière ▭ ◊	quarry
la caverne	cave
la chasse	hunting; shooting
la chaumière ◊	(thatched) cottage
la chute d'eau	waterfall
la :haie ◊	hedge
les jumelles ◊	binoculars
la lande ◊ ▭	moor, heath
la mare	pond
la moisson ◊	harvest

IN THE COUNTRY

IMPORTANT WORDS (f) (cont)

la plaine	plain
la récolte ✧	crop, harvest
la rive	bank (*of river*)
les ruines	ruins
la source	spring, source
la vendange	grape harvest

USEFUL WORDS (f)

la berge	bank (*of river*)
la cabane	hut, cabin
la cascade	waterfall
une écluse	lock (gate)
la garrigue	scrubland
la grotte ✧	cave
la montagnarde	mountain dweller
la parcelle de terre	plot of land
les ronces	brambles, thorns
la villageoise	villager

en aval downstream; downhill
boueux(euse) muddy
campagnard(e) country
faire la moisson to bring in the harvest
faire les vendanges to harvest the grapes
en plein air in the open air
je connais le chemin du village I know the way to the village
ils ont fait tout le chemin à pied/en bicyclette they walked/cycled the whole way
nous avons fait un pique-nique we went for a picnic
traverser un pont to cross a bridge
à la campagne on trouve ... in the country you find ...
aller à la campagne to go into the country
habiter la campagne/la ville to live in the country/in the town
la rivière/le ruisseau coule the river/the stream flows
cultiver la terre to cultivate *or* till the land
se diriger vers to make one's way towards

ESSENTIAL WORDS (m)

l'âge	age
un air ◇	appearance
le bouton ◇	spot, pimple
le caractère ◇	character, nature
les cheveux	hair
le teint	complexion, colouring
les verres (de contact)	contact lenses
les yeux	eyes

quel âge avez-vous? how old are you?

j'ai 15 ans, mon frère a 13 ans I'm 15, my brother is 13

il vient d'avoir ses 17 ans he's just (turned) 17

un homme/une femme d'un certain âge a middle-aged man/woman

il/elle a l'air triste he/she looks sad

il/elle a l'air sympa or **sympathique** he/she looks nice or friendly

il/elle a l'air fatigué(e) he/she looks tired

de quelle couleur sont tes yeux/tes cheveux? what colour are your eyes/is your hair?

j'ai les cheveux blonds I have blond or fair hair

j'ai les yeux bleus/verts I have blue eyes/green eyes

les cheveux bouclés/ondulés curly/wavy hair

les cheveux bruns dark or brown hair

les cheveux châtains chestnut-coloured hair

les cheveux frisés curly hair

les cheveux roux/noirs/gris red/black/grey hair

les cheveux teints dyed hair

court(e) short; **long(ue)** long

à mon avis in my opinion

joli(e) pretty; **laid(e)** ugly; **affreux(euse)** hideous

beau (and **bel** before a vowel or aspirate h) handsome; **belle** beautiful

grand(e) tall; **petit(e)** small

jeune young; **vieux** (and **vieil** before a vowel or aspirate h), **vieille** old

gros(se) fat; **mince** slim, thin

maigre skinny, thin

barbu bearded, with a beard; **chauve** bald

il pleurait he was crying; **il souriait** he was smiling

il avait les larmes aux yeux he had tears in his eyes

un homme de taille moyenne a man of average height

je mesure or **je fais 1 mètre 70** I am 1 metre 70 tall

il pèse 60 kilos his weight is 60 kilos

DESCRIBING PEOPLE

IMPORTANT WORDS (m)

le défaut	fault; bad quality
le dentier 🔲	(set of) false teeth
le géant	giant
le geste	movement, gesture
le grain de beauté 🔲	mole, beauty spot
le poids	weight

USEFUL WORDS (m)

un abruti	moron
un accent	accent
un albinos (pl inv)	albino
un âne ◇	ass, fool
l' aplomb	composure, self-assurance
un arnaqueur	swindler
un arriviste	go-getter
un aveugle	blind person
un bec-de-lièvre (pl ~s ~~)	harelip
le bon sens	common sense
le bonhomme [bɔnɔm] (pl bonshommes)	chap, fellow, bloke
le bosseur	hard worker
le bossu	hunchback
le chignon	bun (in hair)
le colosse	giant
le comportement	behaviour
un couche-tard (pl inv)	late-bedder
un couche-tôt (pl inv)	early-bedder
les couettes	bunches (in hair)
le don	gift, talent
le droitier	right-handed person
l' enfantillage	childishness
un épi (de cheveux)	tuft (of hair)
un ermite	hermit
un érudit	scholar

il a bon caractère he is good-natured or good-tempered
il a mauvais caractère he is ill-natured or bad-tempered
avoir le teint jaune/pâle to have a sallow/pale complexion
porter des lunettes/des verres de contact to wear glasses/contact lenses

---

ESSENTIAL WORDS (f)

la barbe	beard
la beauté	beauty
la confiance	confidence
la conscience	conscience
la couleur ▭	colour
la curiosité ▭	curiosity
une expression	expression
l'habitude	habit
l'humeur	mood, humour
la laideur	ugliness
la larme	tear
les lunettes	glasses
la moustache	moustache
la personne	person
la pièce d'identité ◊ ▭	(means of) identification
la qualité	(good) quality
la taille ◊	height, size; waist

agréable/désagréable pleasant/unpleasant
aimable nice
amusant(e) amusing, entertaining
bête stupid
calme/agité(e) calm/excited
célèbre famous
charmant(e) charming
clair(e) fair (*of skin*), light (*of hair, eyes*)
content(e)/mécontent(e) pleased/displeased
dégoûtant(e) disgusting
drôle funny
formidable great, fantastic
gai(e)/sérieux(euse) cheerful/serious
gentil(le) kind
heureux(euse) happy; **malheureux(euse)** unhappy, unfortunate
important(e) important
méchant(e) naughty
nerveux(euse) nervous, tense
optimiste/pessimiste optimistic/pessimistic
poli polite
sage well-behaved
timide shy

USEFUL WORDS (m) (cont)

l'esprit	wit
le fainéant	idler, loafer
un fanfaron	braggard
les favoris	sideburns
le fayot	crawler, boot-licker
le flatteur	flatterer
le frimeur	poser
le gamin	kid
un garçon manqué	tomboy
le gars [gɑ]	lad; guy
le goujat	boor
l'hippie	hippie
l'hypocrite	hypocrite
un individu	individual
un introverti	introvert
un ivrogne	drunkard
un lève-tard (*pl inv*)	late riser
un lève-tôt (*pl inv*)	early riser
le bohémien	gipsy
le marginal	dropout
le mec	guy, bloke
le menteur	liar
le nain	dwarf
un octogénaire	man in his eighties
le physionomiste	person who has a good memory for faces
le pique-assiette (*pl inv*)	scrounger
le point faible	weak spot
un quadragénaire	man in his forties
un quinquagénaire	man in his fifties
le rabat-joie (*pl inv*)	killjoy
le reclus	recluse
le rentier	person of private *or* independent means
le rêveur	dreamer
le romanichel	gipsy
le septuagénaire	seventy-year-old man
le sexagénaire	sixty-year-old man
le sexiste	sexist
le signe du zodiaque	sign of the zodiac

IMPORTANT WORDS (f)

une allure 🕮	walk, gait
la boucle	curl
la cicatrice	scar
la fossette	dimple
la frange	fringe
la :honte ◇	shame
les lentilles	contact lenses
la permanente	perm
la ressemblance	resemblance, similarity
la ride	wrinkle
la sueur	sweat
la tache de rousseur	freckle
la tache de son 🕮	freckle
la timidité	shyness, timidity

USEFUL WORDS (f)

une abrutie	moron
une albinos (*pl inv*)	albino
une allumeuse	tease, vamp
une andouille ◇	clot, dummy
une arriviste	go-getter
l'assiduité	assiduousness
une aveugle	blind person
la balafre	scar
la bohémienne	gipsy
la bonté	kindness
la bosseuse	hard worker
la bossue	hunchback
la calvitie	baldness
la carrure	build (*of person*)
les cernes	(dark) rings, shadows (under the eyes)

---

c'est une bonne personne he *or* she is a good person
je suis toujours de bonne humeur I am always in a good mood
il est de mauvaise humeur he is in a bad mood
il s'est mis en colère he got angry
elle ressemble à sa mère she looks like her mother
il a l'habitude de se ronger les ongles he has a habit of biting his nails

---

73

DESCRIBING PEOPLE

les **signes particuliers**	distinguishing marks
le **simple d'esprit**	simpleton
le **solitaire**	recluse, loner
le **sosie**	double
le **sourd**	deaf man
le **sourd-muet** (pl ~**s**~**s**)	deaf-mute
le **style de vie**	lifestyle
le **surnom**	nickname
le **tatouage**	tattoo
le **tic**	(nervous) twitch
le **tricheur**	cheat
un **unijambiste**	one-legged man
un **vieux garçon**	bachelor
le **zézaiement**	lisp

aux cheveux oxygénés with bleached hair
avoir un don pour to have a gift for
avoir bonne/mauvaise mine to look well/poorly
avoir des œillères to wear blinkers, be blinkered
avoir la quarantaine to be around forty
avoir de la repartie to be quick at repartee
des mauvaises fréquentations bad company
être d'un abord facile to be approachable
homme de belle/forte carrure well-built/burly man
il a une apparence négligée he is shabby-looking
il bégaye he has a stutter
il mue his voice is breaking
Monsieur/Madame Untel Mr/Mrs so-and-so
(le) torse nu stripped to the waist
(les) bras nus barearmed
nu-jambes, (les) jambes nues barelegged
nu-pieds, (les) pieds nus barefoot
nu-tête, (la) tête nue bareheaded
prendre de l'embonpoint to grow stout
sans apprêt unaffected
se faire faire des mèches to have one's hair streaked
se faire faire une coloration to have one's hair dyed
se faire faire une mise en plis to have one's hair set
se faire faire un brushing to have one's hair blow-dried
un menton saillant prominent chin
souffrir d'un dédoublement de la personnalité to suffer from a split personality

USEFUL WORDS (f) (cont)

la commère	gossip
la crapule	villain
la droitière	right-handed person
une érudite	scholar
la fainéante	idler, loafer
une fanfaronne	braggard
la fillette	(little) girl
la flatteuse	flatterer
la frimeuse	poser
la frisette	little curl
la gamine	kid
la garce	bitch
la gonzesse	chick, bird
une grande personne	grown-up
l'hippie	hippie
la :houppe	tuft (*of hair*)
l'hypocrite	hypocrite
une introvertie	introvert
une ivrogne	drunkard
une lève-tard (*pl inv*)	late riser
une lève-tôt (*pl inv*)	early riser
la mèche	lock (*of hair*)
la marginale	dropout
la menteuse	liar
la naine	dwarf
la nana	bird, chick
la natte	plait
une octogénaire	woman in her eighties
les personnes âgées	the elderly
une quadragénaire	woman in her forties
la queue de cheval	ponytail
une quinquagénaire	woman in her fifties
la raie	parting (*of hair*)
la recluse	recluse
la rentière	person of private *or* independent means
la rêveuse	dreamer
la romanichelle	gipsy
la septuagénaire	seventy-year-old woman
la sexagénaire	sixty-year-old woman

DESCRIBING PEOPLE

la sexiste	sexist
la silhouette	figure
la sourde	deaf woman
la sourde-muette (*pl* ~**s**~**s**)	deaf-mute
la tache de vin	strawberry mark
la tresse	braid, plait
la tricheuse	cheat
une unijambiste	one-legged woman

des pommettes saillantes high cheekbones
avoir la soixantaine to be around sixty
hardi(e) bold, daring; **alerte** agile, nimble
ambitieux(euse) ambitious
anticonformiste nonconformist
arriéré(e) backward; **autodidacte** self-taught
borné(e) narrow-minded; **candide** ingenuous, naïve
boudeur(euse) sullen, sulky
chahuteur(euse) rowdy; **chauvin(e)** chauvinistic
coquet(te) smart; appearance-conscious
daltonien(ne) colour-blind
débrouillard(e) smart, resourceful
décontracté(e) relaxed; laid back
désinvolte casual, off-hand
droitier(ière) right-handed; **gaucher(ère)** left-handed
effronté(e) cheeky, insolent
égoïste selfish; **entêté(e)** stubborn
espiègle mischievous; **excentrique** eccentric
étourdi(e) scatterbrained, absent-minded
frileux(euse) sensitive to (the) cold
galant(e) courteous, gentlemanly
gâteux(euse) senile; **honnête** honest
maladroit(e) clumsy; **muet(te)** dumb
misogyne misogynous, woman-hating
myope short-sighted; **nu(e)** naked
oisif(ive) idle; **paresseux(euse)** lazy
pince-sans-rire *inv* deadpan; **prétentieux(euse)** pretentious
puéril(e) childish; **ras(e)** close-cropped
réfléchi(e) thoughtful; **réservé(e)** reserved
rougir to blush; **sadique** sadistic
sauvage unsociable; **séduisant(e)** seductive; attractive
sénile senile; **sensé(e)** sensible
sensible sensitive; **snob** snobbish

SIGNS OF THE ZODIAC

l'horoscope   horoscope

Bélier	Aries
Taureau	Taurus
Gémeaux	Gemini
Cancer	Cancer
Lion	Leo
Vierge	Virgo
Balance	Libra
Scorpion	Scorpio
Sagittaire	Sagittarius
Capricorne	Capricorn
Verseau	Aquarius
Poissons	Pisces

être (du) Taureau to be Taurus *or* a Taurean
elle est (des) Poissons she is Pisces *or* a Piscean

soigneux(euse) tidy, neat; meticulous
sot(te) silly, foolish; **svelte** slender, slim
sympathique nice, likeable
tatillon(e) pernickety; **téméraire** reckless, rash
têtu(e) stubborn; **trapu(e)** squat, stocky
vaniteux(euse) vain, conceited; **vantard(e)** boastful
vieux jeu *inv* old-fashioned, behind the times
virile manly, virile; **voûté(e)** bent, stooped
xénophobe xenophobic

EDUCATION

ESSENTIAL WORDS (m)

un absent	absentee
l'allemand	German
un ami	friend
l'anglais	English
le baccalauréat, bac ◇ ▭	French school-leaving certificate/exam
le brevet ▭	exam taken at end of 4th form
le bulletin ▭	report
le camarade (de classe)	(school) friend
le certificat	certificate
le CES ▭ (collège d'enseignement secondaire)	comprehensive school
le club	club
le collège	secondary school
le concert ◇	concert
le concours ◇	competitive exam
le copain	pal
le couloir ▭	corridor
les cours	lessons
les cours commerciaux ▭	secretarial studies
le dessin	drawing (subject, work)
le devoir	homework exercise
les devoirs	homework
le diplôme ▭	diploma
le directeur ◇	headmaster
le dortoir ▭	dormitory
un échange	exchange
un écolier	schoolboy
l'électronique ◇ ▭	electronics
un élève	pupil, schoolboy
un emploi du temps ▭	timetable

aimer to like; **détester** to detest; **préférer** to prefer
depuis combien de temps apprenez-vous le français? how long have you been learning French?
j'apprends le français depuis 3 ans I've been learning French for 3 years
apprendre qch par cœur to learn sth off by heart
j'ai des devoirs tous les soirs I have homework every evening
ma petite sœur va à l'école – moi, je vais au collège my little sister goes to primary school – I go to secondary school

ESSENTIAL WORDS (f)

une absence	absence
une absente	absentee
une amie	friend
la biologie	biology
la camarade (de classe)	(school) friend
la cantine	dining hall, canteen
la chimie	chemistry
la classe ▭	class; year; classroom
la conférence	lecture
la copine	pal
la cour ◇ (de récréation)	playground
la cuisine ◇	cookery
la directrice ◇	headmistress
une école (primaire)	(primary) school
une écolière	schoolgirl
l'éducation physique	physical education, P.E.
l'électronique ◇ ▭	electronics
une élève	pupil, schoolgirl
une erreur ◇	mistake, error
l'étude (de) ▭	study (of)
les études ▭	studies
une étudiante ▭	student
une excursion	trip, outing
une expérience ◇ ▭	experiment
la faute ◇ ▭	mistake
la géographie	geography
les grandes vacances	summer holidays
la gymnastique	gym
l'histoire	history; story
une institutrice	primary schoolteacher
la journée ◇	(whole) day; daytime
les langues ◇ (vivantes)	(modern) languages
la leçon (de français)	(French) lesson
la lecture	reading
les mathématiques, math(s)	mathematics, maths
la matière	(school) subject
la musique ◇	music

je vais repasser la leçon demain I'll go over the lesson again tomorrow
repasser ses leçons, réviser to revise

EDUCATION

l'enseignement 📖	education, teaching
l'espagnol	Spanish
un étudiant 📖	student
un examen	exam, examination
le français	French
le groupe	group
un instituteur	primary schoolteacher
l'italien	Italian
le jour de congé	day off, holiday
le laboratoire 📖	laboratory
le lycée	secondary school
le mot	word
le prix ◊	prize
le professeur (*m+f*)	(secondary school) teacher
le progrès 📖	progress
le règlement ◊	rule
le résultat	result
le travail	work
les travaux manuels	handicrafts

un(e) élève sérieux(euse)/paresseux(euse) a serious/lazy pupil
j'aimerais enseigner le français I would like to teach French
le professeur d'allemand the German teacher
en fin de trimestre j'ai gagné un prix I won a prize at the end of term
j'ai dû faire des progrès I must have made progress
bientôt il me faudra passer un examen soon I'll have to sit an exam
est-ce que je vais être reçu(e)? – est-ce que je vais échouer? will I pass? – will I fail?
facile/difficile easy/difficult
intéressant(e) interesting; **ennuyeux(euse)** boring
lire to read; **écrire** to write; **écouter** to listen (to); **regarder** to look at, watch
répéter to repeat; **répondre** to reply; **parler** to speak
elle est (la) première/dernière de la classe she is top/bottom of the class
entrer en classe to go into the classroom
quand je fais une erreur je l'efface et je la corrige when I make a mistake I rub it out and correct it
quelquefois nous faisons des excursions sometimes we go on trips
j'ai fait une faute de grammaire I made a grammatical mistake
ce n'est pas de ma faute it's not my fault
j'ai eu une bonne note I got a good mark *or* good marks
répondez à la question! answer the question!

ESSENTIAL WORDS (f) (cont)

la natation 🕮	swimming
la note ◇ 🕮	mark
la phrase	sentence
la physique	physics
la piscine ◇	swimming pool
la question ◇	question
la récréation	break, interval
la règle ◇	rule
la rentrée (des classes)	beginning of term
la réponse ◇	answer, reply
la salle de classe	classroom
la salle des professeurs	staffroom
la science	science
la traduction	translation (technique, exercise)
une université 🕮	university
les vacances ◇	holidays
la version	(unseen) translation (from French)

CLASSES

sixième (f)	first year of secondary school
cinquième (f)	second year of secondary school
quatrième (f)	third year of secondary school
troisième (f)	fourth year of secondary school
seconde (f)	fifth year of secondary school
première (f)	penultimate year of secondary school
terminale (f)	final year of secondary school

en sixième in first year, in the first form
en première in sixth year, in the sixth form
en terminale in final year

You may want to talk about British concepts of head boy/head girl and prefects. In French these are:
l'élève (*m/f*) **de terminale chargé(e) d'un certain nombre de responsabilités**
and:
l'élève (*m/f*) **des grandes classes chargé(e) de la discipline**

EDUCATION

IMPORTANT WORDS (m)

les arts ménagers	domestic science, homecraft
le brouillon	rough copy
le collège technique	technical college
le couvent	convent; convent school
le demi-pensionnaire (pl ~s)	day-boy
un examinateur	examiner
un exercice	exercise
un externe	day-boy
le grec	Greek
un internat	boarding school
un interne	boarder
le latin	Latin
le lycéen	secondary school pupil
le pensionnaire ◇	boarder
le principal	headmaster (of collège)
le proviseur	headmaster (of lycée)
le rang	row (of seats etc)
le russe	Russian
le test	test
le thème	prose translation
le trimestre	term
le vestiaire	cloakroom
le vocabulaire	vocabulary

USEFUL WORDS (m)

l' ABC	rudiments
un agrégé	holder of the agrégation
un amphithéâtre	lecture theatre
un analphabète	illiterate
l' appel	register
un auditeur libre	unregistered student (attending lectures)
le bachelier	holder of the baccalauréat
le bachotage	cramming

présent(e) present; **absent(e)** absent
punir un(e) élève to punish a pupil
mettre une colle à quelqu'un to give somebody detention, keep somebody in
taisez-vous! be quiet!

IMPORTANT WORDS (f)

l'algèbre	algebra
l'arithmétique	arithmetic
la colle ◇	detention
la composition	composition, essay; class exam
la conduite	behaviour
la couture	sewing, needlework
la distribution des prix	prize-giving
une école maternelle	nursery school
une école mixte	mixed school, co-ed
une école normale	College of Education
l'écriture	handwriting
une épreuve	test
la faculté, fac	university
la feuille de présence ▭	absence sheet
la géométrie	geometry
la grammaire	grammar
l'informatique ◇ ▭	computer studies
l'instruction religieuse	religious instruction
une interne	boarder
la lycéenne	secondary school pupil
la menuiserie	woodwork
la moyenne ▭	fifty per cent, half marks
l'orthographe	spelling
la poésie	poetry
la punition	punishment
la retenue	detention
les sciences naturelles	biology, natural history
la tache	blot
la tâche	task

USEFUL WORDS (f)

l'agrégation	highest teaching diploma in France (*competitive examination*)
une agrégée	holder of the agrégation
une analphabète	illiterate
la bachelière	holder of the baccalauréat
la bourse	grant
la boursière	grant-holder
la cité universitaire	(student) halls of residence

USEFUL WORDS (m) (cont)

le bahut	"school"
le bilinguisme	bilingualism
le boursier	grant-holder
le braille	Braille
le calcul	arithmetic
le cancre	dunce
le carnet de notes	school report
le censeur (*m+f*)	deputy head
le collégien	secondary school pupil
le commentaire de texte	commentary
le concurrent ⟡	candidate
le conférencier	lecturer
le conservatoire	school, academy (*of music, drama etc*)
le contrôle	test
le contrôle continu	continuous assessment
le corrigé	correct version
le doyen	dean (*of faculty*)
un échec	failure
un éducateur spécialisé	specialist teacher
l'effectif	(total) number of pupils
un enseignant	teacher
un établissement scolaire	educational establishment
l'externat	day school
les frais de scolarité	school fees
l'inspecteur d'Académie	(regional) director of education
un intendant	bursar
l'interclasse	break (*between classes*)
le livret scolaire	(school) report
le maître auxiliaire (MA)	temporary teacher
le maître d'école	schoolmaster
le maître de conférences	senior lecturer
le maître-assistant (*pl* ~**s**~**s**)	lecturer
le major de la promotion	first in one's year
le mot d'excuse	note from one's parents (*to explain absence etc*)
le partiel	class exam
le pensionnat	boarding school
le polycopié	handout, duplicated notes
le préau (*pl* -**x**)	covered playground

la collégienne	secondary school pupil
la commission d'examen	board of examiners
la concurrente	candidate
la conférencière	lecturer
la dictée	dictation
la dispense (d'un examen)	exemption (from an exam)
la dissertation	essay
la doyenne	dean (*of faculty*)
l'école maternelle	nursery school
une éducatrice spécialisée	specialist teacher
une encyclopédie	encyclopaedia
une enseignante	teacher
une épreuve d'examen	exam paper
l'étude	study room
la géologie	geology
les grandes écoles	prestigious university-level colleges with competitive entrance examinations
l'infirmerie	sick room
l'inscription	enrolment
l'instruction civique	civics
l'intendance	bursar's office
une intendante	bursar
une interrogation	test
la maître-assistante (*pl* ~s~s)	lecturer
la maîtresse d'école	schoolmistress
la maîtrise	master's degree
la récréation	break
la rédaction	essay, composition
la remplaçante	supply teacher
la résidence universitaire	(university) hall(s) of residence
la stagiaire	trainee
la surdouée	gifted child
la surveillante	monitor; surpervisor
l'unité de valeur (UV)	(university) course, credit

"arrêtez votre bavardage!" ''stop chattering!''
faire l'appel to call the register
il a été recalé he failed

EDUCATION

le premier/second cycle	middle/upper school
le ramassage scolaire	school bus service
le rattrapage	remedial classes
le recteur	(regional) director of education
le réfectoire	refectory
le remplaçant	supply teacher
le restaurant universitaire (RU)	university refectory
le retardataire	latecomer
le secrétariat	(secretary's) office
le stage	training period; training course
le stagiaire	trainee
un sujet d'examen	examination question
le surdoué	gifted child
le surveillant	monitor; supervisor
le télé-enseignement	distance teaching *or* learning

travailler to work; **apprendre** to learn; **étudier** to study
j'ai eu un trou (de mémoire) my mind went blank
matière à option optional subject
se faire exclure de to get o.s. expelled from
un(e) élève brillant(e) a bright pupil
une licence ès lettres/en droit arts/law degree
arriéré(e) backward; **autodidacte** self-taught
décalquer to trace (*a design or map*)
laïque state (*as opposed to private and Roman Catholic*)
redoubler to repeat a year; **retardé(e)** backward
les Français ont congé le mercredi French children have Wednesdays off
mon ami prépare son bac my friend is sitting his school-leaving exam (*like A-levels*)

ESSENTIAL WORDS (m)

l' air ⬦	air
l' aluminium	aluminium
les Amis de la Terre	Friends of the Earth
les animaux	animals
les arbres	trees
un article	article
l' avenir ⬦	future
le bois ⬦ ▭	wood
le climat ▭	climate
le déodorant	deodorant
le détergent	detergent
le(s) dommage(s)	damage
un écologiste	environmentalist, ecologist
l' environnement ▭	environment
un événement	event
le fleuve ⬦	river
les fruits ⬦	fruit
le gas-oil ⬦ ▭	diesel
le gaz ⬦	gas
le gouvernement ⬦	government
les habitants	inhabitants
le journal ⬦ (pl journaux)	newspaper
le lac ⬦	lake
les légumes ⬦	vegetables
le magazine	magazine
le monde ▭	world
le pays ⬦	country
les poissons	fish
le polluant ▭	pollutant
le temps ⬦	weather; time
le trou	hole
le verre ⬦	glass
les Verts	the Greens

j'aimerais faire le tour du monde I'd like to go round the world
le meilleur (la meilleure) du monde the best in the world
il y a beaucoup de monde there are lots of people
à l'avenir in the future
polluer to pollute; détruire to destroy

THE ENVIRONMENT

IMPORTANT WORDS (m)

un atomiseur	aerosol
le canal (*pl* canaux)	canal
le chercheur ◇	researcher
les chlorofluorocarbures (CFCs)	chlorofluorocarbons (CFCs)
le combustible	fuel
le continent	continent
les déchets nucléaires/industriels	nuclear/industrial waste
le dépotoir ▭	dumping ground
le désert	desert
un engrais (chimique) ▭	(artificial) fertilizer
un océan ◇	ocean
le pot catalytique ▭	catalytic converter
le produit	product
les produits chimiques	chemicals
le réchauffement de la terre	global warming
les scientifiques	scientists
l'univers	universe

USEFUL WORDS (m)

un additif	additive
l'affaissement	subsidence
l'aménagement du territoire	town and country planning
l'assainissement	purification; decontamination
le barrage	dam
le colorant	colouring
le détritus	rubbish, refuse
un écologiste	environmentalist, ecologist
l'écosystème	ecosystem
l'effet de serre	greenhouse effect
le gaspillage	waste
un insecticide	insecticide
l'oxyde de carbone	carbon monoxide
un pesticide	pesticide
le réacteur nucléaire	nuclear reactor
le recyclage	recycling
le règne végétal/animal	vegetable/animal kingdom
le sourcier	water diviner

ESSENTIAL WORDS (f)

les **autos**	cars
les **bouteilles**	bottles
la **carte** ◊	map
la **chaleur**	heat
la **côte** ◊	coast
la **crise**	crisis
l'**eau** ◊	water
l'**essence** ◊ ▭	petrol
les **fleurs**	flowers
la **forêt** ◊	forest
une **île** ◊	island
les **informations** ◊ ▭	news
la **lessive** ◊	washing powder; washing
la **mer** ◊	sea
la **montagne** ◊ ▭	mountain
la **nourriture**	food
la **plage**	beach
la **planète**	planet
les **plantes**	plants
la **pluie** ◊	rain
la **pollution** ▭	pollution
la **question** ◊	question
la **région**	region, area
la **rivière** ◊	river
la **solution**	solution
la **taxe** ◊ ▭	tax
la **température** ◊	temperature
la **terre** ◊	earth
une **usine** ◊	factory
la **zone** ▭	zone

contaminer to contaminate; **interdire qch** to ban sth
sauver to save; **recycler** to recycle
vert(e) green; **organique** organic; **biodégradable** biodegradable
nocif(ive) pour l'environnement harmful to the environment
bon(ne) pour la nature environment-friendly
l'**essence sans plomb** unleaded petrol
écologique environmentally friendly
la **consommation d'énergie** power consumption

THE ENVIRONMENT

IMPORTANT WORDS (f)

la **catastrophe**	catastrophe
la **couche d'ozone**	ozone layer
la **forêt tropicale humide**	tropical rainforest
la **lune**	moon
la **nocivité** ⌁	harmfulness
les **pluies acides**	acid rain
la **population**	population
les **vidanges**	sewage

USEFUL WORDS (f)

la **centrale nucléaire**	nuclear power station
la **décharge**	dump; landfill site
la **décomposition**	breakdown of matter
la **défense de l'environnement**	conservation
la **disparition**	disappearance, extinction
une **écologiste**	environmentalist, ecologist
les **économies d'énergie**	energy conservation
l' **élimination des déchets**	waste disposal
l' **érosion**	erosion
la **faune**	wildlife, fauna
la **flore**	flora
la **fuite**	leakage
la **fumée** ◇	smoke
l' **irradiation**	radiation
l' **irrigation**	irrigation
la **mesure antipollution**	anti-pollution measure
les **normes**	standards
la **radioactivité**	radioactivity
la **récupération**	salvage, reprocessing
les **ressources naturelles**	natural resources
les **retombées (radioactives)**	(radioactive) fallout
la **substance toxique**	noxious substance

l'énergie électrique/mécanique/nucléaire/éolienne electrical/mechanical/
  nuclear/wind power *or* energy
la plate-forme de forage/pétrolière drilling/oil rig
la pollution par le bruit noise pollution
qui ne détruit pas l'ozone ozone-friendly
un risque pour la santé a health hazard

ESSENTIAL WORDS (m)

un adolescent	teenager
les adultes	adults
l'âge	age
l'aîné	elder, eldest
le beau-père (pl ~x~s)	father-in-law; stepfather
le bébé 🕮	baby
le cadet	younger, youngest
le célibataire	bachelor
le cousin 🕮	cousin
un enfant	child
l'époux	husband, spouse
le fiancé	fiancé
le fils [fis]	son
le frère	brother
le garçon ◇	boy
les gens 🕮	people
le grand-père (pl ~s~s)	grandfather
les grands-parents	grandparents
l'homme	man
le jeune homme	youth, young man
le mari 🕮	husband
le neveu	nephew
le nom	name
le nom de famille	surname
un oncle	uncle
le parent	parent; relation, relative
les parents	parents; relations, relatives
le père	father
le petit-fils (pl ~s~)	grandson
les petits-enfants [pətizɑ̃fɑ̃]	grandchildren
le prénom	first or Christian name
le veuf	widower
le voisin	neighbour

naître to be born; vivre to live; mourir to die
je suis né(e) en 1980 I was born in 1980
ma grand-mère est morte my grandmother is dead
elle est morte en 1985 she died in 1985
il/elle est célibataire he/she is not married, he is a bachelor/she is a spinster
il est veuf he is a widower; elle est veuve she is a widow

THE FAMILY

IMPORTANT WORDS (m)

le beau-fils [bofis] (pl ~**x**~**s**)	son-in-law
le beau-frère (pl ~**x**~**s**)	brother-in-law
le couple	couple
le demi-frère (pl ~**s**)	half-brother
le gendre	son-in-law
le gosse	kid
les jumeaux	twins
le marié	bridegroom
les nouveaux mariés	newly-weds
un orphelin	orphan
le parrain	godfather
le retraité	(old age) pensioner
le surnom	nickname
les triplés	triplets
le vieillard	old man

USEFUL WORDS (m)

un aïeul	grandfather
les aïeux	forefathers, ancestors
un ancêtre	ancestor
l'arrière-grand-père (pl ~~**s**~**s**)	great-grandfather
les arrière-grands-parents	great-grandparents
l'arrière-petit-fils (pl ~~**s**~)	great-grandson
les arrière-petits-enfants	great-grandchildren
le bambin	little child
les beaux-parents	in-laws
le benjamin ✧	youngest child
le bisaïeul	great-grandfather
le conjoint	spouse
le cousin germain	first cousin
l'entourage	family (circle)
les époux	(married) couple
l'extrait de naissance	birth certificate
le filleul	godson
le grand frère	older brother
le grand-oncle	great uncle
l'héritage	inheritance
un héritier	heir
l'inceste	incest

92

ESSENTIAL WORDS (f)

une adolescente	teenager
l'aînée	elder, eldest
l'allocation familiale 📖	child benefit
la belle-mère (pl ~s~s)	mother-in-law; stepmother
la cadette	younger, youngest
la célibataire	spinster
la cousine 📖	cousin
la dame ◇	lady
une enfant	child
une épouse	wife, spouse
la famille	family
la femme	woman; wife
la fiancée	fiancée
la fille	daughter
la grand-mère (pl ~(s)~s)	grandmother
les grandes personnes	grown-ups
la jeune fille	girl
la jeune fille au pair	au pair girl
la jeunesse	youth (of life); young people
la mère	mother
la nièce	niece
la personne	person; (in plural) people
la petite-fille (pl ~s~s)	granddaughter
la sœur	sister
la tante	aunt
la veuve	widow
la voisine ◇	neighbour

maman! mummy!; **papa!** daddy!
j'ai un frère et une sœur I have one brother and one sister
plus âgé(e) que moi older than me
plus jeune que moi younger than me
je n'ai pas de frères/de sœurs I don't have any brothers/sisters
je suis enfant unique I am an only child
toute la famille the whole family
grandir to grow; **vieillir** to get old
les jeunes, les jeunes gens young people
je m'entends bien avec mes parents I get on well with my parents
compréhensif(ive) understanding
j'ai des disputes avec ma sœur I have arguments with my sister

THE FAMILY

le ménage	(married) couple
le nourrisson	(unweaned) infant
un orphelinat	orphanage
le porte-bébé (*pl*~**s**)	baby sling *or* carrier
les proches	close relatives, next of kin
les quadruplés	quadruplets, quads
les quintuplés	quintuplets, quins
la situation de famille	marital status
le vieux garçon	bachelor

un(e) des voisins one of the neighbours
quel âge avez-vous? how old are you?
j'ai 15 ans – il a 40 ans I'm 15 – he is 40
comment vous appelez-vous? what is your name?
je m'appelle Robert my name is Robert
il s'appelle Jean-Pierre his name is Jean-Pierre
fiancé(e) engaged; **marié(e)** married; **divorcé(e)** divorced; **séparé(e)** separated
épouser qn, se marier avec qn to marry sb
se marier to get married; **divorcer** to get divorced
quel est votre nom/votre nom de famille/votre prénom? what is your name/
  your surname/your first name?
nom de jeune fille maiden name

IMPORTANT WORDS (f)

la belle-fille (*pl* ~s~s)	daughter-in-law
la belle-sœur (*pl* ~s~s)	sister-in-law
la demi-sœur (*pl* ~s)	half-sister
la femme au foyer ◇	housewife
la gosse	kid
la jeune mariée	bride
les jumelles ◇	twins, twin sisters
la marraine	godmother
la ménagère	housewife
la nurse	nanny
une orpheline	orphan
la retraitée	(old age) pensioner
la vieillesse	old age

USEFUL WORDS (f)

une aide familiale	mother's help
une aïeule	grandmother
une ancêtre	ancestor
l'arrière-grand-mère (*pl* ~~~s)	great-grandmother
l'arrière-petite-fille (*pl* ~~s~s)	great-granddaughter
les attaches	ties, connections
la belle-famille (*pl* ~s~s)	in-laws
la benjamine	youngest child
la bisaïeule	great-grandmother
la cagnotte	kitty; nest egg
la conjointe	spouse
la cousine germaine	first cousin
la crèche	crèche, day nursery
la dot	dowry
la fessée	spanking
la fille-mère (*pl* ~s~s)	unmarried mother
la filleule	goddaughter
la garderie	day nursery, crèche
la gouvernante	governess
la grand-tante (*pl* ~s~s)	great aunt
une héritière	heiress
la nourrice	nanny
la pension alimentaire	maintenance allowance, alimony
la personne à charge	dependent

THE FAMILY

USEFUL WORDS (f) (cont)

les quadruplées	quadruplets, quads
les quintuplées	quintuplets, quins
la vieille fille	spinster

ma mère travaille au dehors my mother goes out to work
la nurse s'occupe des enfants the nanny looks after the children
avoir la garde des enfants to have custody of the children
l'acte de mariage/naissance/baptême/décès marriage/birth/baptismal/death certificate
le milieu familial the family circle
un enfant illégitime an illegitimate child
un enfant adoptif/naturel adopted/natural child
neveu/tante par alliance nephew/aunt by marriage
le frère/la sœur de lait foster brother/sister
les parents éloignés distant relatives
feu son père *inv* his/her late father
maternel(le) motherly; maternal
paternel(le) fatherly; paternal

ESSENTIAL WORDS (m)

un **agneau** (pl -**x**)	lamb
un **animal** (pl **animaux**)	animal
le **bœuf** ◇ [bœf] (pl -**s** [bø])	ox
le **canard**	duck
le **champ**	field
le **chat**	cat
le **cheval** (pl **chevaux**)	horse
le **chien**	dog
le **cochon**	pig
le **coq**	cock
le **dindon** ◇	turkey
le **fermier**	farmer
le **mouton** ◇	sheep
le **pays** ◇	country; district
le **paysan** ◇	country person, peasant
le **poulet**	chicken
le **tas**	heap, pile
le **tracteur**	tractor
le **veau** ◇ (pl -**x**)	calf
le **village**	village

IMPORTANT WORDS (m)

un **âne**	donkey
le **bélier**	ram
le **berger**	shepherd
le **bétail**	cattle
le **blé**	corn; wheat
le **chevreau** ▭ (pl -**x**)	kid
un **épouvantail**	scarecrow
un **étang**	pond
le **foin**	hay
le **fossé**	ditch
le **fumier**	manure
le **grain**	grain, seed

un champ de blé a field of corn
cultiver les champs to plough the fields
le chien de berger the sheepdog

FARMING AND AGRICULTURE

le grenier ♢	loft
le :hangar ▱	shed, barn
le laboureur	ploughman
le maïs [ma-is]	maize
le moulin (à vent)	(wind)mill
le porc ♢ [pɔʀ]	pig
le poulailler ♢	henhouse, hen coop
le poulain	foal
le poussin	chick, chicken
le pré	meadow
le puits	well
le ruisseau ♢ (*pl* -**x**)	stream
le seau ♢ (*pl* -**x**)	bucket, pail
le seigle	rye
le sillon	furrow
le sol	ground, earth, land
le taureau (*pl* -**x**)	bull
le troupeau (*pl* -**x**)	flock (*of sheep*); herd (*of cattle*)

USEFUL WORDS (m)

un abattoir	slaughterhouse
l'accouplement	mating
le bétail	cattle
le cheptel	livestock
le colza	rape(seed)
le cultivateur	farmer
l'élevage	cattle breeding
un éleveur	stockbreeder
un exploitant	farmer
le fourrage	fodder
le froment	wheat
le gardeur de chèvres	goatherd
le gardeur de vaches	cowherd
le gardian	cowboy (*in the Camargue*)
le grainetier	seed merchant

s'occuper des animaux to look after the animals
ils mangent du foin et boivent de l'eau they eat hay and drink water

la barrière ◇	gate; fence
la camionnette ◇	(small) van
la campagne	country
la colline	hill
la ferme	farm, farmhouse
la fermière	farmer's wife
la forêt ◇	forest
la paysanne	country woman, peasant
la poule ◇ ▭	hen
la poussière ◇	dust
la terre ◇	earth, ground
la vache	cow

l' avoine	oats
la baratte ▭	churn
la basse-cour (*pl* ~s~s)	farmyard
la boue ◇	mud
la céréale	cereal crop
la charrette	cart
la charrue	plough
la chaumière ◇	(thatched) cottage
la chèvre	goat
une échelle ◇	ladder
une écurie	stable
une étable	cow-shed, byre
la fièvre aphteuse ▭	foot and mouth disease
la gerbe ▭	sheaf
la grange	barn
la lande ◇ ▭	moor, heath
la meule de foin	haystack
la moisson ◇	harvest
la moissonneuse-batteuse (*pl* ~s~s)	combine harvester

vivre à la campagne to live in the country
travailler dans une ferme to work on a farm
la ferme est située au milieu d'un champ the farm is in the middle of a field

FARMING AND AGRICULTURE

USEFUL WORDS (m) (cont)

le :haras	stud farm
l'herbage	pasture
le :houblon	hops
le labour/labourage	ploughing
le maraîcher	market gardener
le maréchal-ferrant	
(pl maréchaux-ferrants)	blacksmith
le métayer	tenant farmer
le meunier	miller
le palefrenier	groom
le pâturage	pasture
la porcelet	piglet
le vendangeur	grape-picker

au chant du coq at cockcrow
faucher to reap
traire to milk
la plantation de café, de coton *etc* coffee, cotton *etc* plantation

IMPORTANT WORDS (f) (cont)

une **oie**	goose
l'**orge**	barley
la **paille** ◇	straw
la **palissade**	fence
la **porcherie**	pigsty
la **récolte** ◇	crop
la **vigne**	vine

USEFUL WORDS (f)

une **auge**	trough
la **bananeraie**	banana plantation
la **bergère**	shepherdess
la **bergerie**	sheep fold
la **cultivatrice**	farmer
une **éleveuse**	stockbreeder
la **faucille**	sickle
la **fromagerie**	cheese dairy
la **gardeuse de chèvres**	goatherd
la **gardeuse de vaches**	cowherd
la **mangeoire**	trough, manger
la **maraîchère**	market gardener
la **métayère**	tenant farmer
la **pintade**	guinea-fowl
la **pisciculture**	fish farming
la **polyculture**	mixed farming
la **(poule) pondeuse**	laying hen
la **tonte**	shearing
la **tourbe**	peat
la **trayeuse**	milking machine
la **vendange**	grape harvest
la **vendangeuse**	grape-picker

rentrer la moisson to bring in the harvest
faire la récolte to bring in the crops

FASHION AND CLOTHES

ESSENTIAL WORDS (m)

un anorak	anorak
le blouson	bomber jacket
le bouton ◊	button
le chapeau (pl -x)	hat
le chemisier	blouse
le col	collar
le collant	(pair of) tights
le complet	suit
le costume ◊	suit (*for man*); costume
le gant	glove
un imper(méable)	raincoat
le jean ◊ [dʒin], jeans	(pair of) jeans
le maillot ◊ (de bain)	swimming costume *or* trunks
le manteau (pl -x)	coat
le mouchoir	hankie, handkerchief
le pantalon	(pair of) trousers
le parapluie ▭	umbrella
le pardessus	overcoat
le pull-over, pull	sweater, jumper, pullover
le pyjama ▭	(pair of) pyjamas
le sac à main	handbag
le sac ◊	bag
le short	(pair of) shorts
le slip ▭	(under)pants
le slip de bain	swimming *or* bathing trunks
le soulier	shoe
le tricot ◊ ▭	jumper, jersey
le T-shirt, tee-shirt	T-shirt, tee-shirt
un uniforme	uniform
le veston	jacket (*for man*)
les vêtements	clothes, clothing

IMPORTANT WORDS (m)

les accessoires	accessories
les bas	stockings
le béret	beret
le bermuda	Bermuda shorts
le(s) bleu(s) de travail	overalls, dungarees

ESSENTIAL WORDS (f)

la botte	boot
la ceinture	belt
la chaussette	sock
la chaussure	shoe
la chemise	shirt
la chemise de nuit	nightie, nightdress
la cravate	tie
la jupe	skirt
la mode 🕮	fashion
la pantoufle	slipper
la poche ◇	pocket
la pointure 🕮	(shoe) size
la robe	dress
la sandale	sandal
la taille ◇	size; waist
la veste	jacket (*for man or woman*)

IMPORTANT WORDS (f)

la blouse	smock, overall
la boutonnière	buttonhole
les bretelles	braces
la cabine d'essayage 🕮	changing cubicle
la canne ◇	cane, (walking) stick
la casquette	cap
la création	model (*garment*)

à la mode in fashion
démodé(e) old-fashioned
cela fait très chic that's very smart
cela vous va bien/mal that suits/doesn't suit you
quelle est votre pointure? what (shoe) size do you take?
quelle est votre taille? what size do you take?
le matin je m'habille in the morning I get dressed
le soir je me déshabille in the evening I get undressed
puis je me rhabille then I get dressed again
porter to wear; **mettre** to put on
j'essaie un béret I try on a beret
puis je l'enlève then I take it off
quand je rentre du lycée je me change when I get home from school I get changed
des soldats en uniforme soldiers in uniform

IMPORTANT WORDS (m) (cont)

le caleçon	(under)pants
le chandail	(thick) jumper
le chapeau (pl -x) melon ⌑	bowler hat
le cuissard	cycle pants or shorts
un ensemble pantalon	trouser suit
le foulard	scarf, headsquare
le gilet	waistcoat; cardigan
le gilet de corps or de peau	vest
l'habit	evening dress, tails
les haillons: en haillons	in rags
les hauts talons	high heels
le jupon	underskirt, petticoat
le képi	(military) cap
le lacet	(shoe)lace
le linge ◇	washing (*items to be washed*)
le nœud papillon	bow tie
le ruban	ribbon
le sac à bandoulière ⌑	shoulder bag
le salon d'essayage	changing room
le soutien-gorge (pl~**s**~)	bra, brassiere
le survêtement	track suit
le sweat [swit]	sweatshirt
le tablier	apron
le tailleur ◇	woman's suit
les talons aiguilles	stiletto heels
les trainings	trainers, training shoes
le tricot de corps	vest

USEFUL WORDS (m)

l'accoutrement	get-up, rig-out
un accroc [akRo]	tear
un après-ski (pl inv)	snow boot
le bandeau (pl -x)	headband
les baskets	trainers
les bas résille	fishnet stockings
le bavoir	bib (*of baby*)
le bonnet	hat
le bonnet de bain	swimming cap
le bouton-pression (pl~**s**~)	press stud

IMPORTANT WORDS (f) (cont)

la culotte	pants (*for child*)
une écharpe ◇	scarf
une espadrille	rope-soled sandal, espadrille
la fermeture éclair	zip
la :haute couture	haute couture
la jaquette	woman's jacket
la jupe-culotte (*pl* ~**s**~**s**)	culottes
la manche	sleeve
la présentation de mode ▭	fashion show
la robe de chambre	dressing gown
la robe de mariée	wedding dress
la robe du soir	evening dress (*for woman*)
la salopette	dungarees, overalls; (ski) salopettes

USEFUL WORDS (f)

la barrette	(hair) slide
la bottine	(ankle) boot
la braguette	fly, flies (*of trousers*)
la cagoule	hood, cowl
la canadienne	fur-lined jacket
la cape	cape; cloak
la capuche	hood (*of a coat*)
la chemisette	short-sleeved shirt
la coiffe	headdress
la combinaison	slip
les cuissardes	thigh boots
la doublure ◇	lining
une échancrure	plunging neckline
une emmanchure	armhole
une encolure en V	V-neck
une épaulette	shoulder strap; shoulder pad
les fringues	clothes
les fripes	second-hand clothes
la gaine	girdle
la godasse	"shoe"
les guenilles	rags
la guêtre	gaiter
la jarretelle	suspender

FASHION AND CLOTHES

le cache-nez (pl inv)	scarf
le caleçon de bain	(swimming) trunks
le châle	shawl
le chausson	slipper
le ciré	oilskin
le corsage	blouse
le décolleté	low neck(line)
le décolleté plongeant	plunging neckline
le déguisement	fancy dress
le demi-bas (pl inv)	kneesock
le déshabillé	négligée
un écusson	badge
un escarpin	court shoe
un éventail	fan
le fichu	(head)scarf
le foulard	scarf
le fuseau (pl -x)	(ski)pants
l' habillement	clothes
les habits	clothes
le :haut-de-forme (pl ~s~~)	top hat
l' henné	henna
le lainage	woollen garment
le maillot une pièce	one-piece swimsuit
le maillot deux pièces	two-piece swimsuit, bikini
le modéliste	(dress) designer
le monokini	topless swimsuit
le nettoyage à sec	dry cleaning
l' ourlet	hem
le pan de chemise	shirt tail
le peignoir de bain	bathrobe
le pli	pleat; crease
le prêt-à-porter	ready-to-wear or off-the-peg clothes
le revers	lapel
le sabot ◇	clog
le smoking	dinner or evening suit
le sous-pull (pl -s)	thin poloneck sweater
les sous-vêtements	underwear
le tailleur-pantalon (pl ~s~s)	trouser suit
le voile	veil

USEFUL WORDS (f) (cont)

la jarretière	garter
la jupe à fronces	gathered skirt
la lingerie	lingerie, underwear
la liseuse	bedjacket
la manchette	cuff
la minijupe	miniskirt
la modéliste	(dress) designer
la modiste	milliner
la moufle	mitt(en)
la paillette	sequin, spangle
la panoplie (d'Indien)	(Red Indian) outfit
la pochette	breast pocket; breast pocket handkerchief
la queue-de-pie (pl ~s~~)	tails, tailcoat
la retouche	alteration
la robe chasuble	pinafore dress
la robe de grossesse	maternity dress
la saharienne	safari jacket
la semelle	sole
la socquette	ankle sock
la tache	stain, mark
la talonnette	heelpiece; stirrup
les tennis	tennis shoes; trainers
la tenue de soirée	evening dress
la voilette	(hat) veil

être/se mettre sur son trente et un to be/get dressed to kill
branché(e) trendy; **étanche** waterproof
rapiécer to patch; **recoudre** to sew back on; **repriser** to darn
retrousser to roll up (*sleeves, trousers*)
long(ue) long; **court(e)** short
une robe à manches courtes/longues a short-sleeved/long-sleeved dress
serré(e) tight; **vague** loose; **ras du cou** crew-neck
une jupe serrée/large a tight/full skirt
rayé striped; **à carreaux** checked; **à pois** spotted
une jupe à plis a pleated skirt; **en tenue de soirée** in evening dress
les vêtements de détente *or* **de loisir** casual clothes
des vêtements de rechange a change of clothes
à l'envers inside out; **des souliers vernis** patent leather shoes
chaussures à semelles compensées platform shoes

FEELINGS AND RELATIONSHIPS

ESSENTIAL WORDS (m)

un amant	lover
l'amour	love
le bonheur	happiness
le divorce	divorce
le sentiment	feeling

IMPORTANT WORDS (m)

l'agacement 📖	irritation, annoyance
le dégoût	disgust
le désaccord	disagreement; conflict, clash
le préjugé	prejudice
le ressentiment	resentment
le soulagement	relief

USEFUL WORDS (m)

l'adultère	adultery
l'affolement	panic
l'amour-propre	self-esteem, pride
le compagnon	companion
le dépaysement	disorientation, feeling of strangeness
le diminutif	pet name
le divorcé	divorcee
l'effarement	alarm, trepidation
l'effarouchement	alarm
l'effroi	terror, dread
l'émerveillement	wonder
le flirt	flirting; (*person*) boyfriend, girlfriend
les inséparables	lovebirds
un intime	close friend
le malentendu	misunderstanding
le ménage à trois	love triangle
le réconfort	comfort

avoir de l'estime pour qn to think highly of sb
avoir la frousse to be scared stiff

108

ESSENTIAL WORDS (f)

l'amitié	friendship
la déception	disappointment
l'émotion	emotion
la :haine	hatred
la :honte ◇	shame
la pitié	pity
la tristesse	sadness

IMPORTANT WORDS (f)

l'anxiété	anxiety
la fidélité	faithfulness
l'horreur	horror
l'impatience	impatience
l'infidélité	unfaithfulness
la patience	patience
la querelle	quarrel
la rancune ▭	grudge, rancour
la revanche	revenge

USEFUL WORDS (f)

l'agressivité	aggressiveness
l'allégresse	elation, exhilaration
une amourette	passing fancy
une arrière-pensée (*pl* ~**s**)	ulterior motive
l'attirance	attraction
l'attraction	attraction
l'audace	daring, audacity
la compagne	companion
la divorcée	divorcee
l'extase	ecstasy
la gaffe	blunder
la :hantise	obsessive fear
une injure	insult, abuse
une insulte	insult
une intime	close friend

FEELINGS AND RELATIONSHIPS

le rival	rival
le tutoiement	use of familiar "tu" form
le vouvoiement	use of formal "vous" form

fidèle faithful
gêné(e) embarrassed
grisant(e) intoxicating, exhilarating
inquiet(inquiète) worried
réagir to react
avoir des remords to feel remorse
avoir de la sympathie pour qn to like sb
avoir la conscience tranquille to have a clear conscience
donner l'accolade à qn to embrace sb
donner/faire un câlin à qn to give sb a cuddle
donner des émotions à qn to give sb a (nasty) fright
en émoi agitated, excited
être aux anges to be in seventh heaven
être fleur bleue to be soppy *or* sentimental

USEFUL WORDS (f) (cont)

la liaison	affair
la maîtresse	mistress
la rivale	rival
la rivalité	rivalry
la rupture	break-up, split
la stupeur	astonishment, amazement
la tendresse	tenderness
la vengeance	vengeance, revenge

garder/perdre son sang-froid to keep/lose one's cool
se réjouir de qch/de faire qch to be delighted about sth/to do sth
semer la zizanie to stir up ill-feeling
vivre séparé to be separated, live apart
un sujet de dispute cause for dispute
une scène de ménage domestic fight
amoureux(euse) in love
contrarier to annoy; bother
convoiter to covet, lust after
énerver to irritate, annoy
envieux(euse) envious
réprimer to suppress
s'énerver to get excited, get worked up
s'entendre (bien/mal) to get on (well/badly)
trahir to betray

FISH AND SHELLFISH

ESSENTIAL WORDS (m)

le crabe	crab
les fruits de mer 🕮	shellfish, seafood
le poisson ◇	fish
le poisson rouge	goldfish

IMPORTANT WORDS (m)

le brochet 🕮	pike
le calmar	squid
le :haddock	haddock
le :hareng	herring
le :homard	lobster
le merlan 🕮	whiting
le poulpe	octopus
le requin	shark
le saumon	salmon
le têtard	tadpole
le thon	tuna

USEFUL WORDS (m)

l' appât	bait
un asticot	maggot
le carrelet	plaice
le colin	hake
les crustacés	shellfish
l' églefin	haddock
un espadon	swordfish
le goujon	gudgeon
le :hameçon	(fish)hook
l' hippocampe	sea horse
le maquereau (*pl* -**x**)	mackerel
le pêcheur ◇	fisherman; angler
le poisson-chat (*pl* ~**s**~**s**)	catfish
le poisson-scie (*pl* ~**s**~**s**)	sawfish
le rouget	mullet
le ver ◇	maggot
le vivier	fish tank; fishpond

112

ESSENTIAL WORDS (f)

l'eau ◊	water
la queue ◊	tail
la sardine	sardine
la truite	trout

IMPORTANT WORDS (f)

une anguille	eel
la crevette	shrimp
l'huître	oyster
la langouste	crawfish, crayfish
les langoustines	scampi
la méduse	jellyfish
la morue	cod
la moule	mussel
la pieuvre 📖	octopus
la sole	sole

USEFUL WORDS (f)

la coquille St-Jacques	scallop
la daurade	sea bream
une écaille	scale
une écrevisse	crayfish
une épuisette	shrimping net
la limande	dab
la limande-sole (*pl* ~s~s)	lemon sole
la lotte	burbot; monkfish
la méduse	jellyfish
la nageoire	fin
la palourde	clam
la raie	skate, ray
la rascasse	scorpion fish

nager dans l'eau to swim in the water
nous allons à la pêche we're going fishing

FOOD AND DRINK

ESSENTIAL WORDS (m)

l'agneau	lamb (*meat*)
un apéritif ▭	aperitif
le bar ▭	bar
le beurre	butter
le bifteck ▭	steak
le biscuit	biscuit
le bœuf ◇	beef
le bol ◇	bowl
les bonbons	sweets
le briquet	lighter
le café ◇	coffee; café
le cendrier	ashtray
le chariot ◇	(supermarket) trolley
le chef ◇ (de cuisine) (*m+f*)	chef, head cook
les chips	crisps
le chocolat (chaud)	(hot) chocolate
le choix ▭	choice
le cidre ▭	cider
le cigare	cigar
le coca	Coke ®, Coca Cola ®
le couteau ◇ (*pl* -x)	knife
le couvert ▭	cover charge; place setting
le croissant	croissant
le croque-monsieur (*pl inv*)	toasted sandwich (*ham/cheese*)
le déjeuner	lunch
le demi	a half (*bottle/litre etc*)
le dessert	dessert
le dîner	dinner
les escargots	snails
le fromage	cheese
un fruit	a piece of fruit, some fruit
les fruits ◇	fruit
les fruits de mer ▭	seafood, shellfish
le garçon ◇	waiter
le gâteau (*pl* -x)	cake

manger to eat; **boire** to drink; **avaler** to swallow
j'aime beaucoup I like; **je déteste** I hate; **je préfère** I prefer
mon repas préféré my favourite meal
qu'est-ce que tu prends à boire? what are you having to drink?

ESSENTIAL WORDS (f)

l'addition ◇	bill
une allumette	match
une assiette ◇	plate
la baguette	French loaf
la bière	beer
la boisson	drink
la boîte	tin, can; box
la bouteille	bottle
la carafe	carafe, jug
la carte ◇	menu
la cigarette	cigarette
la confiture	jam
la confiture d'oranges	marmalade
la côte ◇	chop
la crème ◇	cream
la crêpe ▢	pancake
les crudités ▢	selection of salads
la cuiller, cuillère ◇	spoon
l'eau ◇ (minérale)	(mineral) water
une entrée ◇ ▢	first course
la faim	hunger
la farine	flour
la fourchette ◇	fork
les frites	chips, French fries
la glace ◇	ice cream
l'huile ◇	oil
la limonade	lemonade
la mayonnaise ▢	mayonnaise
la moutarde	mustard
l'odeur	smell

avez-vous du feu? do you have a light?; **une boîte d'allumettes** a box of matches
allumer une cigarette to light (up) a cigarette
"défense de fumer" ''no smoking''; **je ne fume pas** I don't smoke
j'ai arrêté de fumer I've stopped smoking
c'est bon/pas bon it's nice/not nice
déjeuner to have lunch; **dîner** to have dinner; **goûter** to taste
ça sent bon! that smells good!
le vin blanc/rosé/rouge white/rosé/red wine
avoir faim to be hungry; **avoir soif** to be thirsty

FOOD AND DRINK

le goût ⌑	taste
le goûter	tea (*meal*)
le :hamburger	beefburger
les :hors-d'œuvre ⌑	hors d'œuvres, starters
le jambon	ham
le jus de fruit	fruit juice
le lait	milk
le lapin ⌑	rabbit
les légumes ◇	vegetables
le menu	(fixed-price) menu
le mouton ◇	mutton
un œuf [œf] (*pl* -s [ø])	egg
un Orangina	fizzy drink with orange pulp
le pain	bread; loaf
le pain au chocolat	puff pastry bun filled with chocolate
le pain grillé	toast
le parfum ◇ ⌑	flavour
le pâté	pâté
le patron ◇	owner (*of restaurant etc*)
le petit déjeuner ◇	breakfast
le pichet ⌑	jug
le pique-nique (*pl* ~s) ⌑	picnic
le plat	dish; course
le plateau ◇ (*pl* -x)	tray
les plats cuisinés ⌑	cooked dishes
le poisson ◇	fish
le poivre	pepper
le porc ◇	pork
le potage	soup
le poulet (rôti)	(roast) chicken
le pourboire ◇ ⌑	tip
le prix net ⌑	inclusive price
le quart	a quarter (*bottle/litre etc*)
le repas ◇	meal
le restaurant ◇	restaurant
le riz	rice
le rôti ⌑	roast
les salés ⌑	savouries
le sandwich	sandwich

une **olive**	olive
une **omelette**	omelette
la **pâtisserie** ◇ ▭	pastry; pastries
la **pipe**	pipe
la **pizza**	pizza
les **pommes frites**	chips
la **pression** ◇ ▭	draught beer
la **quiche**	quiche
la **recette**	recipe
la **salade**	salad
la **saucisse**	sausage
la **serveuse**	waitress
la **soif**	thirst
la **soucoupe**	saucer
la **soupe**	soup
la **table** ◇	table
la **tarte**	tart
la **tasse** ◇	cup
la **terrine** ▭	terrine, pâté
la **théière**	teapot
la **tranche (de)** ▭	slice (*of*)
la **vaisselle** ◇	dishes
la **viande**	meat

une **assiette anglaise**	selection of cold meats
la **biscotte**	toast (*in packets*)
la **brioche**	bun
la **carte des vins**	wine-list
la **côtelette**	chop
la **crème anglaise**	custard
la **crème Chantilly**	whipped cream
la **cruche**	(milk) jug

ESSENTIAL WORDS (m) (cont)

le saucisson	(*large*) slicing sausage
le sel	salt
le serveur	waiter
le service	service
le sirop	syrup; concentrate
le souper	supper
le steak	steak
le sucre	sugar
les sucrés ⌂	sweet things
le supplément ✧ ⌂	extra charge
le tabac ✧	tobacco; tobacconist's
le thé	tea
le veau ✧ ⌂	veal
le verre ✧	glass
le vin	wine
le vinaigre	vinegar
le yaourt	yoghurt

IMPORTANT WORDS (m)

le bouchon	cork
le cacao	cocoa
le casse-croûte (*pl inv*)	snack
le champagne	champagne
le citron pressé	fresh lemon drink
le cognac	brandy

j'ai faim et j'ai soif I'm hungry and thirsty
mettre le couvert, mettre la table to set *or* lay the table
débarrasser to clear the table
faire la vaisselle to do the dishes *or* the washing-up
délicieux(ieuse) delicious; **appétissant(e)** appetizing; **dégoûtant(e)** disgusting
"plat du jour" ''dish of the day''
"spécialité de la maison" ''speciality of the house''
bon appétit! enjoy your meal!
à votre santé! good health!, cheers!
l'addition s'il vous plaît! the bill please!
est-ce que le service est compris? is service included?
"service (non) compris" ''service (not) included''

IMPORTANT WORDS (f) (cont)

les cuisses de grenouille	frogs' legs
la gelée ◇	jelly
une infusion 💭	herb(al) tea
la margarine	margarine
la miette	crumb
les moules	mussels
la nappe	tablecloth
la nourriture	food
la paille ◇	(drinking) straw
les pâtes	pasta
la purée	mashed potatoes
les rillettes 💭	potted meat (*made of pork or goose*)
la sauce	sauce; gravy
la sauce vinaigrette	vinaigrette *or* French dressing
la serviette ◇	napkin, serviette
la tartine (de beurre)	piece of bread and butter
la tisane	herb(al) tea
les tripes	tripe
la volaille	poultry

USEFUL WORDS (f)

une andouille ◇	sausage made of chitterlings
une arête	(fish)bone
la bouffe	grub
la bouillabaisse	fish soup
la brasserie	pub, brasserie
la brochette	kebab
la canette	bottle (*of beer*)
la cannelle	cinnamon
la capsule	(bottle) cap
les carottes vichy	boiled carrots
la cendre	ash (*of cigarette*)
la cervelle	brain(s)
la chapelure	(dried) breadcrumbs
la chope	tankard
la choucroute	sauerkraut
la ciboulette	chives
la citronnade	lemonade
la collation	light meal

FOOD AND DRINK

IMPORTANT WORDS (m) (cont)

le diplomate (à l'anglaise) ⊞	trifle
le foie ◇	liver
le gibier ◇	game
le glaçon ◇	ice cube
le :haggis	haggis
le ketchup	tomato ketchup
le lard	bacon
les lardons	(chopped) bacon
le miel	honey
le panaché	shandy
le petit pain	roll
le pot à lait	milk jug
le ragoût	stew
les rognons	kidneys
le rosbif	roast beef
le thermos	flask
un toast	slice *or* piece of toast
le whisky	whisky

USEFUL WORDS (m)

les (aliments) surgelés	(deep-)frozen food
les abats	offal; giblets
l'ailloli	garlic mayonnaise
un aloyau (*pl* -**x**)	sirloin
l'amidon	starch
un amuse-gueule (*pl inv*)	appetizer, snack
un anchois (*pl inv*)	anchovy
un arôme	aroma
un arrière-goût (*pl* ~**s**)	aftertaste
l'assaisonnement	seasoning
le basilic	basil
le beignet	fritter; doughnut
le biberon	(feeding) bottle
le Bordeaux	Bordeaux (wine)
le boudin blanc	white pudding
le boudin noir	black pudding
le boudoir ◇	sponge finger (*biscuit*)
le bouillon	broth, stock
le bourgogne	burgundy (wine)

120

la compote de pommes	stewed apples
les conserves	canned *or* tinned foods
la consommation	drink (*in a bar*)
la consommatrice	customer (*in a bar*)
la convive	guest (*at a meal*)
la crêperie	pancake shop
la cuvée	vintage
une dégustation de vin(s)	wine-tasting session
la demi-bouteille (*pl* ~**s**)	half-bottle
l'eau plate	still water
l'eau gazeuse	fizzy water
l'eau-de-vie (*pl* -**x**~~)	brandy
une entrecôte	entrecôte, rib steak
la farce	stuffing
la fine	liqueur brandy
la frangipane	almond paste
la friandise	sweet
la friterie	chip shop
la friture (de poissons)	fried fish
la galette	flat pastry cake; savoury pancake
la gargote	cheap restaurant
la garniture	vegetables
la gastronome	gourmet
la gâterie	little treat
la gaufre	waffle
la gaufrette	wafer
la gorgée	mouthful; sip; gulp
la gourmandise	greed
une gousse d'ail	clove of garlic
la gratinée	onion soup au gratin
la grillade	grill
la guimauve	marshmallow
une habituée	regular customer
la bûche de Noël	Yule log
la liqueur	liqueur
la madeleine	sponge finger cake
la maîtresse de maison	hostess
les matières grasses	fat (content)
la miche	round *or* cob loaf
la mie	inside (*of a loaf*)

FOOD AND DRINK

le cabillaud	cod
le café instantané	instant coffee
le cake [kɛk]	fruit cake
le cassoulet	sausage and bean hotpot, cassoulet
le cerfeuil	chervil
le chausson aux pommes	apple turnover
le chevreuil	venison
un civet de lièvre	jugged hare
le concentré de tomates	tomato purée
le consommateur	customer (*in a bar*)
le contre-filet (*pl ~s*)	sirloin
le convive	guest (*at a meal*)
le cornichon	gherkin
le croque-madame (*pl inv*)	toasted cheese sandwich with a fried egg on top
le croûton	crust (*of bread*)
le cumin	caraway, cumin
le cure-dent (*pl ~s*)	toothpick
un diabolo menthe	mint (cordial) and lemonade
le digestif	(after-dinner) liqueur
un en-cas (*pl inv*)	snack
un entremets	(cream) dessert
un Esquimau (*pl -x*)	ice lolly
le faux-filet (*pl ~s*)	sirloin
le féculent	starchy food
le festin	feast
le flan	custard tart *or* pie
les flocons d'avoine	oatflakes, porridge oats
le friand	(minced) meat pie; small almond cake
le fromage râpé	grated cheese
le fume-cigarette (*pl inv*)	cigarette holder
le fût	barrel, cask

être à la diète to be on a (starvation) diet
faire chauffer au bain-marie (*boîte*) to immerse in boiling water
manger salement to eat dirtily *or* messily
porter à (l')ébullition to bring to the boil

USEFUL WORDS (f) (cont)

la mouillette	finger of bread, soldier
les nouilles	noodles, pasta
une orangeade	orangeade
l'oseille	sorrel
la panure	breadcrumb dressing
la patate	spud
la patate douce	sweet potato
la pâte	pastry
la pâte à choux	choux pastry
la pâte à frire	batter
la pâte à pain	dough
la pâte brisée	shortcrust pastry
la pâte d'amandes	almond paste
la pâte feuilletée	puff *or* flaky pastry
les pommes vapeur	boiled potatoes
la réglisse	liquorice
la restauratrice	restaurant owner
la saumure	brine
la semoule de riz	ground rice
la sucette	lollipop

se gaver de to stuff o.s. with
faire une cure de fruits to go on a fruit diet
servir frais chill before serving
menu à prix fixe set menu
vin d'appellation contrôlée wine guaranteed to be of a certain quality
un steak saignant/à point/bien cuit a rare/medium/well-cooked steak
une rondelle de saucisson a slice of sausage
âcre acrid, pungent
aigre sour
âpre acrid, pungent
comestible edible
croquant(e) crisp, crunchy

le gastronome	gourmet
les germes de soja	beansprouts
le gigot	leg (of mutton or lamb)
le gingembre	ginger
le glaçage	icing
le goudron	tar (of cigarette)
le gourmet	epicure
le gras-double	tripe
le gratin	cheese-(or crumb-)topped dish
les grumeaux	lumps
un habitué	regular customer
le :hareng saur	smoked herring, kipper
le laitage	milk product
le laurier	bay leaves
les macaronis au fromage or au gratin	macaroni cheese
le maître de maison	host
le méchoui	whole sheep barbecue
le mégot	cigarette end or butt
le menu gastronomique	gourmet menu
le mille-feuille (pl ~s)	cream or vanilla slice
le millésime	year; vintage
le moka	mocha coffee; mocha cake
le morceau (pl -x)	piece
le noix de muscade	nutmeg
l'origan	oregano
le pain bis	brown bread
le pain complet	wholemeal bread
le pain de campagne	farmhouse bread
le pain de mie	sandwich loaf
le pain d'épice(s)	gingerbread
le pain de seigle	rye bread
le parmesan	Parmesan (cheese)
le pastis	aniseed-flavoured alcoholic drink
le pâté en croûte	meat pie
le petit pain	roll
le plat à fromages	cheeseboard
le plat cuisiné	pre-cooked meal
le plat de résistance	main course
les plats préparés	convenience food(s)

la **tablette de chocolat**	bar of chocolate
la **tournée**	round (*of drinks*)
la **tourte**	pie
la **truffe**	truffle
la **vanille**	vanilla
la **végétalienne**	vegan
la **végétarienne**	vegetarian
la **verveine**	verbena tea
la **viande hachée**	mince
la **vinaigrette**	vinaigrette, French dressing

un **œuf au plat/poché** fried/poached egg
un **œuf à la coque/dur/mollet** boiled/hard-boiled/soft-boiled egg
des **œufs brouillés** scrambled eggs
au naturel in water; in its own juices
boire au goulot to drink from the bottle
cuit à la vapeur steamed
dîner aux chandelles candlelight dinner
eau (non) potable (non-)drinking water
emballé sous vide vacuum-packed
cru(e) raw
desservir (la table) to clear the table
digérer to digest
filandreux(euse) stringy
garni(e) served with vegetables
glouton(ne) gluttonous, greedy
juteux(euse) juicy
rance rancid
rassis(e) stale
se régaler to have a delicious meal
trinquer to clink glasses
vénéneux(euse) poisonous

FOOD AND DRINK

le porto	port (wine)
le pot-au-feu (*pl inv*)	(beef) stew
le poulet au curry	curried chicken
le pousse-café (*pl inv*)	(after-dinner) liqueur
les rafraîchissements	refreshments
le restaurateur ◇	restaurant owner
le rhum [Rɔm]	rum
le rince-doigts (*pl inv*)	finger bowl
le sablé	shortbread biscuit
le sachet de thé	tea bag
le saindoux	lard
le salon de thé	tearoom
le saumon fumé	smoked salmon
le snack	snack bar
le soja	soya beans
le sucre cristallisé	granulated sugar
le sucre en poudre	caster sugar
le sucre en morceaux	lump sugar
le traiteur	caterer
le végétalien	vegan
le végétarien	vegetarian
le vin de pays	local wine
un zeste de citron	a piece of lemon peel

ESSENTIAL WORDS (m)

un **appareil(-photo)** (*pl* ~**s**~**s**)	camera
l'**argent de poche**	pocket money
le **baby-sitting**	baby-sitting
le **babyfoot**	table football
le **bal**	dance
le **billet** ✧	ticket
le **chanteur (pop)**	(pop) singer
le **cinéma** ✧	cinema
le **club (des jeunes)**	(youth) club
le **concert** ✧	concert
le **concours** ✧	competition
le **correspondant**	pen friend
le **dessin animé**	cartoon
le **disque**	record
le **disque compact** ▭	compact disc, CD
les **échecs**	chess
un **électrophone** ✧	record player
le **feuilleton**	serial; series; ''soap''
le **film**	film
le **:hobby** ▭	hobby
un **intérêt**	interest
le **jeu** ✧ (*pl* -**x**)	game; acting; gambling
le **jouet** ▭	toy
le **journal** ✧ (*pl* **journaux**)	newspaper
les **loisirs**	leisure (activities)
le **magazine**	magazine
le **magnétophone** ✧ **(à cassettes)**	(cassette) recorder
le **magnétoscope**	video (recorder)
le **membre**	member
le **micro-ordinateur** (*pl* ~**s**)	PC, personal computer
le **musée** ✧	museum; art gallery
le **passe-temps** (*pl inv*)	hobby
le **petit ami**	boyfriend
le **programme** ✧	(TV) programme

comment passez-vous le temps? what do you do to pass the time?
je m'intéresse à la musique/aux sports I am interested in music/sport
je sors avec mes amis I go out with my friends
je lis les journaux, je regarde la télévision I read the newspapers, I watch television

127

ESSENTIAL WORDS (m) (cont)

le roman	novel
le son et lumière 📖	sound and light show
le spectacle	show
le télé-journal	TV news
le temps libre	free time, spare time
le théâtre ◇	theatre
le transistor ◇	transistor
le tricot ◇	knitting
le week-end (pl ~s)	weekend; at the weekend

IMPORTANT WORDS (m)

le 33 tours	LP
le 45 tours	single (*record*)
un appareil à sous	one-armed bandit, slot machine
un éclaireur	scout
le fan [fan]	fan
le :hit-parade	charts, hit parade
les mots croisés	crossword puzzle(s)
le palmarès	hit parade
le scout	scout
le vidéoclub	video shop
le Walkman ®	personal stereo

USEFUL WORDS (m)

un adhérent	(club) member
un aoûtien	August holiday-maker
un as (pl inv)	ace
un atout	trump
le baby-sitter (pl ~s)	baby-sitter
le baladeur	personal stereo
le bouquin	book

"avec ou sans filtre?" ''tipped or plain?'' (*of cigarette*)
faire une demande d'admission à un club to apply for membership of a club
faire une balade to go for a walk
faire la grasse matinée to have a lie-in
à court d'argent short of money

ESSENTIAL WORDS (f)

les **actualités**	news
une **affiche** ◇	notice; poster
la **bande** ◇	(recording) tape
la **boum**	party
la **brochure**	leaflet
les **cartes** ◇	cards
la **cassette**	cassette
la **chanson**	singing; song
la **chanteuse** (pop)	(pop) singer
la **collection**	collection
la **correspondante**	pen friend
la **disco(thèque)** ◇	disco
la **distraction**	hobby, entertainment
une **émission**	(TV) progamme
une **excursion**	trip, outing
une **exposition**	exhibition, show
les **informations** ◇ ▭	news
la **lecture**	reading
la **maison des jeunes**	youth club
la **membre**	member
la **musique (pop/classique)**	(pop/classical) music
la **peinture** ◇	painting (*subject, work*)
la **pellicule**	film (*for camera*)
la **petite amie**	girlfriend
la **(petite) annonce**	advert; small ad
la **photo**	photo
la **promenade** ◇	walk; trip, outing
la **publicité** ◇ ▭	publicity
la **radio** ◇	radio
la **randonnée** ▭	walk; hike; drive
la **réunion**	meeting
la **revue** ▭	magazine
la **soirée**	evening
la **surprise-partie** (*pl* ~**s**~**s**)	party

mon hobby préféré my favourite hobby
je m'amuse à bricoler/à faire du baby-sitting I enjoy doing odd jobs/baby-sitting
je joue au football/au tennis/aux cartes I play football/tennis/cards
je joue du piano/de la guitare *etc* I play the piano/guitar *etc*

USEFUL WORDS (m) (cont)

le carreau	diamonds (*in cards*)
le cartomancien	fortune-teller (*who uses cards*)
le centre d'animation	community centre
le cerf-volant [sɛRvɔlɑ̃] (*pl* ~s~s)	kite
le cibiste	CB enthusiast
le ciné-club (*pl* ~s)	film club
le cœur	hearts (*in cards*)
le colin-maillard	blind man's buff
le collectionneur	collector
le coloriage	colouring (*for children*)
le conte	tale, story
le conte de fées	fairy tale
le conteur	storyteller
le damier	draughtboard
le dancing	dance hall
le deltaplane	hang-glider
le divertissement	entertainment
un échiquier	chessboard
le flipper	pinball (machine)
le forfait-vacances	package holiday
le gage	forfeits
le golf miniature	crazy *or* miniature golf
un illustré	illustrated magazine; comic
le jeu de société	parlour game
le manège	roundabout, merry-go-round
le parc d'attractions	amusement park
le pari mutuel urbain (PMU)	system of betting on horses
le parieur	punter
le pique	spades (*in cards*)
le puzzle	jigsaw (puzzle)
le roman d'espionnage	spy novel
le roman noir	thriller
le roman policier	detective novel
le roman-feuilleton (*pl* ~s~s)	serialized novel
le roman-photo (*pl* ~s~s)	(romantic) picture story
les sites touristiques	places of interest
le terrain de jeu	playground
le trèfle ◇	clubs (*in cards*)
le trictrac	backgammon
le valet	jack, knave (*in cards*)

ESSENTIAL WORDS (f) (cont)

la tapisserie ◇	tapestry
la télé(vision) ◇	TV, television
la vedette ◇ (de cinéma) (*m+f*)	(film) star
la vidéocassette	video (cassette)

IMPORTANT WORDS (f)

la boîte de nuit	night club
la chorale	choir
la colonie de vacances	holiday camp
la couture	sewing, needlework
les dames ◇	draughts
la diapositive	slide, transparency
une éclaireuse	girl guide
la grosse radiocassette	ghetto blaster
la photographie	photograph; photography
la planche à roulettes	skateboard

où on se rencontre? where shall we meet?
je passerai chez toi I'll call round for you
faire la sieste to have a snooze *or* nap
faire un tour to go for a walk *or* a stroll
jeu en plein air outdoor games
jouer aux billes to play marbles
jouer à cache-cache to play hide-and-seek
jouer au cerf-volant to fly a kite
j'ai vu à la télévision ... I saw on television ...
j'ai entendu à la radio ... I heard on the radio ...

FREE TIME

USEFUL WORDS (f)

une adhérente	(club) member
l'adhésion	membership
une amicale	association, club
une aoûtienne	August holiday-maker
une arbalète	crossbow
une association	association
la baby-sitter (pl ~s)	baby-sitter
la balançoire	swing
la caméra ◊	cine-camera
la cartomancie	card-reading
la cartomancienne	fortune-teller (*who uses cards*)
la cibiste	CB enthusiast
la collectionneuse	collector
la conteuse	storyteller
la cravache	(riding) crop
la détente	relaxation
les fléchettes	darts
l'histoire	story
la maquette	model; mock-up
la pâte à modeler	Plasticine ®
la pause-café (pl ~s~)	coffee break
la réussite	patience (*cards*)
la roulette russe	Russian roulette
la série noire	(crime) thriller
la vannerie	wickerwork, basketwork

si je m'ennuie je . . . if I get bored I . . .
jouer aux osselets to play jacks; **jouer au pendu** to play hangman
"pile ou face?" ''heads or tails?''; **jouer à pile ou face** to toss up (for it)
jouer à la poupée to play with one's doll
jouer à saute-mouton to play leapfrog
passionnant(e) exciting; **ennuyeux(euse)** boring
amusant(e) funny; **pas mal** not bad, quite good
faire des photos to take photos; **sauter à la corde** to skip (with a rope)
jeu de quilles ninepins, skittles; **divertissant(e)** amusing, entertaining
on se réunit le vendredi we meet on Fridays
je fais des économies pour acheter un Walkman ® I'm saving up to buy a
  Walkman ®
gagner to earn; **emprunter** to borrow; **prêter** to lend; **coûter** to cost; **payer** to pay
acheter to buy; **rembourser** to pay back
flâner to stroll; **"atout pique/trèfle"** ''spades/clubs are trumps''

ESSENTIAL WORDS (m)

un abricot	apricot
un abricotier	apricot tree
un ananas	pineapple
un arbre fruitier	fruit tree
le bananier	banana tree
le cerisier	cherry tree
le citron	lemon
le citronnier	lemon tree
un fruit	a piece of fruit, some fruit
les fruits ◊	fruit
le marron ◊ (grillé)	(roasted) chestnut
le melon	melon
l'oranger	orange tree
le pamplemousse	grapefruit
le pêcher	peach tree
le poirier	pear tree
le pommier	apple tree
le raisin	grape(s)

IMPORTANT WORDS (m)

un avocat ◊	avocado (pear)
le cassis	blackcurrant (*fruit, bush*)
le dattier	date palm
le figuier	fig tree
le fruit de la passion	passion fruit
le kiwi	kiwi fruit
le noisetier ▱	hazel tree
le noyau (*pl* -**x**)	stone (*in fruit*)
le noyer ▱	walnut tree
le pépin	pip (*in fruit*)
le pruneau (*pl* -**x**)	prune
le prunier	plum tree
le verger ◊	orchard
le vignoble	vineyard

un jus d'orange/d'ananas an orange/a pineapple juice
une grappe de raisin a bunch of grapes
les raisins secs raisins
mûr(e) ripe; **pas mûr(e)** unripe

FRUIT

ESSENTIAL WORDS (f)

la banane	banana
la cerise	cherry
la fraise	strawberry
la framboise	raspberry
une orange	orange
la peau ⌑	skin
la pêche ◇	peach
la poire	pear
la pomme	apple
la tomate	tomato; tomato plant

IMPORTANT WORDS (f)

la baie ◇	berry
la datte	date
la figue	fig
la grenade	pomegranate
la groseille	redcurrant
la groseille à maquereau	gooseberry
la mandarine	tangerine
la mûre	blackberry, bramble
la myrtille	bilberry
la noisette	hazelnut
la noix	nut; walnut
la noix de coco	coconut
la prune	plum
la rhubarbe	rhubarb
la vigne	vine

USEFUL WORDS (f)

une amande	almond
une arachide	peanut, monkeynut
la cacahuète	peanut
la clémentine	clementine
la grappe de raisin	bunch of grapes
la mangue	mango
la noix de cajou	cashew nut
la pastèque	watermelon
la pistache	pistachio (nut)

ESSENTIAL WORDS (m)

un **appareil**	appliance; device
un **aspirateur**	vacuum cleaner, Hoover ®
le **buffet** ◇	sideboard
le **bureau** ◇ (*pl* -**x**)	bureau, writing desk
le **canapé**	sofa, settee, couch
le **coffre** ◇	chest
le **congélateur**	freezer
un **électrophone** ◇	record player
le **fauteuil**	armchair
le **frigidaire, frigo** ◇	fridge
le **lecteur de disques**	
compacts ⌑	CD player
le **lit** ◇	bed
le **magnétophone** ◇	tape recorder
le **magnétoscope** ◇	video (recorder)
un **meuble** ⌑	a piece of furniture
les **meubles** ◇ ⌑	furniture
le **miroir** ◇	mirror
le **piano** ◇ ⌑	piano
le **placard** ◇	cupboard
le **radiateur** ◇ ⌑	radiator, heater
le **rayon** ◇	shelf
le **tableau** ◇ (*pl* -**x**)	picture
le **téléphone**	telephone
le **téléviseur** ◇ (**couleur**)	(colour) television
le **transistor** ◇	transistor (radio)

IMPORTANT WORDS (m)

le **berceau** (*pl* -**x**)	cradle
le **cadre** ◇	frame
le **camion de déménagement**	removal van
le **déménagement** ◇	removal
le **déménageur**	removal man
le **lampadaire** ⌑	standard lamp

un appartement meublé/une pièce meublée a furnished flat/room
allumer/éteindre le radiateur to switch on/off the heater
je fais mon lit le matin I make my bed in the morning
s'asseoir to sit down; **asseyez-vous!** (do) sit down!

FURNITURE AND APPLIANCES

IMPORTANT WORDS (m) (cont)

le lit d'enfant	cot
les lits superposés	bunk beds
le matelas	mattress
le mobilier	furniture
le porte-parapluies (*pl inv*)	umbrella stand
le répondeur automatique	telephone answering machine
le sèche-cheveux (*pl inv*)	hair-dryer
le secrétaire ◇ ⊡	writing desk
le siège	seat
le store	blind
le tabouret	stool
le téléphone sans fil	cordless telephone
le tiroir	drawer
le tourne-disque (*pl* ~**s**)	record player

USEFUL WORDS (m)

un abat-jour (*pl inv*)	lampshade
un accoudoir	armrest
le divan	divan
le divan-lit (*pl* ~**s**~**s**)	divan (bed)
le (fauteuil-)relax	reclining chair
le fer à friser	curling tongs
le gadget	thingamajig
un garde-meuble (*pl* ~**s**~(**s**))	furniture depository
le guéridon	pedestal table
le lit à baldaquin	canopied fourposter bed
le lit-cage (*pl* ~**s**~**s**)	folding bed
le lustre	chandelier
le monte-charge (*pl inv*)	goods lift
le paravent	folding screen
le pèse-personne (*pl* ~**s**)	(bathroom) scales
le plafonnier	ceiling light
le portemanteau (*pl* -**x**)	coat rack
le radio-réveil (*pl* ~**s**)	clock radio
le réparateur	repairer
le sèche-mains (*pl inv*)	hand dryer
le vaisselier	dresser
le ventilateur	fan

ESSENTIAL WORDS (f)

une **armoire**	wardrobe
la **bibliothèque** ◇	bookcase
la **chaîne stéréo**	stereo system
la **chaise**	chair, seat
la **glace** ◇	mirror
la **lampe** ◇	lamp
la **machine à laver** ◇ ▭	washing machine
la **maison** ◇	house
la **peinture** ◇	painting
la **pendule**	clock
la **pièce** ◇	room
la **radio** ◇	radio
la **table** ◇	table
la **table basse**	coffee table
la **télévision**	television

IMPORTANT WORDS (f)

la **caméra** ◇	cine camera
la **caméra vidéo**	video camera, camcorder
la **chaîne compacte (stéréo)**	music centre
la **coiffeuse** ◇	dressing table
la **commode**	chest of drawers
une **étagère**	(set of) shelves
la **moquette**	fitted carpet
la **table de chevet**	bedside table
la **table de toilette**	dressing table
la **table roulante**	trolley

USEFUL WORDS (f)

une **applique**	wall lamp
une **essoreuse**	spin-dryer
la **garde-robe** (*pl* ~**s**)	wardrobe
la **glace sans tain**	two-way mirror
la **télécommande**	remote control

c'est un appartement de 4 pièces it's a 4-roomed flat
mettre le couvert, mettre la table to set *or* lay the table
à table, tout le monde! come and eat, everybody!, dinner (*or lunch etc*) is ready!

GEOGRAPHICAL FEATURES

ESSENTIAL WORDS (m)

le **désert**	desert
le **lac** ◇	lake
un **océan** ◇	ocean
le **rocher**	rock

IMPORTANT WORDS (m)

le **delta**	delta
le **fjord**	fjord, fiord
le **fleuve** ◇	river
le **glacier**	glacier
le **golfe**	gulf
le **marais**	marsh, swamp
le **marécage** ▭	marsh, swamp
le **ruisseau** ◇ (pl -**x**)	stream, brook
le **sommet** ◇	summit, top
le **tremblement de terre**	earthquake

USEFUL WORDS (m)

un **abîme**	abyss, gulf
un **affluent**	tributary
un **archipel**	archipelago
l' **arrière-pays** (pl inv)	hinterland
le **col**	(mountain) pass
le **continent**	continent
le **cours d'eau**	waterway
le **cratère**	crater
le **détroit**	strait
l' **équateur**	equator
un **estuaire**	estuary
le **glissement de terrain**	landslide
le **gouffre**	abyss, gulf
un **iceberg** [ajsbɛʀg]	iceberg
le **précipice**	chasm
le **ravin**	gully, ravine
le **récif**	reef
les **sables mouvants**	quicksand(s)
le **vallon**	small valley
le **volcan**	volcano

138

ESSENTIAL WORDS (f)

une île ◇	island
la mer ◇	sea
la montagne ◇	mountain
la rivière ◇	river
la vallée	valley

IMPORTANT WORDS (f)

la chaîne ◇ **(de montagnes)**	(mountain) range
la falaise ◇	cliff
la péninsule	peninsula
la plaine	plain
la presqu'île	peninsula
la roche	rock
la source	spring

USEFUL WORDS (f)

une avalanche	avalanche
la cascade	waterfall
la crevasse	crevasse
la dune	dune
la gorge	gorge
la grotte ◇	cave
la jungle	jungle
la lande ◇	moor
la lave	lava
une oasis	oasis
la secousse sismique	earth tremor

l'hémisphère nord/sud northern/southern hemisphere
en amont upstream; **en aval** downstream

GEOGRAPHICAL NAMES

ESSENTIAL WORDS

les Alpes (*fpl*)	the Alps
l'Atlantique (*m*)	the Atlantic
Bordeaux	Bordeaux
Boulogne	Boulogne
la Bourgogne	Burgundy
la Bretagne	Brittany
Bruxelles	Brussels
la Côte d'Azur	the Cote d'Azur
Dieppe	Dieppe
la Dordogne ⊞	the Dordogne
Douvres	Dover
Édimbourg	Edinburgh
la Garonne	the Garonne
le :Havre	le Havre
la Loire	the Loire
Londres	London
Lyon	Lyons
la Manche	the English Channel
Marseille	Marseilles
le Massif Central	the Massif Central
la (mer) Méditerranee	the Mediterranean
la mer du Nord	the North Sea
le Midi	the Midi, the South of France
la Normandie	Normandy
Paris	Paris
les Pyrénées (*fpl*)	the Pyrenees
Québec ⊞	Quebec (city)
le Québec ⊞	Quebec (state)
le Rhin ⊞	the Rhine
le Rhône	the Rhone
la Seine	the Seine
la Tamise ⊞	the Thames

aujourd'hui je vais à Calais/au Havre today I'm going to Calais/to Le Havre
je viens de Londres/du Massif Central I come from London/from the Massif
Central
je vais en Normandie I'm going to Normandy
la capitale the capital; **le chef-lieu** the main town

IMPORTANT WORDS

Alger	Algiers
Anvers 🕮	Antwerp
Athènes	Athens
Bâle	Basle
Barcelone	Barcelona
Berlin	Berlin
le Caire	Cairo
la Corse	Corsica
l'Extrême-Orient (*m*)	the Far East
Genève	Geneva
la Haye	The Hague
les îles (*fpl*) **anglo-normandes**	the Channel Islands
les îles Britanniques	the British Isles
le Jura	the Jura Mountains
le lac Léman 🕮	Lake Geneva
Lisbonne	Lisbon
Moscou	Moscow
le Moyen-Orient	the Middle East
le Pacifique	the Pacific
Pékin	Beijing
le Pôle nord/sud	the North/South Pole
le Proche-Orient	the Near East
la Sardaigne	Sardinia
Varsovie	Warsaw
Venise	Venice
Vienne (*Autriche*)	Vienna
les Vosges (*fpl*)	the Vosges Mountains

USEFUL WORDS

l' Arménie (*f*)	Armenia
le/la Basque	Basque
les Caraïbes (*fpl*)	the Caribbean
la Champagne	Champagne, the Champagne region
le Chypre	Cyprus
la Crète	Crete
le golfe Persique	the Persian Gulf
le Pays basque	the Basque country

GREETINGS AND INTERJECTIONS

GREETINGS

bonjour hello; good morning; good afternoon
salut hello, hi; goodbye
ça va? how are you?, how's things?
ça va! (*in reply*) fine!
enchanté(e) (de faire votre connaissance) (very) pleased to meet you
allô hello (*on telephone*)
bonsoir good evening, hello; good night
bonne nuit good night (*when going to bed*)
au revoir goodbye
à demain see you tomorrow
à bientôt, à tout à l'heure see you later
adieu goodbye, farewell
faire ses adieux (à qn) to say one's farewells (to sb)
une étreinte embrace, hug
la poignée de main handshake
donner le baisemain à qn to kiss sb's hand
faire une bise à qn to give sb a kiss
serrer la main à qn to shake sb's hand
s'embrasser to kiss each other

BEST WISHES

bon anniversaire happy birthday
bonne fête happy "saint's day"
joyeux Noël merry Christmas
bonne année happy New Year
joyeuses Pâques happy Easter
meilleurs vœux best wishes
félicitations congratulations
les compliments congratulations
bon appétit have a nice meal, enjoy your meal
bon courage all the best, chin up
bonne chance good luck
bons baisers love (and kisses) (*at end of letter*)
grosses bises love (*at end of letter*)
à tes (*or***vos) souhaits** bless you (*after a sneeze*)
à la tienne (*or***la vôtre)** cheers
à ta (*or***votre) santé** good health

GREETINGS AND INTERJECTIONS

mon Dieu my goodness
eh bien, eh ben well
comment?, hein?, eh?, quoi? what (was that?)
ah bon oh, I see
ça, par exemple well, well; my word; really
que de . . . what a lot of . . .
sans blague(?) really(?)
ah oui?, c'est vrai?, vraiment? really?
tu rigoles, tu plaisantes you're kidding *or* joking
quelle chance! what a stroke of luck!
tiens! well, well!

s'il vous (*or* te) plaît please; excuse me (*when approaching stranger*)
merci thank you; no, thank you
non merci no thank you; **oui merci** yes please
de rien, je vous en prie, il n'y a pas de quoi not at all, it's quite all right, don't
  mention it
volontiers willingly, with pleasure
présenter ses hommages à une dame to pay one's respects to a lady

oui yes
mais oui, bien sûr of course
d'accord O.K., all right
bon, bien fine, O.K.
c'est entendu(?) agreed(?)
soit! [swa] so be it, agreed
justement exactly, that's just it
tant mieux so much the better
ça m'est égal I don't mind, it's all the same to me

GREETINGS AND INTERJECTIONS

non no; **ah non alors!** oh no!, no no!
mais non no (*contradicting a positive statement*)
si, mais si yes (*contradicting a negative statement*)
bien sûr que non of course not
jamais de la vie never, not on your life
pas du tout not at all, far from it
au contraire on the contrary
tant pis too bad
oh mais non, vraiment really (*exasperated*)
ça, par exemple well I never, well really
quel culot, quel toupet what a cheek, what a nerve
mêlez-vous de vos affaires mind your own business
cela dépend that depends, it all depends
quand même even so; really (*exasperated*), that's a bit much
à bas ... down with ...

à l'aide! help!
au secours help; **au feu** fire; **aïe** ouch, ow
hélas alas, oh dear
pardon (I'm) sorry, excuse me, I beg your pardon
je m'excuse I'm sorry (*for having done*)
je regrette I'm sorry
les condoléances condolences
désolé(e) I'm (really) sorry
c'est dommage, quel dommage what a pity
zut, flûte, mince alors drat, dash, bother; **mince alors** dash it
j'en ai marre I'm fed up with it
c'en est trop it's (just) too much
je n'en peux plus I can't stand it any more
oh là là oh dear
quel bazar!, quelle pagaille! what a shambles!
quelle horreur what a thought; how awful
que faire? what shall I (*or* we) do?
à quoi bon ... (+ *infinitive*) what's the use of ...?
que je suis (fatigué etc**)** how (tired *etc*) I am
c'est embêtant (de ...) it's embarrassing (to ...)
ça m'embête it bothers me
ça m'agace it annoys me, it gets on my nerves

attention watch, be careful
halte-là stop
hep *or* **eh** , **vous là-bas** hey, you there
fiche-moi le camp clear off, clear out
chut shhhh
ça suffit that's enough
défense de (fumer *etc***)** no (smoking *etc*)
doucement gently, go easy, easy does it
allons go on, come on
allons-y let's go
allez-y, vas-y on you go, go on, go ahead

ah bon oh well, O.K.
et alors well (*threatening*); so what?, so?
eh bien . . . well . . .
aucune idée no idea
peut-être perhaps, maybe
je ne sais pas I don't know
vous désirez? can I help you?
voici, tiens (or**tenez)** here, here you are
voilà there, there you are
j'arrive just coming
ne t'en fais pas don't worry
mettez-vous à l'aise make yourself comfortable
ce n'est pas la peine it's not worth it
à propos by the way
dis donc (or**dites donc)** listen, I say
chéri(e) darling
le (or**la) pauvre** poor thing
vivement les vacances! I can't wait for the holidays!

HEALTH

l' accident	accident
le brancard	stretcher
le cabinet (de consultation) ⌒	surgery
le cachet	tablet
le comprimé	tablet
le coton hydrophile	cotton wool
un coup de soleil	sunburn
le dentiste (m+f)	dentist
le docteur ⌒ (m+f)	doctor
l' hôpital (pl hôpitaux)	hospital
un infirmier ◇ ⌒	(male) nurse
le lit ◇	bed
le malade	patient
le médecin (m+f)	doctor
le médicament	medicine, drug
le pansement	dressing; bandage
le patient ⌒	patient
le pharmacien ◇	chemist
le plâtre ◇	plaster (cast)
le remède ⌒	remedy, cure
le rendez-vous (pl inv)	appointment
un rhume	cold
le sang ⌒	blood
le sirop	syrup
le sommeil ⌒	sleep
le sparadrap	sticking plaster
le ventre	stomach

il y a eu un accident there's been an accident
être admis(e) à l'hôpital to be admitted to hospital
vous devez rester au lit you must stay in bed
se sentir malade, être souffrant(e) to feel ill
se sentir mieux to feel better
j'ai chaud/froid I'm hot/cold
ça me fait mal au cœur it makes me feel sick
maigrir to lose weight; **grossir** to put on weight
avaler to swallow; **saigner** to bleed
se reposer to rest; **guérir** to cure
gravement blessé(e) seriously injured
sous surveillance médicale under medical supervision

146

ESSENTIAL WORDS (f)

une **ambulance** ◊	ambulance
une **aspirine**	aspirin
l'**assurance** ▭	insurance
la **blessure**	injury, wound
la **clinique**	clinic, hospital
la **crème** ◊	cream, ointment
la **cuillerée** ▭	spoonful
la **diarrhée**	diarrhoea
la **douleur**	pain
la **fièvre**	fever, (high) temperature
la **grippe**	flu, influenza
une **infirmière** ▭	nurse
une **insolation** ▭	(a touch of) sunstroke
la **maladie**	illness
la **médecine**	(*science of*) medicine
une **opération** ▭	operation
une **ordonnance** ◊	prescription
la **pastille**	lozenge
la **patiente** ▭	patient
la **pharmacie** ◊	chemist's (shop)
la **pilule**	pill; the Pill
la **piqûre**	injection; sting
la **salle de consultation**	surgery
la **santé**	health
la **température** ◊	temperature

je me suis blessé(e), je me suis fait (du) mal I have hurt myself
il s'est cassé le bras *etc* he has broken his arm *etc*
je me suis brûlé la main I have burnt my hand
elle s'est coupé le doigt she has cut her finger
j'ai mal à la gorge/mal aux dents/mal à la tête/mal au ventre I've got a sore
  throat/toothache/a headache/a stomach ache
êtes-vous assuré(e)? are you insured?
remets-toi vite! get well soon!
aller à la consultation to go to the surgery
avoir des aigreurs d'estomac to have heartburn
avoir une attaque to have a heart attack; to have a stroke
avoir des battements de cœur to have *or* get palpitations
avoir des bourdonnements d'oreilles to have a buzzing (noise) in one's ears
opérer qn des amygdales to take sb's tonsils out

IMPORTANT WORDS (m)

un abcès	abscess
un accès	fit
le bandage	bandage
le bleu ◇	bruise
le cancer	cancer
le choc	shock
le dentier	(set of) false teeth
le fauteuil roulant	wheelchair
le fortifiant ▭	tonic
le microbe	germ
le nerf	nerve
un œil (*pl* **yeux**) poché	black eye
les oreillons	mumps
le poison	poison
le pouls [pu]	pulse
les premiers secours *or*	
les premiers soins	first aid
le régime	diet
le repos	rest
le rhume des fcins	hayfever
le Sida, SIDA	Aids, AIDS
le sidéen	Aids victim
le vertige	(attack of) dizziness
le virus HIV	HIV virus

USEFUL WORDS (m)

l' abus de boisson	excessive drinking
l' accouchement	delivery
l' accouchement naturel	natural childbirth
un alcoolique	alcoholic
l' allaitement maternel	breast-feeding
l' allaitement au biberon	bottle-feeding
un ambulancier ◇	ambulanceman
les antécédents médicaux	past medical history
un antibiotique	antibiotic
un anticorps	antibody
un aphte	mouth ulcer
l' asthme	asthma
un avortement	abortion

IMPORTANT WORDS (f)

une ampoule ◇	blister
une angine	tonsillitis
une appendicite	appendicitis
la bande ◇	bandage
la béquille ◇	crutch
la cicatrice	scar
la coqueluche 📖	whooping cough
la crise cardiaque	heart attack
une écharde 📖	splinter
une écharpe ◇	sling
une égratignure	scratch
une épidémie	epidemic
la guérison	recovery
une intervention	operation
la maison de retraite	old folks' home
la meurtrissure	bruise
la migraine	migraine
la nausée	sickness, vomiting
l' ouate (hydrophile)	cotton wool
la plaie	wound
la pommade	ointment
la radio(graphie)	X-ray
la rougeole	measles
la rubéole	German measles
la salle ◇ (d'hôpital)	ward
la toux	cough
la transfusion sanguine	blood transfusion
la typhoïde	typhoid
la varicelle	chickenpox
la variole	smallpox

avoir des ganglions to have swollen glands
avoir des insomnies to suffer from insomnia
avoir un malaise to feel faint *or* dizzy; **avoir mal aux reins** to have backache
avoir de la tension to have high blood pressure
c'est contagieux it's contagious; **être cardiaque** to have a heart condition
elle s'est cassé le col du fémur she has broken her hip
enceinte (de six mois) (6 months) pregnant
se fêler le bras to crack a bone in one's arm
se fouler la cheville to sprain one's ankle

le barbiturique	barbiturate
le baume	balm, balsam
le bébé-éprouvette (pl~**s**~)	test-tube baby
un bilan de santé	check-up
le brancardier	stretcher-bearer
le caillot	(blood) clot
le calmant	painkiller
le cancérologue	cancer specialist
le cardiologue	cardiologist
le cataplasme	poultice
le claquage	pulled *or* strained muscle
le collutoire	throat spray
le collyre	eye lotion
le contraceptif	contraceptive
le contrepoison	antidote
le cor (au pied)	corn
le curiste	person taking the waters (*at a spa*)
le débile mental	mental defective
le dépistage	screening
le désinfectant	disinfectant
le diabète	diabetes
le diabétique	diabetic
le diagnostic	diagnosis
le dispensaire	community clinic
l'eczéma	eczema
un élancement	shooting pain
un électrocardiogramme	electrocardiogram
l'électrochoc	electric shock treatment
l'empoisonnement	poisoning
un estropié	cripple
un étourdissement	blackout; dizzy spell
un excitant	stimulant
le fémur	thighbone
le fluor	fluorine
les fourmillements	pins and needles
le frottis	smear
le furoncle	boil
le généraliste	general practitioner
le goutte-à-goutte (pl inv)	drip

l'ablation	removal
une accoucheuse	midwife
une accoutumance	addiction
l'acné	acne
l'aggravation	worsening
l'agonie	death pangs
une alcoolique	alcoholic
une allergie	allergy
une ambulancière	ambulance woman
l'anesthésie	anaesthetic
l'arthrite	arthritis
l'arthrose	osteoarthritis
une attelle	splint
la bactérie	bacterium
la bile	bile
la boulimie	bulimia
la bronchite	bronchitis
la brûlure	burn
les brûlures d'estomac	heartburn
la cancérologue	cancer specialist
la cardiologue	cardiologist
la carence	deficiency
une carence vitaminique	vitamin deficiency
la carie	caries
la carie dentaire	tooth decay
la cécité	blindness
la césarienne	Caesarean (section)
la chimio	chemotherapy
la chimiothérapie	chemotherapy
la chirurgie	surgery
la chute des cheveux	hair loss
la civière	stretcher
la cloque	blister
la commotion cérébrale	concussion
la congestion (cérébrale)	stroke
la congestion pulmonaire	congestion of the lungs
la conjonctivite	conjunctivitis
la constipation	constipation

USEFUL WORDS (m) (cont)

un grand malade	very sick person
les grands blessés/brûlés	the severely injured/burned
le guérisseur	healer
le gynécologue	gynaecologist
le :handicapé	physically (or mentally) handicapped person
un hémophile	haemophiliac
un héroïnomane	heroin addict
le :hoquet	hiccough
l'hospice	home (for the old and the sick)
un implant	implant
un infirme	disabled person
un infirme du travail	industrially disabled person
un invalide	disabled person
le kyste	cyst
le laxatif	laxative
les lépreux	lepers
le massage	massage
le mourant	dying man
un oculiste	eye specialist
l'oligo-élément (pl ~s)	trace element
un opiomane	opium addict
un oto-rhino-laryngologiste (pl ~s)	ear, nose and throat specialist
le pédiatre	paediatrician
le pédicure	chiropodist
le pestiféré	plague victim
le planning familial	family planning
le plombage	filling (in tooth)
le point de suture	stitch
le prématuré	premature baby

être dans le coma to be in a coma
être plein(e) de courbatures to be aching all over
être faible to be weak; **faire une chute** to have a fall
faire une cure thermale to take the waters (at a spa)
faire une cure de désintoxication to undergo treatment for alcoholism (or drug addiction)
faire un prélèvement de sang to take a blood sample
faire de la rééducation to undergo or have physiotherapy
reprendre connaissance to come to, regain consciousness

la contre-indication (pl ~s)	contra-indication
la convalescence	convalescence
la coupure	cut
la courbature	ache
la couveuse	incubator
la croissance	growth
la cure	course of treatment
la curiste	person taking the waters (*at a spa*)
la cuti-réaction (pl ~s)	skin test
la cystite	cystitis
la débile mentale	mental defective
la déchirure musculaire	torn muscle
la dépression	depression
la déprime	depression
la déshydratation	dehydration
la diabétique	diabetic
la doctoresse	lady doctor
une échographie	ultrasound (scan)
l'électrocution	electrocution
une élongation	strained muscle
une engelure	chilblain
une entorse	sprain
une épidémie	epidemic
l'espérance de vie	life expectancy
une estropiée	cripple
l'euthanasie	euthanasia
l'extinction de voix	loss of voice
la fatigue	tiredness
la fausse couche	miscarriage
la fécondation in vitro	in vitro fertilization
une fracture du crâne	fractured skull
une fracture de la jambe	broken leg
la gale	scabies
une garde-malade (pl ~s~(s))	home nurse
la gélule	capsule
les gelures	frostbite

il n'est pas dans son assiette aujourd'hui he's feeling a bit off-colour today
interner qn (dans un hôpital psychiatrique) to confine sb (to a mental hospital)

153

USEFUL WORDS (m) (cont)

le préservatif	condom
le psychanalyste	psychoanalyst
le psychiatre	psychiatrist
le psychopathe	psychopath
le pus [py]	pus
le rachitisme	rickets
le rappel	booster
le refroidissement	chill
le remontant	tonic, pick-me-up
le rétablissement	recovery
le saignement de nez	nosebleed
le secourisme	first aid
le secouriste	first aid worker
le service de réanimation	intensive care unit
le service des urgences	casualty department
les soins	treatment, medical attention
le somnifère	sleeping drug; sleeping pill
le souffle au cœur	heart murmur
le stress	stress
le symptôme	symptom
le tabagisme	addiction to smoking
le tétanos	tetanus
le toxicomane	drug addict
le tranquillisant	tranquillizer
un ulcère	ulcer
le zona	shingles

enfler to swell; **éternuer** to sneeze
presbyte long-sighted
rauque hoarse
réanimer to resuscitate
renifler to sniff
vomir to vomit, be sick
mortel(le) deadly, lethal
stérile sterile
ça me fait mal! that hurts!
faible weak; **fort(e)** strong
respirer to breathe; **hors d'haleine** out of breath
s'évanouir to faint; **tousser** to cough; **mourir** to die
perdre connaissance to lose consciousness

USEFUL WORDS (f) (cont)

la généraliste	general practitioner
la gerçure	crack
la glaire	phlegm
la glande	gland
la greffe	transplant
la griffure	scratch
la grossesse	pregnancy
la grosseur	lump
la guérisseuse	healer
la gynécologue	gynaecologist
une hallucination	hallucination
la :handicapée	physically (or mentally) handicapped person
une hémorragie	bleeding, haemorrhage
l'hernie	hernia
une héroïnomane	heroin addict
les heures de consultation	surgery hours
l'homéopathie	homeopathy
l'hypertension	high blood pressure
l'hypnose	hypnosis
l'hypotension	low blood pressure
l'immunisation	immunization
l'indigestion	indigestion
une indisposition	(slight) illness
une infection	infection
une infirme	disabled person
une infirmité	disability
une injection	injection
l'intoxication alimentaire	food poisoning
une intraveineuse	intravenous injection
une invalide	disabled person
la jaunisse	jaundice
la lèpre	leprosy
la laryngite	laryngitis
les lésions cérébrales	brain damage
la leucémie	leukaemia
la luxation	dislocation
les maladies vénériennes	venereal diseases, VD
la meningite	meningitis
la ménopause	menopause

la menstruation	menstruation
la mourante	dying woman
la névrose	neurosis
la nicotine	nicotine
l'obésité	obesity
une opiomane	opium addict
une otite	ear infection
une oto-rhino-laryngologiste (pl ~s)	ear, nose and throat specialist
la pédiatre	paediatrician
la pédicure	chiropodist
la peste	plague
la phobie	phobia
la phtisie	consumption
la physiothérapie	natural medicine, alternative medicine
la pneumonie	pneumonia
la pointe de côté	stitch (pain)
la policlinique	outpatients' clinic
la posologie	directions for use, dosage
la pression artérielle	blood pressure
la prothèse	artificial limb
la polyclinique	private general hospital
la psychanalyste	psychoanalyst
la psychiatre	psychiatrist
la psychopathe	psychopath
la rage	rabies
la rage de dents	(raging) toothache
la rechute	relapse
la sage-femme (pl ~s~s)	midwife
la salle d'attente ✧	waiting room
la salle d'opération	operating theatre
la secouriste	first aid worker
la seringue	syringe
la table d'opération	operating table
la tentative de suicide	suicide attempt
la toxicomane	drug addict
la tuberculose	tuberculosis, TB
la tumeur	growth, tumour
la vaccination	vaccination
la varice	varicose vein

ESSENTIAL WORDS (m)

l'accueil ⊡	welcome; reception (desk)
l'ascenseur	lift
les bagages ◇	luggage
le balcon ◇	balcony
le bar ⊡	bar
le bouton ◇	switch
le bruit ⊡	noise
le cabinet de toilette ◇	toilet
le chef ◇ (de cuisine) (m+f)	chef, head cook
le chèque ◇	cheque
le client ◇	resident, guest
le confort ⊡	comfort
le déjeuner	lunch
le directeur ◇	manager
l'escalier	stairs, staircase
un étage ◇	floor; storey
le garçon ◇	waiter
le grand lit	double bed
le guide	guide-book
l'hôtel ◇	hotel
un incendie ⊡	fire
le jour	day
le Michelin rouge ⊡	(red) Michelin guide
le numéro ◇	number
le passeport ◇	passport
le petit déjeuner ◇	breakfast
le porteur ◇ ⊡	porter
le pourboire ◇ ⊡	tip
le prix ◇	price
le prix maximum ⊡	maximum price
le prix minimum ⊡	minimum price
le prix net ⊡	inclusive price
le réceptionniste ⊡	receptionist
le reçu	receipt
le repas ◇	meal
le restaurant ◇	restaurant
le rez-de-chaussée (pl inv)	ground floor
le séjour ⊡	stay

ESSENTIAL WORDS (m) (cont)

le **tarif** ◇ ▭	scale of charges, tariff
le **téléphone**	telephone
le **téléviseur (couleur)**	(colour) television
les **W.-C.** ◇ ▭	toilet(s)

IMPORTANT WORDS (m)

le **cabaret**	cabaret
le **chasseur** ◇	page(-boy)
le **cuisinier**	cook
un **estaminet**	"pub"
le **foyer**	foyer
l'**hôtelier**	hotelier
le **maître d'hôtel**	head waiter
le **pensionnaire** ◇	resident, guest (*at boarding house*)
le **portier**	doorman
le **sommelier**	wine waiter

une chambre pour deux personnes a double room
un hôtel de grand luxe a luxury hotel
remplissez cette fiche fill in this form
avez-vous une pièce d'identité? do you have any means of identification?
on a monté les bagages we took the luggage up
on s'est installé we got settled in
occupé(e) occupied; **libre** vacant
propre clean; **sale** dirty

ESSENTIAL WORDS (f)

l'addition ◊	bill
les arrhes ◊ ▭	deposit
une **auberge** ◊	inn
la **chambre**	room
la **clé, clef** ◊	key
la **cliente** ◊	resident, guest
la **date**	date
la **demi-pension** (*pl* ~**s**)	half-board
la **directrice** ◊	manageress
la **douche** ◊	shower
l'**entrée** ◊	entrance
une **étoile** ▭	star
la **femme de chambre**	chambermaid
la **fiche** ◊ ▭	form, slip
l'**hospitalité**	hospitality
la **(petite) monnaie** ▭	(small) change
la **note** ◊	bill
la **nuit** ◊	night
la **pension**	guest-house, boarding house
la **pension complète**	full board
la **piscine** ◊	swimming pool
la **réception** ▭	reception (desk)
la **réceptionniste** ▭	receptionist
la **réclamation** ▭	complaint
la **réponse** ◊	reply
la **salle de bains** ◊	bathroom
la **salle de télévision**	television lounge
la **semaine**	week
la **serveuse**	waitress
la **sortie de secours** ◊ ▭	fire escape
la **télévision** ◊	television
les **toilettes** ◊	toilets, ''ladies'', ''gents''
la **valise** ◊	case, suitcase
la **vue** ◊ ▭	view

je voudrais réserver une chambre I would like to book a room
une chambre avec douche/avec salle de bains a room with a shower/with a bathroom
une chambre pour une personne a single room

159

AT THE HOTEL

IMPORTANT WORDS (f)

la pension de famille	guest-house, boarding house
la pensionnaire	resident, guest (*at boarding house*)
la terrasse	terrace, pavement outside a café

dormir to sleep; **se réveiller** to wake
"tirez" ''pull''; **"poussez"** ''push''; **"appuyez"** ''press''
"tout confort" ''with all facilities''
une chambre donnant sur la mer a room overlooking the sea
chambre sans pension room (with no meals)
chambre avec demi-pension bed, breakfast and evening meal
on nous a servis à la terrasse we were served outside

ESSENTIAL WORDS (m)

l'aménagement ⌑	fitting out; conversion
l'ameublement ⌑	furniture, furnishing(s)
un appartement	flat
un ascenseur ⌑	lift
le balcon ◇	balcony
le bâtiment ◇	building
le cabinet de toilette ◇	toilet
le chauffage central	central heating
le concierge	caretaker
le confort ⌑	comfort
le couloir ⌑	corridor
le débarras ⌑	box room, junk room
le déménagement ◇	removal
l'entretien ⌑	upkeep; maintenance
un escalier	stairs, staircase
un étage ◇	floor; storey
l'extérieur ⌑	exterior, outside
le garage ◇	garage
le grand ensemble ⌑	housing estate
un :HLM ⌑ (habitation à loyer modéré)	council flat or house
un immeuble	block of flats
l'intérieur ⌑	interior, inside
le jardin	garden
le logement ⌑	lodgings, accommodation
le loyer ⌑	rent
le meublé ⌑	furnished flat or room
un meuble ⌑	a piece of furniture
les meubles ◇ ⌑	furniture
le mur ⌑	wall
le numéro de téléphone	phone number
le palier ⌑	landing
le parking ◇	parking space
le propriétaire	owner; landlord
le rez-de-chaussée (pl inv)	ground level, ground floor
le salon	lounge, living room
le sous-sol ⌑ (pl ~s)	basement
le terrain ◇ ⌑	plot of land
le toit	roof
le voisin	neighbour

THE HOUSE – GENERAL

IMPORTANT WORDS (m)

le cabinet de travail	study
le carreau (*pl* **-x**)	(floor) tile; (window) pane
le décor ♢	decoration
le grenier ♢	attic
le locataire	tenant; lodger
le parquet	(parquet *or* wooden) floor
le pavillon ♢ ▭	small (detached) house
le plafond	ceiling
le plancher	floor
le seuil	doorstep
le store	blind
le studio	(one-roomed) flatlet
le tuyau (*pl* **-x**)	pipe
le vestibule	hall
le volet	shutter

USEFUL WORDS (m)

l'appui de fenêtre	window sill, ledge
l'âtre	hearth
un auvent	canopy
le bail [baj] (*pl* **baux** [bo])	lease
le boudoir ♢	boudoir
le carrelage	tiles, tiling
le cellier	storeroom (*for wine and food*)
le climatiseur	air conditioner
le court-circuit (*pl* **~s~s**)	short(-circuit)
le dallage	paving
un deux-pièces (*pl inv*)	two-roomed flat
l'éclairage	lighting
l'emménagement	moving in
un escalier en colimaçon	spiral staircase
le fourre-tout (*pl inv*)	junk room (*or* cupboard)
le gîte	holiday home
le gratte-ciel (*pl inv*)	skyscraper
l'interphone	intercom
le judas	spy-hole
le lambris	panelling
le lino(léum)	lino(leum)
le logeur	landlord

ESSENTIAL WORDS (f)

une **adresse** ✧	address
une **allée**	lane
une **avenue**	avenue
la **barrière** ✧	gate; fence
la **cave** ⌑	cellar
la **chambre (à coucher)**	bedroom
la **cheminée** ✧ ⌑	chimney; fireplace; mantelpiece
la **clé, clef** ✧	key
la **concierge**	caretaker
la **cour** ✧	yard; courtyard
la **cuisine** ✧	kitchen; cooking
la **douche** ✧	shower
l' **entrée** ✧	entrance (hall)
la **famille**	family
la **femme de ménage** ✧	cleaning woman
la **fenêtre**	window
la **fumée** ✧	smoke
une **HLM** ⌑ **(habitation à loyer modéré)**	council flat *or* house
la **maison** ✧	house
la **pelouse**	lawn
la **pièce** ✧	room
la **porte (d'entrée)**	(front) door
la **propriétaire**	owner; landlady
la **rue**	street
la **salle à manger** ✧	dining room
la **salle** ✧	room
la **salle de bains** ✧	bathroom
la **salle de séjour**	living room
les **toilettes** ✧	toilet
la **voisine** ✧	neighbour
la **vue** ✧ ⌑	view

j'habite un appartement/une maison jumelle I live in a flat/a semi-detached
monter/descendre (l'escalier) to go upstairs/downstairs
en haut upstairs; **en bas** downstairs; **à la maison** at home, in the house
regarder par la fenêtre to look out of the window
chez moi/toi/nous/lui *etc* at my/your/our/his *etc* house
déménager to move house; **s'installer** to settle in

THE HOUSE – GENERAL

le lotissement	housing development
le manoir	manor *or* country house
le mas [mɑ]	traditional house *or* farm in Provence
le meublé	furnished room; furnished flat
le paratonnerre	lightning conductor
le pâté de maisons	block (of houses)
le perron	steps (*in front of a mansion etc*)
le portail	gate
le réduit	tiny room; recess
le soupirail	(small) basement window
le survitrage	double glazing
le trou de la serrure	keyhole
le trousseau de clés (*pl* **-x**)	bunch of keys
le vasistas	fanlight
le verrou	bolt
le vide-ordures (*pl inv*)	(rubbish) chute
le village	village
le voisin de palier	neighbour across the landing
le voisinage	neighbourhood

louer une maison to rent a house
faire construire une maison to have a house built
les chambres à l'étage the rooms upstairs, the upstairs rooms
de l'extérieur from the outside; **à l'intérieur** on the inside
jusqu'au plafond up to the ceiling
faire du rangement to tidy up
pendre la crémaillère to have a house-warming party
sentir le renfermé to smell stuffy; **délabré(e)** dilapidated
quand je rentre à la maison when I go home
quand je suis entré(e) dans la salle when I went into the room

IMPORTANT WORDS (f)

une antenne	aerial
une ardoise	slate
la boue ◇	mud
la chambre d'amis	spare room
la chaudière	boiler
la chaumière ◇	(thatched) cottage
la façade	front (of house)
la :haie ◇	hedge
la locataire	tenant; lodger
la loge ◇	caretaker's room
la lucarne ▭	skylight
la maison jumelle	semi-detached house
la maison secondaire	second or holiday home
la mansarde	attic
la marche	step
la ménagère	housewife
la parroi ▭	partition
la porte-fenêtre (pl ~s~s)	French window
la sonnette	(door)bell
la tuile	(roof) tile
la vitre	(window) pane

USEFUL WORDS (f)

l'aération	ventilation
une agence immobilière ◇	estate agent's (office)
l'arrière-cour (pl ~s)	backyard
l'arrière-cuisine (pl ~s)	scullery
la balustrade	railing, handrail
une bouche d'aération	air vent
la buanderie	laundry (room)
la canalisation	(main) pipe
la chambre meublée	bedsit
la cheminée ◇	chimney
la climatisation	air conditioning
la cloison	partition
la coupure de courant	power cut
la dalle	paving stone, flag(stone)
l'eau courante	running water
l'embrasure de la porte	doorway

THE HOUSE – GENERAL

la fissure	crack
les fondations	foundations
la fuite	leak
la garçonnière	bachelor flat
la gentilhommière	(small) manor house
la gouttière	gutter
la grille	gate; railings
l'hypothèque	mortgage
l'insonorisation	soundproofing
la logeuse	landlady
la maison à colombage	half-timbered house
la maisonnette	small house, cottage
la masure	tumbledown cottage
la mezzanine	mezzanine (floor)
la moisissure	mould; mildew
les persiennes	(slatted) shutters
la poutre	beam
la résidence principale	main home
la résidence secondaire	second home
la tour	high-rise block
la véranda	veranda(h)
la verrière	glass roof
la villa	villa, (detached) house
la ville	town

vétuste dilapidated
un toit en ardoise a slate roof
frapper à la porte to knock at the door
on a sonné somebody rang (the doorbell)

ESSENTIAL WORDS (m)

un aspirateur	vacuum cleaner, Hoover ®
le bain ◇	bath
le bidet	bidet
le bouton ◇	switch
le cendrier	ashtray
le dentifrice	toothpaste
le drap ◇ ⌑	sheet
un électrophone ◇	record player
un essuie-mains (pl inv)	hand towel
un évier ⌑	sink
le feu (pl -x)	fire
le four	oven
le frigidaire, frigo ◇	fridge
le gaz ◇	gas
le lavabo	washbasin
le lave-vaisselle (pl inv)	dishwasher
le linge ◇	bedclothes; washing
le machin	thing, contraption
le magnétophone à cassettes	cassette recorder
le magnétoscope ◇	video (recorder)
le ménage	housework
le miroir ◇	mirror
un oreiller ⌑	pillow
le placard ◇	cupboard
le plateau ◇ (pl -x)	tray
le poster	poster
le radiateur ◇ ⌑	radiator; heater
le réveil, réveille-matin ◇ (pl inv)	alarm clock
les rideaux ⌑	curtains
le robinet ⌑	tap
le savon	soap
le tableau ◇	picture
le tapis	carpet, rug
le téléviseur ◇	television set
le transistor ◇	transistor

prendre un bain, se baigner to have a bath
prendre une douche to have a shower
"faire cuire à feu doux" "cook on a low heat"

IMPORTANT WORDS (m)

le balai	brush, broom
le balai mécanique	carpet sweeper
le bibelot 📖	ornament
le chiffon	duster; rag
le cintre	coat hanger
le coussin	cushion
le couvercle	lid
le fer (à repasser)	iron
le four à micro-ondes	microwave oven
le grille-pain (pl inv)	toaster
un interrupteur	switch
le mixeur	(electric) mixer
le moulin à café	coffee grinder
le papier peint	wallpaper
le radiateur à accumulation	storage heater
le seau ◊ (pl -x)	bucket
le torchon	dishcloth
le traversin 📖	bolster
le vase	vase

USEFUL WORDS (m)

un aiguisoir	sharpener
un antimite	moth repellent
le balai-brosse (pl ~s)	(long-handled) scrubbing brush
le bougeoir	candlestick
le chandelier	candlestick
le chauffage d'appoint	back-up heating
le chauffe-eau (pl inv)	water heater
le chauffe-plats (pl inv)	dish-warmer
le couvre-lit (pl ~s)	bedspread
le désodorisant	air freshener
le dessous-de-plat (pl inv)	table mat
le dessus-de-lit (pl ~s)	bedspread
le drap-housse (pl ~s~s)	fitted sheet
un édredon	eiderdown
un extincteur d'incendie	fire extinguisher
le fusible	fuse
le garde-feu (pl inv)	fender
le paillasson	doormat

ESSENTIAL WORDS (f)

les affaires ✧	things
une ampoule ✧ (électrique)	light bulb
une armoire	wardrobe
la baignoire	bath
la balance	weighing scales
la boîte aux lettres ✧	letterbox
la brosse	brush
la cafetière	coffee pot; coffee maker
la casserole	pan, saucepan
la couverture	rug; blanket; cover
la cuisinière ✧ ⌑	cooker
la douche ✧	shower
l'eau ✧	water
l'électricité	electricity
la femme de ménage ✧	cleaning woman
la glace ✧	mirror
la lampe ✧	lamp
la lessive ✧	washing powder; washing
la lumière ✧ ⌑	light
la machine à laver ✧ ⌑	washing machine
la peinture ✧	paint; painting
la photo	photo
la poêle	frying pan
la poubelle ✧	dustbin
la poussière ✧	dust
la prise de courant ✧ ⌑	socket, power point
la recette	recipe
la serrure ⌑	lock
la serviette ✧	towel; napkin, serviette
la télévision ✧	television
la vaisselle ✧	dishes

faire le ménage to do the housework
j'aime faire la cuisine I like (doing the) cooking
faire cuire qch dans une casserole to cook sth in a pan
regarder la télévision to watch television; **à la télévision** on television
allumer/éteindre la télé to switch on/off the TV
jeter qch à la poubelle to throw sth in the dustbin
ouvrir/fermer la lumière to switch on/off the light
faire la vaisselle to do the dishes *or* the washing-up

THE HOUSE – PARTICULAR

le **pare-feu** (*pl inv*)	fireguard
le **plumeau** (*pl* -**x**)	feather duster
le **porte-savon** (*pl* ~(**s**))	soapdish
le **porte-serviettes** (*pl inv*)	towel rail
le **produit d'entretien**	cleaning product
le **repassage**	ironing
le **sèche-linge** (*pl inv*)	tumble dryer
le **sommier**	bed base

brancher/débrancher to plug in/to unplug
passer l'aspirateur to hoover round
laver le linge, faire la lessive to do the washing
épousseter to dust
faire le repassage/le nettoyage to do the ironing/the cleaning
balayer to sweep (up); **nettoyer** to clean
ranger ses affaires to tidy away one's things
laisser traîner ses affaires to leave one's things lying about

IMPORTANT WORDS (f)

la **boîte à ordures**	dustbin
la **bouilloire**	kettle
la **cocotte-minute** ® (*pl* ~**s**~)	pressure cooker
la **corbeille** ◊ (à papier)	waste paper basket
la **couette**	continental quilt, duvet
la **couverture chauffante**	electric blanket
la **descente de lit**	bedside rug
la **discothèque** ◊	record cabinet *or* rack
une **échelle** ◊	ladder
une **éponge**	sponge
la **marmite**	pot
la **moquette**	fitted carpet
les **ordures**	rubbish, refuse
la **planche à repasser**	ironing board
la **poignée** ◊	handle
la **tapisserie** ◊	wallpaper

USEFUL WORDS (f)

une **alèse**	undersheet
l' **argenterie**	silverware
la **balayette**	small brush
la **bassine**	bowl, basin
la **bougie**	candle
la **bouillotte**	hot-water bottle
la **carpette**	rug
la **charnière**	hinge
la **cheminée** ◊	fireplace
la **cuvette**	basin
l' **eau calcaire**	hard water
la **:housse de couette**	duvet cover
la **jardinière**	window box
la **literie**	bedding
la **patère**	(coat-)peg
la **penderie**	walk-in cupboard; wardrobe
la **pince à linge**	clothes peg
la **prise multiple**	adaptor
la **sirène d'alarme** ◊	fire alarm
la **taie (d'oreiller)**	pillowslip, pillowcase

THE HUMAN BODY

ESSENTIAL WORDS (m)

le bras	arm
les cheveux	hair
le cœur ⌑	heart
le corps ⌑	body
le côté	side
le cou	neck
le doigt	finger
le dos	back
l'estomac ⌑	stomach
le front	forehead
le genou (pl -x)	knee
le menton	chin
le nez	nose
un œil (pl yeux)	eye
le pied	foot
le pouce	thumb
le sang ⌑	blood
le sourcil	eyebrow
le ventre	stomach
le visage ⌑	face
les yeux	eyes

debout standing; **assis(e)** sitting; **couché(e)** lying
je me suis cassé le bras/la jambe I have broken my arm/my leg
je me suis coupé le doigt I have cut my finger
je vais me faire couper les cheveux I am going to have my hair cut
son cœur battait his *or* her heart was beating
jeter un coup d'œil à qn to glance at sb
en un clin d'œil in the twinkling of an eye
(j'y vais) à pied (I'm going) on foot
un coup de pied a kick
il m'a donné un coup de pied he kicked me
ouvrir/fermer la bouche to open/close one's mouth
se taire to keep quiet; **taisez-vous!, tais-toi!** be quiet!
j'ai mal à la gorge I have a sore throat
j'ai mal au ventre I have a sore stomach, I've got stomach ache
ils se sont serré la main they shook hands
de la tête aux pieds from head to foot
lever la tête *or* **les yeux** to look up

THE HUMAN BODY

ESSENTIAL WORDS (f)

la bouche	mouth
la cheville 🕮	ankle
la dent	tooth
une épaule	shoulder
la figure	face
la gorge	throat
la jambe	leg
la joue	cheek
la langue ◇	tongue
la main	hand
une oreille	ear
la peau 🕮	skin
la poitrine 🕮	chest, bust
la tête	head
la voix	voice

IMPORTANT WORDS (f)

une artère	artery
la chair	flesh
la colonne vertébrale	spine
la côte ◇	rib
la cuisse	thigh
la :hanche	hip
la lèvre	lip
la mâchoire	jaw
la nuque	nape of the neck
la paupière	eyelid
la plante du pied	sole of the foot
la prunelle 🕮	pupil (*of the eye*)
la taille ◇	figure; waist
la tempe 🕮	temple
la veine ◇	vein

je me suis foulé la cheville I have sprained my ankle
"tour de poitrine" "chest *or* bust measurement"
parlez plus fort! speak louder!

173

THE HUMAN BODY

le cerveau	brain
le cil [sil]	eyelash
le coude	elbow
le derrière	bottom
les doigts de pied	toes
le foie ◊	liver
le geste	gesture, movement
le gros orteil	big toe
un index	forefinger
le mollet	calf (of leg)
le muscle	muscle
un ongle	nail
un orteil	toe
un os [ɔs] (pl [o])	bone
le poignet	wrist
le poing	fist
le poumon	lung
le rein	kidney
le sein	breast
le squelette	skeleton
le talon	heel
le teint	complexion
le trait	feature

l'abdomen	abdomen
l'annulaire	ring finger
l'appendice	appendix
l'auriculaire	little finger
l'avant-bras (pl inv)	forearm
le bassin	pelvis
le bas-ventre (pl ~s)	stomach, guts
le biceps	biceps
le cartilage	cartilage
le cérumen	(ear)wax
le crâne	skull
un embryon	embryo
le fœtus [fetys]	foetus
le frémissement	shiver

USEFUL WORDS (f)

l'aine	groin
l'aisselle	armpit
les amygdales [amidal]	tonsils
l'arcade sourcilière	arch of the eyebrows
l'articulation	joint
la balafre	scar
les bronches	bronchial tubes
la canine	canine (tooth), eye tooth
la chirurgie esthétique	plastic surgery
la clavicule	collarbone, clavicle
la crampe	cramp
la démangeaison	itching
une ecchymose	bruise
une écorchure	scratch; graze
une engelure	chilblain
une éraflure	scratch
les fesses	bottom, buttocks
la gencive	gum
la génétique	genetics
l'haleine	breath
l'incisive	incisor
les mensurations	measurements
le moelle épinière	spinal chord
la molaire	molar
la narine	nostril
l'omoplate	shoulder blade
l'ouïe	hearing
la paume	palm
la pommette	cheekbone
la prémolaire	premolar
la prothèse dentaire	denture(s), false teeth
la pupille	pupil
les règles	(menstrual) period
la respiration	breathing
la rotule	kneecap
la souplesse	suppleness
la sueur	sweat
la verrue	wart, verruca
la vessie	bladder
la vue ⋄	(eye)sight

THE HUMAN BODY

le frisson	shudder
le frissonnement	shudder
le gène	gene
le goût	(sense of) taste
le gros intestin	large intestine
l'index	index finger
le lifting	face lift
le ligament	ligament
le majeur	middle finger
le mamelon	nipple
le nerf [nɛʀ]	nerve
le nombril	navel
l'odorat	(sense of) smell
le palais	palate
le pouls [pu]	pulse
le renvoi	belch
le sinus	sinus
le tartre	tartar (*on teeth*)
le tendon	tendon, sinew
le tibia	shin; shinbone, tibia
le torse	chest
le toucher	(sense of) touch
le tympan	eardrum

sourd(e) deaf; **aveugle** blind; **muet(te)** dumb
handicapé(e) handicapped; **handicapé(e) mental(e)** mentally handicapped
un coup de poing a punch
il m'a donné un coup de poing he punched me
à pleins poumons at the top of one's voice
avoir mauvaise haleine to have bad breath
avoir l'onglée to have fingers numb with cold
avoir le torticolis to have a stiff neck
avoir le hoquet to have (the) hiccoughs
se donner un tour de reins to strain *or* sprain one's back
surveiller sa ligne to watch one's figure
une dent de lait/sagesse milk/wisdom tooth
"tour de hanches" ''hip measurement''
"tour de taille" ''waist measurement''

ESSENTIAL WORDS (m)

un **annuaire**	telephone directory
le **billet** ◇	ticket; (bank)note
le **bureau** ◇ (*pl* -**x**) **de change** ▭	bureau de change
le **bureau** ◇ **de poste** ▭	post office
le **bureau de renseignements** ◇	information desk
le **bureau** ◇ **des objets trouvés**	lost property office
le **carnet de chèques** ◇	cheque book
le **centime**	centime
le **chèque**	cheque
le **chèque de voyage**	traveller's cheque
le **code postal**	post code
le **colis** ▭	parcel, packet
le **compte** ▭	account
le **coup de téléphone** ▭	phone call
le **courrier** ▭	mail, letters
le **crédit** ▭	credit
le **domicile** ▭	home address
un **employé** ◇ ▭	counter clerk
le **facteur** ◇ ▭	postman
le **formulaire**	form
le **franc**	franc
le **guichet** ◇ ▭	counter
le **jeton** ▭	token (*for telephone etc*)
le **nom**	name
le **numéro** ◇	number
le **paiement** ▭	payment
le **papier à lettres**	writing paper
le **paquet**	parcel, packet
le **passeport** ◇	passport
le **portefeuille** ◇	wallet
le **porte-monnaie** ◇ (*pl inv*)	purse
le **prix** ◇	price
le **PCV** ▭	reverse-charge call
les **renseignements** ◇	information; directory enquiries
le **stylo**	pen
le **supplément** ◇	extra charge
le **syndicat d'initiative, SI** ◇	tourist information office
le **tarif** ◇ ▭	(postage) rate
le **télégramme**	telegram
le **téléphone**	telephone

ESSENTIAL WORDS (m) (cont)

| le timbre ⋄, timbre-poste (*pl*~**s**~) | (postage) stamp |

IMPORTANT WORDS (m)

un aérogramme	airmail letter
l'annuaire des professions	the Yellow Pages
le Bottin	telephone directory
le cadran ⋄	dial
le combiné	(*telephone*) receiver
le destinataire	addressee
l'expéditeur	sender
les imprimés	printed matter
le mandat(-poste) (*pl*~**s**~-(**s**))	postal order
le papier d'emballage	wrapping paper
le papier gris	brown paper
le récepteur	(*telephone*) receiver
le standardiste	(*telephone*) operator

USEFUL WORDS (m)

un abonné	subscriber
un abonnement	subscription
l'affranchissement	postage
le combiné	(phone) receiver
l'indicatif	dialling code
le mode d'emploi	directions for use
l'office du tourisme	tourist information office
le photomaton	photo-booth
le prénom	first name
le prospectus	leaflet, brochure
le relevé de compte	bank statement
le sigle	acronym, (set of) initials
le virement bancaire	credit transfer
le virement postal	(National) Giro transfer
le visa	visa

on m'a coupé I've been cut off; **la ligne est occupée** the line is engaged
ne quittez pas hold the line; **patientez, monsieur** *or* **mademoiselle** please wait
je me suis trompé(e) de numéro I got the wrong number; **raccrocher** to hang up

---

ESSENTIAL WORDS (f)

une **adresse** ◇	address
les **arrhes** ◇ ▭	deposit
la **banque** ◇	bank
la **boîte aux lettres** ◇	postbox, pillarbox
la **cabine téléphonique**	callbox
la **caisse** ◇ ▭	cash desk; check-out
la **carte bancaire** ▭	bank card
la **carte postale**	postcard
la **dépense** ▭	expense
une **enveloppe**	envelope
une **erreur** ◇	mistake, error
la **fente** ▭	slot
la **fiche** ◇ ▭	form
la **lettre**	letter
la **livre** ◇ **sterling**	pound sterling
la **monnaie** ▭	change
une **opératrice** ▭	operator
la **pièce** ◇	coin
la **pièce d'identité** ◇ ▭	(means of) identification
la **poste** ◇	post office; post
la **poste restante**	poste restante
les **PTT** ▭	*French post and phones*
la **récompense**	reward
la **réduction** ◇ ▭	reduction
la **réponse** ◇	reply
la **signature** ▭	signature
la **taxe** ◇ ▭	tax

je voudrais me renseigner I would like some information
la banque la plus proche the nearest bank
je voudrais encaisser un chèque/changer de l'argent/envoyer une lettre I would
like to cash a cheque/change some money/send a letter
un coup de téléphone *or* **de fil** a phone call
je vais téléphoner à mon père I'm going to phone my father
décrocher to lift the receiver
la tonalité the dialling tone
composer le numéro to dial (the number)
l'indicatif (*m*) the (dialling) code
le signal d'appel the ringing tone
allô – ici Jean *or* **c'est Jean à l'appareil** hello – this is John

INFORMATION AND SERVICES

IMPORTANT WORDS (f)

la bande ⇨	wrapper
la carte-lettre (*pl* ~s~s)	letter-card
la communication interurbaine	trunk call
la communication locale	local call
la dépêche	wire, telegram
la distribution ⇨	delivery (*of mail*)
l'horloge parlante	the speaking clock, TIM
la lettre recommandée	registered letter
la majuscule	block *or* capital letter
la poste aérienne	airmail
la sonnerie	bell; ringing
la standardiste	switchboard operator
la télécarte	phone card

USEFUL WORDS (f)

une abonnée	subscriber
une abréviation	abbreviation
la date d'expiration	expiry date
les initiales	initials
la notice explicative	explanatory leaflet
la photo d'identité	passport photograph
la redevance	(telephone) rental charge; (TV) licence fee
la réexpédition	forwarding; return
la sono	PA system
la tonalité	dialling tone

j'ai perdu mon portefeuille – l'avez-vous trouvé? I've lost my wallet – have you found it?
remplir une fiche *or* **une formule** to fill in a form
en majuscules in block letters
"télécarte: en vente ici" ''phonecards on sale here''
"rayer la mention inutile" ''delete as appropriate''
je vous serais reconnaissant(e) de bien vouloir ... I should be most grateful if you would (kindly) ...

quelle est votre address? what is your address?
comment cela s'écrit? how do you write (*or* spell) that?
avez-vous la monnaie de ...? do you have change of ...?
écrire to write; **répondre** to reply; **signer** to sign
est-ce que vous pouvez m'aider? can you help me please?
pour aller à la gare ...? how do I get to the station?
tout droit straight on
à droite to *or* on the right; **à gauche** to *or* on the left
derrière behind; **devant** in front (+ of *when prep*)
en face (+ **de** *when prep*) opposite; **vers** towards

le nord: au nord	north: in *or* to the north
le sud: au sud	south: in *or* to the south
l'est (*m*): **à l'est**	east: in *or* to the east
l'ouest (*m*): **à l'ouest**	west: in *or* to the west

LETTERS

Cher Robert Dear Robert; **Chère Anne** Dear Anne
Cher Monsieur Dear Sir; **Chère Madame** (*or* **Mademoiselle**) Dear Madam
amitiés very best wishes *or* regards
bien affectueusement (à vous) yours affectionately
bien amicalement *or* **cordialement (à vous)** yours ever
bons baisers love and kisses; **ton ami(e)** your friend
veuillez agréer mes (*or* **nos**) **salutations distinguées** yours faithfully
je vous prie d'agréer, Monsieur (*or* **Madame** *etc*) **l'expression de mes sentiments**
  les meilleurs yours sincerely
T.S.V.P. P.T.O.

PRONUNCIATION GUIDE

When you are talking on the phone or giving details to someone you are often asked to spell something out. This is how you go about it in French. For further information on the International Phonetic Alphabet (IPA) symbols used in column 2, see page 5.

	Phonetically	*Pronounced approximately as*
A	[a]	**ah**
B	[be]	**bay**
C	[se]	**say**
D	[de]	**day**
E	[ə]	**uh**
F	[ɛf]	**ef**
G	[ʒe]	**zhay**
H	[aʃ]	**ash**
I	[i]	**ee**
J	[ʒi]	**zhee**
K	[ka]	**kah**
L	[ɛl]	**el**
M	[ɛm]	**em**
N	[ɛn]	**en**
O	[o]	**oh**
P	[pe]	**pay**
Q	[ky]	**koo**
R	[ɛr]	**air**
S	[ɛs]	**ess**
T	[te]	**tay**
U	[y]	**oo**
V	[ve]	**vay**
W	[dublə ve]	**dooble-vay**
X	[iks]	**eeks**
Y	[i grek]	**ee grek**
Z	[zɛd]	**zed**

Try it out with your own name and the names of some friends.

THE TELEPHONE ALPHABET

When you are making a telephone call, you may want to spell your name, your address or some other word for the benefit of the person you are speaking to. The conventional French and English telephone alphabets are as follows:

A	comme	Anatole	A	for	Andrew
B	comme	Bertha	B	for	Benjamin
C	comme	Célestin	C	for	Charlie
D	comme	Désiré	D	for	David
E	comme	Eugène	E	for	Edward
F	comme	François	F	for	Frederick
G	comme	Gaston	G	for	George
H	comme	Henri	H	for	Harry
I	comme	Irma	I	for	Isaac
J	comme	Joseph	J	for	Jack
K	comme	Kléber	K	for	King
L	comme	Louis	L	for	Lucy
M	comme	Marcel	M	for	Mike
N	comme	Nicolas	N	for	Nelly
O	comme	Oscar	O	for	Oliver
P	comme	Pierre	P	for	Peter
Q	comme	Quintal	Q	for	Queen
R	comme	Raoul	R	for	Robert
S	comme	Suzanne	S	for	Sugar
T	comme	Thérèse	T	for	Tommy
U	comme	Ursule	U	for	Uncle
V	comme	Victor	V	for	Victor
W	comme	William	W	for	William
X	comme	Xavier	X	for	Xmas
Y	comme	Yvonne	Y	for	Yellow
Z	comme	Zoé	Z	for	Zebra

PUNCTUATION AND ACCENTS

un accent grâve/aigu/circonflexe	acute/grave/circumflex (accent)
la barre oblique	slash, oblique
la cédille	cedilla
les crochets (*mpl*)	square brackets
le deux-points (*pl inv*)	colon
les guillemets (*mpl*)	inverted commas
les parenthèses (*fpl*)	brackets
le point	full stop
le point d'exclamation	exclamation mark
le point d'interrogation	question mark
les points (*mpl*) **de suspension**	suspense marks
le point-virgule (*pl ~s~s*)	semicolon
le tiret	dash
le trait d'union	hyphen
le tréma	dieresis
la virgule	comma

souligner to underline

ESSENTIAL WORDS (m)

un **appareil**	appliance; device
le **bol** ◇	bowl
le **congélateur**	freezer
le **frigidaire, frigo** ◇	fridge
le **placard** ◇	cupboard
le **verre** ◇	glass

IMPORTANT WORDS (m)

le **four**	oven
le **pot à lait**	milk jug

USEFUL WORDS (m)

le **beurrier**	butter dish
le **butane**	calor gas
le **casse-noix** (*pl inv*)	nutcrackers
le **compotier**	fruit dish *or* bowl
le **coquetier**	egg cup
le **décapsuleur**	bottle-opener
le **dénoyauteur**	stoner
un **égouttoir**	draining rack
un **épluche-légumes** (*pl inv*)	potato peeler
un **éplucheur**	(automatic) peeler
l'**essuie-tout** (*pl inv*)	kitchen paper
le **fait-tout** (*pl inv*)	stewpot
le **filtre à café**	coffee filter
le **fouet**	whisk
le **freezer**	freezing compartment
le **garde-manger** (*pl inv*)	meatsafe; pantry, larder
le **gaufrier**	waffle iron
le **gril**	steak *or* grill pan
le **gros sel**	cooking salt
le **:hache-légumes** (*pl inv*)	vegetable chopper
le **:hache-viande** (*pl inv*)	(meat) mincer
le **:hachoir**	chopper; (meat) mincer
le **minuteur**	timer
le **moule à tarte**	pie dish, flan dish
le **moule à gâteaux**	cake tin

IN THE KITCHEN

le papier (d')aluminium	tinfoil
le pilon	pestle
le presse-citron (*pl inv*)	lemon squeezer
le presse-purée (*pl inv*)	potato masher
le ramequin	ramekin
le ravier	hors d'œuvre dish
le récipient	container
le robot de cuisine	food processor
le rouleau à pâtisserie	rolling pin
le sablier ◇	egg timer
le saladier	(salad) bowl
le sucrier	sugar bowl
le tournebroche	roasting spit
un ustensile de cuisine	kitchen utensil
le vide-pomme (*pl inv*)	apple corer

pétrir to knead
préchauffer to preheat
mettre qch au four to put sth in the oven

ESSENTIAL WORDS (f)

une assiette ◇	plate
la casserole	saucepan
la cuiller, cuillère ◇	spoon
la cuisinière ◇ ▭ (électrique/à gaz)	(electric/gas) cooker
la fourchette ◇	fork
la poêle (à frire)	frying pan
la soucoupe	saucer
la table ◇	table
la tasse ◇	cup
la théière	teapot
la vaisselle ◇	dishes

USEFUL WORDS (f)

une anse	handle (*of a cup*)
une assiette à dessert	dessert plate
une assiette creuse	soup plate
une assiettée	plateful
une assiette plate	(dinner) plate
la centrifugeuse	juice extractor
la cruche	(milk) jug
l'eau de Javel ®	bleach
une écuelle	bowl
la friteuse	chip pan
une :hotte aspirante	cooker hood
la lavette	dish cloth; dish mop
la louche	ladle
la moulinette ®	(vegetable) shredder
la passoire	sieve; colander; strainer
la pelle à tarte	cake *or* pie server
la planche à découper	chopping board
la plaque chauffante	hot plate
la poivrière	pepperpot, pepper shaker
la râpe	grater
la saucière	sauceboat; gravy boat
la sorbetière	ice-cream maker
la soupière	(soup) tureen
la sous-tasse (*pl* ~s)	saucer
la yaourtière	yoghurt-maker

THE LAW

ESSENTIAL WORDS (m)

un accident	accident
un agent (de police) ◇	policeman
l'argent ◇	silver; money
le budget ▢	budget
le bulletin d'informations	news bulletin
le bureau des objets trouvés	lost property office
le cambrioleur	burglar, robber
le chèque (de voyage)	(traveller's) cheque
le commissariat de police	police station
le constat	report
le consulat	consulate
un espion	spy
le gendarme	gendarme
le gouvernement ◇	government
un incendie	fire
le manifestant	demonstrator
le mort ◇	dead man
l'or	gold
le portefeuille ◇	wallet
le porte-monnaie ◇ (pl inv)	purse
le poste de police	police station
le problème	problem
le propriétaire	owner
le témoin ▢	witness
le type	fellow, chap
le vol	robbery
le voleur	robber, thief

IMPORTANT WORDS (m)

un agent secret	secret agent
un assassin	murderer
le butin ▢	loot
le cadavre	corpse
le coup (de fusil)	(gun)shot

voler to steal; to rob; **cambrioler** to burgle
j'ai été volé! I've been robbed!

188

ESSENTIAL WORDS (f)

une **amende** 💬	fine
une **armée**	army
la **bande** ◇	gang
la **banque** ◇	bank
la **faute** ◇ 💬	fault
la **gendarmerie**	headquarters of gendarmes
une **identité**	identity
la **manifestation** 💬	demonstration
la **mort** ◇	death
la **morte**	dead woman
la **peine de mort**	death penalty
la **permission** ◇	permission
la **pièce d'identité** ◇ 📖	(means of) identification
la **police d'assurance**	insurance policy
la **police-secours**	emergency services
la **propriétaire**	owner
la **récompense**	reward
la **taxe** ◇ 💬	tax

IMPORTANT WORDS (f)

l' **accusation**	the prosecution
une **accusation**	charge; accusation
une **agglomération** ◇ 💬	built-up area
une **arme**	weapon
une **arrestation**	arrest
la **bagarre**	fight, scuffle
la **bombe**	bomb
la **cellule**	cell

contre la loi against the law; illegal
ce n'est pas de ma faute it's not my fault
au secours! help!; **à l'assassin!** murder!
au voleur! stop thief!; **au feu!** fire!
haut les mains! hands up!
dévaliser une banque to rob a bank
manifester to demonstrate, stage a demonstration
récompenser to reward

THE LAW

IMPORTANT WORDS (m) (cont)

le courage	bravery
le crime	crime
le criminel	criminal
le détective privé	private detective
le détournement	hijacking
le drogué	drug addict
un enlèvement	kidnapping
un escroc [ɛskʀo]	crook
le flic	''cop''
le fusil [fyzi]	gun
le gangster	gangster
le garde	guard
le gardien ◇	guard; warden, attendant
le :héros	hero
un hold-up (pl inv)	hold-up
le juge	judge
le jury	jury
le meurtre	murder
le meurtrier	murderer
un otage	hostage
le palais de justice	law courts
le pirate de l'air	hijacker
le policier	policeman
le prisonnier	prisoner
le procès	trial
le reportage	report
le révolutionnaire	revolutionary
le revolver [ʀevɔlvɛʀ]	revolver
le sauvetage	rescue
le terrorisme	terrorism
le terroriste	terrorist
le voyou	hooligan

attaquer qn en diffamation to sue sb for slander
commettre des actes de brigandage to engage in robbery with violence
condamné à 5 mois (de prison) avec sursis given a 5 month suspended (prison) sentence

IMPORTANT WORDS (f) (cont)

la **défense** ◇	defence
la **déposition**	statement
la **dispute**	argument, dispute
la **droguée**	drug addict
les **drogues**	drugs
une **émeute**	uprising
une **enquête**	inquiry
une **évasion**	escape
l'**héroïne**	heroine
l'**incarcération**	imprisonment
la **loi**	law
une **ordonnance** ◇	decree, police order
la **pancarte**	placard
la **preuve**	proof
la **prise (de)**	capture (of)
la **prison**	prison
la **rafle**	raid
la **rançon**	ransom
la **révolution**	revolution
la **tentative**	attempt

USEFUL WORDS (f)

une **affaire** ◇	case
l'**aide judiciaire**	legal aid
une **amnistie**	amnesty
une **audience**	hearing
une **audition**	examination
la **calomnie**	slander; libel
la **complice**	accomplice
la **condamnation**	sentence; conviction
la **condamnée**	convict
la **contrebande**	smuggling
la **contrebandière**	smuggler
la **contrefaçon**	counterfeiting; forgery
la **cour d'appel**	Court of Appeal

en état d'arrestation under arrest
en flagrant délit in the act, red-handed
en liberté provisoire/surveillée/conditionnelle on bail/probation/parole

THE LAW

USEFUL WORDS (m)

l' accusé	accused; defendant
un acquittement	acquittal
un alibi	alibi
un appel	appeal
un arrêté	decree
un assassinat	murder
un attentat à la pudeur	indecent exposure; indecent assault
un aveu	confession
le bagnard	convict
le bagne	penal colony
le bandit	gangster, thief
le banditisme	violent crime
le bourreau (pl -x)	executioner
le brigand	brigand
le cachot	dungeon
le cambriolage	burglary
le chantage	blackmail
le commissaire	(police) superintendent
le complice	accomplice
le condamné	convict
le contrebandier	smuggler
le dédommagement	compensation
le délinquant	delinquent
le délit	(criminal) offence
le détenu	prisoner
le détournement de fonds	embezzlement or misappropriation of funds
le détournement de mineur	corruption of a minor
un échafaud	scaffold
le faussaire	forger
le faux	fake, forgery
le faux-monnayeur (pl ~s)	counterfeiter, forger
le faux témoignage	perjury
le forçat	convict; galley slave
le fric-frac	break-in
le fugitif	fugitive, runaway
le galérien	galley slave
le garde des Sceaux	Lord Chancellor
le geôlier	jailer

la cour d'assises	Crown Court, court of assizes
la cour de cassation	(final) Court of Appeal
la délinquance	criminality
la délinquance juvénile	juvenile delinquency
la délinquante	delinquent
la déposition	statement, deposition
la détenue	prisoner
une empreinte digitale	fingerprint
une escroquerie	swindle
l'évasion	escape
la faussaire	forger
la fraude fiscale	tax evasion
la fugitive	fugitive, runaway
la galère	galley
la garde à vue	police custody
la guillotine	guillotine
une informatrice	informant
la jurée	juror
la juriste	jurist, lawyer
la kleptomane	kleptomaniac
la machination	scheming, frame-up
la maison de redressement	reformatory
la majeure	person who has come of age
les menottes	handcuffs
la partie civile	party claiming damages
la pègre	underworld
la pendaison	hanging
la perquisition	(police) search
la plaidoirie	speech for the defence
la plainte	complaint
les poursuites	legal proceedings
la préfecture de police	police headquarters
la ravisseuse	abductor, kidnapper
les recherches	investigations
la récidive	second (*or* subsequent) offence
la récidiviste	second (*or* habitual) offender
la reconstitution	reconstruction
la séquestration	illegal confinement
la suspecte	suspect
la tentative d'évasion	escape bid

THE LAW

le greffier	clerk of the court
l'homicide	murder
l'homicide involontaire	manslaughter
le :hors-la-loi (pl inv)	outlaw
l'huissier	bailiff
l'indice	clue; piece of evidence
un informateur	informant
l'interrogatoire	questioning; cross-examination
le juré	juror
le juriste	jurist, lawyer
le justicier	judge, righter of wrongs
le kleptomane	kleptomaniac
le casier judiciaire	criminal record
le magistrat	magistrate
le maître chanteur	blackmailer
le majeur	person who has come of age
le malfaiteur	lawbreaker, criminal; thief
le mandat de perquisition	search warrant
le mandat d'arrêt	warrant for arrest
le mineur ⬦	minor
le parloir	visiting room (of prison)
le portrait-robot (pl ~s~s)	Identikit ® or Photo-fit picture
le pot-de-vin (pl ~s~~)	bribe
le préfet de police	Chief Constable
le procureur	public prosecutor
le rapt	abduction
le ravisseur	abductor, kidnapper
le recel	receiving (stolen goods)
le récidiviste	second (or habitual) offender
le recours en grâce	plea for clemency
le signalement	description, particulars
le suspect	suspect
le témoignage	testimony, evidence
le tribunal	court
le tribunal d'instance	magistrates' court
le tribunal de grande instance	high court
le tueur à gages	contract killer
le verdict	verdict
le viol	rape
le violeur	rapist

le vol à main armée	armed robbery
le voyeur	peeping Tom

en résidence surveillée under house arrest
être porté disparu to be reported missing
être en infraction to be in breach of the law
faire subir un contre-interrogatoire à qn to cross-examine sb
faire une fugue to run away, abscond
mettre une loi en application to enforce a law
prendre qn en filature to shadow sb
réclusion à perpétuité life imprisonment
s'introduire par effraction dans to break into
sous l'inculpation de on a charge of
traduire en justice to bring before the courts
en détention préventive remanded in custody, on remand
coupable guilty
gracier to pardon
kidnapper to kidnap
libérer to release
prêter serment to take an *or* the oath
s'évader to escape
une attaque à main armée an armed robbery *or* hold-up
détourner un avion to hijack a plane
enlever un enfant to kidnap *or* abduct a child
se battre to fight; **se disputer** to quarrel
une bande de voyous a bunch of hooligans
en prison in prison

MATERIALS

ESSENTIAL WORDS (m)

l'aluminium	aluminium
l'argent ◇	silver
le bois ◇ ▭	wood
le coton ▭	cotton
le coton hydrophile	cotton wool
le cuir	leather
l'état	condition
le gas-oil ◇ ▭	diesel
le gaz ◇	gas
le jean	denim
le métal ▭ (pl métaux)	metal
le nylon ▭	nylon
l'or	gold
le papier ◇	paper
le pétrole	oil, petroleum; paraffin
le plastique ▭	plastic
le verre ◇	glass

IMPORTANT WORDS (m)

l'acier	steel
l'acrylique	acrylic (fibre)
le béton	concrete
le bronze	bronze
le caoutchouc [kautʃu]	rubber
le caoutchouc mousse	foam rubber
le carton	cardboard
le charbon	coal
le ciment	cement
le cristal	crystal

une chaise *etc* **de** *or* **en bois** a wooden chair *etc*
une boîte en plastique a plastic box
une bague d'or *or* **en or/d'argent** a gold/silver ring
en bon état in good condition; **en mauvais état** in bad condition
les bottes (*fpl*) **de caoutchouc** wellington boots
le papier d'étain tinfoil, silver paper
le papier hygiénique toilet paper
le fer forgé wrought iron

ESSENTIAL WORDS (f)

la brique	brick
la corde ◇	rope
l'essence ◇ 📖	petrol
la fourrure ◇	fur
l'huile ◇	oil
la laine 📖	wool
la pierre ◇	stone
la soie	silk

IMPORTANT WORDS (f)

l'argile	clay
la cire	wax
la colle ◇	glue
la dentelle	lace
l'étoffe	material
la faïence	earthenware, pottery
la ficelle	string
la :houille	(industrial) coal
la paille ◇	straw
la peau de mouton	sheepskin
la peau de porc	pigskin
la porcelaine	porcelain, china
la toile	linen; canvas

USEFUL WORDS (f)

une auréole	ring
la chaux	lime
l'ébonite	vulcanite, ebonite
une émeraude	emerald
la ferraille	scrap iron
la feutrine	(lightweight) felt

un manteau en fourrure a fur coat
un pull en laine a woolly jumper
un bout de ficelle a piece of string
un chapeau de paille a straw hat

MATERIALS

le cuivre	copper
le cuivre jaune	brass
le daim	suede
le drap ◇	woollen cloth
l'étain	tin; pewter
le fer	iron
le fer-blanc ⌐ (pl ~s~s)	tin, tinplate
le fil	thread
le fil de fer	wire
le granit	granite
le lin ⌐	flax
le liquide	liquid
le marbre	marble
les matériaux	materials
l'osier ⌐	wickerwork
le plâtre ◇	plaster
le plomb	lead
le satin	satin
le suède	suede
le tergal ®	terylene ®
le tissu	cloth, material
le tweed	tweed
le velours	velvet
le velours côtelé	cord, corduroy
le vinyle	vinyl

USEFUL WORDS (m)

l'acajou	mahogany
un alliage	alloy
le bitume	asphalt, tarmac ®
le contre-plaqué	plywood
le crin	horse hair
l'ébène	ebony
l'émail	enamel
le fer forgé	wrought iron
le goudron	tar(mac ®)
le grès	sandstone; stoneware
l'inox(ydable)	stainless steel
l'ivoire	ivory

---

la **fibre de verre**	fibre glass
la **fonte**	cast iron
la **glaise**	clay
la **mousseline**	muslin
la **nacre**	mother-of-pearl
la **pâte à papier**	paper pulp
la **pépite**	nugget
la **pierre ponce**	pumice stone
la **rouille**	rust
la **soude**	soda
la **terre cuite**	earthenware; terracotta
la **tôle ondulée**	corrugated iron

adhésif(ive) adhesive, sticky
rêche rough; **résistant(e)** strong, hard-wearing
rugueux(euse) rough (*wood etc*)
soyeux(euse) silky

MATERIALS

le jade	jade
le jais	jet
le jaspe	jasper
le lainage	woollen material
le laiton	brass
le liège	cork
le macadam	tarmac ®
le madrier	beam
le mastic	putty
le minerai	ore
le mortier	mortar
le papier de verre	sandpaper
le platine	platinum
le raphia	raffia
le rotin	rattan (cane)
le silex	flint
le similicuir	imitation leather
le soufre	sulphur
le tissu-éponge (*pl* ~**s**~)	(terry) towelling

plaqué or/argent gold-/silver-plated

ESSENTIAL WORDS (m)

un **article**	article
le **journal** ◇ (*pl* **journaux**)	newspaper
le **journaliste**	journalist
le **magazine**	magazine
le **reportage**	report; story; article
le **reporter**	reporter

IMPORTANT WORDS (m)

un **attaché de presse**	press officer
un **auteur à succès**	bestselling author
le **bestseller**	bestseller
le **communiqué de presse**	press release
le **documentaire**	documentary
les **droits d'auteur**	royalties
un **exemplaire**	copy
l'**indice d'écoute** ▭	ratings
le **logo**	logo
le **périodique**	periodical
le **quotidien populaire**	tabloid
le **reportage exclusif**	exclusive (story)
les **romans à sensation** ▭	pulp fiction
les **romans de qualité** ▭	quality fiction
le **slogan**	slogan
le **spot publicitaire**	commercial break
le **tirage**	circulation

grandes ondes long wave(s)
ondes courtes short wave(s)
petites ondes, ondes moyennes medium wave(s)
le journal du matin/du soir/du dimanche the morning/evening/Sunday paper
diffuser to broadcast
en direct live; **en différé** (pre-)recorded
allumer, mettre to switch on
éteindre, arrêter to switch off
passer à la télé/à la radio to be on TV/on the radio

MEDIA

USEFUL WORDS (m)

un animateur ◇	compère
un applaudimètre	clapometer
un auditeur	member of the audience (*at a conference*); listener (*radio*)
un auditorium	public studio
le chroniqueur	columnist
le clip	pop (*or* promotional) video
le critique	critic
le documentaire	documentary
l'éditorial	leading article, editorial
un éditorialiste	leader *or* editorial writer
un enregistrement	recording
un envoyé	correspondent
le feuilleton	serial
un flash (*pl* ~**es**)	newsflash
le gros titre	headline
l'hebdo, hebdomadaire	weekly
un illustré	illustrated magazine; comic
le journal télévisé	television news
le magnétoscope ◇	video recorder
les mass(-)media	mass media
le mensuel	monthly
le panneau publicitaire	hoarding
le présentateur	presenter
le quotidien	daily (paper)
le réabonnement	renewal of subscription
le scoop	scoop, exclusive
le téléfilm	TV film

ESSENTIAL WORDS (f)

la chaîne ◇	channel
une émission	programme, broadcast
la journaliste	journalist
la presse	press
la publicité ◇	advertising
la radio ◇	radio
la télévision ◇	television

IMPORTANT WORDS (f)

une affiche ◇	poster
une attachée de presse	press officer
l'avant-première (pl ~s)	preview
la campagne de publicité	advertising campaign
la conférence de presse	press conference
une étude d'opinion 📖	audience research
l'image de marque 📖	brand image
la légende	caption
la pub [pyb]	ad
la revue (de luxe)	(glossy) magazine
la série	series
la suite	sequel

USEFUL WORDS (f)

une animatrice	compère
une auditrice	member of the audience (*at a conference*); listener (*radio*)
la censure	censorship
la chronique	column, page
la chronique sportive	sport review
la chronique théâtrale	theatre review
la critique	critic; review
la désinformation	disinformation
une éditorialiste	leader *or* editorial writer
une envoyée	correspondent
la liberté de la presse	freedom of the press
la mondovision	television broadcast by satellite
la nécrologie	obituary

MEDIA

les **petites annonces**	the classified ads
la **présentatrice**	presenter
la **réclame**	advertisement
la **rédaction**	editorial staff; editorial office
la **rediffusion**	repeat (*programme*)
la **réédition**	new edition
la **réimpression**	reprinting; reprint
la **reprise**	repeat
la **rubrique**	column
la **une**	front page, page one

bas de gamme down-market
haut de gamme up-market
grand public mass market
trimestriel(le) quarterly
la télévision par câble/par satellite cable/satellite TV
la télévision en couleurs/en noir et blanc colour/black and white television
les heures de grande écoute prime time

ESSENTIAL WORDS (m)

le **combat**	fight; fighting
le **soldat**	soldier

IMPORTANT WORDS (m)

le **blindé** ▭	armoured car; tank
le **cessez-le-feu** (*pl inv*)	ceasefire
le **défilé** ◇	parade
le **déserteur**	deserter
un **obus** [ɔby] ▭	shell
le **régiment**	regiment
le **service militaire**	military service

USEFUL WORDS (m)

un **adjudant**	warrant officer
un **adjudant-chef** (*pl* ~**s**~**s**)	warrant officer 1st class
un **amiral**	admiral
un **ancien combattant**	ex-serviceman; war veteran
un **appelé**	conscript
les **baraquements**	camp
le **bataillon**	batallion
le **bombardement**	bombing
le **bombardier**	bomber
le **camp** [kɑ̃]	camp
le **canon**	cannon
le **capitaine**	captain
le **caporal** (*pl* **caporaux**)	lance-corporal
le **caporal-chef** (*pl* **caporaux**~**s**)	corporal
le **cavalier**	cavalryman
le **chasseur** ◇	fighter (plane)
le **château fort**	stronghold, fortified castle
le **civil**	civilian
le **colonel**	colonel; (air force) group captain
le **colt**	revolver, Colt ®
le **commandant**	major; squadron leader; captain
le **contingent**	contingent
le **couvre-feu** (*pl* -**x**)	curfew
le **démineur**	bomb disposal expert

MILITARY MATTERS

un éclaireur	scout
un engagé	enlisted man
un engagé volontaire	volunteer
un envahisseur	invader
un escadron	squadron
l'état-major (pl ~s~s)	staff
le fantassin	infantryman
le fusil-mitrailleur (pl ~s~s)	machine gun
le galon	stripe
le général (d'armée)	general; air chief marshall
le général de brigade	brigadier; air commodore
le général de corps d'armée	lieutenant general; air marshall
le général de division	major general; air vice-marshall
le général en chef	general-in-chief, general-in-command
un gilet pare-balles	bullet-proof jacket
le grade	rank
le grenadier	grenadier
le guérillero	guerrilla
le guerrier	warrior
le guet-apens (pl ~s~s)	ambush
le guetteur	look-out
un infirme de guerre	war cripple
le lance-flammes (pl inv)	flame-thrower
le lance-missiles (pl inv)	missile launcher
le lance-pierres (pl inv)	catapult
le lance-torpilles (pl inv)	torpedo tube
le légionnaire	legionnaire
le lieutenant	lieutenant; flying officer
le lieutenant-colonel (pl ~s~s)	lieutenant-colonel; wing officer
le major	adjutant
le maréchal (pl maréchaux)	field marshal
le maréchal des logis	sergeant
le mess	mess
le militaire	serviceman
le mirador	watchtower
un objecteur de conscience	conscientious objector
un observatoire	observation or look-out post
l'occupant	the occupying forces
le para	para

ESSENTIAL WORDS (f)

une **arme**	weapon
l'**armée**	army
l'**armée de l'air**	Air Force
la **guerre**	war
la **marine**	navy
la **paix**	peace

IMPORTANT WORDS (f)

la **bombe**	bomb
la **caserne**	barracks
la **défense** ◇	defence
la **recrue**	recruit

USEFUL WORDS (f)

une **alerte**	warning, alarm
l'**armure**	armour
la **brigade**	brigade
la **carabine**	rifle
la **cartouche**	cartridge
la **cavalerie**	cavalry
la **cavalière**	cavalrywoman
la **cible**	target
la **civile**	civilian
la **corvée**	fatigue (duty)
la **dynamite**	dynamite
une **échauffourée**	skirmish
une **embuscade**	ambush
une **épée**	sword
une **estafette**	courier
la **flotte**	fleet
la **forteresse**	fortress
les **fortifications**	fortifications
la **frégate**	frigate
la **fusillade**	gunfire, shooting; gun battle
la **gâchette**	trigger
la **garnison**	garrison
la **grenade lacrymogène**	teargas grenade
la **guérilla**	guerrilla warfare

MILITARY MATTERS

le parachutiste	paratrooper
le peloton d'exécution	firing squad
le permissionnaire	soldier on leave
le pistolet	pistol, gun
le poignard	dagger
le report d'incorporation	deferment
le sergent	sergeant
le sous-officier (pl ~s)	non-commissioned officer (NCO)
le tireur d'élite	marksman, sharp shooter
le torpilleur	torpedo boat

faire le guet to be on the watch *or* look-out
faire le parcours du combattant to go round an assault course
il s'est fait réformer he was declared unfit for service
passer à l'offensive to go into the attack
passer en conseil de guerre to be court-martialled
s'enrôler dans l'armée to enlist in the army
se replier to withdraw, fall back

la guerrière	warrior
l'infanterie	infantry
l'invasion	invasion
la lance	spear
la légion	legion
la Légion étrangère	Foreign Legion
la milice	militia
la mitraillette	submachine gun
la mitrailleuse	machine gun
les munitions	ammunition
une offensive	offensive
une ogive nucléaire	nuclear warhead
la patrouille	patrol
la permission ◊	leave
la reddition	surrender
les représailles	reprisals, retaliation
la sentinelle	sentry
la sirène d'alarme ◊	air-raid siren
la torpille	torpedo
la trêve	truce

MUSIC

ESSENTIAL WORDS (m)

le chef d'orchestre	conductor
le groupe	group
un instrument de musique ▭	musical instrument
le musicien ▭	musician
un orchestre	orchestra
le piano ✿	piano
le saxophone	saxophone
le trombone	trombone
le violon	violin, fiddle

IMPORTANT WORDS (m)

un accord ✿	chord
un accordéon	accordion
le basson	bassoon
le bâton ✿	conductor's baton
le clairon ▭	bugle
le cor d'harmonie	French horn
l'harmonica	harmonica, mouth organ
le :hautbois	oboe
le jazz [dʒaz]	jazz
un orgue	organ
le soliste	soloist
le tambour	drum
le tambourin	tambourine
le triangle	triangle
le violoncelle	cello
le xylophone [ksilɔfɔn]	xylophone

USEFUL WORDS (m)

l'accompagnement	accompaniment
un accordéoniste	accordionist
un alto	viola
un ampli(ficateur)	amplifier
un archet	bow
un auteur-compositeur (pl ~s-s)	composer-songwriter
le baryton	baritone
le bassiste	(double) bass player

ESSENTIAL WORDS (f)

la **clarinette**	clarinet
la **flûte**	flute
la **flûte à bec**	recorder
la **guitare**	guitar
la **musique** ◇	music

IMPORTANT WORDS (f)

la **batterie** ◇	drums, drum kit
la **contrebasse**	double bass
la **corde** ◇	string
la **cornemuse**	bagpipes
les **cymbales**	cymbals
la **fanfare**	brass band; fanfare
la **grosse caisse**	big drum, bass drum
la **:harpe**	harp
la **note** ◇	note
la **salle des fêtes**	concert hall
la **soliste**	soloist
la **touche** ◇ ▭	(piano) key
la **trompette**	trumpet

THE SCALE

do	do(h)	C
ré	re	D
mi	mi	E
fa	fa	F
sol	so(h)	G
la	la	A
si	ti, te	B

écoutez la musique! listen to the music!; **rayé(e)** scratched (*record etc*)
jouer du piano/de la guitare/du violon/de la batterie to play the piano/the guitar/the violin/the drums
travailler son piano to practise the piano; **une fausse note** a wrong note
jouer *or* **interpréter un morceau** to play a piece
jouer fort to play loudly; **jouer doucement** to play softly
jouer/chanter juste to play/sing in tune; **jouer/chanter faux** to play/sing off key

MUSIC

USEFUL WORDS (m) (cont)

le batteur	drummer
le chœur	choir
le choriste	choir member
le clarinettiste	clarinettist
le clavecin	harpsichord
le claveciniste	harpsichordist
le compositeur	composer
le contrebassiste	(double) bass player
le duo	duet
un enregistrement	recording
un exécutant	performer
le flûtiste	flute player, flautist
le guitariste	guitarist
l' harmonium	harmonium
le :harpiste	harpist
un homme-orchestre (pl ~s~s)	one-man band
un imprésario	impresario
le luth	lute
le luthier	(stringed-)instrument maker
le mélomane	music lover
le micro(phone)	mike, microphone
le microsillon	long-playing record
le phonographe	(wind-up) gramophone
le pianiste	pianist
le play-back	miming
le pot-pourri (pl ~s~s)	potpourri, medley
le quarante-cinq tours	single
le quartette	jazz quartet(te)
le quatuor	quartet(te)
le quintette	quintet(te)
le refrain	refrain, chorus; tune
le slow	slow number
le solfège	musical theory
le solo (pl soli)	solo
le synthétiseur	synthesizer
le tam-tam (pl ~s)	tomtom
le trente-trois tours	LP
le trompettiste	trumpet player
le violoncelliste	cellist, cello player
le violoniste	violinist, violin player

une accordéoniste	accordionist
une alto	(contr)alto
une auteur-compositeur (*pl* ~**s**~**s**)	composer-songwriter
la ballade	ballad
la basse	bass
la bassiste	(double) bass player
la berceuse	lullaby
la cassette vierge	blank tape
la choriste	choir member
la cithare	zither
la clarinettiste	clarinettist
la claveciniste	harpsichordist
la comptine	nursery rhyme
la contrebassiste	(double) bass player
une enceinte (acoustique)	speaker
une exécutante	performer
la flûte de Pan	panpipes
la flûtiste	flute player, flautist
la gamme	scale
la guitare basse	bass guitar
la guitariste	guitarist
la :harpiste	harpist
la :hi-fi [hifi]	hi-fi
la lyre	lyre
la mandoline	mandolin(e)
la mélomane	music lover
la musique classique	classical music
les paroles	lyrics
la partition	score
la percussion	percussion
la pianiste	pianist
la platine	turntable
la platine laser	compact disc player
la pochette de disque	record sleeve
la tournée	tour (*of artist*)
la trompettiste	trumpet player
la violoncelliste	cellist, cello player
la violoniste	violinist, violin player
la vocalise	singing exercise

NUMBERS AND QUANTITIES

CARDINAL NUMBERS

nought	0	zéro
one	1	(*m*) un, (*f*) une
two	2	deux
three	3	trois
four	4	quatre
five	5	cinq
six	6	six
seven	7	sept
eight	8	huit
nine	9	neuf
ten	10	dix
eleven	11	onze
twelve	12	douze
thirteen	13	treize
fourteen	14	quatorze
fifteen	15	quinze
sixteen	16	seize
seventeen	17	dix-sept
eighteen	18	dix-huit
nineteen	19	dix-neuf
twenty	20	vingt
twenty-one	21	vingt et un
twenty-two	22	vingt-deux
twenty-three	23	vingt-trois
thirty	30	trente
thirty-one	31	trente et un
thirty-two	32	trente-deux
forty	40	quarante
fifty	50	cinquante
sixty	60	soixante
seventy	70	soixante-dix
seventy-one	71	soixante-et-onze
eighty	80	quatre-vingts
eight-one	81	quatre-vingt-un
ninety	90	quatre-vingt-dix
ninety-one	91	quatre-vingt-onze
a (*or* one) hundred	100	cent
a hundred and one	101	cent un
a hundred and two	102	cent deux
a hundred and ten	110	cent dix

CARDINAL NUMBERS (cont)

a hundred and eighty-two	182	cent-quatre-vingt-deux
two hundred	200	deux cents
two hundred and one	201	deux cent un
two hundred and two	202	deux cent deux
three hundred	300	trois cents
four hundred	400	quatre cents
five hundred	500	cinq cents
six hundred	600	six cents
seven hundred	700	sept cents
eight hundred	800	huit cents
nine hundred	900	neuf cents
a (*or* one) thousand	1000	mille
a thousand and one	1001	mille un
a thousand and two	1002	mille deux
two thousand	2000	deux mille
ten thousand	10000	dix mille
a (*or* one) hundred thousand	100000	cent mille
a (*or* one) million	1000000	un million
two million	2000000	deux millions

N.B. 1000000: In French, the word *million* is a noun, so the numeral takes *de* when there is a following noun: *un million de gens, trois millions de maisons*

les nombres pairs/impairs even/odd numbers
une assiette de a plate of
une bande de a group *or* gang of; a flock of (*birds*)
beaucoup de (monde) lots of (people)
une boîte de a tin *or* can of; a box of
un bol de a bowl of
une bouchée de a mouthful of
un bout de papier a bit *or* piece of paper
une bouteille de a bottle of
cent grammes (*mpl*) de a hundred grammes of
une centaine de (about) a hundred
une cuillerée de a spoonful of
un demi de bière half a litre of beer, ''a half''
une demi-douzaine de half a dozen

NUMBERS AND QUANTITIES

ORDINAL NUMBERS

first	1	(*m*) premier, (*f*) -ière
second	2	deuxième
third	3	troisième
fourth	4	quatrième
fifth	5	cinquième
sixth	6	sixième
seventh	7	septième
eighth	8	huitième
ninth	9	neuvième
tenth	10	dixième
eleventh	11	onzième
twelfth	12	douzième
thirteenth	13	treizième
fourteenth	14	quatorzième
fifteenth	15	quinzième
sixteenth	16	seizième
seventeenth	17	dix-septième
eighteenth	18	dix-huitième
nineteenth	19	dix-neuvième
twentieth	20	vingtième
twenty-first	21	vingt et unième
twenty-second	22	vingt-deuxième
thirtieth	30	trentième
thirty-first	31	trente et unième
fortieth	40	quarantième
fiftieth	50	cinquantième
sixtieth	60	soixantième
seventieth	70	soixante-dixième
eightieth	80	quatre-vingtième
ninetieth	90	quatre-vingt-dixième
hundredth	100	centième
hundred and first	101	cent unième
hundred and tenth	110	cent-dixième
two hundredth	200	deux centième
three hundredth	300	trois centième
four hundredth	400	quatre centième
five hundredth	500	cinq centième
six hundredth	600	six centième
seven hundredth	700	sept centième
eight hundredth	800	huit centième

ORDINAL NUMBERS (cont)

nine hundredth	**900**	neuf centième
thousandth	**1000**	millième
two thousandth	**2000**	deux millième
millionth	**1000000**	millionième
two millionth	**2000000**	deux millionième

a half	½	(m) un demi, (f) une demie
one and a half helpings	1½	une portion et demie
two and a half kilos	2½	deux kilos et demi
a third	⅓	un tiers
two thirds	⅔	deux tiers
a quarter	¼	un quart
three quarters	¾	trois quarts
a sixth	⅙	un sixième
five and five sixths	5⅚	cinq et cinq sixièmes
a twelfth	¹/₁₂	un douzième
seven twelfths	⁷/₁₂	sept douzièmes
a hundredth	¹/₁₀₀	un centième
a thousandth	¹/₁₀₀₀	un millième

un demi-kilo de half a kilo of
un demi-litre de half a litre of
une demi-livre de half a pound of
tous (f toutes) les deux both of them
une dizaine de (about) ten
une douzaine de a dozen
une foule de a crowd of, crowds of, heaps of, masses of
un kilo(gramme) de a kilo(gramme) of
à quelques kilomètres de a few kilometres from
un litre de a litre of
une livre ◇ de a pound of
un mètre de a metre of
à quelques mètres de a few metres from
des milliers de thousands of
la moitié de half of
un morceau de sucre a lump of sugar
un morceau de gâteau a piece or slice of cake
une paire de a pair of
un paquet de a packet of

NUMBERS AND QUANTITIES

une partie ⟡ **de** a part of
une pelletée de a shovelful of
un peu de a little
une pile de a pile of
la plupart de or **des** most (of)
plusieurs (des) several (of)
une poignée ⟡ **de** a handful of
une portion de a portion or helping of
un pot de a pot or tub of; a jar of
(une) quantité de a lot of, many; a quantity of
un quart de a quarter of
une rasade de a glassful of
une soixantaine de sixty or so, about sixty
une tablette de a bar of (*chocolate*)
un tas de a heap of, heaps of
une tasse de a cup(ful) of
un tonneau de a barrel of
une tranche de a slice of
trois quarts de three quarters of
un troupeau de a herd of (*cattle*); a flock of (*sheep*)
un verre de a glass of

ESSENTIAL WORDS (m)

l' argent ◇	silver; money
le bijou (pl -x)	jewel
le bracelet	bracelet, bangle
le déodorant	deodorant
le gant de toilette	face flannel
le maquillage 📖	make-up
le miroir ◇	mirror
l' or	gold
le parfum ◇ 📖	perfume, scent
le peigne	comb
le rasoir 📖	razor
le salon de beauté	beauty salon or parlour
le shampooing	shampoo

IMPORTANT WORDS (m)

le bigoudi 📖	curler, roller
le blaireau (pl -x) 📖	shaving brush
le bouton de manchette 📖	cufflink
le collier	necklace, beads
le diamant	diamond
le dissolvant	nail varnish remover
les effets personnels	personal effects
le fard	make-up
le fard à paupières	eye-shadow
le fond de teint	foundation
le kleenex ®	(paper) tissue
le pendentif 📖	pendant
le porte-clefs (pl inv)	key-ring
le poudrier	(powder) compact
le rimmel ®	mascara
le rouge à lèvres	lipstick
le vernis à ongles	nail varnish, nail polish

se **laver** to get washed; **s'habiller** to get dressed
se **farder**, se **maquiller** to put on one's make-up
se **démaquiller** to take off one's make-up
se **coiffer** to do one's hair
se **brosser les cheveux** to brush one's hair
se **peigner** to comb one's hair

PERSONAL ITEMS

USEFUL WORDS (m)

un agenda ⟡	diary
un animal en peluche	soft toy, fluffy animal
l'attirail	gear
le bracelet-montre (*pl* ~s~s)	wristwatch
le coupe-ongles (*pl inv*)	nail clippers
le démaquillant	make-up remover
un écrin	case, box (*for silver, jewels*)
un étui à lunettes	glasses case
un eye-liner	eyeliner
le nounours	teddy (bear)
les objets de valeur	valuables, articles of value
le porte-bonheur (*pl inv*)	lucky charm
le rubis	ruby
le saphir	sapphire
le talc	talc, talcum powder

ESSENTIAL WORDS (f)

la **bague**	ring
la **beauté**	beauty
la **brosse à dents**	toothbrush
la **chaîne**	chain
la **chaînette**	chain
la **crème de beauté**	face cream
l' **eau de toilette**	toilet water
la **glace** ◇	mirror
la **montre** ◇	watch
la **pâte dentifrice**	toothpaste

IMPORTANT WORDS (f)

une **alliance**	wedding ring
la **boucle d'oreille** (pl ~s d'oreille)	earring
la **broche**	brooch
la **coiffure**	hairstyle
la **crème à raser**	shaving cream
une **éponge**	sponge
la **gourmette** 📖	identity bracelet
la **perle**	pearl
la **perruque**	wig
la **poudre (de riz)**	face powder

USEFUL WORDS (f)

la **chevalière**	signet ring
la **lame de rasoir**	razor blade
la **laque**	hair spray
la **lotion après rasage**	aftershave
la **pince à épiler**	tweezers
la **serviette périodique**	sanitary towel
la **tirelire**	moneybox; piggy bank
la **trousse de toilette**	toilet bag, sponge bag

se raser to shave; **se brosser les dents** to brush one's teeth
prêt(e) à partir ready to leave
une valeur sentimentale sentimental value
bijou (de) fantaisie fancy jewellery
il est arrivé avec tout son attirail he arrived with all his paraphernalia

PLANTS AND GARDENS

un arbre ◇	tree
le banc (de jardin)	(garden) seat
le bouquet de fleurs	bunch of flowers
le jardin	garden
le jardinage	gardening
le jardinier	gardener
les légumes ◇	vegetables
le parfum ◇ ▭	perfume, scent
le soleil ◇	sun

un arbuste ▭	shrub, bush
un arrosoir	watering can
le bassin	(ornamental) pool
le bourgeon	bud
le bouton-d'or (pl ~s~)	buttercup
le buisson ◇	bush
le chèvrefeuille ▭	honeysuckle
le chrysanthème	chrysanthemum
le coquelicot ▭	poppy
le crocus	crocus
le feuillage ◇	leaves
le gazon	lawn; turf
l'hortensia ▭	hydrangea
le jardin potager	vegetable garden
le lierre	ivy

un jardin entouré d'arbres a garden surrounded by trees
offrir un bouquet de fleurs à qn to give sb a bunch of flowers
tondre le gazon to mow the lawn
"défense de marcher sur le gazon" ''keep off the grass''
mon père aime jardiner my father likes gardening
planter to plant; **déplanter** to dig up

ESSENTIAL WORDS (f)

une **abeille**	bee
la **barrière** ◇	gate; fence
la **branche**	branch
la **culture** ◇	cultivation
la **feuille** ◇	leaf
la **fleur**	flower
la **guêpe**	wasp
l' **herbe** 📖	grass
la **pelouse**	lawn
la **pierre** ◇	stone, rock
la **plante**	plant
la **pluie** ◇	rain
la **rose** ◇	rose
la **terre** ◇	earth, ground

IMPORTANT WORDS (f)

une **allée**	path
la **baie** ◇	berry
la **brouette**	wheelbarrow
la **clôture**	fence
une **échelle** ◇	ladder
une **épine**	thorn
la **giroflée jaune** 📖	wallflower
les **graines**	seeds
la **:haie** ◇	hedge
la **jacinthe**	hyacinth
la **jonquille**	daffodil
la **marguerite**	daisy
les **mauvaises herbes**	weeds
une **ombre**	shadow

les fleurs poussent the flowers grow
par terre on the ground
cueillir des fleurs to pick flowers
se mettre à l'ombre to go into the shade
rester à l'ombre to remain in the shade
à l'ombre d'un arbre in the shade of a tree
la guêpe va vous piquer the wasp is going to sting you

PLANTS AND GARDENS

IMPORTANT WORDS (m) (cont)

le lilas	lilac
le lis [lis]	lily
le muguet	lily of the valley
un œillet	carnation
un outil ◇	tool
le papillon	butterfly
le parterre ◇	border, flower bed
le pavillon ◇	summer house
le pavot	poppy
le perce-neige (*pl inv*)	snowdrop
le pissenlit	dandelion
le pois de senteur ▢	sweet pea
le rosier	rose bush
le sol	earth, soil
le soleil ◇, tournesol	sunflower
le tronc	trunk (*of tree*)
le tuyau d'arrosage	hose
le ver ◇	worm
le verger ◇	orchard

USEFUL WORDS (m)

l'ajonc	gorse
un arbrisseau (*pl* -**x**)	shrub
l'arrosage	watering
le bleuet	cornflower
le chardon	thistle
le chiendent	couch grass
le désherbant	weedkiller
un églantier	wild *or* dog rose (bush)
l'estragon	tarragon
le genêt	broom (*plant*)
le genévrier	juniper
le glaïeul	gladiola
le gravier	(loose) gravel
les gravillons	(loose) gravel
le grillage	wire netting; wire fencing
le gui	mistletoe
un horticulteur	horticulturalist
un iris	iris

IMPORTANT WORDS (f) (cont)

une **orchidée**	orchid
la **pâquerette**	daisy
la **pensée** ◇	pansy
la **pivoine** ▥	peony
la **plate-bande** (*pl* ~**s**~**s**)	flower bed
la **primevère**	primrose
la **racine**	root
la **renoncule** ▥	buttercup
la **rocaille**	rockery, rock garden
la **rosée**	dew
la **semence**	seed (*in general*)
la **serre**	greenhouse
la **tige**	stalk
la **tondeuse**	lawnmower
la **tulipe**	tulip
la **violette**	violet

USEFUL WORDS (f)

une **aubépine**	hawthorn
la **bouture**	cutting
la **capucine**	nasturtium
une **églantine**	wild *or* dog rose
une **épine**	thorn
les **floralies**	flower show
la **gentiane**	gentian
la **glycine**	wisteria
la **greffe**	graft
la **gueule-de-loup** (*pl* ~**s**~~)	snapdragon
une **horticultrice**	horticulturalist
la **lavande**	lavender
la **marjolaine**	marjoram
la **menthe**	mint
la **mousse**	moss
une **ortie**	(stinging) nettle
la **pépinière**	nursery
la **pervenche**	periwinkle
la **roseraie**	rose garden
la **verdure**	greenery
la **vigne vierge**	Virginia creeper

PLANTS AND GARDENS

USEFUL WORDS (m) (cont)

le jardin d'acclimatation	zoological garden
le jardin potager	kitchen *or* vegetable garden
le laurier	laurel
le laurier-rose (*pl* ~**s**~)	oleander
le magnolia	magnolia
le mimosa	mimosa
le myosotis	forget-me-not
le narcisse	narcissus
le nénuphar	water lily
le paysagiste ◇	landscape gardener
le rhododendron	rhododendron
le terreau	compost
le tourniquet	sprinkler
le trèfle ◇	clover
le troène	privet

en fleur in blossom
faire des boutures to take cuttings
élaguer to prune
fané(e) faded; **piquant(e)** prickly
rempoter to repot; **repiquer** to plant out

ESSENTIAL WORDS (m)

le chef d'état	head of state
le député ⬦	Member of Parliament
le gouvernement ⬦	government
le politicien ⬦	politician
le premier ministre	Prime Minister

IMPORTANT WORDS (m)

le citoyen ⬦	citizen
le dirigeant	leader (*of party, country, union*)
le fonctionnaire ⬦	state employee; civil servant
le réfugié	refugee
le régime	régime
les sans-abri	the homeless
le Tiers-Monde	the Third World
le vote	vote

USEFUL WORDS (m)

l'affairisme	(political) racketeering
l'appauvrissement	impoverishment
un arrêt de travail	stoppage (*of work*)
un assisté	person receiving aid from the State
un attentat à la bombe	bomb attack
l'attentisme	wait-and-see policy
le ballottage	second ballot
le bandit	gangster, thief

de gauche/droite left-/right-wing
être partisan(e) de qch/de faire qch to be in favour of sth/of doing sth
le bilan d'une catastrophe the final toll of a disaster
le niveau de vie standard of living
mettre de l'argent de côté to save up
poser la question de confiance to ask for a vote of confidence
prendre des sanctions contre to impose sanctions on
un gouvernement fantoche a puppet government

le bipartisme	bipartisanship
le civisme	public-spiritedness
le colon	settler
le combat de rues	street fighting
le conseiller municipal	town councillor
le conservateur	Conservative
le contestataire	(anti-establishment) protester
le contribuable	taxpayer
le coût de la vie	the cost of living
le débat	discussion, debate
le dépouillement du scrutin	counting the votes
les déshérités	the underprivileged, the deprived
le discours ◇	speech
le droit d'asile	(political) asylum
l'électorat	electorate
un élu	member of parliament; elected representative
un émigrant	emigrant
un émigré	expatriate
un empereur	emperor
un empire	empire
l'état d'urgence	state of emergency
l'état de siège	state of siege
l'État-providence	welfare state
l'exode des cerveaux	brain drain
un expatrié	expatriate
le fascisme	fascism
le gauchiste	leftist
le génocide	genocide
le ghetto	ghetto
le gouverneur	governor
le grand public	general public
l'hémicycle	the benches (in French parliament)
un homme d'État	statesman
un homologue	counterpart, opposite number
l'hôtel Matignon	French prime minister's offices
un immigré	immigrant
l'impôt sur le revenu	income tax
l'impôt foncier	land tax

ESSENTIAL WORDS (f)

la **droite**	the right (wing)
l' **économie**	economy
la **gauche**	the left (wing)
les **législatives**	general election
la **politicienne** ◇	politician
la **politique** ◇	politics; policy

IMPORTANT WORDS (f)

l' **aide sociale**	social security
la **circonscription électorale**	constituency
la **citoyenne** ◇	citizen
l' **égalité**	equality
la **fonctionnaire**	state employee; civil servant
l' **inflation**	inflation
la **manifestation**	demonstration
la **nationalisation**	nationalization
la **réfugiée**	refugee
les **relations internationales**	international relations
la **reprise économique**	economic recovery
la **sécurité sociale**	social security
la **superpuissance**	superpower

USEFUL WORDS (f)

les **affaires étrangères**	foreign affairs
une **allocation**	allowance
l' **allocation (de) chômage**	unemployment benefit
l' **allocation (de) logement**	rent allowance
l' **allocation de maternité**	maternity benefit
les **allocations familiales**	child benefit

voter par procuration to vote by proxy
les pays en voie de développement developing countries
le scrutin proportionnel/majoritaire election on a proportional/majority basis
le scrutin à deux tours poll with two ballots
nationaliser to nationalize
privatiser to privatize
manifester to demonstrate

229

l'impôt sur la fortune	wealth tax
les impôts locaux	rates
un indépendantiste	separatist
l'inspecteur des finances	tax inspector
l'interventionnisme	interventionism
l'isoloir	polling booth
l'Élysée	official residence of the French President
le ministère de l'Intérieur	Home Office
le ministre de la Défense nationale	Defence Minister
le notable	prominent citizen
un opposant	opponent
le parlement	parliament
les partis de droite	the right-wing parties
le passeur de drogues	drug smuggler
les pays non-alignés	nonaligned countries
le percepteur	tax collector
le porte-parole (pl inv)	spokesperson
les pourparlers	talks, negotiations
le pouvoir d'achat	purchasing power
le prestataire	person receiving benefits
un projet de loi	(government) bill
le racket	racketeering
le rapatriement	repatriation
le rationnement	rationing
le rebondissement	new development
le recensement	census
le référendum	referendum
le régime totalitaire	totalitarian régime
le règne	reign
le remaniement ministériel	cabinet reshuffle
le renversement	overthrow (of government)
les rescapés	survivors
le ressortissant	national
le revenu	income
le scrutin	ballot; poll
le septennat	seven-year term (of office)
le sondage (d'opinion)	opinion poll
le statu quo	status quo

USEFUL WORDS (f) (cont)

une ambassade	embassy
l' Assemblée nationale (AN)	French National Assembly
une assistée	person receiving aid from the State
l' autarcie	self-sufficiency
l' autodétermination	self-determination
la bourgeoisie	middle classes, bourgeoisie
la citoyenneté	citizenship
la classe ouvrière	working class
la conjoncture économique	economic climate
la conseillère municipale	town councillor
la conservatrice	Conservative
la contestataire	(anti-establishment) protester
la contribuable	taxpayer
la course aux armements	arms race
la député	Member of Parliament
la dictature	dictatorship
la dirigeante	leader (of party, country, union)
la discrimination	discrimination
l' Éducation nationale	Department of Education
une élection partielle	by-election
une élue	member of parliament; elected representative
une émeute	riot
une émigrante	emigrant
l' émigration	emigration
une émigrée	expatriate
une ethnie	ethnic group
une expatriée	expatriate
la famine	famine
la fiscalité	tax system; taxation
la fonction publique	the civil service
la gauchiste	leftist
l' homologue	counterpart, opposite number
l' immigration	immigration
une immigrée	immigrant
une impératrice	empress
l' importation ⊳	import
une indemnisation	indemnity, compensation
une indemnité parlementaire	MP's salary

USEFUL WORDS (m) (cont)

le surarmement	massive stock of weapons
le surpeuplement	overpopulation
le sympathisant	sympathizer
le taux de mortalité	mortality rate
le téléphone rouge	hot line
le tortionnaire	torturer
le totalitarianisme	totalitarianism
le trafic d'armes	arms dealing
le trafic de drogues	drugs trafficking
le trafiquant	trafficker; dealer
le vote (à bulletin) secret	secret ballot
le vote à main levée	vote by a show of hands
le vote par correspondance	postal vote

une indemnité de logement	housing allowance
l'indépendance	independence
une indépendantiste	separatist
l'insertion sociale	(social) integration
l'insurrection	insurrection, revolt
l'investiture	nomination
la législature	term of office
la liberté syndicale	union rights
la liberté	freedom
la liberté d'opinion	freedom of thought
les libertés publiques	civil rights
les libertés individuelles	personal freedom
les mœurs	customs, habits
la Maf(f)ia	the Maf(f)ia
la motion de censure	vote of no confidence
une opposante	opponent
l'Organisation des Nations Unies (ONU)	United Nations (Organization) (UN, UNO)
l'Organisation du Traité de l'Atlantique Nord (OTAN)	North Atlantic Treaty Organization (NATO)
l'Organisation mondiale de la santé (OMS)	World Health Organization (WHO)
la pénurie	shortage
la perception	tax (collector's) office
la petite bourgeoisie	lower middle classes
la polémique	controversy
la politique étrangère/intérieure	foreign/domestic policy
la population active	working population
les présidentielles	presidential elections
la prestataire	person receiving benefits
la prise d'otages	hostage-taking
la proposition de loi	private bill
la réforme	reform
la répression	repression
la revendication	claim, demand
la ségrégation	segregation
la surpopulation	overpopulation
la sympathisante	sympathizer
la torture	torture
l'urne (électorale)	ballot box

RELIGION AND PHILOSOPHY

ESSENTIAL WORDS (m)

Allah	Allah
un **athée**	atheist
Bouddha	Buddha
le **croyant**	believer
Dieu	God
le **péché**	sin

IMPORTANT WORDS (m)

un **adepte**	follower
le **clergé**	clergy
les **fidèles**	the faithful; the congregation

USEFUL WORDS (m)

un **abbé**	priest; abbot
un **ange**	angel
un **apôtre**	apostle, disciple
un **archevêque**	archbishop
un **autel**	altar
le **bénitier**	font
le **bouddhisme**	Buddhism
le **bouddhiste**	Buddhist
le **catholicisme**	(Roman) Catholicism
le **catholique**	(Roman) Catholic
le **chapelet**	rosary
le **chiromancien**	palmist
le **chœur**	choir
le **chrétien**	Christian
le **christianisme**	Christianity
le **ciel** ◇	heaven
le **cierge**	candle
le **cloître**	cloister

de bon/mauvais augure of good/ill omen
M le curé Vicar
M l'abbé Father
tirer les cartes à qn to read sb's cards
le siècle des lumières Age of Enlightenment

ESSENTIAL WORDS (f)

une **athée**	atheist
la **bible**	bible
la **croyante**	believer
une **église**	church
la **religion**	religion

IMPORTANT WORDS (f)

une **adepte**	follower
la **communion**	communion
la **confession**	confession
la **croyance**	belief
l'**Ecriture (sainte), les Ecritures**	the Scriptures
la **messe**	mass
la **mosquée**	mosque
la **Réforme**	the Reformation

USEFUL WORDS (f)

une **abbaye**	abbey
une **abbesse**	abbess
l'**apothéose**	apotheosis
l'**assemblée des fidèles**	congregation
l'**aumône**	alms
une **auréole**	halo
la **basilique**	basilica
la **bouddhiste**	Buddhist
la **cathédrale**	cathedral
la **catholique**	(Roman) Catholic
la **chapelle**	chapel
la **chiromancie**	palmistry
la **chiromancienne**	palmist
la **chrétienne**	Christian
la **communiante**	communicant
la **conformiste**	conformist

faire la quête to take the collection
jeter un sort to cast a spell
se racheter to redeem o.s.
prier to pray

RELIGION AND PHILOSOPHY

le communiant	communicant
le confessionnal	confessional
(pl **confessionnaux**)	
le conformisme	conformity
le conformiste	conformist
le crucifix	crucifix
le curé	parish priest
le diable	the Devil
le dieu	god
le disciple	disciple
un ecclésiastique	ecclesiastic, clergyman
l'Éden	Eden
l'égalitarisme	egalitarianism
un encensoir	censer, thurible
l'endoctrinement	indoctrination
l'enfer	hell
l'épiscopat	episcopate
l'esprit	spirit
un esthète	aesthete
l'évangile	gospel
un évêché	bishop's palace; bishopric
un évêque	bishop
le fantôme	ghost
un franc-maçon (pl ~**s**~**s**)	freemason
l'hindou	Hindu
l'hindouisme	Hinduism
l'horoscope	horoscope
l'intégrisme	fundamentalism
un intégriste	fundamentalist
Islam	Islam
le jésuite	Jesuit
Jésus-Christ	Jesus Christ
le jeûne	fast
le judaïsme	Judaism
le juif	Jew
le maléfice	evil spell
le méthodiste	Methodist
le miracle	miracle
le moine	monk, friar
le monastère	monastery

236

USEFUL WORDS (f) (cont)

la **crucifixion**	crucifixion
la **déesse**	goddess
l'**eau bénite**	holy water
une **esthète**	aesthete
la **foi**	faith
la **franc-maçonnerie**	freemasonry
la **genèse**	genesis
l'**hindoue**	Hindu
l'**hostie**	host
une **intégriste**	fundamentalist
la **juive**	Jew, Jewess
la **laïcité**	secularity, secularism
la **liberté du culte**	freedom of worship
la **madone**	madonna
la **magie**	magic
la **méthodiste**	Methodist
la **musulmane**	Moslem, Muslim
la **nonne**	nun
la **païenne**	pagan, heathen
la **papauté**	papacy
la **paroisse**	parish
la **paroissienne**	parishioner
la **philosophe**	philosopher
la **possédée**	person possessed
la **rédemption**	redemption
la **réincarnation**	reincarnation
la **religieuse** ◇	nun
la **réprouvée**	reprobate
la **revenante**	ghost
la **Sainte Vierge**	the Blessed Virgin
la **secte**	sect
la **sorcellerie**	witchcraft
la **sorcière**	witch
la **synagogue**	synagogue
l'**utopie**	Utopia
une **utopiste**	Utopian
les **vêpres**	vespers
la **Vierge**	the Virgin
la **voyance**	clairvoyance
la **voyante**	clairvoyant

USEFUL WORDS (m) (cont)

le musulman	Moslem, Muslim
l'office	service
le païen	pagan, heathen
le pape	pope
le Paradis terrestre	Garden of Eden
le paroissien	parishioner
le pasteur	minister, pastor
le pèlerin	pilgrim
le pèlerinage	pilgrimage
le penseur	thinker
le philosophe	philosopher
le possédé	person possessed
le prêcheur	preacher
le premier communiant	child making his first communion
le présage	omen
le purgatoire	purgatory
le rabbin	rabbi
le réprouvé	reprobate
le revenant	ghost
le rite	rite; ritual
le sacristain	sacristan; sexton
le Saint-Esprit	the Holy Spirit *or* Ghost
le sermon	sermon
le sionisme	Zionism
le sorcier	sorcerer
le sort	fate
le sortilège	(magic) spell
le tabou	taboo
le temple	temple: (protestant) church
un utopiste	Utopian
le Verbe	the Word
le vicaire	curate

ESSENTIAL WORDS (m)

un **accident (de la route)**	(road) accident
un **agent (de police)** ✧	policeman
un **automobiliste**	motorist
l'**auto-stop**	hitch-hiking
un **auto-stoppeur** (*pl* ~**s**)	hitch-hiker
le **camion**	lorry, truck
le **carrefour**	crossroads
le **chauffeur** ✧ (*m+f*)	driver; chauffeur
le **code de la route** ▭	highway code
le **coffre** ✧	boot
le **conducteur** ▭	driver
le **cycliste** ▭	cyclist
le **deux-temps** ▭ (*pl inv*)	two-stroke (engine)
le(s) **dommage(s)**	damage
un **embouteillage** ▭	traffic jam
l'**embrayage** ▭	clutch; letting in the clutch
le **feu rouge** ▭	traffic lights, red light
les **feux (de circulation)**	traffic lights
le **frein** ✧ ▭	brake
le **garage** ✧	garage
le **garagiste** ▭	mechanic; garage owner
le **gas-oil** ✧ ▭	diesel (oil)
le **kilomètre**	kilometre
le **klaxon**	horn, hooter
le **lavage** ▭	(car) wash
le **litre**	litre
le **mécanicien** ✧ ▭	mechanic
le **mort** ✧	dead man
le **moteur**	engine
le **motocycliste**	motorcyclist
le **numéro** ✧	number
l'**ordinaire**	2-star petrol

faire de l'auto-stop to go hitch-hiking
déposer un auto-stoppeur to drop off a hitch-hiker
s'arrêter au feu rouge to stop at the red light
freiner brusquement to brake sharply
100 kilomètres à l'heure 100 kilometres an hour

ESSENTIAL WORDS (m) (cont)

les **papiers**	official papers, documents
le **parking** ◇	car park
le **péage** 🕮	toll
le **permis de conduire** 🕮	driving licence
le **phare** ◇ 🕮	headlight; headlamp
le **piéton**	pedestrian
le **plan** ◇ (de la ville)	street map
le **pneu**	tyre
le **pompiste** 🕮	petrol pump attendant
le **rond-point** (*pl* ~**s**~**s**)	roundabout
le **sens unique** 🕮	one-way street
le **stationnement** 🕮	parking
le **super**	4-star petrol
le **voyage** ◇	journey

IMPORTANT WORDS (m)

un **accélérateur**	accelerator
un **arrêt d'urgence**	emergency stop
le **blessé**	casualty
le **capot**	bonnet
le **carburateur**	carburettor
le **clignotant**	indicator
le **compteur de vitesse**	speedometer
le **conducteur débutant**	learner driver
le **contractuel**	traffic warden

crever, avoir un pneu crevé to have a puncture
être à plat to have a flat tyre
sais-tu conduire une auto? can you drive a car?
on va faire une promenade en voiture we're going for a drive (in the car)
faites le plein (d'essence) fill her up please!
l'essence sans plomb unleaded petrol
la route nationale the trunk *or* main road
prenez la route de Lyon take the road to Lyons
perdre/retrouver sa route to lose/find one's way
c'est un voyage de 3 heures it's a 3-hour journey
allez, en route! let's go!, let's be off!
faire un créneau to reverse into a parking space
faire une déclaration d'accident to file an accident claim

ESSENTIAL WORDS (f)

une amende 🖅	fine
l'assurance 🖅	insurance
une auto, automobile	car
une auto-école (*pl* ~**s**)	driving school
une autoroute	motorway
une autoroute à péage 🖅	toll motorway
une auto-stoppeuse (*pl* ~**s**)	hitch-hiker
la batterie ◇	battery
la caravane ◇	caravan
la carte routière	road map
la ceinture de sécurité 🖅	seat belt
la circulation	traffic
la collision	collision
la crevaison	puncture
la déviation 🖅	diversion
la direction ◇ 🖅	direction
la distance 🖅	distance
l'eau ◇	water
l'essence ◇ 🖅	petrol
la frontière	border, frontier
l'huile ◇	oil
la marque 🖅	make (*of car*)
la mort ◇	death
la panne	breakdown
la pièce de rechange	spare part
la police ◇	police
la police d'assurance	insurance policy
la pompiste 🖅	petrol pump attendant
la portière	(car) door
la priorité	priority
la roue	wheel
la roue de secours 🖅	spare wheel
la route ◇	road
la station-service (*pl* ~ **s** ~)	service *or* filling station
la vitesse ◇	speed; gear
la voiture ◇	car
la voiture de dépannage ◇	breakdown van
la zone 🖅	zone, area

IMPORTANT WORDS (m) (cont)

le démarreur	starter
le détour	detour
un essuie-glace (*pl inv*)	windscreen wiper
le lave-auto (*pl* **~s**)	car wash
le motard □	motorcycle cop
le panneau (*pl* **-x**)	road sign
le parc(o)mètre	parking meter
le pare-brise (*pl inv*)	windscreen
le pare-chocs (*pl inv*)	bumper
le périphérique	ring road
le poste d'essence	filling station
le procès-verbal, P.-V. (*pl* **--verbaux**)	fine, (parking) ticket
le rétroviseur	rear-view *or* driving mirror
le routier	long-distance lorry driver
le starter	choke
le tournant, le virage	turning, bend
le volant	steering wheel

USEFUL WORDS (m)

un accrochage	minor collision
l'alco(o)test	Breathalyser ®
l'allumage	ignition
un allume-cigare (*pl inv*)	cigar lighter
un amortisseur	shock absorber
l'antigel	antifreeze
un antivol	anti-theft device
un appui-tête (*pl inv*)	headrest

l'accident a fait 6 blessés/morts 6 people were injured/killed in the accident
il faut faire un détour we have to make a detour; **sabler** to grit
une contravention pour excès de vitesse a fine for speeding
dresser un P.-V. contre un conducteur to book a driver
"priorité à droite" ''give way to the right''
"serrez à droite" ''keep to the right''
"accès interdit" ''no entry''
"stationnement interdit" ''no parking''
"travaux" ''roadworks''
"passage protégé" *road having priority status*

IMPORTANT WORDS (f)

une **agglomération** ◇	built-up area
une **aire de services**	service area
une **aire de stationnement**	lay-by
la **bagnole** ▭	(old) car, banger
la **bande médiane**	central reservation
la **boîte de vitesses**	gearbox
la **bretelle d'accès** *or* de **raccordement** ▭	access road (*to motorway*)
la **caisse** ◇	body, bodywork
la **capote**	hood
la **consommation d'essence**	petrol consumption
la **contractuelle**	traffic warden
la **contravention**	traffic offence
la **dépanneuse**	breakdown van
la **file (de voitures)**	line (of cars), lane
la **galerie** ◇	roof rack
la **leçon de conduite**	driving lesson
la **limitation de vitesse**	speed limit, speed restriction
la **pédale**	pedal
la **plaque d'immatriculation** *or* **minéralogique**	number plate
la **pression** ◇	pressure
la **remorque** ▭	trailer
la **voie** ◇	way, road; lane (*on road*)
la **voie de raccordement** ▭	slip road

---

bonne route! have a good journey!
en route nous avons vu … on the way we saw …
doubler *or* **dépasser une voiture** to overtake a car
faire demi-tour to do a U-turn
garer (la voiture) to park (the car)
je vais faire réparer la voiture I'm going to have the car fixed
d'abord on met le moteur en marche first you switch on the engine
le moteur démarre the engine starts up
la voiture démarre the car moves off
on roule we're driving along
accélérer to accelerate; **continuer** to continue
ralentir to slow down; **s'arrêter** to stop
stationner to park; to be parked

---

l'argus	guide to second-hand car prices
l'avertisseur	horn
le bas-côté (pl ~s)	verge
le bidon à essence	petrol can
le bonus	no-claims bonus (car insurance)
le boulevard périphérique	ring road
le cahot	jolt, bump
le carambolage	multiple crash, pile-up
le carburant	(motor) fuel
le chauffard	reckless driver
le constat d'accident	accident report
le cric	jack
le croisement	crossroads, junction
le déflecteur	quarterlight
le dégivrage	de-icing (of windscreen)
le dégivreur	de-icer
le démarrage en côte	hill start
le diesel	diesel
un embranchement	junction
un enjoliveur	hub cap
l'excès de vitesse	speeding
le fléchage	signposting
le gabarit	size (of car)
le garde-barrière (pl ~s~(s))	level crossing keeper
le gyrophare	revolving (flashing) light
le :hayon	tailgate
l'itinéraire	itinerary, route
le kilométrage	number of kilometres travelled; mileage
le lave-glace (pl ~s)	windscreen washer
le phare antibrouillard	fog lamp
le plaid	(tartan) car rug
un pont en dos-d'âne	humpback bridge
le pont suspendu	suspension bridge
le pot d'échappement	exhaust pipe
le restoroute ®	motorway restaurant
le service/camion dépannage	breakdown service/truck
le tableau (pl -x) de bord	dashboard
le toboggan	flyover
le toit ouvrant	sun roof

l'adhérence à la route	roadholding
une artère	main road
une autoradio	car radio
la bifurcation	fork (*in road*)
la borne kilométrique	kilometre-marker
la bougie	spark(ing) plug
la garde-barrière (*pl* ~**s**~(**s**))	level crossing keeper
la glissière de sécurité	crash barrier
l'immatriculation	registration
la jante	(wheel) rim
la jauge (de niveau) d'huile	dipstick
une ornière	rut
la prévention routière	road safety
la signalisation	road signs
la veilleuse	sidelight
la vignette	(road) tax disc
la voiture de sport	sports car
la voiture d'occasion	second-hand car

au point mort in neutral (gear); **passer au rouge** to go through a red light
en état d'ivresse under the influence of drink
faire subir l'alco(o)test à qn to breathalyse sb
faire un appel de phares to flash one's headlights
prendre la file de droite to move into the right-hand lane
stationner en double file to double-park
une route accidentée an uneven road; **une voiture fiable** a reliable car
traction avant/arrière front-wheel/rear-wheel drive
débrayer to declutch; **dégivrer** to de-ice (*windscreen*)
dégonflé(e) flat (*tyre*); **gonfler** to inflate, blow up
reculer to reverse; **remorquer** to tow
"dépassement interdit" ''no overtaking''
couper le moteur to switch off the engine
il y a eu un accident there's been an accident
vos papiers, s'il vous plaît your identification please
aux heures d'affluence at the rush hour, at the peak period
il a eu 100 francs d'amende he got a 100-franc fine
êtes-vous assuré(e)? are you insured?; **à la frontière** at the border
n'oubliez pas de mettre vos ceintures don't forget to put on your seat belts
être *or* **tomber en panne** to break down, have a breakdown
la roue avant/arrière the front/back wheel
je suis tombé(e) en panne sèche I've run out of petrol

SCHOOL AND OFFICE EQUIPMENT

ESSENTIAL WORDS (m)

le bureau ◇	desk
le carnet ◇	notebook
le classeur	folder, file
le crayon	pencil
le livre ◇	book
le magnétophone ◇	tape recorder
un ordinateur ◇	computer
le papier ◇	paper
le stylo (à encre)	(fountain) pen
le tableau ◇ (noir)	blackboard

IMPORTANT WORDS (m)

le bic	ballpoint pen
le cahier	exercise book, jotter
le cartable	satchel
le dictionnaire	dictionary
le feutre	felt-tip pen
le pupitre	desk
le stylo à bille	ballpoint pen
le stylo feutre	felt-tip pen
le stylomine	propelling pencil
le taille-crayon(s) (pl ~(s))	pencil sharpener
le torchon	duster

USEFUL WORDS (m)

un agenda ◇	diary
le bloc-notes (pl ~s~)	notepad
le buvard	blotting paper; blotter
le calepin	notebook
le calque	tracing paper
le carnet d'adresses	address book
le casier	pigeonhole
le compas	(pair of) compasses
le dossier	file
les fournitures de bureau	office supplies
les fournitures scolaires	school stationery
le magnétoscope	video (recorder)
le marqueur	marker pen

ESSENTIAL WORDS (f)

la **carte** ◇	map
la **gomme**	rubber
la **règle** ◇	ruler

IMPORTANT WORDS (f)

la **craie**	chalk
l' **encre**	ink
la **machine à calculer**	calculator
la **machine à écrire**	typewriter
la **machine de traitement de texte** ◇	word processor
la **sacoche** ◇	schoolbag, satchel
la **serviette** ◇	briefcase

USEFUL WORDS (f)

une **agrafe**	staple
une **agrafeuse**	stapler
la **calculatrice**	calculator
la **calculette**	pocket calculator
une **enveloppe autocollante**	self-seal envelope
une **équerre**	set square
la **fiche intercalaire, l'intercalaire**	divider
la **loupe**	magnifying glass
la **mappemonde**	globe
la **microfiche**	microfiche
la **perforeuse**	punch
la **photocopieuse**	(photo)copier
la **rame (de papier)**	ream (of paper)
la **trousse (d'écolier)**	pencil case

réglable adjustable

le mémento	appointment diary
le microscope	microscope
le papier à en-tête	headed notepaper
le papier calque	tracing paper
le papier de brouillon	rough *or* scrap paper
le papier machine	typing paper
le papier quadrillé	squared paper
le plumier	pencil box
le presse-papiers (*pl inv*)	paperweight
le protège-cahier (*pl ~s*)	exercise book cover
le signet	bookmark
le sous-main (*pl inv*)	desk blotter
le surligneur	highlighter (pen)
le tampon encreur	inking pad
le Tipp-Ex ®	Tipp-Ex ®

le baigneur	bather, swimmer
le bain ◊ (de mer)	bathe (*in sea*), swim
le bateau (*pl* -**x**) de pêche	fishing boat
le bikini	bikini
le bord de la mer	seaside
le château ◊ (*pl* -**x**) de sable	sandcastle
le coup de soleil	sunstroke
le crabe	crab
le fond	bottom
l'horizon	horizon
le maillot ◊ (de bain)	swimming costume *or* trunks
le mal de mer	seasickness
le matelas pneumatique	airbed, lilo
le passager ◊	passenger
le pêcheur ◊	fisherman
le pique-nique (*pl* ~**s**) ⌑	picnic
le pont ◊	deck (*of ship*)
le port	port, harbour
le prix du billet ◊	fare
le quai ◊	quay, quayside
le sable	sand
le slip de bain	swimming *or* bathing trunks
le téléscope	telescope
le vacancier	holiday-maker

l'air marin	sea air
un aviron	oar
le bac ◊	ferry(-boat)
le caillou (*pl* -**x**)	pebble
le cap [kap]	point
le coquillage	shell
le courant	current
un équipage	crew
les flots	waves
le gouvernail	rudder
le maître nageur	lifeguard
le marin ◊	sailor
le mât ◊	mast

AT THE SEASIDE

le matelot	sailor
le naufrage	shipwreck
les naufragés	people who are shipwrecked
un océan ◇	ocean
le pavillon ◇	flag
le pédalo	pedal-boat
le phare ◇	lighthouse
le port de plaisance	marina
le radeau (pl -x)	raft
le rivage	coast, shore
le rocher	rock
le seau ◇ (pl -x)	bucket
le vaisseau (pl -x)	vessel
le vapeur ◇	steamer

USEFUL WORDS (m)

le corail (pl **coraux**)	coral
les embruns	sea spray
les estivants	summer visitors, holiday-makers
le galet	pebble
le garde-côte (pl ~**s**~(**s**))	coastguard boat
le garde-pêche (pl inv)	water bailiff; fisheries protection ship
le goéland	(sea)gull
le :hamac	hammock
le :hors-bord (pl inv)	speedboat (with outboard motor)
le lagon	lagoon
le noyé	drowned man
un oursin	sea urchin
le parasol	parasol, sunshade
le plagiste	beach attendant
le raz-de-marée (pl inv)	tidal wave
le transat	deckchair
le varech	wrack, kelp

ESSENTIAL WORDS (f)

une **agence de voyages** ✧	travel agent's
la **brochure**	brochure
la **chaise longue**	deckchair
la **côte** ✧	coast
la **crème solaire**	sun(tan) cream
l'**eau** ✧	water
une **île** ✧	island
les **lunettes de soleil**	sunglasses
la **mer** ✧	sea
la **natation** ▭	swimming
la **passagère**	passenger
la **pierre** ✧	stone, rock
la **plage**	beach
la **promenade** ✧	trip, outing; walk
la **serviette** ✧	towel
la **traversée**	crossing

IMPORTANT WORDS (f)

les **algues**	seaweed
une **ancre**	anchor
la **baie** ✧	bay
la **barque**	small boat
la **bouée**	buoy
la **cargaison**	cargo
la **ceinture de sauvetage**	lifebelt
la **cheminée** ✧	funnel

au bord de la mer at the seaside
faire un pique-nique to go for a picnic
à l'horizon on the horizon; **se bronzer** to get a tan
il a le mal de mer he is (feeling) sea-sick
nager to swim; **se noyer** to drown
regarder les brochures to look at brochures
nous allons à la côte aujourd'hui we're going to the coast today
je vais me baigner I'm going for a swim
plonger dans l'eau to dive into the water; **flotter** to float
au fond de la mer at the bottom of the sea
à la plage on the beach; to the beach
faire la traversée en bateau to cross over by boat

AT THE SEASIDE

la croisière	cruise
l'écume	foam
une embouchure	mouth (*of river*)
une épave	wreck
la falaise ◇	cliff
la flotte	fleet
une insolation	(touch of) sunstroke
la jetée	pier, jetty
les jumelles ◇	binoculars
la marée	tide
la marine	navy
la mouette	seagull
la passerelle	gangway; bridge (*of ship*)
la pelle ◇	spade
la rame	oar
la vague	wave
la voile ◇	sail; sailing

USEFUL WORDS (f)

les amarres	moorings
la crique	creek, inlet
la dune	dune
la :houle	swell
la lagune	lagoon
la longue-vue (*pl* ~**s**~**s**)	telescope
la morte-saison (*pl* ~**s**~**s**)	slack *or* off season
la noyée	drowned woman
la rabane	raffia (matting)
la station balnéaire	seaside resort

se promener au bord des falaises to walk along the edge of the cliffs
j'ai eu une insolation I had a touch of sunstroke
à marée basse/haute at low/high tide; **faire de la voile** to go sailing
le flux et le reflux the ebb and flow
"baignade interdite" ''no bathing''

ESSENTIAL WORDS (m)

l'argent ◇	money
un article	article
un ascenseur ⊞	lift
le boucher ⊞	butcher
le boulanger ⊞	baker
le bureau (*pl* -**x**) de poste	post office
le bureau de tabac	tobacconist's (shop)
le cabinet de consultation	surgery
le cadeau (*pl* -**x**)	present
le café ◇	café
le café-tabac	café (*which sells tobacco*)
le centime	centime
le centre commercial ⊞	shopping centre
le charcutier ⊞	pork butcher
le chèque ◇	cheque
le client ◇	customer, client
le coiffeur ◇	hairdresser; barber
le commerçant ◇ ⊞	tradesman
le commerce ◇	trade, business
le comptoir ⊞	counter
le cordonnier ⊞	cobbler
un employé ◇ ⊞	employee; clerk
un épicier ⊞	grocer
un escalier roulant ◇ ⊞	escalator
un étage ◇	floor
le franc	franc
le gérant ◇ ⊞	manager
le grand magasin	department store
l'hypermarché ⊞	hypermarket
le libre-service ⊞ (*pl* ~**s**~**s**)	self-service store *or* restaurant
le magasin	shop
le magasin de chaussures	shoe shop
le marchand de fruits ⊞	fruiterer
le marchand de légumes ⊞	greengrocer
le marché ◇	market; deal
le pâtissier	confectioner, pastrycook
le portefeuille ◇	wallet
le porte-monnaie ◇ (*pl inv*)	purse
le prix ◇	price
le rayon ◇ ⊞	department, counter

SHOPPING

ESSENTIAL WORDS (m) (cont)

le reçu	receipt
le rez-de-chaussée (*pl inv*)	ground level, ground floor
les soldes ⌑	sales; bargains
le sous-sol ⌑ (*pl ~s*)	basement
le souvenir	souvenir
le supermarché	supermarket
le tabac ◇	tobacconist's
le vendeur ◇ ⌑	shop assistant, salesman

IMPORTANT WORDS (m)

un agent de tourisme	travel agent
un agent immobilier	estate agent
le bibliothécaire	librarian
le bijoutier	jeweller
le bon	form, coupon
le bookmaker	bookmaker
le coloris	colour
le confiseur	confectioner
le débit de fritures	fish-and-chip shop
le débit de tabac	tobacconist's
le disquaire	record-dealer
l'horloger	watchmaker
le libraire	bookseller
le mannequin ◇	dummy, model
le marchand de biens	estate agent
le marchand de journaux	newsagent
le marchand de nouveautés	draper
le marchand de poissons	fishmonger
le marchand des quatre saisons	barrow-boy, costermonger
un opticien ◇	optician
le produit	product; (*pl*) produce
le pub	pub
le quincaillier	ironmonger
le tailleur ◇	tailor
le vidéoclub	video shop
le zinc	counter (*of bar or pub*)

ça fait combien? how much does that come to?
je l'ai payé(e) 5 francs I paid 5 francs for it

ESSENTIAL WORDS (f)

l'addition ◊	bill
une agence de voyages ◊	travel agent's
une alimentation ▱	food store
la banque ◊	bank
la bibliothèque ◊	library
la boucherie	butcher's (shop)
la boulangerie	baker's (shop)
la boutique ◊ ▱	small shop
la caisse ▱	till; cash desk; check-out
la charcuterie ▱	pork butcher's
la cliente ◊	customer, client
la cordonnerie	cobbler's
la crémerie ▱	dairy
une employée ◊ ▱	employee
une épicerie	grocer's (shop)
une erreur ◊	mistake, error
la laverie automatique	launderette
la librairie	bookshop
la liste	list
la parfumerie ▱	perfume shop/counter/department
la pâtisserie ◊	cake shop, confectioner's
la (petite) monnaie ▱	(small) change
la pharmacie ◊	chemist's (shop)
la pointure ▱	(shoe) size
la poste ◊	post office
la promotion ▱	special offer
la réclamation ▱	complaint
la réduction ◊	reduction
la saison des soldes	sales-time
la taille ◊	size
la vendeuse ▱	shop assistant, salesgirl
la vitrine	shop window

acheter/vendre qch to buy/sell sth
il a envie d'acheter une voiture/de vendre sa voiture he would like to buy a car/to sell his car
quel est le prix de ce manteau? what is the price of this coat?
ça coûte combien? how much does this cost?

SHOPPING

USEFUL WORDS (m)

un achat	purchase
un acheteur	purchaser
le bazar	general store
le bouquiniste	second-hand bookseller (*especially along the Seine in Paris*)
le brocanteur	secondhand (furniture) dealer
le buraliste	tobacconist
le caddie	(supermarket) trolley
le chariot ◇	trolley
le chausseur	footwear specialist, shoemaker
le chéquier	cheque book
le coiffeur ◇	hairdresser
les comestibles	(fine) foods, delicatessen
le commerçant ◇	shopkeeper, trader
le commis	shop assistant
le détaillant	retailer
le distributeur automatique	vending machine
le droguiste	keeper of a hardware shop
un échantillon	sample
l'emballage	packaging; wrapping
un escompte	discount
un étal	stall
un étalage	display
le fourrier	furrier
le gérant ◇	manager
le grossiste	wholesaler
le joaillier	jeweller
le marchand de journaux	newsagent
le mercier	haberdasher
un orfèvre	goldsmith, silversmith
le paquet-cadeau (*pl* ~**s**~**x**)	gift-wrapped parcel
le poissonnier	fishmonger
le pressing	dry-cleaner's
le rabais	reduction, discount
le salon d'essayage	fitting room
le service après-vente	after-sales service
le teinturier	dry cleaner

IMPORTANT WORDS (f)

une **agence immobilière** ◊	estate agent's
la **bijouterie**	jeweller's (shop)
la **blanchisserie**	laundry, dry cleaner's
la **boutique d'animaux** ◊	pet shop
la **caisse d'épargne**	savings bank
les **commissions**	shopping
la **compagnie**	company
la **compagnie d'assurance**	insurance company
la **confiserie**	sweetshop, confectioner's
une **course** ◊	errand
les **courses**	shopping
la **devanture**	shop window; display
la **droguerie**	dispensing chemist's
une **encolure**	collar size
l' **horlogerie**	watchmaker's
la **laiterie**	dairy
la **maison de commerce**	firm
la **maison de couture**	fashion house
les **marchandises**	goods, wares
la **papeterie**	stationer's
la **queue** ◊ [kø]	queue
la **quincaillerie**	ironmonger's, hardware shop
la **société d'assurance**	insurance company
la **société de crédit immobilier**	building society
la **succursale**	branch
la **teinturerie**	dry-cleaner's
la **vente** ◊	sale; selling; sales

je ne fais que regarder I'm just looking
c'est trop cher it's too expensive
quelque chose de moins cher something cheaper
c'est bon marché it's (very) cheap
c'est mieux marché it's cheaper
"payez à la caisse" ''pay at the cash desk''
j'ai trop dépensé I've spent too much money
c'est pour offrir? is it for a present? (*i.e. would you like it gift-wrapped?*)
avec ça? anything else?
S.A. (société anonyme) Ltd.
S.A.R.L. (société à responsabilité limitée) limited liability company
et Cie & Co.

une antiquité	antique
les arrhes ◇	deposit
l'arrière-boutique (pl ~**s**)	back shop
la bouchère	(woman) butcher, butcher's wife
la boulangère	(woman) baker, baker's wife
la boulangerie-pâtisserie (pl ~**s**~**s**)	baker's and confectioner's (shop)
la bouquiniste	second-hand bookseller (*especially along the Seine in Paris*)
la braderie	clearance sale, street sale
la brocante	second-hand goods
la brocanteuse	second-hand (furniture) dealer
la buraliste	tobacconist
la clientèle	customers, clientèle
la coiffeuse ◇	hairdresser
la démarque	mark-down
la détaillante	retailer
la droguiste	keeper of a hardware shop
une étiquette	label
la file d'attente	queue
la friperie	second-hand clothes shop
la gérante	manageress
la grande surface	hypermarket, superstore
les :halles	central food market
l'herboristerie	herbalist's shop
la librairie-papeterie (pl ~**s**~**s**)	bookseller's and stationer's
la liquidation	clearance (sale)
la marchande de journaux	newsagent
la maroquinerie	leather shop
la mercerie	haberdasher's shop

verser un acompte to pay a deposit
vêtement de confection ready-to-wear garment
"baisse sur la viande" ''meat prices down''

USEFUL WORDS (f) (cont)

la **mercière**	haberdasher
la **nocturne**	late opening
la **poissonnerie**	fishmonger's
la **poissonnière**	fishmonger
les **primeurs**	early fruit and vegetables
les **réclamations**	complaints department
la **réserve**	storeroom
la **teinturière**	dry cleaner
la **vente de charité**	charity sale

chez le boucher/le boulanger at the butcher's/baker's
il doit y avoir une erreur there must be some mistake
faire les courses to go shopping
acheter qch à la brocante to buy sth at the flea market
acheter à crédit to buy on credit
article en réclame special offer
le rapport qualité-prix value (for money)
livraison à domicile home delivery
magasin de farces et attrapes joke (and novelty) shop
payer en trois versements to pay in three instalments
"en vente ici" "on sale here"
"maison à vendre" "house for sale"
"appartement à louer" "flat to rent"
"souris à donner" "mice free to good home"
une voiture d'occasion a second-hand car

SOUNDS

le battement	banging; thud; beating; flapping
le borborygme	rumble, rumbling noise
le boucan	din, racket
le boum	bang
le bourdonnement	buzzing; buzz
le braillement	bawling; yelling
le bruissement	rustle, rustling
le bruit	sound, noise
le chahut	uproar, rumpus
la clameur	clamour
le clapotement	lap(ping)
le clapotis	lap(ping)
la claque	slap
le claquement	banging, slamming
le cliquetis	jingle, clink
le cognement	banging; knocking
le crachotement	crackling (*of a radio*)
le craquement	crack, snap; creak
le crépitement	sputtering, spluttering; crackling
le cri	cry; shout; scream
le crissement	crunch(ing); rustle, rustling; screech(ing)
le déclic	click
la détonation	bang
un écho	echo
un éclat de rire	burst of laughter
les éclats de voix	shouts
les flonflons	blare
le fracas	din; crash
la friture	crackle, crackling (*of radio*)
le frottement	rubbing, scraping
le gargarisme	gargle
le gargouillis	gurgling, rumbling
le gazouillis	chirp
le geignement	groaning, moaning
le gémissement	groaning, moaning
le glas	knell, toll
le glouglou	gurgling
le gloussement	chuckle
le grattement	scratching (noise)

le grésillement	sizzling; crackling
le grincement	grating (noise); creaking (noise)
le grondement	rumble, growl
l'hululement	hooting, screeching
le :hurlement	howling, howl; yelling, yell
le martèlement	hammering
le miaou	miaow
le miaulement	mewing
le murmure	murmur
la plainte	moan, groan
le raclement	scraping (noise)
le râle	groan
le ronflement	snore, snoring; hum(ming)
le ronronnement	purr(ing); hum(ming)
le sifflement	whistle, whistling
le soupir	sigh
le tapage	din, uproar
le tic-tac (*pl inv*)	tick-tock, ticking
le tintement	ringing; chiming
le vacarme	row, din
le vagissement	cry, wail
les vociférations	cries of rage, screams
le vrombissement	humming

résonner to reverberate, resound
retentir to ring out

ESSENTIAL WORDS (m)

le badminton	badminton
le ballon ◇	(foot)ball
le basket(ball)	basketball
le billard	billiards
le but ◇	goal
le champion	champion
le championnat	championship
le cricket	cricket
le cyclisme ◇ ⌑	cycling
le football	football (*game*)
le gardien de but	goalkeeper
le golf	golf
le :hockey	hockey
le jeu ◇ (*pl* -x)	game; play
le joueur	player
le maillot ◇	(football) jersey
le match (*pl* matches)	game; match
le netball	netball
le résultat	result
le rugby	rugby
le ski	skiing; ski
le sport	sport
le stade	stadium
le tennis	tennis; tennis court
le terrain ◇ (de sports)	ground; pitch; course
le Tour de France ◇	Tour de France (*cycle race*)
le volley-ball (*pl* ~s)	volleyball

jouer au football/au tennis *etc* to play football/tennis *etc*
marquer un but/un point to score a goal/a point
marquer les points to keep the score
le champion du monde the world champion
gagner/perdre un match to win/lose a match
j'ai gagné/perdu! I won/lost!
premier au classement général first overall
prendre son/de l'élancement to take a run up, gather speed
quarts de finale quarter finals
simple messieurs/dames men's/ladies singles
sponsoriser to sponsor

ESSENTIAL WORDS (f)

la boule	bowl; billiard ball
les boules	bowls
la championne	champion
les courses de chevaux	horse-racing
la défense ◊	defence
une équipe	team
l'équitation	horse-riding
la gymnastique	gymnastics
la joueuse	player
la natation ▭	swimming
la partie ◊	game
la pêche ◊	fishing
la piscine ◊	swimming pool
la piste ◊	ski slope; track
la planche à voile	windsurfing; windsurfer (*board*)
la promenade ◊	walk
la rencontre ◊	match
la réunion	meeting
la voile ◊	sailing

IMPORTANT WORDS (f)

une adversaire	opponent
la balle	(*tennis etc*) ball; bullet
la boxe	boxing
la canne ◊	golf club
la chasse	hunting

faire match nul to draw (*in a match*)
mon sport préféré my favourite sport
courir to run; **sauter** to jump; **lancer, jeter** to throw
battre qn to beat sb; **s'entraîner** to train
mener to be in the lead
je suis un supporter du Liverpool I support Liverpool
une partie de tennis a game of tennis
il fait partie d'un club he belongs to a club
aller à la pêche to go fishing
aller à la piscine to go to the swimming pool
sais-tu nager? can you swim?

SPORT AND KEEPING FIT

IMPORTANT WORDS (m)

un adversaire	opponent
l'alpinisme	mountaineering
un arbitre	referee; (*tennis*) umpire
l'athlétisme	athletics
le canotage	rowing
le catch	wrestling
le champ de course	race course
le chronomètre	stopwatch
le chronométreur	timekeeper
le débutant	beginner
le détenteur (du titre)	(title-)holder
un entraîneur	trainer, coach
le filet ◊	net
le footing	jogging
le gymnase	gymnasium, gym
l'hippisme	horse-racing; horse-riding
le javelot	javelin
le patin (à roulettes)	(roller) skate
le rallye (automobile)	(car) rally
le saut en hauteur	high jump
le saut en longueur	long jump
le score	score
le spectateur	spectator
le squash	squash
le tir	shooting
le tir à l'arc	archery
le toboggan	toboggan; water slide, flume
le vol libre	hang-gliding

USEFUL WORDS (m)

un ailier	winger
l'arbitrage	refereeing
un athlète	athlete
l'avant-centre (*pl* ~s)	centre-forward
le bâton de ski	ski stick
le benjamin ◊	under-13
le classement	placing
le coéquipier ◊	team mate
le concurrent ◊	competitor

IMPORTANT WORDS (f) (cont)

la coupe	cup
la course ◇	running; racing; race
la débutante	beginner
la détentrice du titre	(title-)holder
une éliminatoire	heat
l'escrime	fencing
une étape	stage; stopping point
la finale	final
la gagnante	winner
la luge	sledge; sledging
la lutte ◇	wrestling
la lutte à la corde	tug-of-war
la mêlée	scrum
la mi-temps (pl inv)	half-time
une paire de tennis	pair of tennis or gym shoes
la patinoire	ice rink, skating rink
la perdante	loser
la première mi-temps	the first half
la prolongation	extra time
la raquette	(tennis) racket
la réunion hippique	race meeting
la spectatrice	spectator
la station de sports d'hiver	winter sports resort
la touche ◇	touch
la tribune	stand

faire une promenade en vélo to go for a ride on one's bike
faire de la voile to go sailing
faire du footing/de l'alpinisme to go jogging/climbing
16èmes/8èmes de finale 1st/2nd round (in 5-round knock-out competition)
c'est l'égalisation they've scored the equalizer
faire des abdominaux to do exercises for the stomach muscles
faire des haltères to do weightlifting
faire un revers to play a backhand shot
faire la roue to do a cartwheel
gagner par forfait to win by default
nage libre freestyle (of swimming)
nager la brasse to swim breast-stroke

USEFUL WORDS (m) (cont)

le coureur	runner
le coureur automobile	racing driver
le coureur cycliste	racing cyclist
le court de tennis	tennis court
le crawl [krol]	crawl
le culturisme	body-building
le culturiste	body-builder
le dopage	doping
le dopant	dope
le dos crawlé	backstroke
le dossard	number (*worn by competitor*)
l' échauffement	warm-up
l' entraînement	training
un équipier	team member
les exercices d'assouplissement	limbering up exercises
le fart	(ski) wax
le fondeur	long-distance skier
le footballeur	football player
les gradins	terracing
le grand écart	splits
le grimpeur	climber
le gymnaste	gymnast
le :handball	handball
l' hippodrome	racecourse
le :hors-piste(s)	cross-country (skiing)
les Jeux olympiques (JO)	Olympic Games
le judo	judo
le justaucorps (*pl inv*)	leotard
le karaté	karate
le kayak	kayak
le lancer du poids	putting the shot
le lutteur	wrestler
le maître nageur ⇨	lifeguard
le manager	manager
le manège	riding school
le marathon	marathon
le nageur	swimmer
le parrainage	sponsorship
le patin à glace	ice skate
le patinage artistique	figure skating

une **athlète**	athlete
la **benjamine**	under-13
la **brasse**	breast-stroke
la **brasse papillon**	butterfly(-stroke)
la **combinaison de plongée**	wet suit
la **compétition**	event
la **concurrente**	competitor
la **coureuse**	runner
la **culturiste**	body-builder
la **demi-finale** (*pl* ~**s**)	semifinal
une **éliminatoire**	heat
l'**endurance**	endurance
une **épreuve sportive**	sports event
une **équipière**	team member
l'**escalade**	climbing
la **fondeuse**	long-distance skier
la **footballeuse**	football player
la **genouillère**	kneepad
la **grimpeuse**	climber
la **gymnaste**	gymnast
les **jambières**	shin pads
la **ligue**	league
la **lutteuse**	wrestler
la **nageuse**	swimmer
la **palme**	flipper (*for swimming*)
la **patineuse**	skater
la **planchiste**	windsurfer (*person*)
la **plongée**	diving
les **régates**	regatta
la **remontée mécanique**	ski lift
une **séance d'aérobic**	aerobics class
la **skieuse**	skier
la **volleyeuse**	volleyball player
la **voltige**	acrobatics

USEFUL WORDS (m) (cont)

le patinage de vitesse	speed skating
le patineur	skater
le penalty (pl **penalties**)	penalty (kick)
le perchiste	pole vaulter
le pilote de course	racing driver
le ping-pong	table tennis
le piolet	ice axe
le planchiste	windsurfer (*person*)
le plongeoir	diving board
le plongeon	dive
le plongeur	diver
le pronostic	forecast
le record	record
le remonte-pente (pl ~**s**)	ski tow
le saut à la perche	pole vaulting
le saut périlleux	somersault
le ski de fond	cross-country skiing
le ski de piste	downhill skiing
le ski nautique	water skiing
le skieur	skier
le sponsor	sponsor
les sports nautiques	water sports
le téléski	ski lift, ski tow
le tennisman (pl **tennismen**)	tennis player
le vainqueur	winner
le volleyeur	volleyball player
le yoga	yoga

ESSENTIAL WORDS (m)

un acteur ▭	actor
le balcon ◇	dress circle
le ballet ▭	ballet
le billet ◇	ticket
le cinéma ◇	cinema
le cirque ▭	circus
le clown ▭	clown
le comédien ▭	actor; comedian
le concert ◇	concert
le costume ◇	costume
un entracte ▭	interval
l'espionnage ▭	spying
le film	film
le guichet ◇ ▭	box office
le jeu ◇ ▭	acting
le maquillage ▭	make-up
un opéra	opera
un orchestre	orchestra; (seat in the) stalls
le pourboire ◇ ▭	tip
le programme ◇	programme (*leaflet*)
le public	audience
le rideau (*pl* ~**x**)	curtain
le sous-titre ▭ (*pl* ~**s**)	sub-title
le spectacle	show
le théâtre ◇	theatre
le ticket ▭	ticket
le titre ▭	title
le western ▭	western

IMPORTANT WORDS (m)

les applaudissements	applause
un auditoire	audience
le cercle dramatique	dramatic society
le décor ◇	scenery
le dramaturge	playwright, dramatist
un écran	screen
le foyer	foyer
le metteur en scène	producer
le parterre ◇	stalls

IMPORTANT WORDS (m) (cont)

le **personnage**	character, person (*in play*)
le **poulailler** ◊	the ''gods''
le **producteur**	(film) producer
le **projecteur**	spotlight
le **réalisateur**	director
le **régisseur**	stage manager
le **rôle**	role, part
le **scénario**	script
le **souffleur**	prompter
le **spectateur**	member of the audience
le **texte**	text; lines
le **vestiaire**	cloakroom

USEFUL WORDS (m)

un **accessoire**	prop
un **accessoiriste**	property man
un **acte**	act
un **animateur** ◊	animator
un **aparté**	aside
le **bouffon**	clown; jester
le **bruitage**	sound effects
le **cadreur**	cameraman
le **cascadeur**	stuntman
le **chef-d'œuvre** (*pl* ~**s**~)	masterpiece
le **cinéaste**	film-maker
le **cinéma muet**	silent cinema
le **cinéphile**	film buff
le **comique**	comedian
le **court métrage**	short film
le **danseur**	ballet dancer
le **doublage**	dubbing
un **éclairagiste**	lighting engineer
les **effets spéciaux**	special effects
un **entrechat**	leap (*in ballet*)
le **fakir**	wizard
le **figurant**	walk-on; extra

ESSENTIAL WORDS (f)

une **actrice** 💷	actress
une **affiche** ◇	notice; poster
l'**ambiance** 💷	atmosphere
la **comédie**	comedy
la **critique**	review; the critics
une **entrée** ◇	entrance
la **guerre** 💷	war
la **location** ◇ 💷	booking; box office
la **musique** ◇	music
une **ouvreuse**	usherette
la **pièce** ◇ **(de théâtre)** 💷	play
la **place** ◇	seat
la **réduction** ◇	reduction
la **salle** ◇ 💷	house; audience
la **séance** 💷	performance; showing
la **sortie** ◇	exit, way out
la **vedette** ◇ (m+f)	(film) star

IMPORTANT WORDS (f)

la **corbeille** ◇	circle
les **coulisses**	wings
la **distribution** ◇	cast (on programme)
une **estrade**	platform
la **farce**	farce
la **fosse (d'orchestre)**	(orchestra) pit
une **intrigue**	plot
les **jumelles** ◇ **de théâtre**	opera glasses
la **loge** ◇	box
la **mise en scène**	production
la **pièce à sensation**	thriller
la **rampe**	footlights
la **répétition**	rehearsal
la **répétition générale**	dress rehearsal

aller au théâtre/au cinéma to go to the theatre/to the cinema
acheter un ticket to buy a ticket
réserver une place to book a seat
un fauteuil d'orchestre a seat in the stalls

le film d'épouvante	horror film
le funambule	tightrope walker
le générique	credits, credit titles
le guignol	Punch and Judy show
un illusionniste	conjuror
un imitateur	impersonator
le jongleur	juggler
le long métrage	feature film
le machiniste	scene shifter, stagehand
le magicien	magician
le maquilleur	make-up artist
le polichinelle	Punch
le rappel	curtain call
le sketch (pl ~es)	sketch
le spectacle de variétés	variety show
le strapontin	jump or foldaway seat
le théâtre lyrique	opera house (for light opera)
le tournage	shooting
le trac	stage fright
le trapèze	trapeze
le trapéziste	trapeze artist
le truquage	special effects
le vaudeville	vaudeville, light comedy
le ventriloque	ventriloquist

pendant l'entracte during the interval
offrir un pourboire à l'ouvreuse to give the usherette a tip
entrer sur scène to come on stage
jouer le rôle de to play the part of

IMPORTANT WORDS (f) (cont)

la représentation	performance
la scène	stage; scene
la tragédie	tragedy

USEFUL WORDS (f)

une accessoiriste	property woman
une adaptation	adaptation
une animatrice	animator
l'apothéose	grand finale
l'assistance	audience
une audience	audience
une audition	audition
une avant-première (pl ~s)	preview
la ballerine	ballet dancer
la bande-annonce (pl ~s~s)	trailer
la bande-son	soundtrack
la caméra	camera
la cantatrice	(opera) singer
la cascadeuse	stuntwoman
la cinéaste	film-maker
la cinémathèque	film archives or library
la cinéphile	film buff
les claquettes	tap-dancing
la comédie lyrique	comic opera

mon acteur préféré/mon actrice préférée my favourite actor/actress
jouer to play; **danser** to dance; **chanter** to sing
il a joué le rôle de Rambo he played the part of Rambo
tourner un film to shoot a film
"prochaine séance: 9 heures" ''next showing: 9 o'clock''
"version originale" ''in the original language''
"sous-titré" ''with subtitles''
attendre qn à l'entrée/à la sortie to wait for sb at the entrance/at the exit
l'auditoire applaudit the audience applauds
bis! encore!; **bravo!** bravo!, well done!
faire salle comble to have a full house
film passant en exclusivité à film showing only at
un film classé X X film, 18 film

la comédie musicale	musical
la danseuse	ballet dancer
la doublure ◇	understudy; stuntman
une éclairagiste	lighting engineer
une épopée	epic
la figurante	walk-on; extra
la figuration	walk-on parts; extras
l'habilleuse	dresser
les :huées	boos
une illusionniste	conjuror
une imitatrice	impersonator
l'issue de secours	emergency exit
la jongleuse	juggler
la lorgnette	opera glasses
la magicienne	magician
la magie	magic
la maquilleuse	make-up artist
la marionnette	puppet
la mime	mime
une opérette	operetta, light opera
la pantomime	mime show
la réplique	line
la superproduction	spectacular
la tête d'affiche	top of the bill
la trapéziste	trapeze artist
la troupe de théatre	theatrical company
la valse	waltz

ESSENTIAL WORDS (m)

un an	year
un après-midi (*pl inv*)	afternoon
l'avenir ◇	future
un instant	moment
le jour	day
le lendemain	the next day, the day after
le matin	morning
le midi	mid-day, noon
le minuit	midnight
le mois	month
le moment	moment
le quart d'heure	quarter of an hour
le retard	delay; lateness
le réveil, réveille-matin ◇ (*pl inv*)	alarm clock
le siècle	century; age
le soir ◇	evening
le surlendemain	two days later, the day after next
le temps ◇	time
le week-end (*pl ~s*)	weekend

à midi at mid-day, at noon
à minuit at midnight
aujourd'hui today
demain tomorrow
hier yesterday
il a 22 ans he is 22 (years old)
j'ai passé l'après-midi à ranger ma chambre I spent the afternoon tidying up my
  room
il y a 2 jours 2 days ago
dans 2 jours in 2 days, in 2 days' time
huit jours a week; **quinze jours** a fortnight
tous les jours every day
quel jour sommes-nous? what day is it?
c'est le combien?, le combien sommes-nous? what's the date?
en ce moment at the moment, at present, just now
3 heures moins le quart a quarter to 3
3 heures et quart a quarter past 3
au 20ème siècle in the 20th century
hier soir last night, yesterday evening

TIME

IMPORTANT WORDS (m)

le cadran ◇ — face (*of clock, etc*), dial
le calendrier — calendar
le chronomètre — stopwatch
le futur — future; the future tense
un intervalle — interval (*of time*)
le passé — the past; the past tense
le présent — present (time); present tense

USEFUL WORDS (m)

l'après-guerre — post-war years
le décalage horaire — time difference (*between time zones*)
l'équinoxe — equinox
le fuseau horaire — time zone
le millénaire — millennium
le sablier ◇ — hourglass

le jour férié public holiday, bank holiday
le jour ouvrable week-day
par un jour de pluie on a rainy day, one rainy day
au lever du jour at dawn, at daybreak
le lendemain matin/soir the following morning/evening
à présent at present, now; nowadays
vous êtes en retard you are late
cette montre avance/retarde this watch is fast/slow
le cours du soir evening class
il passe tout son temps à travailler he spends all his time working
arriver à temps, arriver à l'heure to arrive on time
pour combien de temps …? how long …?
avancer/retarder l'horloge to put the clock(s) forward/back
faire la grasse matinée to have a long lie, have a lie-in
d'une minute à l'autre any minute now

ESSENTIAL WORDS (f)

une année	a (whole) year
une après-midi (*pl inv*)	a (whole) afternoon
une demi-heure (*pl* ~**s**)	half an hour, a half hour
la fois	time, occasion
l'heure	time (*in general*)
une heure	hour
l'horloge	(large) clock
la journée ⟡	(whole) day; daytime
la matinée	(whole) morning
la minute	minute
la montre ⟡	watch
la nuit ⟡	night
la pendule	clock
la quinzaine	fortnight
la seconde	second
la semaine	week
la soirée	the (whole) evening
la veille	the day before, the eve

l'année dernière/prochaine last/next year
dans une demi-heure in half an hour
une fois/deux fois/trois fois once/twice/three times
plusieurs fois several times
3 fois par an 3 times a year
9 fois sur 10 9 times out of 10
il était une fois ..., il y avait une fois ... once upon a time there was ...
10 à la fois 10 at one time, 10 at the same time
quelle heure est-il? what time is it?
avez-vous l'heure (exacte *or* juste)? have you got the (right) time?
il est 6 heures/6 heures moins 10/6 heures et demie it is 6 o'clock/10 to 6/half
past 6
tout à l'heure (*past*) a short while ago; (*future*) soon, shortly
tôt, de bonne heure early; **tard** late
cette nuit (*already past*) last night; (*still to come*) tonight
après-demain the day after tomorrow
avant-hier the day before yesterday
à l'avenir in (the) future
être en retard to be late
le jour de congé day off, holiday

TIME

IMPORTANT WORDS (f)

une **aiguille** ⬦	hand (*of clock etc*)
une **année bissextile**	leap year
l' **avant-veille** (*pl* ~**s**)	two days before *or* previously
la **décennie**	decade
une **époque**	epoch; (*particular*) time
une **horloge normande**	grandfather clock
la **pendule à coucou**	cuckoo clock

USEFUL WORDS (f)

l' **aurore**	dawn
la **décade**	(period of) ten days
la **demi-journée** (*pl* ~**s**)	half a day, a half-day
l' **enfance**	childhood
une **ère**	era
la **pénombre**	half-light
la **trotteuse**	second hand (*of clock*)

aujourd'hui en huit a week today
le veille de Noël (on) Christmas Eve
la veille au soir the previous evening, the night before
à cette époque(-là) at that time, in those days
à heure fixe at a set time
à la tombée de la nuit at nightfall
dans le sens des aiguilles d'une montre clockwise
dans le sens invers des aiguilles d'une montre anticlockwise
en semaine during the week, on weekdays
faire le pont to take the extra day (off), make a long weekend
il fait grand jour it is broad daylight
les heures de bureau office hours
les heures creuses off-peak periods
vingt-quatre heures sur vingt-quatre twenty-four hours a day

ESSENTIAL WORDS (m)

un atelier	workshop
le bricolage	D.I.Y., do-it-yourself
le bricoleur	home handyman
le machin	thing, contraption
un ouvre-boîte(s) ◇ (pl **ouvre-boîtes**)	tin opener
le tire-bouchon (pl ~**s**)	corkscrew

IMPORTANT WORDS (m)

le cadenas	padlock
le chantier	construction site
le ciseau (pl -**x**)	chisel
les ciseaux	scissors
le clou	nail
l'échafaudage	scaffolding
un élastique	rubber band, elastic band
un escabeau (pl -**x**)	stepladder, pair of steps
le fil de fer (barbelé)	(barbed) wire
le foret	drill
le marteau (pl -**x**)	hammer
le marteau-piqueur	pneumatic drill
un outil ◇	tool
le pic ◇	pick, pickaxe
le pinceau (pl -**x**)	paintbrush
le ressort	spring
le scotch	sellotape ®, adhesive tape
le tournevis	screwdriver

USEFUL WORDS (m)

un aimant	magnet
le boulon	bolt
le canif	penknife

faire du bricolage to do odd jobs
enfoncer un clou to hammer in a nail
"attention à la peinture!", "peinture fraîche" ''wet paint''
peindre to paint; **tapisser** to wallpaper
"chantier interdit" ''construction site: keep out''

TOOLS

USEFUL WORDS (m) (cont)

le chalumeau (pl -**x**)	blowlamp
le chausse-pied (pl ~**s**)	shoehorn
le coupe-papier (pl inv)	paper knife
le crochet	hook
un écrou	nut
un entonnoir	funnel
un établi	(work) bench
un étau (pl -**x**)	vice
le loquet	latch
le rabot	plane
le râteau (pl -**x**)	rake
le soufflet	bellows
le tendeur	wire strainer

ESSENTIAL WORDS (f)

la clé, clef ◇	key
la corde ◇	rope
la machine	machine
la serrure 🔲	lock

IMPORTANT WORDS (f)

une aiguille ◇	needle
la bêche	spade
la boîte à outils	toolbox
la boîte à ouvrage	workbox
la clef anglaise	spanner
la colle ◇	glue
une échelle ◇	ladder
la fourche	(garden) fork
la lime	file
la pelle ◇	shovel
la perceuse	drill
la pile	battery
les pinces	pliers
la pioche	pick, pickaxe
la planche	plank
la punaise ◇	drawing pin, thumbtack
la scie	saw
la vis [vis]	screw

USEFUL WORDS (f)

la boussole	compass
la chignole	drill
les cisailles	shears
une enclume	anvil

utile useful; **inutile** useless
pratique handy
casser to break; **couper** to cut; **réparer** to mend
fermer à clé to lock
fixer avec une vis to screw (in); **dévisser** to unscrew
une épingle de nourrice or **de sûreté** safety pin; nappy pin

TOOLS

une épingle	pin
la :hache	axe
la :hachette	hatchet
la machine-outil (*pl* ~**s**~**s**)	machine-tool
la manivelle	crank
la pince-monseigneur (*pl* ~**s**~)	crowbar
la ponceuse	sander
les tenailles	pliers, pincers
la torche	torch
la tronçonneuse	chain saw
la trousse à outils	toolkit
la truelle	trowel
la ventouse	plunger
la vrille	gimlet

ESSENTIAL WORDS (m)

un agent (de police) ◇	policeman
un arrêt (de bus)	bus stop
le bâtiment ◇	building
le bureau ◇ (pl -x)	office
le bureau ◇ (pl -x) de poste ▭	post office
le carnet ◇ (de tickets)	book of tickets
le carrefour	crossroads
le centre-ville (pl ~s~s)	town centre
le château ◇ (pl -x)	castle
le cinéma ◇	cinema
le coin	corner
le commissariat de police	police station
le département	(like British "region")
un embouteillage ▭	traffic jam
un endroit	place
les environs	surroundings, outskirts
l'habitant	inhabitant
le :HLM ▭ (habitation à loyer modéré)	council flat or house
l'hôtel ◇	hotel; mansion
l'hôtel de ville	town hall
un immeuble	block of flats
le jardin public	public park
le jardin zoologique	zoo
le kiosque (à journaux)	(newspaper) stall
le lieu (pl -x)	place
le magasin	shop
le maire	mayor
le marché ◇	market
le métro ◇	underground
le monument ◇	monument

acheter un carnet de tickets to buy a book of tickets
circuler to move (along)
visiter la ville to go sight-seeing (*in the town*)
regarder un plan de la ville to look at a map of the town
industriel(le) industrial; **historique** historic
joli(e) pretty; **laid(e)** ugly
propre clean; **sale** dirty

ESSENTIAL WORDS (m) (cont)

le **musée** ◇ ▭	museum; art gallery
le parc	park
le parking ◇	car park
le passant	passer-by
le piéton	pedestrian
le pont ◇	bridge
le quartier	district
le restaurant ◇	restaurant
le **sens unique** ▭	one-way street
le syndicat d'initiative, SI ◇	tourist information office
le taxi ◇	taxi
le théâtre ◇	theatre
le tour ◇	tour
le touriste	tourist
le trottoir	pavement
le **véhicule** ▭	vehicle

IMPORTANT WORDS (m)

un abribus	bus shelter
un arrondissement	district
un autobus à/sans impériale	double-/single-decker bus
le bistrot	café
le cimetière	cemetery, graveyard
le citadin	town dweller
le citoyen ◇	citizen
le comté	county
le conseil municipal	town council
le défilé ◇	procession, parade
le dépliant	leaflet
un édifice	building
un égout	sewer
le faubourg	suburb
le gratte-ciel (*pl inv*)	skyscraper
le panneau (*pl* -**x**)	roadsign
le passage clouté	pedestrian crossing
le pavé	cobblestone; paving
le refuge	traffic island
le réverbère	street lamp

ESSENTIAL WORDS (f)

une **affiche** ✧	notice; poster
une **auto**	car
la **banlieue**	suburbs
la **banque** ✧	bank
la **bibliothèque** ✧	library
la **boutique** ✧ ▭	(small) shop
la **cathédrale**	cathedral
la **chaussée** ✧	roadway
la **circulation**	traffic
une **église**	church
la **gare**	(train) station
la **gare routière**	coach station
la **:HLM** ▭ **(habitation à loyer modéré)**	council flat *or* house
la **mairie**	town hall
la **piscine** ✧	swimming pool
la **place** ✧	square
la **police** ✧	police
la **pollution** ▭	air pollution
la **poste** ✧	post office
la **route** ✧	road
la **rue**	street
la **rue principale**	main street
la **station de taxis**	taxi stand *or* rank
la **station-service** (*pl* ~**s**~)	service station, garage
la **tour** ✧	tower
une **usine** ✧	factory
la **ville**	town, city
la **voiture** ✧	car
la **vue** ✧ ▭	view

je vais en ville I'm going into town
au centre-ville in the town centre
sur la place in the square
une rue à sens unique a one-way street
traverser la rue to cross the street
au coin de la rue at the corner of the street
habiter la banlieue to live in the suburbs
marcher to walk
prendre le bus/le métro *etc* to take the bus/the underground *etc*

IN THE TOWN

les **signaux routiers**	roadsigns
le **sondage d'opinion**	opinion poll
le **square**	square (*with gardens*)
le **tournant**, le **virage**	turning, bend

USEFUL WORDS (m)

un **aire de stationnement**	parking area
le **balayeur**	roadsweeper (*person*)
le **banlieusard**	suburbanite, commuter
le **beffroi**	belfry
le **bidonville**	shanty town
le **bourg**	market town
le **camelot**	street pedlar
le **caniveau** (*pl* **-x**)	gutter
le **casino**	casino
le **clochard**	down-and-out, tramp
le **clocher**	church tower; steeple
le **concitoyen**	fellow citizen
le **coupe-gorge** (*pl inv*)	dangerous back-alley
le **crieur de journaux**	newspaper seller
le **demi-tarif** (*pl ~s*)	half-fare
un **écriteau** (*pl* **-x**)	notice, sign
le **gardien de musée**	museum attendant
le **graffiti**	graffiti
l' **horodateur**	parking ticket machine
le **jumelage**	twinning
le **lavoir**	wash house
le **mendiant**	beggar
le **parvis**	square (*in front of church*)
le **passage souterrain**	subway, underpass
le **réverbère**	street lamp
le **riverain**	local resident

la desserte de la ville est assurée par autocar there is a coach service to the town

IN THE TOWN

IMPORTANT WORDS (f)

|---|---|
une agglomération ◇	built-up area
la camionnette de livraison	delivery van
la caserne de pompiers	fire station
la cité	city (*old part*)
la cité universitaire	university halls of residence
les curiosités	sights, places of interest
la flèche	spire; arrow
la foule	crowd
la galerie ◇	art gallery
la grand'route	main road
la grand-rue	main street
une impasse	dead end
la piste cyclable	cycle path
la population	population
la prison	prison
la queue ◇ [kø]	queue
la statue	statue
la voiture d'enfant	pram

USEFUL WORDS (f)

|---|---|
les arcades	arcade
la balayeuse	roadsweeper (*machine*)
la banlieusarde	suburbanite, commuter
la billetterie	cash dispenser
la chaussée ◇	road, roadway
la cité	city; town
la cité-dortoir (*pl* ~s~s)	dormitory town
la cité ouvrière	(workers') housing estate
la citoyenne ◇	fellow citizen
la clocharde	down-and-out, tramp
la crieuse de journaux	newspaper seller
la fontaine	fountain
la levée	collection (*mail*)
la mendiante	beggar
la riveraine	local resident
la rue sans issue	dead-end street, cul-de-sac
la ruelle	alley(way)
la ville champignon	boom town
la zone industrielle (ZI)	industrial estate

TRAINS

ESSENTIAL WORDS (m)

un aller-retour	return ticket
un aller-simple	single ticket
les bagages ◇	luggage
le billet ◇	ticket
le buffet ◇	station buffet
le carnet ◇	book of tickets
le chemin de fer ▭	railway
le compartiment ▭	compartment
le conducteur ▭	(train) driver
le départ ▭	departure
le douanier ▭	customs officer
un escalier roulant ◇ ▭	escalator
un express ▭	fast train
le frein ◇ ▭	brake
le guichet ◇ ▭	booking *or* ticket office
l'horaire ▭	timetable
le mécanicien ◇ ▭	engine-driver
le métro ◇	underground (railway)
le numéro ◇	number
les objets trouvés	lost and found
un omnibus	slow train
le passeport ◇	passport
le plan ◇	plan, map
le pont ◇	bridge
le porteur ◇ ▭	porter
le pourboire ◇ ▭	tip
le prix du billet ◇	fare
le prix du ticket	fare
le quai ◇	platform
le rapide ▭	express train
les renseignements ◇	information
le retard	delay
le sac ◇	bag
le supplément ◇ ▭	extra charge
le tarif ◇ ▭	rate, fare
le taxi ◇	taxi
le ticket ▭	ticket
le train	train
le train express ▭	fast train
le train omnibus	slow train

ESSENTIAL WORDS (f)

une **arrivée** 🔲	arrival
la **barrière** ◇	barrier
la **bicyclette** ◇ 🔲	bicycle
la **classe** 🔲	class
la **consigne** ◇	left-luggage office
la **consigne automatique** 🔲	left-luggage locker
la **correspondance** 🔲	connection
la **couchette**	couchette, sleeping car
la **destination**	destination
la **direction** ◇ 🔲	direction
la **douane** ◇ 🔲	customs
la **durée**	length, duration
une **entrée** ◇	entrance
la **frontière**	border, frontier
la **gare**	station
l'**horloge**	(large) clock
la **ligne** 🔲	line, track
la **place** ◇	seat
la **portière**	(carriage) door
la **réduction** ◇	reduction
la **réservation** 🔲	reservation, booking
la **salle d'attente** ◇	waiting room
la **section** 🔲	fare stage (*on bus*)
la **SNCF**	French Railways
la **sortie** ◇	exit
la **station (de métro)**	underground *or* subway station
la **station (de taxis)**	taxi stand *or* rank
la **valise** ◇	case, suitcase
la **voie** ◇ 🔲	track, line
la **voiture** ◇	carriage, coach

demander des renseignements to ask for information
réserver une place to book a seat
payer un supplément to pay an extra charge
faire/défaire ses bagages to pack/unpack (one's luggage)
j'aime voyager par le train I like travelling by train
prendre le train to take *or* catch the train; **manquer le train** to miss the train
monter dans le train/bus to get into the train/onto the bus
descendre du train/bus to get off the train/bus
c'est pris?/libre? is this seat taken?/free?

TRAINS

ESSENTIAL WORDS (m) (cont)

le train rapide 📖	express train
le **vélo** ◇	bike
le **voyage** ◇	journey
le voyageur 📖	traveller
le **wagon-lit** (pl ~**s**~**s**)	sleeping car
le **wagon-restaurant** (pl ~**s**~**s**)	dining car

IMPORTANT WORDS (m)

le **chauffeur** ◇	fireman, stoker
le **chef de gare**	stationmaster
le **chef de train**	guard
le **cheminot**	railwayman
le **contrôleur**	ticket collector
le **coup de sifflet**	blast on whistle
le **déraillement**	derailment
le **filet** ◇	luggage rack
le **fourgon du chef de train**	guard's van
un **indicateur**	timetable
le **passage à niveau**	level crossing
les **rails**	rails
le **signal d'alarme**	alarm, communication cord
le **train de marchandises**	goods train
le **trajet**	journey
le **wagon**	carriage, coach

USEFUL WORDS (m)

un **autorail**	railcar
le **distributeur de billets**	ticket machine
le **talus**	embankment

le train est en retard the train is late
un compartiment fumeur/non-fumeur a smoking/non-smoking compartment
"défense de se pencher au dehors" ''do not lean out of the window''

290

IMPORTANT WORDS (f)

la banquette	seat
la carte d'abonnement	season ticket
une étiquette	label
la locomotive ◇	locomotive, engine
la malle	trunk
la salle des pas perdus	waiting room
la sonnette d'alarme	alarm, communication cord
la voie ferrée	(railway) line *or* track

USEFUL WORDS (f)

les grandes lignes	main lines

je t'accompagnerai à la gare I'll go to the station with you
je viendrai te chercher à la gare I'll come and fetch you from the station
je passerai te prendre à la gare I'll come and pick you up at the station
le train de 10 heures à destination de Paris/en provenance de Paris the 10 o'clock
 train to Paris/from Paris

ESSENTIAL WORDS (m)

un arbre ◇	tree
un arbre de Noël	Christmas tree
le bois ◇ ▥	wood

IMPORTANT WORDS (m)

un arbre fruitier	fruit tree
le bouleau (pl -x)	birch
le bourgeon	bud
le buis	box tree
le buisson ◇	bush
le châtaignier	chestnut tree
le chêne	oak
un érable	maple
le feuillage ◇	leaves, foliage
le frêne	ash
le :hêtre	beech
le :hêtre rouge	copper beech
le :houx	holly
un if	yew
le marronnier	(horse) chestnut tree
un orme	elm
le peuplier	poplar
le pin	pine
le platane	plane tree
le rameau (pl -x)	branch
le sapin	fir tree
le saule (pleureur)	(weeping) willow
le tilleul	lime tree
le tronc	trunk
le verger ◇	orchard
le vignoble	vineyard

USEFUL WORDS (m)

le bosquet	copse, grove
le bûcheron	woodcutter, lumberjack
le cèdre	cedar (tree)
le conifère	conifer

ESSENTIAL WORDS (f)

la branche	branch
la feuille ◇	leaf
la forêt	forest

IMPORTANT WORDS (f)

une aubépine ◇	hawthorn
la baie ◇	berry
l'écorce	bark
la racine	root

USEFUL WORDS (f)

les broussailles	undergrowth
la bûche	log
la cerisaie	cherry orchard
la châtaigne	(sweet) chestnut
la cime d'un arbre	treetop
la clairière	clearing
la fougère	fern
la futaie	forest, plantation
une oliveraie	olive grove
une orangeraie	orange grove
la pinède	pinewood, pine forest
la pomme de pin	pine or fir cone
la sève	sap
la souche	stump

une chaise de or **en bois** a wooden chair
à l'ombre d'un arbre in the shade of a tree
les feuilles jaunissent en automne the leaves turn yellow in autumn
déraciner to uproot

USEFUL WORDS (m) (cont)

le cyprès [sipʀɛ]	cypress
le déboisement	deforestation
le défrichement	clearance
le feuillu	broad-leaved tree
le frêne	ash (tree)
le gland	acorn
le merisier	wild cherry tree
un olivier	olive tree
le reboisement	reafforestation
le sous-bois (pl inv)	undergrowth
le sureau (pl -x)	elder (tree)
le taillis	copse

ESSENTIAL WORDS (m)

le champignon 📖	mushroom
le chou 📖 (*pl* -**x**)	cabbage
le chou-fleur 📖 (*pl* ~**x**~**s**)	cauliflower
le :haricot	bean
le :haricot vert	French bean
les légumes ◇	vegetables
un oignon 📖	onion
les petits pois	(garden) peas

IMPORTANT WORDS (m)

l'ail [aj]	garlic
un artichaut	artichoke
le céléri	celery
le chou (*pl* -**x**) **de Bruxelles**	Brussels sprout
le concombre	cucumber
le cresson	cress
un épi de maïs [ma-is]	corn on the cob
les épinards	spinach
le navet	turnip
le persil [pɛrsi]	parsley
le piment doux	(sweet) pepper
le poireau (*pl* -**x**)	leek
le poivron	(sweet) pepper
le radis	radish

USEFUL WORDS (m)

le chou-rave (*pl* -**x**~**s**)	kohlrabi
le fenouil	fennel
le flageolet	flageolet, dwarf kidney bean
le maïs ◇	sweetcorn
le panais	parsnip
le piment rouge	chilli
le pois chiche	chickpea
les pois cassés	split peas
le potiron	pumpkin
le romarin	rosemary
le rutabaga	swede
le safran	saffron
le thym	thyme

VEGETABLES

ESSENTIAL WORDS (f)

la **carotte** 🕮	carrot
les **crudités** 🕮	*selection of salads*
la **pomme de terre** (*pl* ~**s de terre**)	potato
la **salade (verte)**	(green) salad
la **tomate**	tomato; tomato plant

IMPORTANT WORDS (f)

les **asperges**	asparagus
une **aubergine**	aubergine
la **betterave**	beetroot
la **chicorée**	endive
la **courge**	marrow
la **courgette**	courgette
une **endive**	chicory
la **laitue**	lettuce

USEFUL WORDS (f)

une **asperge**	asparagus
la **citrouille**	pumpkin
une **échalote**	shallot
une **épice**	spice
la **fève**	broad bean
les **lentilles**	lentils
la **sarriette**	savory
la **sauge**	sage

aimer to like; **détester** to hate; **préférer** to prefer
cultiver des légumes to grow vegetables
carottes râpées grated carrot
choucroute garnie sauerkraut with meat
pommes persillées potatoes with parsley
pommes frites chips; **pommes vapeur** boiled potatoes
rouge comme une tomate as red as a beetroot
organique organic
végétarien(ne) vegetarian

ESSENTIAL WORDS (m)

l'arrière ⌐	back
un autobus ⌐	bus
un autocar ⌐	coach
l'avant ⌐	front
un avion	plane, aeroplane
le ballon ◇	balloon
le bateau (pl -x)	boat
le bateau à rames/à voiles	rowing/sailing boat
le bus	bus
le camion	lorry, truck
le car	coach
le casque ⌐	helmet
le ferry	ferry
l'hélicoptère	helicopter
l'hovercraft	hovercraft
le métro ◇	underground
le moyen de transport	means of transport
le poids lourd ⌐	heavy lorry, juggernaut
le prix du billet ◇	fare (any mode of transport)
le prix du ticket	fare (boat, plane)
le risque	risk
le scooter ⌐	scooter
le taxi ◇	taxi
le train	train
le véhicule ⌐	vehicle
le vélo ◇	bike
le vélomoteur	moped

voyager to travel
il est allé à Paris en avion he went to Paris by air, he flew to Paris
prendre le bus/le métro/le train to take the bus/the metro/the train
faire de la bicyclette to go cycling
appelez l'ambulance! call an ambulance!
on peut y aller en voiture we can go there by car *or* in the car
conduire une voiture to drive (a car)
une promenade en voiture a drive
une voiture de location a hired *or* rented car
une voiture de sport a sports car
une voiture de course a racing car
une voiture de fonction a company car

VEHICLES

IMPORTANT WORDS (m)

un aéroglisseur	hovercraft
un astronef	spaceship
le bac ◊	ferry (boat)
le bateau-mouche (*pl* -**x**~**s**)	*tour boat on the Seine*
le break [brɛk]	estate car
le bulldozer [buldozœr]	bulldozer
le camion-citerne (*pl*~**s**~**s**)	tanker (*lorry*)
le canoë [kanɔe]	canoe
le canot	rowing boat
le canot de sauvetage	lifeboat
le char (d'assaut)	tank
le cyclomoteur	moped
le dirigeable	airship
le funiculaire	funicular (railway)
l'hydravion	seaplane
le navire	ship
un OVNI (objet volant non identifié)	UFO, unidentified flying object
le paquebot	passenger steamer, liner
le pétrolier	oil tanker (*ship*)
le planeur	glider
le porte-avions (*pl inv*)	aircraft carrier
le remorqueur	tug, tugboat
le semi-remorque (*pl*~**s**)	articulated lorry
le sous-marin (*pl*~**s**)	submarine
le téléphérique	cable car
le télésiège	chairlift
le tramway	tram
le vaisseau (*pl* -**x**)	vessel
le vapeur ◊	steamer
le yacht [jɔt]	yacht

USEFUL WORDS (m)

un avion-cargo (*pl*~**s**~**s**)	air freighter
un avion-citerne (*pl*~**s**~**s**)	air tanker
le bateau-citerne (*pl* -**x**~**s**)	tanker (*ship*)
le bibliobus	mobile library van
le bolide	racing car
le cabriolet	convertible

ESSENTIAL WORDS (f)

une **ambulance** ◇	ambulance
la **bicyclette** ◇ ▭	bicycle
la **camionnette** ◇	(small) van
la **caravane** ◇	caravan
la **distance** ▭	distance
la **moto, motocyclette**	motorbike, motorcycle
la **voiture** ◇	car; coach, carriage
la **voiture de dépannage** ◇	breakdown van
la **voiture de pompiers**	fire engine

IMPORTANT WORDS (f)

la **camionnette de livraison**	delivery van
la **charrette**	cart
la **fusée**	rocket
la **jeep**	jeep
la **locomotive** ◇	engine, locomotive
la **mobylette**	moped
la **péniche**	barge
la **remorque**	trailer
la **soucoupe volante**	flying saucer
la **vedette** ◇	speedboat
la **voiture d'enfant**	pram
la **voiture pie**	Panda car

USEFUL WORDS (f)

la **bétaillère**	livestock truck
la **calèche**	horse-drawn carriage
la **carrosserie**	body, coachwork
la **fourgonnette**	delivery van
la **goélette**	schooner
la **grue**	crane
la **navette spatiale**	space shuttle
la **pelleteuse**	mechanical digger, excavator
la **péniche**	barge
la **pirogue**	dugout (canoe)
la **poussette**	pushchair
la **révision**	service; overhaul

VEHICLES

le Canadair	fire-fighting plane
le carrosse	(horse-drawn) coach
le chalutier	trawler
le corbillard	hearse
un deux-roues (*pl inv*)	two-wheeled vehicle
un engin	heavy vehicle
le fiacre	(hackney) cab
le fourgon	van
un gilet de sauvetage	life jacket
l'hydroglisseur	hydroplane
le landau	pram
le minibus	minibus
le monoplace	single-seater
le traîneau	sleigh, sledge
les transports en commun	public transport
le trimaran	trimaran
le van	horsebox
le voilier	sailing ship; sailing boat

"voitures d'occasion" ''second-hand cars''
les transports en commun public transport
une 6 cylindres a 6-cylinder car
une grosse cylindrée big-engined car

ESSENTIAL WORDS (m)

l'air ◇	air
un an	year
un après-midi (*pl inv*)	afternoon
l'automne	autumn
le brouillard	fog
le bulletin de la météo	weather report
le changement	change
le ciel ◇ 🕮	sky
le climat 🕮	climate
le coucher du soleil	sunset
le degré 🕮	degree
l'endroit	place
l'est	east
l'été	summer
le froid	cold
l'hiver	winter
le lever du soleil	sunrise
le matin	morning
le mois	month
le monde 🕮	world
le nord	north
le nuage 🕮	cloud
un orage	thunderstorm
l'ouest	west
le parapluie 🕮	umbrella
le pays ◇	country
le printemps	spring
le soir ◇	evening
le soleil ◇	sun; sunshine
le sud	south
le temps ◇	weather
le vent	wind

quel temps fait-il? what's the weather like?
il fait chaud/froid it's hot/cold; **il fait beau** it's a lovely day
il fait mauvais (temps) it's a horrible day
il fait du soleil/du vent it's sunny/windy
en plein air in the open air; **il fait du brouillard** it's foggy
écouter la météo *or* **les prévisions** to listen to the forecast
pleuvoir to rain; **neiger** to snow

WEATHER

IMPORTANT WORDS (m)

un **amoncellement de neige**	snowdrift
un **arc-en-ciel** (pl ~**s**~~)	rainbow
le **baromètre**	barometer
le **chasse-neige** (pl inv)	snowplough
le **clair de lune**	moonlight
le **coup de tonnerre**	thunderclap
le **coup de vent**	gust of wind
le **courant d'air**	draught
le **crépuscule**	twilight
les **dégâts**	damage, destruction
le **dégel**	thaw
le **déluge**	downpour
un **éclair**	flash of lightning
le **flocon de neige**	snowflake
le **gel**	frost
le **givre**	frost
le **glaçon** ◇	icicle
un **ouragan**	hurricane
le **paratonnerre**	lightning conductor
le **point de congélation**	freezing point
le **rayon** ◇ **(de soleil)**	ray (of sunshine)
le **smog**	smog
le **tonnerre**	thunder
le **tremblement de terre**	earthquake
le **verglas**	black ice

USEFUL WORDS (m)

le **crachin**	drizzle
le **cyclone**	cyclone; hurricane
l' **enneigement**	snow coverage
l' **ensoleillement**	hours of sunshine
le **grêlon**	hailstone
le **grésil**	(fine) hail
le **microclimat**	microclimate
le **radoucissement**	milder period, better weather
le **tourbillon**	whirlwind
le **typhon**	typhoon
le **vent de tempête**	gale
le **zénith**	zenith

ESSENTIAL WORDS (f)

une **amélioration** 🕮	improvement
une **après-midi** (*pl inv*)	afternoon
une **averse** 🕮	shower
la **chaleur**	heat
la **côte** ◇	coast
une **éclaircie** 🕮	bright period
une **étoile** 🕮	star
la **fumée** ◇	smoke
la **glace** ◇	ice
une **île** ◇	island
la **journée** ◇	(whole) day; daytime
la **lumière** ◇ 🕮	light
la **météo**	(weather) forecast
la **montagne** ◇ 🕮	mountain
la **neige**	snow
la **nuit** ◇	night
la **pluie** ◇	rain
la **poussière** ◇	dust
la **précipitation** 🕮	rainfall
les **prévisions (météorologiques)**	(weather) forecast
la **région**	region, area
la **saison** 🕮	season
la **température** ◇	temperature
la **tempête** 🕮	tempest, gale, storm
la **visibilité** 🕮	visibility

il pleut it's raining; **il neige** it's snowing
le soleil brille the sun is shining
le vent souffle the wind is blowing
il gèle it's freezing; **geler** to freeze; **fondre** to melt
ensoleillé sunny; **neigeux(euse)** snowy
orageux(euse) stormy; **pluvieux(euse)** rainy, wet
frais (fraîche) cool; **variable** changeable; **humide** humid; damp
il faisait une chaleur intenable the heat was unbearable
il pleut à verse it's pouring; **se mettre à l'abri** to shelter
le ciel est nuageux/couvert the sky is cloudy/overcast
mouillé(e) wet

WEATHER

IMPORTANT WORDS (f)

l'atmosphère	atmosphere
l'aube	dawn
la brise	breeze
la brume 📖	mist
la canicule	heatwave
la chute de neige	snowfall
la congère	snowdrift
la flaque d'eau	puddle
les fleurs de givre	frost patterns (*on window*)
la foudre	lightning
la gelée ✧	frost
la goutte de pluie	raindrop
la grêle	hail
une inondation	flood
la lune	moon
l'obscurité	darkness
une ombre	shadow
la rafale	squall
la rosée	dew
la sécheresse	drought
les ténèbres	darkness
la vague de chaleur	heatwave

USEFUL WORDS (f)

une accalmie	lull
l'acclimatation	acclimatization
la bourrasque	gust of wind, squall
la bruine	drizzle
la fonte des neiges	(spring) thaw
une giboulée	sudden shower
la girouette	weather vane *or* cock
les intempéries	bad weather
la mousson	monsoon
une ondée	shower
la perturbation (atmosphérique)	atmospheric disturbance
la pluviosité	raininess, wetness; (average) rainfall
la tornade	tornado
la vague de froid	cold spell

ESSENTIAL WORDS (m)

le bureau ◇ (pl -**x**)	office
le dîner	dinner
le dortoir ▯	dormitory
le drap ◇ ▯	sheet
le garçon ◇	boy
le guide	guide-book
le linge ◇	bedclothes, bedding; washing
le lit ◇	bed
le petit déjeuner ◇	breakfast
le règlement ◇	rule
le repas ◇	meal
le repas préparé	prepared meal
le sac à dos	backpack, rucksack
le sac de couchage	sleeping bag
le séjour ▯	stay
le silence ▯	silence
le tarif ◇ ▯	rate(s)
le visiteur ▯	visitor
les W.-C. ◇ ▯	toilet(s)

je voudrais louer un sac de couchage I would like to hire a sleeping bag

ESSENTIAL WORDS (f)

une auberge de jeunesse	youth hostel
la carte ◇	map; card
la carte d'adhérent	membership card
la cuisine ◇	kitchen; cooking
la douche ◇	shower
la fille	girl
la gourde	flask
la nuit ◇	night
la place ◇	room; place
la poubelle ◇	dustbin
la randonnée ⌑	walk; hike; drive
la salle à manger ◇	dining room
la salle de bains ◇	bathroom
la salle de jeux ⌑	games room
les toilettes ◇	toilet(s)
les vacances ◇	holidays

passer une nuit à l'auberge de jeunesse to spend a night at the youth hostel

The vocabulary items on pages 307 to 334 have been grouped under parts of speech rather than topics because they can apply in a wide range of circumstances. You should learn to use them just as freely as the vocabulary already given.

CONJUNCTIONS

CONJUNCTIONS

alors que when, as, while
aussi so, therefore
aussi ... que as ... as
avant de + *infinitive* before
car for, because
cependant however
c'est-à-dire that is to say
comme as
comment how
depuis que (ever) since
dès que as soon as
donc so; then
et and
et alors? so what!
et lui? what about him?
lorsque when, as
maintenant que now (that)
mais but
mais non! of course not!
au moment où (just) as

ne ... que only
ni ... ni neither ... nor
or now
ou or
ou ... ou either ... or
ou bien or (else)
parce que because
pendant que while
pourquoi why
pourvu que + *subj* provided that, so long as
puisque since, because
quand when
que that; than
si if
sinon otherwise; other than, except
tandis que whilst
tant que so long as, while
vu que seeing (that); in view of the fact that

ADJECTIVES

abordable within reach
abrégé(e) shortened
absurde absurd
accessoire of secondary importance; incidental
actif, active active
actuel(le) present (*time*)
aérien(ne) aerial
affectueux, -euse affectionate
affreux, -euse frightful
âgé(e) old
agité restless; busy; (*street*); stormy (*sea*)
agréable pleasant
agricole agricultural
aigu, aiguë acute; piercing
aimable kind, nice
aîné(e) elder, eldest
amer, amère bitter
amusant(e) amusing, enjoyable
ancien(ne) old, former
animé(e) busy, crowded
annuel(le) annual
anonyme anonymous
anormal(e) abnormal, unusual
anxieux, -euse anxious, worried
appliqué(e) diligent
apte capable
arrière: siège *m* **arrière** back seat
assis(e) sitting, seated
aucun(e) any, no, not any
automatique automatic
autre other
avant: siège *m* **avant** front seat
barbu bearded
bas(se) low
beau (bel), belle beautiful, fine
bête silly
bien fine, well; comfortable
bienvenu(e) welcome

bizarre strange, odd
blessé(e) injured
bon(ne) good
bon marché *inv* cheap
bordé(e) de lined with
bouillant(e) boiling
bouleversé(e) thrown into confusion
brave fine, good
bref, brève brief
brillant(e) bright, brilliant; shiny
bruyant(e) noisy
calme calm
capable capable
carré(e) square
célèbre famous
certain(e) sure, certain
chaque each, every
chargé(e) de loaded with; responsible for
charmant(e) delightful
chatoyant(e) glistening; shimmering
chaud(e) warm; hot; *see* **avoir, faire**
cher, chère dear; expensive
chic smart
choquant(e) shocking
chouette great, brilliant
clair(e) clear; light
classique classical
climatisé(e) air-conditioned
commode convenient
complet, complète complete; full
compliqué(e) complicated
composé(e) de comprising
compris(e) understood; including
confortable comfortable
contemporaine(e) contemporary
content(e) happy

continuel(le) continuing
convenable suitable
correct(e) correct
couché(e) lying down
courageux, -euse courageous
court(e) short
couvert(e) de covered with
créé(e) created, established
cruel(le) cruel
cuit(e) cooked; **bien cuit** well done (*of steak*)
culturel(le) cultural
curieux, -euse curious, strange
dangereux, -euse dangerous
debout standing (up)
décevant(e) disappointing
déchiré(e) torn
découragé(e) discouraged
déçu(e) disappointed
dégoûté(e) disgusted
délicat(e) delicate
délicieux, -ieuse delicious
dernier, dernière last, latest
désagréable unpleasant
désert(e) deserted
désespéré(e) desperate
désolé(e) desolate; sorry
détestable foul, ghastly
détruit(e) destroyed
différent(e) different
difficile difficult
digne worthy
direct(e) direct
disponible available
distingué(e) distinguished
distrait(e) absent-minded
divers(e) different
divertissant(e) entertaining
divin(e) divine
divisé(e) divided
doré(e) golden; gilt
doux, douce gentle; sweet; soft
droit(e) straight; right(hand)

drôle funny
dur(e) hard
éclairé(e): bien éclairé(e) well lit
économique economic; economical
effrayé(e) frightened
égal(e) equal; even; steady
électrique electric
élégant(e) elegant
élevé(e) high; **bien élevé(e)** well-mannered
embêtant(e) annoying
enchanté(e) delighted
ennuyé(e) bothered; annoyed
ennuyeux, -euse boring
énorme huge
ensoleillé(e) sunny
entendu(e) agreed; **bien entendu** of course
entier, entière whole
épais(se) thick
épouvantable terrible
épuisé(e) exhausted, worn out
essentiel(le) essential
essoufflé(e) out of breath
étendu(e) stretched out
étonnant(e) astonishing
étonné(e) astonished; **d'un air étonné** in astonishment
étrange strange
étranger, étrangère foreign
étroit(e) narrow; strict
éveillé(e) awake
évident(e) evident, obvious
exact(e) exact
excellent(e) excellent
expérimenté(e) experienced
extra *inv* first-rate; top quality
extraordinaire extraordinary
fâché(e) angry
facile easy
faible weak; faint
fatigant(e) tiring

ADJECTIVES

fatigué(e) tired
faux, fausse false, wrong
favori(te) favourite
fermé(e) closed, shut; off (*of tap etc*)
féroce fierce
fier, fière proud
fin(e) fine; thin
final(e) final
fondé(e) founded
formidable tremendous, magnificent; great
fort(e) strong; hard
fou, folle mad; **un succès fou** a great success
fragile fragile; frail
frais, fraîche fresh, cool
froid(e) cold; *see* **avoir, faire**
furieux, -euse furious
futur(e) future; **future maman** *f* mother-to-be
gai(e) gay
gauche left(hand)
général(e) general
gentil(le) kind, nice
gonflé(e) blown up
gracieux, -ieuse graceful
grand(e) big, great; tall; high
gratuit(e) free
grave serious
gros(se) big; fat
habile skilful
habitué(e) à used to
habituel(le) usual
haut(e) high; tall
heureux, -euse happy
historique historic(al)
honnête honest
identique identical
illuminé(e) lit; floodlit
illustré(e) illustrated
imaginaire imaginary
immense huge, immense

immobile still, motionless
important(e) important
impossible impossible
impressionnant(e) impressive
imprévu(e) unforeseen
inattendu(e) unexpected
incapable (de) incapable (of)
inconnu(e) unknown
incroyable unbelievable
indispensable indispensable
industriel(le) industrial
inondé(e) flooded
inquiet, inquiète anxious, worried
insouciant(e) carefree
insupportable horrid, unbearable
intelligent(e) intelligent
interdit(e) prohibited
intéressant(e) interesting
interminable endless
interrompu(e) interrupted
inutile useless
irrité(e) annoyed
isolé(e) isolated
jaloux, -ouse jealous
jeune young
joli(e) pretty
joyeux, -euse merry, cheerful
juste just; correct
lâche cowardly
laid(e) ugly
large wide; broad
léger, légère light
lent(e) slow
leur/leurs their
libre free, vacant
local(e) local
long(ue) long
lourd(e) heavy
de luxe luxurious, luxury
magique magic; magical
magnifique magnificent
maigre thin

malade ill
malheureux, -euse unhappy, unfortunate
malhonnête dishonest
mauvais(e) bad; **à la mauvaise ligne** on the wrong line; **de mauvaise humeur** in a bad temper
mécanique mechanical
méchant(e) naughty
mécontent(e) unhappy
médical(e) medical
meilleur(e) better, best
même same
merveilleux, -euse marvellous
militaire military
minable pathetic, pitiful
mince slim, slender
mobile mobile; moving; movable
moche ugly; rotten, bad
moderne modern
moindre least
mon/ma/mes my
montagneux, -euse mountainous
mort(e) dead
mouillé(e) wet through
mouvementé(e) lively
moyen(ne) average
mû, mue (par) moved (by)
multicolore multicoloured
muni(e) de provided with
municipal(e) municipal, town
mûr(e) ripe
musclé(e) muscular, brawny
musical(e) musical
mystérieux, -euse mysterious
natal(e) native
national(e) national
naturel(le) natural
né(e) born
nécessaire necessary
nerveux, -euse nervous
net(te) clear, sharp

neuf, neuve new; **tout(e) neuf (neuve)** brand new
nombreux, -euse numerous
normal(e) normal
notre/nos our
nouveau (nouvel), nouvelle new
noyé(e) drowned
nul: match nul draw
obligatoire compulsory
obligé(e) de obliged to
occupé(e) engaged, taken (*of room*); busy (*of person*); engaged (*of phone*)
officiel(le) official
ordinaire ordinary
original(e) original
orné(e) de decorated with
outré(e) outraged, appalled
ouvert(e) open; on (*of tap etc*)
paisible peaceful
pâle pale
pareil(le) similar, same; **une somme pareille** such a sum
paresseux, -euse lazy
parfait(e) perfect
particulier, particulière particular; private
passionnant(e) exciting
passionné(e) passionate
patient(e) patient
pauvre poor
pénible painful
permanent(e) permanent
perpétuel(le) perpetual
personnel(le) personal
petit(e) small, little
pittoresque picturesque
plat(e) flat
plein(e) (de) full (of); **en plein air** in the open air; **en plein jour** in broad daylight
plusieurs several
pneumatique inflatable

ADJECTIVES

poli(e) polite; polished
populaire popular
portatif, -ive portable
possible possible
pratique practical; handy
précédent(e) previous
précieux, -euse precious
précis(e) precise; **à cinq heures précises** at exactly five o'clock
préféré(e) favourite
premier, première first
pressant(e) urgent
pressé(e): être pressé(e) to be in a hurry
prêt(e) ready; **prêt à porter** ready to wear, off-the-peg
primaire primary
privé(e) private
privilégié(e) privileged
prochain(e) next
proche nearby; close
profond(e) deep
propre own; clean
prudent(e) cautious
public, publique public
publicitaire publicity
quel(le) what
quelque(s) some
rafraîchissant(e) refreshing
rangé(e): bien rangé(e) neat and tidy
rapide fast, quick, rapid
rare rare
ravi(e) delighted
récent(e) recent
reconnaissant(e) grateful
rectangulaire rectangular
religieux, -euse religious
réservé(e) reserved
responsable (de) responsible (for)
rêveur, -euse dreamy
riche rich, wealthy

ridicule ridiculous
rond(e) round
roulé(e) rolled up
rusé(e) cunning
sage good, well-behaved; wise
sain et sauf safe and sound
sale dirty; **un sale temps** terrible weather
sanitaire sanitary
satisfait(e) (de) satisfied (with)
sauvage uncivilized; wild
scolaire school (*year etc*)
sec, sèche dry
second(e) second
secondaire secondary
secret, secrète secret
sensass great, fantastic
sensationnel(le) sensational
sérieux, -euse serious
serré(e) tight, close
seul(e) alone; lonely; single
sévère severe, strict
simple simple, plain
sincère sincere
sinistre sinister
situé(e) situated
social(e) social
solennel(le) solemn
solide solid
sombre dark
son/sa/ses his, her, its, one's
peu soucieux (soucieuse) unconcerned
soudain(e) sudden
soupçonneux, -euse suspicious
souriant(e) smiling
sous-marin(e) underwater
spécial(e) special
suivant(e) following
suivi(e) de followed by
super super, great
superbe magnificent
supérieur(e) upper; advanced

supplémentaire extra
supportable bearable
sûr(e) sure
surprenant(e) surprising
sympa(thique) nice, likeable
technique technical
tel(le) such
temporaire temporary
terrible terrible; great
théâtral(e) theatrical
tiède lukewarm, tepid
timide shy
ton/ta/tes your
touristique tourist (*area etc*)
tout/toute/toutes all
traditionnel(le) traditional
tranquille quiet, peaceful
trempé soaked
triste sad
troublé(e) disturbed

typique typical
uni(e) plain
unique only (*hope etc*); unique
urbain(e) urban
urgent(e) urgent
utile useful
varié(e) varied; various
vaste vast
véritable real, genuine
vide empty
vieux (vieil), vieille old
vif, vive keen; vivid; bright
vilain(e) naughty; ugly; nasty
violent(e) violent
vivant(e) alive; lively
voisin(e) neighbouring
votre/vos your
vrai(e) real, true
vraisemblable likely, plausible

ADVERBS AND PREPOSITIONS

à to, at
d'abord first, at first
tout d'abord first of all
aux abords de alongside
au premier abord at first sight
absolument absolutely
actuellement at present
admirablement admirably
afin de so as to
ailleurs elsewhere
d'ailleurs moreover
ainsi thus
ainsi que as well as
aux alentours de in the neighbourhood of; round about
alors then; while
anxieusement anxiously
après after
après-demain the day after tomorrow
d'après according to
avec à-propos suitably
assez fairly, quite
assez de enough
aujourd'hui today
auparavant previously
auprès de by, close to, next to
aussi also, too; as
aussitôt at once
autant (de) as much; as many
d'autant plus (que) all the more (since)
autour (de) around
autrefois formerly
autrement otherwise, differently
autrement dit in other words
autrement que other than
à l'avance in advance
avant (de) before
avec with

en bas downstairs, at the bottom
beaucoup a lot; much, far
beaucoup de a lot of; many
bien well
bien entendu of course
bientôt soon
à bord (de) on board
au bord de beside
au bout de after (*of time*); at the end of
bref ''to cut a long story short''
brusquement abruptly, sharply
cependant however
certainement certainly
sans cesse without stopping, unceasingly
chez at (*or* to) the house of
chez moi/toi/lui/elle at my/your/his/her house
combien (de) how much, how many
comme as, like
comme d'habitude as usual
comme toujours as usual
comment? how?
complètement completely
y compris including
par conséquent as a result
continuellement continually
contre against
ci-contre opposite (this)
par contre on the other hand
à côté de next to, beside
de ce côté (de) on this side (of)
de l'autre côté (de) on the other side (of)
juste à côté next door
couramment fluently
dans in, into
davantage (de) more

de of, from
debout standing
dedans inside
(au) dehors outside
déjà already
demain tomorrow
après-demain the day after
  tomorrow
depuis since, for
depuis lors since then
derrière behind
dès from (*time*)
dès que as soon as
dessous underneath, beneath
ci-dessous below (this)
dessus on top
au-dessus (de) above
ci-dessus above (this)
devant in front (of)
doucement quietly; gently, softly
tout droit straight (on)
à droite on the right, to the right
dur: travailler dur to work hard
en effet indeed, as a matter of fact
également also; equally
encore still; again
encore une fois once again
enfin finally, at last
énormément (de) a lot (of)
ensemble together
ensuite then, next; later
entièrement entirely
entre between
environ about
éventuellement possibly,
  perhaps
évidemment evidently; obviously
exactement exactly
exprès on purpose, deliberately
à l'extérieur (de) outside
extrêmement extremely
face à facing; faced with
en face (de) opposite

facilement easily
de façon à so as to
fidèlement faithfully
finalement finally, in the end;
  after all
fort hard
franchement frankly, honestly
à gauche on the left, to the left
en général usually
généralement generally
gentiment nicely
grâce à thanks to
gravement gravely; seriously
ne ... guère hardly
à gogo galore
d'habitude usually
comme d'habitude as usual
par hasard by chance
au hasard at random
en haut (de) at the top (of)
de haut en bas from top to
  bottom
à l'heure on time
de bonne heure early
heureusement fortunately
hier yesterday
avant-hier the day before
  yesterday
ici here
immédiatement immediately
n'importe où anywhere
intellectuellement intellectually
à l'intérieur (de) inside
jadis formerly, once
jamais ever
ne ... jamais never
jusqu'à until; as far as, up to
jusqu'ici so far, until now
jusque-là until then
justement exactly
là there
là-bas over there, down there
là-haut up there

ADVERBS AND PREPOSITIONS

légèrement slightly; lightly
le lendemain the next day
le lendemain matin the next morning
lentement slowly
loin (de) far (from), a long way (from)
le long de along
longtemps (for) a long time
lourdement heavily
depuis lors since then
maintenant now
mal badly
malgré in spite of, despite
malheureusement unfortunately
manuellement manually
au maximum at (the) most; to the utmost
même same; even
même pas not even
quand même even so
mentalement mentally
mieux better
le mieux best
au milieu de in the middle of
moins less, minus
moins de less than, fewer than
au moins at least (*quantity*)
du moins at least
mystérieusement mysteriously
naturellement of course, naturally
nerveusement nervously
normalement normally
notamment especially
de nouveau again
nulle part nowhere
ne ... nullement in no way
où where
n'importe où anywhere
en outre furthermore
paisiblement peacefully
par by; through

par terre on the ground
par-dessous under(neath)
par-dessus over (the top) (of)
parfaitement perfectly
parfois sometimes
parmi among
à part apart (from)
nulle part nowhere
quelque part somewhere
en particulier in particular
particulièrement particularly
partiellement partially
à partir de from
partout everywhere
pas du tout not at all
pas loin de not far from
patiemment patiently
à peine scarcely, hardly, barely
pendant during, for
en perspective in prospect
peu à peu little by little
à peu près about, approximately
peut-être perhaps, maybe
poliment politely
plus [plys] plus
en plus [plys] moreover
plus de (pommes) [ply] no more (apples)
plus de (dix) [ply] more than (ten)
de plus [plys] moreover
de plus en plus [dəplyzãply] more and more
ne ... plus [ply] no more, no longer
plus tard [ply] later
non plus [ply] neither, either
moi non plus! nor me!
plutôt rather
pour for; in order to
pourtant yet, nevertheless
près de near (to)
à présent at present
presque almost, nearly

à proximité de near to
puis then, next
quand when
quand même however, even so, nevertheless
quant à (moi) as for (me)
quelquefois sometimes
quelque part somewhere
rapidement quickly
rarement rarely, seldom
récemment recently
régulièrement regularly
en retard late
sans without
sans cesse without stopping, ceaselessly
sauf except (for)
selon according to
sérieusement seriously
seul(e) alone
seulement only
simplement simply
soigneusement carefully
soudain suddenly
sous under
souvent often
"suite" "continued"
à la suite de following
suivant according to, following
"à suivre" "to be continued"
sur on
sûrement certainly, surely
sur-le-champ at once

surtout especially
sus: en sus in addition
tant de so much, so many
tard late
plus tard later
trop tard too late
tellement so; so much
de temps à autre from time to time
de temps en temps now and then, from time to time
en même temps at the same time
tôt early
trop tôt too soon, too early
le plus tôt possible as soon as possible
toujours always; still
en tout in all
tout d'abord first of all
tout à coup suddenly
tout à fait completely, quite
tout près (de) quite close (to)
tout de suite at once
à travers through
très very
trop too; too much
trop de too much, too many
uniquement only
un à un one by one
vers towards; about (*of time*)
vite quickly, fast
vraiment really
y there, to that place, in that place

NOUNS

SOME EXTRA NOUNS

un **accord** ▷ agreement
un **accueil** reception
l'**action** f action
l'**activité** f activity
une **affaire** matter
affût: à l'affût (de) on the lookout for
l'**âge** m age
l'**agrandissement** m enlargement
un **ajout** addition
l'**ajustage** m fitting
l'**ajustement** m adjustment
l'**alarme** f alarm
les **aléas** mpl hazards
un **amas** (pl inv) heap, pile
l'**ambition** f ambition
l'**âme** f soul
une **amélioration** improvement
l'**amour** m love
l'**ampleur** f scale, extent
l'**ancêtre de** m the forerunner of
une **ânerie** stupid comment
l'**angoisse** f anguish, distress
une **annonce** advertisement
l'**anonymat** m anonymity
l'**antériorité** f precedence (in time)
un **anthropophage** cannibal
une **anthropophage** cannibal
un **aperçu** general survey; insight
l'**apesanteur** f weightlessness
l'**aplomb** m balance
appui: à l'appui in support of this
l'**argot** m slang
une **armature** frame, framework
les **armoiries** fpl coat of arms
l'**arrière** m back, rear
l'**arrière-plan** m (pl ~s) background
un **(nouvel) arrivant** newcomer

une **(nouvelle) arrivante** newcomer
l'**arrivée** f arrival
à mon arrivée when I arrived
l'**articulation** f articulation
l'**asile** m refuge
l'**assistance** f aid, assistance
l'**assujettissement** m subjection
un **astre** star
une **astuce** trick
un **atout** asset
atteinte: hors d'atteinte out of reach
l'**attention** f attention; see **faire**
à l'attention de for the attention of
une **attestation** certificate
un **attrait** attraction
un **attroupement** mob
une **aubaine** godsend; windfall
l'**autocensure** f self-censorship
un **autocollant** sticker
l'**autorité** f authority
un **avantage** advantage
avant-dernier(ière) (pl ~s) last but one
un **avant-goût** (pl ~s) foretaste
un **avant-propos** (pl inv) foreword
une **aventure** adventure
un **avertissement** warning
un **avis** notice; opinion
à mon avis in my opinion
azimut: tous azimuts omnidirectional
le **bâillement** warning
la **banderole** streamer
la **bataille** battle
le **bâton** stick
la **beauté** beauty
le **besoin** see **avoir**

318

la **bêtise** stupidity
le **bien** good
la **blague** joke
le **bonheur** happiness, good luck
la **bonne volonté** goodwill, willingness
la **bousculade** bustle
le **bout** end
un **brin de** a touch of, a bit of
le **bruit** noise
le **but** ◊ aim; goal
la **cachette** hiding place
le **calcul** calculation
le **calme** peace, calm
le **candidat** candidate
le **caractère** ◊ character, nature; letter
le **cas** case
en **cas de** in case of, in the event of
en tout **cas** in any case
la **catastrophe** disaster
le **cauchemar** nightmare
la **cause** cause
à **cause de** because of
le **centre** centre
le **cercle** circle
la **certitude** certainty
le **chagrin** distress
la **chance** luck
la **chapelle** chapel
le **chapitre** chapter
le **charme** charm
le **charnier** mass grave
le **chef** ◊ chief, head, boss
le **chiffre** figure; numeral
le **choix** choice
la **chose** thing
le **chuchotement** whispering
le **cirage** (shoe)polish
la **citation** quotation
la **civilisation** civilization
la **clarté** brightness; clearness; lightness

le **classement** classification
un **clin d'œil** wink
le **clocher** steeple
le **coin** corner
la **colère** anger; see **mettre**
la **colonne** column
le **commencement** beginning
la **comparaison** comparison; see **soutenir**
le **complot** plot
le **compte** calculation
la **conclusion** conclusion
la **confiance** confidence
le **confort** comfort
la **connaissance** see **faire**
la **conscience** conscience
le **conseil** (piece of) advice
le **contemporain** contemporary
la **contemporaine** contemporary
la **construction** construction
le **contraire** the opposite
au **contraire** on the contrary
le **contrecoup** repercussions
la **copie** copy
la **corbeille** basket
le/la **correspondant(e)** correspondent
le **Coton-Tige** ® (*pl inv*) cotton bud
la **couche** nappy
la **couche-culotte** (*pl~s~s*) disposable nappy
le **coup** blow, bang, knock
le **couplet** verse
le **courage** courage, bravery
la **couronne** crown
cours: au cours de during, in the course of
en **cours** in progress
la **coutume** custom
la **crainte** fear
la **crasse** filth
le **cri** cry

NOUNS

le **critère** criterion
la **cruauté** cruelty
la **culture** ⟡ culture
la **curiosité** curiosity
le **danger** danger
les **déboires** setbacks
les **débris** wreckage
le **début** beginning
la **décision** decision
la **découverte** discovery
le **défi** challenge
les **dégâts** damage
le **demi-sommeil** half-sleep
le **demi-tarif** half-price
la **dépilation** hair removal
le **désarmement** disarmament
le **désastre** disaster
le **désavantage** disadvantage
le **désir** desire, wish
le **désordre** disorder
le **destin** destiny
le **détachant** stain remover
le **détail** detail
la **détresse** distress
la **déveine** bad luck
le **diagramme** chart, graph
le **(bon) Dieu** God
la **différence** difference
quelle est la différence entre X et Y? what is the difference between X and Y?
la **difficulté** difficulty
la **dimension** dimension
la **direction** direction
la **discipline** discipline
le **dispositif** device
disposition: être à la disposition de qn to be at sb's disposal
la **dispute** argument, dispute
la **distance** distance
le **doute** doubt
sans doute no doubt; probably
le **droit** right

la **durée** time
un **échange** exchange; *see* **taux**
en échange de in exchange for
l'**économie** f economy; saving
un **effet** effect
l'**efficacité** f efficiency; effectiveness
un **effort** effort
un **électeur** elector
une **élection** election
l'**élégance** f elegance
un **empêchement** (unexpected) obstacle, hitch
une **empreinte** (foot)print
un **endroit** place
l'**énergie** f energy
l'**engagement** m: "sans engagement" "without commitment"
une **énigme** riddle
l'**ennemi** m enemy
l'**ennui** m annoyance, boredom
une **enseigne** sign
un **ensemble** group (*of buildings etc*)
l'**enthousiasme** m enthusiasm
un **entretien** conversation, discussion
envie *see* **avoir**
les **environs** mpl surrounding district
l'**épaisseur** f thickness
l'**équilibre** m balance
une **erreur** mistake
l'**esclavage** m slavery
un **esclave** slave
une **esclave** slave
l'**espace** m space
une **espèce** sort, kind, species
en espèces in cash
un **espoir** hope
l'**essentiel** m the main thing
une **étape** ⟡ stage; stopping point

un état state
l'étendue *f* extent
une étincelle spark
l'étonnement *m* astonishment
un événement event
un excès excess
un exemplaire copy
en deux exemplaires in duplicate
un exemple example
par exemple for example
l'exil *m* exile
l'expérience ◊ *f* experience
un expert expert
une explication explanation
une exposition exhibition
un extrait extract
un extra-terrestre extraterrestrial
une extra-terrestre extraterrestrial
la fabrication manufacture
la façon way, method, manner
de cette façon in this way
le fait fact
le fantôme ghost
la farce practical joke
la faute ◊ fault
c'est de ma faute it's my fault
la fermeté firmness
la fermeture closure
la fin end
le fléau scourge, curse
la flèche arrow
la foi faith
la fois time
la folie madness
le fond background; bottom
la force strength
le format size
la forme form, shape
la foule crowd; heap
la fraîcheur freshness
les frais *mpl* expenses
le franc franc
le fric (*fam*) cash

la gaieté, la gaîté gaiety
le genre type, kind, sort
la gentillesse kindness
une gifle slap (in the face)
les goûts *mpl* interests
chacun son goût every man to his taste
le gouvernement government
grand-chose *nm/f inv*: **pas grand-chose** nothing much
la grandeur size
le gros lot first prize (*in lottery*)
un gros mot coarse word
la grossièreté coarseness, rudeness
le groupe group
la guerre war
le guide guide
l'habileté *f* skill
l'habitude *see* **avoir**
la :halte stop, break; halt
faire halte to stop
l'harmonie *f* harmony
un :haut-le-cœur (*pl inv*) retch, heave
un :haut-le-corps (*pl inv*) start, jump
le :haut-parleur (*pl ~s*) loudspeaker
la :hauteur height
l'hébergement *m* accommodation, lodging
le :hochet rattle
l'hommage *m* tribute
un homme-grenouille (*pl ~s~s*) frogman
l'honneur *m* honour
les honoraires *mpl* fees
la :honte shame
l'humeur *f* humour, mood
l'hygiène *f* hygiene
l'hypothèse *f* hypothesis
une idée idea

NOUNS

un/une idiot(e) idiot
une image picture
l'imagination f imagination
un/une imbécile idiot, imbecile
l'inconvénient m disadvantage
l'importance f importance
une impression impression
un/une inconnu(e) stranger
un inconvénient disadvantage
les informations fpl news
un inspecteur inspector
les instructions fpl instructions
l'intention f see **avoir**
l'intérêt m interest
une interruption break, interruption
une interview interview
la jalousie jealousy, envy
la joie joy
le jouet toy
le journal (pl **journaux**) newspaper
le juron curse, swearword
le laissez-passer (pl inv) pass
le lancement launching
la largeur width
la larme tear
le lecteur reader
la légende caption
le lieu (pl **-x**) place; see **avoir**
au lieu de instead of, in place of
la ligne line
la limite boundary, limit
la liste list
la litote understatement
la littérature literature
la livre (sterling) pound (sterling)
la location ⟡ hire, rental
le loisir leisure
la longueur length
la Loterie Nationale National Lottery
la lumière light

le lutin imp, goblin
la lutte ⟡ struggle
le magazine magazine
la malchance bad luck
le malheur misfortune
la manière way, method
le manque (de) lack (of)
le maximum maximum
le mélange mixture
le membre member
la mémoire memory
la méthode method, way
le mieux best; see **faire**
le milieu (pl **-x**) centre, middle
le minimum minimum
le Ministère de the Ministry of
le mot word; note, message
sans mot dire without saying a word
le moyen (de) the means (of)
au moyen de by means of
le mystère mystery
négatif: au négatif in the negative
le niveau (pl **-x**) level
le nombre number
la nouvelle (piece of) news
une objection objection
un objet object
une observation remark
une occasion opportunity; occasion
les œuvres fpl works
une opinion opinion
un ordre order
l'orgueil m pride
l'ouverture f opening
la page page
la paire pair
le panier basket
le panneau (pl **-x**) sign, notice
le pari bet
la parole word
la part part

de la part de on behalf of; from
de ma part on my behalf; from me
pour ma part for my part
le partenaire partner
la partie ◇ part; *see* **faire**
le pas footstep
le passager clandestin stowaway
la patience patience
la peine difficulty
la pensée ◇ thought
la permission permission
la personne person
la phrase sentence
la pièce (de 10 centimes) (10-centime) coin
la plaisanterie joke
le plaisir pleasure
le plan ◇ plan; map
au premier plan in the foreground
à l'arrière plan in the background
le plateau ◇ (*pl* **-x**) plateau
la plupart de *or* **des** most (of)
le poids weight
le point point, mark
le point de départ starting point
le point de vue point of view
la politesse politeness
la politique politics
portée: à portée de la main within arm's reach
le portrait portrait
positif: au positif in the positive
la position position
le possesseur owner
la possibilité possibility, opportunity
la poupée doll
le pouvoir power
les préparatifs *mpl* preparations
la préparation preparation
la présence presence
le pressentiment feeling

le principe principle
en principe as a rule; in principle
le problème problem
le produit product; produce
la profondeur depth
le projet plan
la propreté cleanliness
la prospérité prosperity
les provisions provisions
la prudence caution
avec prudence carefully; cautiously
le pseudonyme fictitious name; pen name; stage name
la publicité publicity
la qualité quality
la question question
le raccourci short-cut
la raison reason; *see* **avoir**
le rapport connection
la rature deletion, erasure
la recharge refill
la récompense reward
la recrudescence fresh outbreak
la réinsertion rehabilitation
la religion religion
les remerciements *mpl* thanks
le remue-ménage (*pl inv***)** stir, hullaballoo
la rencontre ◇ meeting
le rendez-vous appointment; date; meeting place
les renseignements *mpl* information
la réponse reply
la reprise resumption
la réputation reputation
le rescapé survivor
le réseau (*pl* **-x**) network
la résolution resolution
le respect respect
les restes *mpl* remains
le résultat result

NOUNS

le retour return
de retour back
la réussite success
le rêve dream; dreaming
de rêve: une maison de rêve a
  dream house
la révolution revolution
le révolutionnaire revolutionary
la rime rhyme
le rythme rhythm
la saleté dirtiness
le sang-froid calmness
le sanglot sob
le schéma diagram, plan
le secours help
le secret secret
la section section
la sécurité security
le séjour stay
la sélection selection
le sens sense
la sensation sensation; see faire
la série series
le service service
de service on duty
hors service not in use; out of
  order
le signal de détresse distress
  signal
le signe sign; see faire
le silence silence
la similitude similarity
le sinistre disaster
la situation situation
la société society
la solution solution
la somme sum
le somnambule sleepwalker
le son sound
le sort fate
la sorte sort, kind
la sottise stupidity, foolishness;
  silly remark

le souhait wish
la suie soot
le soupçon suspicion
le sourire smile
le sous-entendu (pl ~s) innuendo,
  insinuation
le souvenir souvenir
le spectateur spectator
le stéréotype stereotype
le style style
le succès success
le sujet subject, matter
au sujet de about
la surprise surprise
la surveillance supervision;
  watch
le système system
la tâche task
le talent talent
le taux de change exchange rate
la taxe tax
la tentative attempt
le terme term, expression
la tétine (baby's) dummy
le texte text
la théorie theory
la timidité shyness
le tonneau barrel
la toupie (spinning) top
le tour ⟡ turn; trick
c'est ton tour it's your turn
le tournoi tournament
la trace sign, trace
la tragédie tragedy
la tristesse sadness
le truc thingumajig, whatsit
le tube tube; hit song or record
le type fellow, chap, sort, kind
le va-et-vient coming and going
la valeur value
la vapeur ⟡ steam
le vaporisateur spray, atomizer
la veine ⟡ luck

la version version
le verso back (*of page*)
la victoire victory
la vie life
les vœux *mpl* wishes

le voyage journey
la vue view
de vue by sight
en vue de with a view to

VERBS

abandonner to abandon
abîmer to spoil
aboutir to end
s'abriter to shelter
accepter to accept
accompagner to go with
accomplir to accomplish
s'accoutumer à to become accustomed to
accrocher to hang (up); to catch (*à* on)
accueillir to welcome
accuser to accuse
acheter to buy
achever to finish
acquiescer (à qch) to assent (to sth)
acquitter to endorse
admettre to admit
adorer to adore
s'adresser à to apply to; to speak to
affecter (de faire qch) to pretend (to do sth)
afficher to display
affirmer to maintain, assert
agacer to irritate, aggravate
agir to act, behave
il s'agit de it is a question of
agiter le bras to wave
s'agrandir to grow
agrémenter (de) to adorn (with)
aider qn à to help sb to
aimer to like, love
aimer bien to like
aimer mieux to prefer
ajouter to add
aller to go
aller chercher qn to fetch sb, go and meet sb

aller voir to go and see
s'en aller to go away
allumer to switch on; to light
amener to bring; to bring about
s'amuser to enjoy oneself
annoncer to announce
annuler to cancel
s'apercevoir de to notice
appartenir (à) to belong (to)
appeler to call
s'appeler to be called
apporter to bring
apprécier to appreciate
apprendre (à faire) to learn (to do)
apprendre qch à qn to teach sb sth
(s')approcher de to approach
approuver to agree with; to approve (of)
appuyer to press; to lean (*object*)
s'appuyer to lean
arracher to pull out; to snatch; to tear
s'arranger: cela s'arrangera it will be all right
arrêter to stop; to arrest
s'arrêter to stop
arriver to arrive; to happen
s'asseoir to sit down
assister à to attend, be present at, go to
s'assoupir to doze off
assurer to assure; to insure; to ensure
attacher to tie, fasten
attaquer to attack
atteindre to reach
attendre to wait (for); to expect
attirer to attract

attraper to catch
augmenter to increase
(s')avancer to go forward
avoir to have
avoir l'air (de) to seem (to)
avoir besoin de to need
avoir chaud/froid to be hot/cold (*person*)
avoir envie de to want to
avoir l'habitude de to be in the habit of
avoir honte (de) to be ashamed (of)
avoir l'intention de to intend to
avoir lieu to take place, to occur
avoir du mal à to have difficulty in
en avoir marre to be fed up
avoir peur to be afraid
avoir raison/tort to be right/wrong
avouer to confess
baisser to lower
balbutier to stammer
barrer to block
bâtir to build
battre to beat
se battre to fight
bavarder to gossip, chat
bloquer to block
bouger to move
bouleverser to startle, shatter
bricoler to potter about, do odd jobs
briller to shine; to sparkle
briser to break, smash
brûler to burn
(se) cacher to hide
(se) calmer to calm down
casser to break
causer to cause; to chat
cesser (de) to stop
changer d'avis to change one's mind
chanter to sing
charger (de) to load with
chasser to chase (off); to get rid of
chatouiller to tickle
chauffer to warm up, heat up
chercher to look for; *see* **aller,** **envoyer**
choisir to choose
chuchoter to whisper
circuler to move (*of vehicles*)
cirer to polish
collaborer to collaborate
collectionner to collect
coller to stick
commander to order
commencer (à) to begin (to)
compenser to compensate for, make up for
comporter to comprise
composer to compose; to make up; to dial
composter to date-stamp; to punch
comprendre to understand
compter to count; to intend to
concerner to concern
conclure to conclude
conduire to drive
condamner to condemn; to sentence
se conduire to behave
confectionner to make
confesser to confess
confirmer to confirm
connaître to know (*person, place*)
consacrer to devote (*time*)
conseiller to advise
conserver to keep
(se) considérer to consider (oneself)
consister to consist
consommer to consume

VERBS

constater to establish; to state
constituer to constitute, make up
construire: faire construire une maison to have a house built
consulter to consult
contacter to contact, get in touch with
contempler to contemplate
contenir to contain
continuer to continue
convenir to be suitable
copier to copy
se coucher to go to bed; to lie down
coudre to sew
couler to flow
couper to cut (off)
courir to run
couvrir to cover
craindre to be afraid of, fear
créer to create
crever to have a puncture
crier to shout, cry
critiquer to criticize; to assess
croire to think; to believe
cueillir to pick; to capture
cultiver to grow, cultivate
danser to dance
déborder to overflow; to boil over
se débrouiller to manage
décharger to unload
déchirer to tear
décider (de) to decide (to)
se décider (à) to make up one's mind(to)
déclarer to declare
se décourager to become discouraged
découvrir to discover
décrire to describe
défendre to forbid; to defend
dégager to clear; to extricate
se déguiser to disguise oneself

demander qch à qn to ask sb for sth
demander à qn de faire qch to ask sb to do sth
se demander to wonder
demeurer to live
démolir to demolish
dépasser to overtake; to exceed
se dépêcher to hurry
dépendre de to depend on
déplaire: cela me déplaît I don't like it
déposer to put down
déranger to disturb
désapprouver to disapprove of
descendre to come *or* go down; to get off (*train etc*); to take down
désirer to desire, want
dessiner to draw
détester to detest
détourner to divert
détruire to destroy
développer to develop
devenir to become
devoir to have to (*must*)
différer (de) to differ (from), be different (from)
diminuer to diminish, reduce
dire to say, to tell
à vrai dire as a matter of fact
diriger to direct
se diriger vers to go towards
discuter to discuss
disparaître to disappear
se disputer to argue, have an argument
dissimuler to conceal
distinguer to distinguish
distribuer to distribute
diviser to divide
dominer to overcome; to dominate
donner to give
donner sur to overlook

dormir to sleep
doter (de) to endow (with)
se doucher to have a shower
douter (de) to doubt, have one's doubts about
dresser to set up, erect
se dresser to stand (up)
durer to last
échanger to exchange
s'échapper (de) to escape (from)
éclairer to light (up)
éclater de rire to burst out laughing
économiser to save
écouter to listen (to)
écraser to crush
s'écraser to crash
s'écrier to exclaim, cry out
écrire to write
effectuer to carry out
effrayer to frighten
s'élancer to rush, dash
élever to erect; to raise
s'élever to rise
(s')embrasser to kiss
emmener to take
empêcher (de) to prevent (from)
employer to use; to employ
emporter to take; to carry
emprunter qch à qn to borrow sth from sb
encourager qn à faire to encourage sb to do
s'endormir to fall asleep
enfermer to imprison
s'enfuir to flee
enlever to take away; to get rid of; to take off
s'ennuyer to be or get bored
enregistrer to record
ensevelir to bury
entasser to stack
entendre to hear

qu'entendez-vous par …? what do you mean (or understand) by …?
entendre parler de to hear about
s'entendre to agree, get on
entourer (de) to surround (with or by)
entrer (dans) to enter, go or come in(to)
envahir to invade
envelopper to wrap (up)
envoyer to send
envoyer chercher qn to send for sb
éprouver to experience, feel
espérer to hope
essayer (de faire qch) to try (to do sth)
essuyer to wipe
établir to establish, set up
étaler to spread out
éteindre to put out, extinguish; to switch off
(s')étendre to extend; to stretch out
étonner to astonish
s'étonner to be astonished
étouffer to suffocate; to be stifled
étrangler to strangle
être to be
être assis(e) to be sitting
être obligé(e) de to be obliged to
être de retour to be back
être sur le point de to be on the point of, be just about to
être en train de faire qch to be (busy) doing sth
étudier to study
(s')éveiller to wake up
éviter (de faire) to avoid (doing)
exagérer to exaggerate; to go too far
examiner to examine

VERBS

s'excuser (de) to apologize (for)
exister to exist
expliquer to explain
exprimer to express
fabriquer to manufacture, make
se fâcher to become angry
faillir: il a failli tomber he almost fell
faire to do; to make
faire attention to be careful
faire son autocritique to criticize o.s.
faire chaud/froid to be hot/cold (*weather*)
faire la connaissance de to meet
faire contrepoids to act as a counterbalance
faire entrer quelqu'un to let somebody in
se faire couper les cheveux to have one's hair cut
faire du mal (à) to harm
faire de même to do the same
faire partie de to belong to (*club etc*)
faire de son mieux (pour) to do one's best (to)
faire l'éloge de to praise
faire des démarches auprès de qn to approach sb
faire une promenade to go for a walk
faire remarquer to mention, point out
se faire remarquer to be noticed
faire semblant de to pretend to
faire sensation to cause a sensation
faire signe to signal, wave
il faut one must *etc*
falloir to be necessary
féliciter to congratulate
(se) fermer to close, shut

fermer à clef to lock
se figurer to imagine
finir to finish
fixer to stare at; to fix
flâner to stroll, lounge about
fonctionner to work (*of machine etc*)
faire fonctionner to operate
former to form
fouiller to search
fournir to provide
frapper to hit, strike, knock
fréquenter to frequent (*place*); to see (*person*)
gagner to win; to earn
garantir to guarantee
garder to keep
gâter to spoil
se gâter to go wrong
gémir to groan
gêner to bother
glisser to slip, slide
gratter to scratch
grimper to climb
guetter to watch
habiter to live in
hésiter to hesitate
heurter to bump into
ignorer not to know
imaginer to imagine
imprimer to print
indiquer qch à qn to inform sb of sth
s'inquiéter to worry
ne vous inquiétez pas! don't worry!
inscrire to inscribe
s'inscrire to register
installer to fix (up)
s'installer to settle, sit (down)
s'instruire to educate oneself
insulter to insult
interdire to prohibit
"interdit de fumer" "no

smoking''
intéresser to interest
s'intéresser à qch to be interested in sth
interroger to question
interrompre to interrupt
interviewer to interview
introduire to introduce
inviter to invite
jeter to throw (away)
joindre to join
jurer to swear
laisser to leave; to let; to allow
laisser tomber to drop
lancer to throw
(se) laver to wash
lever to lift; to raise
se lever to get up; to stand up
lire to read
loger (chez) to lodge (with), live (with)
louer to hire, rent
lutter to struggle
manœuvrer to manoeuvre; to operate
manquer to miss; to be lacking
marcher to walk; to work (*of object*)
se marier (avec qn) to marry (sb)
marquer to mark; to write down; to score
mêler to mix
se mêler (à qch) to be involved (in sth)
menacer to threaten
mener to lead
mentir to lie, tell a lie
mériter to deserve
tu l'as mérité! you deserved it!
mesurer to measure
mettre to put (on); to take (*time*)
mettre qch au point to bring sth about; to get sth ready

mettre qn à la porte to throw sb out
mettre qch à la poste to post sth
se mettre à l'abri to take shelter
se mettre en colère to get angry
se mettre en route to set off
monter to come *or* go up; (*+ dans*) to get into (*car etc*); to take up
montrer to show; to point out
se moquer de to make fun of
multiplier to multiply
noter to note
nourrir to nourish; to cherish
obliger qn à faire to force *or* oblige sb to do
observer to observe; to keep
obtenir to obtain
s'occuper à to occupy oneself *or* keep oneself busy (with)
s'occuper de to attend to; to be concerned (with)
offrir to give, offer
s'opposer à to be opposed to
ordonner to order, command
organiser to organize
orner (de) to decorate (with)
oser (faire qch) to dare (to do sth)
oublier to forget
(s')ouvrir to open; to switch on
paraître to appear
parier (sur) to bet (on)
parler to speak, talk
partager to share
participer (à) to take part in; to share in
partir to leave, depart, go away
à partir de from
passer to pass; to spend (*time*)
passer un examen to sit an exam
se passer to happen
passionner to excite
pavoiser to decorate with flags
payer to pay

peindre to paint
pénétrer (dans) to enter, make one's way into
penser (à) to think (about)
penser de to have an opinion of
perdre to lose
perdre qn de vue to lose sight of sb
permettre (à qn de faire) to allow or permit (sb to do)
persuader to persuade
peser to weigh
photographier to photograph
placer to place, put
se plaindre (de) to complain (about)
plaire (à) to please
cela me plaît I like that
plaisanter to joke
pleurer to cry
plier to fold
porter to carry; to wear; to take
poser to put (down)
poser des questions to ask questions
posséder to possess
postillonner to sp(l)utter
poursuivre to pursue
pousser to push; to grow
pousser un cri to utter a cry
pouvoir to be able to (*can*)
pratiquer to go in for
précipiter to hurl
se précipiter dans to rush into
prédire to predict
préférer to prefer
prendre to take; to have
prendre feu to catch fire
prendre part à to take part in
prendre qch à qn to take sth from sb
prendre soin (de) to take care (to)
préparer to prepare

présenter to present; to introduce
se présenter to appear; to introduce oneself
prêter qch à qn to lend sb sth
prévoir to foresee
prier to request
je vous en prie please, don't mention it
priver qn de qch to deprive sb of sth
produire to produce
se produire to happen, occur
profiter (de) to take advantage (of)
se promener to go for a walk
promettre (à qn de faire qch) to promise (sb to do sth)
prononcer to pronounce
prononcer un discours to make a speech
proposer (de faire) to suggest (doing)
protéger to protect
protester to protest
prouver to prove
provoquer to cause
puer to stink
se quereller to quarrel
quitter to leave
raccommoder to mend, repair
raconter to tell
ralentir to slow down
ramasser to pick up
ramener to bring or take back
ranger to arrange, tidy
se rappeler to remember
rapporter to report; to bring back
rater to miss; to fail
rattraper qn to catch up with sb
recevoir to receive
réchauffer to warm (up)
recommander to recommend; to register (*letter*)

recommencer to begin again
reconnaître to recognize
recouvrir (de) to cover (with)
reculer to move back; to reverse
redescendre to come *or* go down again
refaire to re-do, do again
refermer to close again
réfléchir to think, reflect
refuser (de) to refuse (to)
regagner to go back to
regarder to look (at)
régler to adjust; to direct (*traffic*); to settle (*bill*)
regretter (que) to be sorry (that)
rejoindre to meet; to rejoin; to reach
se relever to get up again
relier to connect
relire to read again
remarquer to notice
rembourser to refund
remercier (de) to thank (for)
remettre to put back; to take back; to postpone
remonter dans to get back into
remplacer to replace
remplir (de) to fill (with)
remuer to stir
rencontrer to meet
se rencontrer to meet; to collide
rendre to give back
rendre visite à to visit
se rendre to surrender, give oneself up
se rendre à to visit (*place*)
se rendre compte to realize
(se) renfermer to shut (oneself) in
renseigner to inform
se renseigner (sur) to inquire (about)
rentrer to return
renverser to overturn, knock over

renvoyer to send back
réparer to repair
repasser to press, iron
répéter to repeat
répondre to reply
se reporter à to refer to
se reposer to rest
reprendre to resume
représenter to represent
réserver to book, reserve
résoudre to solve
respecter to respect
ressembler à to resemble
ressortir to bring *or* take out
rester to stay, remain
retenir to book, reserve
retentir to sound
retourner to return
se retourner to turn round
retrouver to meet; to find (again)
se réunir to meet
réussir (à faire) to succeed (in doing)
se réveiller to waken up
révéler to reveal
revenir to come back
rêver to dream
revoir to see again
au revoir goodbye
rigoler, rire to laugh
risquer (de) to risk
ronfler to snore
rougir to blush
rouler to drive (along)
saisir to seize, grasp; to catch, understand
salir to dirty
se salir to get dirty
saluer to greet
sangloter to sob
sauter to jump
sauver to save
se sauver to run off

VERBS

savoir to know (*fact*)
sécher to dry
secouer to shake
sélectionner to select
sembler to seem
sentir to smell
se sentir (mal) to feel (ill)
séparer to separate
se serrer la main to shake hands
(se) servir to serve (oneself)
se servir de qch to use sth
signaler to point out
signer to sign
somnoler to doze
sonner to ring
sortir to go *or* come out; to take out
se soucier de to worry about
souffrir to suffer; to bear, stand
souhaiter to wish
soulager to relieve
soulever to lift
soupçonner to suspect
soupirer to sigh
sourire to smile
soutenir la comparaison avec to bear comparison with
se souvenir de qch to remember sth
sucer to suck
suffire to be sufficient
suggérer to suggest
suivre to follow
supposer to suppose
à supposer que . . . supposing that . . .
surprendre to surprise
sursauter to give a jump
se taire to be quiet
taquiner to tease
tâter to taste; to sample
téléphoner (à) to telephone
tendre to hold out
tenir to hold; to run (*shop*)

tenter de to attempt to
(se) terminer to finish
tirer to pull; to let off (*fireworks*); to shoot
tomber to fall
laisser tomber to drop
tomber en panne to break down
toucher (à) qch to touch sth
toucher de l'argent to receive money
tourner to turn; to shoot (*film*)
se tourner vers to turn towards
traduire to translate
trahir to betray
traîner to drag, pull
travailler to work
traverser to cross; to go through; to go over
tromper to outwit
se tromper to be mistaken
troubler to worry
trouver to find
se trouver to be (situated)
tuer to kill
unir to unite
utiliser to use
vaincre to conquer
valoir to be worth
vendre to sell
venir to come
venir de faire qch to have just done sth
vérifier to check
verser to pour
visiter to visit
vivre to live
voir to see
voler to steal; to fly
vouloir to want
vouloir bien (+ *infinitive*) to be happy to
vouloir dire to mean
voyager to travel

334

The following French words can have more than one translation, depending on context. If you do not already know these translations, check them up on the pages shown.

ENGLISH INDEX

The vocabulary lists on the following pages cover all of the English nouns in the first two levels of the book, i.e. ESSENTIAL and IMPORTANT.

ENGLISH INDEX

ENGLISH INDEX

348

ENGLISH INDEX

ENGLISH INDEX

ENGLISH INDEX

ENGLISH INDEX

The vocabulary lists on the following pages cover all of the French nouns in the first two levels of the book, i.e. ESSENTIAL and IMPORTANT.

FRENCH INDEX

FRENCH INDEX

FRENCH INDEX

FRENCH INDEX

FRENCH INDEX

FRENCH INDEX

When David pulled in ju... ... jumped off her tricycle and ran to him. Without so much as a glance at his daughter, he walked straight into the apartment building. He didn't seem angry or in a hurry. Pat picked up Andrea, grabbed Christine by the hand, and followed. By the time she reached the apartment, David was already emptying his closet, holding as many hangers as he could in his left hand. He seemed cool, methodical, almost as if he were packing for a business trip . . .

From Richard Rashke, prize-winning author of *The Killing of Karen Silkwood* and *Capitol Hill in Black and White*, an inspiring true story of women and family, commitment and courage, as told to him by the people who lived it . . .

RUNAWAY FATHER

"COMPELLING!" —*Orlando Sentinel*

"A TIMELY, DRAMATIC ILLUSTRATION OF A NATIONAL SHAME."
—*New York City Tribune*

RUNAWAY FATHER

THE TRUE STORY OF PAT BENNETT,
HER DAUGHTERS, AND THEIR
SEVENTEEN-YEAR SEARCH

RICHARD RASHKE

BERKLEY BOOKS, NEW YORK

This Berkley book contains the complete text
of the original hardcover edition. It has been
completely reset in a typeface designed
for easy reading and was printed from new film.

RUNAWAY FATHER

A Berkley Book / published by arrangement with
Harcourt Brace Jovanovich, Inc.

PRINTING HISTORY
Harcourt Brace Jovanovich edition published 1988
Berkley edition / March 1990

All rights reserved.
Copyright © 1988 by Patricia Ann Bennett.
This book may not be reproduced in whole or in part, by
mimeograph or any other means, without permission.
For information address: Harcourt Brace Jovanovich
Publishers, Orlando, Florida 32887.

ISBN: 0-425-12009-0

A BERKLEY BOOK® TM 757,375
Berkley Books are published by The Berkley Publishing Group,
200 Madison Avenue, New York, New York 10016.
The name "BERKLEY" and the "B" logo
are trademarks belonging to Berkley Publishing Corporation.

PRINTED IN THE UNITED STATES OF AMERICA

10 9 8 7 6

For abandoned and
abused children everywhere

*The quality of a civilization
may be measured by how it cares for
its elderly. Just as surely, the
future of a society may be forecast
by how it cares for its young. . . .*

—Daniel Patrick Moynihan

Contents

▼

Author's Note

▼

THE FIRST NAMES of two people have been changed for reasons of privacy—Lenora, the woman James Parker "married" after he abandoned his wife and daughters; and Beth, a family friend. Pat Bennett's lawyer's name has been changed to Victoria Gordon. The first name of Pat Bennett's cousin, David, has been changed to Joe, his middle name, to avoid confusion.

Unfortunately, the runaway father himself, James C. Parker, has declined repeated requests through his attorneys to be interviewed. Information about him comes from court records, public and subpoenaed documents, his interviews with the press, and my interviews with those who knew him.

—R.R.

Part
One

SURVIVAL

1

▼

DAVID HAD NOT come home all night. Pat waited up for him, holding dinner as long as she could. Then she cleaned the kitchen, put Christine and Andrea to bed, and crawled between the cool sheets, exhausted. Pregnant for the third time, she felt listless as August. Anemic again, she thought as her eyes blinked closed. I must remember to tell Dr. May.

In spite of her fatigue, Pat awakened every few hours, hoping to feel the security of David's warmth and hear the rhythm of his breathing. Each time she realized he hadn't come, she checked the clock, then drifted into yet another anxious dream.

Andrea began whimpering at six that morning as usual. Without opening her eyes, Pat reached over and felt David's side of the bed. It was empty, unrumpled. She tried to hold back the day with a few more minutes of sleep, but Andrea soon wailed for her bottle and woke up Christine, who padded into her parents' room in her footed pajamas.

"Daddy?" Christine said in a disappointed voice when she saw her father wasn't in bed. "Daddy?"

So the day began.

When Pat's eyes finally opened, she greeted the morning with an anger so hot it melted her pain. It had been months since David had stayed out all night, and she had talked her-

self into believing that he had finally sown the last of his wild
oats. Now she realized for the first time in her three and a
half years of marriage that what she had been calling his
"restlessness" was nothing less than adultery. The admission
was hard to grasp. Why would David want another woman
when she was eager for him? If he loved her, how could he
hurt her? And if he no longer cared, why did he still make
love to her?

Pat eased herself out of bed and began her morning routine.

It was a small but comfortable two-bedroom apartment with
red oak floors and plenty of light. Disney-character placemats
hung on the walls in the girls' bedroom—Donald Duck, Pluto,
Snow White, and Dopey. Above Christine's bed stretched a
heavy cardboard choo-choo train seven feet long, which Pat
had bought in a toy store. Up to a height of two feet, the
walls were covered with crayon scribbles. In the middle of
the room sat a tiny table and two chairs surrounded by toys.
A picture window overlooked a wide strip of lawn out back,
with picnic tables, a life-size toy stagecoach, and Jungle-Gym
bars. Beyond the lawn lay thick woods. In the evenings, rab-
bits and groundhogs ventured out to feed on the grass.

The apartment was furnished with the things Pat and David
had bought on credit for four hundred dollars: a matching
brown tweed easy chair and couch with two imitation walnut
end tables, a formica-topped dinette table with light blue
vinyl-backed chairs to accent the navy blue living-room rug,
a double bed with a bookcase headboard and matching
dresser. Scattered throughout the apartment were mementos
marking the mileposts of Pat's twenty-three years. On the
bookcase, next to her old college textbooks, sat two beer
mugs, one bearing the word "Bermuda," where David had
proposed to her; the other reading "Immaculata College,"
which she had attended for three semesters. The Boston
rocker in one corner of the living room had been a gift from
her friends at Jackson Memorial Hospital in Miami, where
she had worked until she was eight months pregnant with
Andrea. Standing somewhat out of place on an inexpensive
tea cart was her grandmother's antique silver tea service.

Pat changed the girls, gave Andrea her bottle, and put her
in the playpen against the wall in the living room. Then she

gave Christine her early morning bath. It was one of the joys of her day and not even David's night out could rob her of that pleasure.

She had been six months pregnant with Christine when David stayed out all night for the first time. Married just over a year and a half, they were living in a cheap, off-base apartment in Camp Lejeune, North Carolina, where David was stationed as an enlisted Marine. That first time, unable to accept the possibility that David might be with another woman, Pat told herself that a soon-to-be father needed a night out with the boys. But six weeks after Christine's birth, a pregnant teenager knocked on her door, claiming David as the father and asking for four hundred dollars to cover expenses in a home for unwed mothers. Pat was shattered. She rushed into the bedroom and brought out Christine. Clutching the proof of David's love, she rocked the baby in her arms as if the touch and smell of their own child could prove the pregnant girl a liar. But as Pat paced the floor and wept, she sensed that the girl was telling the truth.

Composing herself, Pat told the teenager she would be willing to help financially once Christine was old enough to allow her to go back to work. The girl declined the offer. She had come to make David suffer, she said, not his wife.

Later, when Pat confronted him, David argued with quick, cold logic. Girls come to Lejeune all the time to shake down Marine wives by claiming to be pregnant when they aren't, he explained. They demand money and promise to leave town forever. How could she fall for such an obvious scam?

In Miami a year later, after David's discharge from the Marines and while Pat was carrying Andrea, David began staying out all night again. One day, Christine pulled out a package of condoms from the glove compartment of the car; but even then, Pat could not admit to herself that David was actually using them. A month after Andrea was born, however, a woman phoned and asked for David. As soon as Pat identified herself as David's wife, the woman's voice froze. Begging the caller not to hang up, Pat asked, was she David's girlfriend? The woman admitted she was, but said she hadn't known David was married. A few days later, Pat got a package in the mail: a stack of love letters signed "David" and a gift of fifty dollars for Andrea.

The letters burned like acid. As she raced through each page, Pat's anger rose around her like a steel wall. She went looking for David and found him in the shower. Without a word, she slid back the glass door and tossed the letters in.

This time he couldn't talk his way out of it like he had at Camp Lejeune, nor was she prepared to let him try. But what should she do? She had two children now and no job or money. Worse, she still loved David and needed him for a string of reasons she only dimly understood. She had always been the obedient, doting wife, bolstering her marriage with every available excuse. Yet after three years, even she had to admit failure, and the realization made her afraid. If David was capable of change, she would have to shock him into it.

For the first time since she had left home, Pat called her parents collect and asked for help. They agreed to send airplane tickets for her and the children and offered to hire a van to bring her things back to Washington. They promised to find Pat an apartment and cover all her expenses until Andrea was old enough to allow her to go back to work. She accepted the offer as a loan.

Pat waited until David was on a training flight for his private pilot's license. Then she had the movers empty the house of everything except David's clothes and a few pieces of furniture. She wanted him to come home to bare rooms and a lipstick message on the bathroom mirror: ''Go fly a kite!''

David walked in before she could leave for the airport, and she could sense his shock. When he finally realized that she was serious about leaving, he agreed to drive her and the children to the airport.

Pat settled into a two-bedroom apartment in northern Virginia and waited for David's next move. Common sense told her he would never change. Even if he did, she knew she would never completely trust him again. But she was lonely, in love, and insecure without him. When David finally asked to join her and promised to be faithful, she decided to give him a second chance. For a few weeks all was well. But now she was pregnant again. And he had stayed out all night.

For the first time, Pat began to see why she put up with his behavior. David stayed out all night only when she was most vulnerable—either pregnant or caring for a new baby. What could she do? Her children needed a father. She *had* to believe she still loved him. If she didn't, she could never live with him. And if she walked out, where would she go? What would she do once she got there? How could she pay her way?

Now, as she waited to face him, Pat finally understood the survival game she had been playing—a game that defied logic, although millions of women had played it before her. She had convinced herself that her husband was faithful in spite of the evidence, but subconsciously she had vowed never to trust him again.

No more, she told herself. David wasn't restless, he was cheating. And he was doing it when she felt most helpless and needy. Pregnant or not, she wouldn't stand for one more night of it.

When David walked in just after seven that morning, Pat was feeding Andrea at the kitchen table. Christine sat in her little rocker in the living room, and when she saw her father, her face broke into a sunny smile.

"Daddy," she cried. "Daddy!"

Christine adored her father. The most difficult moment of her day was when he would kiss her good-bye and drive off to work. The sight of his car pulling up in front of the apartment at dusk was her reward for missing him all day. Even though she was not quite two years old, his unpredictable comings and goings the last few weeks had unsettled her. She cried more, laughed less, and seemed irritable and anxious.

This morning, David ignored Christine and headed straight for the bedroom without saying a word.

"David, where were you?" Pat demanded as she wiped cereal from Andrea's face. "I want to know where you were!"

Ignoring Pat's questions, David walked out of the bedroom and into the bathroom. Pat put Andrea back in the playpen and, while David showered, she went through his suitcoat pockets. There she found a motel receipt dated August 28, 1968. She felt her anger rise. Last night she had held his dinner, waited up as long as she could, and worried most of the night, only to find that he had spent money they could ill afford for a motel room and who knew what else. Without bothering to knock, she yanked the bathroom door open.

"What the hell is this?" she shouted, waving the motel slip in his face. When she got no answer, she tossed the piece of paper at him in disgust and slammed the door. She was not surprised at his silence. A few months earlier in Miami, David had also refused to discuss his love letters. Tearing them into tiny pieces, he had simply flushed them down the toilet. As if that would make the problem go away.

After showering, David walked back into the bedroom and began putting on his tailor-made blue suit and a clean white shirt that Pat had carefully starched the way he liked it. Pat stood just inside the door fighting back a familiar and growing panic.

"Why do you have to sleep with someone else?" she asked sadly, surprised at the sound of her voice. "What's wrong with me?"

Unruffled, David stood before the mirror and straightened his blue-and-maroon-striped necktie. No answer.

"You make me sick," Pat said, finally allowing her anger to overcome her fear and insecurity. "How can I even want you to touch me!"

David stepped out of the bedroom without a word of explanation, walked past Christine, whose eyes never left him, and slipped out the apartment door. He had not stopped long enough even to hug or kiss his daughters good-bye.

Christine stared at the door, sobbing. Pat picked her up and held her tightly. It was only seven-thirty and it promised to be a very long day.

2

THE MORNING DRAGGED. By the time Pat straightened the apartment, dressed the girls, and settled down Karen and Michael, two children whom she babysat, it was ten o'clock. That was the hour when the young mothers in the building gathered on the front stoop and turned their kids loose. There were often as many as fifteen women huddled together watching twenty-five children run around the lawn like gophers.

The stoop was a place to kill time and gossip, a maternal commune with each woman keeping an eye on her neighbors' children. On muggy mornings and evenings, the women sat on the cool cement steps. In the afternoons, they sprawled on blankets under a sugar maple whose branches brushed the building when a strong wind blew. It was a pleasant place to wait for husbands to come home.

Fairmont Gardens in Annandale, Virginia, sat parklike amid apple trees, maples, and Virginia pines planted in haphazard care on stretches of weedless grass. A ribbon of blacktop wound through the lawns and flowerbeds to a four-lane highway linking the development to the rest of the world. Although there were nearly four hundred apartments in a string of two-story brick buildings, the planners had designed the space so well it was hard to tell so many people lived there.

Since David took the car to work and he and Pat rarely went out together, she felt isolated and unchallenged most of the time. Chatting with the other women, even if it was only to swap gossip, made her feel like an adult. All about the same age and all facing the same struggles, the women understood each other like sisters. This morning, sensing Pat was moody, they left her to Andrea and her private thoughts and kept a lookout for Christine, Michael, and Karen, who played on the sidewalk.

With eight anxious hours to wait for David's next move and feeling frightened and insecure, Pat slipped back into blaming herself for his behavior, no longer certain about the conclusions she had reached earlier that morning. He had stayed out all night and was angry at her, she reasoned, because she had not made a perfect home for him as a wife should.

Perfect was what she sensed David wanted. An only child raised in a tidy foster home, her husband had grown into a tidy man. He liked clean, starched white shirts. A home free of clutter. A nicely set table and dinner, hot and waiting, served by a smiling wife in a dress and makeup. And he wanted children who cried only when he wasn't home, and who didn't spit up, soil diapers, or throw toys.

Pat, on the other hand, was one of five children born to parents for whom clutter was life. She grew up feeling comfortable with dishes in the sink, babies screaming, and toys scattered on the floor. Although the neatness issue had always created sparks between her and David, she had managed to keep things on shelves and in closets until Andrea was born nine months earlier. With two children of her own, two more to sit, and a baby on the way, she was finding it increasingly difficult to have perfect children in a perfect apartment and still look attractive herself. Besides, housework was an insult. At first she had accepted it as part of the fine print of "I do." But when she couldn't keep up with the endless chores, and David complained without so much as stooping to pick up a toy, she began to show her resentment. On days when she felt especially harried or bushed, she wouldn't even try to keep up the illusion of a perfect home. If David wanted one so badly, he'd simply have to help. Or learn to put up with the mess.

The previous week, Pat knew, had almost driven David

mad. Her parents had left town for a few days, and she had agreed to look after her teenage sister and ten-year-old brother, along with babysitting Karen and Michael. That gave her six children and a husband to worry about. She knew David would be unhappy with the added commotion, but she had had no choice. She couldn't turn her parents down after all they had done for her, and she and David needed the twenty dollars a week babysitting money. Pat felt the tension building between her and David all that week. It was the ironing board, however, that brought things to a head.

David had walked through the door after work one evening to the usual baby bottles in the sink and toys on the floor. Andrea was crying in the playpen as she had been doing for much of that noisy week, and the ironing board was still up between the living room and the dining area. Overwhelmed with housework, Pat had either forgotten to take it down or had left it up in unconscious protest, she couldn't say which. The clothes she had already ironed were folded and piled on the couch. In the basket on the floor sat the things that still needed ironing. On a doorknob hung David's freshly pressed shirts which had first been starched, then put in the freezer until she was ready to press them. David took one look around and walked back out the door. He returned later that night when the apartment was quiet and neat.

If only she had taken the time to fold the ironing board! Pat felt a stab of guilt as sharp as a labor pain. As usual, the guilt quickly turned to panic. Any thought of losing David left her numb. Without him to define her, she seemed to have no sense of herself. He had hinted he might take a month's furlough from the marriage to think things over, and she had even found a stack of apartment brochures he hadn't bothered to hide. But he had never talked about permanent separation, thank God. David loved Christine too much to do that. She had always been his "buddy." When he washed the car, she'd stand next to him with a little rag. When he went out, she'd beg to go along, clinging to his pants leg.

On top of it all, Pat felt so unattractive these days. Five feet four inches tall, with light blue eyes and shoulder-length blonde hair flipped up at the ends, she had a slim, hourglass figure and, even four months pregnant, weighed only 120 pounds. But now that she was showing, she felt undesirable.

When she had begun to thicken with Christine and Andrea, David seemed to lose interest in her. Maybe that was why he spent last night in a motel, Pat thought. Maybe her body disgusted him.

Or maybe it was the business about college. Pat had been pushing David to get a degree ever since they married. She was determined to do everything she could, even go back to work, to give him a chance to get an education and better their lives. At Lejeune, they had taken courses in English and history and had studied together in the evenings. She found it fulfilling, fun even. When David got his discharge, she had suggested they move to Greenville and finish college together at East Carolina University on the GI Bill. But David had decided to move to Miami instead. It was a big disappointment for her; she could not understand his lack of interest in school.

Turning it over in her mind now, Pat realized that college was her ambition, not David's. Perhaps being pushed had bothered him more than she realized.

Then there was the matter of intimacy. Pat was a toucher whose eyes couldn't hide her emotions. David, on the other hand, rarely said how he felt. During their courtship, he had always found it easier to express his feelings in letters than face to face.

She had met him at his going-away party in January 1963. She was eighteen, a senior in an all-girl Catholic high school and so shy, she blushed at the slightest provocation. Pat liked David immediately. Nineteen and on his way to Marine Corps boot camp, he was tall, muscular, and meticulously dressed. He wouldn't dance with anyone else at the party and didn't want her to either. Never having had a real boyfriend before, she enjoyed feeling like the only girl in the room. At the Catholic mixers she had gone to, she had grown used to boys passing her by. She knew she had a good figure but thought her face was plain. A boy's wolf whistle would startle her; she was sure that if he saw her close up, he'd walk the other way.

David changed all that in one night. He asked her out and afterward kissed her goodnight. Their two-year courtship was a blend of love letters and occasional dates during his home leaves. The dates were fun, the letters warm and intimate. Pat married the David who wrote letters.

Once married, David seemed to slide into a pattern of emotional coolness. He disliked being fussed over and would frequently withdraw into himself. Pat often attributed his aloofness to his mother's decision to send him to his aunt to raise when he was two years old. Why she had given only him away and not his sister seemed to bother him.

Now, waiting on the front stoop, Pat grew more anxious by the hour. Before she knew it, it was lunchtime, and one by one the women began to drift away. Pat brought the four children back inside and fed them. At nap time she put Karen and Michael in the double bed, Andrea in her crib, then lay down next to Christine. While Christine slept, Pat usually dozed, but this afternoon she was too edgy to rest; she dreaded David's return yet wished he would hurry. As soon as Christine's breathing grew heavy, Pat slipped out of bed, grabbed a basket of dirty diapers, and raced to the laundry room in the basement before someone else beat her to the washers.

At four o'clock, Karen and Michael's father picked them up, and Pat began to prepare dinner. She loved baking pies and breads and experimenting with new recipes. The kitchen, with its Pepto Bismol-pink refrigerator, stove, and countertops, was the only place she had felt creative lately. Normally, she had the table set and dinner waiting when David walked in; the ritual was important to her. When Pat was a child, her father had worked two jobs and never came home for supper on weeknights. Having missed that family tradition herself, she now insisted on it for her daughters.

Lately though, David had been coming home at such unpredictable hours. She peeled the potatoes, washed the vegetables, and trimmed and seasoned the meat. Then she dressed Christine. Although Pat always made her older daughter look pretty for her father, today she took special care. She put Christine in a frilly red-and-white gingham dress and pinned her long, reddish-orange hair back with red barrettes. Then she brought Christine and Andrea outside to play with the other children.

After a week of record-breaking heat and humidity, it was an unusually pleasant August afternoon. Pat and Andrea joined the other women on a blanket under the maple while Christine waited for her father's car to turn the corner and pull up in front of the stoop. As soon as she saw the car, she would run down the sidewalk shouting, "Daddy! Daddy!" It was a beautiful moment and Pat always looked forward to it.

But not that afternoon. No matter how much she tried, Pat found it impossible to shake a sense of impending doom. None of the problems in their marriage was insurmountable, she argued to herself. Once the baby was born, she wouldn't be so tired and listless; her stomach would be flat again, and she'd exercise to tone her muscles. She would work harder at keeping the place neat for David, and in return, perhaps, he would be just a little more tolerant when she failed. If she was too clinging, she would learn to be more restrained, and maybe David would try to be more expressive. If he didn't want college, she wouldn't push him. And once the new baby was old enough, she would go back to work if he felt overwhelmed by the responsibility of three children.

When David pulled in just after six, Christine jumped off her tricycle and ran to him. Without so much as a glance at his daughter, he walked straight into the apartment building. He didn't seem angry or in a hurry. Pat picked up Andrea, grabbed Christine by the hand, and followed. By the time she reached the apartment, David was already emptying his closet, holding as many hangers as he could in his left hand.

Pat watched in resignation. There was nothing to say. When his arms were full, David walked back out to the car and returned for another load. On his second trip, Pat snatched his car keys from the dining-room table and rushed across the hall to the apartment of her friend Lorraine, who was also pregnant.

"He's leaving," Pat said. She wasn't surprised he was going, but she was furious at the way he was doing it. No explanation. No word where he was going or how long he intended to stay away. "He's taking his clothes. I'm going to keep his keys so he can't go."

"Don't, Pat!" Lorraine advised. "Don't do that. Give him the keys and let him go. You can't hold on to someone by force."

Pat went back to her apartment, put the keys on the table, and watched David empty his dresser drawer. The apartment seemed as still as a grave. Pat wasn't crying, David didn't look angry or sad, Andrea was sitting in the playpen, and Christine was watching her father pack with the same curiosity as she would watch him polish the car. David seemed cool, methodical, almost as if he were packing for a business trip.

Pat felt too defeated and worthless even to try wringing an explanation from him. If she asked, she knew she would get upset, the kids would cry, and she would not get a straight answer anyway.

After his fourth trip to the car, David didn't come back. Numb and in shock, Pat called her mother.

3

"DAVID LEFT," PAT told her mother. She wasn't crying or shaking. She was just imparting information with a matter-of-factness that surprised even her. "He took his clothes. I guess he was fed up. I'm sure he'll be back in a couple of days. What do you think I should do?"

Pat's mother had opposed her marrying David. Twenty was too young to begin a family, especially for a girl so naïve and impressionable. She herself had never regretted waiting until she was twenty-six before settling down. And she didn't like her daughter's choice of an enlisted man with no trade or education to fall back on. When Pat had called her mother from Bermuda, while visiting David, and said he wanted to marry her then and there, Pat's mother had tried to talk her into waiting until David got a discharge and a decent job.

"Come home and give it a rest," she had advised. "If you still want to marry him after that, your father and I will give you a church wedding with all the trimmings."

Caught between David and her mother and confused, Pat chose to listen to her mother. But she had had to face David's anger; he wouldn't even drive her to the airport. Three months and a dozen letters later, Pat dropped forty-four quarters into a pay phone to talk to David for three minutes. Afraid she might lose him if she didn't agree to marry immediately, Pat told him she had changed her mind. He said he'd be home in two weeks. Pat's mother was not happy with her daughter's decision, especially since she had only one semester left in her two-year course at Immaculata College in Washington. But realizing she couldn't stop her, she gave Pat her blessing and her written consent.

When, after three years, her daughter brought the children back to northern Virginia, Pat's mother thought the marriage was dead. Pat's reunion with David three months later left her skeptical. She had seen enough of men to know that once they walked out, they frequently kept right on going. And David, she sensed, was the walking kind.

This time, when she got Pat's call, she spoke her mind. "Get yourself a lawyer, Patsy. In the meantime, don't worry. Your daddy isn't going to leave you and the babies without."

Her mother's words made Pat realize the corner she was in. It was almost David's payday, time to do the heavy shopping. There was no milk in the refrigerator, she was nearly out of baby food, she didn't have a car, and the only store within walking distance was McDonald's. She and David had about fifty dollars in their joint checking account.

The more she thought about Andrea and Christine, the more Pat worried. If only David had left some money or promised to give her some on payday or see to it that the rent was paid. But he had said nothing; he had just left her dangling. Although she had no reason to doubt that he would take care of her and the children, especially now that she was pregnant, she didn't know how or when.

Pat put the girls to bed, waited until they were asleep, then joined Lorraine on the front stoop, feeling guilty and depressed. The evening was growing pleasantly cool and the maple leaves fluttered in a gentle breeze. Other women were inside with their husbands. Lorraine's was still at work.

"You're better off without him," Lorraine said. Gentle but firm, she told Pat the truth she didn't want to hear. "If he gets whatever it is out of his system, he might come back. If not . . . you don't need him."

Pat had looked up to Lorraine from the first day she moved into Fairmont Gardens. Slender and striking, Lorraine had the poise and self-confidence Pat lacked. Pat said little, convinced her new neighbor would think she was dull. But Lorraine found Pat bright and warm with a good sense of humor. They quickly became close friends.

Although she knew Lorraine was right, Pat couldn't bear the thought of losing David. Alone in the apartment later that evening, she convinced herself he'd be back. In a few days, he'll walk through the door, arms full of groceries as if nothing had happened, she told herself as she waited for sleep. "You look pretty," he'd say. "I missed you."

Anxious to look her best when he did come back, Pat went to the Fairmont Gardens beauty parlor the next morning for a haircut and a permanent. A twenty-five-dollar extravagance, she thought as she wrote out the check—more than a week's babysitting money—but worth it. She needed to face David with confidence, not feeling fat and beaten. Later in the day, her father dropped in with bags of groceries and baby food. Although she was grateful, Pat was embarrassed and felt a flash of anger. But guilt quickly smothered it. Her father was working two jobs to support her mother, brother, and sister. Now he had to take care of a grown daughter whose husband had decided to take a vacation from fatherhood.

Although David didn't come back that first day or the next, Pat's check did. The beauty parlor called to say it had bounced: insufficient funds. Instead of being angry at David, Pat felt ashamed. How could she tell the beautician that her husband had cleaned out their checking account and left her and two children without even enough money to wash and dry a load of diapers?

Too humiliated to call on her father again, Pat phoned Father Finley, associate pastor at Saint Michael's Church, where she had gone to grade school and where she and David had been married. It was beginning to dawn on her that she might be in worse trouble than she had imagined. If David planned to stay away for only a few days, why had he cleaned out the checking account just before payday?

Like her mother, the priest was practical. "See an attorney right away," he advised. "I suggest Phil Brophy. He's a good Catholic."

Pat was relieved to hear the priest mention an attorney. The thought of David *not* coming back had begun to creep into her mind at unguarded moments. She didn't know the church's position on legal separation, or how to go about getting one.

Religion was one of her few comforts, and she didn't want to lose that too. As a child, she had prayed the rosary daily; at Camp Lejeune she frequently went to Mass and Communion during the week, and she still confessed weekly. Even though the president of Immaculata had asked her to return her school ring and had refused to let her complete the last semester of her two-year course of studies because she had gotten married, Pat had not allowed the narrow-mindedness of one nun to shake her faith.

With no idea what an attorney would advise or what he would charge, Pat could not have done better than Philip Brophy. The father of thirteen who wasn't embarrassed to drive to court in a clunker, he was so outraged at Pat's story that he took her case for twenty-five dollars.

"You have a problem," Brophy told her. "You're broke and have no income. It may be some time before your husband pays child support. What are you going to live on in the meantime?"

Recognizing that Pat was in a state of shock, Brophy told her exactly what to do. Her problem wasn't new and he told her the same thing he had told many women before. "First, move back in with your parents," he said. "Second, go out to the Juvenile and Domestic Relations Court in Fairfax and sign a petition for child support. Third, go to the county services office and apply for welfare."

Brophy's words shook the fear right out of Pat. Welfare? She didn't need welfare. David would send her money. After all, he was the father of their children. They were his responsibility and he knew it. Move back in with her parents? Never! To live with them again would be to admit total failure as a wife and mother. She would not give up what little independence she had and become a burden to them.

"In the meantime," Brophy continued. "I'll see if your husband has an attorney. Maybe we can speed things up and settle the dollars and cents out of court."

Eight days after David walked out, Pat went to the Juvenile and Domestic Relations Court wearing her prettiest maternity dress and feeling like a criminal. The counselor who helped her file a two-page petition for child support sensed her guilt.

"You're different from most of the women who come in here," he told her. "I can tell you're going to make it. Don't ever forget that. You're smart. And with those beautiful blue eyes of yours, you'll find someone.''

Pat cried for the first time since David had left. The counselor's words had pierced the armor of her shock. She couldn't believe she was actually asking the law to order her husband to pay money to feed their children. But the counselor had also told her she was smart and pretty when she felt naïve and undesirable. His words were a comfort she would summon again and again during the next few months.

If Pat felt degraded asking the court for help, it was nothing like taking a number and waiting in the welfare office. No one in her family, whose history she had traced back to the 1700s, had ever received charity or public assistance even if it had meant working two jobs as her father did. She was the first on the dole. And after spending almost two years in college with women who had moved on to careers or comfortable marriages. What would her classmates think if they saw her now? She stared at the floor, convinced that everyone in the waiting room was looking at her. Finally a clerk called her number.

Her ordeal had been for nothing. The welfare counselor told her she didn't qualify for public assistance because she had not lived in Virginia a full year.

''But I've lived here most of my life,'' Pat objected.

''You left the state,'' the counselor explained. ''And you've been back less than a year. You'll have to wait three more months until mid-January. We'll do all the paperwork today. Then, as soon as you fulfill the Virginia residency requirement, you'll begin receiving your checks.''

The prospect of court-ordered support, welfare, and food stamps left Pat more depressed than the thought of life without a husband. Her family's pride didn't help matters. Her mother resented the fact that Pat would even consider taking public assistance. She and her husband had always taken care of their own and always would. ''Daddy will support you,'' she told Pat. There was an edge of anger to her voice. ''We don't want you on welfare.''

Philip Brophy moved as if Pat were his most important client. And to him, she was. She had young children who needed help, and it had already been three weeks since her husband walked out. He got a subpoena for David to appear in court so a judge could determine the amount of child support he'd have to pay. David immediately hired an attorney and agreed to settle out of court. Delighted with the news, Brophy called Pat.

It was Christine's second birthday and there were so many kids laughing and shouting in the apartment that Pat had a hard time hearing Brophy. She had gone out of her way to make the day special for Christine, who missed her father and had been crying constantly. When Christine played on the front lawn, she frequently ran up to parked cars, calling in her small voice, "Daddy! Daddy!" as if she expected the door to swing open and her father to step out. When Christine's loss became too painful to watch, Pat took her to a pediatrician, Dr. Carl Hanfling, who said, "Even though Christine's only two, she can understand the truth. So you might as well tell it to her." Pat took his advice, and whenever Christine cried for her father, Pat simply explained that Daddy wouldn't be coming home for a while. Now, momentarily caught up in the excitement of birthday cake, ice cream, and Kool Aid, Christine looked happy.

"David's agreed to half his paycheck," Brophy said. "That's ninety-nine dollars and eleven cents every two weeks. If you agree, I'll ask the court to write up an order."

The news made Pat lighthearted, almost happy. Although Christine was too young to understand, her father had just given her a wonderful birthday present. Half of David's salary seemed so generous; still, Pat wished that he made more than $396 a month. Her rent came to $142.50. That would leave her with $1.86 a day for food, clothes, and medical expenses. And she had no idea when David would come back. One month? Three? Well, however long he needed to think things through, she would survive and be waiting.

With babysitting money, she calculated, she could make it until early January when she would begin getting welfare to supplement David's child-support payments, if necessary. If her parents were humiliated by her receiving public assistance, well, they would simply have to swallow their pride. The new baby was due in late January. Pat figured that by mid-March, when the baby was six weeks old, she could get a job and drop off the dole. If the plan worked, all she had to do was grit her teeth for six more months at most. Back on her feet, she'd repay her parents every single dime they were giving her for food and rent. Philip Brophy had already agreed to accept a dollar a month until she had paid his twenty-five-dollar fee. She began to feel a sense of hope again. The court counselor was right. She'd make it.

The Juvenile and Domestic Relations Court accepted the settlement, ordering David to make his first payment by October 3, in effect giving him a free month. It also scheduled a hearing on December 30 to review Pat's case. But before October 3 came, Pat got a phone call from the Beneficial Finance Company demanding that she repay her $461 loan and threatening to repossess her new furniture.

"What loan?" Pat asked. "What new furniture?"

4

PAT LEARNED THAT after she left him in Miami nine months earlier, David had taken out a $745 loan in her name—for furniture.

Pat was so angry when the skip-chaser read her the loan application that she could hardly talk. It was one thing for David to clean out their checking account to buy time to think. But sticking her with a forged loan! How stupid did he think she was? The more she allowed herself to feel her anger, the more frightened of it she became. Sensing it would consume her if she let it, she quickly slammed a lid down over the feeling.

Pat knew where David worked but not where he was living. Concerned that she might get him in trouble if she called his office, she decided to ask his best friend, Bill Daniels, where David was staying. It was Bill who had thrown David's going-away party, where Pat had first met David.

Since Bill didn't have a phone, Pat called his mother, who lived next door to him. "Do you know where David is?" she asked. "He left me with the girls . . . and I'm pregnant."

"Yes, indeedy, I know where he is," Bill's mother said. It sounded as if she was speaking through clenched teeth. "Livin' right next door with my Billy. . . . You just forget

David, you hear? I brought up six kids on a waitress salary. You kin do it, too.''

"I only want to talk to him," Pat said.

"Well, if you must . . . I'll go and call 'im.''

Bill's mother got back on the line a few minutes later. "He won't come to the phone," she said in disgust. "He says he don't want to talk to you.''

Pat had left David alone for three weeks while she lived on charity. She had been willing to give him time, even to wait until October 3 for rent and food money. But getting stuck with a forged loan—when she had to borrow change just to use the washer and dryer—was the last straw.

That evening Pat asked Lorraine to drive her to Bill's house. She didn't dare ask her father, for fear he'd cause a scene.

"Don't go," Lorraine warned Pat. She knew that if Pat was torn between anger and love, her seeing David was a bad idea, loan or no loan. She could only get hurt more deeply. "Let him be.''

"I can't," Pat said.

Parked next to Bill's car was a new white Chevy Nova Supersport that said David all over it. Pat's anger blew like an oil well. David had taken the few dollars they shared out of their checking account, he had walked out just before payday, he had left her without enough money even for milk, he had stuck her with an unpaid loan that amounted to more than three months' rent—and now he had bought himself a new car! His monthly payments had to be more than half of the court-ordered child support he owed.

Bill Daniels met Pat at the back door and saw the fire in her eyes. "Hi, Pat," he said sheepishly. "I guess I'm in the middle.''

"I guess you are! Where is he?" Hearing the threatening tone in her voice, Bill stepped aside.

David drove Pat back to the apartment in his new car as calmly as if he were taking her home after a date. Pleased just to have him at her side like old times, Pat had buried her anger once again under a fragile feeling of security. When they got to the apartment and put the children to bed, they chatted. In spite of the reassuring words, a sadness filled the room.

David said he'd be back soon. She didn't want him to come

home for the wrong reasons, did she? In the meantime, she and the girls wouldn't starve; her parents would see to that. The new car? Well, he had no choice, the old one died. She shouldn't worry about the loan, he'd handle it.

David took a few bills from his wallet, laid them on the table, and headed for the door. Pat counted the money: sixty-five dollars. Her warmth for David boiled into hot anger. She'd be damned if he could turn his back on her! He'd bought a new car that must be costing at least one hundred dollars a month and he'd given her sixty-five dollars for the children as if he were the most generous father in the world!

Pat ran after David shouting, "Sixty-five dollars! What the hell is that? You're not going to get away with this."

Catching up with him, Pat grabbed David by the shoulder and tried to swing him around. When he shrugged her away, she tore his shirt, then ran past him and turned to face him. Six months pregnant and afraid, Pat directed her anger into her bare right foot. She kicked David hard in the shins. She wanted to hurt him, make him cry out in pain, watch him walk away limping—anything just so he'd react to her.

But it was Pat who let out a yelp, and David walked away without a word. She spent the next two weeks on crutches with a sprained ankle. When mid-October rolled by and she still had not received any court-ordered support, Philip Brophy called Associates Finance, where David worked. He had been fired. No forwarding address.

Things were now bleaker than ever. Pat lapsed into a depression so severe she thought she might be having a nervous breakdown. Her marriage appeared to be over, and she felt she was to blame because she had failed to keep the family together. She had little to offer her daughters now but love. Among her many anxieties, she worried about getting to the hospital to have her baby, even though her father had assured her he would be on call day and night. She slept fitfully, and when she finally drifted off late at night, it was with a prayer that she would never wake up.

The end of October came and went. No child support. Likewise, Thanksgiving. At the end of November, Philip Brophy asked the court to subpoena David to explain why he had failed to support Christine and Andrea for eight weeks. The court issued the subpoena, but the sheriff was unable to serve it. He couldn't find David. Bill had asked David to move out and Pat didn't know where he was living or working.

David's foster mother apparently did. She invited Pat and her granddaughters over for Christmas, saying David would be there.

It never crossed Pat's mind to tell the sheriff where David would be celebrating the holiday. She could hardly have her children's father arrested during Christmas dinner.

Pat was tempted to stay home herself. She was sick with the flu and hated the thought of watching her mother-in-law shield David. The baby was due in a month and she felt as big as a house. She hadn't had money to get her hair done for the holidays and was depressed after spending Christmas Eve with two children and no husband. It was her twenty-third birthday; the next day would be her and David's fourth wedding anniversary. And as much as she wished it weren't so, she still loved him.

When Pat walked into her in-laws' home, she knew it was a terrible mistake. David was already there, trim and relaxed in an expensive three-piece suit, his white Nova parked outside. He spent the afternoon sipping bourbon and eating ham and turkey as if he hadn't a care in the world. If he knew the sheriff was after him, he didn't show it. He gave Christine and Andrea huge stuffed elephants, which they loved. Their mother had only given them clothes and plastic toys.

All Christmas Day Pat felt defeated and helpless. She was in David's family home, watching his foster mother dote on him. Everyone at dinner, it seemed, was on his side. She felt too depressed to cry. She realized David had a hold on her she couldn't shake. Away from him, she could think of things to say, feelings to express, demands to make. Around him, she faded into a shadow.

Soon after Christmas, Pat started getting phone calls from a repossessor working for the company that had financed David's new Chevy. He had missed so many payments that the company wanted the car back, but it couldn't find him. Did she know where David was living or working?

Pat told the repossessor she knew nothing and why. "If you find him, will you let me or the sheriff know?" she asked.

She wanted David to feel the pinch of the law and to hear the court lecture him. "The judge wants to talk to him, too."

On January 14, the repossessor called again. "I found him," he said.

"You did? Where?"

Pat was excited. If David was arrested and forced to face the judge, maybe he would learn that failing to support one's children was a matter the courts took seriously. More than that, Pat wanted David to experience the same humiliation and fear she was feeling. He had made her suffer; now she wanted to see him squirm. As her attorney had told her, "A month on the road gang in the middle of July would do him a world of good." She not only believed it, she prayed for it without the slightest trace of guilt. The law, not she, would punish him.

"He's working at Victory Van Lines in Alexandria," the repossessor said.

"What are you going to do?" Pat asked.

"Repossess the car."

"Not so fast," Pat said. "Someone should notify the sheriff."

"I have to tell the police I'm taking the car so I don't get arrested for stealing," the repossessor said. "I'll make sure the sheriff is there."

"Let me know?" Pat asked.

"As soon as it's over."

Late afternoon the next day, Pat got the call. "He's been arrested," the repossessor said. He went on to explain what had happened.

The repossessor had waited for the police across the street from Victory Van Lines. The sheriff had pulled up in a marked car and had gone in. Shortly afterward he had come out with David and handcuffed him. The sheriff had fished David's car keys out of his pocket and handed them to the repossessor, who unlocked the Nova, got in, and leisurely drove off.

"He was standing there in cuffs," the repossessor said. "He looked shocked to death—and he couldn't do a damn thing. It was great."

Pat felt a sweet revenge as she listened. There was only one thing David loved more than himself—his car. To take it was to cut off a leg. Good! It was about time he got a taste of what helplessness felt like. Convinced that the law had finally scared responsibility into him, Pat was sure things would be different. She was wrong.

David's foster mother paid the five-hundred-dollar bond and bailed him out of jail that evening. The next day, the judge sentenced him to ten days in jail for contempt, suspending all but two days. Victory Van Lines fired him. When he got out of the county jail, his foster mother was waiting for him with another car.

Pat dreamed of a hundred ways to get even. Slash his tires. Steal his false teeth. Hound him. Too weak to confront him directly, she phoned the mother of the teenager he was dating—the girl had signed credit card slips using David and Pat's card. She told the teenager's mother that David was married and had two children with a third due any day. She knew she was being bitchy, but she didn't care. The woman promised to keep her daughter from seeing David again. Then Pat turned all her pent-up anger on her mother-in-law. She told David's foster mother she was low class. She had spoiled David and made him the kind of father and husband he was. It was all her fault; she was as irresponsible as he was. She had hidden him from the law as if it were some kind of game, then bailed him out of jail, where he belonged, and bought him another car. She had rewarded him for deserting his children. After all that, how could she expect Pat to keep bringing Christine and Andrea over to visit!

Three days after David got out of jail in January of 1969, his third child was born. It was Richard Nixon's inauguration day, and by late afternoon the streets and sidewalks were slick with ice. Pat's parents came over to her apartment for dinner. Her mother had been helping with the cooking and cleaning for weeks. At four that afternoon, Pat began to feel labor pains even though the baby was not due for two more weeks. Her parents took her by the elbows, walked her down the icy sidewalk to their car, and drove her to her obstetrician's office. After examining her, Dr. Russell May sent her to Fairfax General Hospital. "I'll be there shortly," he said.

Pat was in labor for four hours and Dr. May spent every minute of them at her bedside, holding her hand. When he wasn't talking to her gently, he was reading a magazine, turning the pages awkwardly with his free hand.

"We talked about an anesthetic before," he told Pat at one point. During one of her checkups, he had suggested an epidural, a spinal injection. "Is that what you want?"

"How much will it cost?" Pat asked.

Although her limited insurance would cover 80 percent of the hospital bill, it would not pay for the anesthetic or for Dr. May's fee, which came to $210. He had agreed to accept five dollars a month until she paid it off. Since she was paying another dollar a month to her attorney, Pat was concerned about getting too deeply into debt.

"I don't know, but I think around seventy dollars," Dr. May said. He seemed surprised she had asked.

"I think I'll do without."

Because she had been given an anesthetic when Christine and Andrea were born, Pat didn't realize what she was letting herself in for. She had never read anything about natural childbirth nor had she taken any classes. When the hard pains began, she changed her mind as fast as she had made it up.

"I'll take the shot," she told Dr. May.

"It's too late," he told her. "The baby's almost here."

Pat watched her baby being born in the big overhead mirror. She never knew anything could be so painful and beautiful at the same time. If she hadn't been so poor, she thought when the pain stopped, she would have missed the whole thing.

"It's another girl," Dr. May told her. He put the unwashed infant on her stomach. Pat started to laugh and couldn't stop. She felt relief that it was all over. That her daughter was normal.

A nurse wheeled Pat into the hallway where two other women who had just given birth lay on gurneys. Their husbands were at their sides, smiling and attentive. Seeing their pride and love, Pat began to cry. Even with her mother nearby, she felt alone and abandoned.

Pat dozed off. When she opened her eyes David was standing there. Convinced he had come only to humiliate and hurt her, she quickly turned her face to the wall.

"I went down to the nursery to see her," David said.

"She's the healthiest-looking one. What are you going to call her?"

Pat was surprised he wanted to know. When she had seen him on Christmas Day, she had asked what he wanted to call the baby, since he had chosen both Christine's and Andrea's names. He had told her then that if she wanted a name, she should go to the phone book and pick one. It was a cruel thing to say and it had struck her with all the brutality of an ice pick.

"Marcia Ann," she said to the wall.

It seemed David had come just to spoil a special night. Pat realized he was the last person she wanted with her. He was Marcia's deserter, not her father.

"What are you doing here anyway?" she demanded. David didn't have to see her face to know she was angry. "You didn't stick around while I was carrying her. Now you want to see what she looks like. Well, you don't have a right to be here—I want you to go!"

When Pat finally stopped crying and got settled in the recovery room, a nurse came by and picked up her chart. "Oh, I see you're separated," she said. "Are you going to keep the baby?"

The nurse said "separated" as if it were a dirty word, something Pat had done that was wrong. How could anyone think she would give up Marcia after all they had already gone through together? Almost nine months of suffering and worry, fear and anger.

"Keep her?" Pat said. "Of course I'm going to *keep* her. She's my baby."

5

EARLY IN 1969, Pat began receiving $249 a month from Aid to Dependent Children. David's $198-a-month child support was to go directly to the court, which would then reimburse the state. Pat would never see it. Besides the monthly check, she also got sixteen dollars' worth of free food stamps. As long as David paid the court, Pat figured she was actually accepting only sixty-seven dollars a month in public assistance. If she could just swallow her pride for a few more weeks, she was sure she could find a job as a medical secretary and make more than welfare was paying her.

But if welfare was humiliating, Pat found the food-stamp system utterly degrading. Soon after getting out of the hospital, she began combining trips to the supermarket in a borrowed car with visits to her doctor or bank. Wearing makeup and her best dress was the only way she could face the world outside Fairmont Gardens with dignity. If she didn't preserve her pride, she was afraid she'd slip deeper into dependency. With three children and no husband or job, it was her only hedge.

But Pat quickly learned that the nicer she looked in the supermarket line, the nastier the cashiers became when she pulled out food stamps to pay her bill. They would eye her from head to toe, then say, "Boy, that must be nice!"

In a way, Pat couldn't blame them for being hostile. She was young, well dressed, and looked healthy. If they had to work behind a checkout counter, why couldn't she do the same? Grocery shopping became a weekly humiliation. In the supermarket Pat would say over and over, "For my children, for my children." Finally, she stopped dressing up and took Christine, Andrea, and Marcia shopping with her. Although she still got dirty looks, she heard fewer unkind remarks.

The supermarket experience made her even more determined to get off welfare before she became so demoralized she could no longer fight back. David's walking out that way had all but destroyed her self-confidence as a woman and mother. Food stamps robbed her of her last shred of dignity.

As Pat saw it, she had only two choices—get back together with David, whom she still loved in spite of everything, or go to work. She tried David first. She phoned David's foster mother, asking her to have David call. When he did, she invited him to the apartment, no strings attached. Pat made it a point not to tell her parents or friends what she was doing because she knew they would get angry and try to talk her out of it. Every time she broke down in tears and said, "But I love him," they would say, "Any man who would do that to you once will do it again!"

At the apartment David seemed kind and friendly, but he didn't want to talk about coming back to live. When Pat asked if he was paying child support to the court, he said he was, but her question seemed to make him suspicious.

"Do you get those payments?" he asked.

"No," she said. "They go from the court to the welfare office."

"So you never even see them?"

Pat knew she had said the wrong thing and could almost hear him thinking, Why should I pay, if she doesn't get the money?

Then David started blaming Pat. If he was a delinquent father, he said, it was her fault. She had made Victory Van Lines fire him. What did she expect when she had him arrested in front of his boss? How could he pay if he was in jail? How could he work if she had his car repossessed? But in spite of her meddling, he said, he had found another job in the finance business. Feeling beaten and guilty, Pat didn't press him to tell her where he was now working.

Just before he left, David went into the bedroom and took the model car set he kept under their bed. As she watched him pack it up, Pat knew he wouldn't be coming back. He picked up Christine, gave her a big hug and kiss, and let her have a sip of his ginger ale. Then he put her to bed and walked out for good.

Pat went job hunting. Although she preferred to stay home with the children, she needed to become independent and useful as soon as possible. Comforted somewhat by the thought that she could find a good sitter in Fairmont Gardens, Pat set up an interview with the personnel director at Fairfax General Hospital, where there were openings for medical secretaries and transcribers.

The director seemed impressed by Pat's qualifications. But from there on, it was downhill.

"I note on your application you have children," he said. "What are their birth dates?

"What does your husband do?

"I see. . . . Who will take care of them when you're at work?

"Well, what if they get sick?

"I see. . . . I'm sorry, but we have no openings at this time."

Pat drove home close to tears. She got the message. Who wanted to hire a single mother of three, two of whom were still babies? Not sure what to do and discouraged that it was already March and she didn't have a decent job, she called the Juvenile and Domestic Relations Court to make sure David was paying his child support.

David had made only two of his twelve payments to date, she learned, and the court wanted to talk to him but couldn't find him. Pat felt another surge of rage, and this time she was in no hurry to bury it. Counting food stamps, she had actually been receiving $265 a month in public assistance, not $67 as she had thought. She wasn't going to put up with that for one more day. If the sheriff couldn't find David, she would. And when she did, she'd turn him in faster than he could say "run."

Recalling that David had said he was working for a finance company, Pat drafted her friend Lorraine, whose voice David would not recognize. She flipped through the *Yellow Pages* to "Finance Companies." "You might as well start at the top of the list," she told Lorraine. "Ask to speak to David. If it's him on the line, hang up. If it's not, wait and see if he works there."

Pleased that Pat was looking for David not to get back together with him but to make him pay, Lorraine was glad to play sleuth. And it didn't take her long to score. When she called Credit Recovery and asked for David by name, the receptionist said, "One moment please." Lorraine slammed down the receiver, grinning. "Nothing to it," she said.

Now that Pat knew where David worked, she called Bill Daniels to ask where David lived. Bill had always been a friend she could count on. Since David had left, she spoke to him nearly every night for emotional support. Warm and understanding, he listened without telling her, as everyone else did, to forget about David.

It wasn't just revenge she wanted, Pat told Bill. It was important for her dignity that David pay child support. She knew where he was working. Did Bill know where he was staying?

Pat could tell from the sheepish, almost guilty tone in Bill's voice that he knew, but his loyalty toward David was standing in the way. Sensing that if she got mad, Bill might clam up completely, she played a game she was very good at. "Please, Bill," she said in her best little-girl voice. "It's important."

Bill wavered, then compromised. He said he and David had had dinner recently in a Mexican restaurant near David's apartment, but he would say no more. If he thought he was protecting David while pacifying Pat, Bill had miscalculated. He had offered her a challenge, and she grabbed it. Knowing which bus Bill took to work each day, Pat borrowed a car and drove the entire route looking for a Mexican restaurant. She eventually found one not far from a bus stop and two apartment buildings. Not wanting to meet David in an apartment lobby or risk having the desk clerk say a blonde woman was looking for him, she called Bill back.

"I know where David is staying," she bluffed.

"You do? How did you—Where?"

Choosing the apartment building that looked like it would suit David best, she said, "In the Duchess Gardens."

"Well, I'll be damned." Bill was impressed. First, Pat had chased a lead and found out where David was working. Now she had followed a hint and traced him to his apartment. "What are you going to do now?"

"Call Phil Brophy."

Brophy told the court where David was working and living. It issued another subpoena for him to appear before the bench on April 14 and show cause why he should not be punished for failing to pay the more than one thousand dollars in support he owed his children. The sheriff went to Credit Recovery to serve him. David wasn't there. The sheriff said he'd be back later that day. When the sheriff returned, David was gone again. Not surprisingly, no one at Credit Recovery could say where he had gone or when he might be back. Later that night, the sheriff rapped on David's door in the Duchess Gardens apartments, but David's roommate said he had just moved out. No forwarding address.

When David failed to show up in court on April 14, the judge issued a warrant for his arrest. Pat did not take the news calmly. She was convinced the sheriff had allowed David to slip away, and she couldn't understand why. Deserting one's children was a crime in Virginia. Yet the sheriff, who had taken an oath to uphold the law, had done everything but make an appointment for David's arrest. Having pinned her hopes for justice on the court and the law, Pat was devastated.

Although her parents and friends were convinced that David was finally gone for good and glad of it, Pat was not. She gave the law one more chance and reported David as a missing person to the Fairfax County Police, which sent an officer to interview her. While she told her story and answered his questions, the officer took notes. She gave him a picture of David and he promised to file a missing-person report and send out an alert. Pat grew uneasy, however, when the same officer came back to her apartment several times to ask the same questions. After he made a pass at her, she gave up on the Fairfax County Police. The officer had not filed a single report, she learned later.

About a month after David had disappeared, Pat got a phone call from one of his friends, who had received a postcard from David from somewhere in the Midwest, saying he was on his way to California. Pat finally admitted to herself that David would not be coming back for a long time, if ever, and that she had better do what everyone had been advising—plan a life without him.

The first step, she knew, was to figure out a way to get off welfare. Although she didn't consider herself poor, she knew she ran the risk of becoming permanently dependent. She had read somewhere that poverty is an acid that eats away pride until all pride is gone. She believed that. Welfare was only a fragile lifejacket. She either had to use it to help herself swim to shore or spend her life bobbing in the sea, looking for rescuers who would never come. The longer she waited to swim, the weaker she would become.

The first step was to break David's hold on her life. Although he had apparently run so far away that she doubted she would ever see him again, he still controlled her feelings and, in some vague way, cast a shadow on her future. Having abandoned his children, he nevertheless continued to sap vital energy that she and they needed to survive. The only way to deal with him was to bury her anger and her ache for justice as deep as she could under her determination to make it on her own. The pain of those feelings stood in the way of her future. She couldn't afford to use up any energy now on David.

It also became clear to Pat that as long as Marcia and Andrea were babies, she'd never get a job that paid more than welfare paid. And once the children started school, Pat knew, her expenses would go up. That meant she would need an even better paying job to support them without public assistance. The best, and maybe the only, way to ensure a decent job with a future was more education—her ticket out of the welfare ghetto. While her children were growing up, she could go back to school and take courses in business, maybe finish her second year of college. That ought to give her an edge in the job market.

Instead of encouraging and supporting her, Pat's welfare case officer all but killed her enthusiasm. None of the mothers he counseled had ever asked to go to college, he told her. He wasn't sure his supervisor would approve it. All he could promise was to pitch it as hard as he could.

Pat was stunned. She had come up with a way to get off welfare permanently, to save the taxpayers money while regaining her pride and dignity, and her counselor wasn't sure his supervisor would allow it. She could have wept with frustration. Having three young children limited where, when, and how long she could work. This in turn meant she was confined to a childlike dependence on her own parents. Was there anything about her life she could still control?

The social worker returned the following week with a grin. No one in the welfare department, he said, knew of any recipient in the state who had asked to go to college; therefore, there was no policy. But the department had decided to make hers a test case. Although it would not raise her monthly allowance to help her, it would permit her to go to school as long as she did not use welfare money for books or tuition. She'd have to get a full scholarship and student aid through the normal channels. If he could help her with references, of course, he'd be happy to.

Pat was too pleased to be discouraged. Welfare's permission to go to school was the first positive thing that had happened to her since David walked out. Wasting no time, she targeted George Mason University, part of Virginia's state college system. It was close to Fairmont Gardens and it was new, so it was still trying to build its student body. Pat applied for a scholarship to cover tuition for the first five-week session of summer school and financial aid to help with books and gas. Intrigued by the idea of setting a precedent for welfare recipients, the university granted the scholarship and helped her get a federal student-poverty grant. The school further recognized most of her credits from Immaculata and East Carolina, which amounted to more than one and a half years of college. Pat's father bought her an old Dodge Dart. She hired her sister, Maureen, who was still in high school, to babysit for fifteen dollars a week, with payments spread over twelve months.

Pat's routine was punishing. Up at six each morning to feed and dress Christine, Andrea, and Marcia, she would leave for school by half past seven for an eight o'clock class. At half past twelve she would get home in time to join the other mothers and kids out front for a half hour. Then there was a midafternoon nap with the children, a visit on the stoop, and another meal for the kids at six. She would begin studying at eight, put the girls to bed at nine, and study until midnight. Often she would wake up in the middle of the night to Marcia's crying. Then she would rock her back to sleep, worried about how her youngest would survive knowing her father had abandoned her. If she was lucky, she would catch a few hours' sleep before she was up again at six.

Sometimes Lorraine would watch the children after dinner so Pat could have an extra hour with the books and get to bed earlier. But long before the summer session was over, Pat had ugly bags under her eyes. She was convinced she would flunk out. David's walkout had destroyed her confidence on every level. She felt stupid, unattractive, and worthless. And she began to doubt that she was a good mother. School was stealing time from her daughters. Smart enough to recognize their competition, the girls would sit on her books to get more attention.

Pat was torn. She felt guilty, especially about Marcia who was only five months old. She had held and rocked both Christine and Andrea a lot when they were small, but as a student she had less time for Marcia. On the other hand, more study and better grades would lead to a better job, which would help her and her daughters in the long run. Caught between guilt and her determination to get off welfare, she found herself snapping and yelling at the girls and relieved when Lorraine would take them off her hands.

Sometimes the gnawings of guilt almost drove her to quit school. All she had ever wanted was to be a good wife and mother. She had already failed at the one and was beginning to fail at the other. Was she just being selfish? Was she merely using school to distract her from her problems and give her a sense of control over her life? Then Pat would remember standing in the supermarket line with food stamps; she would remember waiting for her number to come up in the welfare office; she would remember the handouts from her parents. Better the guilt than the shame. At least the guilt would buy a future for her children. The shame was worthless.

If the routine was killing and the guilt painful, school itself was confusing. She couldn't shake thinking of herself as a loser: a college dropout, a wife without a husband, a mother with three fatherless children, a medical secretary without a job, a ward of the county. She was afraid of failing again. What would happen to her plan for independence if she flunked? How could she face the future if she lost her one hope?

Pat also discovered she was angry at men, and George Mason was full of them. They were the enemy she couldn't trust, each a potential David. Equating closeness with dependency, she didn't want to risk getting involved. Never again would she give a man control over the tiniest piece of her life—she would support herself and her children alone. At the same time, however, Pat felt lonely and hungered for sharing and tenderness.

Moreover, Pat was different from her classmates. Most of them had either just graduated from high school or were just back from Vietnam. She felt like a curiosity item. A mother on welfare going to college? Some students and teachers resented her. She was abusing the taxpayers' money, they told her to her face. If she could find time to go to school, she could find time to work. Why wasn't she home taking care of her kids? What kind of mother was she?

She felt isolated and confused. Although she didn't wear rags or panhandle on street corners, she knew she could easily slide into permanent poverty and degradation. That fear haunted her. She was certain her classmates were aware she had only three outfits, which she carefully rotated. She quickly learned to skip meals; she couldn't afford them. Saying she wasn't hungry, she'd have only a cup of coffee or a piece of pie. A few friendly classmates encouraged her not to give up, helped her with homework, loaned her books, even teased her until she blushed. She was afraid to let them become real friends, however, because she had no time to socialize. School and children were all she could manage.

Back at Fairmont Gardens, Pat often felt sad. School had changed her relationship with the women there. Before, her apartment had been a neighborhood social center. She had organized an informal morning exercise class for three or four women in her living room. In the evenings, one or two women would stop in to chat. But once Pat started school, the exercise classes ended and she told her friends not to visit at night because she had to study.

When her grades came in the mail, Pat was afraid to look,

certain she had failed. Her classmates were brighter and had more time to study. They would push her to the bottom of the grading curve. When she finally ripped open the envelope, the two Bs shocked her. Maybe she wasn't as stupid as she thought. Maybe she should take a second summer session while she still had the courage. It would only be for five weeks.

By the time she finished summer school, Pat was exhausted. But it had been worth it. She had gained confidence and felt ready to try the job market once again. Employers should find it harder to turn her down, given her two years of college. Even if she did have three children.

Before she could fill out her first job application and get on with her life, however, Pat got news of David.

6

▼

PAT AND LORRAINE had just finished putting the girls to bed
and cleaning up after Christine's third birthday party. Christine in particular had been flushed with excitement and difficult to get in bed, so when the phone rang, Pat grabbed it
before it could wake anybody up. The call was from David's
foster mother. In tears she told Pat she had just gotten a call
from a man in Atlanta. She didn't know who he was and
hadn't thought to ask his name. He said David had been killed
in a plane crash.

It had been five months since David had disappeared, and
in spite of her demanding schedule and her resolve to erase
him from her mind, Pat still thought of him often. Where was
he? What was he doing? How did he feel? Did he ever think
about her and his daughters? She thought she still loved him,
even though she knew he had fled the state. She had received
two Mobil credit card receipts—one from Gainesville, Virginia, the ''gateway west,'' issued the day the sheriff had
tried to arrest him, and one from Kansas.

By the time she hung up the receiver, Pat was shaking.
Then she began to cry uncontrollably. ''He's dead,'' she kept
telling Lorraine. ''He's dead. All those rotten things I said
about him. Now he's—''

Once she calmed down, Pat began calling every airport in

and around Atlanta. That he might have been in a fatal plane crash didn't strike her as odd. Maybe he had finally passed his flight test in the Midwest and had gotten a job as a pilot. But when no one, including the Federal Aviation Administration, could tell her anything, Pat concluded that the phone call to David's foster mother had been a hoax. She felt relieved, for as long as David was alive, he might come back. She still could not accept the fact that he would abandon her and his children forever. Nor could she admit that David might have perpetrated the hoax himself. He would never be so cruel as to fake his own death on Christine's birthday.

Faced with an unrelated but important decision in her own life, Pat soon stopped worrying about the bogus plane crash. One of her George Mason classmates had suggested that she try school full-time in the fall, just for one semester to see what it was like.

After a good start, Pat was torn. Her summer grades had only been average. However, they proved that she could at least pass and meet the demands of single motherhood at the same time. But she was also sure that she had managed to limp through summer school only because she could tell herself the session would be over after five weeks. But five courses for five months? Now that her sister was back in high school, Pat couldn't afford a sitter. And if she managed to hire one and the welfare department found out, it could cut her off. No welfare money for school—that was the deal.

On the other hand, Pat knew she had to begin living her own life and preparing for an independent future. As long as she was on welfare, every monthly check would have David's face printed on it. She knew she'd find a job if she looked for one, but she wanted more than a job—she wanted a real life for herself and her children, not just existence without welfare. She wanted a career.

Pat's next-door neighbor Joan made up her mind for her. Joan had four children and worked from four until midnight. She agreed to watch Andrea and Marcia from eight in the morning until three in the afternoon. In turn, Pat agreed to sit Joan's children from three until ten at night, when Joan's husband would pick them up. That meant minding and feeding seven kids after class for seven hours every day while still trying to find time to study. It also meant finding a place during the day for Christine, who was so active that no one wanted to sit her. If Pat was going to attend school, she would have to send Christine to a day-care center.

Too ashamed to ask her parents for more help, Pat called her parish priest, Father Finley, who had been supportive ever since David left. She needed seventy-five dollars to send Christine to nursery school for one semester, she said. Could Saint Michael's parish help? Her parents had been contributing to the church weekly for more than fifteen years, and she'd pay the money back someday.

Although Father Finley was eager to help, the pastor was not. He called Pat's mother. "Why should the church pay?" he scolded her. "Can't you take care of your own daughter?" Reluctantly, Pat accepted another loan from her parents for Christine's day-care. George Mason awarded her a scholarship and a student loan and secured another federal grant.

Pat decided to major in business and planned to look for a job in hospital administration after semester exams in January. The semester turned out to be even more difficult than she had anticipated. She left for school before eight and returned home at three. When she wasn't in class, she was studying in the library. To concentrate on her books at home, she taught herself to tune the children out. But when she did, she felt she was neglecting them. Between these emotions and the seven kids for seven hours every day, she was drained to the point of exhaustion.

When her grades came in the mail in January 1970, however, Pat knew she could do it. She had passed all five courses, even though there had been days when she couldn't find time to study for tests she was not prepared to take. Although she still didn't feel as bright as her classmates, she felt for the first time that it might be *possible* to graduate. She signed up for another semester—then for both summer sessions. By the end of the summer of 1970, a year and a half after David had run away, she had completed her third year of college. Graduation was no longer just a dream.

Although still distrustful of men, Pat felt the edges of her anger blunted. Men were flirting with her, and she began to think of herself as attractive. When a fellow student asked her for a date, she was surprised—and thrilled. It was her first night out in almost a year. Her date brought her home, ripped her blouse, and tried to rape her. Shocked and mortified, she cried for days. Then she began feeling guilty, as if the attack was her fault, just like David's leaving.

Months passed before Pat could bring herself to date again. The second time, the man was gentle and loving. He and Pat began seeing more and more of each other until he suggested serious involvement. Pat balked. She could manage her family and school, she told him, but nothing more for the time being. He stopped calling.

Her responsibilities were not the only reason Pat refused to get involved after David ran away. She was afraid that a serious relationship would make her dependent again. With three children to support, she wanted to become so self-reliant that she would never have to trust a man with her life again. She was determined to allow nothing to stand in the way of her education and her independence—not even loneliness. If it meant living like a nun until she graduated and got a job, then that's what she would do.

The only way Pat could go back for her final year of college, in the fall of 1970, was to find a better babysitting arrangement. The thought of another year of coming home from school and caring for seven children was overwhelming. Fortunately, the Welfare Department softened and agreed to give her the same day-care assistance it offered working mothers. Her happiness lasted until she visited the center chosen for Christine, Andrea, and Marcia. It was in an airless church basement—a smelly place, ugly and depressing. It offered no classes and no playground. What's more, almost every child in the cramped school was a welfare kid. She had worked hard to protect her children from the indignities of a monthly welfare check and food stamps, and subjecting them to the ''welfare brat'' label was something she would not tolerate.

Pat began visiting nearby day-care centers until she found Annandale Springfield Country Day School, a real school with real teachers. The children there wore clean, attractive uniforms; they sang, studied French, danced, looked healthy. Pat told Welfare she wanted her daughters to go there. When the department refused, she recruited the school's director, Jinks Roach, to help her. They pleaded, argued, and won.

Soon a school bus was picking up the girls each morning before Pat left for her first class; they returned at five-thirty in the evening, an arrangement that gave her two whole hours of uninterrupted study after classes. To her surprise, she was feeling no guilt at leaving them. Christine, no longer the cheerful, smiling child she had been before her father ran away, had become a withdrawn and moody four-year-old at home and around adults. At school with children her own age, she seemed happier. In fact, she liked Annandale Springfield so much that she bounced up the bus steps each morning and didn't want to come home in the evening. Christine's aloofness with adults seemed to be her way of saying, "I don't trust grown-ups. I loved my father and look what happened."

Three-year-old Andrea, on the other hand, didn't want to leave her mother or the apartment, the only place she seemed to feel safe. She would cry when Pat put her on the bus, but once at school she created few problems and played quietly—mostly alone. It was as if Andrea were saying, "The only person I can count on is me."

Marcia, almost two, also fought school. She didn't want to get up on school mornings, resisted getting dressed, and began crying even before Pat put her on the bus. As soon as she got to school, she would roll down her gray knee socks, pull her blouse out of her skirt, and muss up her hair. She spent most of the day playing with boys. Marcia didn't seem to like who she was. At times Pat even felt that Marcia wished she were a boy.

One of Pat's courses at George Mason that fall of 1970 was federal taxation. Her teacher invited an Internal Revenue Service recruiter to speak to the class. The IRS sounded so exciting that Pat applied for a job as either a grade-five tax auditor, which paid just under seven thousand dollars a year or, if she was lucky, a grade-seven revenue agent, at just over nine thousand dollars. The IRS seemed ideal. It was as stable as the government itself and offered an almost unlimited opportunity for growth. A grade seven would get her off welfare immediately and for good. Besides, she liked people; accounting was her favorite subject; and she had a natural aptitude for investigative work. She went in for an interview dressed in a new brown suit her mother had bought her, then waited anxiously to hear the results.

Pat's goals for her final semester of college that began in February 1971 were ambitious, even for her. She planned to take the CPA exam immediately after graduation in June. The certificate would help her advance more quickly at the IRS, if they hired her, and she was certain they would. To qualify for the exam, however, she needed three more credits in accounting. Since George Mason didn't have the course she needed, she decided to enroll at the University of Virginia extension in her area. That meant taking eighteen credits instead of the usual fifteen. Pat was sure she could handle the work—after all, it was only for one semester. She would simply make herself do it because the CPA certificate would guarantee her daughters and her a better future.

To take the extra course, however, Pat needed permission from her accounting professor at George Mason. On a cold, icy February day, Pat made her way to his office to explain how important the CPA certificate was for her.

"Plain stupid," the professor said, refusing permission. "A full load here is more than you can handle."

The refusal meant that, to qualify for the exam, Pat would have to go to night school after graduation while holding a full-time job and caring for three children. She seriously doubted that she and her daughters could take that much punishment. But the harder she pleaded, the more stupid she felt and the more her self-confidence began to waver. By the time she left his office, she was quaking with anger and doubt. The man had no right to say that, she told herself. And he called himself a teacher. He was supposed to encourage her dreams, not kill them. "Stupid" was what David had called her.

"If that ignorant man thinks he can get away with this, he's in for one hell of a surprise. I'll go over his head—I'll fight him all the way to the top if I have to. I'm not going to let a sparrow-brained professor tucked away in the business department of some little school stop me!"

Pat was in tears as she drove to her parents' home to pick up the children. As she turned off the busy road into her parents' driveway, still furious at her humiliation, a tractor trailer behind her skidded on a patch of ice, and slammed her car into the front yard. While Christine, Andrea, and Marcia watched from their grandparents' window, paramedics arrived, lifted Pat into an ambulance and drove off, red lights flashing and sirens screaming.

7

▼

PAT WAS BEDRIDDEN for three weeks, in constant pain, and on medication. Fortunately, her mother was able to help with the children. When she finally returned to school, she was behind in all her courses and still in a great deal of pain. Four of her five professors allowed her to make up homework and tests, but her accounting teacher refused, giving her an F for whatever she had missed. Mixed with the bitter, however, was a sweet piece of news. The IRS had hired her as a tax auditor, grade five. Her salary would be less than seven thousand dollars a year and she would still need some public assistance until she got a promotion, but at least she had a career waiting as soon as she finished school.

Graduation on June 6, 1971, offered no special thrill. Pat was too exhausted to feel proud. Still disappointed that she hadn't made grade-seven revenue agent, she began work the next day without even a weekend to rest. She was anxious about her new job and wondered how much time and energy she'd have left for the girls after a full day in the office.

But Pat could be happy about one thing: she was beginning her new life debt-free. At six dollars a month, she had finally paid Dr. May and Phil Brophy. And her four thousand dollars of insurance money from the truck accident had repaid her parents, cleaned up a backlog of small bills, and bought some new clothes for work. Now, at the age of twenty-five, she was ready to begin a new life, a little over two years after David had walked out. The final step was to get off welfare completely.

The day after graduation Pat began a six-week IRS training course in Baltimore. The service arranged for all students to stay in a motel near the school, but Pat decided to commute so she wouldn't be away from the children. The routine was worse than school had ever been. Up at four-thirty or five each morning, she would drive an hour to suburban Maryland to catch the train to Baltimore, get home by seven-thirty or eight, and play with the children until bedtime. Her friend Vi usually brought over some dinner. "Just a few leftovers," she'd say.

Pat discovered that her course in taxation law at George Mason had pushed her ahead of most of her IRS classmates. It was fortunate, for she slept through a good part of those six weeks. The teachers, who knew her circumstances, were firm but understanding. When they awakened her with a question, she would ask them to repeat it. They would do so with patience and a suppressed smile, but she had enough correct answers to get her through the course comfortably.

Pat's grade-five take-home pay was $315.46 every month, or 46 cents more than she was getting from Fairfax County. The Welfare Department decided that since her expenses had increased now that she was working, it would supplement her IRS income by $58.50 a month. It also continued to pay for day-care for Christine, Andrea, and Marcia. Pat's first welfare check in July after she had received her IRS paycheck was $157 too much. With a great sense of satisfaction, she returned the money. She didn't want one penny more than she needed; what she wanted was the raise that would get her off the dole forever.

As an IRS auditor, Pat interviewed taxpayers to see if they owed the government money. It was a stressful position and the attrition rate was high. Still shy, at first she had so little confidence and blushed so easily that red blotches appeared on her neck. To cover them, she usually wore high-necked blouses. Exemption cases for women became her favorites. Having lived on welfare and stretched dollars herself, she had a special understanding of poor women. When a single mother said she had spent nothing on clothes all year, Pat knew she was probably telling the truth.

Eight months after Pet started working for the IRS, the service promoted her to revenue agent. Four months after that, she advanced to grade seven. Although she was still eligible for some public assistance after her two-thousand-dollar-a-year raise, she asked to be removed from the welfare rolls. It was one of the proudest days of her life. She had made it. She was free.

Finally independent and with a promising future, Pat felt she was now ready for a relationship. In 1972, one year after she began working for the IRS and three years after David had disappeared, Pat divorced David and married an IRS attorney, Eugene Bennett. She changed her children's names to his. Twelve years older than she and with a son from a previous marriage, Gene Bennett had what she wanted most from a mate at that point in her life—stability and a sense of responsibility. Soon after her wedding, however, Pat began to realize that her strongest motive in marrying Gene was to provide a father for her girls.

As hard as she tried to keep David pinned in the past, he kept intruding on her marriage. Besides the bogus airplane crash, she had heard about him again in 1970 while she was still in school. She and the girls were visiting David's foster mother as they frequently did. Even though Pat hadn't quite forgiven the woman for shielding David, she knew that David's running away without a word had hurt her deeply. Besides, she was still the girls' grandmother and they loved visiting her.

The phone rang while they were sitting in the living room sipping coffee. David's foster mother went into the bedroom to answer it. When she returned, her face was white and she was shaking. ''Patsy, Patsy,'' she said, ''pick up the phone. There's someone who says she knows David.''

Her name was Lenora Parker. She was calling from Dallas and spoke with a lilting Southern accent. The woman told Pat she was married to a Jim Parker, whom she believed to be David. She said she had married him in November of the previous year—seven months after he had abandoned Pat and his children.

Jim Parker had walked out on her two weeks ago, she said.

It was a total shock. While poring over the papers he left behind, she had found the name of his sister in Miami who, she knew, had married a doctor. She located the doctor through directory assistance. He had given her the phone number of David's foster parents.

Pat was trembling. When she steadied herself enough to speak, she and Lenora compared notes—height, weight, face, appendix scar, bridgework, voice, habits. There was no doubt that David and Jim Parker were the same person. Since David was still married to Pat, he was a bigamist.

Pat and Lenora both started crying. Pat felt sorry for the woman and so angry at David she wanted to kick him again. Knowing exactly what Lenora was going through, she tried to console the woman as best she could. After promising to send Pat a copy of her marriage certificate, Lenora hung up.

The next few weeks were traumatic for Pat. Her conversation with Lenora Parker had opened old wounds and revived both good and bad memories. She couldn't help but wonder again where David was, what he was doing, and why he had left the way he did. She called the FBI, hoping it would be able to find him. She explained to an FBI agent who interviewed her that David was a runaway father and a bigamist, wanted for contempt of a court order to pay child support. She asked the agent to file a missing-persons report. She was convinced that he was hiding in another city, probably married to another woman. Personally sympathetic but professionally uninterested, the agent told her that David would be on the bureau's active list of missing persons for four years. If his fingerprints turned up anywhere, the bureau would notify her.

To Pat, it sounded like a bureaucratic brush-off. Maybe the FBI would find him, probably not. If it did, she would deal with David then. In the meantime, she was not about to spend another dime or expend another ounce of energy looking for him. Pat assumed David had adopted a new identity and moved to yet another city, and she returned her attention to her children, school, and career.

But David still lurked in the shadows of Pat's life. She sought his face in every crowd, scanning the streets for a tall man with David's distinctive gait. And she would turn her head as cars passed, looking for a tall man behind the wheel.

Despite years of intense, repressed anger, she found herself confused, with tender feelings and gentle memories welling within her.

Eight years passed. In 1978 the FBI was still insisting David's name had never flashed up on its missing-persons computer. And in all that time his foster mother—once very close to him—heard nothing. Like everyone else, Pat now concluded David was dead. On that presumption, she applied to the Social Security Administration for death benefits for Christine, Andrea, and Marcia. As far as Pat could calculate, those benefits would amount to nearly seventy thousand dollars by the time Marcia turned eighteen.

When it comes to presumption of death, however, Pat found the Social Security Administration as cautious as the Kremlin. The SSA denied her request, arguing that before it would pay, Pat would have to prove David was "unexplainably unheard of" for seven years. From six sworn statements, a Social Security claims representative concluded that David had good reason to disappear and then hide: he didn't want to pay child support, and since he had changed his name and committed bigamy, he was afraid of arrest.

Her request denied, Pat asked for a reconsideration. Two years after she had first applied and without any further investigation, a second claims representative reviewed her case and upheld the denial. Pat then requested a hearing before an administrative law judge. While preparing for the hearing, she studied decisions on similar presumption-of-death cases and could not find a single instance in which an original decision, reconsidered and upheld, had been reversed by an administrative law judge. Concluding that it would be wiser to leave her file open, in case incontrovertible proof of David's death was found, Pat withdrew her request for a hearing.

Initially, Pat felt somewhat at peace because at least she had done everything she could to settle David's official and legal status.

But far from laying David to rest, she had created a new uncertainty and ambivalence that began troubling her sleep in a recurring dream: There'd be a knock at the door. She'd open it dressed in an evening gown. It would be David. She'd invite him inside and they'd sit at the kitchen table. She had been four months pregnant when he ran away, and her hair had lost its sheen. But in her dream she'd be slim, her hair full and shiny. When he ran away, a baby was crying and there were toys, diapers, and baby bottles all over the small apartment. In her dream, the large house would be empty, spotless, and quiet. He would seem surprised, as if he expected a bedraggled woman in a tiny cluttered place.

"Where have you been?" she'd ask without bitterness or anger.

"I can't tell you," he'd say.

"What have you been doing all these years?" she'd ask.

"I can't tell you."

He'd try to hide how impressed he was by her looks and the elegance of her house, but she'd know he was thinking, How did I ever leave her?

In her dream she'd feel his desertion had been her fault—that he had run away because she wasn't perfect, hoping to prove that she'd never make it without him. So she'd feel a sense of forgiveness toward him. But she'd also be firm, silently telling him with her eyes, "Yes, I know, but you can't have what you see. I don't need you anymore. I'm happy now and I want you to know it."

She'd wake from the dream feeling somewhat satisfied; she had shown him how well she had done without him, and he had understood. But ultimately the dream raised more questions for Pat than it resolved. Why did she feel forgiving and not consumed with anger? What *was* he doing all those years? Why wouldn't he tell her?

The longer Pat was married to Gene Bennett, the longer David's shadow became. Her relationship to Gene, they both recognized, rested in part on an unreasonable but very real fear of abandonment and an exaggerated need for independence and control. Woven into the fabric of their commitment was a foreboding that Gene might run away as David had. As a protection, Pat always held back a piece of herself. She decided to continue working just in case Gene left. And when she finally talked herself into quitting her job so she could spend more time with her daughters, it didn't last. A year later, she was back at work. She felt too dependent and insecure without a job.

Gene was quick to recognize how destructively David haunted his marriage. "I'm not going to pay for *his* sins," he'd tell Pat. After ten years of marriage and two years of counseling, they separated by mutual agreement. They remained friends.

The year after the separation Pat received a master's degree in business administration from Marymount College in suburban Washington and was promoted to grade thirteen at the IRS. Pat at last felt free of fear. But a sense of sadness pervaded her freedom. Her daughters had learned to love Gene as a father, and now, thirteen years after their abandonment, they were fatherless once more.

Part
Two

THE SEARCH

8

THE SUMMER OF 1984 began with promise. The scars of Pat's separation from Gene had healed and David's memory faded like an almost-forgotten nightmare. But beneath the welcome peace, Pat felt a vague, persistent tug to face and resolve her past. Perhaps some people could live comfortably surrounded by questions and doubts. She could not. As an accountant, she liked tidy ledgers.

Pat knew part of the problem was David. Although she did not allow herself to feel angry at him and never talked about the abandonment, she was still stung by curiosity. She had heard nothing from or about him for fourteen years. Was he dead or alive? Was he hiding under another assumed name in another city, married to still another woman?

The state of Virginia had officially declared David dead at the request of his foster mother, and his insurance company had paid the woman over eleven thousand dollars in death benefits without even challenging the state. Hoping to lay her own doubts to rest, Pat refiled her petition with the Social Security Administration. If the FBI couldn't solve the dead-or-alive question once and for all, maybe SSA would.

For a second time the Social Security Administration denied both her request and reconsideration. As far as it was concerned, Pat decided, David was alive until she mailed in

his jawbone. She appealed the decision again on the slim
hope that an impartial hearing judge would give more weight
to the new facts than the claims representatives had. In many
ways, the hearing had become a symbol, the last step in her
journey to bury David emotionally and psychologically. If she
lost the appeal that summer as she expected, then so be it.
She could at least officially declare David dead in her own
mind.

Three weeks before the hearing, the IRS sent Pat to San
Francisco to help the Western Regional Office evaluate its
accounting procedures. She planned her free time carefully.
While in San Francisco, she would look up her cousin Joe,
whose whereabouts, she had discovered only recently after
twenty-three years, and Cheryl, an old classmate from Immaculata College. On the way home and at her own expense,
she would stop in Salt Lake City to see Vi, an old friend from
Fairmont Gardens, and then touch down in Denver to visit
Arlene, her closest friend during her difficult year in Miami.

Even though she had seen her older cousin Joe only one
week each summer during the family's annual vacation in
Indianapolis, he had been tremendously important to her.
Unlike her teachers and classmates, Joe had always accepted
her as an equal and a friend, caring enough to listen as she
chattered about her feelings and dreams. He didn't seem to
think she was unattractive even though she did, and he seemed
to like her just as she was. The week with Joe during summer
vacations loomed so large that for the first six months after
she returned from Indianapolis each year, she'd replay it in
bed each night. Come January, she'd begin spinning dreams
for the summer ahead.

After the death of Pat's grandparents, her aunt stopped
speaking to her mother and the visits with her cousin suddenly ended. She never heard from or saw Joe again. The
petty behavior of grown-ups contesting her grandfather's will
had driven a wedge between them. As she grew older and
discovered how rare were friendships such as Joe's and hers,
Pat buried her loss deep inside. Now, after twenty-three years,
Joe was a piece of unfinished business, another man who had
meant a great deal to Pat and then suddenly disappeared.

With an irrational fear gnawing in her, she dialed Joe's
home from her hotel room in San Francisco. His wife an-

swered. "He'll be so pleased to hear from you, Pat," she said. "Call him at the office. Here's the number."

"Would you warn him I'll be calling?" Pat asked. In spite of the reassurance, she was afraid that he might hang up on her, or pause in embarrassment because he couldn't remember her, or tell her he was too busy to talk. This way, if he didn't want to see her, he could let her down easily. She didn't think she could bear rejection from the man who, in her mind, was still the boy who had accepted her, listened to her, and cared about her.

She recognized his voice immediately. "Did your wife tell you I was going to call?"

"Yes, she did, Patsy. Where are you? It's so *good* to hear from you again."

She didn't try to stop the tears of relief. "In San Francisco . . . Do you really remember me, Joe?"

"Of course I remember you. The last I heard, you were married to a Marine."

Joe called her back so she wouldn't run up a huge phone bill. They talked for over an hour with Pat doing most of the talking. Feelings and stories poured out as if it were another summer visit. "I needed to talk to you so much over those years," she said.

"Well, I'm here now and we'll never be separated again," he said. She could tell he meant it.

That evening, Pat rode the subway down the bay to Daly City and climbed the escalator, looking for gray slacks and a blue blazer. Joe was standing at the top—she could have picked him out anywhere. He hugged her and she said through her tears, "It wasn't fair. It just wasn't fair."

They talked through most of the night, long after Joe's wife went to bed, bringing each other up to date about family and children. Talking to him still gave Pat a deep feeling of calm: the twenty-three years fell away easily. As she said good-bye the next morning, she felt like the child who left Indianapolis each summer. She clung to Joe and the security he represented, as if she had a premonition that a storm lay ahead.

The night before she left San Francisco, Pat did the town with Cheryl. Back at Pat's hotel later that night, the conversation drifted to Immaculata and to how devastated Pat had been when the college expelled her for marrying David and demanded that she return her class ring. Pat told Cheryl she had finally figured out why the school had punished her. The nuns assumed she had married David during the Christmas break because she was pregnant, and they didn't want the evidence of her sin showing in their school. Recently, Pat had written the new president of Immaculata explaining what had happened and why. The nun wrote her a touching letter of apology and enclosed a new black onyx school ring engraved with her initials. The return of her ring dissolved the last traces of bitterness toward the school.

"Remember," Cheryl asked, "when I stopped you after class and asked what it felt like to lose your virginity? And your face turned as red as the Sacred Heart?" They both laughed.

"What ever happened to David?" Cheryl asked.

Pat told her how he had changed his name to Jim Parker after he abandoned her and her daughters and how he had married Lenora. She hadn't heard a whisper about him in fourteen years, she said, and had concluded he was dead. The state of Virginia had declared him dead and she was asking the Social Security Administration to do the same.

"Well, I don't think he's dead," Cheryl said.

Her reply left Pat shaken. Everyone she had talked to about David so far had agreed he must be dead. But Cheryl argued like an SSA claims representative, and coming from her friend, the logic was more convincing.

The way Cheryl saw it, David had a good reason to run and an even better one to hide once he had. Why should he risk everything by calling or writing his foster mother, who had already collected life insurance money? Wouldn't it be to his advantage if everyone, especially the woman who raised him, actually believed he was really dead?

"You just may be right," Pat finally admitted. And with her admission, her old doubts returned like a toothache.

Pat left San Francisco for Utah, her link with Immaculata renewed and the twenty-three-year-old silence between her and Joe finally broken. But the fourteen-year-old problem of David festered unresolved.

Pat's old friend Vi was waiting for her at the airport in Salt Lake City. Along with Lorraine, Vi had watched the girls at night so that Pat could study for her courses at George Mason. Pat and Vi lunched at the Snow Bird ski resort above the city and talked and laughed about the old days in Fairmont Gardens. It was Vi who had first advised Pat to apply to the Social Security Administration for death benefits for her daughters. To the practical Vi, it was immaterial whether David was actually dead or alive. No one had heard from him for fourteen years, so in all the important ways, he *was* dead. Let the bureaucrats take it from there.

Meeting Vi and remembering, even laughing about, those nightmarish years reminded Pat of something she tended to forget: if pressed, she could be tough, and when the time came to fight or bear pain, she always managed to find inner resources. She left Salt Lake City for Denver, and Arlene, asking herself, "Does it really make any difference whether David is dead or alive? Shouldn't I just take the money and run if I can get it? Shouldn't I, in effect, bury David alive?"

Arlene had never liked David and couldn't understand why Pat put up with him. Like Lorraine, she believed David had done his wife a favor when he ran away. And like Cheryl, she was convinced that David was still alive, probably doing to another woman what he had done to Pat.

Yet in spite of her dislike for David, which she did not try to hide, Arlene stirred up emotions and memories Pat did not want to face: all those happy times before there was any hint of trouble. The tiny apartment in Lejeune, studying history together then making love, her long-awaited pregnancy, the birth of Christine—tender feelings washed over Pat. She had loved David so much and still loved him the day he walked out. How could she reconcile her feelings when the man who had given her so much happiness was the same man who had abandoned her? Love and anger wrestled, but neither won.

On the flight from Denver back to Washington, exhausted from emotion and from lack of sleep, Pat was overwhelmed by what had happened in four short days. For years she had been afraid to face the past and suffer again, but on this trip she had found that pain remembered is often a healing salve.

Pat came home determined to face it all—herself, her feelings toward David, and her anger at what he had done to her and her daughters. Legally defining him—dead or alive—was the first simple step, and her Social Security Administration hearing suddenly took on new meaning.

9

▼

BACK IN WASHINGTON it took Pat only a few minutes from her lunch hour to photocopy the seventy-one pages in David's Social Security Administration file. As she fed the copier, she glanced at each page. Along with the documents she herself had submitted, there were five affidavits, including the one that she was itching to read—Bill's. From what she had already learned, Bill's sworn statement more than anything had convinced the claims representatives that David was probably still alive.

Her curiosity smoldering, Pat fidgeted throughout the IRS reception she had to attend that afternoon. When the speeches began, she slipped back to her office. She had half an hour to read the affidavits before the rest of the staff returned. Pat barely glanced at her mother's; she already knew what was in it: a statement claiming David had to be dead because he had made no attempt to contact those closest to him, his foster parents. David's foster mother's affidavit did not surprise Pat either: he must be dead because normally, he either came home once a month or wrote or called when he couldn't. His sister's statement held no revelations: if David was alive, he would have no reason to hide from his family.

But the affidavit of David's *real* mother was as puzzling as the others had been predictable. She had a ''feeling'' he wasn't dead, his real mother wrote, and no idea why he wouldn't reveal his whereabouts. He was an insurance salesman, and she had not seen or heard from him since July 1968, when he had run away.

What puzzled Pat was that David had never sold insurance before or during their marriage. Was his real mother confused, or did she know something she didn't want to talk about? The more Pat studied the standard two-page form, sloppily written and filled with minor inaccuracies, the more she questioned it. Maybe David's real mother hadn't heard *from* her son after he ran away, but it sure sounded as if she might have heard *about* him.

Pat saved Bill's affadavit until last. If the sworn statement of David's real mother puzzled her, Bill's angered her. David was dead, Bill had written, but if he wasn't, he was hiding to "avoid child support and alimony."

Why the hell didn't Bill just argue one way or the other? Either he thought David was dead or he thought he was alive—not both at the same time. No wonder the Social Security Administration had denied the claim. If David's closest friend had agreed with everyone else that David must be dead because he hadn't tried to contact family or friends, the issue would have been settled years ago. Bill was taking David's side again. The good old boy network was still alive and well.

Pat found it difficult to concentrate on IRS business that afternoon; new questions arose and her anger toward Bill simmered. Where did David's mother get that insurance salesman idea, and why was she so convinced her son wasn't dead? What would Pat find in David's file if she began looking for clues suggesting he was *alive* instead of dead?

Too curious even to change her clothes when she got home that evening, Pat kicked off her shoes and spread the file out on the kitchen table. Trying to be the objective IRS revenue agent, she began analyzing the SSA summary reports.

Evidence in support of the "dead" theory: David's foster parents had not heard from him since he disappeared. But of course, they stood to gain over eleven thousand dollars in insurance money if he was declared dead. Also, David's fingerprints had not turned up on the FBI computer, meaning he had not been arrested and police had not found his prints at the scene of a serious crime.

Evidence in support of the "alive" theory: It would be in David's best interest to hide. As Bill had pointed out, David was anxious to avoid child support. His only reasons for surfacing would be to meet his daughters, to talk to his foster parents, or to stop running.

Next, Pat studied the affidavits. Everyone, including her, agreed on two key points—David had had no previous history of disappearing, and he had always kept in touch with his family. That the family had not heard from him in sixteen years seemed to suggest he was dead. But there was a huge hole in that argument. If David hadn't felt the need to contact family or friends between 1968, when he ran away, and 1970, when Lenora had called and confirmed David was alive, why would he do so later on? He had changed his name and covered his trail like an escaped convict. Would loneliness or guilt or curiosity be strong enough motives to drive him above ground? Or was it more logical to assume that his behavior had remained consistent and that he was still hiding somewhere with a new name and a new wife?

Included in the Social Security investigative file was a copy of Lenora's marriage certificate to James Clinton Parker, which Pat had already seen. Lenora had sent her a copy fourteen years ago and she hadn't really looked at it since. The SSA file document was in fact a copy Pat had submitted when she first applied for death benefits.

As she studied the certificate, it struck her as odd that Social Security had never bothered to ask Lenora for a sworn statement. After all, she was David's "wife" and the last person known to have seen him alive. Pat had assumed that SSA claims representatives or FBI agents had interviewed the woman. She had always felt that if David was still alive, his real mother and Lenora would be the two people to know, not his foster mother, who saw her granddaughters regularly and could let slip that she had heard from their father.

Pat also found it strange that there was nothing in the file to suggest that SSA had searched for James Clinton Parker on its computer. If he wasn't currently listed as a Social Security contributor, wouldn't that be an important fact to note? And if he was in their computer, couldn't a claims representative easily determine if he was the same man Lenora had married?

The last line on Lenora's marriage license suddenly leapt out at Pat. She could not believe she had never noticed it before: Place of birth of female—Mamou, Louisiana. She ran to get her road atlas. Lenora's maiden name was not a common one, she reasoned, and Mamou couldn't be very big. Lenora must have family there. She thumbed through the atlas to Louisiana, then down the alphabetical list of towns to Mamou—population 3,275.

It was Thursday, and her hearing was scheduled for the following Wednesday, June 20. If anyone could confirm that David was dead or have any leads if he was alive, it would be Lenora. Should Pat do what the Social Security Administration had failed to do—call the woman?

Pat hesitated for a moment. If Lenora had any leads for her, Pat knew she would *have* to pursue them no matter how long it took or where they might end. If she didn't, they'd gnaw at her forever. Pat grabbed the phone and called the Louisiana operator. She had no choice: there was an odor clinging to those affidavits and she had to find out where it came from and why.

"Which city?" a woman drawled.

"Mamou," Pat said. She gave the operator Lenora's maiden name and waited.

"There are several listed," the operator said. "But no Lenora."

"The names and numbers, please." Pat tingled, knowing somebody on that list would lead her to David's "wife."

"I can't do that," the operator said. "I can give you two numbers. Which ones do you want?" She recited the list.

Pat took the first two names and dialed one quickly before she could lose her nerve. She didn't like the idea of intruding on Lenora's life again. Like Pat, the woman wouldn't be happy about someone prying into her past.

"I'm looking for Lenora," she told the woman who answered the phone. "I wonder if you know how I can—"

"Why, yes. She's outside next door mowin' the lawn." The woman's voice was soft and lilting. Pat placed her in her late fifties. "I'm her cousin. You want me ta yell for her?"

"Could you give me her number?" Pat asked. "I'll call her later."

"She should be in the house in about five minutes," she said. "I'll tell her ta expect a call."

After she hung up, Pat paced the floor, replaying in her mind the day Lenora had called fourteen years earlier. In spite of her own shock, she had felt sorry for the woman who sounded so sweet and innocent. The last Pat had heard, Lenora was trying to get her marriage annulled.

Pat waited ten minutes, then dialed the number. From the first gentle, cautious hello, Pat knew it was Lenora. Afraid to alarm her, Pat spoke calmly and slowly as she tried to hide the tremor in her own voice. She wanted the woman to feel she was not out to hurt her; she only wanted information about David.

"Lenora? This is Pat," she said. "Do you remember me?"

"Yes, I do. How could I forget?" Lenora said. She seemed surprised.

Pat was nervous. For Lenora to hear her voice after all this time, she knew, was painful, and what Lenora might tell her about David could hurt even more.

"I thought about you all these years, Lenora, and I wondered what happened to you," Pat said. "I'm trying to get Social Security benefits for my three daughters and I'll be going to a hearing next week. David was declared legally dead in Virginia last year. Even so, I don't want to go to the hearing if there's a chance he is still alive."

Pat paused to let the shock wear off and the message sink in. "I need to ask you a couple of questions," she continued. "Anything you might know could really help me settle this thing once and for all."

It worked. Lenora began to tell her story, slowly, quietly, and without further coaxing. After talking to Pat in 1970, she said, she had her marriage to Jim annulled. A few months later, in January 1971, Jim came to her door. He was out of work, he said, the bank had repossessed his car in Houston, where he had been living, and he wanted to move back in with her. Would she take him? She was leery, but he charmed his way back into her home. It worked out fine. Hoping to start fresh, they moved to Jacksonville, Florida, where Jim managed a men's clothing store. Then they moved to Tampa, where he walked out on her for the second time, in 1975. They had no children.

The more Pat heard, the angrier she became. She had asked Lenora in 1970 to call her if she ever heard from David again. She had told her then that she had three babies to support, was on welfare, and needed help badly. Lenora had promised she would call. Now Pat knew Lenora not only hadn't contacted her, but had moved right back in with the runaway father of her children. Pat tried not to let her emotions show in her voice.

"He left you in 1975?" Pat asked, with an appropriate note of surprise.

"Yes. And he kept in contact with me until 1976."

Now Pat was overwhelmed with anger and confusion. She needed time to sort through what she had just heard and to get her feelings under control. If she showed hostility, Lenora would snap a double bolt over the past.

"Can I call you back?" Pat asked. "I have to take Marcia to diving practice at the pool. She's my youngest."

Lenora hesitated as if to say, What else can I tell you? When she finally said yes, it was almost a sigh.

Pat drove Marcia to the pool, careful not to let her daughter suspect whom she had been talking to, or why. Marcia had grown into a sensitive fifteen-year-old with reddish brown hair and dark brown eyes that mirrored her every feeling. She spoke in rapid fire as if unable to express her thoughts fast enough to suit her, and she said exactly what was on her mind.

Although each of her daughters had been hurt by David, Marcia's pain was special. When the truck had rammed Pat's car in front of her mother's house that winter afternoon in 1971, Marcia, who was two years old at the time, had seen the paramedics lift her mother into an ambulance and drive off. Although she knew better from discussions around the house in later years, Marcia had talked herself into believing that her father had been killed in that terrible scene. She couldn't accept the fact that he had abandoned her before she was born, and Pat did not discourage the accident story because for all she knew David *was* dead.

By the time she was ten, Marcia finally accepted the fact that her father didn't die in that car accident but had run away from her and her sisters. For the next few years, she'd creep into Pat's bed at night to cry and be cuddled. "If only I could hear Daddy's voice,'' she'd say. ''I wish I knew what he sounded like.'' Then her guilt feelings would pour out. ''If only you didn't have *me*,'' she'd whimper. ''You'd still have Daddy, and so would Christine and Andrea. Why was I ever born?'' There was little Pat could do but hold her daughter tightly to make her feel wanted and secure and to encourage the tears to flow.

By the time Marcia was fourteen, anger had replaced feelings of guilt, even though she did not understand the roots of her anger. With a hostility that went well beyond the usual teenage rebellion, Marcia began needling Pat about the smallest thing as if to punish her because she couldn't punish her father. There were temper tantrums and outbursts for almost no reason, and her school grades began to slip.

Now, at fifteen, Marcia was beginning to snap out of her angry phase and settle down. She still flew into rages, but they didn't last as long and they were tempered by other admirable qualities. Marcia was a leader in sports, which she loved, and in organizing activities. She stood up for her rights fiercely. And most important as far as Pat was concerned, she chose her friends carefully, and once she did, she committed herself to them tenaciously. When a friendship broke up, which was rare, she mourned its loss as if it were a death. Marcia seemed to be trying to be as loyal and caring as her father had been disloyal and uncaring.

Pat also watched Marcia become more and more domestic. She made dinner for her mother every night. She baked and made cookies for parties and for her friends, just as Pat had done in her apartment after David had run away. Coupled with her domesticity, Pat noted with concern, was a dependency on her mother, a kind of clinging that Marcia didn't seem to be outgrowing. It was almost as if her daughter was telling her, ''I want to stay close to you so you won't leave me too.''

With this puzzling dependency and the smoldering anger she was still working through, how would her youngest daughter react if she found out the object of her anger was still alive?

Yes, Pat concluded as she dropped Marcia off at the pool, it was best to wait until the last minute to tell her.

On the way home, her feelings somewhat under control,

Pat mulled over what Lenora had said. The whole picture had changed completely with one phone call. She had phoned Lenora expecting to dig up facts to support presumption of death and had found instead evidence pointing to presumption of life.

Pat rehearsed the additional questions she wanted to ask Lenora, then dialed Mamou again with a vague sense that she was about to set out on another journey. She thought of her cousin Joe and felt a renewed strength. She would listen, probe, and then weigh what she learned before deciding what to do next. One thing was already clear: in spite of her shock and anger, she would cancel the SSA hearing if she seriously doubted David was dead—even though she wanted and needed the death benefits for her daughters.

Pat began with chitchat, then said, "Lenora, he left you in 1975 in Tampa—why?"

"Well, you know how he was." Lenora sounded defensive and embarrassed. "I lived from day to day not knowing whether he would come home. Then one evening, he said, 'I have other plans for my life and they don't include you.' "

"Weren't you upset?" Pat asked, trying to keep Lenora talking.

"Yes, but what was I to do?"

"Didn't you try to stop him?"

"No," Lenora said. "I even helped him move his furniture. I stayed in Tampa for a while, then came back home."

"Then what?"

"Jim went to Baton Rouge for a while, then moved on to San Antonio. That's the last I heard of him."

"Do you have his address in San Antonio?"

Lenora gave her a number on Gardendale Drive, then said, "I've often wondered myself whether he's dead or alive. There isn't a day I don't think about him."

"Lenora, are you still in love with him?" Pat asked gently.

"Well, I do think about him a lot."

The realization that Lenora still loved James Parker helped Pat frame her next questions. Like an attorney probing a hostile witness, she began picking the story apart, looking for details, clues, leads, all the while taking notes furiously. When she sensed that Lenora was being evasive, she didn't press the point. Slowly the facts began to pile up:

The name of the shop in Jacksonville where David had worked was the Suburban Men's Store. When its owners decided to move to South Carolina, David stayed in Florida. He took a job with the Safeco Insurance Company's branch office in Jacksonville. In 1973 Safeco transferred him to Sarasota, then to Tampa, in 1974. In March 1975 he left Lenora for good.

Although there was no reason to disbelieve what Lenora told her, Pat sensed there was a lot she had left out. Did Lenora know he was alive and was she protecting him? Or did she really lose track of David after 1975?

Pat probed a few more times, and when she felt resistance she asked the question she had been saving for last. "Lenora, please believe me when I say that all I want to do is find out if David's dead or alive. If he's dead, I'll go through with my hearing for death benefits for his children. If he's alive, I'll ask the child-support office to help me. Is there anything else you can tell me?"

"No," she said. "I told you all there is."

"Can you give me his Social Security number?" Pat asked. That alone would solve the mystery quickly and easily.

"I don't have that," Lenora said. But from the way she said it, Pat knew Lenora would not tell her, even if she did have it.

Nonetheless, Pat asked again in a pleading voice. When Lenora began crying, Pat thanked her and hung up, still not sure what the woman was hiding.

Pat found it hard to sort out how she felt. She was sorry she had made Lenora cry. Yet she was angry at her for going back to David after learning he had abandoned a young wife and three children. She also felt pity for the woman; obviously Lenora was still in love with David and hadn't gotten over the pain after ten years. And, of course, she was angry at herself for her own anger. Above all, Pat was afraid of what she had to do next.

David's trail was only eight years old now, and she had two good leads—an address in San Antonio and the name of an employer. And she had every reason to believe David was alive. She would cancel the hearing in the morning and then try to find him. She didn't want to think about what she'd do if she actually did.

That night, when she wasn't staring at the ceiling, she tossed and turned. The next morning, her thoughts were clearer, even if her feelings weren't. Shortly after nine, when the Social Security Administration offices opened, she canceled the hearing. All afternoon she chafed to get home and take the next fateful step.

10

PAT BURST THROUGH the kitchen door that evening. It was only four-thirty in Texas, so she had half an hour to dig around before the work week ended. She didn't think she could stand the tension of waiting until Monday.

Pat called the operator in San Antonio and asked for the listing for James C. Parker who lived on Gardendale. No one by that name. Disappointed but not surprised, she redialed and asked another San Antonio operator for the phone number of the Safeco Insurance Company. Quickly she called that number.

"May I speak to James Parker, please?" she asked the receptionist.

"There is no James Parker here," the woman said. "But there is one in our Dallas office. Would you like that number?"

Bingo, Pat thought, her heart thumping. She couldn't believe how easy it was. She called Dallas. "One moment, please," a cool voice said. Pat held her breath. A man came on the line. "This is James Parker," he said. "Can I help you?"

Pat felt relieved. It was the voice of a young black man. Drained from the emotional stress, she hung up and sat down to catch her breath. When she felt calm again, she took stock.

One of her clues—David's last known address—was a blind alley. But given the number of moves he had made between 1970, when he had married Lenora, and 1976, when Lenora had last talked to him, it was unlikely he'd lived at the same address for eight years. And that he wasn't working for Safeco in San Antonio or Dallas didn't surprise her either. He still could be living in San Antonio at another address and no longer working for Safeco. Or he could still be with Safeco—there might be more than one James Parker in a big company—and they had transferred him. Hadn't they moved him from Jacksonville to Sarasota to Baton Rouge to San Antonio like a piece on a Monopoly board?

It was after five o'clock in Texas. Before searching any further, Pat decided to tell her daughter, Christine. She felt the need to share her secret and wanted someone to confide in. Christine was the oldest, and Pat knew it would please the eighteen-year-old that her mother trusted her not to leak a word to her younger sisters.

Tall and striking, Christine had long auburn hair and freckles. Her brown eyes, shaded by thick brows, had a tentative, sad look. But when she smiled, they became suddenly warm and friendly. Like her father, she had large hands and a gait so distinctive that Pat could pick her out of any crowd.

Unlike her sisters, Christine remembered her father. Abandonment had hurt her deeply even though she was only two years old at the time. Today, reserved and introspective, Christine held everything inside, seldom expressing her true feelings, especially her anger. While Marcia was impulsive and challenging, Christine thought before she spoke. A peacemaker, she looked for everyone's best side and was almost always warm and considerate, if somewhat naïve.

All through high school, Christine worked hard at her grades and at part-time jobs, but she seldom dated. At five feet ten, she felt different. And like her mother at that age, she was so shy and insecure that she seemed surprised when boys showed interest. Although she wanted to be noticed, she didn't like dealing with the attention. As a compromise she took up dancing; on stage she could have it both ways—be seen but at a safe distance.

When she started to date seriously after graduating from high school, Christine developed an interesting pattern. If she cared about a young man, she clung to him and wanted to be with him constantly. But she only managed to develop relationships with men who lived in cities far from home, making intimacy possible only on the phone and in letters. She sensed that her habit of long-distance loving had something to do with her father and it bothered her, but she wasn't sure how the pieces fit together.

When Pat told Christine that her father might still be alive, Christine was neither surprised nor curious. If he showed up after sixteen years, he couldn't undo what he had done, and she didn't want to pick up their relationship where he had left off. Finding and meeting her father would only bring more disappointment, so why get excited?

Given Christine's tendency to bury tough issues, Pat was not surprised at her lack of emotion. She merely noted it and went on to explain that she didn't want David's foster mother to find out about the lead because she might know where he was and alert him. Then he'd burrow so deep they'd never find him.

"Well, what do you think?" Pat asked finally, trying to get her daughter to share some of her thoughts, if not her feelings. But Christine's brown eyes, so expressive when she wanted them to be, showed nothing.

She said only, "Mom, you better not tell Marcia; she'll freak out. And don't tell Andrea or she'll say something to Grandma."

Nevertheless, Christine was flattered by her mother's confidence, and like co-conspirators, they set up Pat's bedroom as a command post where they would plan the search and share the news. Then, nervous and excited, Pat continued the chase.

Hoping David was still in San Antonio, Pat made several phone calls to the operator and put together a list of all the James, Jim, Jimmy, and J. Parkers in the city. She ended up with twenty-eight. Dallas was worse, with sixty-four. Pat concocted a cover story. Using the name of a girlfriend, she would ask to speak to Mr. Parker. She would say she was looking for a James Parker who worked for an insurance company, then explain she was with the Executive Research Corporation in Andover, Massachusetts, a recruiting agency with several management jobs open in the insurance field. If Mr.

Parker was interested in applying, she would send him a questionnaire. In the event she actually located David, she would have special stationery and a questionnaire printed and ask a friend who did not live in the Washington area to mail it to him.

After three San Antonio blanks, she hit a live one.

"In insurance? How long ago?" a Mrs. Parker asked.

"I'm not sure," Pat said. "We have a list of people who used to work for insurance companies. And we have an old San Antonio address for a James Parker." Nervously, Pat fed the woman details about her "company" in hopes of wheedling more information.

"The reason I ask," the woman said, "is that my husband did work in insurance several years ago—like eight or nine years ago."

"It's been that long?" Pat was disappointed. "Well, it's still possible he's our man."

"He's not here right now," the woman said. "He's due back in about thirty minutes."

"Do you think he would be interested in talking?"

"I don't know because I don't have any idea what you have in mind."

"Well, if he's interested, I can't guarantee anything because we don't guarantee jobs. But—" Pat fumbled to explain precisely what the Executive Research Corporation of Andover would do for James Parker.

"Is this strictly door-to-door sales?" the woman asked. She sounded suspicious.

"No, no, these are *executive* positions. We have an application—"

"Is this a full-time job?"

Pat's heart was pounding so fast and her voice became so breathy she hardly heard the woman's questions. More out of nervousness than anything else, she began running through the "history" of the company, how it recruited and for whom, making it up as fast as she could. "We've been very successful with people who have left the business," she explained. "I can't say I have a particular job in mind for your husband. He'd have to fill out our application and tell us where he wants to work and we'll try to match him with an executive job on our list."

"Well, my husband is retiring soon," the woman said. "And he's thinking of doing something on the side."

Retiring! Pat's heart began to sink. "Just how old *is* he?"

"Sixty-five. You might give him a call."

Pat suddenly felt exhausted.

"Generally, we are interested in people under thirty-five," she said lamely.

"Well, if you can't find anyone," the woman volunteered, "give him a call."

Not sure she could take any more false alarms, Pat nevertheless forced herself to phone the other Parkers on her San Antonio list just to get them out of the way. She got nowhere. It was nine o'clock on Friday night when she finished. It didn't seem worthwhile even to try the Parkers on her Dallas list, for she had no evidence that David worked there.

Drained but not completely discouraged, Pat called Richard Froemming, a private investigator she had met a few months earlier at Boomerangs, a singles watering hole where young professionals gathered. Richard was a former D.C. cop who had quit the force and started his own company, Shamus, Inc. He and Pat had dated a few times and frequently chatted on the phone. Richard already knew the story of Pat's former husband.

When Pat called on Friday night and told him about her San Antonio phone calls the day before and why she thought David was still alive, Richard was amazed at how far she had come in just a few days.

"Will you find him for me?" she asked.

As an investigator, Richard worked on the principle that as long as there are leads, there's hope. Pat had at least one good lead, and she was bright and determined. "Why pay me?" he said. "You're doing just fine."

"But I'm stuck," she complained. "I don't know what to do next."

"Begin with Safeco," he suggested. "Find out where its headquarters are. Call Personnel and take it from there."

It would be a long wait until Monday, Pat thought.

11

▼

PAT WAITED UNTIL after work on Monday to call Safeco's corporate offices in Seattle. Deciding to play it straight, she asked to speak to the personnel director. When he came on the line, she told him she was looking for her husband, who had disappeared twice, the second time eight years ago. "At that time," she said, "he was working for you in San Antonio. I'd appreciate any information you can give me."

"I'll help as much as I can," the personnel director promised. "But privacy laws are pretty strict. About all I can do is confirm or deny. What's his name? I'll see if we have his file."

"James Clinton Parker."

"Hold on a minute," he said.

To Pat, it seemed like a long wait. The man was cautious and if he felt sorry for her, his voice didn't show it. Pat wasn't used to that. Most people went out of their way to help once they understood what she was after and why.

"Yes, we have a file for a James C. Parker," he said finally. Again Pat tried to read something in his voice, but it was flat and businesslike. "Do you have an address?"

She read him the San Antonio address on Gardendale.

"That's the address we have in his file. He left Safeco in 1976. Do you have his Social Security number?"

''No,'' she said, thinking of Lenora who might have been able to give it to her. How easy it would have been if she had.

''Date of birth?''

She gave him the one on the marriage certificate Lenora had sent. It was not David's real date of birth but it was close.

''It's not the same,'' he said.

''What do you have?'' she asked. It looked as if David was trying to cover his trail again. If he had changed his date of birth a second time, she thought, he had probably taken a different Social Security number as well.

''I'm sorry, but I can't give you that,'' the Safeco man said. ''Describe him to me.''

Pat went into detail.

''The height and weight match,'' he said.

Without saying as much, they both concluded that Safeco's James C. Parker was Lenora's Jim and Pat's David. She tried to coax more information out of the personnel director, but he showed no sign of weakening. Finally, she thanked him and hung up. Except for the different date of birth, a minor discrepancy, all the pieces fit.

Pat called Richard. She told him what she had learned and how frustrating it was to be so close yet so far. Richard encouraged her. That was an important call, he said. It confirmed that David had worked for Safeco and had been an insurance man for six years. And if he had *been* in insurance, Richard pointed out, he was probably still in insurance.

Pat was not impressed. ''There must be ten thousand insurance companies,'' she said.

''Probably . . . but only fifty state licensing offices.''

The insurance business was tightly controlled, Richard explained, and every legitimate insurance agent had to be licensed in the state or states where he or she sold insurance. Licenses had to be renewed periodically—the information was public.

Now Pat's strategy became clear. Fifty phone calls at most. If David was still in insurance and still using the name James C. Parker—two very big *if*s—she'd find him. If not—well, she'd face that when she got there.

Pat made a list of the state capitals she wanted to call. She knew David had worked for Safeco in Texas, Louisiana, and

Florida. So she would call the insurance licensing offices in Austin, Baton Rouge, and Tallahassee. Then, figuring that if she couldn't find him there, he would probably still be working in the South, she added Montgomery, Little Rock, Jackson, and Atlanta to the list.

Before calling it a night, she decided to lean on Safeco once more. This time she explained to the personnel director that when her husband had deserted her sixteen years ago he had left her with three babies. She had thought he was dead, she said, but now, there was every reason to believe that the James C. Parker in Safeco's files was her former husband. She and her children needed to be certain for their peace of mind.

"Has anyone requested employment references for James C. Parker?" she asked. Surely someone had, and the information would be a fresh lead.

"I can't give you that information," the Safeco man said. "You'll need a court order for his personnel file."

Frustrated, she tried a few more questions and once again asked for Parker's Social Security number. From his voice, the hemming and hawing, and the shuffling of papers, she got the impression that Safeco knew where David was. His refusal to help her only confirmed that she was on the right trail. If Safeco knew, others must know as well.

Pat took leave on Tuesday so she could call the state capitals on her list. It was not a difficult job, but there was always a bureaucracy to cut through, going from one clerk to another until she found the right person, and long waits on the phone while files were checked. She drew blanks in Texas and Louisiana.

When she got to Florida, Pat changed her tactic. Instead of going directly to the central office in the capital, she decided to try the regional office in Jacksonville, where James C. Parker had once worked. "Yes, we show a James C. Parker licensed . . . but in Tampa," the Jacksonville clerk said. "I suggest you call our Tampa office."

When Pat hung up she was trembling. She knew she had found David even though there was no reason to be so sure. She paced the kitchen floor, trying to summon enough courage to get back on the phone. Then she dialed the Tampa number. "You'll have to call the central office in Tallahassee," another clerk said. "We don't keep licenses here."

The Tallahassee clerk was very helpful. She pulled James C. Parker's file and read Pat the information on his license application that she was permitted by law to reveal: the date on which James C. Parker's license had been renewed, his Tampa address, and his date and place of birth. The birth date and place were different from David's real ones and different from the information on Lenora's marriage certificate, but again they were close enough to convince Pat she might have found the right man.

She was now in mild shock. If she had just found David, she had found a piece of herself as well. Her feelings were so confused that she didn't even try to sort them out. What should she do now? Tell Andrea and Marcia? Or wait until she was sure?

Reason prevailed, and she called the clerk in the insurance licensing office in Tallahassee once more. Woman to woman, she explained that David had deserted his babies sixteen years ago and that Virginia had declared him dead. She said she was convinced that James C. Parker was her former husband, but she needed to be absolutely certain before she could tell her teenage daughters that she had found their father.

"Can't you give me any more information?" she pleaded. The clerk had told her she was permitted to reveal only public information. That meant there *was* private information.

There was a long pause. Pat could hear the clerk draw a deep breath. "I could lose my job for this," came the voice finally.

"Don't worry. I don't even know your name," Pat said.

"Hang on."

A moment later, the clerk returned with Parker's file and began reading it almost in a whisper. Every detail matched: James C. Parker had spent four years in the Marine Corps as David had, but the service dates, like his birthdates, didn't quite match. He had worked at Suburban's Men's Store in Jacksonville in 1971, as Lenora had said, and he had begun working for the Safeco Insurance Company in 1972, as both Lenora and Safeco had agreed.

There was no doubt in Pat's mind now that James C. Parker was the man who had married Lenora. And the man who had married Lenora was the father of her children. She was amazed at how easy it had been to find him, after all those years when she had been wondering whether he was dead or alive, whether she hated or loved him.

As soon as Pat hung up, however, she felt sick to her stomach. She began pacing the floor and hyperventilating. She found herself saying over and over, "What am I going to do? What am I going to do?" She struggled with an urge to call the licensing clerk back and make her prove that she had made a mistake, that the James C. Parker in her file was not David. But it was too late. She knew she had found him.

Pat called Richard instead. "You won't believe this," she said. Words began spilling out.

"Calm down," Richard ordered. "Slow down and begin again."

Pat told him what she had learned and how. "I want to hire you," she said, placing the responsibility for the next step on his shoulders.

"You don't need me, Pat," Richard said. "You've already found him."

"Well, I want you to *prove* it's him," she said. "Go down there and tail him. Follow him into a restaurant. Get him to touch a glass and then take it and dust it for prints. Maybe you can—"

Richard laughed. "You watch too many movies," he said. "What would I do with fingerprints? I'll send someone down there to get pictures of him and his house, and they can poke around in the court records. If it's him, you'll know when you see the pictures."

Richard asked his partner, Rick Hager, who was finishing a surveillance job in Miami, to stop in Tampa on his way home. It was a breeze assignment: find Parker's house and snap pictures, get the make and tag number of his car, check the courthouse for anything on Parker in the public domain, and get pictures of the man himself. Not a boring assignment, and not interesting either. One day's work, then a day or two on the beach.

A former police officer like Richard, Hager was used to the methodical background checking that makes up a large part of any investigation. He rented a car in Tampa and bought a local street map, but Foxwood Drive, where James Clinton

Parker lived, wasn't on it. And Parker's company, Frontier Adjusters, was just a number in the Tampa phone directory. No help there. Next, Hager checked at the post office and found out there was no Foxwood Drive inside the Tampa city limits. Figuring it must be in a nearby suburb, Hager walked over to the Hillsborough County Sheriff's office, where he discovered two Foxwood Drives in two different towns outside Tampa. He chose one and found the street without much trouble, but there was no house with Parker's number. By that time, it was almost dark.

The next morning, Hager drove out to the second Foxwood Drive in the suburb of Lutz, about a half hour from downtown Tampa. He found James Parker's house in the Cypress Cove development, a typical single-family home sitting on a corner lot: blue with white trim, a chalet roof with two dormers, and an attached garage. A grove of cypress trees shaded the rear of the house. There was a swing and slide set in the backyard. Parked in the driveway were a blue Chevy Camaro, a red Dodge Diplomat, a blue Honda, and a Chevy truck. Hager guessed that Parker worked out of his home, as most insurance adjusters do, and that was why there was no address in the phone book for Frontier Adjusters.

Hager also concluded that Cypress Cove was not the place to play photographer. The houses were nestled close together, separated only by small patches of green; with no cars parked on the street, someone was sure to get suspicious of a stranger watching and waiting. Besides, Hager found it almost impossible to cover both exits from Cypress Cove. He couldn't be sure of catching sight of James Parker, much less of freezing him on film. So he copied down the license numbers of all the cars in the driveway and left.

Hager checked into a Holiday Inn down the road and then drove over to the Pasco County Courthouse nearby to find out who owned the house and whether James C. Parker had a criminal record. He learned that Parker was renting and was clean. Next, Hager drove back to Tampa to check the Department of Motor Vehicles. The red Dodge was registered to James C. Parker, he found out, and the truck to Frontier Adjusters. Neither had a lien on it. The other two cars were registered in the name of Parker's business partner.

Finally, Hager visited the bureau of marriage licenses and

found out that James C. Parker had married a nineteen-year-old woman in January 1979. Noting she was sixteen years younger than Parker, Hager bought a certified copy of the marriage license. He could forget that day in the sun.

That night Hager began to plan his sting. That was the fun part of being a private eye, outsmarting the mark. Betting that the best way to reach Parker would be through his pocketbook, Hager worked on a hook until it was fish-bone sharp: "My name is Bill Henderson and I'm a businessman from Philadelphia. Someone rear-ended my new Cadillac Seville. How much would you charge to take pictures of the damage and do an adjustment? I have to drive back home today and I'm worried. If I get into another accident, I won't be able to figure out which one caused which dents."

Hager smiled in satisfaction. It was a good hook and he knew it would take. The first thing the next morning, he called Frontier Adjusters. A man answered. Hager tossed the bait.

"Why don't you take your car into a local Cadillac dealer," the man said after he heard Hager out. "They'll do it for nothing."

Hager was staggered. He never figured Parker would follow the bait so closely but refuse to take it. Had he misjudged the man? Thanking him for the suggestion, he asked, "By the way, who am I speaking to?"

"Jim Parker."

Hager hung up. Over a cup of coffee, he tied a second barb on his hook and called Parker back. "I'm in a hurry to get back to Philadelphia and I don't have time to check in with a Cadillac dealer. How much will you charge to look at the car, take pictures, then drive out to the scene of the accident to photograph that too? I'll pay cash."

Hager didn't think Parker would pass up tax-free money.

"At least fifty," Parker said.

"Fine. Come on over. I'm at the Holiday Inn in Lutz and I'm getting ready to check out. I'll be waiting for you in the lobby."

Hager gave Parker a phony description of himself. Parker said he'd be there in ten minutes. He was six foot one, he said, and would be wearing a tan shirt and tan slacks and driving a red Dodge Diplomat.

Hager picked up his camera bag and rushed out to his white compact car parked about twenty-five yards from the motel's front entrance. He selected a 200-mm lens and waited. Less than ten minutes later, Parker rolled into the lot and slowly drove around the motel looking for a black Cadillac. Then he went around a second time. When he started his third loop, Hager was afraid he might drive right out of the lot and go home. He sighed in relief when the Diplomat turned the corner again and slipped into a parking place out front. Hager fired a series of clean shots—Parker getting out of his car under a "Prime Rib $10.95 All You Can Eat" sign, Parker walking toward the lobby, and Parker returning to his car.

Hager pulled out of the lot before Parker had climbed back into his car, and tooled over to the house on Foxwood Drive, where he snapped another series. On the way back to the motel, he passed Parker, jaw set and hands tightly gripping the wheel. Hager sensed that Parker wasn't the least bit suspicious, just mad as hell that fifty bucks had slipped through his fingers.

Hager smiled to himself. He had pulled it off neatly, cleanly, and with no fuss. Tidy investigations always gave him a great sense of accomplishment and pride. He couldn't wait to call Richard, who had been following the Parker case as it unfolded.

Back in Washington, Pat worked in a daze. She'd call Richard during her lunch hour and from home at night. When he was on a stakeout, she'd reach him on his van telephone. Hungry for details, she grilled the investigator: "Describe the house! What did his voice sound like? What did he look like? What did he say—exactly? Tell me again."

The more Pat heard, the more she felt her emotional tension mount. She was surprised that David lived in a nice house, even if he didn't own it, for she could only remember him the way he was when he left her—barely scraping along. She was shocked to hear that he had married a woman just a few years older than Christine and that he had said on his license application that he had never been married before. The wife complicated matters for Pat. Hadn't enough people been hurt already? Did she want a broken marriage on her conscience?

When some of the shock and numbness wore off, she made

a decision. Why shouldn't she finish what she had begun? Her first obligation was toward her daughters and herself. Besides, she argued, she'd be doing the woman a favor if she ripped the mask off James C. Parker. If David had walked out on her and on Lenora, he would probably abandon his present wife too. Better for her to find out now, while she's young.

But it was the slide and swing set that really took the wind out of Pat. Although it had crossed her mind when she first began looking for David that he might be married, she never allowed herself to think that he could have more children as well. Richard tried to reassure her. Other than the swing and slide behind the house, he explained, there was no evidence that Parker had children. And since he was renting, the back-yard set was probably not his.

Pat fretted for two days. If Hager proved Richard wrong, she had decided she would let go of the whole thing. To embarrass David and shock his wife who apparently didn't know his background was one thing. They were adults and could cope. But to hurt children? Who would protect them? Christine, Andrea, and Marcia were three casualties too many. Pat didn't think she could add any more to the list.

Looking for legal advice about what to do next, Pat called an attorney friend, Victoria Gordon. Go to the Juvenile and Domestic Relations Court, Victoria advised, and ask the clerk for a certified copy of the sixteen-year-old court order telling David he had to pay $99.11 every two weeks. Then call back.

What Victoria didn't tell Pat was that without a certified copy of the original order she could never prove to the court that David owed her daughters sixteen years of back child support. The best she could hope for then would be a new judgment ordering David to begin paying for Marcia, who was fifteen, and Andrea, who was seventeen. Christine would turn eighteen in three months, at which time she would cease to be David's responsibility. And Victoria also didn't tell Pat that the chances of finding the original court order after six-teen years were slim indeed.

12

THE FAIRFAX COUNTY Juvenile and Domestic Relations Court was housed in an old two-story brick building in downtown Fairfax. It had been the hub of the county's entire judicial system until the commonwealth attorney, his staff of prosecutors, and their judges had moved down the street to a new glass high-rise befitting one of the richest counties in the nation. As for the old, asbestos-ridden building, Fairfax had given it to its women and children and the professionals who try to help them.

The Juvenile and Domestic Relations Court intake office, where all the court's paperwork began and ended, was located in an airless beige corridor that desperately needed a new coat of paint. A few hard chairs and benches lined one wall for the hard-luck cases who came for help. Taped on the wall next to the intake desk was a list of phone numbers for treatment centers. Most of the court's domestic relations counselors worked in tiny basement offices with unfinished walls of painted brick and exposed pipes.

A door from the back parking lot of the old building led into the juvenile holding tank. Its reception area, where prisoners were logged in, and where the guards sat around chatting on slow days, was dirty; cigarette butts littered the floor. Behind the reception area were the cells where juveniles waited to be called into the courtrooms upstairs. The two rows of cubicles, one for boys and one for girls, were stuffy, dreary, and smelled of urine. Near the cells was a counseling cubbyhole with paint peeling from the walls and asbestos flaking from the pipes. A bare bulb dangled from the ceiling. Under it stood a small table on which the initials of half the teenagers in the county seemed to have been carved.

When Pat walked into the intake office late in the afternoon, the day after she had talked to Victoria, Linda Schnatterly was working at her station behind a counter. On her desk sat a typewriter so old that county service had condemned it, promising her a new one within twelve months. For four years, Linda had been supervising the clerical staff of six women who processed the papers for all child custody and support cases, disputes over visitation rights, and domestic criminal activity. The clerks also scheduled the twenty to thirty daily counseling appointments with the professional staff, tried to help the ten or so walk-ins that showed up each day, and handled 150 to 200 phone calls daily. A single file clerk maintained the center's 128,000 records. Linda, who had been working for Fairfax County for fifteen years, also drove eighteen-wheel semis part-time; she had to supplement her income to support herself and her two children.

After one quick look, Linda knew Pat was in a highly emotional state. She seemed confused and her face was ashen and drawn. Linda listened as a garbled story began to tumble out. She tried to slow Pat down, for part of her job was to pinpoint the problem so she could direct her client to the right help quickly. After a few questions and some jumbled answers, she concluded she was dealing with a child-support case.

"Where's the father?" Linda asked.

"In Florida," Pat said. "I finally found him."

Good luck, lady, Linda thought. You'll have to file an interstate court action and by the time it's settled, if it ever is, your kids will be grandmothers. And Florida of all places.

Linda told Pat that she would have to file for child support for her children under eighteen. If Pat wanted to do that, Linda said, she would make an appointment for her with a counselor.

"That won't work," Pat said. "He doesn't know I've found him and if he hears I have, he'll run again."

You're right on that score, Linda agreed silently. Deadbeat dads and runaway fathers got so much advance notice from legal filings that they could easily keep a step ahead of the lead-footed law.

"I have a child-support order and an arrest warrant," Pat said. "But they're sixteen years old and I don't have certified copies."

Linda shook her head as she fired up her computer. She would have liked to believe that the 128,000 names and case numbers in the computer were complete and accurate, but she knew they weren't. Some files had been lost; others never got on the list because a clerk had misplaced them or a tired keyboard operator had overlooked them or entered them incorrectly. If a woman's husband wasn't on the computer correctly, she'd never find his file.

Linda keyed in David's name and hit the search code. His case number flashed on the screen—15-292. "You're in luck," she told Pat. "It's stored in the basement. But don't hold your breath while I'm gone."

Linda figured that after sixteen years and frequent reorganizations, there was about a fifty-fifty chance that file 15-292 would be collecting dust where it was supposed to be. If it was filed out of sequence, it was probably lost forever. Even if it *was* sitting between 15-291 and 15-293, there was no guarantee that the court order and arrest warrant would be in the file. And if they were, would the papers and the judge's signature still be legible after sixteen years?

Linda walked down two flights of stairs to the basement and into the brightly lit file room lined with rows of identical folders on gray steel shelves. She went over to the 15-200s—and there it was. She couldn't believe it. She opened file 15-292 and began flipping through the twenty pages inside. Each was as crisp and clear as if it had been typed the day before. God must be with you, lady, Linda thought as she carried the file back upstairs.

Pat sat on a wooden bench in the intake corridor. Her stomach began to knot as she read the file Linda had given her— the court order of October 7, 1968, signed by Judge Frank Deierhoi; a second support order for fifty dollars a week signed by Judge Richard Jamborsky four months later; and the arrest warrant of April 1, 1969. The file tapped a deep well of sadness, like a death remembered. When Pat returned the file to Linda, she was crying quietly. They were the first tears she had shed over David in more than ten years, and in spite of the pain they brought, they felt good. Following Victoria's advice, still not sure why, she asked for certified copies of the support order and arrest warrant.

"Now, let's just go over this again," Linda suggested.

Pat started once more from the beginning, coherently this time, and it became clear to Linda that David had been missing for sixteen years, living under an assumed identity, and that Pat had actually gone out and found him. She had never heard this sort of child-support case before. By the time Pat finished her story, the other clerks and women waiting for intake services had gathered around her in disbelief.

Linda studied the old child-support order for a minute. "At fifty dollars a week, that's twenty-six hundred dollars a year. . . . My God, that's almost forty-two thousand dollars in back child support. He owes you forty-two thousand dollars!"

Linda began to boil as her thoughts turned inward. Her own father had left her and her three younger brothers for several years. They were nightmarish years for the family, and Linda never forgot what it was like to be a fatherless child. Besides her own two children, she always seemed to have a stray or two around the house—scared, battered, abandoned kids, unwanted and in trouble with nowhere to go. Over the years she had sheltered more than fifty of them, some just overnight or for a weekend until they could get professional help; others for as long as two years. One of the saddest cases had been the twelve-year-old she accepted for a weekend.

Late one Friday as she sat at home recovering from surgery, Linda had gotten a call from a probation officer she knew. The officer had a twelve-year-old on his hands and needed a place for him until Monday morning, when the court convened. Would Linda take him for the weekend?

She agreed, and the probation officer dropped the boy off at her doorstep early Friday evening. From the start, Linda knew the child was deeply disturbed. He acted like a wild animal. He didn't talk, he looked at her and her two boys with strange wariness, and he crept about the house staring as if he had never seen one before. At mealtimes he didn't know how to eat at the table, and he couldn't seem to get enough food into his stomach.

It was only after a social worker picked the boy up Monday morning that she got the full story. He and his younger brother, who had spent the weekend at another foster home, had been abandoned by their parents. To survive, they had dug a hole in a field and made a roof over it out of old boards and tin. They stole clothes off clotheslines, raided garbage cans, fought dogs for scraps, and broke into houses for food and blankets. They scrounged for a year before someone finally spotted them and called the Fairfax County Police. No one knew where the parents were or why they had left. The court issued a warrant for their arrest, but the police never found them.

Linda still had nightmares about that boy ten years later. She was less angry at runaway parents than at the thoughtless system that let them get away with it. They have their fun, make their babies, walk out when the going gets tough, and nothing ever happens to them. But not Pat's husband. Pat was special. After sixteen years, she'd actually found the son of a bitch. Good for you, lady, Linda thought. Go for him. Even if all you get out of it is a fistful of money. Send a message to other runaway fathers: "Hey, Dad, if we can get you in Florida, we can nail you anyplace."

Although she was neither an attorney nor a counselor, Linda understood how badly the system was stacked against women and children. Fail to pay your income taxes, and you commit a felony. The IRS doesn't let up even if it costs them two hundred thousand dollars to collect ten thousand dollars in back taxes. Imagine what would happen if word leaked that the IRS wasn't bothering with delinquent taxpayers anymore. Fail to pay your bill at Sears, and the company hires bill collectors or takes you to court even if it loses money. Imagine what would happen if word got around that Sears wasn't bothering to collect unpaid bills. Fail to pay your tag fee, and the county tows your car away or refuses to renew your license. But steal forty-two thousand dollars from your kids, and the system looks the other way or slaps your wrist. Runaway dads were giving the court the finger, and the system was winking at them.

Although she felt sorry for Pat, Linda's heart went out most of all to Pat's daughters. Mothers could usually survive; they could wait on tables if they had to, seek counseling, even find a new husband or lover. But what about the kids? They didn't choose their parents. They weren't responsible for the failure. And they weren't mature enough to understand or handle it. It wasn't easy to grow up an abandoned child. Linda knew that.

Convinced that the case was important and unusual, Linda introduced Pat to Kathleen Meredith, supervisor of Domestic Relations. Meredith was just as impressed, but for a different reason. She couldn't believe that Pat would still be fighting after sixteen years. Most women simply didn't have the mental and physical stamina, professional guidance, and money to do what Pat had done. And few, if any, would unearth a sixteen-year-old child-support order in perfect condition. Her case was, to put it mildly, intriguing.

Assuming Pat wanted to do something about the unpaid child support, Meredith quickly calculated the options: file for criminal prosecution on the grounds of desertion and nonsupport; seek a civil judgment for back child support based on the sixteen-year-old court order and then try to collect the money; or try both. None of the choices was simple.

Leading Pat from the intake office on the second floor to her own basement office, where they could explore the alternatives, Meredith bumped into a judge in the Juvenile and Domestic Relations court, Michael Valentine. Meredith knew Pat could find no better court ally than Judge Valentine. She would also be willing to bet a week's salary on what Judge Valentine would advise her to do.

"This lady's husband has been missing for sixteen years and she just found him," Meredith explained to Judge Valentine. "He's never paid child support. Linda had the file upstairs. Will you listen to her story and see if there's anything you can do?"

Soft-spoken and friendly, with sympathetic brown eyes that couldn't hide his underlying moral toughness, Judge Michael Valentine seemed born to sit on the bench of the Juvenile and Domestic Relations Court. With degrees in both foreign service and law, he had interned in Fairfax County's legal-aid program for the poor. After passing the bar, he slipped easily into a general practice centered around juvenile and domestic relations cases. In 1980, after ten years as an attorney, he was named to the bench in the court where he now practiced.

Married and the father of two, Judge Valentine believed children deserved a lot more than their parents, the county, and its prosecutors were giving them. He had appointed himself their spokesman. Surrounded by clerks, bailiffs, counselors, and child-support case files stuffed in tomato boxes, he had a reputation dispensing as much justice as the law allowed, as patiently and as quickly as he could.

On child-support day, Judge Valentine saw them all: Men arguing they weren't the fathers of children even though court-ordered blood tests showed a 99.8-percent probability they were. Women who had finally found their former husbands and were asking for court orders to attach their wages. Mothers seeking child support for the first time, and fathers saying they'd pay but not that much and only if the court guaranteed that the mothers wouldn't spend the money on themselves. Women making false charges out of spite. Mothers in tears, clutching unpaid bills, begging the court to make the fathers of their children pay the back child support they owed even if it was only twenty-five dollars a month.

Through it all, case after sad case of broken relationships, anger and mistrust, selfishness and poverty, Judge Valentine never seemed to lose sight of the absent children. "Do you have health insurance for your daughter?" he'd ask a mother with concern. Then, hoping to reach a settlement, he'd tell a father, "She's only asking for two hundred twenty-five dollars a month. Don't you know a good deal when you see one?"

A sense of urgency and fairness seemed to hang over his court. "Just tell me what you want me to do for you," he'd say to a woman who couldn't make up her mind how much child support she needed. "Turn around and look at all those people out there waiting for me to do something for them." He'd order a blood test in a paternity case and tell the couple to pay half of the fee each. "If the child turns out to be yours," he'd tell the man, "you'll reimburse her. If it doesn't, she'll reimburse you."

If Judge Valentine had learned anything in his years on the

bench, it was that delinquent fathers who didn't understand words like "justice" and "duty" knew the meaning of the word "jail." Threaten them with it and they mysteriously found money to feed their kids. If they didn't have it, their girlfriends, buddies, or new wives waiting outside the courtroom did. Valentine used that fear of the jail cell on fathers in contempt of court for not paying. "But Judge," they'd say like tape recordings, "I don't have four hundred dollars. And how am I going to get it if I'm in jail?"

Valentine showed no sympathy. After cheating their children and insulting his court, they deserved to be paid in kind. "I'm here to enforce the law," he'd lecture. "You were warned. You had a chance to appeal. Now you have only two choices—pay or lose your freedom. Do you have the four hundred dollars?" He'd pause. "You don't have it?" His face would redden and his voice turn to granite. "Then I sentence you to ten days in the county jail." Out would come the bailiff with handcuffs. Next case! The courtroom hum would break into ripples of excitement, and word would trickle back to Linda and the staff that Mike had just nailed another bastard.

Valentine was proud of his record. His jail sentences had scared as much as nine thousand dollars out of fathers who claimed to be broke, and he wished the law were even tougher. He had sent half a dozen outrageously delinquent fathers to jail for up to a year for criminal desertion and nonsupport. And even though other judges had commuted those sentences under appeal, he had made his point: Give the law the finger in my court, and it's jail time.

Judge Valentine was not without critics, many of them judges and prosecutors. They'd tell him, "It's not fair to put a father in jail just for not paying child support." He'd argue back: "We'd toss him in jail for drunk driving because he has endangered society, wouldn't we? Well, for him to neglect his children is far worse. They'll be deprived of a good education and be emotionally scarred. We'll see a lot of them right back here in juvenile court someday."

As he listened to Pat's story, Judge Valentine's face turned a delicate pink. In his fifteen years in juvenile and domestic relations work, he had rarely seen such blatant criminal desertion. Although he had sat on cases where a father had burrowed somewhere in Virginia for a few years before being caught, he had seldom dealt with a father who had skipped the state and assumed a new identity to avoid paying, or who had been found after sixteen years. He wanted James Parker before his bench. If Pat's facts were correct, he'd throw the book at him; the man had committed a crime for which he deserved to be punished. By listening to Pat Bennett, however, Valentine knew he had prejudiced himself. Should Parker come to Fairfax, some other judge would get him.

"This guy's a criminal," Valentine told Pat, who didn't know yet that he was a judge. "You can't let him get away with it. You *have* to do something. I suggest you file a petition for criminal desertion and nonsupport."

"Nothing will happen to him," Pat said. "The judge'll just slap his wrist and let him go."

"Oh no, he won't," Valentine said. "We'll extradite him back to Virginia to stand trial. He'll go to jail and still have to pay what he owes." He explained the system step by step:

Pat would first meet with a counselor who would help her fill out a petition to prosecute for criminal desertion and nonsupport. As soon as the petition came to the judge's desk, a warrant for Parker's arrest would be issued. The commonwealth attorney would recommend extradition to Virginia's governor, who would ask Florida's governor to send Parker back. The sheriff in Tampa would arrest him, and Fairfax County Police officers would fly down to get him and bring him back to face charges. Criminal desertion and nonsupport in Virginia carried a maximum penalty of one year in jail and a fine of one thousand dollars.

Judge Valentine promised Pat he'd do everything he could to speed the case up. He didn't tell her that, to his knowledge, the state of Virginia had never requested another state to extradite a runaway father for criminal desertion and nonsupport.

Still not realizing that Valentine was a judge, but encouraged by his confidence, Pat agreed to file. But first, she said, she wanted to see pictures of James C. Parker to make sure he was really David.

"When you need me," Valentine said, "I'll be here."

Linda was standing nearby listening. "Who is that man?" Pat asked her.

"That's Judge Michael Valentine," Linda said.

"Oh, my God!" Pat said. "And I told him that the judge wouldn't do anything to David even if he ever appeared in court."

"Don't worry," Linda laughed. "He's the best . . . and he's heard worse."

Pat left the Juvenile and Domestic Relations Court that afternoon with her mind made up. Finding the sixteen-year-old child-support order and talking to Judge Valentine had cleared her head. She wasn't going to let David get away with what he had done to her and her daughters. He had been summoned before the judge sixteen years ago to explain why he wasn't paying the fifty-dollar-a-week child support the court had ordered, but he had never kept that date. For all those years, she had been powerless to make him do so. No more. With the support of people who cared, like Linda, Kitty Meredith, and Judge Valentine, she'd have him brought back to face the same court. She'd listen to a judge shame and sentence him, and then enter the punishment into the record. Until she did that, David would still have some control over her life. Even if her daughters never received the forty-two thousand dollars their father owed them, it was important to set the record straight. It was time to tell them.

13

ANDREA AND MARCIA were in their rooms when Pat got home. With no easy way to begin, she called them both into the hallway and simply said, "I've got some news for you. It's about your father . . . I'm almost certain he's still alive and I think I've found him in Florida." Then she waited.

"Oh, my God, my God!" Marcia screamed. "He's still alive!" She put her hands over her face and began to cry hysterically. "I want to see him . . . I want to see him. Where is he? Give me his phone number. I have to call him—now!"

Trying to calm Marcia down, Pat explained that she couldn't phone her father because if she did, he'd probably run away again and they would never find him. But Marcia's feelings were deaf to logic, and when Pat refused to give her the phone number, she turned on her mother: "Why can't I call him?" she demanded. "He's *my* father. You have no right to keep his phone number to yourself. . . . Please, Mom!"

Andrea listened to her sister with disdain as if to say, "When are you going to grow up, Marcia?" Pat wasn't surprised. Now a cool, pencil-thin seventeen-year-old with dark brown hair, Andrea was conscious of her good looks and how to use them, and she had a sharp mind and a tongue to match. She received the news that her father was still alive with icy coldness, then anger.

"The asshole," she said. "He didn't stay around to raise me. He's not my father, and I don't care if he's dead or alive."

Pat knew Andrea meant every word, and allowed her to vent her feelings, wishing Christine could do the same.

"Put his ass in jail, Mom," Andrea said. "How can he get away with this? Can't you do something?"

"I'm working on it."

Pat explained Judge Valentine's recommendation. She'd probably go to Florida to identify their father for the sheriff, she said. The girls would see him when the police brought him back to Fairfax.

"No way!" Andrea exploded. "You're not going down there without me. And how come you told Christine first? That wasn't fair. I had a *right* to know."

The tense day ended with Marcia pestering her mother for her father's phone number, with Andrea threatening to tell his foster mother, and with more crying and silence and anger. If it's this bad now, Pat thought, what's it going to be like when they actually *see* him?

Private investigator Richard Froemming sat watching for Pat from inside his surveillance van parked in the lot of the Landmark Shopping Mall in Alexandria. It was early evening and he was waiting to give her the Parker pictures before going to work on another case.

Knowing how deeply David had hurt Pat, Richard admired her fierce determination to face her old feelings. He knew she had been in love with David the day he left her, and that the image of her former husband she had been carrying in her mind for sixteen years was of a young and handsome man who had silently taken his clothes out to his car and driven off. Richard knew the photographs of James Parker he had sitting on his dashboard would shock her, and he wasn't looking forward to handing them over. Showing clients pictures of the man or woman they had hired him to watch was never fun. There was always anger or tears. He felt Pat Bennett would be no exception. The photos would be her first undeniable evidence that David was really alive. All the facts she had unearthed so far were only pieces of an intellectual puzzle that happened to fit perfectly. But the pictures were real. They would hurt.

Richard watched Pat park her blue Oldsmobile and get out. In the spill of parking-lot lights, her face looked pale and drawn. She barely said hello as she climbed into the van and sat beside him. He gave her three clearly labeled manila envelopes—one with pictures of James C. Parker, one with photos of his house, and one with all the negatives. Her hands trembled slightly, Richard noted, as she opened the first envelope slowly, gingerly, as if it would break. The pack of photos slid out. She turned over each one in silence. Her face wrinkled in puzzlement as she studied the middle-aged man with a dark beard, sunglasses, the hint of a paunch, and a balding head. Reading disappointment and shock, Richard almost expected Pat to say, "Hey, Richard, Hager got the wrong man." Each time she leafed through the pictures, she'd stop at the shot of James Parker walking toward the entrance of the Holiday Inn in a long, sure stride, his head bent forward slightly, his arms swinging, and his shoulders back. But there were no tears or labored breathing, no "I finally caught you, you son of a bitch!" A kind of softness seemed to light her face. A youthfulness, Richard thought, as if she were reliving moments of happiness and feeling their loss.

"It's him," she finally said. "I'd know his walk anywhere."

When he was a Marine, she used to pick him out of a crowd of a hundred uniforms, so distinctive was his gait and bearing. Christine had inherited some of those same features. Pat's voice was sad, almost tender, as if she was giving up something precious.

"He's lost his hair," she said. "He's aged. He's forty years old."

Richard could feel Pat trying to bridge sixteen years in ten minutes. It was too much, too fast.

Thanking Richard quietly, Pat climbed back into her own car. She was numb. She felt no anger or hatred. No love or warmth. Just an indefinable sadness and shock. For sixteen years she had been scanning crowds, looking at faces in bus windows and in passing cars, searching for a handsome twenty-three-year-old former Marine who didn't exist anywhere but in her mind. Beneath the painful sense of void there was a great relief.

As she drove home, doubts began to return. Maybe Parker

wasn't David after all? Maybe she just wanted to believe he was David, just as she wanted to believe David had no other children? Torn with indecision, she stopped at her mother's house and showed the photos to her mother and sister.

"That's him," her mother said.

"Definitely him," her sister echoed.

But Pat was still not satisfied; she wanted to show the photos to one more person before she filed a petition to prosecute David.

Bill Daniels had just moved up from Florida, and Pat was anxious to see him again for a lot of reasons. She would always remember how he had supported her emotionally during those hard months after David had run away. But she could neither forget nor forgive Bill for giving David a place to stay when he ran out and for keeping David's whereabouts a secret, all the while knowing how humiliating it was for her to be on welfare. Over the years, she and Bill had often discussed what might have happened to David, and Bill had always seemed curious. She called and told him she had found David and how.

"Well, I'll be damned," he said.

"I've got pictures of him, Bill," she said. "Wait till you see them. You won't believe it."

Pat was in Boomerangs with half a dozen of her friends when Bill walked in. Trim and self-assured, with a hint of gray in his curly blond hair and mustache, he was hands-down the most handsome man in the place that night, Pat thought, but she gave no sign she recognized him.

Bill ordered a drink and soon spotted Pat seated at the bar, as they'd arranged. Leaning over a railing that separated one part of the bar from another, he said to her, "Excuse me, don't I know you from somewhere?"

Barely giving him a glance, Pat said huffily, "I've never seen you before. You guys are all alike—you think you can just walk in and pick anybody up."

"All I did was say hello," Bill said. "What's your problem, lady?"

"Really," Pat sniffed, "just because you look like Paul Newman you think every woman is going to fall at your feet."

Pat's friends gaped. The act was a bit of fun she and Bill

had cooked up on the phone. When the introductions were finally made, there was a gale of laughter.

Later, when the merriment died down, Pat excused herself. She and Bill found a quieter corner. After giving him a detailed account of her investigation, she handed Bill the package of photographs. "Tell me what you think."

Bill studied the pictures almost as intently as Pat had. Finally, he said, "It doesn't look like him, but it is."

"How do you know?" Pat asked. If she had any doubt, it was gone now.

"There"—Bill pointed—"look at the way he's standing. Look at how he's carrying his shoulders. I'd know that walk anywhere."

"You sure?" she asked.

"Positive."

It was the beard and the baldness that had made both of them hesitate. Pat fished out of her purse some old snapshots of David as well as the more recent pictures of Jim Parker that Lenora had sent her. Hunched over the photos spread out on the cocktail table and straining to see in the dim light, they compared noses and faces, noting that on Lenora's pictures, David's hair was already beginning to thin and his hairline had receded.

Bill turned serious. "Pat," he advised, "you better let sleeping dogs lie. You don't know what you're getting into. You don't know his frame of mind. You could answer a knock on the door and face a shotgun."

Bill wasn't trying to frighten her. His concern was genuine. The David who ran away, changed his name, and became a bigamist was not the David he grew up with. Bill felt he really didn't know the man in the photographs anymore. Weren't the newspapers full of stories about husbands and wives shooting each other in rages of anger or jealousy? He couldn't imagine that David would be pleased with Pat for having unmasked him. He was married. He had a business.

In fact, he was thinking that if she went down to Tampa, he wouldn't be surprised to get a call saying David had killed her and the girls and then committed suicide.

Misreading his concern, Pat thought Bill was feeling sorrier for David than for her and her daughters. Not about to back down, especially not because of anything Bill told her, she said she was going to Florida not only to identify David but to have him extradited to Virginia and hauled before a Fairfax judge for criminal desertion.

"Why mess up his life?" Bill argued. "Why not just call him up? The kids want to meet their father. So set up a time and place."

"Because he'll disappear again."

"You don't know that. Why not give him a chance? For God's sake, Pat, you're going to ruin his life."

"You just don't understand, do you, Bill?" Pat was getting angry now. "What about what he did to me and the girls? Should I just let him walk away from that?"

"He probably doesn't even have any money," Bill said. He was getting upset, too. Money was no reason to crush a man and ruin his life. "You can't leave well enough alone, can you? You know he's alive. You know where he is. You know what he looks like. So just drop it. Aren't you going to feel rotten if he has to spend a year in jail?"

Same old Bill, Pat thought. Still taking David's side no matter what. When you nab a burglar, you don't decline to press charges because he and his family might find jail a hardship.

"Come on, Bill," Pat said. "You don't really believe he's going to jail for deserting his kids, do you? Nothing ever happens to guys like that and you know it. He'll just stand before the bench, the judge will say, 'naughty, naughty,' the girls will see him—end of story. I'm sure he doesn't have any money, either."

Pat unleashed her anger on Bill. "You were a wimp, Bill. You took his part sixteen years ago. You took him in when you knew I was looking for him. I was just a pregnant kid on welfare. But you couldn't stand up to David and tell him he was wrong, could you? You're still a wimp."

"Well, I was wrong back then and I regret it," Bill admitted to Pat for the first time. In fact, he had always felt guilty about taking rent money from David when David's children were getting nothing. "But this is now."

Pat left Boomerangs that night with a lot to think about. It had been only a week since she had phoned Lenora, but it seemed like a whole summer. In those seven days, she had found David, located a sixteen-year-old court order, had an audience with a judge, looked at photographs of a husband she barely recognized, and watched her daughters try to cope with the shock that their father was still alive. During that hectic week, she had never really asked herself what extradition would do to David. Would it really ruin his life?

Pat felt torn. Whose advice should she follow? Judge Valentine's or Bill's? Bill's solution seemed simpler and less painful. But she knew it was short-term and ultimately unacceptable. To jail or not to jail, to pay or not to pay, to destroy or not to destroy were red herrings. The real issue was—to resolve or not to resolve. Put that way, she knew she had no choice. David had robbed her of inner peace for sixteen years, and she would never get it back until she confronted him personally and legally and gave her daughters the chance to do the same.

She would request extradition the next day, Pat decided. But first, she'd show her daughters the pictures of their father. As Andrea would say, they had a right to see them.

Pat called the girls into the kitchen later that night and told them she had photos of their father. Marcia almost ripped them out of her hand. "Let me see," she cried. "Let me see!" Christine was tentative and silent. Andrea was hostile and indifferent, as if afraid to admit she was curious.

If Pat was shocked at seeing David, she knew her daughters would be, too. Like her, they had been carrying an image of him in their minds for years. For Christine and Marcia, at least, it was a romantic one. Tall and good looking. Someone to be proud of. They had fantasized about him coming to their graduations or escorting them to a school activity, impressing all their classmates and friends. "See, we told you he was handsome," they would say.

At first, Christine, Andrea, and Marcia all reacted the same way. After a moment of silence, they appeared let down and somehow cheated.

"That's *him*?" they asked with the general disdain of youth for middle age. "That's him? He's almost bald! He's so old. Yuk, he's ugly."

As she listened to them work through their initial disappointment, Pat noted subtle differences in her daughters' responses. Christine seemed almost relieved that her father wasn't mounted on a white charger. The ordinary forty-year-old man she saw only reassured her that there was no reason why she should care about him or go out of her way to meet him.

To Andrea, the pictures also came as a relief, and Pat could hear her sigh inwardly. It would have been more difficult for Andrea to be angry at a father who was dashing. To her, his looks reflected what she felt. "What a sleazebag," she said.

Marcia seemed genuinely disappointed. She kept looking at the pictures trying to find something she could relate to. Finally, she said, "Christine stands just like him."

Pat smiled to herself. She had asked Richard to get pictures of James Parker so she could make a positive identification. She always knew she'd show them to the girls if he turned out to be David, but she had never thought about how the first glimpse of their father might affect them. She couldn't have been more pleased, for the pictures forced her daughters to face their real father and to come to terms with their fantasy father. With "I wonder what he looks like" out of the way, maybe they could start dealing with the deeper questions she knew were troubling them.

14

▼

No LONGER DOUBTING that James Parker was David, Pat went to see Nanette Hoback, an intake officer in the Juvenile and Domestic Relations Court, after dinner the following night. At Hoback's office Pat signed a sworn affidavit stating that David had failed to pay child support for sixteen years, and that he had gone to extremes to hide his identity by changing his name, Social Security number, and date and place of birth, as well as inventing a fictitious background. She requested in the affidavit that David, alias James C. Parker, be ordered to show cause why he should not be held in contempt.

The court moved as swiftly as a greyhound. The next day, Linda called Pat at work to say that a petition asking the court to prosecute David for criminal desertion and nonsupport was waiting in the intake office for her signature. Pat signed it that night after work. The next morning Judge Valentine issued a warrant for the arrest of David aka James C. Parker on the grounds that he "as a spouse and without just cause, deserted or willfully neglected, refused or failed to provide for the support and maintenance of his children under the ages of 18 years." At the same time, Judge Valentine asked Fairfax County's commonwealth attorney to recommend to the governor that Parker be extradited.

The Virginia code, like most state codes, provides for extradition for criminal desertion and nonsupport, but prosecutors have rarely invoked that power—with good reason. Whether a father owes his children one hundred dollars or forty-two thousand dollars, the law defines the crime as only a class-A misdemeanor. Criminal desertion is put on a par with shoplifting. By relegating desertion and nonsupport to the category of misdemeanor, lawmakers ensured that prosecutors would not take it seriously. The state of Missouri is an exception. There, nonsupport is a class-A misdemeanor "unless the actor leaves the state for the purpose of avoiding his obligations to support, in which case it is a class-D felony."

To Judge Valentine, the law was a sad commentary on how society values its children. He preferred a statute that made criminal desertion and nonsupport a felony once the amount a parent owed reached a certain limit. Valentine didn't care much whether lawmakers drew the line at one thousand or three thousand dollars, as long as there was a clearly defined line. Until then, runaway fathers would continue to ignore the toothless snarl of the law.

By sending his request for extradition to the commonwealth attorney, Judge Valentine was asking for an exception to Fairfax County practice, an exception he believed was justified by Parker's outrageous flouting of the law. Valentine knew that in Virginia petitioners like Pat Bennett had to exhaust all *civil* remedies in child-support cases before requesting extradition, unless civil proceedings "would be of no avail." Since Bennett's former husband had deserted her and their three daughters and had hidden under an assumed name for sixteen years, there was good reason to believe that civil action would be "of no avail" in her case.

Valentine had no illusions about how effective an out-of-state "civil proceeding" would be. James Parker would get a letter from the court, saying in effect: "Dear Sir: Your former wife has found you and wants you to appear in court so she can collect the forty-two thousand dollars you owe your children. She has a valid sixteen-year-old court order for the money, and there is a warrant for your arrest in Virginia should you decide to return. The warrant, however, is no good outside the state. If you appear and fail to pay, you can be prosecuted for criminal desertion and nonsupport, which carries a penalty in Virginia of up to one year in jail. The court is giving you thirty days to tell us what you intend to do.''

Of course, Parker would just sit right down, pull out his checkbook, and write a check for forty-two thousand dollars.

The final decision on extradition rested with Fairfax's commonwealth attorney. If he recommended extradition to the governor, Valentine knew the governor would routinely sign the order. Otherwise, it was impossible. The whole matter simply boiled down to, Would the commonwealth attorney, an elected official, be willing to set a county precedent in desertion and nonsupport cases?

As Fairfax County's commonwealth attorney for twenty years, Robert Horan was a powerful man, and not simply by virtue of his office. Over the years, the rotating crop of assistant prosecutors who had served under him had matured into an influential and loyal network of lawyers, judges, business executives, and politicians throughout the state. Horan loved big cases and headlines and had few critics in the media, in part because he was one of the finest prosecutors in Virginia. The prosecutor had a mind like a steel trap and could argue with logic as hard and as cold. Not many people in the state wanted to challenge him or find themselves on his bad side.

An exception to that rule was Judge Valentine, who fought with Horan constantly in private and in the press over how poorly the Commonwealth Attorney's Office treated the Juvenile and Domestic Relations Court. At the heart of the squabble was the role of the county prosecutors. Valentine wanted Horan to assign full-time assistant commonwealth attorneys to his court. Horan always refused. Across the Potomac, in Washington, there were twenty-seven full-time prosecutors in the family division, serving a population of 650,000. Serving just as many people, Fairfax County did not have a single full-time prosecutor in its family division. Although Valentine yelled and screamed, he got nowhere. If Horan didn't have enough assistants, Valentine would argue, he should hire more. After all, wasn't Fairfax the fifth-richest county in the nation? But Horan was as stubborn as he was bright. Sometimes the situation got so ridiculous that Valentine was forced to throw cases out of court because there simply weren't any prosecutors to try them, which left the judge angry, the police bewildered, and the victims wondering where they'd have to go to get justice.

If Judge Valentine was hard on Horan, child-support specialists were even tougher. They had learned that the Commonwealth Attorney's Office held a rigid party line: child support was a civil matter, not a criminal one; it was the job of Juvenile and Domestic Relations Court counselors to investigate all child-support cases and prepare all paperwork; if a prosecutor was eventually needed, he or she was not obligated to study the case file before entering the courtroom; prosecutors were not to get involved with the collection or enforcement.

In following that line of legal and administrative thinking, the Fairfax County Commonwealth Attorney's Office was, like James Parker, thumbing its nose at the law, which mandates that each state prosecute *diligently* and represent its clients at *all* hearings. In Fairfax County, despite the law, mothers routinely stood before the bench without legal counsel. And should the Commonwealth Attorney's Office manage to send a prosecutor to handle a case, the lawyer was generally one of the least experienced on the staff, someone profoundly ignorant of the complex and fluid body of child-support law. To compound that ignorance, the assigned prosecutor rarely reviewed the case file until a few minutes before entering the hearing and facing an experienced defense attorney. Unembarrassed by his lack of preparation—especially since most hearings involving children were private and thus closed to peers and the press—the prosecutor then proceeded to anger by his incompetence the judge who sat on the case.

Through bitter experience, Fairfax child-support experts had learned to expect the Commonwealth Attorney's Office to push child support to the bottom of its list of concerns: chasing delinquent fathers reaped few if any political benefits.

As he signed his letter requesting extradition, Judge Valentine wasn't sure how Horan would handle the Bennett case, which required his personal signature. To make sure his letter would not end up in a slush pile, Valentine called Horan's right-hand man, Assistant Commonwealth Attorney Britt Richardson.

After summarizing the Bennett story, he told Richardson that he knew Horan did not recommend extradition in desertion and nonsupport cases on principle, but that Bennett was a clear exception. "A perfect case," he said.

To Judge Valentine's delighted surprise, Richardson agreed. "It seems to me that this is the kind of case we ought to do something about," he told the judge. "I'll take care of it."

When she got home after signing her petition to prosecute David, Pat called Beth, an old friend who had also been abandoned with an infant son by her husband. Like David, her husband had vanished, and Beth had not heard from him for more than ten years. Pat and Beth had become like sisters in spirit.

"Beth, I found David," Pat blurted.

"But why?" Beth was genuinely confused, for she knew Pat had asked the Social Security Administration for a death-benefits hearing. "I don't understand what in the hell you're doing. First, you want him declared dead. Now you're telling me you found him."

"I'm going to have him arrested for desertion," Pat said.

"I can't believe you're doing this," Beth said. There was a touch of panic in her voice. "For the first time in your life, everything is going well. Now you're going to— This makes me sick to my stomach. I can't talk about it. I don't even want to hear about it."

"But you don't understand—"

"I can't talk about it!"

Beth hung up, leaving Pat shaken. Her closest friend, who knew what it was like to be deserted and to bring up a child without knowing where the father was, wouldn't even hear her out. Feeling abandoned herself, she called Beth back, but her friend refused to talk and hung up a second time.

Realizing that Beth's rejection must have something to do with her own former husband, Pat called a third time. "I've *got* to talk to you," she said. "Don't hang up on me, Beth. Why are you acting this way?"

"I simply don't want to talk about it," Beth said.

"Well, I think I'm hitting close to home. You don't want to face your own past, and you're angry at me because I'm facing mine!"

Pat waited for Beth to slam the receiver down again. She knew she was on the right track, and she sensed she had just hit a nerve. There was a long silence, then Beth said quietly, ''There's more to it than that.''

What was really bothering her was that her son, who was Marcia's age, was begging her to find his father so he could meet him for the first time. But Beth kept putting him off because she didn't think she could go through with it. Then Pat called to say she had just done for her daughters what Beth's son was asking her to do.

''I can't,'' Beth said. ''I just can't. Please don't call anymore.''

Pat was crying when she hung up. Both for herself and for Beth. She realized that the shared experience that had formed the foundation of their friendship had just shattered it.

Beth was the first woman Pat had met who seemed threatened by her refusal to let runaway fathers hide, but she knew there would be others, and she had begun to understand why. Before Pat had decided to look for David, she had been a victim with whom most women could identify—dumped on, wronged, and hurt by a husband, and abused by a legal system created and run by men. But by challenging David and the system, she became a threat to those women who wouldn't, or couldn't, do the same. To them she was a victimizer not a victim. A cold, castrating, greedy bitch.

Although saddened and shaken by Beth's rejection, Pat was not about to call Judge Valentine and say she wanted to back out. Instead, over the weekend, she sketched out a plan.

Monday morning, she would call the Tampa sheriff to let him know she was coming and why, and to ask his full cooperation. She knew this would be dangerous because Florida sheriffs and their deputies had earned a reputation for helping runaway and delinquent fathers escape. But she felt she had little choice. With the help of Judge Valentine, she would make sure the warrant for Parker's arrest would not be on the national computer listing lest someone see it and alert David.

A week later, July 2, she would fly to Tampa with Victoria in tow as her attorney in case David fought extradition and her friend Stewart, a former Washington Redskin, as her bodyguard. Extradition order in hand, she would ask the sheriff to arrest Parker that night. The next day, July 3, she'd attend the extradition hearing and identify James Parker as David. Then she'd bask on the beach over the Fourth of July and return to Washington on the fifth in time for David's hearing in Juvenile and Domestic Relations Court on Friday, July 6. Christine, Andrea, and Marcia would see their father when he arrived in Fairfax, in a private conference room she hoped, instead of in court or in jail. But if they had to meet him for the first time in handcuffs, or behind bars, or facing a judge, then that's the way it would have to be.

The plan was clean, simple, and fast. It would all be over in just seven more days.

Pat made reservations on Piedmont Airlines for herself, Victoria, and Stewart. On Monday she called the sheriff in Tampa. He listened to her story and promised to be ready and waiting with cuffs. "It's very important that nothing go wrong or he'll disappear again," Pat said.

"Don't worry, I won't say a word," the sheriff promised.

All Pat needed now was the extradition order. A preprinted form. Just fill in the blanks, Mr. Horan, and ask the governor to sign.

If Pat was comfortable with her plan, the six counselors at the Juvenile and Domestic Relations Court were not. The male counselors tended to agree with Pat's decision to sic the law on David. The women, especially Kitty Meredith, were cautious, more concerned about how justice would affect Pat and her daughters than about justice itself. Meredith recognized that Pat craved satisfaction and resolution more than money, and she respected those deep needs. She felt Pat had a right to see her former husband stand before the bench, watch the court peel away the layer of lies, and hear a judge say he was a criminal and had to pay. The troubling question was, In this case, was justice worth the risk?

Meredith was worried. It was possible that prosecuting her former husband might resolve nothing for Pat. In fact, it might awaken in her a bitterness and thirst for revenge that could dog her for the rest of her life. In the end, she might have less peace than she had before. Meredith had watched that happen to other women. Just seeing their former husbands and listening to them make excuses for their criminal neglect often turned them into bitter women, thirsting for legal and financial blood.

Kitty Meredith was worried even more about Christine, Andrea, and Marcia. They had adjusted to being abandoned sixteen years ago and had learned to live without a father. True, they would be scarred for life and might always feel a sense of loss, hurt, and self-doubt. But each had probably created a fantasy father all her own. What would it do to them if they met their father for the first time in jail, in handcuffs, or standing before the court like a criminal? Was Pat taking pleasure in turning her daughters against David, using them to punish him? As volatile teenagers, they were quite capable of turning against Pat at any point, accusing her of a vendetta. They could even end up taking their father's side against her saying, "Now we know why he abandoned us. You drove him away."

Or it could go the other way. Meredith knew that if Pat could become bitter and angry in her search for justice, her children could too. If they did, any hope of a relationship with the only father they had, no matter how bad they might think he was, could be dashed. They could even go through a period of hating all men.

Then again, it could all turn out well. In Meredith's business, not everyone who skated on thin ice fell through. In the end, all she could do was encourage people to test the ice before they put their skates on. She was prepared to explore the risks with Pat if she wanted to talk about them, but Pat never opened up. All she had said was, "Kitty, do you think I should do this?" Sensing that Pat's mind was already made up and that she was just looking for support, Kitty replied, "Pat, you'll have to decide this one for yourself."

Pat took leave on Monday, July 2. Everything was ready but Robert Horan's signature on the request to extradite. Her plane left for Tampa at 5:45 that evening. Victoria was on hold. Stewart was ready to go. Her bags were packed and sitting by the kitchen door next to the carport. She was keyed up and kept calling Linda every hour to see if Horan had signed yet. One moment, she was pleased that it would soon be over. The next, she was afraid something might go wrong. Afraid of David. Afraid of herself.

At four o'clock, Linda finally called with news. "Horan has a problem with the papers," she said. "He won't sign."

Pat was crushed. She had always assumed that if she ever

found David, Virginia would see to it that he faced the judge. She never believed he'd really be punished, but she never doubted she'd have her day in court.

Pat called Piedmont and canceled her reservations. Then she hung up the phone and cried. "Nobody cares," she sobbed. "Nobody cares!"

15

▼

PAT BROKE THE news to Victoria Gordon, who was home in bed recuperating from a jaw operation and bored to distraction. Although she was in pain, her doctor couldn't find wires and screws strong enough to stop her from talking.

An independent woman, Victoria graduated from law school in Fairfax and hung out her own shingle. She didn't want to spend years doing someone else's research at a lawyer factory in Washington. Finding corporate law cold and remote from life, she easily slipped into the practice of family law. A high-energy person who lived on adrenaline, Victoria didn't have the patience to wait her turn in court. Born for the stage or the soapbox, front and center and before the bench was where she wanted to be.

It came as no surprise to Victoria that Horan had refused to sign the extradition papers. She had called him earlier in the day to say that Pat had airline reservations that evening for Tampa, where the sheriff was waiting. Horan spouted like a sperm whale because Pat had dared to assume he would sign. Victoria tossed all the arguments in her arsenal at him:

Pat would lose months if she sought civil redress as Horan demanded, instead of criminal sanctions as Judge Valentine suggested. James Parker might flee, and if Pat Bennett ever found him again, Marcia would probably have turned eighteen, making it even more difficult to seek justice. Even if Parker didn't flee, the Florida judge might reduce the amount of unpaid child support. Finally Victoria assured him that if the cost of extradition posed a problem for the county, Pat Bennett had volunteered to pay the cost herself.

Horan wouldn't budge.

In one sense, Victoria was relieved. She thought that Pat's game plan was unrealistic and made no legal sense. Ninety percent emotion and 10 percent strategy. For one thing, it was unlikely that Parker would be arrested one day and face an extradition hearing the next. If by some judicial witchcraft he did, Victoria felt she didn't have enough documentation to prove David's identity absolutely if James Parker contested it. Besides, her jaw was so sore that the only tempting thing about Tampa was the beach.

Victoria's alternate plan was, she thought, much more practical: get Horan to sign the extradition request as soon as possible; have Parker arrested immediately; then, after a preliminary bond hearing, put off the extradition fight for thirty days to give her time to prepare her case.

Pat sounded so disappointed and angry after Horan's resounding "No" that Victoria put in an immediate conference call to Judge Valentine so they could assess the damage and discuss what to do next. Valentine and Victoria did all the talking.

Like Victoria, Judge Valentine was angry with Horan's decision, but not shocked. As far as he was concerned, the commonwealth attorney had just kicked the state of Virginia in the legal groin. When Victoria told Valentine she had tried to lean on Horan earlier that day, he was frankly annoyed.

"Why did you do that?" he scolded.

"I wanted to make sure the request was signed," Victoria explained.

"Well, he might have signed it without noticing whom it was for," Valentine said. "But you just called his attention to it."

Valentine told Victoria that as far as extradition was concerned, he had done everything he could without jeopardizing his position. The rest was up to her and Pat. He'd always be there if they needed him.

Too angry and depressed to be alone, Pat drove over to

Victoria's townhouse more as a friend than a client. Victoria switched on her new word processor, and she and Pat huddled in front of the screen, pouring out their frustration in a letter to Horan—nine single-spaced pages of angry words. Written in Pat's name, the letter ended: "I believe there is a difference between revenge and justice. I seek the latter. . . . The number [of men] who have fled to avoid child support is a disgrace in this country. I want to make a statement to all such men who believe that risking the penalties of the law is a better alternative to meeting their legal obligation to pay child support. Mr. Horan, I ask you, please give this request your utmost consideration." Although the letter made them both feel better, they didn't bother to revise or mail it because they knew it wouldn't help.

Since Victoria was in pain, Pat suggested that the attorney spend the night at her house. And since next to talking, eating was Victoria's favorite pastime, Pat ordered a giant pizza. Forced by her aching jaw to exercise some culinary imagination, Victoria scraped the topping off her half of the pizza, put it in a blender, and settled down to a serious evening of drinking pizza and looking for new ways to get Pat her day in court.

The next morning, Pat took Victoria out for a breakfast of blueberry pancakes floating in maple syrup. "I don't know any other attorney," Victoria said through slightly clenched teeth, "who'd work for pizza and blueberry pancakes."

Emotion caught up with Pat the following weekend at a pool party. Buoyed by a few drinks, the feeling she had been suppressing rose to the surface like bubbles and burst. Fortunately, Bill Daniels was there, and he did what he could to help her through it.

She was determined to be so tough, Pat told Bill. After David ran away, she had vowed never to depend on anyone again. Yet she felt like a little girl who needed her father's arms around her. She didn't think she could wear a brave face for even one more day. Her daughters and her friends thought she could handle anything, but she couldn't any longer. She was so tired—of carrying the whole burden alone, of always struggling, of fighting. And she was afraid too. Afraid of what she had found. Afraid of herself. Afraid of what she'd

have to do next. Afraid of how it would all end. Now it was
too late to turn back.

"I'm so scared," she sobbed as Bill held her. "Oh, my
God, what have I done?"

But there was more to it than just being scared. Pat knew
she should be angry at David. She should want him to suffer,
go to jail, pay in pain and in kind. Instead, she found herself
feeling sorry for him, and that made her mad at herself. She
didn't want to feel anything *for* David, only something *at*
him. Why did everything have to be so emotionally complicated when it was all so logical and simple?

Bill was touched. In the twenty years he had known Pat,
he had never seen her afraid before. And although he had
watched her cry many times, it was never the kind of weeping
that grabs the body and doesn't want to stop. For a moment,
she was the young Pat he had known when she was dating
David. The little girl without pretense, unsure of herself, vulnerable.

After he had seen Pat's pictures of Jim Parker, Bill had had
a long talk with his mother and she had taken Pat's side. She
made Bill change his mind—to a point. David should be
caught and punished, he concluded, but Pat was going about
it the wrong way. What she was feeling now was just a taste
of what was to come. Bill thought that she was obsessed with
confronting David and bringing him to justice even though
she was confused about how she felt toward him. Since she
wasn't about to give up, the best thing he could do would be
to support her.

Bill held her until the last sob ended, then said, "I understand, Pat. I was wrong to try and put you off. Go through
with it. I knew from the moment you told me you found
David that you wouldn't give up."

For the next two months, Pat called the Commonwealth
Attorney's Office almost every day, asking to speak to Robert
Horan. She never got through. Assistant Commonwealth Attorney Mindy Norton was assigned to return her calls. Although she was sympathetic, Norton firmly held to the party
line. Pat sensed that Norton felt David ought to be extradited
but couldn't say so because she had to be loyal to her boss.
Pat was right in a way. Norton had told Judge Valentine that

she would prosecute the case herself should Horan decide to recommend extradition.

Victoria also called Mindy Norton, whom she had known at law school. She had seen Norton work in court many times and found her a good, conscientious prosecutor, totally professional and cautiously friendly. Norton told Victoria that Pat had sent so many mixed signals that Norton was no longer sure why Pat wanted the county to extradite her former husband. First it sounded as if she had a personal vendetta against the man, Norton said. Then it seemed as if she might drop the charges against him if she ever got him into court. One minute it sounded as if all she wanted was justice; the next, as if she was merely using the state to get the man back to Virginia so her children could see him.

Victoria tried to convince Norton that Pat was balanced and serious, and that her motives, although complex, were honest.

"Well, I'll have to talk to Bob," Norton said. But she didn't sound as if she'd be talking very loudly.

Pat dug in for a long siege. She eventually got through to Britt Richardson, who was just as firm as Norton but not as sympathetic. After listening to her and explaining Horan's position, he finally said, "We've already spent too much time on this case. We have rapes, murders, and burglaries to deal with."

"What about the taxpayers?" Pat argued. "Doesn't the state want its money back?"

Pat had been on welfare for two years because David had refused to support his children. In effect, he had pocketed more than ten thousand dollars of the taxpayers' money. If she could collect the forty-two thousand dollars David owed his children, the state would be first in line for its share.

Richardson was annoyed. "Mr. Horan asked me to call you and to say *for* him that he will not see you and that his decision is final. He thought you understood that from previous conversations."

Pat would not let Richardson off that easily. "It makes no sense for me to file for civil action. My former husband has fled before and he'll run again. Virginia law covers situations like that. I've drafted a letter to the state attorney general and—"

"We're independent here and can't be swayed by the attorney general's office. It's the policy of the governor that all other means have to be exhausted before he'll agree to extradition."

"The IRS prosecutes tax cheaters to keep the rest of the country honest," Pat continued. "Can't you use this case as an example for others?"

"We don't make an example of one person!" Richardson's voice was getting louder, higher, and more emphatic.

"You sound angry and defensive," Pat said.

"Well, I'm not," he said and hung up.

Not convinced that Robert Horan, an elected official, stood above political pressure, Pat decided to try a little muscle as a last resort. If logic and pleading wouldn't work, maybe power would. Both she and Victoria spoke to Tyke Miller in the attorney general's office in Richmond. He was anxious to extradite. Virginia had a good national reputation for collecting support for its children, and Miller wanted to protect it. "You have Horan call me," he told Pat. "I'll tell him that if he signs the request we will definitely recommend extradition to the governor."

Next, Pat leaned on State Senator Clive DuVal, one of the most powerful politicians in northern Virginia. If you want something done, the word went, go see Clive. They spoke for an hour. "How could anyone just walk out on those children like that?" DuVal kept saying. In the end, he promised to talk to Horan on her behalf.

Pat waited a few days, then called Horan again. This time she got through. "I told your attorney to exhaust all civil remedies," he told her. He spoke as if he were in court, loud, self-assured, and righteous. "You're making this whole thing more complicated than it really is."

"If I file civilly, it'll take a year if not longer," Pat pleaded. By that time, Marcia would be eighteen, and because Pat would no longer have any minors, Horan would not have to represent her by law.

"Well, then, you better get started," he said.

"If I do, they'll give him notice. They'll send him a letter. He'll just disappear again."

"There are ways to handle that," Horan said obliquely.

"I realize you know more than I do about these matters,"

Pat said, fanning his ego. "The attorney general's office said it would recommend extradition if you asked for it."

"I don't know how they can say that." Horan was getting impatient. "We don't extradite for this."

"But would you talk to Tyke Miller?"

Grudgingly, Horan agreed.

"If he says he'll recommend extradition to the governor, will you then sign off on it?"

Horan didn't answer. Pat asked the question two more times. Still no answer. "I'll talk to him," was all Horan would promise.

"Would it help if I got ten thousand signatures on a petition to the governor?" Pat pressed. She had already drafted a letter and was ready to go door-to-door to get signatures. Even if it took a month of evenings, she knew she could do it. But Horan wouldn't answer that question either.

"Mr. Horan, I am *not* going to go away!" Pat burst out in frustration. It was the only threat she had uttered. "This case is important. It will help other women. And I know it will get a lot of publicity—"

"This case isn't going to help anybody," Horan said and hung up sounding as angry and defensive as Richardson.

Although Horan talked to Miller, it made little difference; he wouldn't change his mind. Pat was left with no choice. It was the civil route or nothing. Where it would lead her, how long it would take, and what it would cost in emotion and money, she didn't know. One thing was certain—she was not about to let one commonwealth attorney stop her now.

16

As SHE HAD done so often in the past when facing a crisis or in need of strength, Pat decided to visit the site of the old farmhouse that had been so special to her as a child. She needed to hear what the place had to say to her now more than ever before. As soon as she turned onto Robin Lane, Pat began to feel a gentle sadness. It was the ghost of her childhood drawing her back as it had so often done before.

Her blue Oldsmobile bounced over the potholes past the row of ugly brick houses built just before she had moved away, almost thirty years ago. When the blacktop took a sharp turn to the left, she kept straight ahead, edging the car slowly down the same dirt road she had walked as a child. She came out into an open field surrounded by woods. Behind the trees in the distance stretched a ribbon of fast-food places and gas pumps, and beyond them the beltway connecting Washington, Maryland, and Virginia.

The twin holly trees with ice-cream-cone crowns still stood side by side in the empty field, but the old house, no longer worth the cost of repairs, was long since gone. So were the small red barn where she had played and the pear tree she used to climb.

She got out of the car, stood in the tall grass where the vegetable garden had once been, and gazed slowly about her.

Other than a thinning of the treeline and a new school which had gobbled up part of the woods, the old place looked the same.

She was in Camp Springs, Maryland, a few miles southeast of Washington. Her parents had moved there from Georgetown more than thirty years ago before Georgetown was an address to brag about. At thirty-five dollars a month, the farmhouse had been a bargain even then and a relief from an apartment too small for a family of five. Sitting on cinder blocks and covered with fake brick siding, it had a large living room and kitchen, and two bedrooms upstairs. Bare lead pipes ran across the ceilings and down the walls, and a single wood-coal stove in the kitchen had struggled to heat the upstairs in the winter and usually failed. Renting that place, half a century old, while her father worked as an auto-parts salesman by day and a government electrician on the four-to-midnight shift, was the only way her parents could provide space for their growing family and still save for a down payment on a proper house of their own.

Pat had shared a bedroom with her younger sister, while her older brother slept on the downstairs couch in the winter and, in the summer, on a daybed on the porch, which her father had closed in.

It hadn't taken Pat long to learn that in some ways her family was poor, for all her neighbors and classmates, it seemed, lived in nicer homes. And just a mile behind the woods lay Manchester Estates, a manicured reminder that not everyone's house sat on cinder blocks.

But in other ways, important to a child, she understood she was rich. A one-hundred-acre farm ringed her house, turning her backyard into a private park on the edge of a cramped and noisy city. In the fields all around grew grass so thick and tall that she could weave caves and tunnels to hide in. The oak and maple woods that filtered out the hum of nearby traffic were a magic forest through which trickled a dark and mysterious creek. There were frogs and turtles and crayfish. And in back of the woods to the south was White's Store, where a nickel bought the world.

Each spring her father had ploughed an acre next to the house with a cultivator rigged up to an old car motor, and the family pitched in, planting, hoeing, and picking. Her

strawberry patch, her friends told her, was the biggest in all
of Camp Springs, and that made her feel proud. When the
summer began to wane, there'd be days upon days of canning
the fruit and vegetables and jams she'd eat all winter.

Standing there now in the summer of 1984, Pat was intensely aware that the field where the house had stood was
not just a plot of ground where she had once lived, but the
place that had molded her into the woman she was. Her deepest feelings she could trace back to the old farm. What she
craved most in life, she found there. And whatever drove her
onward had its roots in those five acres. It was as if she could
read her whole life there, where she had been, where she was
going, and why.

She remembered how she had prayed the rosary each night,
kneeling on the hard wooden floor next to her mother as vigil
lights cast spooky shadows on the walls. They had asked God
for another baby and a new house of their own, and to send
her father home safely from work. Far from comforting her,
the Hail Marys only reminded her each night that maybe her
father wouldn't be back, that maybe he'd get into an accident
and go to a hospital, that maybe he'd die. A nagging fear she
didn't understand as a child but understood now, tugged at
her. She remembered how sometimes, when her father was
late, she'd hear her mother crying in the next bedroom, how
she'd go to comfort her, and how together they'd drop to their
knees. Beads in hand, each with a different terror, they'd
pray, ''Please, God, bring him home safely.'' God always
heard that prayer, but the fear of being left alone never went
away.

For the first time, standing at the old place, Pat understood
that when David ran away, leaving her pregnant with two
other babies, he had made that childhood fear a reality.

Pat had cried when her family had moved twenty-five miles
around the beltway into Virginia to a real house on their own
suburban acre. For her parents, the move was a hard-earned
slice of the American dream; for Pat it was the greatest loss
of her young life, and even now, almost thirty years later, the
memory of it brought tears to her eyes.

Even as an eleven-year-old she had understood she was
losing a freedom she'd never find in her new home, and it
struck her as odd that one of the things they had been praying

the rosary for every night for five years, and which God had finally given them, could cause so much pain. Her parents thought the memory of the old place would fade for her as it had for her sister, but it never did. She missed it so much that when she got her driver's license at sixteen, she drove right over to Robin Lane.

Now, with an extraordinary vividness, Pat remembered a vacation in Indianapolis when she was four years old. Her grandparents had taken the children to the State Fair, and like kids everywhere, they had run straight for the ferris wheel, hoping to see the whole world from its top. But when it was time to sit in the wooden seat and let the attendant snap the holding bar in place, Pat had become too frightened to get on. Instead, she stood below holding her grandmother's hand while her brother, sister, and two cousins rode the giant circle round and round. She listened to them squeal and laugh and returned their waves feeling ashamed and jealous.

Those childhood emotions came back to her now as she stood where the old house used to be, wishing she could fly back in time to the State Fair and take that ride after all. She remembered how timid and shy she had remained for nearly twenty-five more years, still a "fraidy cat," until one day she recognized that the fear of the ferris wheel had run much of her life. It was then that she made up her mind never again to refuse a ride simply because she was afraid. From that point on, challenging the ferris wheel fear had meant meeting issues head on and refusing to let others control her life. And now that she had found David, she was not about to back off from the ride, whatever might happen.

But more than for herself, Pat was afraid for her daughters. Warnings from friends to the contrary, she felt she owed them the chance, if they wanted it, to talk to the father they never knew. But she sensed all too clearly that his would be a painful gift to them. They seemed almost too cavalier about it now, unaware of how angry and hurt they really were. Like her, they would have to face their feelings or bury them even deeper. Either way, there lay a very real danger.

She worried about Christine, who seemed to bottle up everything inside, to push away the memory of her father so that she wouldn't have to face the pain. Would meeting him finally resolve things for her or tear open old wounds that would never heal?

She worried about Andrea, who seemed angry at the whole world and wrapped herself in an armor of indifference toward her father. Would seeing him help her face that anger or encourage her to bury it beyond reach?

She worried about Marcia, so volatile and sensitive. Her need for love and acceptance was as strong as Christine's withdrawal and Andrea's anger. How would she react if her father rejected her as a teenager the way he had rejected her as an unborn child?

It was just plain wrong, the old place was reminding her, for the world to be indifferent to the injustice done to her and her children, or to say by its silence, "It's okay, David, that you ran out on your daughters, reduced them to poverty, robbed them of opportunity, and covered them with layers of insecurity, guilt, and fear. It's okay."

It's *not* okay, the old place was telling her. Fathers couldn't just be allowed to desert helpless children. If love and responsibility wouldn't shame them into supporting their families, then fear of the law should. You owe that much to your daughters, the old place was saying, and you owe it to other abandoned and hurting children.

As she climbed back into her car, Pat was aware of a profound upheaval within her. The tears were coming again but under them she felt a new strength and wholeness. Part of it was the energy of this place that fused past, present, and future for her. But part, she knew, came from a new bond she felt with mothers and children everywhere who were abandoned and suffering and voiceless.

Pat drove slowly back down Robin Lane to the beltway. Facing David and demanding justice was her only real choice.

17

▼

JUDGE VALENTINE KNEW that if Pat Bennett tried to thread her way through civil court, she'd need more than Victoria Gordon to guide her. Child-support laws and procedures were not only complex and confusing; they varied so much from state to state that it was hard to find two people who'd agree on anything. And one small mistake could cost Bennett months.

Judge Valentine could think of no better guide than Betty Murphy, who had been wading through the legal swamp for years. She already knew more about the child-support tangle than most judges and attorneys, and he admired her dedication and guts. He frequently attended the meetings of the support group she had founded called VOICES—Virginians Organized to Insure Children's Entitlement to Support.

Valentine met Murphy in the courthouse one day not long after Horan had slammed the door on Pat's extradition request. "Betty, there's a case you ought to look at," he told her. "I can't give you the name of the woman, but I can tell you who her attorney is—Victoria Gordon."

Not one to sit back when she could help another deserted mother, Murphy found Victoria and through her, Pat. Over the next year, she shared what she knew, offered suggestions, and encouraged Pat—for free. The picture she drew was dismal but realistic.

If Pat wanted to collect and have David face a judge, she had two basic choices within the civil court system: hire an attorney to pursue David in Florida under the laws of that state, or ask the state of Virginia to help her collect. If she asked Virginia's assistance, she could do it through the counselors at the Fairfax County Juvenile and Domestic Relations Court, or through the Virginia State Child Support Office.

If Pat chose to get help from court counselors, as Betty Murphy had, Kitty Meredith would interview her, gather the necessary documents, and then set a hearing date.

If everything went well, Pat would be in court in two months.

After a brief hearing to review the validity of her facts and documents, the judge would order that a notice be sent to the circuit court in Pasco County, Florida, saying that Fairfax was requesting its assistance under the Uniform Reciprocal Enforcement Support Act (URESA), passed in 1958 and strengthened in 1968 and 1984. Fairfax would also send David a statement specifying that he owed more than forty-two thousand dollars and was still under court order to pay current child support.

If Pat was lucky, phase two would also take two months.

The circuit court clerk in the county where David lived would receive Fairfax's notice and send it to the prosecuting attorney. If Pat pestered the prosecutor's office during this critical phase, refused to be intimidated, threatened to call in the media, or was lucky enough to find at least one person who cared, she might get action in six months.

Even if the prosecutor decided to move on her case within a week, the nightmare was just beginning. Since David would be notified that Pat was after him, he could simply move out of the county that had subpoenaed him to appear in court. In that case, the prosecutor could either send the notice back to Fairfax saying David didn't live there any more, or could request the new county to take over. Since such transfers required time and paperwork and yielded few votes at the polls, most prosecutors refused. If the notice came back to Fairfax, the court would then have to redraft and resend papers to the court in the new county and to David. David could migrate across Florida until Pat and the court gave up. With each refiling, he would gain another six months to a year.

Even if David lived at the address Pat furnished to the court and made no attempt to move, Florida law required the sheriff or his deputy to personally serve the subpoena. Since David would be given advance notice, he could elude them a hundred different ways, enlisting the help of his friends, employer, or business associates. Mothers trying to subpoena delinquent dads faced this all the time.

If David was actually served, he wouldn't even have to appear in court. The prosecutor could negotiate with him or his attorney over the phone without notifying Pat. Then—again without notifying her—the prosecutor could settle with David the amount of arrearage he actually had to pay, and when and how he would pay it. David could end up paying as little as twenty dollars a month on the arrearage; at that rate, Marcia would be 187 years old when she got her last check. Because the prosecutor didn't have to notify her, Pat could lose her right to appeal the settlement. Thousands of women before her had been ill served by prosecutors who, anxious to get the cases settled without fuss, often bargained away essential support for children.

Finally, if Pat's case ever reached a courtroom, the prosecutor would not have to notify her of the time and place, even if she specifically asked to be told. And the hearing judge could make whatever demands he wanted from David, including cutting as much arrearage as he wished and lowering the amount of support to be paid in the future. It happened all the time.

Although Pat would have a constitutional right to appeal any judge's decision, she might never get the chance. There is a specified time within which she must appeal, even though there is no specified time within which Florida must inform her of the court's decision.

If Pat wanted the state of Virginia to help her collect, her other option involved the Virginia State Child Support Office. There the collection process would be essentially the same, except she'd have to pay a processing fee based on her income and assets, and it would take longer.

Collecting from Florida, moreover, might prove difficult. Florida had long been considered by child-support specialists to be one of the hardest states in which to collect child support. ''Florida is a cesspool of runaway fathers and deadbeat dads from all over the country,'' as one expert put it. Florida laws sound good on paper, but the old-boy network among prosecutors, judges, clerks, sheriffs, and their deputies is stronger than the pull of justice. And the State Office of Child Support Enforcement charges children hefty fees.

After listening to everyone, Pat Bennett decided to hire her own attorneys to corral David into court, not just to keep control over her case, but to make sure her daughters got a chance to see him. It would not be easy. The entire legal deck was stacked against her. She would need one attorney in Virginia and another in Florida. With luck and a few sympathetic people in the right places, she just might be able to resolve her case within a year, while Marcia was still a minor.

18

▼

TERRY KELLOGG, PAT'S cousin, passed through Washington at the end of September on his way to conduct a family therapy workshop in Lancaster, Pennsylvania. Since Pat had not seen him for more than twenty years, she was looking forward to his visit. The timing was perfect for the Bennett household was tense with growing doubts and fears.

A low-key, nontraditional family-systems therapist who wasn't afraid to give advice, Terry was a good listener, and his approach to what was happening to Pat and her daughters, and why, was fresh. Terry disagreed with traditional Freudians, who believe that the root of an individual's problem lies within deeply buried conflicts of the person, and that these conflicts are related to early experiences with one's parents. He believed that problems were a symptom of a disturbance of emotional forces deep within the family itself. If you wanted to know why you were feeling or acting a certain way, family-systems therapists advised, don't focus on yourself or your childhood, or on your mother and father. Look at your whole family and how each member in it acts and reacts.

After they had brought each other up to date on family and careers, Pat told Terry how she had found David, what she planned to do, and why. She had chatted with her cousin off and on over the years, and he had always been easy to talk to, understanding, and helpful. Now she poured out her doubts and fears.

Her biggest concern, Pat told Terry, was her daughters. Now that they were closer to a meeting with their father, she could see they were beginning to feel anxious even if they didn't admit it. Christine was expressing a greater than usual indifference to her father, while accusing Pat of being obsessed and vengeful. Christine's indifference disturbed Pat. She knew her oldest daughter must be feeling some deep anger or hurt that she couldn't express. Christine's nonchalance even bothered her younger sisters, who had begun calling her a wimp.

Andrea's aggressive behavior and open hostility worried Pat almost as much, she told her cousin. So did Marcia's obvious confusion and extreme emotional response to anything connected with her father. The two younger girls were constantly needling their mother because the law, courts, and lawyers were moving so slowly. They couldn't understand how someone who had committed what seemed such a horrendous crime could be walking the streets. As if to prove a point, Andrea had gotten herself arrested for disturbing the peace. She had waited for the police to arrive and almost begged to be handcuffed. The arresting officers had wanted to let her go with a warning, but she put out her wrists and insisted on going to jail. "My father is Jim Parker," she told anyone who would listen. "He deserted me and is still free. I'm the one who's going to jail."

Pat admitted she was pushing her daughters to meet their father, and that in some ways, it was cruel because it was so painful for them. But she wanted her daughters to be independent and free of the emotional burden she had carried most of her adult life.

"Maybe I'm wrong," she told Terry. "Maybe they'll be so devastated by all this that they'll fall apart emotionally and never recover. Am I making a mistake? Should I go to Florida alone?"

There was no doubt in Terry's mind that not only was Pat doing the right thing by facing David and urging her daughters to do the same; she was being courageous. He knew she was hoping the media would pick up on her case and that somehow it might help others, and he approved. In fact, he believed that what she was trying to do for other abandoned wives and children by exposing the rotten child-support system bordered on heroic. She was using her anger to bring about change while at the same time carrying out an act of justice for her children. Nothing could be healthier. He was delighted to give her any advice and support he could.

"It can't backfire," Terry reassured Pat. "Facing the anger and pain is healthier than sitting on your emotions. And meeting their father can only bring some degree of resolution to the girls' lives. You are offering them a chance to recover, Pat. That's a wonderful gift for a mother to give. Few deserted wives have the courage and strength to do that."

Terry went on to explain that abandoned children repeated the past by either abandoning others or setting themselves up to be abandoned over and over. They could only break the cycle by facing their feelings of anger, guilt, worthlessness, shame, and fear. That was the first step to recovery.

"The girls were devastated a long time ago," he said, "and have been living with the pain ever since. Meeting their father can't make that pain any worse. It may bring their anger to the surface so it looks worse, but it won't be. That's healthy. Even though they may not have expressed the anger yet, they know there's plenty to go around. They've been feeling yours for years. Besides, they have a *right* to see who their father is and what he looks like."

Pat smiled: Terry sounded like Andrea.

Terry went on to share with Pat his insights about her daughters, based on what she had told him and on his experience with other abandoned children. As the firstborn and a child who actually remembered her father, Christine had, in many ways, been hurt the deepest, Terry explained. What she was feeling was closer to rage than anger. She didn't know she was angry because she'd always been that way. Anger was her natural state, and she didn't know what it would be like not to feel it. Her indifference toward her father was the ultimate expression of her rage. It was her way of killing him, of saying, "You don't exist." To Christine, her rage was so terrifying, she was afraid to face it lest it destroy her. Instead, she found little ways to sublimate it and get temporary relief. Only by facing her rage could Christine release it.

As the secondborn child, Andrea was closer to Pat than to her father. Because of that closeness, she was very sensitive to her mother's feelings and tended to be protective of her. Andrea had a tremendous fear of abandonment—even more than Christine or Marcia. All her life she had felt her own fear of it *and* her mother's as well. She carried a double load. Fear of abandonment had almost become an obsession with her, and she reenacted it in her relationships. What you didn't resolve, you tended to reenact. She denied it on one level, then acted it out on another. She constantly set herself up to be rejected. She picked relationships that were doomed. She didn't know how or when to let go. She entered where she wasn't wanted. Expressing her anger at her father was the first step to breaking the cycle.

Marcia, more than Christine or Andrea, felt responsible for the pain of her mother and sisters. She might say that she no longer felt guilty or that she had worked it through, but she hadn't. She had turned her shame on herself and reenacted her abandonment by wanting to be punished and treated as worthless. Many of her problems in school stemmed from this. She underachieved as if to prove to herself she was no good. She tended to be *too* loyal in her relationships and she set up expectations that couldn't be met. Her conflicting feelings confused her. Facing her guilt could only help her accept that her father's abandonment of her mother and sisters wasn't her fault.

Relieved that her instincts about her daughters and their needs had been sound, Pat wanted to be sure she was doing the right thing for herself. Dr. Charles Crotty, whom she had known for years and who was more like a friend than a therapist, had told her it was even more important to resolve her own conflict than to give her children a chance to meet their father. Was she obsessed, as Christine seemed to think? Was she really doing the right thing for herself by confronting David and her darkest feelings in the process?

Terry once again encouraged her. She had never had the chance to resolve her relationship with David in 1968, he said. His running away was like cutting off her oxygen. There had been no discussion, no argument, no explanation.

Pat began to cry. She told Terry that for sixteen years she couldn't talk about what had happened in 1968. She held it all in as if it had never occurred. When she finally began to face it, the feeling of panic at having two babies with another on the way, and no food or money, came back to haunt her. It was foolish, she knew. She had a good job now, but the fear of being abandoned and penniless was still there, as she put it, "like a knife running through me."

The more Pat brought up the past, the more tears poured out. Terry told Pat that there was more than anger and fear behind her tears. She was a victim, he explained, and like most victims, she was tormented by guilt: Was she responsible for David running away from his children? Was she responsible for their pain? If she was, how could she live with herself? Like most victims, too, she felt worthless: Perhaps she deserved the treatment David had given her? If not, would he have done that to her? And like most victims, Terry continued, she felt a deep sense of shame about what had happened to her.

Pat was driven more by these feelings of guilt, shame, and worthlessness than by anger, Terry continued. Her tremendous drive to find David was her way of trying to resolve her feelings. She needed to hear a judge say that David had wronged her and must pay for his crime because—hard as it may be for others to understand—a jail sentence and reparations would finally confirm her value as a person and as a member of society.

"Going after David," Terry summed up, "is your way of finally telling yourself after all these years of guilt, 'I'm worth something.' "

It all made sense to Pat: For sixteen years she had had to steel herself against those powerful feelings so they wouldn't overwhelm her. But now it was time to resolve them. The more she faced her feelings, the less they would control her.

"In order to get on with your life," Terry advised, "you have to face David's rejection of you, and you can only do that by going back emotionally to 1968 in order to do now what you couldn't do then. You have to confront him and you have to do it face to face. When you do, the anger you repressed for sixteen years can begin to come out. Only then can you grow beyond it."

Terry added a word of caution: "Maybe you'll resolve this whole thing when you face David," he said. "Maybe not.

But you'll never know until you take the risk. Look at it as part of growing up and taking control of your life.''

Terry's words were like a balm. Ever since David had left, Pat's feeling toward men had been mixed. She wanted a committed, loving relationship, but she was afraid of being deserted once again. She wanted to share her life, but she could never allow anyone to have the power over her that David once had.

Encouraged by Terry's gentleness and understanding, Pat expressed a fear she found difficult to talk about. ''What really bothers me,'' she said, ''is that when I see David, I may feel sorry for him—even worse, I may find I still love him.''

Terry minced no words. ''Maybe you'll feel sorry for him,'' he said. ''But it's unlikely you'll still love him. If you feel sympathy or affection, take it as a positive sign of your ability to love and care for people. But you won't know until you try. If you don't try, your doubts will never be resolved.''

There was one more thing.

''What if my daughters meet David and turn against me?'' Pat asked. She didn't think she could go on if they did. ''What if they don't see him for what he is and put all the blame on me? What if they want to live with him instead of with me?''

Even though he recognized her terror as real, Terry knew that Pat didn't really believe she'd lose her daughters.

''If the girls really become angry and need to express it,'' Terry said, ''they may direct it at you. If they do, ignore it. It'll pass. They will recognize that *you* were the one who stayed with them, cared for them, and loved them—not their father. He was the one who abandoned them. Believe me, Pat, it *can't* backfire and it won't. In the end, the girls may decide they want a relationship with their father. Fine. Then they can have one with both of you.''

Pat asked Terry if he would talk to the girls alone. It was important, she said, that they have a chance to express how they felt about meeting their father. Also, it would be good for them to know Terry better so that if a problem came up later, they would feel comfortable talking to him on the phone. Terry agreed.

Terry and the three girls spent the evening sprawled in the rec room. The girls asked him about his teenage children and wanted to know if they had messy rooms, too. When he said they did, they asked him to look at theirs and judge whose was the messiest. They took him around and there were a lot of giggles and groans.

"It's a tie," Terry said when the tour was over. "Anything growing in there?"

The room inspection was a good icebreaker, almost a test in a way, and the girls felt Terry was open-minded enough to talk to. It didn't take them long to turn to the topic of their father. Marcia and Andrea did most of the talking, saying more about what they expected then how they felt. Marcia said she was excited and told Terry that finally seeing her father and hearing his voice would be terrific; she had so many questions to ask him. Andrea spoke with coolness and nonchalance. She seemed to be trying to deal with him from a safe distance—close enough to satisfy her curiosity but not close enough to really be touched. Terry didn't push. He heard them out, then gave them an informal but important lecture.

"I want you all to remember one thing," he said. It sounded more like an order than advice. "If you see or talk to your father, you are to say *anything* that comes to your mind. You are to say *every* single thing you ever wanted to say but never had the chance. Don't be concerned about your father or how he feels. You have the right to say what you want, and it's very important that you do just that. Even though you were too little to remember, you had feelings as babies. Those feelings stayed with you. Get them out in the open so you can look at them."

Terry's words got to Christine and she brought up an issue that had been troubling her for a long time. She had a boyfriend who lived in Mexico, she said, and her relationship with him was very dependent. Although she knew he loved her, she constantly wanted him to say it and prove it. When he did, she couldn't believe him. And as far as she was concerned, he couldn't ever love her enough. "All my friendships with boys seem to turn out that way," she said. Could being abandoned as a baby have something to do with it?

Terry encouraged Christine to talk about each of her serious relationships. Although she was reluctant to discuss her father, she liked talking about her boyfriends. As Terry picked and probed, Christine began to see that each of her relationships followed the same pattern—long-distance and overly dependent.

"You're deliberately choosing relationships that are doomed," Terry told Christine when he sensed she was ready to hear it. "You are setting them up so that the man *will* leave you. One of your strongest and earliest feelings is that of being abandoned. You're reenacting it with each relationship. Part of you wants to go back to those feelings. They hurt but they are safe because you know you can handle them. You have to break that cycle by facing up to what your father did to you."

Pat drove Terry to the airport the next morning. She felt that nothing could stop her from facing David now. She had her cousin Joe for strength, Judge Valentine for support, Betty Murphy for advice, and now Terry for understanding and reassurance on the deepest level.

As she drove back from the airport, Pat mulled over something that Terry had said when she asked if David ought to be punished. He had told her, "Being someone like that *is* punishment. He was always a runaway father about to happen."

Terry's remark reminded Pat of what Dr. Crotty had told her about abandonment being generational, and that it would be good therapy to dig into David's family history for clues to understanding why he would run away. Crotty had studied under Dr. Murray Bowen at Georgetown University, a pioneer in family-systems therapy. Dr. Bowen taught that a patient's problem is the product of imperfections in his or her parents, and the parents' imperfections are a product of imperfections in the grandparents, continuing back generation after generation. Each generation was probably doing the best it could considering its stresses and its resources.

Pat knew David's mother had given him to her sister to raise, but she didn't know why. Was that a form of abandonment? She had also heard that David's grandfather had abandoned his children and disappeared. Was that true? If it was, and if Dr. Bowen's theory was correct, why should *she* feel guilty because David ran away? Why should *she* accept responsibility for "a runaway father about to happen"?

19

▼

ALTHOUGH DAVID HAD used the last name of his foster parents, Pat had heard him mention his real last name. Never having seen it written out, she assumed it was spelled T-A-L-B-O-T. She also remembered David telling her that his grandfather and grandmother had worked in cotton mills, but he had never said where. She recalled that David's real mother had stated in her sworn affidavit to the Social Security Administration that David's father, Oscar David, was from Morrisville, Pennsylvania.

The hunt was on.

This time Pat wasn't trying to discover *where* David was but *who* David was. She started with the telephone operator in Morrisville, Pennsylvania. Although there were no Talbots in the area, there were two mills. She called them and asked Personnel to check mill records to see if an Oscar David Talbot—or any other Talbot—ever worked for them. She drew blanks at both.

Pat knew that David's real mother and her sister (David's foster mother) had grown up in or around Concord, North Carolina. Hoping that Oscar David, or O.D., as everyone called him, had married David's mother in Concord, she asked the marriage license office there to run a check on him.

She gave an approximate year of marriage. There was no record.

Next, Pat called every Talbot listed in the Concord and Charlotte phone books. No one had ever heard of an Oscar David. As a last resort, she called all the cemeteries in Concord. No luck.

By that time, Pat knew something was wrong. If she had been poking in the right places and asking the right questions, she would at least have found a clue. There was only one way for her to get back on track. She knew the name and address of David's real mother from her sworn affidavit. Pat got the woman's number from the operator and called. After a somewhat strained chat about how Christine, Andrea, and Marcia were doing, Pat told David's mother she was drawing a family tree and wanted to talk to David's father. Did she know where he was?

David's mother said she hadn't talked to her former husband in almost twenty years and wasn't even sure if he was still alive.

"How do you spell his last name?" Pat asked on a hunch.

"Why, T-A-L-B-E-R-T."

Pat almost jumped out of her skin and couldn't wait to hang up. On her first phone call back to Concord, she scored. The Talbert she had fished out of the phone book told her that although he didn't recall any Oscar David in the family, that didn't mean there wasn't any. The Talbert clan in North Carolina was old and big. He said his sister-in-law was also working on a family tree and gave Pat her number. "You might want to talk to the retired mailman, too," he added. "He knows everyone in town. Why, just the other day, he was asking about the Talberts in the grocery store." He gave Pat the man's name and number as well.

When she hung up, Pat knew it was just a matter of time. From now on, finding O.D. would be like tracking a deer in fresh snow.

The sister-in-law turned out to be a history book. There was an O.D. on her family tree, she said, but he wasn't closely related to her side of the Talbert family. Although she didn't know where O.D. was living, she filled Pat in on the family background:

No one knew for sure when the Talberts came to America

or from where. But census records showed they lived in Pennsylvania in the mid-1700s. In the late 1700s, they moved to Chesterfield County, South Carolina, to farm. One part of the Talbert clan stayed in South Carolina; another part, including David's side, moved to North Carolina in 1845. David's great grandfather, William, and his grandfather, Oscar Duberry Talbert, were born there.

Pat thanked the woman and hung up. She knew she had the right limb on the Talbert tree because David, his father, and his grandfather all had the same initials—O.D. She called the retired mailman, who was said to collect bits and pieces of information about old Concord families the way some people collect stamps. Like most local historians, he was delighted and proud to share what he knew.

He remembered the Oscar Duberry Talbert family well, he said, because he went to school with one of the Talbert girls and he later delivered mail to their small house near the train station on Depot Street. The Cannon Mills Company, founded in 1887, owned the house, which was a short walk from the mill where Mrs. Talbert worked. "She had a mess of kids," the mailman told Pat, "and there was never a man around."

"Do you know where any of them are living now?" Pat asked.

As far as he could tell, he said, they all moved out of town except the Talbert girl he went to school with. She married a man from Concord, but he couldn't remember the man's name.

Pat called the marriage license office once again. With the woman's first name and the correct spelling of her maiden name, it was easy to find out whom she had married. Fortunately, the man still lived in Concord. Pat called him.

He had divorced his first wife many years ago, he said. He thought her family was from Mooresville, down the road a piece. Bingo! O.D. was from *Mooresville*, North Carolina, not Morrisville, Pennsylvania. Several calls to Mooresville later, Pat was speaking to O.D. himself. She traced him to The Corral, a restaurant-bar he managed in nearby Charlotte. After making sure he was Oscar David Talbert, she asked, "Do you have a son named David and a daughter named Betty?"

"Why, yes," he said. He sounded more curious than cautious.

"Well, let me tell you who I am—it will probably shock you," Pat said. "I'm your son's first wife, Pat. And I have three teenage daughters—your grandchildren."

"Well, great day in the mornin', honey!" O.D. sounded genuinely excited. "I didn't know. I just didn't know!"

"I've spent days trying to track you down," Pat said. "No one in the family would ever tell me anything about you. My children want to meet their grandfather."

"I wanna meet the children too, baby," O.D. said. His voice sounded sincere and much younger than it was. "I'd give my life ta see you and the babies. No one ever told me. Honey, I don't have any grandchildren—I—I do *now*."

"They're sixteen, seventeen, and eighteen years old," Pat explained. "I think it's a shame that no one ever told me about you. . . . Your mother's dead?"

"Yes, in '81," he said. "She was a beautiful, beautiful—the nicest person you'd ever wanta meet."

"She was my daughters' great grandmother," Pat said. "I'm sad they never got to meet her. When was the last time you talked to David?"

"When he was fixin' ta go into the Marine Corps," he said. "He came to the plant and we talked. I heard from Betty he disappeared some time ago."

"Well, I found him—"

"You did?" O.D. was very excited now. He hadn't talked to his son for over twenty years. "Where is he?"

"In Florida. He changed his name and everything about himself. He didn't want to be found."

"He's still my son," O.D. said. "It don't make any difference—I love him."

"David told me that your father had deserted you, too," Pat said. "Is it true?" She wasn't sure whether he'd want to talk about his own father, but he was as open as the sky. It was a sad, almost uncanny story.

As O.D. told it, David's great grandfather William was a horse trader. He left Concord and moved to Texarkana, Texas. There, he married a cousin, Lilly Polk (a relative, some say, of President James Polk). The couple had five children, one of whom was David's grandfather, Oscar Duberry Talbert. Some Talberts say William murdered Lilly with a clothes iron and buried her in the backyard; others say she died in Texarkana of blackwater fever. Whatever the case, William packed his children in a covered wagon and took them to Columbus, South Carolina. There, he was eventually convicted of murdering his cousin and sent to prison. After the governor pardoned him (no one knows why), he moved to Concord, North Carolina, where he remarried and had four more children.

David's grandfather Oscar Duberry stayed in South Carolina and married Haley Dunman in 1905. She was just fifteen and he was a twenty-year-old tenant farmer. In the early 1920s, he got caught stealing cotton. While he was in jail, Haley relocated closer to her husband's family in Concord, North Carolina, where she got a job as a spinner in a Cannon mill. She eventually had nine children. David's father, O.D., born in 1925, was her eighth.

David's grandfather Oscar Duberry had the habit of running away for a time, then coming back home. Sometimes he'd be gone for as long as a year. Once he left with a woman called Blossom. Another time, he and three other men skipped town when a girl they all knew turned up pregnant. Once he bought a new Whippet coupe on credit and headed for Texas. When the car dealer couldn't collect from Haley, he dropped charges. David's grandfather returned. On August 17, 1928, when David's father, O.D., was three years old and the youngest child was nine months old, Oscar Duberry ran away for good.

Haley cried for six months. Her brother helped her get a better job and a mill house in Concord on Depot Street. The county wanted to put the children in an orphanage, but she insisted on keeping her family together. She worked ten hours a day, six days a week; her oldest sons helped with food and money; people left clothes on her porch when she was at work; and the Salvation Army gave her children hot lunches and shoes. But no matter how hard she tried, she couldn't control her younger sons. Several, including David's father, O.D., had to attend a correctional school—The Stonewall Jackson Manual Training and Industrial School for Boys. Haley never remarried or even divorced David's grandfather.

After he left Haley for good, Oscar Duberry changed his name to James Ellis Jordan and bought a farm outside Mobile, Alabama. He "remarried" and had one daughter. In 1957, twenty-nine years after he had run away, he wrote to his sister, asking for a copy of his birth certificate so he could start collecting Social Security. His sister told her nephews where he was. Two of David's uncles went down to see him, and found him in his yard. "Do you know me?" one asked him. "No," he said. "I don't reckin I do, but I'm scairt I might."

His sons brought him back to North Carolina for six weeks so the rest of his children could meet him. The sons were happy he was back, but his daughters refused to talk to him. So did Haley. During his visit, he never told his sons he was sorry for deserting them. He had run away, he said, because they were becoming too difficult to handle. Over the twenty-nine years he was gone, he said, he had returned many times, parked down the street, and watched his children play in the yard.

Two years after David's grandfather returned to Mobile, he died of heart failure. Haley outlived him by twenty-two years. She died at the ripe age of ninety in a house in Mooresville her children bought for her after she retired from the mill.

"We're goin' ta have ta meet," O.D. said after he finished his story, " 'cuz I wanna see you and my grandchildren. Tell the babies I love 'em and wanna see 'em just as soon as I can."

O.D. wasn't trying to be polite, and the sense of urgency he communicated was real. Although Pat didn't know it, he was dying of brown lung disease from all the cotton dust he had breathed over the years. He told her he'd fly up to Washington or pay for their trip down to North Carolina, and he begged her to send him pictures of herself and the girls as soon as she could.

Pat promised she would. When she hung up, she was in a mild state of shock. Both Dr. Crotty and Terry had told her that abandonment tends to be generational. The doctor had said that the only way to break the cycle was to face the issue and the feelings and emotions that surround it. He was right, and the parallels between David and his grandfather rocked her: Both had run away in the month of August and almost on the same day; both hid in the South, changed their names, and became bigamists; neither attempted to pay child support, even indirectly; both were assumed to be dead; and both were found years later by a family member.

Andrea and Marcia—Christine was out of town—knew Pat was looking for their real grandfather. When she told them that night that she had found him in North Carolina, they weren't interested in hearing what she had learned about him and the Talberts. They wanted to talk to him directly. Marcia was so excited she insisted on calling O.D. immediately and Pat agreed.

"Can I speak to O.D. Talbert?" Marcia asked the man who answered the phone at The Corral. She could hear the jukebox playing in the background. Pat stood by nervously, hoping O.D. would say the right things. She didn't think her daughters could handle another rejection.

"You got him, ma'am," O.D. said.

"This is Marcia Bennett." Her voice was unsteady. "I'm your granddaughter."

"I know," O.D. said. There was tenderness in his voice. He paused. He was evidently choked up and close to tears. "I know—and I can't wait ta see you and your sisters and your mother. You see, I have a family I didn't even know I had."

"Me too." Marcia began to cry.

"Oh God, I can hardly wait," O.D. said. "Tell your mother ta get pictures in the mail just as soon as she can so I kin show 'em off all around the joint here. I'll have some big ones made and put 'em right here on the wall."

O.D. began to brag to impress Marcia, almost as if he were afraid that she'd reject him if he didn't. "I got a home on the lake," he said. "A hunting lodge in Maine on Lake George. I run this lounge and I have another home in the Dominican Republic. I have my own company—a loom service. We overhaul and repair all kinds a looms. . . ." O.D. paused self-consciously, sensing he was building himself up larger than life. "When you see me, you may not like me," he added.

"Don't say that!" Marcia said.

"I weigh around two twenty," O.D. said. "Six two. Hair

is thinnin' on the top. I got a gray mustache, curly on the ends.''

''I'm five seven and a half,'' Marcia said. ''I don't know how much I weigh. I have long hair and—You'll see pictures of us.'' She was crying so hard it was difficult for her to speak. ''I don't know you, but I guess I love you.''

''When you see this mug of mine,'' O.D. said, ''you probably won't. I'm as ugly as a mud fence.''

''I don't care,'' Marcia said.

''But I *am* your grandfather. There's no doubt about that.''

''I was tickled ta death when your mother called me tonight.''

''Were you?'' It was as if Marcia couldn't believe it. ''Were you really?''

''I sure was,'' O.D. said. ''I've been telling everyone in the lounge I have three beautiful granddaughters. Don't you worry none. I know you're bound ta be a beautiful little lady.''

''Thank you,'' Marcia said through her sobs. She sounded like a little girl.

''I wanna see you so bad I can hardly stand it,'' O.D. said.

''Please fly up here,'' she pleaded. ''I want to see you. That would make me *so* happy.''

Andrea grabbed the phone.

''Oh gracious,'' O.D. said. ''I don't know what in the world ta say. I'm overwhelmed. I didn't know.''

''Really?'' Andrea said. ''You didn't know about us. Oh my God!''

''I know you belong ta me now.''

''Our dad really messed up,'' Andrea said. ''But we're glad we found you.''

''You better believe it.''

''How old are you?''

''Sixty. I have emphysema,'' he lied, ''but I git along just fine.''

''I'm seventeen,'' Andrea said. She could hear Marcia hyperventilating in the background, sucking and gulping air as if she couldn't get enough.

''I've always wanted to know who my father is,'' Andrea said. There was no anger in her voice nor the touch of hardness she frequently used to protect herself. Like Marcia, she sounded like a child. ''Ever since we were little, we would talk about him and blame him. . . . I'd like to send you a picture of me.''

"And write me a long letter," O.D. said.

"Believe me, I will." She felt the emotion in his voice. A kind of long-distance caress. "Are we upsetting you?"

"Nope, I hope I'm not upsettin' you."

"I've been upset all my life," Andrea said. "But this is the best upset I've ever been."

O.D. laughed. "You found yourself a grandfather and I found what I know are three beautiful girls."

"I hope I look like you," Andrea said. "I look like David."

"Dark hair—"

"He had those thick eyebrows. I have those."

"I got pictures of him when he was a little feller," O.D. said. "I'll bring 'em."

"I have a boyfriend," Andrea said. She was trying to cram her whole life into five minutes. "I've been dating him for about a year."

"Well, honey, you tell him if he's not good to you, your grandfather will come up there and skin 'im like a cat."

"If I get married, and I walk down the aisle and stuff," Andrea said, "you can give me away, if you want to." Andrea was crying, too.

"I'd love it," O.D. said. "I'd love it."

"I'm really confused now," Andrea said. "Maybe when I straighten things out we can talk some more. I'm so confused."

Breathing normally again, Marcia took the phone and said, "Granddaddy? I don't know you, but I love you. I love your son in a way, too. And I hate him in a way, you know. We all have to forgive . . . You better come. I want to see you *so* bad. I'm glad my mom did this for us. I'm glad we found you. I'm glad we know who you are. Now you know, too. You have three granddaughters."

"You're mine," O.D. said. "You belong ta me."

"We're going to make it worth it," Marcia said and hung up.

Pat could feel how much Andrea and Marcia were reaching out for O.D.'s love. They were like starved, greedy kids, and they kept pressing her to invite him to Washington or take them to North Carolina. They kept wondering what their grandfather looked like, where he lived, if they looked like him.

In the end, Pat decided to drive the girls to North Carolina the following week so they could see the house where their great grandmother Haley had lived and the mill where she had worked, and meet as many aunts, uncles, nieces, and nephews as they could. But still worried that O.D. might reject her daughters, she wrote him a long letter in which she came close to pleading with him not to push her daughters away.

"When the girls talked to you they were very afraid and nervous," she wrote.

You couldn't tell, but they were crying. After they talked to you, we stayed up till after two, talking. Andrea said, "Mom, that is the first man that hasn't rejected us. And he told us he loved us." They thought you sounded very honest. They have heard so many lies all their lives that they couldn't believe someone would tell them the truth. . . .

It's all very sad for them—the years they did without a father. You must understand because your own father did the same thing. They do not forgive David—they are bitter toward him because he hurt them so much.

But now they have a chance to know you, their real grandfather, and they want to meet you. All they want is for someone to love them and not leave them. . . . They need a relationship with someone who won't disappoint them—that is all they want. My girls will give you back more love than you've ever had because they want to love you as their granddaddy. They called you "granddaddy" on the phone and they liked the way that sounded.

They left for North Carolina on Friday. When they arrived in Mooresville, O.D.'s brother was waiting. "O.D.'s scairt a meetin' you," he explained as he drove them out to O.D.'s modest home on Lake Norman. "But he's real excited. He's dyin' of brown lung, you know, but he's proud and don't want anyone to know it."

O.D. was sleeping when they pulled into his driveway, and it took his brother five minutes of knocking to awaken him. They sat in the living room and talked for an hour. O.D. looked weak and tired, and he found it difficult to breathe and talk. Every now and then he squirted medication into his mouth from a vaporizer to clear his lungs.

O.D. was overwhelmed. He hugged the girls, stroked their hair, and held their hands like a sponge soaking up every drop of affection they and Pat showed him. "My granddaughters," he kept saying. "My grandbabies. If only I'd known you sooner I'da taken walks with you, gone fishin' . . . Why didn't I know?"

The more he looked at his grandchildren and touched them, the angrier at David he became. "You let me know when that trial is," he ordered Pat. "I'm goin' down there with ya. I wanna sit in the front row with my arms around my grandbabies. No one can do this to 'em. I'll tell David what a louse he is. I'll never turn *my* back on my grandbabies. I swear. You promise me now, you'll tell me!"

Pat promised. Then O.D. hung his head in guilt and shame. "I wasn't around to raise 'im," he said softly. "I wasn't around to tell 'im right from wrong."

That night, Pat and the girls played cards with O.D.'s brother until two in the morning, sitting around the kitchen table in Haley Talbert's old white frame house. Haley's children had left it just the way it was when she died four years earlier. O.D.'s brother was as lively and talkative as O.D. was tired and quiet. All night long, he told funny stories about the Talbert family and about growing up in a mill town.

The next day, Pat and the girls met more aunts, uncles, nieces, and nephews. By the time they settled down with O.D. for a steak dinner that night, they had a good sense of who the Talberts were. O.D. was very quiet during dinner, exhausted and drained by all the emotions that had flowed so freely during the visit.

Although she was glad she and her daughters had come to Mooresville, Pat left for Washington the next morning with mixed emotions. It was clear that O.D. felt nothing but affection for her daughters—it shined in his eyes and she could hear it in his voice, and she was grateful for that. She had merely hoped that O.D. wouldn't reject them and would find that he really loved them. But he was so sick and exhausted that he didn't have the energy to demonstrate the love he felt. She sensed that her daughters ended up giving him more than they had received. And like O.D., she felt sad they had found him at the end of his life.

Pat was also pleased that she had learned so much about David's family. Who they were. How they lived. How they had felt about being abandoned by their father. She had uncovered a history of early marriages, divorces, and abandonment unlike anything on her side of the family. It helped her understand why David would think of running away. But she was also disappointed that, after talking to O.D. and his relatives, she had no clear answer as to why David's mother had given him away and why she had kept his sister, Betty.

All she learned was that O.D. was sixteen years old when he married David's mother, whose own father had deserted her and her five brothers and sisters, just as O.D.'s father had deserted him. O.D. admitted walking out on his wife and two children, when he was twenty. While he was gone, his wife gave David to her sister and brother-in-law, who were childless. When he returned after a year, O.D. sued his wife for divorce—the grounds for his suit were unclear. O.D. said he had such great respect for his brother-in-law that when the man asked if he could keep David, O.D. said yes. David's foster parents legally changed David's name to theirs.

Pat returned home, disturbed as well as pleased by the visit. O.D. looked just like David. He moved like David. Walked like him. Even shared some of David's speech patterns. She felt a deep surge of affection for him, not because he was a likable old man, or was dying, or was the grandfather of her children, but because he reminded her of David. She didn't want to feel any warmth for David, even if it was through his father. She wanted him out of her life for good. My God, she thought, if I feel loving toward O.D. because he reminds me of David, what will I feel for David himself when I meet him?

If that wasn't bad enough, Pat had begun to feel a sympathy for David. It wasn't that she was about to excuse David for what he had done to her and his daughters, just because abandonment seemed to run in his blood. But she felt sad because of what he had missed. "If only David had known all this," she said to herself. "He had a whole family—a real history. And he didn't even know his own father."

O.D. died eight months later, and Pat and Christine went to the funeral. David wasn't there and probably didn't even know his father was dead.

Part
Three

CONFRONTATION

20

▼

OCTOBER AND NOVEMBER turned out to be so busy for Pat that she hardly had time to think about David. Swept up in a new IRS training program, she had few spare moments to search for the documents needed to prove that James Parker was really David. Although she could go to Florida in December, Christine, Andrea, and Marcia didn't want to see their father jailed until after Christmas. The girls still weren't sure whether he had any other children, and since Christmas was so special to them, they didn't want to destroy their own or anyone else's. Pat agreed to go down in early January 1985—six months after she had found David.

If October and November flew by, December crawled. Pat grew so anxious as her trip to Florida approached, she found it almost impossible to sleep. She'd get into bed at one o'clock, only to wake up at three, unable to drift off again. She became so exhausted, she couldn't work or give her daughters the attention they needed.

It wasn't just Pat who was anxious. With each passing week, the girls were getting more tense as they sensed their mother's fear and began facing their own. They argued more with her over trivial things, almost as if they were looking for an excuse to pick a fight, and they squabbled more and more among themselves. Their comments never changed:

"When are we going? Why not now? I can't wait. Give me his phone number. Why is everyone so slow? Doesn't anyone care?"

Marcia in particular was frightened, and although she didn't say what bothered her the most, Pat knew. Marcia felt trapped between two painful alternatives. On the one hand, she feared her father might reject her a second time; on the other, she feared she might love her father and sensed that this would hurt her mother. Pat felt there was little she could do to help Marcia except be there if her youngest needed her.

One evening, as Pat and her daughters sat around the kitchen table reminiscing over the photos Pat was putting together, the girls decided to take an album to Florida to share pieces of their lives with their father. Since each was proud of her athletic achievements, they chose an album filled with sports pictures. Their unspoken motive was: See what you missed? See what you left behind? See how well we did without you?

The girls concocted a plan to meet their father at his home because they didn't want to see him for the first time in handcuffs or in jail. It was Andrea's idea and Pat welcomed it. They would rent an old car and fake a breakdown in front of his house. Pat and the sheriff would be in another car down the street. The girls would go to the door, using the names of their three best girlfriends for cover—Kim, Laura, and Sharon. Andrea would do all the talking. "Our car broke down," she would tell her father. "Can we use your phone?"

The plan was riddled with holes. "Andrea, you talk too much," Marcia said. "You'd blow it."

"What if he wants to come out and fix the car?" Christine said.

"Maybe we should tell him we ran out of gas," Andrea suggested.

Bill Daniels walked in during the discussion and killed the whole idea. "David will know," he said. "Three girls all about the ages of his daughters. And look at Andrea—she looks just like him!"

Even though she was taking a sedative, the tense weeks of waiting wore Pat down. She started to have bad dreams about the trip. In one of them, she found herself sitting in her Florida attorney's office waiting for him to finish a conversation with David's attorney. Then she went outside for some fresh air and a stroll. When she came back, she saw David's attorney getting into a car. She forced her way in beside him and asked what was going on. He smiled and said her own attorney would tell her; she would be very pleased. Realizing they had made a deal behind her back, she began crying. Then she screamed, "You don't understand, there's supposed to be a judge! Jim Parker is supposed to be here!" David's attorney replied, "But he's going to pay all the money." She began to panic: "But the girls are supposed to see him!" She got out of the car and started running down the street. Then she woke up.

To help ease her tension, Pat wrote David a letter she planned to give him before his daughters could ask to see him. She would wait in her attorney's car down the street from David's house. As soon as the sheriff arrested him, she'd rush over and give him the letter, saying, "The children want to meet their father, David. It's important that you don't reject them. Read this and then read it again!"

The letter, a plea not to abandon the girls a second time, read:

Dear David,

I realize that my finding you after sixteen years must come as a great shock. I believe, however, that it is something you have anticipated, or you would not have gone to the extremes you have to avoid being discovered. I can only guess what you may have felt during those years. Maybe you even tried to put this day out of your mind, believing that your past did not exist. I would like to believe, however, that from time to time you thought of your three daughters and maybe wondered what they looked like or what kind of life they had. I cannot begin to recount what has happened to them. There have been times of joy—of sadness. They were sick, sometimes depressed. In the hospital after auto accidents. They've laughed. They've cried.

I'm very proud of them. They are three very beautiful daughters.

Since I told them where you were, it was all I could do to keep them from telephoning you. They wanted to call so badly, but I thought that might only frighten you into running again, so I would not let them. I knew the only chance they would have of seeing you was to arrive unexpectedly and hope that you would meet them. They were very upset before this trip and are having a hard time coping. Marcia has been very depressed.

I do not believe that you, yourself, have been without pain, David. I know that this letter is a very emotional one for you as well as for me. Hopefully, you will understand its importance. If you do, you will bury your own fears and react in a manner that is best for the children.

Our daughters are here with me in Tampa, and I have gone to a great deal of effort and expense to get them here—not for myself, but for them. They desperately want to see who their father is. They have things they want to say to him—to you—things they have dreamed about for years, things they have practiced over and over. They all have their own individual feelings, but I can tell you, a visit with you is the most important thing in all their lives. They have spent their childhood and teenage years not knowing if you were dead or alive. They have been hurt deeply, and all have feelings of being abandoned. They often told me how they wanted to become famous so you would see them and get in touch with them. So many times, they came to me in the night crying for want of you. They would say to me, "If only I could see him once just to know what he looks like, what he sounds like." No matter how much consolation I gave them, the hurt remained.

You must understand their feelings, David, for you were abandoned, too. Perhaps that was the biggest hurt in your life and it caused you to run from those closest to you. You are forty—too old to keep running. Well, you can stop looking over your shoulder.

Now—you have an opportunity to do something for your daughters. You cannot erase the years. You cannot erase their hurt. But you can meet them and your responsibility to support them. It is so important for them to face you. When you see them, you will only realize what you've missed.

They deserved better than they got out of life, David. They have carried your guilt by believing it was somehow their fault that you abandoned them. Especially Marcia. She feels that if she had been a boy you would not have left. I've had to get them counseling to help them realize it wasn't their fault. I would not have brought them with me or put them through this if I did not believe it was important for them.

I don't know what the outcome will be. But I believe they cannot be hurt any more than they already have. They are very afraid right now, as I am sure you are, too. They don't know how to react, but I do know that if you reject them again, they will be devastated. How they will feel in the end depends on you.

Our daughters are beautiful young ladies, grown up in many respects, but they are hurting inside deeply. You've missed them growing up, and I am sure that's something you must think about. They went through everything without you there to share it with them. They were cheerleaders, played soccer, were on the diving and swimming teams. They each have dreams of going to college. Christine's a freshman now. But they must resolve their conflicts of who they are and who their father is before going on with their lives.

I am writing this letter so that you will realize the importance of this meeting, so that you will put aside your own fears and do what is right for them—not for me. The past cannot be undone, but I ask that you do not perpetuate the suffering of our daughters. It's up to you, David, to give your daughters a father.

21

PAT COULD SEE it now. He would walk into the courtroom and tell the judge, "I don't know what she's talking about. I don't know her, and I've never heard of any David. I'm Jim Parker and here's my birth certificate to prove it."

Pat wasn't about to risk that. To clear all doubt about James Parker's real identity, she called the FBI for a copy of David's fingerprints, which she knew were on file; but the bureau said the Privacy Act of 1974 prevented it from releasing them to her.

A small hurdle. By this time, Pat knew how to play the game. She simply asked Judge Valentine to issue a Subpoena Duces Tecum for them. That way, the prints would go directly to the court, not to her.

"Anything else you need?" Valentine asked after he signed the subpoena.

"Could you get David's personnel file from Safeco?" she asked. She really didn't need the file to prove his identity if she had the prints, but she wanted to document how hard he had tried to hide from the court and the law, just in case.

Somewhat skeptical whether Safeco would respond to an out-of-state subpoena in a juvenile and domestic relations case, Judge Valentine signed it anyway. Corporate attorneys frequently advised companies to ignore such requests, since they knew that, with few exceptions, J and D courts didn't have time to force them to comply.

While waiting for the FBI and Safeco to respond, Pat began studying the papers David left behind when he ran away. Among them, she found a twenty-year-old traffic ticket that he and a fellow Marine had picked up in North Carolina. The name of the other Marine was James Parker.

Safeco sent James Clinton Richard Parker's file the day after it received Judge Valentine's express-mail subpoena. Pat devoured it. In his job application papers, Parker had claimed that he was born in New York on August 30, 1944 (David's real date of birth was July 17, 1944); that his father worked for the U.S. Foreign Service; that he attended primary and secondary schools in Fair Lawn, New Jersey; that he had graduated from Rutgers University in 1967 with a B.S. in Food Science; and that he had been in the Marines, Camp Lejeune, from 1967 to 1971 (these dates were not accurate) and had won a Bronze Star in Vietnam.

Of course, little in Parker's job application was true. David's father, O.D., was never in the Foreign Service; David was born in Virginia, not in New York; he had gone to primary and secondary schools in Virginia, not in New Jersey; he had never been to Vietnam or won a Bronze Star; and he had never gone to Rutgers.

The Rutgers connection intrigued Pat so much that she called the Rutgers University Alumni Association to see if a James Parker had actually graduated in 1967.

"Yes," a clerk told Pat after she checked the records. "There was a James R. Parker, born August 30, 1944, who graduated in 1967 with a B.S. in agriculture. He is listed as a food chemist and now lives in Oregon."

"Can you give me his address or phone number?" Pat asked.

"I'm sorry."

"Can you tell me anything else about him?"

"I'm sorry."

Pat asked Judge Valentine to subpoena James R. Parker's student file from the alumni association. While she was waiting for the reply, David's fingerprints arrived. "A name check of the files of the FBI Identification Division disclosed a United States Marine Corps enlistment fingerprint card," the bureau wrote Judge Valentine. "A copy of this fingerprint card is enclosed for your release to Ms. Patricia Ann Bennett."

Although she should have felt relieved at having David's prints, Pat was in such a state of anxiety that she feared the worst. The FBI wasn't perfect, was it? It had made mistakes before. What if it had sent the wrong card? David would walk out of the court laughing.

When the alumni association file arrived, Pat learned a few more details: The middle name of the James Parker who had graduated in 1967 was Rothery, not Richard; he graduated from Fair Lawn primary and secondary schools; and his father had been in the Foreign Service.

During the first week of January 1985, Pat and Victoria Gordon met in Pat's home to piece together their identity case and to decide exactly what they hoped to accomplish in Florida the following week. Pat knew that David had assumed the name James Parker soon after he had run away, because he had used James Parker—without a middle initial—on his marriage certificate to Lenora the following year. Pat guessed that he took the middle name Clinton from Clinton, Maryland, where he had flunked his private pilot's exam after he had been discharged from the Marines. She assumed that he later found the name James R. Parker and added the name Richard to Clinton.

The more they talked that night, the clearer their Florida legal goals became: first, positively identify Parker as David; second, get the Florida court to accept the Virginia decree for over forty-two thousand dollars in arrearage and to enter it as a judgment; third, hold David in contempt of court for not having obeyed the Virginia court order for child support; and fourth, amend the order to cover Marcia, who wasn't born when Fairfax issued the order almost seventeen years ago.

Pat and Victoria both recognized that although their legal strategy sounded fine on paper, it failed to address the main reason why the Bennetts were going to Florida in the first place. The money was secondary at this point. Pat neither expected to get forty-two thousand dollars, nor would she insist on it. She would settle for ten thousand dollars—enough to cover the trip to Tampa and her legal expenses—provided she and her daughters had the chance to face David. And there was the rub: If Victoria filed any petition in Tampa, David would be duly notified. If he was notified, he could flee. And even if he didn't run, his attorneys could line up so many legal straw men that it might be months before he would have to stand before a judge—if he ever had to.

Pat's Florida attorney, Frank de la Grana, who had been looking for a way to have James Parker arrested long enough for Pat and her daughters to meet him, saved the day. Why not post a bond and ask the court for a Writ of Ne Exeat? he suggested. That would allow the sheriff to arrest James Parker without prior notice and hold him in jail until he paid in full the cash bond the judge set, or until he had a hearing. Even though it wasn't certain a judge would sign the writ, which was an extraordinary legal measure founded in old English law, it was worth trying. The writ was designed precisely for cases like Pat's—someone owes money and threatens to flee to avoid paying, or the petitioner has reason to believe the debtor might flee.

The problem with a Writ of Ne Exeat was that the burden of proof fell on Pat. She would have to convince the court that David might flee if he found out she was looking for him. If she drew a grumpy judge or one of those Florida good old boys, she might never get a signature. At best, it would be a legal lottery.

If Pat managed to secure the writ, however, the sheriff could arrest David at night, when he was sure to be home and when the banks were closed. If he couldn't raise the cash for bail immediately, he'd have to spend the night behind bars. Pat and his daughters could then try to see him.

The plan was set. Christine would leave Saturday, January 11, for her summer job in Orlando. She would meet her mother, her two sisters, and Victoria at the airport Sunday afternoon and drive them to Tampa in her 1978 Camaro so Pat would not have to rent a car. Richard Froemming, who was in Miami on a surveillance job, would join them in Tampa on Tuesday or Wednesday. Not only was Richard pleased to help, he had declined to charge for his services and insisted on paying his own expenses.

The legal drafts from de la Grana arrived by courier late

Friday afternoon—thirty-six hours before Pat's plane was to
take off. She and Victoria worked all day Saturday in Victoria's office in downtown Washington, sharpening the motion
and petition on Victoria's word processor. After breaking for
dinner around eight, they went back to the word processor
until three o'clock Sunday morning. Neither had done any
packing and their plane left at eight a.m. But at least they
had the paperwork neatly tied up.

The legal motion argued that David had a history of running and hiding to avoid his responsibility to pay child support, and that his pattern of behavior indicated a probability
he might run again if notified. It asked the court to set cash
bond at forty-two thousand dollars—the amount of arrearage.

The petition asked that the court recognize and enforce the
sixteen-year-old Virginia child-support order as a Florida
judgment and enter it against David in the amount of forty-
two thousand dollars, find David in contempt of the court
order and enforce the maximum penalty of the law, amend
the Virginia order to include Marcia and raise the amount
David had to pay from two hundred dollars to at least five
hundred dollars a month, and order David to pay Pat's court
and investigative costs as well as her attorneys' fees.

When Pat got home shortly before four that morning, tense
and exhausted, Marcia was waiting in a state of near hysteria.
She lit into Pat as soon as her mother walked through the
door.

"Where were you?" she screamed. "Why did you leave
me alone? I needed you. I'm so-o-o scared."

"We're leaving in a couple of hours," Pat said firmly.
Emotionally drained and raw, she was angry that Marcia was
needling her after she had worked all night. "I haven't
packed. I'm exhausted. Why don't you go to sleep and leave
me alone!"

Pat went into her bedroom and closed the door. After tossing a few clothes in a suitcase, she lay down on the bed for
an hour or two of sleep. But before she could drift off, Marcia
barged in crying and yelling. She grabbed Pat's favorite lamp
and threw it on the floor, screaming that Pat had no right to
leave her alone when she was so frightened. She made such
a commotion that she woke her sister across the hall.

Andrea flew into the room. "Mom, you have to do something about Marcia," she yelled. "She's flipping out!"

Her nerves close to shattering, Pat couldn't think. She kept worrying about the hundred things that could go wrong. On top of all that, Marcia was now blaming her for not being there, and Andrea was blaming her for not keeping the lid on Marcia. What did they expect of her? She was only human, and as scared as they were.

"Look, I'm wiped out, Marcia," Pat yelled back. "Just be quiet, leave me alone, and go to bed."

Pat slid off the bed to nudge the girls out of the room and to close the door again. But Marcia was so out of control that she hit Pat on the shoulder and shoved her back toward the bed. Then Marcia drew back and slugged Andrea in the nose.

Pat pushed both daughters out the door and sat on the bed so tired she could barely grasp what was happening. Across the hallway, she could hear Marcia crying hysterically, "I hit my mom! I can't believe I hit my mom!"

The shock over what she had done brought Marcia to her senses like a splash of ice water, and she went back into Pat's room. "I'm so sorry, Mom," she said. She was crying softly now. "I didn't mean it. I don't want to go."

"You don't have to go," Pat said gently.

"Part of me wants to love him, Mom," she said. "Part of me wants to hate him. And I'm scared I will love him."

Pat put her arms around Marcia and hugged her tightly. They were both weeping now, more out of relief than hurt or anger.

"I'm scared, too," Pat said. "And for the same reason. I don't want to love him either."

"Well, what if I *do*?" Marcia seemed to feel less alone now that she knew her mother had the same hidden fear.

"I don't know," Pat said. "But I have to find out for myself; you don't. You don't have to come if you don't want to."

Andrea came back into the room and sat on the bed. My God, what have I done? Pat thought. What right do I have to put them through this? They'll never get over it. What a mistake! It's out of control, and it's all my fault.

They held each other. A mother and two daughters closer together than they had ever been.

"Can I call Victoria?" Marcia asked suddenly.

Pat told her it would be all right. She was convinced that Marcia wanted to tell Victoria she wasn't going, but she would deal with that later. Right now, it was four o'clock, time for at least one good hour of sleep and peace.

Marcia called, and Victoria's sleepy voice came on the line. "I'm so scared," Marcia began. A jumble of words and emotions spilled over the phone as she tried to explain to the older woman how she felt. "I love him even though I don't know him. I'm afraid that's going to hurt my mother. I hate him. I don't want to love him. I don't want to go. I don't know what's going to happen down there. I'm staying home. I'm angry at her. She left me alone. She won't talk to me."

"Honey, don't get mad at your mother," Victoria said gently. "She's very tired. It's four in the morning. She loves you and she's doing this for you too. Not just for herself."

"I know she's been working hard," Marcia said through her tears. "And I love her. But I feel left out."

It was plain to Victoria that the girls were hoping for too much from their father. They expected him to be as eager to meet them as they were to see him. In reality, he might refuse to talk to them. They expected him to say how sorry he was that he had deserted them, how pretty they were, how sad he was because of what he had missed, and that if he had a chance to do it all over again, he'd love them and never leave them. In reality, he might not be the least bit sorry, just embarrassed that he had got caught.

Victoria knew that whatever David said, did, or felt, he was not going to be the father they wanted. She chose her words with care.

"I can see how tough it's been growing up without a father. You have all those dreams of what he must be like. But listen, honey, maybe he's not like the dad in your dreams. Maybe he's different—maybe not as nice. Maybe he won't want to see you and that's what's scaring you."

Marcia thought it over for a second. "What's he going to be like, Victoria?" she asked. "Will he love mé? I don't want to go."

"Don't worry, honey, Victoria will be there." She felt

touched and overwhelmed by the depth of Marcia's feelings and how completely vulnerable the girl was. Although she wanted to hold and protect Marcia, she knew no one could shield her from what she had to face. "I won't leave you, honey," she said.

22

CHRISTINE WAS WAITING in Orlando when her mother, her sisters, and Victoria landed at noon. Christine wasn't happy to be leaving, even for a short time. She felt that her mother was obsessed with David, and she didn't think any good would come out of the trip for anyone, including David—so why get excited? Besides, Christine resented being pushed and put under such pressure. But she had agreed to drive everyone to Tampa and see her father, rather than risk upsetting her mother and have her sisters call her a wimp.

When Victoria saw Christine's old Camaro, however, she had second thoughts about the plane travel plans. She rented her own car and the group split up. Marcia rode with Christine, since she got along better with her older sister than Andrea did. Pat and Andrea joined Victoria.

Traveling in convoy, they got lost in Tampa, and by the time they found Frank de la Grana's office, it was almost six. To help Pat trim expenses, Frank had arranged the free use of a condo belonging to an attorney in Frank's office, at Indian Rock Beach near Clearwater, about an hour's drive from downtown Tampa. Frank drove Pat, Andrea, and Victoria out to the beach house in his gray BMW while Christine and Marcia followed.

Soft-spoken, laid back, and with the pure bloodline of an

old and respected Spanish family, Frank knew his way around Tampa's courts and judges as well as Victoria did around Fairfax's. But unlike Victoria's practice, Frank's was mostly criminal defense. Though criminal law paid the bills, family law was really Frank's first love, and he wished he could do more of it.

On the drive to the balmy gulf beach, Frank was stunned by Victoria's energy. If someone hadn't told him, he would never have believed she had had only a few hours of sleep the night before. Without pausing for breath, she chattered about the case, the motion, the petition, and the likelihood she'd get the Writ of Ne Exeat. Then she bombarded Frank with questions—what was the court system like in Tampa? Who were the good judges? How far was the courthouse from Frank's office? All the while, Pat sat exhausted in the back seat, depressed because she felt like a stranger to her own case. She didn't like not being in control, and it was clear that Victoria had appointed herself commander-in-chief.

The condominium where they would be staying, in a development called Pelican Pointe, was a two-story, two-bedroom home tastefully done in a nautical decor. Victoria hardly seemed to notice. Glancing around and nodding her approval, she spread out her papers on the table across from the bar while the girls checked out each room and argued about who was going to sleep where.

Frank listened patiently as he resigned himself to a Sunday evening lecture on the law. He had left a family gathering to meet the noisy two-car caravan in the street below his office, and he was eager to return home. Finally, at nine-thirty he got up to leave. Reminding Victoria that he was in the middle of a federal narcotics trial, Frank said he would not have much time to spare that week, but that he would make sure someone showed her the legal ropes around town.

By the time Frank left the condo, the girls were tired, hungry, and cranky. Like Pat, they felt left out, not sure what was going to happen, and uncertain where or when they would see their father. Eventually, they settled in front of the TV with a bucket of Southern Fried Chicken. It was a quiet but tense evening. With the sleeping arrangements finally negotiated, they all turned in.

Around noon the next day, Monday, Pat and Victoria drove

to Frank's office on the thirtieth floor of the First Florida Tower, overlooking Tampa, the Hillsboro River, and Frank's new home—a gleaming white speck on the riverbank. They spent most of the afternoon holed up in the conference room working out procedures: where to go, whom to see, how to file. By the end of the day, they had agreed on a strategy.

At Frank's suggestion, they would make an appointment the next day, Tuesday, to talk to a judge he knew, Julio Gonzalez. Like Judge Valentine, Judge Gonzalez would be sympathetic and in a good position to advise and guide them. Tuesday evening, they would meet with Richard Froemming to coordinate plans. Assuming Richard found Jim Parker in town Wednesday morning, they would file the papers and Victoria would plead for a Writ of Ne Exeat before a judge that day. Since judges on the Hillsborough County Circuit Court rotated their assignments, there was no predicting whom Victoria would draw. If the judge signed the writ, they would ask the sheriff to arrest Jim Parker Wednesday night. If he didn't sign . . . it was anyone's guess.

Back at the condo, the girls were in a dither. With no clues about what was happening, they sat by the phone all afternoon, waiting for a call from their mother saying that their father was arrested and wanted to meet them. When Pat returned early that evening, she explained that nothing was going to happen for a couple of days, so they might as well get used to the waiting. To appease them, she gave them enough money to buy dinner across the road at the Hungry Fisherman. Then she and Victoria drove back into town to a private club Frank had suggested, for dinner.

Pat and Victoria spent most of Tuesday in the county courthouse; while Victoria met with legal officials behind closed doors, Pat sat on benches outside, growing more anxious by the hour. Judge Gonzalez turned out to be as understanding and helpful as Frank had predicted. After listening to Victoria explain the case, he supported their decision to seek a Writ of Ne Exeat. And he became so intrigued by David's having assumed the identity and college credits of another person that the judge suggested Victoria march down the hall to the prosecutor's office. Maybe David had committed another crime besides desertion and nonsupport.

Equally curious, the prosecutor pulled down his Florida

law books. He had never tried a false-identity case before and wasn't even sure if it was a crime. He found Florida law quite clear: to assume someone's identity to defraud that person of money or property was larceny; but there was no evidence that David had done that. To assume someone's identity to get a job or a credit rating was a misdemeanor of the first degree (like desertion and nonsupport was in Virginia). In Florida, this crime carried a maximum penalty of one year in jail and a fine of up to one thousand dollars. The Hills-borough County prosecutor was no more interested in col-lecting misdemeanor trophies than Fairfax County's Robert Horan had been, even assuming there was hard evidence that David had committed a false-identity crime in Florida.

However, the False Identification Crime Control Act of 1982 made it a federal crime to "possess an identification document that is or appears to be an identification document of the United States which is stolen or produced without au-thority, knowing that such document was stolen or produced without authority." That law listed "birth certificate" as a document of the United States. If David "produced" or fraudulently obtained the birth certificate of the real James R. Parker, he could be fined up to twenty-five thousand dol-lars and could spend up to five years in jail. But no one knew how David had gotten the birth certificate he had furnished Safeco, and there was no copy of it in his Safeco file. Fur-thermore, if a federal crime had been committed, Victoria was talking to the wrong prosecutor in the wrong court. She'd have to see the U.S. attorney for Tampa, and it would take a lot of talking, even for Victoria, to interest him in prosecuting a man who allegedly used a false birth certificate when bigger crooks were getting away because the U.S. attorney didn't have the investigators or money to catch them.

When Pat walked through the door that evening, it was Andrea, not Marcia, who was waiting to turn on her. "You didn't call all day long. What the hell is going on?" she shouted at her mother, who was feeling just as helpless as her daughters. "You don't understand. You just walk in and don't tell us a thing. I'm really pissed."

If Andrea was angry, Marcia was quite calm for a change. The crisis of the day had been what she was going to wear when she saw her father. It was an important question for all three girls because they wanted to look their best. Christine had little trouble picking an outfit, but Andrea and Marcia couldn't decide. Andrea ended up borrowing a beautiful red suit from Victoria. It fit her perfectly, and she knew she looked stunning in it. Pat had given Marcia money to go out and buy a new dress. Since she would be turning seventeen in less than a week, the clothes were an early birthday present.

Marcia had bought a bluish purple dress, which she really seemed to like. That was unusual, for Marcia seldom wore dresses and rarely found one that pleased her. As she modeled it for Pat and Victoria, she appeared light-hearted and excited. After getting the girls settled for the evening, Pat and Victoria drove down the beach to a French seafood restaurant to meet Richard, who had just flown in from Miami.

Richard did not share Pat's fears. He didn't think Parker was dangerous, because he had no history of violence. Nor was Richard concerned that someone might slip Parker a message that Pat was in town. But as a private detective, Richard believed in patterns, and he was convinced that Parker would run if he got wind of what was about to happen. The investigator had agreed to come to Tampa to make sure that this time Parker would find no place to hide.

One look at Pat and Victoria told the whole story. Pat would barely say a word; she seemed tense and drawn, almost numb. Richard had never seen her like that before. Victoria, on the other hand, was so pumped up that even food could not slow her talking.

"What do you want me to do?" Richard asked Pat, between courses.

"Follow him," Pat said.

"That's the worst thing," Richard said. "What if he spots me? He'll run for sure. . . . Here's what I'll do. I'll go out to his place first thing to make sure he's there. Then I'll call you. I'll hang around the pool at the Holiday Inn. When you get your paperwork tied up, page me. I'll see to it he's around for the arrest."

The job wasn't that simple, but Richard would never tell Pat that. Jim Parker worked at home, and Richard knew from his partner's surveillance report that it would be foolish to sit on the street and watch Parker's house. If he did that, he'd run the risk of Parker calling the police or sensing something was afoot and sneaking out the back. If Parker stayed home all day, fine. But if he planned an overnight somewhere, Richard might not see him leave and Pat would be out of luck. Whatever happened, Richard didn't want to hang around Tampa very long. He was busy, and Pat must set the trap or get out of town. Besides, her nerves obviously couldn't take much more of this legal cat and mouse.

"Don't worry, Pat. I'll know where he is when it's time," Richard bluffed. "But just one day. That's it. If you can't get it done tomorrow, tough shit. I'm gone."

23

PAT GOT UP at six the next morning, sat on the carpeted steps, and cried. It wasn't just anxiety and fatigue. She felt totally alone with no one to confide in. She couldn't share her feelings with her daughters. They were part of her problem, and letting them know how desolate and frightened she was would only upset them more. She couldn't talk to Victoria about her feelings, either. Her attorney was swept up in the challenge and drama of the case. Pat thought she could have talked to Richard or Frank, who seemed to calm her just by their presence, but she could never manage a moment alone with either. Who else was there?

She waited until quarter to eight, then called Dr. Charles Crotty, the therapist who had helped her several times after she had found David, and who she knew would be in his office early. Unable to control her sobbing, she wasn't even sure he could understand what she was saying: ". . . biggest mistake of my life . . . girls on edge and fighting . . . they want to come home . . . they're scared . . . it's too late . . . I've done this to them . . . I'm pushing them into it . . . don't think I can make it . . ."

Dr. Crotty listened as he usually did, and Pat responded more to the kind and understanding tone of his voice than to what he actually said. She hung up feeling calmer and ready to face the day.

Richard had gotten up early, too. He drove out to Jim Parker's house and watched. He saw Parker's car in the driveway and, a few minutes later, a man passing in front of the window. Certain the man was Parker, from his photograph, Richard drove to the Holiday Inn where his partner, Rick, had stayed, and called Pat from the lobby.

"He's home," Richard said. "I'll be at the pool. Good luck in court."

Frank had asked his paralegal, Debbie Perez, to take care of the girls while Victoria, Pat, and he went to court to plead for a Writ of Ne Exeat. Debbie didn't know what to expect, but she had heard that Pat's daughters could be as restless as bees.

Victoria, true to form, burst into Frank's office dressed in a white suit, as fresh as if she had just returned from a vacation and ready to tear a hole in the courthouse. "Hi, Debbie," she called over her shoulder as she strode toward Frank's office. Pat, who looked exhausted, trailed a few steps behind; tagging after her were Christine, Andrea, and Marcia, the last two squabbling fiercely over a hair dryer. Oh, my God, Debbie thought.

While Victoria and Pat worked with Frank, Debbie tried to keep tabs on the girls. Christine, who looked quite grown-up in her high heels, was very quiet. Debbie was surprised because she had been expecting three noisy, gangly teenagers. She could see that Christine not only didn't want to be there, but was embarrassed at her sisters, who kept cracking loud jokes, mostly about Victoria's being a walking cosmetic counter. It was also clear to Debbie that they were trying to hide their fear under the string of wisecracks. They reminded Debbie of her own sisters—cute, lovable kids in grown-up clothes. She felt sorry for them because she sensed frcm the few serious comments they had let slip about meeting their father that they were expecting a ride into the sunset with full orchestra. Debbie knew better.

After the girls had explored the office and worn a path to the ladies' room, Debbie suggested lunch. Leading them into Frank's office, she pointed to a golden arch thirty floors below and two blocks away. The girls caucused, then agreed to eat and go back to the beach house to wait. With a sigh of relief, Debbie watched them argue their way out the door.

While the girls were having lunch, Victoria, Frank, and Pat were filing court papers. To hear their plea for the Writ of Ne Exeat, the clerk sent them to Judge Vincent Giglio, who was free. It was three o'clock. Pat held her breath in the hallway while her attorneys went into the judge's small chamber to present their case. After reading the motion with a stony face, Giglio listened to their brief argument, then asked, ''Is there any reason why bond should be more than one thousand dollars?''

The motion before him requested forty-two thousand dollars, the amount of the arrearage. Knowing they had won, both Frank and Victoria argued for more than one thousand dollars, pointing out that if the court set bond too low, Jim Parker might pay on the spot, then flee.

''Ten thousand,'' Giglio said when they finished. ''And good luck.''

The order Judge Giglio signed directed the clerk to issue a Writ of Ne Exeat against James C. Parker, ordering him to post a $10,000 cash bond, stay in Florida, and attend the child support hearing Pat had requested. If Parker refused to or could not post the bond, the Writ further ordered the sheriff ''to arrest him and confine him in the Hillsborough County Jail and to bring him before a judge of this Court within twenty-four hours of his confinement or at the Court's earliest session.''

While Pat, Victoria, and Frank stood in the hallway savoring their victory, Judge Gonzalez walked by. No one had to tell him Bennett had won. ''Yep,'' he said, ''that Writ of Ne Exeat is a *mean* thing! But it's the way to go.''

Pat rushed to the nearest phone. She had been checking in with Richard every couple of hours all day. The last time she had talked to him, he told her Jim Parker was still at home, and that he had seen him standing in his yard watching a construction crew. But Pat hadn't spoken to the girls since noon because there had been nothing to report. Now there was. Within the hour, she and Victoria would be asking the sheriff to arrest their father, and she wanted them to be dressed and ready. She phoned Debbie, who told her the girls had gone back to the beach house to wait. Pat called there.

"Christine took off," Andrea told her. "We don't know where she is."

"But why?"

Pat began to panic. Without Christine and her car, Andrea and Marcia were stranded an hour's drive from Tampa. It *would* be Christine who'd disappear at the eleventh hour, Pat thought. She had never wanted to come in the first place.

"Christine's pissed at Marcia," Andrea explained. Apparently Marcia had spilled water on Christine while she was sunning herself on the deck, and Christine had got so angry, she dressed and drove off.

"Did she say where she was going? When she's coming back?"

"We don't know where she is, Mom," Andrea said.

"Well, I'm going to see the sheriff right now, so sit by the phone!" Pat ordered. "When Christine comes back, go straight to Frank's and wait there."

Pat then called Richard, who was sitting by the swimming pool in the Holiday Inn in Lutz. "Christine's gone," she said. "No one knows where she is. Would you go get Andrea and Marcia if she doesn't come back?"

"It's too far," Richard said. "We'd never make it back here on time."

Pat was in a state of shock as Victoria led her down the polished terrazzo hallway and through the double glass doors of the Hillsborough County Courthouse Annex to the sheriff's office. Captain Richard Frazier stood up to greet them. A big man—six feet tall and two hundred pounds—he wore gold-rimmed glasses and had unusually large hands with neatly manicured nails. His voice was soft and kind, but a little raspy from too many cigarettes over too many years. And he spoke with the slow drawl of a native Floridian.

Dressed in a short-sleeve tan shirt with brown slacks and without a badge or gun, Captain Frazier didn't seem like a sheriff. But one look at the wall behind his huge glass-topped desk and you knew he was a lawman and proud of it. A Florida state flag hung on a pole next to the Stars and Stripes. To one side of it was his favorite picture—a color photo of Tampa in 1938. Although he had had many offers, he wouldn't part with it. Directly behind the desk hung certificates from the FBI National Academy and the Bureau of Prisons.

During his thirty years as a lawman, Frazier had done just about everything: riding patrol, chasing pimps while on the vice squad, investigating homicides as a detective, and preventing prison riots as a warden. He was mighty proud of the fact that he had once made it into *Time* magazine. For the last sixteen years, he had commanded the civil division of the Hillsborough County Sheriff's Office. With regular hours and no street work to keep him on edge, it was the easiest job he had ever had and he liked it.

As Frazier eased back in his chair and listened to Pat's somewhat incoherent story, he felt touched. The woman was decidedly different from most of the wives who walked into his office begging him to arrest their no-good husbands. I wasn't just her tears, which he knew weren't the crocodile variety often used to soften the heart of an old sheriff. From what he could tell of her story, she had walked through hell to find her former husband, and he sensed in her a moral outrage that appealed to his Christian ethic. But whatever she was doing and for whatever reasons, he concluded, it was so important to her that she wouldn't waste his time by melting into a puddle and dropping all charges once he arrested this James C. Parker.

Victoria read Captain Frazier as easily as a billboard. Detecting a rather old-fashioned wisdom and chivalry clinging to his speech and manner, she went to work on him. In her best Virginia drawl—soft and lilting with just a touch of deep Dixie to match his—Victoria launched into her own five-minute version of the Bennett story. When she finished, she handed Frazier the Writ of Ne Exeat, stressing how important it was to arrest James Parker that very night because if he suspected his former wife was looking for him, he'd run again. The papers she and Pat had filed were public record, she pointed out. Someone in the courthouse who knew Parker might alert him, or a reporter who covered the court might sniff out the story and call him for a comment.

A father who prided himself on providing for his children, Frazier had little sympathy for Parker. The more he heard about how the man had treated his daughters, the more he wanted to help the woman in tears. In his mind, James Parker had violated the laws of the land and the rules of the Lord, and belonged behind bars for both. As he studied the writ, Frazier was impressed, and his respect for the lady lawyer from Washington grew by the minute. That Writ of Ne Exeat was a mighty powerful piece of paper and plenty hard to get.

Pat watched as Victoria played on Frazier's sympathies like a master cellist. The more Pat listened to her attorney's stroking, the more impatient she became. After waiting sixteen years to face David, every extra minute was agony. She had three emotionally charged daughters, a writ in hand, a private detective on hold, and an attorney who didn't know what time it was. Pat was so close now, all she needed was Captain Frazier to send a deputy to Lutz, thirty miles away. Every minute of chitchat and flattery was a luxury she could no longer afford.

As Captain Frazier swiveled in his chair, a cigarette dangling from his lips, Pat noticed a curl of smoke drifting lazily up from beneath his seat. God, that was all she needed—fire engines and hoses, while David skipped town!

Victoria saw the smoke, too. "Captain Frazier," she said calmly, "I do believe you're on fire."

Frazier uncoiled himself just as calmly and began brushing his pants legs. "Looks like I'll have to buy me a new pair," he drawled. "I do this about once a week."

Pat had to laugh in spite of herself, and the tension momentarily drained from her body. What in the world am I doing here? she asked herself. I'm facing the biggest crisis of my life, and here I sit, watching slapstick.

"Don't worry none, purdy ladies," Frazier said after he put out the fire on his pants leg. "We'll get that desperado inside of an hour."

Spread out on Frazier's desk were Rick Hager's photos of James C. Parker. When he sat down again, Frazier studied them a moment, admiring Rick's work.

"Who took 'em?" he asked.

"A private detective," Pat said.

"D'ya think he might like to move down to Tampa?" Frazier smiled as he called a deputy into the office. "Look at these pictures the PI done took," he said. "You think you kin get this boy?"

The deputy nodded. He was a trim young man with dark

hair and a mustache to match. On his tan shirt hung a silver
star and a name plate. To Pat, he seemed so nervous that she
wondered if he even knew how to fire the gun hugging his
leg. Not sure exactly where the tiny town of Lutz was, the
deputy went to the outer office to check a county map. A few
minutes later, he was back.

"Lutz isn't in Hillsborough," he announced. "It's more
than a mile into Pasco."

"Well, darn it!"

With disappointment on his face, Captain Frazier explained
to Pat and Victoria that if Lutz were just over the county line,
he could still arrest Parker there without getting into a jurisdictional skirmish. But under the circumstances, the Pasco
County sheriff would have to do the arresting. He was sorry,
but there it was.

"His name's Jim Marsee and you'll find him in the courthouse in Dade City," he told them.

Victoria checked her watch. It was just after four.

"The office closes at five," Frazier said.

Pat turned pale. Dade City was thirty miles away. Victoria
had just wasted more than an hour finding and stroking the
wrong sheriff. Now, as they got ready to make a dash through
Tampa to Dade City, she still didn't know whether Christine
had returned to the condo. If she simply sped off into the
rush hour with Victoria, the girls might miss seeing their
father.

While Pat and Victoria ran for the pay phones in the lobby,
Captain Frazier called the Pasco County Sheriff's Office. Like
good neighbors, Hillsborough and Pasco frequently did fa-
vors for one another. Since Deputy Sheriff Jim Marsee was
out of the office, Frazier left a message: "Expect two ladies
with a Writ of Ne Exeat. Keep the door open. It's important
to me that you arrest him immediately."

While Frazier was leaving his message for Marsee, Victoria was paging Richard at the swimming pool. "Drop everything and race over to Dade City," she told him after she
explained the latest legal wrinkle. "Hold the sheriff until we
get there." On the phone next to her, Pat was ringing the
beach house. No answer. All she could do was pray that the
girls were on their way to Frank's.

After making their calls, Pat and Victoria raced back into

Frazier's office. He was waiting, ready to push them out his private door, which opened onto the parking lot. "Lady lawyer," he told Victoria, "you better fly . . . But don't you worry none—you ladies are too purdy to get arrested for speeding in *my* county . . . North on the freeway to the Land O' Lakes exit sign, Highway 54 . . ."

Victoria and Pat dashed to the white Lincoln parked just outside. "Hold tight!" Victoria yelled as they took off down the street behind an escort car and onto the freeway a few blocks away. Tooling along at eighty miles an hour, they passed the escort, who waved them by like a flagman at the Indy 500.

Victoria was having fun, and her driving scared the anxiety right out of Pat. "Don't worry," Victoria said. "If we get stopped, I'll just ask the officer to lead us right to the Pasco County Courthouse!" She wove in and out of the rush-hour traffic until she saw the Land O' Lakes sign and the Zephyrhills exit. Then she screeched off the freeway and down the ramp to Highway 54. Which way—right or left? Neither Pat nor Victoria could remember. There were no road signs, and no time to check a map.

Across the highway sat a country store with a pickup parked out front and a driver sitting inside munching a sandwich. Victoria cut across the road and slowed down just enough for Pat to jump out. She ran over to the truck and rapped on the window.

"Which way to Dade City?"

"East on Fifty-four to Zephyrhills," the driver said. He pointed right. "About ten miles. Turn left onto Three-oh-one. There's a sign there that says Dade City—about nine miles."

"Where's the Pasco County Courthouse?"

"Can't miss it, lady. Keep driving right into town. Big gray dome on the right side."

Pat pointed east to Victoria, who did a quick U-turn. With the door hanging open and the car still moving, Pat jumped back inside. It was after four-thirty. Victoria stepped on it again, this time racing down a two-lane blacktop that rolled first through pines, marshes, and pastures, then sliced through a suburban sprawl of pizza parlors, trailer parks, and cheap motels.

As the Lincoln bounced over a little crest, they saw a road gang about a mile away, working on what looked like a bridge over a patch of swamp. Sawhorses blocked the left lane. In the right lane stood one man holding a stop sign and another signaling with a red flag. Refusing to slow, Victoria began flashing her lights and tooting her horn while Pat stiffened in fright.

The flagman frantically tried to wave them to a stop. When he saw they weren't about to, he flagged the left lane to a halt. The other worker flipped his sign around to Slow. The Lincoln sped over the bridge like a souped-up squad car. The column of waiting cars slipped by in a rush of wind, and Pat let out a sigh of relief.

As Victoria drove through Zephyrhills, Pat shouted, "There's the sign—Dade City—turn left at the light!"

24

SITTING BY THE pool, bored, with nothing to do, Richard was relieved when he finally got his marching orders from Victoria. He listened to her story about the wrong sheriff in the wrong county courthouse and took it as a bad case of prebattle jitters. Typical Victoria, he concluded after he hung up. Melodrama at its best.

Richard eased into his rented Cadillac and leisurely drove to Dade City just a few miles from the Lutz Holiday Inn. He circled the courthouse, parked in the rear across the street from a string of police cars, then discovered he didn't have change for the meter. He didn't need to be a former cop to know that the easiest place to collect a ticket was right outside a police station. Hoping his luck would hold, Richard bounded up the stairs of the courthouse looking for a sheriff and a couple of quarters.

The Pasco County Courthouse was a relic of the old Florida—before snow-hating yankees had invaded. It was a two-story red brick building with gray cement steps and a clock in the dome. Inside, its ceilings were high and its terrazzo floors chipped. A long bulletin board papered with notices ran down one wall just above the white wainscoting. And at one end of the wide hallway, a double staircase with worn marble steps wound to the second floor, where Deputy Sheriff

Jim Marsee was getting ready to go home to a clam and lobster supper.

Marsee was exactly what Richard expected. Smooth and quiet with a big gut. Richard liked Florida lawmen, whom he found pleasantly different from the cops around Washington. Florida police usually respected PIs and cooperated with them. Washington cops didn't—and who could blame them? Good PIs ran their own show, chose their own cases, made more money, and led lives filled with less danger and more predictability.

After introducing himself, Richard showed Marsee his license, stating that he was a former D.C. special-operations policeman who had been wounded five times. He explained why he was in Dade City and told Marsee two women were on the road somewhere between the courthouse and Tampa with an arrest warrant. Since he planned to leave town that night, Richard was as anxious for Marsee to arrest Jim Parker before dark as Pat and Victoria were.

"I know it's a lot of trouble, Sheriff," Richard said. "And I know it's almost time for supper, but I wish you'd help me out. These women are driving me nuts. We both know the guy will be there tomorrow. But *they* don't believe that. My client will get herself a heart attack if you don't arrest the man tonight."

Marsee was as sweet as pecan pie. Captain Frazier's message had not caught up with him yet, and he wasn't fond of PIs who more often than not came in, stirred the pot, then walked away leaving a mess for the sheriff to clean up. Although Richard seemed responsible, it was almost quitting time and Marsee wasn't eager to make an after-hours arrest for anyone. He told Richard he would wait until the ladies came with the paperwork so he could judge for himself what this was all about.

Richard got change from Marsee's clerk, bought an orange soda from the soft-drink machine downstairs, and walked out of the courthouse toward his parking meter. He was in the middle of the empty street when he caught a white gleam out of the corner of his eye. He heard tires squeal and jumped aside just as the white Lincoln cut the corner of the curb and screeched to a halt. Doors flew open. Victoria and Pat jumped out and began running up the courthouse steps. "Hurry up, Richard," Victoria shouted. "It's five o'clock!"

Richard followed, sipping his soda. By the time he reached the courthouse door, Victoria was already racing up the stairs at the other end, the clicking of her high heels on the marble echoing in the nearly empty hallway. Richard and Pat took the elevator. When they walked into Marsee's small, shabby office, Victoria was standing in front of the glass service window. Behind it, Marsee was studying the Writ of Ne Exeat.

"In fourteen years, I ain't seen anything like this piece of paper," he said. Since it came from Hillsborough County, Marsee wasn't even certain it was valid in Pasco. And Pasco County regulations required him to run the warrant by his superiors before attempting an arrest. He couldn't do that until the next day. "I'm on my way home for supper. I'll take care of this in the mornin'."

"We need to get it served tonight, Sheriff," Victoria purred, her big brown eyes pleading with his. "We need your help. You're the *only* one who can do this for us."

Marsee came out from behind his glass shield and walked over to Pat, trying to size her up. He considered himself a good judge of character, and the lady impressed him as serious. She had been chasing this James C. Parker in Fairfax, then Hillsborough, now Pasco. She had come all the way from Washington with an attorney and that in itself was unusual. In Marsee's experience, it was difficult to get an attorney just to walk across the street for a client. And the lady and her attorney were smart enough to get a Writ of Ne Exeat so the man couldn't run again.

Marsee decided to bend the rules. He'd try to arrest Parker that night without authenticating the Writ of Ne Exeat or settling the jurisdiction question first.

While Marsee was deciding how to handle Pat's case, the office clerk had been eavesdropping. Sensing Marsee's ambivalence, she got up from behind her desk and came over to him. "Deputy," she asked, knowing full well the answer, "is this a child-support case?"

"Yes, it is," Pat nearly shouted.

"Well, then," she told Marsee, "go get that bastard!"

Marsee let out a guffaw. He had been paying child support himself for almost ten years, and not only did he not owe anything, he was paid up two years in advance. He turned to Victoria, straightened to his full height, then let his knees buckle to bring himself down to her level.

"I'm gonna get this boy," he announced.

Pat was so relieved she had to bite back a giggle.

Marsee asked Richard if Jim Parker had a history of violence. When Richard said he didn't know, Marsee said he wouldn't make the arrest without backup. Not wanting to give him an excuse to put off the job until morning, Richard volunteered.

"I'll go right on out there and wait," he said. "If you can't get help, I'll back you."

Marsee thanked Richard. "You be there, but I'll go in alone," he said. "If you see a big ol' fat deputy flying out the door, you know I'm losin'. You jump right in, you hear?"

Marsee turned to Pat and Victoria. "You ladies go on out to the jail and sit. I'll bring 'im in for you." Then, after giving them directions to the jailhouse a few blocks away, Marsee closed up the office and left.

Victoria smiled in triumph. Not only had she just saved the day, she had had fun doing it. In fact, she had had so much fun that she had worked up a Texas appetite. "I'm starved," she told Pat. "Let's eat."

They walked across the street to the Crest Restaurant. Pat phoned Debbie from there to see if she had heard from the girls. For all Pat knew, Christine could be in Orlando now, leaving Marcia and Andrea still standing on the beach.

"They're on their way," Debbie told Pat. "Frank'll drive them to the jail when they get here."

"Christine too?"

"Yes, Christine too."

Pat was so relieved to have all three daughters on their way that she even managed to enjoy her dinner. The hardest part was almost over now. Unless David tried to kill himself or shoot it out with Deputy Marsee, the girls would finally get to meet him. She felt one twinge of regret, however. They would have to see him for the first time in jail.

I have no choice, she told herself. It's that or nothing.

Richard sat in his Cadillac down the street from Jim Parker's house waiting for Marsee to show up. It was growing dark.

His camera with a 200-mm lens was loaded and ready to capture the arrest on film, but there were no street lights. And a flash would never work from so far away.

Richard was doing a slow burn. He knew Pat and Victoria were eating dinner somewhere, and he suspected Marsee had gone home for his supper as well, otherwise he would have been there by now. Everyone seemed to be getting something from this arrest but him. Marsee and Victoria were getting paid, Pat would have the satisfaction of seeing her former husband behind bars, and her daughters would finally meet their father. But him? He got to foot the bill himself for the car he was sitting in, the motel room he slept in, and—if he found time to eat—the food. To top it all off, unless Marsee hurried, Richard would miss his plane to Sarasota.

To make matters worse, Richard knew he couldn't just keep sitting on Parker's empty street. Somebody might call the cops on him and that's all he'd need to make his evening complete. Arrested while waiting for the police. His partner Rick would have a good laugh over that one.

Richard got out of the car and rang the doorbell of a house near Parker's. "Please don't be concerned," he explained to the man who answered. "That's my car over there. I'm supposed to meet a real-estate agent here who's going to show me a house. But she's late."

The man nodded knowingly and Richard went back to his car. This time, he stood outside to make it look as if he was really waiting for someone. He glanced at his watch and, without effort, looked genuinely steamed. Every now and then, he could see Jim Parker or a woman pass by the front window. Richard was worried that Parker might decide to take a ride somewhere, maybe for a six-pack, and he'd have to follow. If that happened, it would be just like Marsee to come by and, when he didn't find Parker, go back home for the evening.

As Richard's anger reached the boiling point, Jim Marsee pulled up to Parker's house in an unmarked car. A squad car with one uniformed officer inside tagged behind. Marsee hadn't gone home to eat as Richard had suspected. Since he couldn't be sure whether James Parker would try to flee or would arm himself, Marsee had decided not to go in alone, no matter what. To get backup, however, he had needed the

approval of his superiors. Then he had driven out to Land O'
Lakes to pick up another deputy. That had taken almost two
hours.

Marsee, who was casually dressed, and the policeman got
out and walked up to Parker's front door and knocked. A
man in his forties answered wearing Bermuda shorts and no
shirt. He let the lawmen in.

"Good evening, Mr. Parker," Marsee said as he pulled
out his ID card. "I'm Jim Marsee with the Pasco County
Sheriff's Office. I need to talk to you briefly."

As Marsee explained why he was there, he watched Parker's face so he could anticipate any move the man might
make. He noted that Parker was surprised at his arrival but
did not seem surprised by the reason. When he called Parker
by his real name, the man didn't wince.

"Obviously, there must be some mistake," Parker said.

His wife came into the room. "What's this all about?" she
asked her husband.

Parker gave her a vague explanation and told her he'd have
to go with the sheriff to clear it all up. He'd be back soon.
She began to cry.

"I need to change," Parker told Marsee.

The deputy sheriff followed Parker upstairs and stood in
the open doorway as Parker put on a shirt, pants, and a pair
of shoes. Marsee watched carefully. Parker might pull a gun
and try to shoot himself. Under these circumstances, men
were unpredictable.

Marsee followed Parker back downstairs, cuffed him, and
led him to the unmarked car. He told his backup he could go
home, then reached for his car radio. First, he called Central
Communications. "Ten-fifteen," he said after identifying
himself. "Ten-fifty-one" (prisoner in custody, en route). Then
he called Warden George Carpenter at the Pasco County Detention Center saying he was on his way and asking Carpenter
to open the back gate.

Richard watched the arrest with mixed emotions. He was
happy for Pat, and relieved that Marsee had finally come. But
through the bay window, he watched a woman enter the room,
and he could imagine what she must be feeling.

He tensed when Parker left to get his shirt. Unable to see

Marsee follow, Richard was appalled at the lawman's apparent carelessness. Any minute he expected to see the back door fly open and Parker race to his car for a quick getaway. By the time Marsee realized he was gone, Parker would have a head start—maybe he would even pull it off. Richard quickly slid back behind the wheel, ready to chase Parker if he tried to slip away. But the man returned a minute later buttoning a shirt.

When Marsee finally drove off with Parker, Richard glanced back at the house. The woman was still standing in the doorway, a silhouette against the soft living-room light. On her left arm, she held a child. She continued to stare down the street long after Marsee had taken her husband away.

The Pasco County Detention Center was a white box surrounded by a seven-foot chain-link and barbed-wire fence. Like the courthouse, it was an old building with chipped white tile walls and, above them, gray painted cement. Sergeant George Carpenter was the deputy warden in charge that night. When Victoria explained who she and Pat were and why they had come, Carpenter led them into the warden's office to make them feel comfortable. It was a slow night in the jailhouse and the drama of Pat's story caught Carpenter's imagination—a wife about to face a husband who had deserted her sixteen years ago; daughters about to see their father for the first time. Within fifteen minutes, all the guards and clerks knew the Bennett story, and there was a buzz of anticipation in the air that both Pat and Victoria could feel.

"Would it be okay for my daughters to talk to their father?" Pat asked Carpenter on one of his visits to the office to see how she was holding up. "They brought their photo album along so they can show him pictures of their childhood."

"If he wants to see them," Carpenter promised, "I'll arrange it." He wasn't so sure the man would. Handcuffs right after dinner, without warning, would shock the talk out of most men.

Warden Carpenter was so solicitous that Pat couldn't believe her luck. She had come to Florida convinced that justice would be hard to find there. After all, wasn't Florida the state where the old-boy network was still alive and doing well? Yet every official she had dealt with—Judges Gonzalez and Giglio, Captain Frazier, and Deputy Sheriff Marsee—had been fair, if not actually kind. And now Sergeant Carpenter and the prison staff were warm and concerned. It was ironic: she was getting more cooperation in Florida based on a sixteen-year-old court order from another state than she had ever received in Virginia.

Half an hour after Pat walked into the jail, Richard called. "They got him," he said. "He should be there soon. Good luck!"

"Aren't you coming?"

"This is your moment, kid," Richard said. "You don't need me there."

All in all, Richard felt pleased. He had just been part of something he knew was important—at least to the mother and three daughters, if no one else. And professionally, he was satisfied by how quickly the collar had gone down. No superfluous motion, just one clean move like a gymnast's routine. Richard checked his watch. If he hurried, he'd catch his plane for Sarasota after all.

Recognizing how anxious Pat was once she learned that Marsee was on his way to the jail, Warden Carpenter unlocked the door to the clerk's office and told her she could wait there so she wouldn't miss anything. Through the large glass window that separated the office from the intake section of the jail, she could see all the way down the hallway to the back door through which Marsee would lead David to be booked. Pat's mouth was as dry as bread crumbs. In her purse was the letter she had written David. She was certain that Warden Carpenter would agree to deliver it to him before David talked to his daughters.

Convinced that the next hour would be the girls' only chance to see their father, Victoria was nervous, too. She held David's FBI fingerprint card in her hand in case Parker denied he was David. Like Carpenter, she doubted he would want to talk to his daughters. Since Warden Carpenter had given her permission to use the prison phone, Victoria called Frank's BMW. "Step on it," she told him. "I don't want them to miss this."

Pat began to cry again once she realized her daughters would not be there when the back door opened. If the girls were lucky, they would have a few minutes to see their father through the window while a guard fingerprinted and photographed him before taking him to his cell. If they missed that as well, and if David refused to talk to them, they might never get the chance to actually see him. And *seeing* him—just that—was important to them.

Victoria tried everything she could think of to keep Pat's mind occupied. She chattered, brought coffee, cracked jokes. Nothing worked. Every time Pat heard a noise, she jumped to the glass window. Doubts began to nag at her again. Maybe David had escaped. What if he wouldn't admit he was David? Maybe the girls wouldn't make it on time. What if they went to pieces? Maybe she should have let them live with their fantasy father instead of pushing them toward their real one.

Her own emotions were in a swirl, too: she felt sorry for David; she hated him; she was ready to forgive him; she wanted to see him punished. Pat was angry at having so many conflicting feelings.

She heard feet shuffling and chains jingling even before the back door swung open. She jumped up and stood by the window, Victoria next to her, her nose almost pressed into it so she wouldn't miss anything. Her heart was pounding. She shivered. Her palms were sweating.

Deputy Sheriff Jim Marsee led David in. His hands were cuffed in front of him, he shuffled down the corridor like an old man, head bowed. As he entered the booking area, he looked up. David studied Victoria's face first. His eyes were wide and filled with confusion. Then he looked at Pat.

Without flinching, her eyes held his. No fear or shame. They didn't plead or question as they would have done sixteen years ago—they challenged. "David, I know who you are," they said. "I know what you did. You got away with it all those years. No more. I'm here and I'm not going away."

In a silent, powerful confrontation her eyes locked on his until he looked down. It was over.

Pat stood at the window and watched an officer book David. A guard led him away to be deloused. She sat down and a nervous giggle overtook her. She was trembling uncontrollably: She had done it. This man wasn't the man she had married and had been afraid to meet. He wasn't the man she had written the letter to. *That* David was her fantasy husband who still lingered in her mind. She had been so concerned that her daughters might not be able to make the leap from fantasy to real father that she'd been blind to how a fantasy David had persisted in her in spite of her common sense, in spite of the photographs, in spite of everything.

At last she felt free. She slipped the letter to her fantasy David back into her purse. The letter sounded foolish now. Whatever she had intended to say to him, she wanted to no longer.

Pat turned to Jim Marsee. "What did he say when you arrested him?"

"Nothing," Marsee said. "His wife asked him, 'What's this all about?' And he said, 'I'll explain later.' Then I told him the charges."

"Did he deny anything?" Pat was still worried that the FBI might have sent her the wrong fingerprint card.

"He didn't deny or admit anything."

"What did he say on the way here?"

"He said he didn't want to discuss it. He was very quiet."

"Did he deny who he *was*?" Pat asked.

"Nope!"

Pat threw her arms around Victoria and they both began to laugh out of sheer relief. "We did it," Pat nearly shouted. "We did it!"

25

THE TRAFFIC ON Highway 301 was light. Not that it made any difference to Frank, who always drove fast and who didn't need Victoria to tell him to step on it. After a full day in federal court, he was tired, but still deeply concerned about the girls and more than curious. He could only imagine what it would be like to be a teenager about to meet your father for the first time. But he didn't have to imagine what it would be like to be a runaway father and have the sheriff knock on your door during dinner waving a Writ of Ne Exeat. A mean piece of paper that, no doubt about it.

Frank could tell that the girls were scared, and he did his best to keep their minds off their father. He cracked jokes whenever he could or picked up on their juvenile humor, trying hard to be one of the gang. Christine was quiet most of the time, somewhat embarrassed by her sisters' behavior. Andrea, clutching the photo album, did most of the talking.

When the car phone rang, Frank was never so glad to hear from Victoria. Within a minute, she managed to turn the BMW into a moving phone booth with everyone shouting. "Did they arrest him?—You hear that? They got him!—Is he there?—Let me talk to Victoria—No, let *me* talk to her—Come on, Frank, give me the phone!"

When at last they hung up, Frank could feel the girls' relief. They now knew that nothing could stop them from finally seeing their father. Frank also sensed they were taking David one step at a time, almost as if that was all they could handle emotionally. Just *seeing* him was uppermost. Talking to him would come later. More relaxed, knowing their father was there at the jail, they changed the conversation to their favorite topic—their mother's attorney. For the next half hour, they roasted Victoria.

Victoria had given Frank directions to the Pasco County Detention Center. Frank had barely turned the motor off before the girls flew out of the car and down the walk to the jailhouse door, Andrea clutching the photo album. Warden Carpenter let them in and Pat, Victoria, and Frank (as well as most of the jail staff) stood back while the three girls peered through a small glass window set in a steel door separating the visitors' section from the prisoners' section. Through it, they could see the fingerprinting room. The timing was perfect. An officer had already taken David's photo and was just beginning to ink his fingers.

The window was too small for three heads, and Andrea and Marcia, who were more aggressive, kept nudging Christine away. "Let me see," Christine kept saying. "Let me see!"

Pat watched with concern, expecting an emotional outburst. Her daughters were excited. It was almost as if they were looking at a new baby through the window in a maternity ward. It didn't seem to bother them that they were seeing their father for the first time in a jail while he was being fingerprinted. What he was doing and where he was made no difference to them. They were totally absorbed in just looking at him, taking in every detail. He was finally real, standing right there before them. Pat was surprised: no one was crying. In fact, the girls were smiling and seemed happy. Suddenly it seemed worth all the energy, pain, and expense for just that moment. A two-minute look at a runaway father through a tiny glass window.

Andrea was quiet, her wall of indifference down for a brief moment. Christine looked at her father, but then stood back to let her sisters have the window to themselves, as if to say, "What's the big deal?" Pat couldn't tell what she was really thinking or feeling. Marcia couldn't tear her eyes away or stop chattering nervously.

"Look, Mom," she said, as if to herself. "I have his nose."

Pat laughed and sighed all at once. In spite of all the threats to back out and all the "I don't cares," her girls had come, they had seen, and they had conquered their fear. They'll be all right now, she thought. No matter what David says or doesn't say, they can handle it. He is no longer a mystery. He's the middle-aged man who fathered them and who's just as scared as they are.

After a guard led David away, Warden Carpenter went to his cell to tell him that his daughters were at the jail and wanted to talk. When he returned, Carpenter told Pat, "He said he doesn't want to see them while he's in jail."

The girls didn't seem upset. They seemed to have had enough excitement for one day. In a way, Pat was relieved as well. It would be easier on all of them if the girls talked to their father privately in the courthouse before or after his upcoming hearing.

"Mom," Christine suggested, "what if we sent our pictures in to him?"

Christine meant the wallet-size photos of themselves they had intended to leave with their father after they had finished talking to him.

Pat collected the pictures, wrote the names and ages on the back, and gave them to Warden Carpenter, who took them to David.

"He wants to keep them," Carpenter said when he returned. Pat smiled. It was Jim Parker's first admission that he was David.

Parker's business partner, John Reynolds, hurried into the detention center shortly after David had been booked, asking to see Victoria and Frank privately. They went into a conference room and closed the door. Thinking Reynolds was David's attorney, Pat waited outside the conference room worried that her lawyers would make a deal without her as they had done in her nightmare, or that Reynolds had brought ten thousand dollars with him and would spring David immediately. If he got out, she was convinced he'd run.

When the meeting was over, Victoria explained to Pat who

Reynolds really was. "He wants to give us three thousand dollars to leave town," she said. "He said, 'You don't want to destroy his business, do you?' "

Pat took the question as a threat: If you destroy Parker's business, how will he pay you? But the offer was laughable, not just because it was so meager, but because if she accepted it, David would avoid facing a judge a second time, just as he had sixteen years before. In her mind, David had to keep that date. She had come to Florida prepared to settle *in* court or *after* court, but not without a court.

"You're not considering that offer, are you?" Pat asked Victoria.

"No way!" Victoria said.

Reynolds introduced himself to Pat. He seemed cool, and if he was worried about his share of the business, he didn't show it.

"Did you know anything about this?" she asked him.

"No," he said. "I had no idea he wasn't Jim Parker or that he had three daughters."

"Does he have any money?" Pat asked. She was more worried about his having enough cash to post bond than his ability to pay his children what he owed.

"He should have," Reynolds said. "We did very well last year."

Pat was almost afraid to ask the next question. "Does he have any children?"

"A two-year-old boy," Reynolds said.

"No!"

The rush of sympathy Pat felt for David's wife and child was even stronger than her own shock. But despite her feelings, she still refused Reynolds's offer. She had come all this way for her day in court and the papers had already been filed. The situation had become more complicated with yet another child who could be hurt.

It had been a long, draining evening and Frank, for one, was ready to put it behind him. With a sense of great relief, he left the girls with Victoria and began the drive back to Tampa alone.

Pat, her daughters, and Victoria sat outside the jail in Victoria's Lincoln Town Car waiting to see if John Reynolds would spring David. It was already eight-thirty and David had been in the jail since seven. Reynolds eventually came out with a message. "I saw Jim," he said. "He wants to see the kids, but not at the jail. Can we arrange something?" Once again, Pat saw the offer as a threat: Drop the charges and he'll talk, otherwise . . .

When David didn't walk through the door by nine, they took off for the beach house, stopping at a Roy Rogers on the way. Victoria called her parents with the news, and Pat phoned her mother.

Everyone felt good. Victoria was pleased that the legal strategy had worked so far. Pat was pleased that David was beginning to pay for what he had done. And the three girls were amazed to have actually *seen* their father.

"Did you see how shook up he looked?" they asked each other. There was no bitterness or glee in their voices. They didn't seem especially glad that their father was being punished, just fired with curiosity.

"What do you think he felt like?"

"I bet he sure was surprised when he saw the sheriff!"

"Maybe he was glad he finally got caught."

The more Christine, Andrea, and Marcia talked about the man they had just watched through the small glass window, the more they wanted to hear his voice, even if he only said a few words so they'd know what he sounded like. Would he have a deep voice? Would it sound frightened?

By the time they pulled up to the beach house, the girls were already planning what they wanted to say when they met their father at the courthouse in the next day or so. Talking to him was a real possibility now, not just a fantasy. Now they had a real father. Hadn't they just seen him? Now they had things to say, questions to ask, and answers to demand.

After settling the girls in at the condo, Pat told them they could have one long-distance phone call each. "Just one," she warned. Then, in a mood to celebrate, she and Victoria took off for the Adams Mark Hotel in Clearwater Beach. Still flying high, they laughed and giggled like schoolgirls as Victoria burned up the beach road. This time, she got caught.

"You know you were doing forty in a twenty-five-mile zone?" the officer asked Victoria after he pulled them over.

Pat jumped in before Victoria could try her wide-eyed Southern belle routine on him. "Officer, I can explain," she said. "This is my attorney and . . ." She condensed the entire sixteen-year saga into three minutes, and when she had finished, the officer was studying her curiously.

"Lady, I've heard a lot of stories in my day, but never one like this before. Still, I can see you're both all wound up. I'll let you go with a warning this time. Have a good time, relax—but slow down."

They thanked him, and when his tail lights had disappeared, they burst out laughing so hard they couldn't stop. They had talked Jim Parker straight into jail, and now they had talked their way out of a ticket. Evidently nothing could stop them.

Pat and Victoria stayed at the Adams Mark until two-thirty the next morning, dancing with two doctors who were in Clearwater for a convention. If someone had told Pat back in Washington that a few hours after seeing David she would be light-hearted, she would have scoffed. Now here she was in a classy beach hotel having a good time at the moment she had feared would destroy her. The evening had turned into a celebration of life. Sixteen years of doubt and fear were finally over. She had left those anxieties with David in the Pasco County Detention Center.

Terry was right, she thought. You had to face it to get it behind you. And until it was behind you, you couldn't get on with your life. Well, she had taken the plunge, and by God, the water wasn't so cold after all.

26

▼

THE NEXT DAY, Thursday, attorneys for both sides drew the battle line. David Rankin, Jim Parker's counsel, filed a motion to reduce bond. Victoria filed one to increase it. A hearing was set for Friday afternoon. Meanwhile, Parker sat in jail, waiting for the wheels of justice to grind Pat down.

Victoria had drawn Judge Julio Gonzalez. But since he had advised Victoria on the case and would open himself up to conflict of interest if he heard the motions, Gonzalez had recused (excused) himself. The hearing shifted to Judge Vernon Evans.

Victoria cornered attorney Rankin in the hallway before he went into Evans's chambers. "I don't think your client knows who my client is," she warned. She could tell from Rankin's motion to reduce bond that Jim Parker wasn't going to go down easily, and she didn't want him or Rankin to get the impression that they could bully Pat. "I think he thinks she's still the little girl he left on welfare. Well, let me tell you—she *isn't*."

Pat told her daughters to wait in the hallway during the hearing, which would be over in less than thirty minutes. She thought David might be present and didn't want emotions to cloud the issue. The girls could talk to their father afterward if he was willing to see them, she said. They didn't object.

It was a small, private hearing room and Jim Parker wasn't in it. The atmosphere was icy and everyone seemed nervous, including Judge Evans. If he had any sympathy for Pat and her daughters, his voice and manner hid it well. "What do I have to do to get this man out of jail?" he asked even before he heard the arguments.

Rankin pleaded that there was no reason for Jim Parker to run. He had been living in Florida since 1972 and, except for business trips, had remained in the state where he had deep personal and economic ties. (Rankin was mistaken: Parker had left Florida in 1976 and hadn't returned until 1981.) Parker and his wife had just bought a house, he argued. And besides owning a "substantial" and ongoing business, he had "numerous assets" in Florida. Why would he want to leave them behind?

Rankin went on to point out to Judge Evans that the Writ of Ne Exeat posed a jurisdictional problem. It was issued in Hillsborough County and served in Pasco. Although he challenged the legality of keeping Jim Parker in jail, Rankin did not make a formal motion to vacate the writ.

Since Frank was in federal court that day, Michael Echevarria, an attorney who shared his office and who had been helping Victoria over the past few days, pleaded for Pat. He argued that not only did Parker have a history of running and hiding, but he was counting on Florida's reputation as a haven for fugitive fathers, as well. Since Parker was such a poor risk and since he owed his children forty-two thousand dollars in back child support—not to mention current support—ten thousand dollars was not enough to encourage him to stay home. Echevarria asked Judge Evans to raise the bond to forty-two thousand dollars.

Judge Evans said he would study the written motions, consider the oral arguments and case law, and make his decision that afternoon. He would call the winning attorney and let him know what it was.

Even though David was still sitting in the Pasco County Detention Center, his wife and son had come to the hearing. Like his daughters, they waited for news in the hallway. Marcia, in particular, had a hard time keeping her eyes off her half brother. "Mom, look!" she said to Pat after the hearing. "There's our brother. He's so cute. He looks like us."

Although Marcia wanted to run over to the baby and ask his mother if she could hold him, she knew better. How could they talk even, with this lawsuit? She began to feel a twinge of jealousy toward the baby as well as guilt. If she had been a boy, her father would never have run away. He hadn't abandoned his new family, had he? Was that because he had a son instead of another daughter?

Everyone went back to Frank's office to wait for Judge Evans's verdict. Sensing they had lost, they expected Evans to lower the bond to one thousand dollars. Parker would come up with the money, get out of jail, and put on his running shoes.

They didn't have long to wait. About an hour after the hearing, Judge Evans called David Rankin with his decision: he was issuing an order to vacate the Writ of Ne Exeat itself, making the question of raising or reducing the bond moot; James C. Parker was free to go home.

Rankin called Frank's office. Although no one was surprised that Rankin had won, no one had been expecting Judge Evans to grant what Rankin had never even asked for—a dismissal of the writ itself. The wording of the decision that Judge Evans called "Order Granting Motion to Vacate Writ of Ne Exeat" was vague. First, there never *was* a motion to vacate; second, the order never explained why it was being vacated. It simply stated, "The Court finds that the evidence presented at the hearing would require vacating of the order in and of itself."

Wasting no time, Victoria grabbed the phone and called the Tampa FBI with a warning that James Clinton Parker, who was wanted in Virginia for criminal desertion and non-support, who owed forty-two thousand dollars in back child support, and who was under court order to pay current child support, might try to flee as he had done before. Would bureau agents keep an eye on him? It was a long shot, but what the hell. Then she called The American Heritage Life Insurance Company, which had paid David's foster parents over eleven thousand dollars after the state of Virginia declared him legally dead. She told a claims officer that David was still alive and might try to play possum again. Shouldn't American Heritage put someone on his tail? If the company lost him again, it would never get its eleven thousand dollars back from David's foster parents, because it could never prove he was still alive.

By the time she got to reporters, Victoria was red hot. Frank didn't want her to attack the court—she, after all, could fly back to Washington the next day, but he'd have to deal with the repercussions. But Victoria had sharpened her tongue for Judge Evans. After accusing him of dealing "in a very, very light-handed and limp-wristed way with a man known to have avoided the courts," she came one word short of calling him incompetent. "It could turn out to be a very grave indiscretion," she warned.

Although Jim Parker got away with a light slap on the wrist, he wasn't happy either. He told the *St. Petersburg Times*, "It was a case of false arrest. It was thrown out in Hillsborough County and somebody's going to pay. They're going to have to stick to their story and somebody's going to pay."

And when the *Washington Post* caught up with him, he said:

It's been devastating. I'm rather angry they would still be pursuing me after all these years. It would seem that after a mistake I made twenty years ago—well, what good is it going to do now, other than persecute me? All they came for was vengeance. . . .

I wouldn't give them the satisfaction of seeing me with leg irons and handcuffs. I think that is a vindictive thing their mother did to try to parade me in front of them like that. . . .

We had a separation, and before I could ever do anything as far as her child support, she ran me out of town. Every time I got a job, she would call up screaming at my employer. I couldn't keep a job. I couldn't support myself, let alone them. . . .

After such a long time hiding from that woman, trying to get my life together, I really didn't feel that I had the right to intrude on their lives. . . . I don't think money is the primary thing. From all appearances, all they are trying to do is discredit me. . . .

It's affecting my family, my business, it's affecting me now. It's been mud and dirt and hurt and vengeance, that's all. And that's all it's been between me and that

woman for twenty years. That's why I've gone to such
extremes to hide from her.

Pat was disappointed but not shaken by Judge Evans's order
to let David go. It was only round one; more bells would
sound. She had accomplished what she had set out to do—
establish Parker's real identity, have him arrested, confront
him, and give her daughters the chance to see him. Victoria
had already filed Pat's Petition to Establish a Foreign Decree
as a Florida Judgment. Pat and David—either through the
court or through their attorneys—would settle on how much
of the forty-two thousand dollars David would have to pay.
Eager to put the whole emotional mess behind her, Pat wanted
to be reasonable. Not exactly a perfect ending, but a satisfying one.

If Pat wasn't upset, her daughters were. "How could they
just let him go?" they demanded. "It's not fair!"

Naïve and inexperienced in the law, they couldn't understand Judge Evans's reasoning. Their father had abandoned
them and avoided child support for sixteen years. He was
wanted in Virginia for criminal desertion. He had committed
bigamy and might have criminally assumed the identity of
another person. Why did the judge let him go after just two
nights in jail? They couldn't grasp the concept that justice
and the law were not the same thing.

That night at about eleven o'clock, Pat crept out of bed,
sensing something was afoot because it was so quiet. She
went downstairs. Marcia had the telephone receiver in her
hand and was about to call her father. Without saying a word,
Pat sat on the couch waiting to see what would happen. What
harm could a phone call do? If they were ready to talk, why
not let them? Hadn't Terry advised them to think only of
themselves, not of their father's feelings? Too bad if he had
had a rough two days. Too bad if it was late and he might be
upset by the phone call.

"Can I speak to my father?" Marcia asked Jim Parker's
wife, who answered the phone.

"He's just been through a terrible ordeal and can't talk
now," she said. "Wait a couple of days and he'll talk to you
then." She hung up.

Andrea was angry. No one had the right to hang up on

them, especially Parker's wife. He should have enough guts to answer his own damn phone. She dialed and got a similar message. Not one to be put off easily, she called again.

"Which one is this?" Parker's wife asked.

"Andrea," she said. "Look, I've been waiting sixteen years to talk to him and I'm not going to wait another day. If he's not man enough to come to the phone, then I'll stay here in Florida until I see him. And I won't stop calling until he talks to me!"

"Just a minute!"

Pat raced upstairs to wake Victoria, then picked up the only other extension. Both she and Victoria listened to the conversation.

"I just want to ask you one question," Andrea told her father when he got on the phone. She wasted no time—it was a question that had been on her mind ever since she realized he had abandoned her. Deep down she knew there was no answer that could possibly satisfy her, but she had to ask it anyway: "Why did you do it?"

David blamed Pat, saying she had had him fired from his job four or five times and then run him out of town.

Andrea wouldn't buy that. She was willing to concede that her parents had had problems and that her mother might not have been the easiest person to live with, but that was all. She went after her father with rapid-fire questions, not even waiting for the answers: "How could someone force you to leave? She's not stronger than you. You're bigger than she is. You mean to tell me that you let *one* little woman ruin your home, your family, your children? Any marriage can fail, but that's no excuse to just get up and run. You're a coward. A wimp!"

Andrea's anger poured out, not loud or volatile, but through the fierce insistence of her questions. She saw through her father, found his excuses thin, and recognized his evasiveness as a sign of weakness. She had him on the mat. This time, *she* held the power to hurt. She struck out, not wildly but with short and painful jabs. And she knew exactly what she was doing.

"I had no choice," David said when she kept asking why he had run away. His voice sounded weak and defeated.

"What do you mean, you had no choice?" Andrea demanded.

Silence.

"What do you mean? That's no answer!"

Silence.

Andrea moved on. "Did you ever feel guilty?" she asked. What she wanted was to hear him say he was terribly sorry, and would she forgive him? But Andrea was smart enough to realize that he really wasn't sorry. Embarrassed, yes—at having been caught. Scared, yes—of facing the consequences. But guilty? No. If he had felt guilty, he would not have been able to live with himself for seventeen years knowing what he had done to three children. Nor would he have been able to marry Lenora, leave her, and marry again.

When he didn't answer directly, Andrea's anger flared. "Don't you see what you've done?" she asked.

"Don't you *see*?" she pressed.

Silence.

Andrea moved on. "Didn't you ever wonder what we looked like all those years?" she asked. "Didn't you ever want to see us?"

Andrea knew what she wanted to hear. That he had missed her and had wondered about her all the time—what she looked like, if she resembled him in any way, how she was doing at school. Although she knew she would never get the answers she wanted, she was driven to keep asking these questions.

David told Andrea that he had thought about his daughters often, but that he hadn't wanted to intrude on their lives. He accepted full responsibility for what he had done, he said. If his daughters thought of him as a good-for-nothing father, he could accept that. When he left Virginia for Texas in 1969, he said, he was so depressed that he could hardly remember that year. For the first ten years, he thought he'd never be found. Then later he began to figure it was a possibility. During the last year, however, he had had a feeling they would find him somehow. He was too old to run now, he said, and would face his responsibilities.

Andrea wasn't satisfied. His answer sounded lame and insincere. If it had been *her* daughter left behind, Andrea knew she would have thought about the child every waking moment.

The issue was important to Andrea. It was one thing to be abandoned, but quite another to be abandoned and never thought of again. That was double rejection and twice as painful. So she asked again, "Didn't you ever want to see us?"

When she heard her father circling the question and choosing not to answer her directly, she struck out at him again. "I don't think you're listening to me," she said. Then she began to lecture him on what it was like to be abandoned.

Pat and Victoria listened to Andrea and David on the extension upstairs. Forgetting for a moment Terry's advice that her daughters were to tell their father whatever they wanted, and not be concerned about his feelings, Pat felt Andrea was talking too much and listening too little. She grabbed a pencil and a paper plate and scratched, "You're not letting him talk. You're lecturing him." Then she gave the plate to Marcia, who ran down the stairs to deliver it to her sister.

Andrea read the note, but didn't take her mother's advice. She continued asking questions and, when she wasn't satisfied with the answers, poured out her own feelings. If it sounded like a lecture, then her mother didn't have to listen. This was *her* father and *her* phone call. If her mother wanted to hear more of David and less of her, she could have the phone next.

Andrea's "whys" came so fast there was hardly time to answer them. Some she asked more than once.

"Why did you leave us?

"Why didn't you contact us?

"Why didn't you pay child support?

"Where did you go?

"You knew we were on welfare. You knew that and you *still* took off.

"Did you know what I went through?

"Weren't you even curious about us? What we looked like? Didn't you even wonder if we were dead or alive? What we were doing? You didn't even know if we were starving to death!"

"I take full responsibility," David said.

"You take responsibility! What kind of answer is that?" Andrea demanded.

David went on the offensive, but as far as Andrea was concerned, he was wasting his time. After explaining how he had been strip-searched in jail and treated like a criminal, he asked, "Why did your mother have to have me arrested? If all you wanted to do was talk to me, all you had to do was call."

As Pat listened on the extension, she found David getting to her the way he used to when they were married. In spite of herself, she felt sorry for him and his wife and what they were going through. Tears began to well up.

But not in Andrea. So the police had treated her father like a criminal. Well, what the hell did he expect? He *was* one in her book.

"If we called, you would have run away again," she said coldly.

"No, I wouldn't. . . . It was a very cruel thing for your mother to do. No way am I going to give her the satisfaction of seeing me in chains and handcuffs."

"Why didn't you just pay the child support?"

"I couldn't. Your mother would have had me arrested."

"You could have sent it from anywhere and no one would know."

"No, she would have found out and come after me. She was always one step behind me. I kept looking over my shoulder the whole time."

Andrea was so angry by this time that she landed a low blow. Knowing how her father had favored Christine, she told him how his old friend Bill came over to the house to help Christine. She knew the jab would hurt, and although she felt bad about tossing it, she couldn't resist.

"Bill fixes Christine's car," Andrea said. She spoke more slowly now, giving each sentence a chance to sting. "Bill and my mom went out on New Year's Eve. . . . He comes over almost every day. . . . Bill and Mom are good friends."

In the end, Andrea hung up the phone neither satisfied nor angry, just disappointed. She felt nothing for her father, just as Pat had felt nothing for David when she saw him in jail. Her indifference surprised her. If he had said the right words, like "I'm so sorry, I'm glad you found me," or "I love you, please forgive me," and if she had believed him, she would have wanted to try to build a relationship, even if that hurt her mother. Now, as far as she was concerned, her father had talked but had said *nothing*.

Andrea realized that for weeks she had been setting herself up for either total acceptance or total rejection. What she had gotten was neither, and she felt as lukewarm to her father as he had sounded to her. With a curious weightless feeling, she realized he wasn't worth hating or loving. And she didn't want anything in between.

All during Andrea's conversation, Marcia was fidgety, and with good reason. She had had two dreams the night before that told her exactly where her heart was. In the first, her father walked into her house. Everyone was at home as if waiting for him. He was gorgeous and smiling, and under his shirt he was wearing a Superman suit. He gave her and her sisters a hug and said he was sorry. In turn, they each told him that they forgave him. Then he looked at her mother. She, too, forgave him. Marcia woke up feeling warm and loved.

In her second dream, her father was standing on the corner fifty yards from the cul-de-sac where her house stood. He was stalking her with a knife, threatening to rape and kill her. She hid in the bushes, shivering from fright. Although her mother and sisters knew he was after her, they couldn't help her. He went from door to door asking for her. When he finally came to her house, he went inside to wait for her. She couldn't hide in the bushes forever and she couldn't go home. Marcia woke up from the second dream in a state of panic.

Besides her anxiety about talking to her father, Marcia was also angry at Andrea. She kept telling her sister, who seemed to be on the phone forever, "Hurry up, I want to talk. You can get back on later." She was afraid that Andrea was being too tough on her father and that he might not want to talk to her.

When she wasn't trying to coax her sister off the phone, Marcia was upstairs with her mother and Victoria, trying to listen on the extension with them. But she found it difficult to concentrate with three ears to one receiver and a constant flow of comments: "Did you hear that?—Can you believe he said that?—Tell Andrea to ask him this!" As far as Marcia was concerned, the phone call was a private business between her, her sisters, and their father. It was the big chance everyone had been promising her. Here he actually was—on the phone—and she couldn't hear, concentrate, or even feel what she wanted to feel without being coached!

Marcia left the bedroom after half an hour and sat next to Andrea at the table, waiting and making up the final list of questions she wanted to ask. She didn't want to repeat Andrea's questions. But she hadn't been able to catch all of her father's answers, and some questions were so important to her that she would never be satisfied with what he had told her sister. She wanted him to answer to *her*. What worried her was that she might lose control of her emotions, and she didn't want to give him the satisfaction of knowing that he could get to her that deeply.

"Hi," Marcia began, "how are you?"

She was so nervous that she kept twisting the phone cord around her hands. But the deeper she got into the conversation, the calmer she became until she could hardly believe it was Marcia Bennett who was talking and listening. She had expected to cry, hyperventilate, perhaps be so overwhelmed that someone would have to hang up for her. Instead, not only was she in control of herself, she dominated the entire conversation, becoming as patient and unrelenting as a prosecutor.

"Did you cheat on Mom?

"Did you ever come to see me in the hospital?

"Weren't you lonely? Scared?

"Did you give a crap about us?"

Unlike Andrea, Marcia waited for answers. If David tried to avoid her, she'd ask again, saying, "You're not answering my question" or "You're trying to get around this." When he wouldn't give her the answer she wanted, she suggested one: "Well, you could have done this or that, couldn't you?" When she felt there was no more to squeeze from the question, she methodically moved on to the next.

Marcia asked her father about his boyhood, his parents, and his foster parents; about Lenora, his current wife, and his son. She and her father even laughed a few times. And when the time felt right, Marcia began to talk about what had been eating away at her for as long as she could remember.

"I always believed you were dead," she said. "And when I knew you were alive, I wanted to call you right away. But Mom wouldn't give me your phone number. I grew up believing that it was *my* fault that you left." She was crying now, not hysterical tears, but quiet ones springing from deep pain. "I thought that if I had only been a boy, you would have stayed. I believed that, all the time I was growing up. I'm over it now, but that's what I used to think."

"How could it be a child's fault?" David said. He seemed close to tears himself. "Well, it wasn't your fault, I assure you."

"You have a son," Marcia said, still crying. "And that's *my* brother. Promise that you won't ever leave him like you left us. Promise!"

"I'm too old to run," David said.

Christine was next. Her voice was soft and warm and she was very nervous. "I missed you," she said.

To Pat, it sounded as if Christine had been holding back those three words for a long time, and she heard her daughter crying inside. So Christine was not indifferent after all. Missing her father for sixteen years and never hearing from him was like being rejected over and over again. Pat began to understand her oldest daughter's pain. Yet in spite of herself, she was annoyed at Christine for what seemed like forgiveness without even a show of anger.

"I remember you," Christine said. "I remember when you left. You gave me a ginger ale, then got your toy car set from under the bed."

"I still remember you," David told her. "I remember what you smelled like. I remember holding you. I thought about you every day. And I missed you, too. I want to see you. I want to see all you girls."

But after asking her father some of the same questions her sisters had asked and hearing the same answers, Christine gave the phone back to Marcia, convinced she still didn't care about her father, and that it hadn't been worth the energy and money to find him. If she wanted to meet him sooner or later, she told herself, it would only be to satisfy her curiosity, nothing more.

Still not satisfied, Marcia began asking the same questions all over again. What she was aching to hear was, "I lost so much when I left you. I love you. Can't I start being your father again? It's not too late. We still have a lifetime. I can't make up for what I did, but I can try. . . ." But her father didn't say that. The more he talked, the more he sounded as if he didn't care about her or what he had done to her. And the more Marcia listened, the angrier she became until, like Andrea, she began verbally pounding him. And when she sensed he was crying silently, she felt good. She wanted him to suffer.

"Look, you don't have to talk to me if you don't want to," Marcia finally said. Her voice was threatening.

"I'll talk as long as you want," David said. He sounded tired and beaten.

"That's not an answer," Marcia objected. "Do you want to continue talking to me?"

"I'll talk as long as you want."

"Look, I really don't see the point in all this," Marcia said. "We've been on the phone for three hours and you haven't said anything about being sorry or that you even *want* to talk to us. I'm going to hang up. Good-bye!"

Marcia ran upstairs to her mother. Pat was proud of her daughters. For three hours, they had said exactly what was on their minds, and each had unburdened herself of a special pain. Andrea had said how angry she was at being abandoned and, more than her sisters, demanded to know why. She wouldn't let her father off easily. Marcia had told her father how she had blamed herself for his actions all those years. Although she said she no longer felt guilty, Pat knew she did. And by telling her father how much she had missed him, Christine had admitted how deeply she had been hurt. She knew, even if she wouldn't say it to her mother and sisters, that she was pushing her father away so he couldn't hurt her again.

"I feel s-o-o good, Mom," Marcia said softly when she joined her mother in the bedroom. "Like the biggest burden has been lifted from my shoulders."

27

▼

Jim Parker didn't run. Instead, he decided to fight with the weapon of Pat's choice, the law—in the arena of her choice, the courtroom. Thirty days after Pat petitioned to have Florida recognize Virginia's child-support order, David's attorney hadn't lifted his pen. Technically, he didn't have to, for Pat's own attorneys had made a procedural error in serving James Parker. Pat would have to refile, serve David again, and wait another thirty days for a response.

Back in Washington, Pat wasn't terribly discouraged at the new delay. Filled with second thoughts about her legal strategy, in the light of Judge Evans's order to free James Parker, she was getting jittery about facing David in Hillsborough County, where she might draw Evans a second time.

But if Pat wasn't discouraged, she was angry. Her feelings of guilt, hurt, and anxiety disappeared, almost as if the face of her anger had frightened them away. Relieved that she had finally let go, she understood in a new way what Terry had told her daughters: before they could put the past behind them, they would have to express their rage.

What sparked the eruption was David's decision to use the system to avoid supporting Andrea and Marcia, who were still minors. Once she had found and exposed him, she had honestly expected him to begin paying current child support at the rate the court had ordered sixteen years before until he and she could renegotiate the amount before a judge. But it became clear to her back in Washington that not only had David chosen to stand in contempt of court as he had in 1969 when he ran away, but that he also intended to fight her on arrearages down to the last dollar. In 1969 he had hidden behind the name of another man. Now, in 1985, he was hiding behind the skirts of the law.

Well, if David wanted a fight, she'd give him one he'd never forget. Never again would she allow him to intimidate her the way he had when he walked out. Never again would he use her fear and guilt to keep her meek and humble. She would not allow him to punish his children a second time nor run from his responsibility again. If a battle was what he wanted, a battle to the finish is what he would get, win or lose. If he believed thirst for vengeance was driving her, as he told the *Washington Post*, so what? Of course she wanted to see him pay. She would even cheer if a Florida judge sent him to jail for a year. And if he was so foolish as to ever put his foot in Virginia again, she would send the sheriff after him for criminal desertion and nonsupport faster than he could say Jim Parker. As sweet as these thoughts were, however, it was not simple vengeance that fired her. She was fighting for her dignity and self-worth. For the right to hold up her head proudly and say, ''No one can step on me and my children—no one!'' It was justice she wanted most now. And next to dignity and justice, vengeance ran a poor third.

Before her Florida experience, Pat had been prepared to settle for five hundred dollars a month current child support for Andrea and Marcia, and ten thousand of the forty-two thousand dollars in arrearage to cover her travel and legal expenses. No longer. She began to rethink the motion Frank and Victoria had filed for her in Hillsborough County. And she talked to Judge Valentine about her anger, the Florida hearing, and her legal options. By mid-March 1985, two months after Judge Evans had let David go free, she made her decision.

She would seek a hearing in Pasco County, not in Hillsborough. For one thing, she didn't want to get into a jurisdictional skirmish that could cause more delay and expense. For another, she didn't want to risk drawing Judge Evans, before whom she was convinced she would never get fair treatment. She had done some checking on how Evans had ruled on other child-support cases, and the pattern she had found disturbed her. Since she couldn't fight him, protected as he was by the bench, she would avoid him.

Next, she would seek a judgment based on the now seventeen-year-old child-support order in Virginia, instead of in Florida, then ask Florida to enforce it. She had enough experience in the Juvenile and Domestic Relations Court in Fairfax to know that no matter which judge heard her case, he or she would at least grant a judgment for the full forty-two thousand dollars in back child support. Florida, on the other hand, had a history of whittling arrearages down to almost nothing just to clear the docket. In a way, Pat wouldn't have blamed Florida if it did that to her. If Virginia didn't take criminal desertion and nonsupport seriously enough to extradite, why should Florida clog its court with an order for huge arrearages that might be difficult to collect?

Finally, she would ask the Virginia court to include attorneys' fees and investigative expenses in the judgment as well as interest on the unpaid child support. Recovering legal and court costs should not be a problem, since attorneys routinely requested them. But to get interest in support cases was unusual. Pat had done enough legal research at the IRS law library on her lunch hours to feel confident that she would at least get a much better hearing on that issue in Virginia than in Florida.

At first, Victoria opposed Pat's plan. She had no argument with filing in Pasco County instead of in Hillsborough, since she wasn't eager to face Judge Evans again, especially after describing him as "limp-wristed" to the *St. Petersburg Times*. But legal sense told her that it would be easier to enforce a Florida judgment in Florida than a Virginia judgment in Florida. Besides, since she was about to leave for a vacation in the Sunshine State, she could file the papers in Pasco County at little cost. But Pat wouldn't budge.

Two weeks after Pat decided to begin the fight in Virginia, David offered through his attorneys to settle out of court—a single cash payment of five thousand dollars within ten days and two hundred dollars a month in current child support for Andrea and Marcia for two years, until Marcia turned eighteen. The offer only served to strengthen Pat's resolve to dig in and do battle in Virginia first.

Victoria made a counteroffer: two hundred dollars a month in current child support and a lump sum of between ten and twenty thousand dollars. Until both parties settled, she suggested, Jim Parker should begin sending the two hundred dollars a month the court had ordered in 1969, "showing his good faith in the event that we do reach an amicable settlement."

When Parker refused to send the two hundred dollars a month or settle for more than five thousand dollars, Victoria drafted a Petition and Affidavit for Rule to Show Cause in which she asked that the Fairfax County Juvenile and Domestic Relations Court summon David to prove that he should not be held in contempt of the 1969 support order, enter a judgment for $42,793 in arrearages plus $34,696 in interest, and grant Pat investigation costs and reasonable attorneys' fees.

Victoria filed the petition in mid-May. The court ordered David to appear on July 11, 1985, one year after Pat had found him in Tampa. Two days before the July hearing, Rankin responded to Pat's petition, arguing that James Parker could not pay the arrearage because he didn't have the assets, and that Virginia no longer had jurisdiction over the case because Pat Bennett had already begun legal proceedings in Florida.

Pat, Victoria, and Marcia, who had insisted on going to the hearing, sat in Judge Michael Valentine's courtroom at nine in the morning on July 11. No one seriously expected James Parker to be present because there was still a valid warrant for his arrest on charges of criminal desertion and nonsupport, and the jail was just down the corridor.

All Pat and Victoria knew for sure was that Judge Valentine would not be hearing their petition for a judgment because he had advised Pat on the case from the very beginning. Shortly after nine-thirty, Valentine called out Pat's name and told her to go to Judge Jane Delbridge's chambers.

"Oh, shit!" Victoria said. She had never argued before Delbridge and didn't know what to expect.

Pat waited on a bench outside Judge Delbridge's small hearing room until eleven. Every now and then she would steal a peek through a window in the door in the hope of catching a glimpse of the woman who could make or break her case. Over the last twelve months, Pat had discovered what most attorneys learn after their first week in the pit. Blind justice is a myth; judges, good and bad, are the reality.

It was eleven-thirty when a bailiff finally ushered Pat, Victoria, and Marcia inside. The room was empty except for a bailiff and Judge Delbridge, who sat up high behind a wooden barrier, like a bishop in a pulpit. Victoria went right to work. After explaining the facts of the Bennett case, she told Delbridge what they had tried to accomplish in Tampa and why they were back in Fairfax. All the while, Pat watched Delbridge, hoping to read something in her face. But there was little to see. Delbridge listened intently to Victoria's story and when she asked a question, her tone was as dispassionate as a lawbook.

When Victoria rested her case, Judge Delbridge peered down at Pat for the first time, then leaned forward. "There's no court reporter here," she said. "Now tell me—how did you find him?"

Pat relaxed and walked over to the bench. As she began her story, she immediately felt at ease; she was simply talking to another woman. She told Judge Delbridge all about the Social Security hearing and Lenora's marriage certificate. How she found Lenora and her conversation with her. How she called Safeco in Seattle to confirm that David had worked for the company, and then how she phoned state insurance license offices in the South until she scored in Tallahassee. Then she told about Richard and Rick and the photographs. About subpoenaing David's fingerprints from the FBI and his personnel records from Safeco, which led to the Rutgers University transcript. And she explained how, through subpoenaed information from Rutgers, she had found the man she believed to be the real James Parker living in Oregon.

"You ought to consider becoming a private eye," Judge Delbridge told Pat when she finished. "You're very good and you'd probably make more than you do now."

Judge Delbridge's decision that afternoon didn't surprise either Pat or Victoria. She granted a judgment for the full $42,793 in arrearages, then asked Victoria if she had prepared a list of Pat's investigative costs and whether she had calculated the interest schedule from 1968 to 1985. Pat had done both. Promising to study them, Delbridge then asked if Victoria had brought a written analysis of decisions where the court had granted interest on arrearages in support cases. Victoria had not.

"Would you do a memorandum?" Judge Delbridge asked.

Both Pat and Victoria felt good after the hearing. Not only did they get a judgment for the total arrearage, but they sensed from Judge Delbridge's questions that she would at least grant *some* of the court and legal fees. And since she had asked for a memo on interest, which amounted to almost thirty-five thousand dollars, it was clear Delbridge was at least open to granting interest if Victoria could satisfy her about the legal grounds for doing so.

Victoria submitted her Supplemental Memorandum two months later, in mid-September. Along with it, she appended a breakdown of Pat's actual child-support expenses from 1968 to 1985, which Pat had worked out in great detail. They came to $359,000. Had David paid the two hundred dollars a month the court had ordered during that same period of time, his share of the actual support would have come to 12.1 percent.

Two more months crawled by after Victoria had submitted the interest memorandum, and Pat still had no word from Judge Delbridge. It had now been one and a half years since she had found David, and Andrea had just turned eighteen. Unable to stand the tension any longer, Pat wrote Delbridge a letter. After explaining the history of her court battle and how two of her daughters had already reached majority with a third one almost there, she said:

I never anticipated in June 1984 that pursuing this issue would leave me so emotionally exhausted and financially burdened. I've mortgaged my house, borrowed from every possible source, and struggled not only to support my family by myself, but now to collect the child support owed. If I didn't believe this to be so important, I would give up just as so many other women have.

Judge Delbridge, I respectfully request that my case be given priority, and that a decision be rendered concerning the issues as presented at the hearing on July 11.

Ten days later, on Saturday, November 23, Pat pulled into the driveway with her cousin Joe from San Francisco in the front seat. She had just driven back from Philadelphia, where Joe had attended a business meeting. He was planning to stay the weekend.

Marcia was waiting.

"You have the judgment!" she screamed. Instructed to open any mail that looked important while her mother was away, she had read the letter from the court. "It's here."

Pat turned pale. Judgment? Was someone suing her? For what? Pat grabbed the envelope Marcia was waving and tore out the judgment. She screamed, then kept shaking her head in disbelief while Joe stood in the driveway thinking all the Bennetts must be crazy.

Jane Delbridge had given Pat everything she had asked for down to the last penny—$79,403.52 for arrearage and interest, $15,388.44 for current fees for Victoria Gordon, $6,100 for Frank de la Grana, and $5,181.62 for investigative and other expenses. She had been so angry and discouraged, feeling that the whole snail-paced child-support system was stacked against her. She had been beaten and bruised in the courts for one and a half years. Now this! The victory tasted as sweet as candy—$106,073.58 worth.

28

▼

THE FOLLOWING MONDAY, Pat took off from work and spent the day at the courthouse getting triple-sealed, certified copies of the judgment for Frank de la Grana to register in Pasco County. First, she obtained the signature of the clerk of the circuit court verifying that her copy of the judgment was true. Next, a signature from the judge of the circuit court verifying that the clerk's signature was valid. Finally, a second signature from the clerk attesting the validity of the judge's signature. That took half a day.

While scurrying around the courthouse, Pat met Judge Jane Delbridge in the ladies' room. Not wanting to compromise Delbridge by discussing the case, Pat merely looked at her and said thank-you quietly. There was a flicker of recognition in Delbridge's eyes, and Pat thought she saw the trace of a smile at the corner of her mouth, but she couldn't be sure.

"Good luck," Judge Delbridge said.

Not realizing at the time just how much luck she would need, Pat gave copies of Delbridge's judgment to Victoria, who, in error, sent them by express mail to Mike Echevarria. They sat in his office for a month before Frank finally found them and requested the Pasco County Circuit Court to register the judgment. Once again, David Rankin had thirty days to respond or the judgment would be binding in Florida. On the thirtieth day, Pat called the court to see what Rankin had done, if anything. The court told Pat it had misplaced her file and that James Parker had not been notified of the judgment. It was now the end of January 1986 and Pat had just lost another sixty days.

When the second thirty-day period had passed without Rankin contesting, Virginia's final judgment for $106,000 became active in Florida. Pat now had two ways to enforce it. She could file a petition with a court of equity asking it to determine how much of that amount and when he should pay. If he didn't pay, he would stand in contempt of the Florida court. Or, she could hire a collection attorney to ask the circuit court for writs of execution to attach Parker's assets (certificates of deposit, savings accounts, cars, stocks, bonds); to place liens on his assets so that if he ever sold them, part or all of the money would come to her; and to garnish his wages. Either choice would be expensive and thorny.

If Pat asked a court of equity to enforce the judgment, she would have to subpoena Parker's financial records to prove he could pay what she was asking. And Rankin would have acres of legal territory in which to stall or maneuver, if that was what Parker wanted.

If she hired a collection attorney, each time Pat wanted to attach, place a lien on, or garnish an asset, her attorney would have to ask the court for a separate writ of execution, and Parker would be notified of her request. That would buy him enough time to bury assets where Pat could never find them.

Frank, Victoria, and Pat all agreed that enforcement through a court of equity was the better choice. The principles on which that court was founded—morality, fairness, justice—had their roots in the ecclesiastical courts of medieval England. And since the moral obligation to support children was more basic than the legal obligation to do so, Pat and her attorneys felt that the court of equity, with its broad discretionary powers, would handle her case simply, fairly, and quickly. If everything went smoothly, Pat could ask the court to force David to pay or go to jail. Given his last brush with Warden Carpenter, she was certain David did not relish the thought of doing more time.

But before Frank could finish writing his Motion to Enforce a Foreign Judgment for the court of equity, Pat learned that

David was leaving for Texas. Afraid he might be planning to run away again, now that he faced a valid $106,000 judgment, she asked Frank to take his sworn deposition quickly.

The meeting took place in Frank's office in mid-April, five months after Judge Delbridge had reduced the arrearage to a judgment. Rankin's associate, Mark Kelly, represented James Parker. Although Frank's main purpose in deposing Parker was to uncover how much money he had and where it was, he also asked some relevant background questions and received some puzzling answers.

"What's your date of birth?" Frank asked. Pat had instructed him to pose the question because David/Parker had been using three different ones.

"July or August of 1944," Parker said. "I'm not sure which."

"Any particular reason why you're not sure?"

"I'm an adopted child."

When he joined the Marines and when he married Pat, David had given July 17, 1944, as his birth date. When he married Lenora, he changed the year to 1943. And when he applied for a job at Safeco a few years later, he gave August 30, 1944—the same birth date as James Parker from Rutgers University.

Frank then asked David when he had abandoned Pat, but Mark Kelly objected. This was a deposition in aid of execution of a money judgment, he argued, and therefore the question was irrelevant. He instructed Parker not to answer.

After David had admitted marrying Lenora in Dallas in 1969, Frank asked if he had divorced Pat first. Once again, Kelly advised him not to answer on the grounds that the question was irrelevant and possibly self-incriminating.

Next, Frank began asking Parker where he had worked, beginning in Florida in the early 1970s.

"I sold clothes in a men's clothing store," David said.

"How long did you do that for?"

"Year and a half."

"And after that, what did you do?"

"I was an insurance adjuster."

"Under what name?"

"James Parker."

"Is your name legally James Parker?"

"Yes."

"When did you change it?"

"Around 1969, 1970."

"What state?"

"Texas."

"What city in Texas?"

"Dallas, I believe."

"Did you have an attorney perform this for you, or did you do it yourself?"

"I had an attorney."

"Do you remember his name?"

"Smith."

"First name?"

"Lynn or Glenn, I'm not sure."

Frank continued taking Parker's employment history. "How long did you work at the Safeco Insurance Company?"

"Three to four years."

"As an adjuster?"

"Yes." Parker went on to explain how Safeco had transferred him from Jacksonville to Tampa to Baton Rouge to San Antonio, where he quit and returned to Jacksonville.

"What did you do after you left Safeco?" Frank asked.

"I had various jobs in and around the automotive industry."

"Such as?"

"Assistant service manager . . . Lee Chevrolet."

"How long did you work at Lee Chevrolet?"

"Approximately six months."

"What did you do after that?"

"I moved back to Tampa and I went to work for Ernie Haire Ford."

"In what capacity?"

"Body shop manager."

"How long?"

"Something over a year."

"After working at Ernie Haire, where did you work?"

"Bob Wilson Dodge . . . Body shop manager."

"How long?"

"Six months."

"After you left Bob Wilson Dodge, where did you go?"

"Back to the Ford dealer."

"How long did you work there?"

"About six months."

"Since leaving Ernie Haire Ford, have you worked in the capacity of an insurance adjuster?"

"Yes, I have . . . 1980 through the present."

"Where?"

"Custard Adjusters."

"How long did you work there?"

"1980, 1981."

"Any reason for leaving?"

"Yes, I got a franchise with another company . . . Frontier Adjusters."

"And have you worked at Frontier Adjusters up until now?"

"No," Parker said. "Approximately a year ago, due to the negative publicity, I lost my franchise."

"Frontier Adjusters took it away from you?"

"Yes."

"How are you presently employed?"

"With the Adjusters Claims Bureau of Tampa."

"How long?"

"One year."

"Since you lost your franchise?"

"Yes."

"Where is Adjusters Claims Bureau located?"

"In my home."

When Pat read the transcripts of David's deposition, she found only four surprises. She had not realized David had bumped around in the auto business after he had left Safeco. Had he not returned to insurance, she might never have found him. Second, she had never before heard that he had been formally adopted. She checked Virginia records and found out that his foster parents had legally changed his name to theirs but had never adopted him. Third, she hadn't been informed that he had lost his franchise with Frontier Adjusters because of the runaway father news stories about him. (She called Frontier. An executive told her that James Parker had not lost the franchise because of the publicity surrounding her case.) And fourth, she was surprised that David had legally changed his name. She asked the clerk of the county court in every city in which he said he had lived—Dallas,

Houston, San Antonio, Baton Rouge, Jacksonville, and Sarasota—to check court records from 1969 (the year he ran away) through 1985 to see if the court had granted him a name change. She received certified reports from each clerk indicating no record of the name change.

Soon after Frank had finished questioning James Parker, Victoria and Pat began preparing for a second, more thorough, sworn deposition. But before they could subpoena David, Rankin asked the court for and received a Protective Order barring further questioning. There was nothing else to do but ask for a hearing. In mid-August 1986, three months after he had deposed Parker and two years after Pat had found him, Frank filed a Motion to Enforce the Foreign Judgment with the Pasco County Circuit Court. The clerk scheduled a hearing before Judge Ray E. Ulmer for October 13, 1986.

As she sat in the small hearing room waiting for Judge Ulmer to open the proceedings, Pat was nervous and disappointed. David wasn't present because the court had seen no reason to subpoena him. Once again, he had managed to evade the judge.

"What can we do for you, Counselors?" Judge Ulmer said as soon as he sat down. Aware that Pat had come all the way from Washington, he seemed friendly and anxious to settle the matter before him.

"For the record," Frank stated, "I would object to the defendant or respondent . . . not being present. I fear his lack of presence here today and the history that he has in the past of avoidance of child support is something that the court should take issue with."

Judge Ulmer nodded but did not respond. "Let's proceed as far as we can, gentlemen," he advised. "You have an opening statement?"

Frank outlined the Bennett story. "This is a court of equity and this court can do what it deems fair under the circumstances," he argued. "So we're asking the court not just to recognize the foreign judgment, but to go ahead and enforce it."

Rankin counterargued that a court of equity has no jurisdiction to enforce a foreign money judgment under Florida law because money judgments have to be enforced through a writ of execution or other collection means. "They are attempting to ask this court, sitting as a court of equity, to do something which it has no jurisdiction to do," Rankin concluded.

Never having practiced law in Pasco County, Frank was surprised that jurisdiction had become the focus of the hearing. In Hillsborough County, child-support matters were routinely handled in a court of equity. Frank was fully prepared to argue that Parker was David and that David was the father of Christine, Andrea, and Marcia, should he deny either fact.

"We're not here to enforce someone for failing to pay a *loan*," Frank argue. "We're not here to enforce [payment for] a car that was repossessed . . . We're here to enforce a judgment that arises from a formal order of child support, Your Honor. I feel there's a big difference."

"What do you want this court to do?" Judge Ulmer asked Frank.

"To enforce the final judgment of the Virginia court and to make the defendant pay a substantial portion of the outstanding judgment . . . And I think this court has the authority and ability to do so."

"All right," Judge Ulmer said. "I'm going to have to ask you gentlemen to drop me a brief on the jurisdiction. I'm not totally persuaded I have [it]. I do not customarily do that, but jurisdiction is an important prerequisite to my being able to do anything, and I have no intention of entering an order in this court that I cannot enforce."

Ulmer gave Frank five days to submit a brief arguing from Florida cases that a court of equity had the authority to enforce child-support payment under its contempt powers. And he gave Rankin five days to respond to Frank. Judge Ulmer would then study both briefs, call another hearing, and rule.

29

CHRISTINE, ANDREA, AND Marcia had come to Dade City for the hearing, hoping to talk to their father. When he didn't show up in Judge Ulmer's chambers in the Pasco County Courthouse, they were angry. Most of the hearing, which dealt with legal technicalities, went right over their heads. With each passing month, they had grown less concerned about arrearages—which they were not convinced their mother would ever collect—and more interested in sitting down with their father to hear what he had to say, face to face, under calmer conditions. All this legal stuff was between their mother and him. That Judge Ulmer had delayed their parents' final confrontation bothered them less than their father's not being present at his own hearing. And though they wouldn't be unhappy if their mother actually got $106,000, it wasn't the most important thing to them.

After the hearing, the three girls stood in the courtyard outside Judge Ulmer's chambers and stewed. It had been a long time since they had telephoned their father from the beach condo, and during that time their attitude about meeting him again had changed. They were willing to give him one more chance. Maybe he wasn't himself when he had first talked to them after being arrested without notice and spending two nights in jail.

Marcia still wanted to meet her father, even more than when she had hung up on him in January 1985. In fact, she had written him a poem and wanted to deliver it personally. Christine and Andrea, both so disappointed in January, soon began itching to look him in the eye at least once. Now, when they felt they were giving him the benefit of the doubt, their father didn't even bother to show up.

Outside the courthouse, Christine stayed close to her mother and Frank, preferring adult company to that of her teenage sisters. Marcia and Andrea paced the flagstones in long, impatient strides. There was fire in their eyes. They walked over to Pat and Frank and announced, "We're going to his house to see him." That they didn't have a car or know exactly where he lived was inconsequential; this wasn't a time for logic. They strode over to Bob Jensen, a *St. Petersburg Times* reporter.

"I'm really ticked," Andrea told him.

"He couldn't face us," Marcia added.

Then back to Pat and Frank, saying they wouldn't take no for an answer. But both Pat and Frank, like Deputy Sheriff Marsee, cautioned them against walking in on David. Pat was still worried about possible violence; Frank didn't want to complicate a simple child-support case with a countersuit for harassment.

Despite threatening to see their father no matter what, the girls left Dade City for Tampa without a meeting. On the tense drive back to Frank's office, Pat could sense their anger.

Andrea was the most upset. She would not accept her mother's final decision not to allow her to see her father. She had come all the way to Tampa to do precisely that. Feeling left out and cheated, she exploded.

"I hate you," she yelled at Pat. "I hate you! All you think about is yourself and your money. I want to see him. I don't care about this stupid case. When we get to the hotel, we're going to rent a car and go!"

Christine and Marcia were shocked. Bitching was one thing, but such an outright attack on their mother, who had always stood by them, was a low blow they couldn't accept. Frank was so shaken he was ready to walk home. Pat was stunned and embarrassed, and only her pride kept her from crying. None of the girls had ever said that to her before. How could Andrea be so cruel?

After a long moment of silence, Marcia finally spoke up. "Shut up, Andrea. How could you say that? I love Mom."

The car phone rang—it was Victoria. Pat had never been so glad to hear from her. Each of the girls wanted to talk to the attorney, who managed to take their minds off their father for the rest of the ride to the city.

But when they reached Frank's office, the girls refused to let up. They wanted to call their father and force him to see them. How they would do that, they didn't know. But they'd find a way. As an attorney, Frank had no objection to their talking to their father or asking to see him. What Frank didn't want was for the girls to go out to Parker's house and beat the door down.

Somewhat reluctantly, Pat also agreed to the phone call and a meeting, but only if David agreed to meet them in a public place and if a third party sat nearby in case David tried something. After a few minutes of discussion, they had a plan: Christine, who was the coolest and least threatening, would make the call and invite David to the coffee shop in the Hilton Hotel, a few blocks from where they were staying. If he agreed, they would call him back later to set the time, after they had found a bodyguard.

"Hi, this is Christine," she began. Frank turned on the speaker phone so Marcia and Andrea could hear their father, too. "How are you doing?"

"Not too well," David said.

"Why's that?"

"I had a bad day," David said. "Someone's out to get me. Someone wants to destroy me—my business partner and my business."

Christine pushed her father's remark aside. "We'd like to see you," she said.

"I'd like to see you, too . . . hold you."

"We can meet you at the Hilton."

"Okay," he said. "I'll come."

"We'll have to call you back and set a time."

Pat and her daughters rushed to the Hyatt. After Pat arranged for a friend to be in the coffee shop when the girls walked in, Christine called her father back. "Let's meet at five," she suggested.

"No," he said. "I can't. My attorney advised against it. Everything I say will end up in the paper."

"Our attorney advised us against it, too," Andrea said. "But we're not wimps."

David hung up.

Jim Parker didn't know or understand his daughters. They were determined to force him to meet them. Angry and frustrated, they ganged up on him, calling him thirty-two times over the next few hours until he finally took his phone off the hook in desperation.

Through it all, Christine was considerate and gentle. Controlled and understanding, she did everything but beg him to see her. In the end, she just gave up and sprawled on the bed while her sisters took over.

Andrea charged at her father like a Doberman. David was no match for her.

"We're your family," she insisted. "How do you suggest we go about this? There is no solution for us. We waited for seventeen years for you to appear on our doorstep. Our dreams and hopes did not include calling you and hearing you say you won't meet us. . . . You and my mother have your own thing to settle; we have ours. I told Mom before we came down here, 'This is his chance—he can take it or leave it.' Well, I mean it! If you can't come to visit, you've had your chance."

David still refused to meet.

"What are we supposed to do?" Andrea continued to pound. "You don't know what it has done to my life. Don't you see? . . . No, I am not yelling at you. . . . Do you know what it was like to see my father for the first time in jail? Do you know how it feels to be rejected a *second* time?"

David hung up.

Marcia grabbed the phone and dialed. "How come you won't see us?" she demanded. "I am *not* hostile. Why are you hostile to me? What did I do to you *ever*? You want to see Christine. Why not me and Andrea?—Damn it, he's hanging up."

It was a long and draining day for Pat. She sat in the semi-dark room, depressed and hurt. Sleep wouldn't come. Hands down, this trip was the worst experience she had had with the girls since she had found David over two years ago. And it wasn't over yet. Rejection had rubbed her daughters raw.

Christine had fallen asleep in Pat's bed as if nothing in the world bothered her. Andrea had finally drifted off as well. Marcia was still awake, crying softly.

Finally, Pat simply couldn't handle it anymore—her own pain and Marcia's as well. She called her cousin Terry, allowing herself the luxury of crying now that two of her daughters were asleep. It was midnight in Minneapolis where Terry lived.

"Hell broke loose down here," Pat began, explaining what had been going on all day. "Terry, they're so hurt. Andrea yelled at me on the way back to the hotel, 'I hate you. I hate you. All you think about is yourself and your money.' They're so angry at me!"

"They should be," Terry said gently but firmly as if he meant it. "Look at it as they do. You married the asshole, didn't you?"

"Thanks a lot!"

"Their anger is healthy," Terry said. "Just try to understand, Pat. They don't mean it. But they don't have a choice. They can't say it to David because he won't let them. That leaves *you*. Let it go in and out. Let them say what they have to."

"Are they really angry at me?"

"Of course," Terry said. "You really *did* marry him, you know. Try to see it this way. Andrea's anger is her gift to you. If she didn't face it, it would smolder and prevent her from having a relationship with you. The more she accepts how deeply she's been hurt, the greater the possibility of forgiveness. Her relationship with you can't be built on her denying her anger at you. If she denies it, she'll drift away. Andrea has opened the door. You should be pleased."

Even though what Terry said was not very comforting at that moment, Pat had to admit it made sense. "Marcia's still very upset and can't stop crying," she said. "Will you listen to her?"

Marcia was eager to talk to someone other than her mother, and Terry was a good choice. "I just want to see him," she told Terry. "Just once."

"Once won't be enough," Terry said. He decided to tell her the hard truth. "You'll want more and more. It will never end because you'll never get back what you lost. You understand?"

"Yes," Marcia said. His voice had calmed her.

"You want to make him understand how you feel and how you hurt," Terry went on. "But Marcia, he'll *never* understand. If he could, he wouldn't have abandoned you in the first place. It would take a miracle for him to see."

"Well, I don't want to end up with someone who will do that to me," Marcia said. Her thoughts were running fast, trying to keep up with her feelings. "I have a very good boyfriend—and David has a little son, you know, my brother—I don't want him to grow up like David—I want to see my brother—"

Marcia started to cry again. Her emotion and confusion were almost too much for her. Terry listened and encouraged her to say whatever came to her mind. He recognized that she was still playing victim, trying to be loyal to her father, who had caused the hurt. She needed to stand up for herself and say, "The hell with you, Dad. You're simply not worth it. Get lost!" She was having a hard time saying that because she was afraid of the pain. It was much easier to punish herself than to attack her father.

But no matter how bad she felt, Marcia always thought of others. "You know, Christine never talks. I know she's hurting, too. But she never says it."

"Christine is probably more angry than anyone," Terry said. He was quick to turn the conversation back to Marcia. "Anger is *good*, Marcia. And you're beginning to feel it. Sooner or later you have to, in order to feel better, and right now it's important that you do. Let it out. If you can't tell your father how you feel because he won't let you, then write him a letter. Write him every day if you have to. Get those feelings out even if he doesn't answer."

"I wrote a poem to give him," Marcia said.

"Will you read it to *me*?" Terry asked. He was touched by how rejected she must be feeling. She had been courageous enough to compose a poem for her father—not, as it turned out, a tough, angry letter, but a poem that connoted care and thoughtfulness—only to have him deny her the

chance to present it. Terry knew it was important for her to
read the poem to someone. Better him than no one.
   "All right," Marcia said.

What could have been going through your mind?
And what made you want to leave?
How could you have been so unkind?
This is still hard for me to believe.

It seems like you had it all so well,
A wife, a family, and a home.
Maybe you were hurting and no one could tell.
Is that why you felt that you had to roam?

The burden and responsibility had to be lightened.
Leaving was the only way you could have dealt.
So you ran away alone, you must have been frightened.
Didn't you think though, how your family felt?

Inevitably this was the way it had to be.
Through the years you would try to forget.
But you had to know you couldn't always be free.
Now, I'm sure running is something you regret.

You were gone for so long, sixteen years.
And you never figured you would get caught.
I'm sure, like me, you've had pain and tears.
But how do you feel now after being sought?

We found you after looking for just days.
There's no getting out of this, nothing for you to do.
If you try to get out of this now, there are no ways.
Well, Dad, it's over. Your running is through.

30

BACK IN WASHINGTON, Pat was still shocked at Judge Ulmer's jurisdictional scruples. She had gone to Dade City expecting to settle everything in one hearing, prepared to some extent to argue that David could afford to pay off the whole $106,000 within three or four years. Looking back at several of Ulmer's courtroom comments, however, Pat sensed that the almost unprecedented size of the arrearage had frightened him into wanting legal certainty before moving ahead.

Well, if the law was muddy, Pat couldn't blame Ulmer for that. What angered her was that there could still be any legal doubt in the United States that child support was a moral issue as well as a legal obligation and, therefore, best enforced by a court of equity. To her, such legal myopia was just one more example of a system that cared more about fathers' pocketbooks than the rights and welfare of their children. Pat anxiously waited for the dust to settle on the debate so that Judge Ulmer could decide. She thought it would be a short wait. She should have known better.

As discouraging as the trip to Florida had been for Pat, it was not a complete waste. David had agreed out of court to pay two hundred dollars a month in child support for Marcia from October through January, when she would turn eighteen, and Judge Ulmer had signed an order reflecting that agreement. It wasn't the eight hundred dollars, which barely covered the airfare to Tampa for her and her daughters, that mattered so much. It was the psychological lift that the decision gave Pat, and the new legal door it opened.

When the first two-hundred-dollar check arrived, Pat sat at the kitchen table and stared at it. She felt good. David had actually paid something. After skipping around the country, avoiding the law, and running for cover under an assumed name for seventeen years, he had finally paid something. It *was* possible! And now, if Judge Ulmer either tossed her case out of court or enforced the judgment unfairly, she could invoke a little-known and even less-used regulation of the IRS code (#301.6305), which instructs federal agents to collect unpaid child support for mothers if requested to do so.

Based on a provision in the Social Security Act, the IRS code orders the district director to enter an assessment against the father as soon as the Office of Child Support Enforcement (OCSE) certifies the amount of arrearage owed. Then the code instructs IRS agents to go after the delinquent father ''in the same manner and with the same powers'' as they pursue delinquent taxpayers.

The state OCSE would determine the total amount of unpaid child support David owed, from 1968 to the date of Pat's request, and would fill out the two-page request form. Pat would have to forgo attorneys' fees and court costs. The state OCSE would then send Pat's request via its central office in Richmond to the federal OCSE regional headquarters in Philadelphia, where the amount due would be certified. The regional OCSE in Philadelphia would send the certified request to the IRS southeast regional office in Atlanta, which handles Tampa. There, a tax specialist would enter the certified amount as an assessment against David and notify him to pay all of it within sixty days. If he failed or refused to pay, the regional office would assign a revenue officer to seize and sell David's property, levy bank accounts, and garnish his wages. If the IRS had reason to believe he might run, it could waive the sixty-day notice.

Whereas the court of equity granted judges leeway in deciding what was or was not fair, the Internal Revenue Code told its collection officer exactly what to do. Although he or she could allow payment through installments, the officer had "no authority to compromise a proceeding by the collection of only part of a certified amount." In addition, code provisions would yank the legal rug right from under David's feet, leaving him no platform to plead from. "No court of the United States," the code says, "has jurisdiction of any legal or equitable action to restrain or review the assessment or collection of certified amounts."

But in order for Pat to ask OCSE to request the IRS to collect for her, she must first have exhausted all other civil means, be able to prove that David could pay the arrearages, and have at least one minor child living at home and a valid court order for that child's support. The Juvenile and Domestic Relations Court had never ordered David to pay child support specifically for Marcia because he had run away just after she was born and before Pat could get him in front of a judge. The new Florida order for child support for Marcia, however, enabled Pat to qualify for the IRS collection.

By the end of October, and within two weeks after the hearing, Frank de la Grana and David Rankin had their briefs on Ulmer's desk. The next move was the court's. On December 8, two months after Pat had first appeared in his court, Ulmer issued a Notice of a Hearing, set for January 8, 1987. Frank subpoenaed James Parker to appear so that, win or lose, Pat's daughters would have one more chance to meet their father face to face.

To prepare for that final hearing, Pat began to subpoena Parker's bank and business records in an attempt to draw a clearer picture of his income and assets. She flew down to Florida just after New Year's and set up an office in her room at the Tampa Hilton. Using tax returns, canceled checks, savings account records, and the patterns of withdrawal and spending they indicated, she worked out a summary for Judge Ulmer and made up a series of exhibits. Fully armed and proud of her thoroughness, she was prepared to ask and argue for $30,000 to be paid within ten days and $2,000 a month for the next three-plus years, until David had paid off the full $106,000. If she had to settle for less, she told Frank, she would be reasonable.

For his part, Frank was amazed at what Pat had put together. If her analysis was correct, Parker had made as much or more money in 1986 than he had. Frank called Victoria to discuss the summary. "We're in the wrong business, Frank," Victoria quipped.

Pat's parents had agreed to drive their granddaughters to the airport on the morning of the hearing. When they arrived at Washington's National Airport, everyone was frazzled. Marcia was tired and tense, Christine was sick with the flu. And Andrea was cranky.

While her daughters were in the air somewhere over North Carolina, Pat got a call from Frank, asking her to come to his office. Something had turned up. She hurried there at once.

"Bad news," he told her after motioning her to a chair. "The hearing's off."

"What do you mean, the hearing's off!"

"Ulmer's reached a decision."

The judge had paged Frank at eleven that morning in Clearwater where Frank was defending a client to say that he had read both briefs for the first time the night before. Based on the cases presented and argued, he had concluded that a court of equity does not have the jurisdiction to enforce child-support judgments. When Frank pointed out that his client and her three daughters had flown all the way from Washington for the hearing, Ulmer asked Frank to extend his apologies for any and all inconvenience.

"You're kidding!" Pat said when Frank finished. "Shit, the kids are on the plane! Why in the hell didn't he think of that before? That's why I made the kids wait until the very last minute before coming down."

"I told him that," Frank said.

"Well, you have to think of a way to still have that hearing—anything, I don't care what. I want David at the courthouse so the girls can see him."

"What's the use?" Frank said.

"I'm going to call Judge Valentine," Pat announced.

"Can you believe this?" she asked, when Michael Valentine came to the phone.

"Why are you surprised?" Valentine said. "You're in Florida. And they're wrong."

"The kids are landing right now. Can you think of anything we can do?" Pat asked.

"Go to the hearing, anyway," Valentine suggested. "Ask

the court to reconsider. The judge hasn't signed an order yet. Make him give you the reason for his decision. Whatever he says will form the basis for an appeal."

Frank was standing next to Pat during the conversation and caught the drift enough to know what Valentine was recommending and why.

"Okay," he told Pat after she hung up. "Let's do it."

Pat was too angry to be discouraged. Ulmer had no excuse for waiting until the night before the hearing to read the arguments for the first time, especially since he knew she would probably come down from Washington. She had just spent two thousand dollars in airfares and hotel bills to learn that she and her daughters shouldn't have bothered to come. She had taken a week of annual leave and had spent another two thousand dollars to subpoena records she would not be able to use. What did she have to do to make David face judgment on the real issue—of right and wrong—instead of just jurisdiction? What did she have to do to get justice?

They met in the same hearing room where they had sat four months earlier. Andrea and Marcia were present. Christine was back at the hotel, too ill to budge. Before Frank could challenge Judge Ulmer's oral decision, Mark Kelly, who represented James Parker, told Ulmer that his associate David Rankin had complied with the subpoena and had brought his client to the courthouse. But in light of Ulmer's phone call and decision, neither he nor Rankin felt Parker had to be present in court. "I have him in the [court] library," Kelly said. "I don't at this state of the proceeding understand the necessity for his presence. For that reason, I have asked him to wait over there."

Judge Ulmer agreed and Frank did not object.

Judge Ulmer, it turned out, had three legal problems with the Bennett case. The Virginia judgment didn't actually order Parker to pay $106,000; it merely stated that he owed that amount. Second, Bennett had not demonstrated that Parker could pay that much. And finally, the cases Frank had presented in his memorandum did not convince the judge that the court of equity actually had jurisdiction to enforce support judgments in Florida.

"I have a judgment here from the Domestic Relations Court

of Fairfax, reducing the matter to judgment in the amount of $106,000 and some change," Ulmer began. "And there's no question but that it has been properly registered here in the State of Florida and this court has jurisdiction of the matter now for that purpose. But I don't find where the man has ever been ordered to pay that amount."

Judge Ulmer's first problem was so thin that a second-year law student could have settled it for him. Pat Bennett stood before his court with a valid seventeen-year-old decree ordering David to pay, an outstanding warrant for his arrest because he hadn't paid, and a valid 1985 document from Judge Jane Delbridge called "Order," holding James Parker in contempt of court and entering a judgment against him, in part, for $79,403.52, "which amount constitutes the amount currently due and owing in child-support arrearages."

Judge Ulmer's second problem was a catch-22 of his own making. During the first hearing, he had not allowed Pat to furnish proof that Parker could pay until the jurisdictional issue was settled. Now Ulmer was arguing that he didn't have jurisdiction because Pat had not proved that Parker could pay.

"Unless he, at this moment as of today, has the present ability to respond to any lawful order that this court might enter," Ulmer said, "it occurs to me that I would be wasting my time and it wouldn't be worth the paper that it's written on."

Frank was unwilling to budge a centimeter. "Your Honor, I understand what you're saying," he argued. "But if you will recall—and if need be we can have the record . . . transcribed—at the previous hearing you basically cut off . . . my client."

"True."

"Once again," Frank continued, "we were prepared prior to our conference call this morning to come in here and to complete proving that gentleman's ability to pay. And if that had been done, then we would be in a position for the court to have jurisdiction to order him to make payment. But we were kind of cut off at the pass this morning . . . We can more than prove his ability to pay, Your Honor."

Frank went on to tell Ulmer that he agreed with the court's assessment that the Bennett case was unusual. "This is not your common everyday support case."

"Well, now, but for the amount of money involved it is," Judge Ulmer said. "That's an unbelievable amount of money alleged to be due."

Pat almost jumped out of her chair. How could Ulmer say "alleged" when he had already accepted the Virginia judgment as valid? It had been properly domesticated in Florida and David had never contested it. Pat sensed she was in deep trouble. Ulmer's statement was clearly biased.

Frank argued back: "I believe that this court is entering an order today or proposing to enter an order today, based on circumstances which have never come to light or have never been able to come to light."

Judge Ulmer gave an inch: "I'm not going to preclude you from any presentation of any evidence that you need . . . Number one, I think it would not be fair not to provide you an opportunity to make a proper proof. And I would never preclude someone from doing that.

"Number two, it very well may be that after you have made the presentation . . . you might very well be entitled to an order ordering this man to make these payments depending upon his present ability to pay. And if he does not do so then you may very well be entitled to the contempt-of-court powers of the court."

But before Frank could even begin demonstrating Parker's ability to pay, Mark Kelly turned Ulmer's attention to the judge's third problem—cases indicating that a court of equity in Florida did or did not have jurisdiction to enforce support judgments. Kelly summarized the cases he had presented that seemed to argue against jurisdiction. Then he, Frank, and Ulmer chased each other in a circle for ten minutes. In the end, ignoring his previous promise to allow Pat the opportunity to prove Parker could pay, Judge Ulmer said: "Okay, gentlemen, we might as well take the bull by the horns and get the matter resolved . . .

"I would find that the contempt authority of this court is not available for us to enforce a foreign judgment for child support as it has been presented to the court in this fashion. Now, if there are other matters that you wish the court to address in these proceedings, I will do so. But if your sole request for the court is to order this man to pay this judgment from a sister state, subject to the contempt powers of this court, I do not feel that I have the authority to do so. And that would be the ruling of the court.

"And I am more persuaded as to the correctness of this, having had the opportunity to be enlightend by counsel. And I appreciate your help . . . The only other comment—it is unnecessary for me to make, but I will make it—is that I am not pleased with this decision. But I don't make the law. I am sworn to uphold it as I see it."

The hearing was over in exactly thirty-five minutes. It had taken Pat Bennett two and a half years to get that far. She had spent fifteen thousand dollars in out-of-pocket expenses. And she had one bill from Frank de la Grana for ten thousand dollars and another from Victoria Gordon for fifteen thousand dollars. David had paid her exactly eight hundred dollars in current child support. Marcia would turn eighteen in twelve days, all but guaranteeing that Robert Horan would never reconsider extraditing David to Virginia to stand trial for criminal desertion and nonsupport.

Pat was so discouraged by Judge Ulmer's final decision that she could not even cry. But she never considered giving up. Hadn't she promised herself to give David a fight to the finish? Hadn't she vowed to see him face a judge? Once again he had wriggled away, protected by an old-boy legal network that made the victim look like the criminal. Now it was no longer David versus her. It was Pat versus the system—and the fight was on.

31

▼

WHEN CHRISTINE HAD walked into the Tampa Hilton on the afternoon of the hearing, she headed straight for the queen-size bed. Her mother felt her hot, damp forehead and told her to skip the hearing. Although she wanted to go to Dade City to meet her father, Christine had to admit she felt somewhat relieved that she wouldn't have to. She also felt as foolish as she did feverish. She had come all this way only to sleep the afternoon and night away in an expensive bed. She had a reservation for a return flight to Washington the next morning so she would not miss work and school. Sick or well, she intended to be on that flight.

Andrea and Marcia made up for their sister's lack of energy. From the moment they had jumped out of Frank's car in the courthouse parking lot, they began searching for their father. "He'll be here, I *know* it," Marcia kept saying. She had brought along her poem, which she had recopied five times on white stationery so it would be in her best handwriting. It was folded inside an envelope addressed "James Parker."

Andrea and Marcia made the courtyard outside Judge Ulmer's hearing room their command post. Every five minutes they would charge out to the parking lot, looking for their father's car.

"He's here," Marcia told her mother after one foray. "I saw his car. I know it's his."

"There's a baby seat inside," Andrea nodded. "Maybe he's in the coffee shop with Kelly." A friend checked for her, but he wasn't there.

Shortly before three-thirty, Marcia and Andrea had followed their mother into the hearing room to wait for Judge Ulmer. When they heard Mark Kelly tell Ulmer that James Parker was waiting in the court library in case he was needed, they were somewhat relieved and satisfied. They at least knew where he was hiding this time. With growing impatience, they waited through all the jurisdictional hair-splitting for Judge Ulmer to rule in their mother's favor, then order Jim Parker before the bench.

But Ulmer ruled against their mother and walked through the hearing-room door to his chambers. At once Andrea and Marcia shifted their attention to cornering their father before he drove off. "You check the parking lot," Marcia told Andrea. "I'll take the library."

Noting that Jim Parker's car was still in the lot, Andrea rushed back to her mother. "He's still here, Mom," she announced. "We're going to go talk to him."

"Of course," Pat said. "If he wants to."

Frank turned to Mark Kelly, who was standing nearby, and asked if it would be all right for Pat's daughters to talk to their father. Kelly agreed, and Frank thanked him. Pat knew he didn't have to grant permission, since the case was still in litigation. He had done the compassionate thing and she was grateful.

In the meantime, Marcia had reached the library. It looked empty. She began walking down the center aisle, which cut through rows of bookcases. After passing two rows, she found her father sitting behind a table in a research alcove. Dressed immaculately in a three-piece blue suit, he was flipping through a book as if to kill time while waiting for someone. Seeing him there stunned her for a moment, for she had half expected him to be on his way home by this time.

"Take a seat," David told her.

Marcia placed the envelope with her poem on the table and immediately backed away. "No . . . no," she said. Frank and Pat had so worried her about jeopardizing the case that she was afraid she would get in trouble. Besides, her father's invitation surprised her. So far, he had always resisted talking to her.

"Wait a minute," David said. "Don't go. I want to talk to you. Please—take a seat."

"Let me go get Andrea first."

Marcia disappeared around the bookshelf and out of the library as quickly as she had come, almost running across the stone courtyard to Andrea and her mother.

"Come on," she said to her sister. "He wants to talk to us. Okay, Mom?" They raced to the library, where David sat looking fidgety and nervous.

"Will you sit down?" he asked.

"Are you going to talk to us?" Andrea said.

"Why wouldn't I?"

"Christine's not here," Andrea said. "She's sick."

Both Andrea and Marcia could read the disappointment in their father's face. They knew Christine was his favorite and sensed that he had only agreed to meet them because he wanted to see Christine. Ever since they had first talked to him, he had not bothered to disguise his preference for her and it hurt. They sat down across the table from him.

"You look like me when I was a boy," David told Andrea. Then he turned to Marcia, "You look more like your mother."

At that moment, Marcia had the strangest experience of her life. After two and a half years of wanting and dreading this meeting, she looked straight into her father's eyes as her mother had done in the county jail and realized that she no longer wanted to talk to him. Her feelings of anxiety, fear, and anger seemed to dissolve. All she wanted to do was go home and put her father and her past behind her. No longer feeling a need to listen to him try to explain away his behavior, she had only one question to ask.

"Did you love my mother?"

"Of course I did," David said.

Drained from the strain of anticipation and lack of sleep, Marcia rested her head on the table and waited for Andrea to finish her business with David. I want nothing from him, Marcia thought. He means no more to me now than a stranger on the street. He is not my dad—or even my father.

Andrea, too, had been surprised that her father had waited to talk to them. She felt it was out of character and wondered why. It didn't take long to find out. She began with the string of questions she had already asked him over the phone in the beach condo, but he stopped her after a few minutes, saying he didn't want to talk about the past. Suddenly, Andrea no longer felt the need to press him. A strange kind of indifference she had never felt before had smothered her anger. She couldn't quite believe it. This indifference was real, not the kind she had frequently put on like armor to protect herself from disappointment. Here she was, sitting across the table from her father and feeling no emotion at all—not even the need to ask one more "why." She had absolutely no curiosity about what he had done during the past seventeen years or how he had felt.

It's gone, Andrea thought. There's nothing there anymore. Not even a possibility.

David widened the gap between Andrea and himself by his blatant attempt to use her to get Pat to drop the suit against him. He began to make promises to Andrea about what he would do for her once the child-support matter was settled out of court. At one point, he admitted that he intended to make sure her mother wouldn't see a nickel of his money, and that he would continue to bleed her pocketbook by legal tactics until she gave up.

Recognizing the game for what it was, Andrea played along for a while, then said, "So you want me to tell my mom that if she drops the suit, you'll give us an allowance each month, help us through school, and give us spending money—okay, I'll tell her."

Marcia had been listening to all of this. Suddenly, she felt so used that she wanted to get away as fast as she could. She could take no more. "This whole think is beat!" she said. "I'm tired and I want to go."

From the look on her father's face, Marcia could see that her remark had cut him, and she was glad. She wanted him to suffer. "Here, this is for you." She shoved her poem, which lay unopened, across the table.

Andrea and Marcia stood up to go. David remained seated. Eyes red, he look tired and close to tears. They both sensed he wanted something more from them. They could see it in his face.

Andrea felt a stab of sympathy for the man sitting in front of her and was tempted to walk around the table and give him a hug. She knew that was what he wanted. But then she thought, I don't owe him a thing. If I deny him a show of affection, I will be punishing him. And I want him to feel how much being rejected hurts.

Marcia also recognized that, for the first time, her father wanted a sign of forgiveness from her. But she didn't feel anything for him and had nothing to give him. She wanted to go home where she belonged.

"I don't know what to say," David finally volunteered, breaking the tension. He seemed awkward just sitting there.

"How about goodbye?" Marcia suggested.

Andrea and Marcia turned their backs on David and quickly walked out of the library.

Part
Four

JUSTICE

32

▼

ON THE LEGAL battlefield, time was on James Parker's side. Marcia would turn eighteen in less than two weeks. That would only complicate Pat's strategy.

Florida law was not clear on whether a judge could order a father to pay arrears of child support after the child had reached majority. And to make matters worse, if Pat wanted the IRS to collect arrearage, at least one daughter had to be a minor on the day she made her request. So the day before Marcia's birthday, Pat signed the petition for an IRS collection, then filed away the rest of the paperwork until she could decide what to do about Judge Ulmer's decision.

On the one hand, Pat wanted to fight. She was convinced that Ulmer had been unfair and had made a legal error. Her case against him was strong and the issue was important. To crumble now just because one elected judge either didn't know the law or feared male-voter backlash was foolish. Women had been doing that for the past century. It was time to take a stand.

On the other hand, justice was expensive. Pat had taken out a second mortgage on her house, owed at least twenty-five thousand dollars in legal expenses, and had borrowed heavily from her parents. It was clear she couldn't afford an

appeal. And attorneys were not standing in line to take her
case pro bono.

If Pat itched to beat Judge Ulmer at his own game, so did
her parents. Being private people who didn't relish dragging
family matters into the limelight, they had not encouraged
their daughter's search. Although they never doubted that the
law would deal firmly with David if it ever caught up with
him, they didn't believe he was worth the inevitable emotional and financial strain. And they couldn't understand Pat's
need to face David and her past before she could get on with
her life. But the more they watched the law at work, the more
shocked and disillusioned they became. To them the issue
was clear: David had abandoned his wife and children; abandonment is against the law; therefore, David must face the
law. Judge Ulmer's decision struck them as irrational, and
they were angrier than their daughter, who had long since
learned the painful difference between the law and justice.

"Your daddy wants you to appeal," Pat's mother told her
when she returned from Tampa. "We'll help."

That was all Pat needed to hear. She called Frank, but he
was not convinced she could win; her daughters had all turned
eighteen. Next, she contacted the Tampa law firm of Pippinger and Tropp, who, she was told, was good on domestic
relations cases. Asking her to send the relevant court documents, the firm told her that if it decided to take the case, it
would require a five-thousand-dollar deposit.

Pat told Pippinger and Tropp that she was looking for an
aggressive attorney who understood the national significance
of her case and who was not afraid of publicity. Explaining
that she was financially exhausted, she asked how the firm
intended to spend the retainer and what the total cost of the
appeal might be. Two days later, Pippinger and Tropp turned
Pat's case down, saying it was primarily a collection matter
and that the firm rarely took collection cases.

Not knowing where else to turn for legal help, Pat finally
decided to write her own brief and argue her own case. It
was the only thing she could afford, and she had nothing to
lose.

She spent most of her free time in February and March of
1987 researching child-support decisions, writing a fifty-page
brief, and answering the brief written by James Parker's at-

torney, Mark Kelly. Gene Bennett read her final drafts. Finding her casework and legal logic thorough, he suggested a few stylistic changes. Then, with nothing to do but wait for the oral argument before the Second District Court of Appeal in Tampa, Pat turned her attention back to the IRS collection.

Although the Internal Revenue Service pursues delinquent fathers much more aggressively than the courts, it gets fewer than one hundred child-support collections a year because it requires a summary of the father's assets. Nine out of ten mothers who know about the IRS collection option and who apply don't know their former husbands' assets or how to find them. Pat did.

When she walked into the Fairfax County Office of Child Support Enforcement (OCSE)—the first step on the IRS collection ladder—Pat had 151 pages of James Parker's financial records, which she had subpoenaed for the hearing before Judge Ulmer, including personal and corporate bank account statements and canceled checks, 1982–85 tax returns, loan applications, credit card information, and property transfers. Based on these certified documents, Pat submitted a financial analysis of Parker's income, known assets and liabilities, and net worth. She asked the IRS to collect the unpaid child support to date. That amounted to $80,303.52.

Pam Powers, the Fairfax County OCSE case officer, concurred that Pat had submitted enough asset information to satisfy the IRS and that the eighty thousand dollars-plus she requested was accurate, given the judgment against David. Powers sent the documents and forms to her district office in Richmond by overnight courier. Then the bureaucratic wheels began to turn:

—At the end of April, a month later, Richmond certified Pat's request and mailed it to the OCSE regional office in Philadelphia for final approval.

—At the end of May, a month later, Philadelphia sent the approved certified request to the IRS Service Center in Atlanta, which covers Tampa.

—At the end of June, a month after that, the IRS notified James Parker that he had sixty days to come up with either $80,303.52 or a payment plan, or the service would begin collecting it from him.

Pat had requested that the IRS waive the sixty-day notice,

as the code allows when there is reason to believe that "assets are in jeopardy." But the IRS apparently had declined to do so. Convinced that David would use the grace period to bury his assets and prevent IRS collection, Pat began to pump herself up for her oral argument in Tampa.

Pat's mouth was dry as she sat on the bench facing Judges Campbell, Danahy, and Threadgill in the Second District Court of Appeal on July 8, 1987. Three years earlier, almost to the day, she had found David. Now she had twenty minutes to argue her case against him. For days people had been offering her advice—a blue dress would be perfect; don't hide your nervousness; let them know you're not an attorney and would appreciate help; keep it simple.

Even though she was afraid of making a fool of herself, Pat could appreciate the irony of the moment. She had started out simply expecting Fairfax County to extradite David to Virginia to stand trial. But Commonwealth Attorney Robert Horan had blocked extradition. Now, three years and more than thirty thousand dollars later, she was sitting nervously before three black-robed judges still looking for justice. It was a page right out of Dickens.

Even more ironic, all Pat had ever wanted was to face David in court and give her daughters the chance to do so as well. Now she found herself waiting for a chance to force the state of Florida to settle a question that affected other people's lives: can a Florida judge hold a father in contempt of court if he refuses to pay a judgment issued in another state?

Using different interpretations, both Pat and Mark Kelly had picked apart the *same* Florida court decisions in their briefs. Now the task of the three judges about to hear the oral arguments was to evaluate their legal logic and decide what the Florida courts had meant in those earlier decisions.

A handful of visitors sat in the four rows of theater chairs in the back of the courtroom. Frank de la Grana was there to wish Pat well and a few journalists were hunched over their notes. Standing confidently at the walnut podium, Mark Kelly spoke as if addressing an appeals court was something he did every day. But from the moment he opened his mouth Judge Campbell began challenging his legal reasoning. Quickly sensing he was getting nowhere after a few critical exchanges,

Kelly changed his tactic. Since Marcia had reached majority six months earlier, he argued, James Parker was no longer required to pay arrearages according to Florida law.

Without denying his argument, Judge Campbell interrupted Kelly again, pointing out that *age* was not the issue before the court.

"I understand, Judge," Kelly said. "But even if we do send it back [to Ulmer] we're going to have to reach that inquiry."

"We don't jump those hurdles up here that haven't been jumped in the trial court yet," Campbell said, almost promising another legal battle ahead.

Blocked a second time, Kelly summarized his position, telling the court he'd be pleased to answer further questions. There weren't any.

For her part, Pat chose to address the social problem rather than the fine points of the law she had already raised in her brief. Clutching the podium, she briefly told the court in a quavering voice how David had abandoned her and his three children, and how his foster parents had had him declared legally dead in Virginia. Sixteen years after he had run away, she said, she found him in Florida living under an assumed name. After a warrant had been issued for his arrest for criminal desertion and nonsupport, she had asked Fairfax County to have him extradited, but the commonwealth attorney declined to do so because desertion was only a misdemeanor in Virginia. At that point, Pat explained, she had two choices—file a URESA [Uniform Reciprocal Enforcement Support Act] action or seek a judgment. She rejected URESA because she was told it would take two years.

"Three years later here I am," she said.

Judge Campbell smiled.

To save her time, Judge Danahy summarized her story. "What you finally did was to get the judgment in Virginia for all of the arrearages?" he asked.

"Correct."

"And you brought that judgment to Florida?"

"That is correct."

"You went to the circuit court here in Florida to enforce it . . . through what we call equitable-type remedies, including contempt?"

"That is correct."

"[Judge Ulmer] refused that and that's why you're here?"

"That's why I'm here."

Judge Threadgill then took over. "What would you ask the trial court to do to [Parker] for not paying the hundred and six thousand dollars?"

"I would like to see the case sent back to the lower court to have another hearing," Pat said. "And for the court to order him to pay whatever the court deems that he *can* pay."

"In failing to pay?" Threadgill asked.

"He would be subject to contempt and imprisonment."

"Jail?"

"Yes," Pat said. "Unfortunately that is one of the only ways some child support can be collected."

If Judge Ulmer's decision was correct, Pat argued, Florida law was contradicting itself. On the one hand, the law required that arrearages like David's be reduced to a final judgment, before a court of equity could enforce collection. But once they were reduced to a final judgment, it was saying that a court of equity had no jurisdiction.

Calling child-support enforcement in the United States a national disgrace, Pat pleaded with the court to help by at least clarifying Florida law. "The decision of this court," she emphasized, "has a very far-reaching effect when you consider the fact that [a large] percentage of the Florida child-support cases are from out of state."

Pointing out that the Tenth Annual Report to Congress ranked Florida close to last for child-support enforcement, she said it was generally accepted in Virginia that if you were a father and wanted to hide from the law, Florida was the place to go. If the court let Ulmer's decision stand, she argued, it would be opening the door to runaway fathers from all over the country.

Pat recapped her own story. "In this eighteen-year time frame, this man has changed his identity," she said. "He has committed bigamy. He has failed to support his children. He has never once gone before a judge to answer . . . There is no amount of money—even if he walked in here today with a check for a hundred and six thousand dollars—that would repay the emotional damage and scars left on my three daughters."

Pat closed by quoting Senator Daniel Patrick Moynihan: "The quality of a civilization may be measured by how it cares for its elderly; just as surely, the future of a society may be forecast by how it cares for its young."

Recognizing the importance of the issue, the Second District Court of Appeal moved with unusual speed. A month after the oral arguments, Pat got a call from the clerk of the court saying she had won. Although she felt a deep sense of satisfaction, Pat was neither surprised nor terribly excited. She had never doubted the logic and strength of her case. After all was said and done, she had merely won the right to buy another ticket to Tampa to pick up the hearing where Judge Ulmer had left it.

The last paragraph of the appeals court's unanimous decision requested the Florida Supreme Court to rule on the decision, whether Parker appealed it or not. If its decision was correct, the Second District Court felt it was important that it be the law in the *whole* state, not just in five of the state's twenty judicial circuits. For Pat, that meant still another trip to the bench.

"This court," Judge Campbell wrote, "certifies to our supreme court as a question of great public importance, the following: Do the circuit courts of this state have jurisdiction to enforce a foreign judgment for arrearages of alimony or child support by means of equitable remedies including contempt?"

No one was more pleased with Pat's victory than Florida's Department of Health and Rehabilitative Services (HRS), which was responsible for prosecuting runaway and deadbeat dads. Florida's reputation for coddling runaway fathers embarrassed HRS and made it look as if it wasn't doing enough to help out-of-state mothers. But without the threat of jail, the fathers HRS was prosecuting were not about to open their wallets. If the Florida Supreme Court upheld the Second District's decision, HRS could quickly dispatch a stack of cases. It immediately petitioned the supreme court with an amicus curiae brief in support of Bennett.

"The issues raised by this appeal are important and far-reaching," William Branch and Chriss Walker, attorneys for HRS, told the supreme court. "This court's decision will literally impact upon millions of persons within and outside the State of Florida.''

The supreme court accepted HRS as the amicus curiae for Pat Bennett.

Recognizing the national significance of the Bennett case, the Legal Defense and Education Fund of the National Organization for Women (NOW) also petitioned the Florida Supreme Court for leave to join as amicus curiae. The organization argued that the Bennett decision was not only important for children of other states whose fathers lived in Florida, but for children in states where the law—like Florida's—needed clarification.

''The poverty rate for female-headed single-parent families is nearly three times the national average,'' NOW attorneys Kathy Chinoy and Sally Goldfarb argued in their motion to the supreme court. ''This trend has disastrous implications for American women and children. . . . The National Advisory Council on Economic Opportunity has estimated that by the year 2000, if current trends continue, virtually all of the Americans living in poverty will be women and children in single-parent families. Inadequate child-support enforcement is a major cause of the spiraling poverty rate among women and children. . . . The question currently before this Court directly addresses this issue.''

The supreme court granted NOW's request to appear as an amicus curiae for Bennett as well as a request from the attorney general of Florida and, ironically, the attorney general of Virginia. John Rupp, Virginia's senior assistant attorney general, argued that his office took a ''strong position in support'' of the issue, which was important to Virginia children whose fathers lived in Florida. What Rupp didn't say, however, was that the Virginia warrant for David's arrest was still valid, that David was still charged in Fairfax County with criminal desertion and nonsupport, and that, in this particular case, the attorney general was not taking a ''strong position in support'' of extradition.

But extradition was the furthest thing from Pat's mind. It was time to prepare for a new hearing in the Pasco County Court, which would now center around two questions—one legal, the other practical: Did Florida require a delinquent parent to pay arrearage if the child was no longer a minor?

And did James Parker have the ability to pay the $106,000 judgment?

If the court ruled that Parker didn't have to pay because Marcia had turned eighteen, it made no difference how much money he had; he was home free.

33

CHRISTINE DROVE FROM Tampa to Dade City half-listening to her mother and Richard Froemming chattering in the back seat, and wondering what she was doing back in Florida. From her sick bed in the Hilton six months earlier, she had listened with total indifference to Andrea and Marcia describe the meeting with their father in the courthouse library. At the time, she had not felt even a twinge of jealousy or sadness. The only emotion that penetrated the wall she had built between herself and her father was a sense of satisfaction that her absence had disappointed him. At least, that's what her sisters had told her. And even though Andrea and Marcia seemed to have settled the score with their father, Christine wasn't convinced he had been worth the energy and money. Now, half a year later, as she drove to what she hoped would be the last in a string of ridiculous hearings, she still wasn't convinced.

Whatever her feelings, Christine's appearance belied her facade of indifference. She wore a simple but striking black dress that made her look even taller than she was and highlighted her pale skin and long, thick auburn hair. Around her neck hung a single sapphire on a chain, a gift from her fiancé. Even if she couldn't admit that impressing her father was important to her in some strange way, she had evidently dressed up for him.

If Christine wasn't sure why she had come to Florida, Richard Froemming knew why *he* was there. Even though the private detective hadn't investigated anything for Pat in the past year, he had followed her case closely and had given her advice whether she asked for it or not. When Pat suggested he come to the hearing as her bodyguard, Richard took her seriously. During his first month on the street as a Washington cop, he had learned that domestic violence can be as vicious as it is unpredictable. And although he joked during the drive to Dade City about a courtroom shootout or knife fight, his adrenaline was flowing. As soon as the car pulled into the courthouse parking lot, the wisecracks stopped. Richard walked a few steps behind Pat and refused to carry her briefcase filled with bank records, so that both his hands would be free. And when Pat and Christine entered the courthouse coffee shop, he cased the place quickly, then made certain the door was in sight the whole time they were there.

Half an hour before the hearing, David Rankin, who was representing James Parker, handed Pat a stack of documents she had requested six weeks earlier. The papers, especially Parker's financial affidavit, were important for her case against him. Using that sworn statement as a foundation, Parker had to prove he was too poor to pay the $106,000 arrearage. Acting as her own attorney, Pat's job was to destroy the credibility of that affidavit.

"You made one mistake," Rankin said as he handed her the pile of documents. "You asked me to mail them to Virginia. Remember that for next time."

Although Florida's Rules of Civil Procedure required that Rankin either produce the documents Pat had asked for or file a motion arguing they were irrelevant, he was not required to mail them outside Pasco County and he hadn't.

This was not the first time Rankin had interpreted the rules in his client's favor, or ignored them altogether. Florida law had also required him to submit the same financial affidavit to Judge Ulmer at least ten days before the first hearing more than a year ago. Not only did Rankin fail to do that, he actually chided Frank de la Grana for being late in submitting Pat's companion affidavit. At that earlier hearing, when he noted that Parker's financial statement was not in the court file, Judge Ulmer had ordered Rankin to produce one within five days. Again, Rankin failed to do so. For the current hearing before Judge Cobb, Florida rules also required Parker to submit to the court the same financial affidavit he gave to Pat, and to do it at least ten days before the actual hearing. Yet Rankin gave the court its copy at the same time Pat got hers.

Naturally, Pat was eager to study the elusive document even if she had less than thirty minutes to do so. What she found in Parker's three-page sworn financial affidavit rocked her. She had spent weeks analyzing his subpoenaed corporate and personal bank records, including canceled checks. According to those records, Adjusters Claims Bureau, which employed Parker and which he co-owned, had paid him around $85,000 a year during 1986 and 1987; and Parker had at least $16,000 in bank accounts in his wife's name. From that information, Pat was expecting Judge Cobb to order Parker to pay at least $25,000 within ten days and $2,000 a month until he had retired the full $106,000 judgment.

But Parker's affidavit claimed that his corporation paid him around $26,000 a year in salary and rent, that he had no cash, and that his current liabilities totaled $166,000. Something was very, very wrong. If canceled checks showed that the corporation had been giving him around $85,000 a year, what had happened to the other $59,000?

Judge Wayne L. Cobb's court was so small that the ABC cameraman pointing a lens across the only table in the room could barely move. A dozen chairs for spectators lined one wall. Christine sat quietly on one of them behind her mother, facing her father just a few feet away.

"Good morning, Mr. Rankin," Judge Cobb began. He looked serious and anxious to dispatch the case once and for all.

"Good morning, Your Honor."

"How are you?"

"Fine."

"Mrs. Bennett, you are still representing yourself?"

"Yes, Your Honor, I am."

The court swore in James Parker, and David Rankin argued

first. After establishing that Parker's financial affidavit bore his true signature and was a true statement, Rankin asked, "Are you the sole source of income to your family?"

"Yes, I am," Parker said. His voice was firm and unemotional. If he was nervous, he didn't show it.

"In the event you were incarcerated . . . would there be any form of income which your family might have benefit of?"

"None."

"Have you recently been contacted by the IRS?" Rankin asked.

Pat froze. She knew that the IRS had begun the collection process at the end of August, nearly four months ago. But she had no idea what it had taken so far, if anything.

"I have," Parker said.

"Did they explain to you why you are being contacted?"

"Yes. They are attempting to collect this judgment."

"Have you paid the Internal Revenue Service money as a result?"

"Yes."

"How much?"

"Six hundred sixty-five dollars and some change."

Pat was not totally surprised at the piddling sum. Parker's bank records pointed to a flurry of money transfers and withdrawals days before the collection began.

"Did you enter into some negotiation with the Internal Revenue Service with regard to [monthly] payment of the outstanding debt?" Rankin asked.

"They wanted five hundred dollars."

"After they had an opportunity to review your financial condition at this time, did they come up with a lesser sum?"

"Yes."

"Had you agreed to pay that lesser sum?"

"I signed an agreement to pay two hundred fifty-six dollars a month. . . . First payment is due on the nineteenth of this month."

"Your Honor," Rankin concluded, "that's all I have of this witness at this time."

"Mrs. Bennett," Cobb asked, "do you have any questions?"

"Yes, I do."

Judge Cobb's question sounded unreal to Pat. Even in her wildest courtroom fantasy, she had always watched a judge humiliate David as he stood before the bench. Never had she dreamed of actually having the power to force him to answer questions she herself would ask. Ever since she had decided to represent herself before Judge Cobb, she had worried about falling apart in court or becoming so emotional that she'd forget why she was there and what she had to accomplish. She had even talked to Dr. Crotty about her fear, and he advised her to write out her basic questions and stick to the script. Then, when it was time to ad lib, he told her, she'd be warmed up.

But Rankin destroyed that game plan when he introduced the IRS collection, forcing Pat to ad lib her initial cross examination of Parker. Without realizing it, Rankin had done her a favor. She was so determined to expose the IRS collection issue as a legal red herring that she forgot to be nervous. From what she knew of Internal Revenue Service procedures, she doubted that the IRS would settle so quickly for $256 a month—only $56 more than the court had ordered David to pay eighteen years ago.

"Do you have a copy of that agreement you made with the Internal Revenue Service?" Pat asked Parker.

"I do not," Parker said.

"Would they not have given you a copy of an agreement?"

"I asked for it and they indicated that it had to be approved."

"So it has not been accepted as yet?" Pat said.

"Well, as I understand it, it hasn't been accepted. It has not been approved."

Having made the point, Pat began questioning Parker about his salary. He didn't know it, but in the briefcase at her feet Pat had copies of all the checks Adjusters Claims Bureau had made out to him; and outside the courtroom, she had a bank officer waiting to attest to the validity of those canceled checks.

"How does the corporation pay you?" Pat asked.

"By check . . . twice a month."

"How much?"

"One thousand dollars each payday."

Pat had noted that Parker owned a 1985 Mercury, which

cost seventeen thousand dollars. She wondered if he was making the three-hundred-dollar-a-month payment or whether his corporation was doing it for him.

"Does the corporation pay for any of your . . . business expenses?" she asked.

"Yes."

"Your car payment?"

"Yes."

"They make your car payment?" Even she seemed surprised. "Whose name is the car titled in?"

"It's jointly held in my and my wife's name."

Having established that Parker was indirectly receiving thirty-six hundred dollars a year from his corporation in car payments—over and above salary and rent for an office in his home—Pat began probing Parker's equity, since ability to borrow helps the court determine what a father can and should pay.

"Have you received any loans since January 1985?" she asked.

"I have borrowed from the corporation."

"How much?"

"Somewhere in the neighborhood of sixty thousand dollars."

Pat was momentarily stunned. So Parker wasn't denying that the corporation had given him around eighty-five thousand dollars a year. He was simply alleging that all the money over and above his twenty-four thousand dollar salary, rent, and odds and ends was loans. Pat doubted that was true. But without proof, she had a weak case.

"Have you made any payments back?" she asked.

"Yes."

"Would you have canceled checks for the payment of the loan?"

"Yes."

"Was this sixty thousand dollars one loan or many loans?"

"Many."

"Do you sign a note with the corporation?"

"More than one kind," Parker said. "Some . . . are short-term loans . . . payable quarterly, and others were long-term loans."

"Does [your partner] borrow the same amount that you have?"

"Yes."

"So you both have borrowed roughly sixty thousand dollars . . . within the same time period?"

"Yes."

"Why do you not consider [the money] salary?"

"Because I borrowed the money and it will have to be paid back sometime."

"Can you prove you are making payments to the corporation?"

"I think I've done that already."

"Do you have any of those records with you?"

"No, I do not."

It was a stalemate. Although Pat had asked Rankin to produce Parker's corporate records six weeks before the hearing, Rankin had argued that they were irrelevant and did not furnish them. They turned out to be not only relevant but the one piece of evidence that could weaken or destroy his case. Naturally, Parker did not bring copies of the notes payable he swore he had signed, or the canceled checks proving he had repaid some loans. If Pat had received Parker's financial affidavit on time, she could have fought for those records and subpoenaed Parker's accountant to explain his bookkeeping to the court.

With no further option than to leave a doubt in Judge Cobb's mind as to how much money Parker was actually making, Pat moved on to Parker's assets. He had told Marcia and Andrea in the courthouse library that he was burying his money where their mother could never find it. Bank records showed that he had kept at least sixteen thousand dollars in various accounts, but that he began withdrawing and moving the money around just before the IRS sixty-day grace period was up.

First, Pat established that within days after his arrest on the Writ of Ne Exeat, Parker had transferred his share in a co-owned property, cashed several co-owned certificates of deposit, and transferred a duplex, which, he claimed, belonged to his wife and her family.

Next, Pat got Parker to admit that he had spent nearly twenty thousand dollars in home improvements during the past year and had purchased a new TV for thirty-two hundred dollars—not exactly the spending habits of a poor man.

Finally, Pat tried to prove Parker was hiding cash. But he swore he no longer had any savings or checking accounts anywhere, and that the cash he had once had was either spent on home improvements, used to pay off a bank loan, or levied by the IRS. In short, James C. Parker claimed he was stone broke and deeply in debt.

"Does your wife have any [accounts]?" Pat asked.

"She may."

"You don't know?"

"I believe she has a checking account."

"Where would the money come from?"

"My pay."

"Does she have a money market account?"

"She did at one time. I'm not sure she still does."

"Does she have a savings account?"

"I don't know."

"You don't know!" Pat was getting frustrated. "Have you opened any new bank accounts in the last six months?"

"I have not."

"Do you deposit your check, or does your wife deposit it?"

"More often she does."

"And you do not know to which account that check goes?"

"Since the IRS levy, the checks have been cashed because I don't have an account."

Requesting time to examine Parker again, Pat rested for the moment. Rankin then took a few minutes to reestablish his client's credibility, focusing on the sixty thousand dollars in loans from the corporation.

"Prior to making those loans," he asked Parker, "did you consult an accountant?"

"Yes . . . he arranged it and made the loan papers."

"So that in his opinion, it was a loan from the corporation?"

"Yes."

As her only witness, Pat called Sandra Mitchell, a records custodian at the Sun Bank of Tampa Bay. Noting that the Parkers had closed their money market account and savings account just before the IRS collection was to begin, she asked Mitchell, "How much was in the money market account?"

"Fourteen thousand, seven hundred forty-four dollars and eighty-four cents," Mitchell said.

"And the money withdrawn from the savings account?"

"One thousand, five hundred sixteen dollars and fourteen cents."

"That is roughly about sixteen thousand dollars withdrawn from both accounts in August of 1987?"

"That's correct."

Next, Pat asked Mitchell to review the canceled checks written to James Parker from Adjusters Claims Bureau from January 1986 through November 19, 1987. For the first time, Parker seemed nervous. He conferred with Rankin several times as Mitchell read the bank record. Pat called the court's attention to March 1987 as Mitchell slowly read the numbers: $8,000 . . . $815 . . . $815 . . . $1,000 . . . $1,000 . . . $2,500.

"Excuse me," Pat interrupted. "What was the amount on the first check?"

"Eight thousand."

"Thank you."

Mitchell continued down the month-by-month list until she came to October 1987, six weeks before the hearing. "Would you read the amounts . . . very slowly please?" Pat asked.

"One thousand dollars . . . one thousand dollars . . . two thousand dollars . . . one thousand dollars . . . two thousand dollars . . . one thousand dollars."

That amounted to eight thousand dollars in six weeks. Under Pat's probing, Mitchell testified that several recent checks had been deposited into another account at the Florida Federal Savings and Loan. Parker had just sworn there were no other accounts.

Recalling Parker after Mitchell's testimony, Rankin quickly established that his client had used most of the fourteen thousand dollars in the money market account to repay a bank loan, and that the large checks Mitchell had read off were the loans Parker had testified to earlier.

Once again, Pat returned to the loans in her recross examination. "You stated earlier that you had [received] approximately sixty thousand dollars in loans from your corporation,'' she asked.

"Yes.''

"But the income level that you state for your corporation for 1986 is negative one thousand, three hundred thirty-four dollars; and for 1985, [a negative] twelve thousand, one hundred fifty-two dollars. How are you able to borrow sixty thousand dollars from a corporation . . . doing so poorly?''

"I can't explain that. I'm not an accountant,'' Parker said, once again denying that the sixty thousand dollars was salary.

Pat pointed out that she had carefully traced the money traveling in and out of his bank accounts before he had cleaned them out. It amounted to $78,298.22 over a one-year period.

"Two thousand a month is what you say you make,'' she argued. "How can you deposit seventy-eight thousand dollars a year in three accounts?''

Parker said that because he was moving the money around, she had counted it three times.

"Do you have another bank account?''

"I do not.''

"Why did those checks say 'for deposit only,' '' she asked, referring to the other account, "and [can you give] the account number of Florida Federal Savings and Loan?''

"I can't answer that.''

"Is the account in your wife's name?''

"My wife has no account.''

"Is it in another name?''

"I have no hidden accounts,'' Parker said, losing his composure for a moment. "I have no Swiss bank accounts. I have *no* hidden accounts, Ms. Bennett.''

Pat was getting nowhere. She was convinced that the sixty thousand dollars was a form of compensation rather than a loan, but she couldn't prove it. And she believed that Parker was hiding cash, but she couldn't find out where. Her frustration began to show. Judge Cobb stepped in after Rankin objected to her badgering his client.

"Ma'am,'' Cobb said, "you have been over this, and I think you are just argumentative at this time.''

"Thank you,'' Pat said. "I have one final question . . .

You met your two daughters, Andrea and Marcia, for the first time last January, is that correct?''

"No, that's not correct."

"For the first time since they were babies."

"That's correct."

"Did you tell your daughters at that time that you had money hidden in places that their mother would never find?"

The question hit like a slap in the face. Parker flushed.

"Absolutely not," he said.

"Do you know who this lady is here?"

Pat pointed to Christine sitting behind her. She had planned that question for weeks and had been looking for the right moment to slip it in. This might be Christine's only confrontation with her father, and Pat thought it best to force her oldest daughter to face him. She had not warned Christine in advance, sensing that surprise might help break down her protective wall of aloofness. Pat had no idea how the confrontation would turn out, and she relied only on her instincts and the knowledge that David could not hurt his daughter any more than he already had.

David looked across the table at Christine, then said without hesitation, "No, I don't."

"She's your daughter," Pat said.

The courtroom grew very quiet, and Judge Cobb let Pat have the one emotional moment of the morning.

"It's too bad you do not know who she is."

"It is," Parker said.

"That's Christine!"

Judge Cobb waited for a long second, then asked, "Any other questions, Mrs. Bennett?"

"No, Your Honor."

Christine had sat through the tedious hearing barely moving a muscle. Naturally, she wanted her mother to win her case and Judge Cobb to order her father to pay. But in cold reality, the money—whether it was a little or a lot—had little to do with her. She was no longer living at home and had been paying her own way for some time now. Furthermore, she had no overwhelming desire to see her father suffer. She neither hated him nor felt sorry for him.

But the more Christine listened to this middle-aged man

with a raspy voice trying to squirm out of his obligations, the more she began struggling with a new set of feelings. Was this the man she had loved so much as a child? Who had always thought she was special? Who had apparently been disappointed when she hadn't come to see him in the courthouse library?

Was this the father she had carried around in her mind for eighteen years?

Her mother's question "Do you know who that is?" both jolted and angered her. Her relationship to her father was a personal and private matter. Her mother had just dragged it into an open court before reporters and a television camera. All at once, she could no longer hide—from her father or from herself.

But if the question made her feel uncomfortable, the answer hit like a harpoon. After the initial numbness, tears welled up in her eyes. She fought them back. Her father didn't even know her! He had asked for her picture in the Pasco County jailhouse and she had sent one back to him. But it had made such a small impression on him that he didn't even recognize her when she sat six feet away. He didn't care about her. He never had. And he never would.

Why should she care about him?

The moment passed quickly for the court, and the hearing moved on to its inevitable conclusion. But for Christine, time stood still.

Rankin directed the court's attention away from money to the fine point of the law: since Marcia was no longer a minor, did her father have to pay the arrearage? Rankin had already argued that muddled issue in his written brief to the Florida Supreme Court and Bennett had answered him in her brief.

After listening patiently to both sides argue, summarize, and reargue, Judge Cobb called a cease-fire. "I don't require any further argument at this time," he said.

It was almost as if Cobb had made up his mind long before the hearing, but had allowed Rankin and Bennett to debate for the record. Throughout the hearing, Cobb had shown a great deal of patience. Most of the time, he overruled Rankin's objections, giving Pat every opportunity to proceed at her own pace. His message was clear: You waited a long time for this day. I don't want you to feel cheated. Although the court had set one hour aside for the hearing, he had allowed it to drag on for nearly three hours with only a single break to clear up several other cases waiting in another courtroom.

The financial question was simple enough. As far as the court was concerned, James Parker had proven he could not pay a lump sum of $106,000. His sworn financial affidavit, which the court accepted as factual unless proven otherwise, made it clear that he was making around $26,000 a year, that he had to support a wife and child on that income, and that he was more than $160,000 in debt, including the judgment.

For her part, Pat Bennett had proved that Parker's corporation had given him around $85,000 a year, and that he had at least $16,000 in cash a few months ago. But she had not proved that the $60,000 Parker identified as loans were not really loans, or that he still had the $16,000 cash.

Judge Cobb knew, however, that no matter how he decided the practical financial question, he would be criticized. If he came down hard on Parker, ordering him to pay a large sum up front and steep monthly payments, he would be accused of trying to squeeze blood from a turnip. If he tailored the payments to fit Parker's pocketbook as described in his sworn financial affidavit, he would be accused of coddling runaway dads. And then, there was the question of the ongoing IRS collection. If Parker had money buried somewhere, wouldn't the IRS find it for Bennett?

The age question was trickier, and Judge Cobb found himself on thin legal ice. Whatever he ruled—and rule he must—he would be challenged by either Bennett or Parker. Ultimately, the Florida Supreme Court would have to settle the issue. All he could do was what the taxpayers paid him to do—interpret the law as fairly as he could.

Cobb bit the bullet. "I find that this order by the Second District on Mrs. Bennett's appeal," he ruled, "survives children reaching the age of majority, that is eighteen, and that this court *does* have contempt authority."

Rankin seemed rattled. No matter what Cobb now ordered his client to pay, he had lost his case—at least for the moment.

"Is there some authority?" Rankin sputtered, his face sunburn pink. "I just don't see any case law. I would be glad—I certainly wouldn't argue with the court unless I—I just didn't see any case law that might support what the court is doing . . ."

Cobb explained his reasoning, in part agreeing with Rankin. "I believe the Second District [Court of Appeals] doesn't give me the authority to do it," he said. "But it gives me *direction* to do it, and I believe they understood. They are intelligent folks over there. They understood the children were getting near eighteen. They have the whole record, and they have said that contempt was the proper mode of enforcement. . . . I therefore find that Mr. Parker has had the ability to make payments on this support and has failed to do so."

Not only had Cobb studied the ruling of the Second District Court of Appeal; he had done his arithmetic. Noting that the $106,000 judgment was over two years old and that Parker had not paid the full amount of current child support during that time, Cobb recalculated Parker's bill and charged 12 percent interest on the unpaid balance. The total now came to $148,536.12.

"I'm going to find that his failure to make payments on this has been willful," Cobb continued, "and order him confined to the Pasco County Jail for a period of thirty days.

"I'm going to allow him to purge himself of that contempt by the payment of fifteen hundred dollars toward that arrearage and order him to pay one hundred dollars a week for the remaining arrearages when he's released. . . .

"Mr. Parker, I'm going to remand you to the custody of the sheriff to begin serving that sentence."

Parker seemed devastated. He kept his back to the television camera hoping it would go away. It wouldn't, and neither would the bailiff.

"We'll have to go now," the bailiff said after giving Parker a minute to compose himself.

As the camera rolled, Parker held out his wrists.

As soon as Judge Cobb walked out of the hearing room, Pat felt an overwhelming urge to run and hide. She didn't have the strength to face reporters. Nor did Christine, who ached to get back to the hotel so she could nurse her wounds.

"Let's go, Christine," Pat said. Brushing by the cameras, they hurried down the hallway and into the ladies' room. Pat was shaking so badly she held onto a sink for support. "Only fifteen hundred!" she sobbed. "I can't believe it! How am I going to pay my mother back? And what am I going to tell the press?"

Christine was pale and sick to her stomach. "They want to know how I feel about David," she said softly. "I don't *know* how I feel."

When they both calmed down, they agreed to tell the media that Cobb's decision was important for all women and children, and not to talk about their personal disappointments. After touching up their makeup, they walked out to the court-yard to face the cameras.

When the last question was asked and answered, Pat felt as alone as she had when facing David in the courtroom. Everyone, from Richard Froemming to the TV reporters, was calling Cobb's decision a big victory. Maybe it was. But she didn't feel victorious. Just exhausted and disappointed.

Back at the hotel later that afternoon, Pat tried to be happy and chatty over drinks with Richard and Frank de la Grana. And although she joined the small group that partied and danced until the early hours of the next morning, she was only going through the motions.

Pat and Christine had reservations for a two o'clock flight back to Washington that day. When they pulled up to the car rental office at the airport, Pat realized she couldn't leave. "You go on by yourself," she told Christine. "I'm not ready to go back yet. I'm exhausted and I need time alone."

Christine was relieved; she wanted nothing more than to be alone, too. Seated next to the airplane window and shielded by anonymity, she finally let out the tears she had held back for so long. Christine cried quietly all the way home and through most of the night. In Tampa, her worst dream had come true. She had always resisted meeting her father because she was afraid he would reject her once again. He had, and it hurt more than she thought it ever could. James Parker had shattered the image of David she had carried for most of her life and with it, any hope of a relationship with him. David *was* really dead after all.

While Christine was on her way home, Pat was driving around aimlessly. She found herself drawn to the sea.

It was late afternoon and chilly as she took off her shoes

and began walking down a deserted beach. Waves lapped the shore, leaving a trace of foam on the wet sand, and the icy water on her feet lent the only reality to the dreamlike day. She walked until her car was a speck in the distance.

Away from everyone, she began to sob uncontrollably. She desperately wanted to leave David behind in Tampa where she had found him. She was tired of courtroom battles, exhausted from pushing and protecting her daughters, raw from facing her own feelings. But she was afraid she wouldn't be able to leave it all there—the bitterness, the obsession, the tiredness.

The more she let go of her emotions, the more she felt the tug of an indefinable sadness. She encouraged the new feeling until it enveloped her like a pool of soothing warm water.

She had never mourned David when he walked out seventeen years ago. By simply disappearing, he had denied her that right. Part of what drove her to find him and drag him before the bench, she finally understood, was the need to arrive at a ritual conclusion. She was burying David at last. Now the mourning that she had put off seventeen long years could begin.

She was ready to go home, to let the sadness run its course, to face the Florida Supreme Court. No matter what happened there, she had already won. She had conquered her fear. She had faced David. She would never dream of him again.

A small white seashell, washed up by a wave, lay gleaming in the sand. She stooped to pick it up, then found two more. David had proposed to her on a beach in Bermuda. Now she had buried him on a beach in Tampa.

Three shells were all she wanted to take home. Three shells, one for each of her daughters.

Epilogue

▼

JAMES PARKER'S WIFE paid fifteen hundred dollars two hours after Judge Cobb's hearing and her husband was set free. Parker began missing his weekly payments four months later. With the threat of contempt, however, he quickly caught up.

The IRS is still trying to collect some or all of the outstanding arrearage.

Pat Bennett argued her case before the Florida Supreme Court on April 1, 1988. A decision is pending. If she loses, Parker can no longer be sent to jail for contempt.

Acknowledgments

▼

MORE THAN FIFTY people, from judges to sheriffs, family friends to child-support experts, have contributed to this book through interviews, expertise, and guidance. Their cooperation has not only enriched the story of the Bennett family but has made it more objective and balanced. I wish to thank them:

Lorraine Baker, Andrea Bennett, Christine Bennett, Eugene Bennett, Marcia Bennett, Arlene Bierbaum, Philip Brophy, William Branch, George Carpenter, Kathy Chinoy, Charles Crotty, Bill Daniels, Marge De Blaay, Elizabeth L. Dribben, Michael Echevarria, Cheryl Fitzpatrick, Richard Frazier, Richard Froemming, Sally Goldfarb, Frank de la Grana, Richard Hager, Carl Hanfling, Ron Haskins, Margaret Campbell-Haynes, Nanette Hoback, Clegg Holliday, Jean Holzhueter, Joyce Jeffers, June Inuzuka, Maureen Kayes, Daniel Kellogg, John Kellogg, Mary Kellogg, Terry Kellogg, Jim Marsee, David Mees, Kathleen Meredith, Debbie Perez, Pam Powers, Jean Samson, Linda Schnatterly, Susan Sheehan, Viola Tesch, Michael Valentine, Chriss Walker, Jill Weber, Beth Weisberg.

I would like especially to thank Betty Murphy, president of the National Child Support Advocacy Coalition, for sharing her knowledge and experience and for evaluating the first draft manuscript; Diane Dodson, child-support specialist, for directing me to resources; Chriss Walker for reviewing the final draft manuscript; and my wife, Paula Kaufmann, for editing draft after draft.

1-800-777-7735